# *The Columbia Guide to African American History Since 1939*

COLUMBIA GUIDES TO AMERICAN HISTORY AND CULTURES

*Columbia Guides to American History and Cultures*

Michael Kort,
*The Columbia Guide to the Cold War*

Catherine Clinton and Christine Lunardini,
*The Columbia Guide to American Women in the Nineteenth Century*

David Farber and Beth Bailey, editors,
*The Columbia Guide to America in the 1960s*

David L. Anderson,
*The Columbia Guide to the Vietnam War*

# *The Columbia Guide to African American History Since 1939*

*Edited by Robert L. Harris Jr. and Rosalyn Terborg-Penn*

COLUMBIA UNIVERSITY PRESS
NEW YORK

Columbia University Press

*Publishers Since 1893*

New York Chichester, West Sussex



Library of Congress Cataloging-in-Publication Data

The Columbia guide to African American history since 1939 / edited by Robert L. Harris Jr. and Rosalyn Terborg-Penn.

p. cm. —(Columbia guides to American history and cultures)

Includes bibliographical references and index.

ISBN 0-231-13810-5 (alk. paper)

1. African Americans—History—1877–1964. 2. African Americans—History—1964–

I. Harris, Robert L., 1943— II. Terborg-Penn, Rosalyn. III. Series.

E185.6.C715 2006

973'.0496073–dc22 2005034370

Columbia University Press books are printed on permanent and durable acid-free paper.

Printed in the United States of America

c 10 9 8 7 6 5 4 3 2 1

*For*

*Anita, Lisa, Leslie, and Lauren*

*and*

*Jeanna C.T. Penn*

CONTENTS

# INTRODUCTION

This guide introduces a general audience to the contours of the African American past since 1939 and serves as a reference for students and scholars to the major themes, events, and persons that dramatize the story. Part I provides a historical narrative that acquaints readers with four chief time frames and that gives them a context within which to place central developments of the post-1939 African American experience. It begins by exploring approaches to the study, interpretation, and teaching of African American history from World War II to the present. African American history began to take on a life of its own after 1939 as black people became more active in the struggle for freedom, justice, and equality and as the nation confronted the contradiction between advocating democracy abroad while practicing racial discrimination and segregation at home. This contradiction stood out in bold relief in 1939, a watershed year in African American history, when some 75,000 Americans, black and white, attended a concert by Marian Anderson on the steps of the Lincoln Memorial in Washington, D.C., after the Daughters of the American Revolution refused to rent its Constitution Hall for her performance. Millions more heard the concert on radio and became aware of the irony that the world's greatest contralto had to perform outdoors because of racial bigotry and discrimination, even as the nation criticized Nazi Germany for its practice of fascism and white supremacy.

Historians have used several approaches to make sense of the African American past, such as revisionist, contributionist, vindicationist, and Afrocentric interpretations. With the triumph of the civil rights movement, scholars broadened their study to include issues of class, sexuality, color, gender, religion, region, and profession. They have begun to probe the multidimensionality of the black population in the United States in ways that were not possible when African Americans had to project a united front against racial subordination. In the process, African American history has become richer, more varied and nuanced in texture.

Readers can use the historical narrative as a guide to the unfolding of African American history since 1939 and as a means of identifying the major issues that black people confronted in their drive for racial equality. They will become familiar with the need for different movements to address those concerns. Moreover, they will begin to understand why the movements took shape and their strengths as well as their weaknesses. Readers will be in a better position to determine for themselves the efficacy of strategies for change. They will realize the differences between the desires of local communities for change and the programs of national organizations. The African American journey since 1939 is much more than the story of a few brave men and women. Although figures such as Ella Baker, Mary McLeod Bethune, Jesse Jackson, Martin Luther King Jr., Malcolm X, Thurgood Marshall, Rosa Parks, A. Philip Randolph, and Eleanor Roosevelt loom large in the story, they were representatives of countless black and white unnamed and often unrecognized participants in the movement.

The present juncture in African American history is much more complex than in the past, with a larger black immigrant population, with the "black" and "white" dichotomy being complicated by the growing Asian and Latino populations, and with the irony of a sizeable black middle class but the persistence of a huge black underclass. The historical narrative identifies and explains these developments as well as issues such as affirmative action, police brutality, and the drive for reparations.

Part II examines some of the key themes for understanding African American history since 1939. Essays in this section explore cultural and political issues of self-designation from colored, Negro, Afro-American, and black to African American, as well as the unsettled aspects of what people of African ancestry in the United States should call themselves at the beginning of the twenty-first century. The postindustrial era since World War II, marked by a decline in manufacturing jobs and the rise of new technologies, has shifted the ground of racial inequality in this country and the best means to address the problem. The military has become both a means for black advancement in American society—especially for black women, who outnumber white women in the armed forces—and a model of greater opportunity for African Americans. Although today African Americans dominate some of the major sports, such as boxing, basketball, football, and track and field, the slow process of desegregation there is still being played out at the management level. Similar to sports, African American literature, art, theater, film, and music have moved more into the mainstream since World War II and have reflected the changing nature of African American and American society. Black business development has also shifted from a traditional black consumer base to a broader market, especially in music and advanced technology.

Each of the thought-provoking essays in Part II includes a list of sources that readers can draw upon for further study. They can engage the issues raised in these essays and generate their own assessments. High school students and undergraduates in particular will acquire greater background and direction for understanding and appreciating the key themes in African American history since 1939. Teachers will find these essays an important starting point for their own instruction, as the essays identify the salient points for making greater sense of the African American past. While Part I provides a context for readers, Part II gives them the specific components that add greater meaning to the whole. In each instance, readers can use the material as a reference to understand the African American past in its different dimensions. They can learn for the first time about certain events and developments, verify information, or refresh their memories.

The chronology in Part III can serve to reinforce knowledge of the main currents in African American history since 1939 and provide a means to spark interest in new topics. History is a process more than an artifact. It is a dynamic means of engaging the present by understanding the past. Each generation adds to our knowledge of the past by using the inflections of their time to identify issues that beg for comprehension. Readers of this guide will enter that process and will find this reference an important tool for their encounter with the past to make better sense of the present. Part IV, with entries on the central persons and organizations that constitute the black experience since World War II, will deepen the reader's awareness of the African American past. The entries in Part IV do not duplicate the events that are highlighted in the historical narrative. They provide biographical and organizational information to gain a better sense of most of the actors that are mentioned in Part I. The work concludes with Part V, a substantial resource guide to textbooks, general references, military records, and materials on some of the major events and eras, such as desegregation of the military, the civil rights movement, black nationalism, urban riots and rebellions, post–civil rights, and the decades of the 1980s and 1990s. The resource guide identifies manuscript collections; film, video, and recordings; libraries, museums, and historical sites; and newspapers, periodicals, and

Web sites. Most of the materials are annotated to introduce the reader to the resources and their significance.

This guide to African American history since 1939 is a comprehensive toolkit for building an appreciation and understanding of the black experience in the United States in its various dimensions. It contains practically everything that the general reader or student will need to learn, study, write, and teach about this pivotal period of the African American past, and it will be a useful resource for teachers and scholars alike.

Collaboration for this project began under a grant from the Ford Foundation to strengthen Africana / Black Studies at Binghamton University, Cornell University, Morgan State University, and Syracuse University through a common graduate seminar, pedagogy workshops, and joint research. We thank the Ford Foundation, our contributors to this volume, Cornell University administrative assistant Patricia Stark, and especially the graduate students who assisted us (Derick Hendricks, Mario Nisbett, Anthony Ratcliffe, and Jade Rogers at Morgan State University and Michelle Scott and Kawsi E. Larbi-Siaw at Cornell University). For assistance with the annotated bibliography, Debra Newman Ham acknowledges Jade Rogers and Mario Nisbett, graduate students at Morgan State University, as well as her colleagues Professors Charles Johnson and JoAnn Robinson, James E. Lewis Museum of Art Director Gabriel Tenabe, Special Collections Librarian Edith Murungi, and Library Technician Elizabeth Gross-Morant. She also thanks Walter Hill at the National Archives and Records Administration, Mary Wolfskill and Ardie Myers at the Library of Congress, James Danke at the Wisconsin Historical Society, and technical specialist Lester J. Ham. The anonymous reviewers of our manuscript provided comprehensive and insightful comments and recommendations for which we are grateful. James Warren and Peter Dimock, our editors at Columbia University Press, helped a concept to become a reality, and Gregory McNamee expertly made the manuscript more cohesive and comprehensible.

# PART I

## *Historical Narrative*

ROBERT L. HARRIS JR. AND ROSALYN TERBORG-PENN

# INTERPRETING AFRICAN AMERICAN HISTORY SINCE 1939

The period of African American history from 1939 to the present is one of the most important for understanding the black struggle for freedom, justice, and equality. The dean of African American history, John Hope Franklin, has affirmed the "interconnection between the history of a people and their drive for first-class citizenship."[1] The writing of African American history has changed over time in relation to the socioeconomic, cultural, and political position of black people in the United States; as Earl E. Thorpe remarks, "It is because the past is a guide with roads pointing in many directions that each generation and epoch must make its own study of history."[2] And Eric Foner has argued that "history always has been and always will be regularly rewritten, in response to new questions, new information, new methodologies, and new political, social, and cultural imperatives."[3] Under the influence of black opposition to racial oppression and segregation, black and white historians, after 1939, began to explore black resistance, agency, and self-determination. For the first time, African American history began to take on a life of its own, as black people became actors rather than pawns in the nation's history. Historians began to develop a periodization for African American history that does not blindly follow the major eras in American history. Colin Palmer has explained that "a people's internal trajectory, particularly that of an oppressed, marginalized group, and one that did not enjoy full citizenship rights, is not coterminous with the political history of the state."[4] As the great essayist and novelist Ralph Ellison wrote, "But can a people . . . live and develop for over three hundred years simply by *reacting*? Are American Negroes simply the creation of white men, or have they at least helped to create themselves out of what they found around them?"[5]

## REVISIONIST, CONTRIBUTIONIST, VINDICATIONIST, AND AFROCENTRIC APPROACHES

Many of the post-1939 historians wrote to revise the errors, omissions, and distortions about black people that appeared in standard histories of the United States. Often, they focused on the contributions that African Americans made to America as a way of incorporating them into the nation's history. Some wrote in what V. P. Franklin and Bettye Collier-Thomas have called a "vindicationist" mode "to deconstruct the discursive structures erected in science, medicine, the law, and historical discourse to uphold the mental and cultural inferiority of African peoples."[6] African American history is central to understanding American history, and there is an ongoing interaction between the two. Thus historians have begun to drill more deeply into the strata of the black past. They have examined black identity and cultural development. This approach to the African American past might be considered Afrocentrist, as an examination of the black experience from the inside out rather than from the outside in. Afrocentricity, as explained by Maghan Keita in *Race and the Writing of History*, is a challenge to the construction of knowledge that supports Western interpretations as universal and that disallows multiple perspectives based on non-Western traditions.[7]

## THE INTEGRATIONIST OR NATIONALIST PARADIGM

In *The Souls of Black Folk*, W. E. B. Du Bois writes about the world African Americans inhabited at the turn of the twentieth century, one that yielded them "no true self-consciousness" and that only let them see themselves "through the revelation of the other world." He suggested that the history of African Americans was the tension between being "an American, a Negro; two souls, two thoughts, two unreconciled strivings; two warring ideals in one dark body."[8] Harold Cruse, in *The Crisis of the Negro Intellectual*, contends that African American history has been either integrationist (focusing on freedom, civil rights, and racial equality) or nationalist (emphasizing group solidarity, self-help, and separatism).[9] According to Kevin Gaines, interpretations of African American history since the 1970s have taken two approaches: the study of elites and middle-class reformers and their organizations on one hand and working-class resistance, mass mobilization, and labor politics on the other. For Gaines, the "framework of integrationism versus nationalism . . . failed to elucidate not only the complicated operations of race and class in social and power relations but their gendered dimension, as well."[10]

## MULTIDIMENSIONALITY

Today, historians such as Earl Lewis have broadened the dilemma posed by Du Bois to include people of African ancestry who have recently immigrated from Africa, the Caribbean, Europe, and Central and South America. The binary that once confronted African Americans (American or Negro, integration or nationalism) has been expanded beyond the United States and Africa to experiences that black people in this country now bring from overlapping diasporas. Moreover, the post–civil rights era has made it possible to consider, as Lewis calls it, the multipositionality of African Americans to probe issues of class, sexuality, color, gender, religion, region, and profession.[11] Prior to the successes of the civil rights movement, it was difficult to examine the multidimensionality of black communities. Primarily for political reasons, African Americans had to put up a united front against racial oppression. As the walls of segregation began to crumble and as many African Americans were able to enter mainstream society, the need for racial unity was no longer as urgent. The study of African American history has become more complex, but also more rewarding, with a rich tapestry, especially for the period since 1939.

## THE USES OF AFRICAN AMERICAN HISTORY

In his insightful essay "Black History's Diversified Clientele," published in 1977, Benjamin Quarles writes that African American history serves at least four publics: the black rank and file, black revolutionary nationalists, black academicians, and the white world (both scholarly and lay).[12] For the black rank and file, the purpose of African American history is to create a sense of racial pride and personal worth. This is African American history that is still written in the contributionist or vindicationist vein. Revolutionary nationalists, who are very critical of the United States and its oppression of African Americans through institutional racism and white supremacy, seek a past that supports a black aesthetic and identity. This approach looks to the past primarily for the purpose of nation building and is the goal of the Afrocentrist school of historiography today. The Afrocentrist school of interpretation places Africa at the center of historical development and examines the past from the cultural and racial unity of people of African ancestry more than their geographical or temporal location. Quarles did not dismiss the revolutionary nationalist school because it brought fresh perspectives by posing challenging questions and provoking multidisciplinary and comparative studies of the past. The black academician, according to Quarles, engages history as "a discipline, an attempt to recapture and mirror the past as accurately as possible." The black academician combines both a citizenship role to improve the condition of African Americans and a scholarly role in the search for truth. The multidimensionality and complexity of African American history with tragedy and triumph, failure and success, stagnation and progress, influences the approach of the black academician. Quarles concludes that African American history is not just the province of African Americans but should be the concern of the white community as well, both scholarly and lay. As W. E. B. DuBois, in *The Souls of Black Folk*, so perceptively writes, "Your country? How came it yours? Before the Pilgrims landed we were here. Here we have brought our three gifts and mingled them with yours: a gift of story and song . . . the gift of sweat and brawn . . . a gift of the Spirit. . . . Actively we have woven ourselves with the very warp and woof of this nation. . . . Would America have been America without her Negro people?"[13]

## MULTIDIMENSIONALITY AND INTRAGROUP RELATIONS

Although the revisionist, contributionist, vindicationist, and Afrocentrist approaches to the research, writing, and teaching of African American history are still prominent, there was a shift during the last decade of the twentieth century to a more multidimensional interpretation of the past. This shift was especially important to move beyond what Nell Painter identified as the "representative 'men' of color" who dominated most of the story about African Americans.[14] Evelyn Books Higginbotham argues that African American history "has failed to examine the differential class and gender positions men and women occupy in black communities—thus uncritically rendering a monolithic 'black community,' 'black experience,' and 'voice of the Negro." While not losing sight of intergroup relations, there has been a change to examine more closely intragroup relations. Higginbotham has helped us to understand that the "metalanguage" of race (a social construction, not a scientific principle) has muted but not silenced conflict among African Americans. Especially with regard to women, she has concluded, "We must problematize much more of what we take for granted. We must bring to light and to coherence the one and the many that we always were in history and still actually are today." There have always been differences among African Americans. Recognizing those differences does not diminish the past but enriches it.[15]

## MAJOR PERIODS OF AFRICAN AMERICAN HISTORY SINCE 1939

This guide to African American history begins in 1939, a watershed year for the black experience in the United States. Marian Anderson's concert on the steps of the Lincoln Memorial was witnessed live by 75,000 black and white Americans and heard on the radio by millions more, who recognized the irony of the world's greatest contralto having to perform outdoors because of racial bigotry and discrimination at a time when the United States criticized Nazi Germany for its doctrines of Aryan supremacy. Moreover, in 1939, the National Association for the Advancement of Colored People (NAACP), the foremost champion of the rights of African Americans, incorporated the NAACP Legal Defense and Educational Fund, which made it possible to receive tax-free contributions for its campaign in the courts against segregation. Prior to 1939, the NAACP had difficulty financing litigation. Now it could employ a dedicated staff of attorneys to battle against segregation and to establish the precedents that would lead to the momentous Supreme Court decision of 1954 that overturned the principle of "separate but equal" that had separated the races, especially in the South, since the rise of Jim Crow in the 1890s.

### 1939–1957

From 1939 to 1957, African Americans set the foundation for the civil rights struggle, which the Montgomery Bus Boycott Movement triggered in 1955 on the heels of the Supreme Court's 1954 *Brown v. Board of Education* decision, which undercut the ground for de jure or legal segregation. With victories in the courts against segregation and momentum building for first-class citizenship for African Americans, supporters of white supremacy identified the NAACP as the main villain, assuming that if they could cripple the organization, they could stem the rising tide for equal rights. In many respects, this strategy backfired. As southern states curtailed the activities of the NAACP, other organizations emerged with a more local base to challenge segregation and disfranchisement.

## 1955–1965

During this period, the civil movement spread throughout the South to crumble the walls of segregation. It was also a catalyst for the nation, as the black freedom movement, according to Vincent Harding, served as a "wedge" that pried open the consciousness not only of African Americans but also of white students, women, Latinos, gays and lesbians, Native Americans, consumers, Asian Americans, environmentalists, and the elderly, to struggle for a more democratic society.

## 1965–1975

In 1965, when the Voting Rights Act passed into law, African Americans entered the post-civil rights era. By 1968, other laws had been placed on the books to recognize the rights of African Americans as first-class citizens of the United States. There were still questions of enforcement that would continue to plague African Americans, but the laws against racial discrimination and segregation were in place. The end of legal segregation, however, confronted African Americans with a stark reality. Although they had the right to public accommodations and transportation, they lacked the wherewithal to afford access, thereby giving the right small meaning. Moreover, African Americans in the North witnessed little change in their lives despite the publicity accorded to the so-called Negro Revolution. Uprisings or riots in the cities, primarily in the North, revealed the depth of deprivation and despair for many African Americans who remained mired in poverty. The Black Power and Black Consciousness movements arose in 1965, and over the next decade addressed the disparity between the promise of racial equality and the reality for most African Americans.

## 1975 *TO THE PRESENT*

After 1975, with the rise of black elected officials, a growing black middle class, and the incorporation of African Americans into many areas of American life—education, business, entertainment, government, and sports—it appeared, in William Julius Wilson's words, that there was a "declining significance of race." Moreover, the United States changed demographically after the 1960s with greater immigration from Africa, Asia, the Caribbean, and Central and South America. As the Advisory Board on Race that President Bill Clinton appointed in 1997 discovered in conversations across the country and reported in *One America in the 21st Century: Forging a New Future*, the face of America had changed with a growing population of Asian ancestry and a Latino community that is now as large as the African American population. America has become an increasingly multicultural nation, marked by ethnic, social, and economic divisions of many kinds. For most of the nation's history, with Native Americans isolated on reservations, the black/white divide had been central to the country's laws and practices, especially in the South. The lingering problems of disproportionate poverty, inadequate education, incarceration, police brutality, racial profiling, and covert discrimination in employment, health care, and housing pose a dilemma for African Americans over whether previous race-based strategies are still appropriate for largely class-based issues. The narrative that follows examines the key periods of African American history since 1939 to the present and provides a context for understanding the changing contours of African American life and culture.

## NOTES

1. John Hope Franklin, "On the Evolution of Scholarship in Afro-American History," in *The State of Afro-American History: Past, Present, and Future*, ed. Darlene Clark Hine (Baton Rouge: Louisiana State University Press, 1986), 22.

2. Earl E. Thorpe, "Philosophy of History: Sources, Truths, and Limitations," *Quarterly Review of Higher Education Among Negroes* 25, no. 3 (July 1957): 172–185.

3. Eric Foner, *Who Owns History? Rethinking the Past in a Changing World* (New York: Hill and Wang, 2002), xvii.

4. Colin A. Palmer, *Passageways: An Interpretive History of Black America* (New York: Harcourt Brace, 1998), 2:x.

5. Ralph Ellison, *Shadow and Act* (New York: Random House, 1953), 315.

6. V. P. Franklin and Bettye Collier-Thomas, "Biography, Race Vindication, and African American Intellectuals," *Journal of Negro History* (Winter 1996): 1.

7. Maghan Keita, *Race and the Writing of History: Riddling the Sphinx* (New York: Oxford University Press, 2000).

8. W. E. B. Du Bois, *The Souls of Black Folk* (New York: Penguin Books, 1996), 5.

9. Harold Cruse, *The Crisis of the Negro Intellectual* (New York: Morrow, 1967).

10. Kevin Gaines, "Rethinking Race and Class in African-American Struggles for Equality, 1885–1941," *American Historical Review* 102 (April 1997): 378–387.

11. Earl Lewis, "To Turn as on a Pivot: Writing African Americans Into a History of Overlapping Diasporas," *American Historical Review* 100, no. 3 (June 1995): 765–787.

12. Benjamin Quarles, "Black History's Diversified Clientele," in *Black Mosaic: Essays in Afro-American History and Historiography* (Amherst: University of Massachusetts Press, 1988), 202–213.

13. Du Bois, *The Souls of Black Folk*, 214–215.

14. Nell Irvin Painter, *Exodusters: Black Migration to Kansas After Reconstruction* (New York: Knopf, 1977), 16.

15. Evelyn Brooks Higginbotham, "African American Women's History and the Metalanguage of Race," *Signs: Journal of Women in History and Culture* 17, no. 2 (Winter 1992): 251–274.

# FOUNDATIONS OF THE MOVEMENT, 1939–57

On Easter Sunday 1939, in Washington, D.C., a crowd estimated at 75,000 stretched from the front of the Lincoln Memorial along the reflecting pool to the base of the Washington Monument to hear a concert by the world-renowned contralto Marian Anderson. The concert had to be staged outdoors because the Daughters of the American Revolution (DAR) refused to rent Constitution Hall for the performance. Howard University, the historically black college in Washington, usually sponsored Marian Anderson's appearances in the nation's capital. As her popularity grew, Howard sought larger quarters for her concert. Constitution Hall, with excellent acoustics and four thousand seats, was the largest concert facility in the District of Columbia. In 1931, the DAR permitted a performance by the black tenor Roland Hayes and a benefit concert by the Hampton Institute Choir. To prevent the prospect of blacks and whites sitting together in the audience, the DAR, in 1932, adopted a policy of renting the facility for performances by white artists only.

When Howard University officials approached the DAR about renting Constitution Hall, African Americans in Washington had grown cautiously optimistic about improvement in race relations in the nation's capital. During the 1930s, under the administration of President Franklin Delano Roosevelt, buses, taxicabs, railroad station dining and waiting rooms, and public libraries had become desegregated, as had meetings, lectures, and concerts in government halls and the Library of Congress. The First Lady, Eleanor Roosevelt, had been an outspoken champion of racial equality. The DAR decision not to rent Constitution Hall for a concert by Marian Anderson became major news nationally and internationally. The famous conductor Arturo Toscanini had hailed Anderson's voice as one heard only once every hundred years. Many newspapers compared the DAR's decision to racial bigotry in Nazi Germany. In her nationally syndicated newspaper column on February 27, Eleanor Roosevelt announced her resignation from the DAR because of its blatant racial discrimination. Although Howard University continued to press the DAR, as a backup the school sought use of the Central High School Auditorium from the Board of Education, which refused on the grounds that it could not permit a commercial performance on school property.

A biracial group formed the Marian Anderson Citizens Committee (MACC) in the law office of Charles Hamilton Houston, NAACP special counsel. Walter White, the NAACP executive secretary, proposed that Anderson sing on the steps of the Lincoln Memorial as a strong statement against racial bigotry and discrimination. Houston threw the MACC's support behind White, who encouraged organizations to send representatives by train to Washington for the concert. Secretary of the Interior Harold L. Ickes endorsed the concert and lent his department's support in making preparations. Members of the Roosevelt administration, Supreme Court justices, and members of Congress were among the dignitaries who assembled on the steps of the Lincoln Memorial for Anderson's concert. Ickes opened the program by exclaiming, "In this great auditorium under the sky, all of us are free. When God gave us this wonderful outdoors and the sun, the moon, and the stars, He made no distinction of race, creed, or color."[1]

## THE CHALLENGE OF RACIAL INEQUALITY

This was a momentous event for the United States, especially as the Nazi menace spread in Germany and war clouds loomed over Europe. The United States would soon have to confront the issue of racial equality in an unprecedented manner, an issue that had not challenged the nation in such a direct way since the abolition of slavery and the Reconstruction Era. After 1896, with the infamous Supreme Court decision of *Plessy v. Ferguson* establishing the doctrine of "separate but equal," African Americans, especially in the South, faced racial separation and discrimination in practically every area of American life, from the cradle to the grave. The Roosevelt administration and the New Deal gave "symbolic" hope to African Americans, inasmuch as it appeared that they had a friend in the White House for the first time since Abraham Lincoln. Desegregation of public facilities in Washington, D.C., and Eleanor Roosevelt's advocacy instilled some confidence that change was on the horizon.

Preparing for that change was Charles Hamilton Houston, who played an instrumental role in facilitating Marian Anderson's concert before the Lincoln Memorial, which would become a popular venue for black protest during the latter half of the twentieth century. Houston, according to his biographer Genna Rae McNeil, laid the groundwork for the successful legal battle against the "separate but equal" doctrine and for the direct action campaign against racial inequality. In 1939, the NAACP incorporated its Legal Defense and Educational Fund, which marked a major shift in the struggle for civil rights. As a nonprofit organization within the NAACP, the Legal Defense and Educational Fund could receive tax-deductible contributions from individuals and foundations to press its legal challenges to racial segregation. Houston, especially as dean of the Howard University Law School from 1929 to 1935 and as NAACP special counsel from 1935 to 1940, established the strategy of judicial precedent building to end the principle of "separate but equal" in education, employment, and transportation.

A Phi Beta Kappa graduate of Amherst College, Charles Hamilton Houston was the first African American to serve as editor of the *Harvard Law Review*. Supreme Court Justice Felix Frankfurter, who taught Houston at Harvard, considered him one of the best law students that he had encountered. Houston later gained a reputation as one of the best trial lawyers in the United States, black or white. He believed that African Americans could employ the Constitution to challenge racial discrimination, injustice, and second-class citizenship by creatively interpreting and using it. At Howard Law School, he was determined to train the black lawyer as a social engineer to lead the struggle for African American freedom, socially, politically, and economically. Houston declared that racial discrimination in education symbolized all the inequalities that African Americans confronted in American life. He planned a strategy to challenge pay differentials for black and white teachers, inequitable transportation—especially in rural areas—that prevented consolidation of schools without regard to race, and inequalities in graduate and professional education. Houston left the NAACP in 1940 to return to private practice. He died in 1950 before seeing his student and fellow special counsel Thurgood Marshall successfully argue against the doctrine of "separate but equal" before the Supreme Court.[2]

## WORLD WAR II

With the outbreak of World War II in Europe in September 1939, the United States finally escaped from the clutches of the Great Depression. America's role, initially as a supplier of war materiel and later as a combatant, set the stage for rapid economic growth, government expansion, and the country's rise as the world's greatest superpower. Industrial expansion and growth of the federal government helped a sizeable portion of the black population enter the middle class, determined to gain first-class citizenship. African Americans traditionally had been the last hired and first fired, a reserve army of labor, to be employed in good times and let go when the economy soured. As companies initiated intensive training programs to produce skilled workers to manufacture war supplies, they excluded black men and women from those programs. Manufacturers and organized labor confined African Americans to unskilled and service positions. The military segregated black men in the Army, restricted them to menial service in the Navy and the Coast Guard, and excluded them from the Marines.

Less than two weeks after President Roosevelt signed the 1940 Selective Service Act into law, the National Urban League's T. Arnold Hill, the Brotherhood of Sleeping Car Porters' A. Philip Randolph, and NAACP's Walter White met with the president to discuss the armed forces' use of black manpower. After the meeting, the War Department affirmed its policy of racial segregation and implied that the black leaders acquiesced in the policy. At a protest rally in Chicago, a black woman suggested that fifty thousand "Negroes" from across the country surround the White House until the president changed his mind. In January 1941, Randolph proposed a "March on Washington" against racial discrimination in defense industries and the military. A March on Washington Committee (MOWC) was organized with offices in Brooklyn, Chicago, Detroit, Harlem, Pittsburgh, St. Louis, San Francisco, and Washington, D.C., to urge African Americans to travel to the nation's capital on July 1 for the demonstration.

## *THE MARCH ON WASHINGTON COMMITTEE*

Because of his experience with the Communist Party in the National Negro Congress during the late 1930s, Randolph excluded whites from participating in the MOWC. The Communist Party of the United States, which was closely tied to the Soviet Union, supported the right of African Americans to self-determination, condemned capitalist exploitation, and was one of the most vigorous opponents of racial inequality during the 1930s. The National Negro Congress was organized in 1936 as a broad coalition of African Americans with white organized labor support to protest against racial segregation. Communists had infiltrated and disrupted the work of the National Negro Congress from which Randolph resigned as president in 1940. He explained that the MOWC was not anti-white but pro-black and that African Americans needed to mobilize themselves to build a sense of self-confidence and self-reliance. Randolph initially planned for 10,000 African Americans to descend on Washington, D.C., a figure that he soon revised upward to 100,000. Numerous black fraternal, labor, civic, and social organizations as well as the black press endorsed the march. Both Eleanor Roosevelt and New York Mayor Fiorello H. LaGuardia tried to persuade the MOWC to cancel the march, but the organizers stood firm. After meeting with Randolph, White, and labor organizers Frank Crosswaith and Layle Lane, President Roosevelt issued Executive Order 8802 on June 25, 1941, banning discrimination in employment by defense industries and the government and establishing a Fair Employment Practices Committee (FEPC) to investigate compliance with the executive order. The MOWC called off the march and formed a coalition of black organizations to keep pressure on the White House to enforce its directive, which many African Americans hailed as the greatest presidential decree since Lincoln's Emancipation Proclamation.[3]

Although the FEPC encountered resistance in its investigation of training programs and employment practices, there was a gradual change in African Americans securing work in defense industries, due in large measure to labor shortages during the war. Substantial numbers of black workers did find employment in skilled, managerial, and clerical positions. Moreover, through the unions of the Congress of Industrial Organizations (CIO), they secured better-paying positions in the automobile, meatpacking, and steel industries. In 1942, the CIO established a Committee to Abolish Racial Discrimination and encouraged its affiliates to work for equal opportunity in employment practices. Once the United States entered the war as a combatant after the Japanese attack on Pearl Harbor of December 7, 1941, African Americans decided to wage a "Double V Campaign" for victory at home as well as abroad. The black press, especially the *Pittsburgh Courier*, pressed the "Double V Campaign." African Americans had temporarily put their grievances behind them during World War I with the expectation that the battle to make the world safe for democracy would bring greater racial equality at home. They were severely disappointed with race riots and increased segregation. They were determined that this war would be different and laid the foundation during the conflict for the civil rights movement.

## *BLACK TROOPS*

More than a million black men and women served in the military during World War II. When the Japanese attacked Pearl Harbor, Dorie Miller, a black cook on the battleship *Arizona*, rushed from below deck, pulled his wounded captain to safety, manned a machine gun without any prior experience, and shot down at least four enemy planes before running out of ammunition. He later received the Navy Cross for his heroism but was still confined to mess duty. Almost a half million black soldiers were stationed overseas during the war, where most served in labor details unloading ships, transporting troops and supplies, building and repairing roads, and clearing fields. Some saw combat such as the 761st Tank Battalion, which fought at the Battle of the Bulge toward the end of the war and in which the United States suffered enormous casualties. There were major changes during the war as the Army integrated its officer candidate schools except those training air force pilots. The number of black commissioned officers, who could only command fellow black troops, was still less than one percent. The Army did create a training program for black pilots at Tuskegee Institute. The 99th Squadron and the 332nd Group had black officers, the most noted of whom was Col. Benjamin O. Davis Jr., who in 1954 became the first African American brigadier general in the military. Davis commanded the 99th Pursuit Squadron, known as the Tuskegee Airmen, which escorted U.S. bombers into German territory and could boast that of more than two hundred missions it did not lose a single one to the enemy. The very existence of the Tuskegee Airmen was a breakthrough because many Americans doubted that black men had the intelligence to fly aircraft or the courage to survive intensive combat.[4]

Black women, many of whom served in the Nurse Corps, also faced racial discrimination during the war. Although the military experienced a shortage of nurses, black nurses could only treat black soldiers and German prisoners of war. Mabel K. Staupers, executive director of the National Association of Colored Graduate Nurses, waged a campaign to lift quotas against black nurses in the Army and their exclusion from the Navy. She organized a letter-writing crusade to protest discrimination against black nurses. In early 1945, the Army ended its quotas and the Navy accepted its first black nurses. More than three hundred black women served in the Army Nurse Corps and some four thousand were members of the Women's Army Corps (WAC).

## *THE HOME FRONT*

On the home front, African Americans volunteered their services to organizations such as the United Services Organization (USO) and the Red Cross, although they protested the latter's practice of keeping the plasma of black and white blood donors separate. Ironically, it was a black physician, Dr. Charles R. Drew, who helped to pioneer the preservation and storage of blood plasma. Drew became medical director of the Red Cross Blood Bank but resigned over the U.S. military's decision to segregate the blood of black donors and to use it only for transfusions to black patients. African Americans organized war bond campaigns and rationed materials that were important to the war effort. Paul Robeson, the world-renowned actor and singer, who later would be ostracized by the U.S. government and prevented from making a living during the Cold War, gave concerts throughout the country to sell war bonds. African Americans refused to stay in their "place" during the war, for which they made sacrifices at home and abroad. On military bases in the U.S., black officers protested exclusion from officers' clubs. Jackie Robinson, who became a second lieutenant and would become the first black major league baseball player in the twentieth century, was court-martialed for refusing to sit in the back of a segregated military bus in Texas. He was acquitted and later received an honorable discharge from the Army.

Attracted by well-paying jobs in war industries, more than a million and a half African Americans migrated from the South to the North and the West during the 1940s. This was the largest migration ever of African Americans from the South. Moreover, by the end of the war, the majority of the black population was urban, a milestone that the white population had reached after World War I. Although it has become a popular and somewhat mythical image, African Americans did not pick up from the fields in the rural South and move immediately to the factories of the urban North. Most African Americans migrated from urban areas of the South to urban areas of the North and the West.

As African Americans moved into northern and western cities, they competed with white residents for employment, housing, and recreation. In Detroit, scene of one of the nation's worst riots, tensions were reaching a boiling point in late spring of 1943. Relations were especially tense between African Americans and the city's police force. Violence erupted on June 20 at the segregated city beaches and an amusement park on Belle Isle in the Detroit River. Fighting between black and white bathers spread to the city, where white men attacked black men and women trying to get home and invaded black neighborhoods. It took federal troops to stop the riot that had more the characteristics of a pogrom or massacre of African Americans, who did fight back. Twenty-five African Americans and nine whites lost their lives in the violence, in which some seven hundred people were injured, with property damage of more than two million dollars. Detroit police killed seventeen of the African Americans who lost their lives—but none of the white men who attacked African Americans and burned their property.

Similar riots took place in Harlem and Los Angeles. In Harlem, violence broke out on August 1 after rumor spread that a white patrolman had shot and killed a black soldier in uniform trying to protect his mother. The rumor had all of the elements to incite a mob. Unlike Detroit, there was not as much interpersonal violence as black Harlemites took out their vengeance on property, not persons. Some 1,450 stores suffered damages and losses, as high as five million dollars, most of it due to looting. In Los Angeles, the "zoot suit" riots took place when white sailors and civilians attacked African American and Latino men who affected a style of dress with bright colors, pegged-leg pants, broad-shouldered and long tapered suit jackets, and wide brim hats that defied the rationing of cloth for the war. These disturbances had a common thread of police brutality that would resurface in riots in the following decades.

## *THE RACE PROBLEM*

An important publication appeared during World War II that together with rejection of the Nazi idea of a master race would begin to change the way in which the United States viewed its "race problem." Gunnar Myrdal's *An American Dilemma: The Negro Problem and Modern Democracy* was published in 1944 and became one of the most influential works of social science ever printed in the United States. The Carnegie Corporation (a foundation) commissioned Myrdal in 1937 to undertake the study. Myrdal, a Swedish political economist, identified a dilemma between the American creed of freedom, justice, and equality and the oppression of African Americans. He warned the country that it could not maintain its international position as the defender of liberty abroad while it practiced racial discrimination at home. Myrdal's study, which was assisted by a number of black scholars, most notably Ralph J. Bunche, the political scientist and Nobel Peace Prize recipient in 1950, helped to make the "race problem" a national issue for the first time. With the massive migration of African Americans to the North and West during World War II, the "race problem" was no longer just a regional or Southern matter. Moreover, Myrdal analyzed the issue as one of white Americans' not living up to the American creed rather than alleged inferiority or innate deficiencies on the part of African Americans, which was the justification for racial segregation in the past. The civil rights movement of the late 1950s and early 1960s would base its strategy of appeal to conscience through nonviolent direct action in large part on Myrdal's premise of the "American Dilemma."[5]

## *GROWTH OF THE NAACP AND CORE*

Historian Richard Dalfiume, in a 1968 essay, referred to the World War II period as the forgotten years of the "Negro Revolution."[6] It was during this period that African Americans laid the base or foundation for the activist phase of the civil rights movement. Historians have started to give this period more scholarly attention. The NAACP, for example, increased its membership from 50,000 members and 35 branches in 1940 to 450,000 members and 1,073 branches by 1946. Most of this phenomenal growth took place in the South and was the result of the indefatigable efforts of Ella Baker, who from 1943 to 1946 served as NAACP director of branches. A coalition of northern whites and African Americans formed the Congress of Racial Equality (CORE) in 1942 to challenge racial segregation, especially in public accommodations in the North. Southern white liberals and African Americans organized the Southern Regional Council in 1944 to research and report on racial inequality. In a series of judicial decisions pressed by the NAACP, the Supreme Court declared in *Smith v. Allwright* (1944) that the "white primary," which had excluded African Americans from voting, was unconstitutional; *Morgan v. Virginia* (1946) ruled against segregation in interstate commerce; and *Shelley v. Kraemer* (1948) outlawed restrictive covenants that blocked African Americans and Jews in particular from owning or occupying property. Moreover, African Americans registered to vote in unprecedented numbers to influence the political system. The number of African Americans registered to vote skyrocketed from 150,000 in 1940 to more than a million by 1952. And black veterans returned from World War II resolute in their determination to gain full rights as American citizens.

## *THE UNITED NATIONS*

African Americans took heart in the formation of the United Nations in 1945 and carefully watched the development of its charter with two goals in mind, racial equality at home and self-determination for colonized peoples abroad. Walter White, NAACP Executive Secretary, explained that "the struggle of the Negro in the United States is part and parcel of the struggle against imperialism and exploitation in India, China, Burma, Africa, the Philippines, Malaysia, the West Indies, and South America."[7] The NAACP, represented by Walter White, W. E. B. Du Bois, and Mary McLeod Bethune, was selected as one of forty-two organizations to consult with the eight member American delegation to the United Nations Conference on International Organization that met in San Francisco in late April 1945 to draft the United Nations charter. They lobbied the American delegation for a strong racial-equality plank in the charter and an end to colonialism. Although they did not receive everything that they desired in the United Nations Charter, especially immediate steps toward decolonization, they did secure references to freedom from discrimination based on race, language, religion, or sex. The United Nations Charter would become one more weapon in the arsenal against racial inequality that was strengthened in 1948 by the General Assembly's adoption of the Genocide Convention against acts intended to destroy in whole or part a national, ethnic, racial, or religious group and the Universal Declaration of Human Rights.

## THE COLD WAR

The twin struggles for racial equality and decolonization, however, were unlinked by the Cold War. The United States and the Soviet Union sought primacy in world affairs for their respective systems of capitalism and communism. They competed for adherence to their economic and political systems by the emerging nations of Asia and Africa. In the United States, support for the Soviet Union and in large measure for the self-determination of colonized nations brought charges of disloyalty. Paul Robeson, Du Bois, and William L. Patterson all lost their passports (which they regained after protracted legal wrangling that lasted as long as eight years) primarily because of their political positions that became unpopular with the American government during the late 1940s and early 1950s. Robeson was a Phi Beta Kappa graduate of Rutgers University, where he became an All-American football player. He graduated from Columbia University Law School but was not hired by any of the major law firms. He became a concert performer and actor on stage and in film. Robeson was a champion of the working class throughout the world and a strong advocate of racial equality and decolonization. At the World Congress of the Defenders of Peace in Paris in 1949, he stated, "It is unthinkable that American Negroes would go to war on behalf of those (the United States) who have oppressed us for generations against a country (the Soviet Union) which in one generation has raised our people to full human dignity of mankind."[8] Because he refused to declare publicly that he was not a member of the Communist Party, the U.S. State Department revoked his passport in 1950. He was blacklisted, and his career was ruined, with concert dates cancelled, recordings removed from stores, and his name eliminated from the college All-American football lists for 1917 and 1918 (the only years for which a ten-member team was listed).

Du Bois, a founder of the NAACP in 1909, was known as the Father of Pan-Africanism for his support of African liberation, especially through the Pan-African Congresses that he organized. The Fifth Pan-African Congress met in Manchester, England, in 1945 and was attended by many Africans who would become prominent in liberation movements. Du Bois connected the freedom of Africa with the freedom of Africa's descendants throughout the world, particularly African Americans. He lost his passport in 1951 for allegedly failing to register as an agent of a foreign government for his role as chairman of the Peace Information Center. While Robeson served as chair, Du Bois was co-chair of the Council on African Affairs, which lobbied for African independence. Many of its members were communists or communist sympathizers. The U.S. Attorney General in 1947 placed the group on the subversive organizations list.[9]

A graduate of the Hastings College of Law in San Francisco, William L. Patterson joined the Communist Party in 1927 to eradicate the capitalist system and economic exploitation that he concluded was the cause of black oppression. He served from 1932 to 1946 as executive director of the International Labor Defense, the legal action arm of the Communist Party, which challenged the NAACP as defender of African American rights. Patterson later headed the Civil Rights Congress, which defended radical political activists and African Americans in court. His passport was revoked in 1950 for refusing to answer questions before the House Un-American Activities Committee.[10] A year later, Patterson and Robeson presented the United Nations with a petition entitled "We Charge Genocide: The Crime of Government Against the Negro People." The National Negro Congress in 1946 had issued a "Petition to the United Nations on Behalf of 13 Million Oppressed Negro Citizens of the United States of America," that was formally presented by Paul Robeson, and the NAACP in 1947 registered "An Appeal to the World: A Statement on the Denial of Human Rights to Minorities in the Case of Citizens of Negro Descent in the United States and an Appeal to the United Nations for Redress," a document drafted by Du Bois.

Du Bois, Patterson, and Robeson came under close government scrutiny and persecution because of their leftist ideas and activities, efforts to internationalize the struggle for racial equality, and strong support of decolonization. Given the example that the government made of Du Bois, Patterson, and Robeson among others, African Americans, in the main, eschewed left-wing politics and international causes for attention to domestic matters. Although still inspired by the United Nations and interested in African independence, they placed less attention on human rights appeals under international law for racial equality and more emphasis on the American Constitution as a means of securing their rights. They tried to avoid any hint of disloyalty to the country that their adversaries might use to discredit the civil rights movement. As his biographer, Juan Williams reveals, Thurgood Marshall, while head of the NAACP's Legal Defense and Educational Fund, tried to make sure that the FBI realized that neither he nor the NAACP had any connection to the communists. Marshall, who later became the first African American Supreme Court justice, secretly supplied the FBI with information about suspected "subversives" within the NAACP. According to Williams, "Marshall's secret ties to the FBI and the information he gave the bureau were justified by the arc of the African-American struggle, dating back to antislavery efforts, to end government-sanctioned racism in America. But once he had made his pact with (J. Edgar) Hoover (head of the FBI) and set himself apart from the likes of Malcolm X, not to mention much of the NAACP, Marshall had all but ended his time as the much-honored legal leader of the movement."[11] It was probably a tortured decision for Marshall. Williams concludes, "In his heart Marshall wanted to protect mainstream civil rights groups from becoming easy targets for attacks that could set back the fight to defeat segregation and win equal rights for all."

## THE AMERICAN COUNCIL ON HUMAN RIGHTS

When six of the eight black fraternities and sororities joined together in 1948 to form the American Council on Human Rights (ACHR), prospective members asked two major questions. They wanted to know if the organization duplicated the work of existing civil rights organizations, particularly the NAACP, and whether the ACHR was on the attorney general's subversive group list. The ACHR played an important role in supporting the development of the civil rights struggle. It represented a constituency of about one hundred thousand college students and college graduates, including a large portion of educators, one of the few professional arenas open to college educated African Americans. They were among the most restive members of the black population, who wanted to do something meaningful for themselves and their fellow citizens to gain full citizenship. The ACHR concentrated its work primarily on the U.S. Congress and the federal government to pass legislation and to develop administrative policies to achieve equal justice and opportunity for all Americans. By 1952, the organization had twenty-six local councils in eighteen states and the District of Columbia. They organized letter writing campaigns, lobbied members of Congress, and provided political education for African Americans. The ACHR sought legislation to protect the right to vote, ban segregation in interstate travel, make lynching a federal crime, abolish the poll tax, and eliminate racial discrimination and segregation in the nation's capital. Through a series of ready reference guides, the ACHR informed African Americans about the political process and how they could become more engaged in it. The organization, which became mainly a consortium of black sororities after the fraternities pulled out by 1957, developed a preparation for integrated living project. The project was created to make black youth aware of the responsibilities that came with full citizenship. ACHR members were principally middle-class African Americans who believed that they should set standards of respectability for all black Americans, especially in interactions with the broader society after the fall of segregation. They held a series of workshops from 1956 to 1960 for black college students on equal opportunity in voting, employment, housing, and education. The workshops also sought to develop leadership skills. Before its demise in 1963, the ACHR assisted black college students who encountered financial problems because of participation in peaceful protest demonstrations against segregation.

## PRESIDENT TRUMAN'S COMMITTEE ON CIVIL RIGHTS

To bolster America's image abroad, allay black concerns about growing racial violence after World War II, and enhance his chances for reelection, President

Harry S. Truman appointed the Committee on Civil Rights on December 5, 1946. Brutal racial violence in the South had shocked and outraged both African Americans and liberal whites and sullied the nation's reputation, especially among the emerging nations who were being courted by the American and Soviet blocs. In Batesburgh, South Carolina, on February 13, 1946, a recently discharged black war veteran, still in uniform, was blinded in an attack by the chief of police after an alleged argument with a white bus driver. The Ku Klux Klan terrorized African Americans in Columbia, Tennessee, for two days the same month. And a white mob in Monroe, Georgia, on July 25, 1946, murdered two black couples. The Committee on Civil Rights found that African Americans were subjected to lynching, police brutality, unequal justice in the courts, and persistent instances of peonage in which they were forced to work. They were denied the right to vote through terror and intimidation, literacy tests, and poll taxes. They faced racial discrimination in the military, employment, education, housing, health care, and public services and accommodations. The committee's most severe criticism was leveled at racial segregation in the nation's capital, where foreign dignitaries were often humiliated when mistaken for African Americans.

For moral, economic, and international reasons, the Committee on Civil Rights in its report "To Secure These Rights," issued on October 29, 1947, urged the federal government to take immediate steps to protect the civil rights of all citizens. The report called for strengthening the Civil Rights Section of the Justice Department and for elevating it to a full division; establishing a permanent Commission on Civil Rights; enacting an antilynching law; eliminating the poll tax; ending segregation in education, housing, health care, the military and public services, and creating a federal fair employment practices act. The report also encouraged a continuous campaign of public education through the Commission on Civil Rights about the need to end racial discrimination. "To Secure These Rights" recognized the major areas of racial inequality, reinforced the grievances of African Americans, and suggested specific remedies, but it would take at least two decades of struggle before the executive, legislative, and judicial branches of government would implement most of its recommendations.

## *DESEGREGATION OF THE MILITARY*

Within his own Democratic Party, President Truman was flanked on the left by former Vice President Henry A. Wallace's Progressive Party and on the right by South Carolina Governor Strom Thurmond's Dixiecrats in his reelection battle against the Republican Thomas E. Dewey. Civil rights had become an important issue in American politics, as President Truman in June 1947 was the first president to address the national convention of the NAACP. The black vote, especially in the North and the Southern border states, was pivotal to Truman's winning the 1948 election. Prior to the election, President Truman had faced the prospect of massive civil disobedience by African Americans after he reinstated the draft in March 1948 in response to the Soviet Union's gaining control of Czechoslovakia. A. Philip Randolph once more threatened huge demonstrations throughout the country and advised black men to face imprisonment rather than serve in a segregated military. On July 26, Truman issued Executive Order 9981 to desegregate the armed forces. The order was not fully implemented until the Korean War (1950–53), when the last all-black military units were dissolved. The fall of Jim Crow in the military, the National Football League in 1946, major league baseball in 1947, and the National Basketball Association in 1950 set the stage for desegregation in other areas of American life. Gunnar Myrdal in *An American Dilemma* had forecast a favorable resolution of the race problem in America because African Americans' rank order of discrimination was parallel but inverse to that of white Americans. Whites were foremost concerned about interracial marriage and sex; social interactions in dining, recreation, and amusements; integration in schools, churches, and transportation; political enfranchisement; equal justice by the courts and the police; discrimination in employment, purchasing land, acquiring credit, and securing public assistance. African Americans' priorities were the reverse: they were interested principally in employment, equal justice, education, and the right to vote. Social interaction and intermarriage ranked low on their scale of interests. Resistance to desegregation would closely follow white America's order of priorities.

## *THE LEGAL CHALLENGE TO SEGREGATION*

The NAACP continued to pursue its attack on Jim Crow through the courts, where it enjoyed some success in chipping away at the doctrine of "separate but equal." In a series of Supreme Court cases, the NAACP challenged segregation in graduate and professional education. In 1948, the University of Oklahoma Law School denied admission to Ada Lois Sipuel because of her race. In *Sipuel v. Oklahoma State Board of Regents,* the Supreme Court ruled that the state had violated Sipuel's right to equal protection under the Fourteenth Amendment. Many southern states paid tuition for black students to attend graduate and professional schools out of state to avoid the expense of creating separate facilities. The NAACP's challenge to this practice led to some states quickly setting up black law schools or separate facilities for black students at white law schools. Three important Supreme Court decisions in 1950 shook the edifice of racial segregation. In *Henderson v. U.S. Interstate Commerce Commission and Southern Railway,* the Court decided that the Southern Railway's practice of separating the races in its dining cars violated the nondiscrimination clause of the Interstate Commerce Commission. Elmer W. Henderson, a field representative for the Fair Employment Practices Committee, initiated his case in 1942, when he traveled from Washington, D.C., to Birmingham, Alabama. En route, he went to the dining car for a meal. Southern Railway's policy was to seat black diners at two tables nearest the kitchen and to draw a curtain to separate them from white diners. When Henderson entered the diner, whites occupied the designated tables and the curtain was open. Although there was a seat available, he was not seated next to the white patrons. Because whites continued to occupy some of the seats, Henderson was never seated before the dining car was taken out of service at 9:00 p.m. He contested this blatant racial discrimination through the Interstate Commerce Commission and the federal district court in Baltimore before the case reached the Supreme Court.

In *Sweatt v. Painter,* the University of Texas at Austin Law School placed Herman Sweatt in a separate basement facility with a small library and instructors who would teach him alone. The Supreme Court ruled that the arrangement did not afford him equal protection and deprived him of an education equal to that offered to other students in the law school with its strong faculty, fellow law students, extensive library, and reputation. In a similar case, G. W. McLaurin successfully gained admission to the University of Oklahoma's graduate school of education. He was separated from white students in the classroom, library, and cafeteria. The Supreme Court, on grounds akin to those in the Sweatt case, deemed the segregation practices unconstitutional. After these path-breaking cases in higher education, black parents in Delaware, the District of Columbia, Kansas, South Carolina, and Virginia filed suits against the doctrine of "separate but equal" in elementary and secondary education.

## *BROWN V. BOARD OF EDUCATION*

The initial challenge was to inequitable allocation of resources, whereby bus transportation was not provided for black children in Clarendon County, South Carolina, but was available for white children. In Farmville, Virginia, black students protested inadequate facilities at their high school, which had no gymnasium or cafeteria, was overcrowded, and had drafty classrooms in which students often had to wear coats. Moreover, unlike the better-equipped white high school, there were no late afternoon buses for students who wanted to play sports or to participate in extracurricular activities. Hockessin, Delaware, a small rural town west of Wilmington, provided school buses for white students, but not for black students, who attended a one-room school. Sarah Bulah, a black parent, resented having to drive her daughter to school each day while a school bus route ran right past her house. In Topeka, Kansas, the city provided bus transportation to black children but not to white youngsters, who generally attended neighborhood schools. Linda Brown had to ride a bus past a white school that was only seven blocks from her home. These four cases started in 1951 and worked their way up to the Supreme Court, where they were combined as *Brown v. Board of Education, Topeka, Kansas.*[12] The NAACP took up these cases under the guidance of Thurgood Marshall as the lead attorney, who believed that this was an opportunity to have the Supreme Court void its 1896 *Plessy v. Ferguson* decision, which had sanctioned the doctrine of "separate but equal."

To strengthen his argument, Marshall used social science evidence, especially the work of black social psychologists Mamie and Kenneth Clark. The argument went beyond less pay for black teachers, greater expenditures for white schools, and inadequate facilities for black schools that in many instances did not have indoor plumbing, let alone science laboratories, libraries, gymnasiums, and auditoriums. The question became not whether separate facilities were equal but how segregation negatively affected black students' self-esteem, instilled in them a sense of inferiority, stunted their educational development, and weakened their motivation for educational achievement. The focus of the cases shifted from the parents' concerns about transportation and equitable facilities to the idea that equal education meant integrated education. Chief Justice Earl Warren, in the unanimous Supreme Court decision of May 17, 1954, supported the NAACP lawyers' argument that separate schools were inherently unequal and that the doctrine of "separate but equal" had no place in public education. Warren stated, "To separate them [black children] from others of similar age and qualifications solely because of their race generates a feeling of inferiority as to the status in the community that may affect their hearts and minds in a way unlikely ever to be undone." The NAACP lawyers' arguments and the Supreme Court ruling seem to suggest that black student achievement was tied directly to school integration.

That assumption has led to great controversy and revisiting of the *Brown* decision. There is general agreement that the case spelled the demise of legally sanctioned segregation in American life. But there is less consensus about the effect of Brown on education. According to historian Raymond Wolters, by the early 1960s, much of the social science research cited in *Brown* had come into question. Educational research by the late 1970s indicated that school integration alone did not increase the academic scores of inner-city black youth and that in some instances the scores actually declined in integrated schools.[13] NAACP General Counsel Robert L. Carter, who organized and presented much of the social science evidence, later questioned the strategy in the *Brown* case. He affirmed his belief in the long-term goal of integration and the positive effect that the decision had on race relations, but he acknowledged the mistaken postulate of their strategy that eliminating enforced segregated education would necessarily result in equal education. Carter, who became a federal district judge in New York, wrote, "If I had to prepare for *Brown* today, instead of looking principally to the social scientists to demonstrate the adverse consequences of segregation, I would seek to recruit educators to formulate a concrete definition of the meaning of equality in education."[14] The *Brown* decision, in many respects, reinforced a "deficit model" of black life that black scholars and activists rebelled against in the 1960s.

## MASSIVE RESISTANCE TO SCHOOL DESEGREGATION

Although the Supreme Court had ruled against school segregation, it did not issue any guidelines for desegregation or set any deadlines. Some states, especially the border states, acted immediately to dismantle their dual school systems. Other states, particularly in the Deep South, dragged their feet or resisted desegregation altogether. Almost a year after the *Brown* decision, the court issued a unanimous decision, in what has become known as *Brown II*, that the district courts were to "enter such orders and decrees consistent with this opinion as are necessary and proper to admit to public schools on a racially nondiscriminatory basis with all deliberate speed the parties to these cases." Although the Supreme Court recommended school desegregation "with all deliberate speed," it would take at least a decade of protracted struggle to bring about more than token desegregation. Many southern states waged a campaign of massive resistance to school desegregation. They tied up the NAACP in costly and time-consuming litigation. The Ku Klux Klan used violence and intimidation, while the White Citizens Councils that were organized in the mid-1950s often employed economic retaliation against African Americans who tried to vote or to send their children to previously all-white schools. White Citizen Council members turned down mortgages, called in loans, denied insurance, and even refused medical care to African Americans who tried to enjoy their rights as American citizens. There were about 250,000 White Citizens Council members in the South by 1957. Nineteen of the twenty-two southern senators and 77 of the 105 representatives signed the "Southern Manifesto" in 1956, accusing the Supreme Court of abusing judicial power and promising to use all lawful means to reverse the Brown decisions and to prevent their implementation. Lyndon Johnson from Texas and Albert Gore and Estes Kefauver of Tennessee were the only southern senators who refused to sign the manifesto.

Many southern states identified the NAACP as their chief adversary and sought to cripple the organization. Alabama in 1956 requested the NAACP's membership lists and fined the group $100,000 for contempt of court when it refused to comply with the order. Virginia passed laws prohibiting the NAACP from soliciting funds for litigation in antidiscrimination cases, barring it from advocating desegregation of public schools, forbidding it from giving financial assistance to anyone involved in lawsuits against the state, and requiring the organization to post its membership lists in public. Georgia accused the NAACP of not paying taxes, even though it was a tax-exempt organization. When the NAACP refused to give Texas its membership lists, the state secured an injunction charging the organization with violating the laws regulating corporations and banning it from operating there. South Carolina legislated that teachers could not belong to the NAACP. These tactics reduced the NAACP's membership in the South from about 130,000 in 1955 to 80,000 by 1957 and caused the loss of some 246 branches. Many branches had to go underground, which reduced their effectiveness as well as their membership. The NAACP successfully fought these restrictions in court, but it was costly and time consuming. The sociologist Aldon D. Morris has suggested that weakening the NAACP contributed to emergence of the activist phase of the civil rights movement. The NAACP was a highly centralized and tightly structured organization that devised strategy at its national headquarters in New York City for implementation at the local level. With its attention focused on survival in the South and with many of its branches underground, the NAACP could not function in its usual manner.[15] Local groups were now free to identify and to address their specific issues with means other than the NAACP's traditional reliance on the courts.

## NOTES

1. Allan Keiler, *Marian Anderson: A Singer's Journey* (New York: Scribner, 2000).

2. Genna Rae McNeil, *Groundwork: Charles Hamilton Houston and the Struggle for Civil Rights* (Philadelphia: University of Pennsylvania Press, 1983).

3. Herbert Garfinkel, *When Negroes March: The March on Washington Movement in the Organizational Politics for FEPC* (New York: Atheneum, 1969).

4. Gerald Astor, *The Right to Fight: A History of African Americans in the Military* (Novato, Calif.: Presidio Press, 1998).

5. Gunnar Myrdal, *An American Dilemma: The Negro Problem and Modern America*, 2 vols. (New York: Harper & Brothers, 1944).

6. Richard M. Dalfiume, "The 'Forgotten Years' of the Negro Revolution," *Journal of American History* 55 (1968): 90–106.

7. Robert L. Harris Jr., "Racial Equality and the United Nations Charter," in *New Directions in Civil Rights Studies*, ed. Armstead L. Robinson and Patricia Sullivan, 126–148 (Charlottesville: University Press of Virginia, 1991).

8. Martin B. Duberman, *Paul Robeson* (New York: Knopf, 1988), 341–350.

9. David Levering Lewis, *W. E. B. Du Bois: The Fight for Equality and the American Century, 1919–1963* (New York: Henry Holt, 2000).

10. William Patterson, *The Man Who Cried Genocide: An Autobiography* (New York: International Publishers, 1971).

11. Juan Williams, *Thurgood Marshall: American Revolutionary* (New York: Times Books, 1998), 283.

12. James T. Patterson, *Brown v. Board of Education: A Civil Rights Milestone and Its Troubled Legacy* (New York: Oxford University Press, 2001).

13. Raymond Wolters, *The Burden of Brown: Thirty Years of School Desegregation* (Knoxville: University of Tennessee Press, 1984).

14. Robert L. Carter, "A Reassessment of Brown v. Board," in *Shades of Brown: New Perspectives on School Desegregation*, ed. Derrick Bell, 21–28 (New York: Teachers College Press, 1980).

15. Aldon D. Morris, *The Origins of the Civil Rights Movement: Black Communities Organizing for Change* (New York: Free Press, 1984).

# THE CIVIL RIGHTS MOVEMENT, 1955–65

Three months before Rosa Parks's refusal to relinquish her seat on a Montgomery, Alabama, bus altered the landscape of the civil rights movement, an event took place in Money, Mississippi, that steeled black determination for change. Emmett Till, a fourteen-year-old black youngster from Chicago, was visiting his uncle for the summer in LeFlore County, Mississippi. Because Till had bragged about having a white girlfriend in the North, defying the conventions of race relations in the South, some of his cousins and friends dared him to ask a young white woman, working in her family's store in the nearby town of Money, for a date. On August 24, the youths traveled to the store where Till went in alone and allegedly squeezed Carolyn Bryant by the hand, grabbed her waist, asked her for a date, and on leaving the store wolf-whistled at her. When Bryant's husband returned from out of town, he and his half-brother abducted Till from his uncle's home on August 28, despite the latter's protestations that "the boy was from up yonder, didn't have good sense" and that he would take care of him. Roy Bryant, especially as a white man in the rural South, felt compelled to protect his honor and to uphold the sanctity of white womanhood. Many black men had been lynched in the South for even the hint of looking lustfully at a white woman, called "reckless eyeballing." In this instance, a black male, despite his youth, had compromised Bryant's wife. They took Till to an abandoned cotton mill, brutally beat him, shot him, tied a cotton gin fan around his neck, and tossed his body into the Tallahatchie River. Till's badly decomposed body surfaced three days later. In an act of immense courage for its time, Till's uncle, Moses Wright, testified against his abductors. An all-white jury acquitted them on grounds that the body was too mangled for a positive identification, although there was a ring on his finger given to Till by his father.

The county sheriff insisted that the casket with Till's body, which was to be transported to Chicago for burial, be sealed. When the casket reached Chicago, Till's mother, Mamie Bradley, insisted that the casket be opened despite the sheriff's order so that she could determine that it was her son's body inside. And later, she wanted the world to see what had happened to her son. The open casket was viewed by thousands in Chicago and millions nationally and internationally as *Jet Magazine* published a picture of Till's brutally battered body on its front cover. Emmett Till's lynching incensed African Americans, although two black men, Rev. George Lee and Lamar Smith, were killed that same year in Mississippi for encouraging African Americans to register and vote. Till's youth, the horrendous manner of his death, and the quick acquittal of his murderers told black America that something had to be done. Amzie Moore, an activist from Cleveland, Mississippi, later remarked that Till's lynching was the beginning of the modern civil rights movement in the state. As Lawrence D. Reddick would write in *Dissent*, at the beginning of the Montgomery bus boycott "the outrage of the Emmett Till murder was alive in everybody's minds."[1]

## THE MONTGOMERY BUS BOYCOTT

December 1, 1955, was not the first time that Rosa Parks, a seamstress at a downtown department store in Montgomery and secretary of the local NAACP branch, had refused to give up her seat on a city bus. But it was the first time that she was arrested and charged specifically with violating the city's transportation ordinances. African Americans, who made up almost three-quarters of the riders on the buses in Montgomery, had long sought better treatment by bus drivers. They were often called derogatory and demeaning names, forced to pay their fares at the front and then get off and board at the rear of the bus, and made to relinquish their seats to white passengers even if the seats across the aisle were empty.

The segregated city bus was the one site of Jim Crow rituals that working-class African Americans in particular found difficult to avoid. They had to take the bus to work, to school, or to shop. Only those African Americans who could afford automobiles could escape the humiliation of segregation on the buses. It was a daily reminder of their "place" in American society as a subordinate group with little control over their lives.

The Women's Political Council (WPC), formed by middle-class black women in 1946, fought for black political rights and for better conditions on the city buses. A year and a half before Parks's action, the WPC threatened a bus boycott if the city did not change its practices by allowing blacks to sit from the rear to the front and whites to sit from the front to the back until all seats were occupied, without blacks having to give up their seats if all the white seats were taken. And they asked simply that African Americans not be forced to reboard the bus after paying their fares. Given the city's refusal to accede to these modest requests, the WPC waited for an opportune moment to challenge the city's bus practices. That spring, a black teenager named Claudette Colvin refused to give up her seat. She cursed the bus driver and the police officers who arrested and charged her with violating the city transportation ordinances. Some WPC members and others thought that Colvin's arrest might be the test case for a bus boycott. They decided not to make her arrest the rallying case when they discovered that she was pregnant and feared that she would be the subject of a legal challenge rather than the real issues of segregation and discourteous treatment.

Rosa Parks's case was perfect. She was a member of the community respected by both blacks and whites. The WPC led by Mary Fair Burks and Jo Ann Gibson Robinson, teachers at historically black Alabama State College in Montgomery, sprang into action and flooded the black community with leaflets asking that black passengers stay off the buses on Monday, December 5. The bus boycott became a topic of conversation in black beauty parlors, barbershops, pool halls, and bars. E. D. Nixon, a member of the Brotherhood of Sleeping Car Porters and former president of the local branch of the NAACP, contacted black ministers about announcing the boycott from their pulpits on Sunday and encouraging their congregations to attend a mass rally that Monday evening. It was Nixon whom Parks called immediately after her arrest, and it was Nixon who arranged for her release on bail with the assistance of Fred D. Gray, a black attorney, and Clifford Durr, a white lawyer, who with his wife Virginia was sympathetic to racial equality. Nixon played a major role in organizing the boycott and in establishing the Montgomery Improvement Association to carry it out. He discussed the boycott with the local NAACP branch president about the prospect that the organization might sponsor the boycott. When he was informed that the local branch would have to check first with headquarters in New York, Nixon decided that the moment would be lost by the time that the NAACP bureaucracy swung into action. After Roy Wilkins, the executive director, received a report on the boycott from one of his field secretaries, he responded that the NAACP could not support such a mild protest that seemed geared more to improving segregation and making it more polite with its demand for first come first served seating with whites from the front to the rear and blacks from the rear to the front.

The Sunday morning edition of the *Montgomery Advertiser*, the city's major newspaper, carried a front-page story on the planned boycott and the mass rally. Now the white community became aware of the boycott. Many white housewives, who feared that their black housekeepers would not be able to get to work on Monday, called and offered them rides. Their concern about having their houses cleaned, clothes washed and ironed, diapers changed, and meals prepared contributed to the success of the boycott, in which almost 95 percent of African Americans stayed off the buses, took cabs, carpooled, walked, and in some instances rode mules. At an afternoon meeting of local leaders to assess the boycott and to plan for the mass rally that evening, the group selected Martin Luther King Jr. to serve as president of the Montgomery Improvement Association (MIA). King had been in Montgomery for only fifteen months as pastor of Dexter Avenue Baptist Church, which served the black middle class, many of whom taught or worked at Alabama State College. He was only twenty-six years old, had become a father just a month before, and had recently completed his doctoral degree in theology at Boston University. He had every reason to decline the position. Yet he was prevailed upon because he was new in town, had not made any enemies, and could bring the community together. Moreover, he was the son of a prominent black Baptist minister in Atlanta and could always return home should the boycott fail.

At the mass rally that evening, King rose to oratorical heights, as would be his wont on many important occasions during the course of the civil rights movement. He brilliantly combined black church culture and American principles of freedom, justice, and equality to describe the bus boycott. He reassured the overflow crowd that they deserved their rights as children of God and as citizens of the United States. These would be twin themes of King's rationale for the movement as well as the methodology of nonviolence. Moreover, the black church, as the only institution controlled by African Americans, became a critical base for the movement. Although black colleges provided many of the foot soldiers for the movement through participation of their students, they were subject to outside pressure, especially the public colleges that depended on allocations from state legislatures for their survival. Even the private colleges were vulnerable, but black students often ignored the warnings of some college presidents who were prompted by white interests to restrain their students, faculty, and staff from participating in demonstrations. Some faculty even lost their jobs for involvement in civil rights activity.

Although the MIA's demands were modest, the bus company absolutely refused to make any adjustments. The city commissioners tried to break the boycott through intimidation and litigation. Primarily through the use of carpools, the MIA was able to sustain the boycott. It also raised funds locally and nationally to purchase gas and tires and to provide maintenance for the privately owned vehicles and black-owned taxicabs that supplied transportation. The MIA modeled its carpool strategy after the successful bus boycott in Baton Rouge, Louisiana, in 1953, which lasted only a week and that resulted in a stable rather than a floating designation of where blacks and whites had to sit on the buses. The Montgomery bus boycott would last almost a year and was maintained through weekly mass meetings that rotated among the black churches, the inspirational leadership of King, and the resolve of African Americans, young and old, middle class and poor, religious or not, to succeed in this attack on racial segregation. That resolve was tested when almost two months into the boycott, someone threw a stick of dynamite on the porch of King's home and later planted a bomb on Nixon's front lawn. King rushed home from one of the mass meetings to find hundreds of angry African Americans assembled around his house, some of them with weapons. After comforting his family, King counseled the crowd to remain nonviolent and to love their enemies. This was the beginning of his journey to Gandhi's technique of nonviolent resistance that remained rooted in Christian philosophy of redemption.

After the bombing of King's home, the MIA decided to file a lawsuit in federal court against segregation on the buses in Montgomery. This was a major step from its earlier request for a milder form of segregation. On June 5, 1956, in the case known as *Browder v. Gayle,* the federal court ruled that racial segregation on the buses violated the equal protection clause of the Fourteenth Amendment. The city appealed to the Supreme Court, which on November 13 affirmed the local federal court ruling. The city asked for a rehearing of the decision, and the Supreme Court on December 20 gave its final order that bus segregation was unconstitutional. The decision was met with resistance as several black churches and homes were bombed. Members of the Ku Klux Klan drove through the city's black neighborhoods in a forty-car caravan, but African Americans did not run in fear and hide in their homes. Instead, they bravely watched as the Klan drove by and even waved to their would-be tormentors. The back of Jim Crow was broken in Montgomery and over the next decade would crack throughout the South.

## BLACK CLASS SOLIDARITY FOR SOCIAL CHANGE

Sociologist William J. Wilson has argued that "it did not take long to realize that the group that had profited the most from the civil rights legislation up to 1965 was middle-class blacks."[2] Although Wilson was foremost concerned about lingering racial inequality, many critics have characterized the civil rights movement as a middle-class movement. The Montgomery bus boycott, however, depended for its success on solidarity among African Americans across class lines. It was basically members of the middle class who volunteered their cars during the early stages of the boycott until the carpools could be organized with some forty-eight dispatch and pickup stations. Later, the MIA purchased a fleet of station wagons with contributions from across the country, assigned ownership to different black churches, hired drivers, and set regular routes. Although these carpools became a substitute for the buses, they were still inconvenient. But poor African Americans who had to depend on them for transportation supported the boycott as much as the middle class, which owned cars. In fact, it was poor and working-class African Americans who benefited from desegregation of the buses, on which they were no longer humiliated. Much depends on how the civil rights movement is analyzed and evaluated, on different goals and objectives, and the reasons why so many Americans, black and white, participated in what has been sometimes called the Second American Revolution because it changed the country almost as much as its independence from Great Britain.

## THE SOUTHERN CHRISTIAN LEADERSHIP CONFERENCE

During the Montgomery bus boycott, young black ministers in cities such as Atlanta, Birmingham, New Orleans, and Tallahassee initiated similar protests. Ella Baker, Stanley Levison, and Bayard Rustin prompted Martin Luther King Jr. to form a regional organization in the South to advance the Montgomery strategy. Baker was a veteran of the civil rights movement and had served with both the NAACP and the New York Urban League. Levison, a white New York attorney, businessman, and former Communist Party member, became one of King's closest advisers and confidants. Rustin, a member of the Young Communist League as a youth, a founder of the Congress of Racial Equality, and a homosexual, worked as race relations secretary for the Fellowship of Reconciliation, a Christian pacifist organization devoted to nonviolent social change through civil disobedience. Baker, Levison, and Rustin had rallied northern support and raised funds for the Montgomery bus boycott. Rustin was a brilliant strategist who advised King for a while in Montgomery but who ran afoul of the homophobia of many black ministers and had to leave. He continued to advise King and was an architect of the Crusade for Citizenship in 1957 and the March on Washington in 1963. Because of his past ties to the Communist Party, Levison came under scrutiny by the FBI, especially as its director, J. Edgar Hoover, later tried to discredit King, whom he labeled as "the most dangerous man in America."

Black leaders from across the South came together in 1957 to form the "Southern Negro Leaders Conference on Transportation and Nonviolent Integration," which eventually became known as the Southern Christian Leadership Conference (SCLC). To avoid competition with the NAACP, SCLC became a coalition of affiliated local organizations rather than a membership group. It focused initially on bus desegregation and the right to vote. Ella Baker helped to organize SCLC's office in Atlanta and served for two years as acting executive director. She resigned the position because the black ministers, who dominated the organization, found it difficult to follow the directions of a black woman.

SCLC's first major campaign was the Crusade for Citizenship. In 1957, Congress enacted the first civil rights legislation since Reconstruction. While the legislation was before Congress, some 27,000 civil rights advocates gathered before the Lincoln Memorial in a "Prayer Pilgrimage for Freedom" on May 17, 1957. As he would do six years later at the same site but before a much larger audience, King reached oratorical ecstasy with the refrain: "Give us the ballot and we will no longer have to worry the Federal Government about our basic rights. Give us the ballot." The Civil Rights Act passed Congress, despite a southern filibuster in the Senate. It empowered the federal government through the Justice Department to bring lawsuits against the denial of voting rights. As President Truman's Committee on Civil Rights had recommended a decade earlier, the law established a Commission on Civil Rights to monitor voting violations and to propose remedies and elevated the Civil Rights Section of the Justice Department to full division status. SCLC's Crusade for Citizenship assumed that the ballot was crucial to school desegregation, employment opportunity, decent housing, and equal access to public accommodations and transportation. Its goal was to double the number of African Americans registered to vote in the South. Southern white racists thwarted that goal through delaying tactics, economic reprisals, gerrymandering, and other devices. It would take more years of struggle, several additional civil rights bills, and a constitutional amendment to achieve the right to vote for most African Americans in the South.

## TWO SIDES OF THE SAME COIN: COLONIALISM IN AFRICA AND SEGREGATION IN THE UNITED STATES

Two months before the Prayer Pilgrimage for Freedom, King, his wife Coretta Scott King, Rep. Adam Clayton Powell Jr., and A. Philip Randolph, among others, had flown to Ghana at the invitation of Kwame Nkrumah, the country's first president, to attend the nation's independence ceremonies on March 5. Because his passport was still under revocation, the father of pan-Africanism,

W. E. B. Du Bois, was not able to be present at the celebration for the first independent African nation in modern times. The Kings also visited Nigeria and Europe, where, in London, they had lunch with C. L. R. James, a Trinidad-born pan-Africanist, socialist, and author of the acclaimed study of the Haitian Revolution, *Black Jacobins*. This was King's first trip outside the United States, and it had a profound effect on him. He recognized that both colonialism and racial segregation were based on white supremacy. Moreover, he noted, "The oppressor never voluntarily gives freedom to the oppressed. . . . Freedom comes only through persistent revolt, through persistent agitation, through persistently rising up against the system of evil." Although King clearly saw the connection between systems of oppression, he would devote himself to the struggle in the United States until he began speaking out against the Vietnam War by 1965, which brought him great opprobrium by putative friends and long-standing enemies.[3]

## LITTLE ROCK, THE MEDIA, AND DRAMATIZATION OF THE STRUGGLE

Desegregation came very slowly as African Americans had to struggle almost every step of the way. When school opened in 1957, the governor of Arkansas, Orville Faubus, stationed soldiers from the National Guard outside Central High School in Little Rock to prevent nine black students from entering. President Dwight D. Eisenhower was lukewarm to civil rights, but he could not tolerate Faubus's open defiance of the Supreme Court decision against school segregation. Eisenhower persuaded Faubus to remove the National Guard, but this left only the local police to protect the black students against a jeering mob of white opponents to desegregation. Daisy Bates, the courageous publisher with her husband of the black newsweekly *Arkansas State Press* and state president of the NAACP, transported the nine black students to school for their first day of classes.

To forestall violence and to mend America's damaged image abroad as the international press carried pictures of the Arkansas National Guard blocking entry of the black students, Eisenhower put the National Guard under federal authority and sent in over a thousand riot-trained troops from the 101st Airborne Division. One of the major grievances of southern states during Reconstruction was the imposition of federal troops on the South to protect the rights of African Americans. Southern historians, in particular, blamed disruption in the South on the presence of federal troops and the federal government's attempt to force black political participation. Eisenhower dreaded sending in federal troops, but he had to gain control of an ugly situation that was featured on the evening television news and in newspapers around the globe. Television was a new medium, and, as historian Vincent Harding has suggested, "the black struggle for freedom in the South was its first major ongoing story."[4]

## ROBERT F. WILLIAMS AND THE RISE OF BLACK NATIONALISM

Television helped to dramatize the civil rights movement and to make the contradiction between democracy and racial oppression visible for the nation. Although the "race problem" was national in scope, attention was focused on the South, and it appeared that it was there that change needed to occur. Few accentuated the need for fundamental change more than Robert F. Williams of Monroe, North Carolina. He was a World War II veteran who also served in the Marines during the mid-1950s. After he was not able to secure employment in his hometown or several other cities across the country, Williams finally got a job near Monroe through the intervention of a white friend, Ray Shute, the former mayor of the town. Because of his outspoken opposition to racial oppression and segregation and publication of a few articles in communist and socialist publications, the FBI considered Williams to be a subversive and a communist. In several instances, the FBI influenced prospective employers against hiring Williams. In Monroe, he became active in the Unitarian Fellowship, helped to start the Union County Council on Human Relations, an interdenominational and interracial group, and revived a moribund NAACP branch of which he became president.

The interracial coalition fell apart when African Americans sought to desegregate a local swimming pool that had been built with federal funds. Several black youngsters had drowned in nearby rivers and lakes because of inadequate recreational facilities. Williams and members of the NAACP branch pressed for a separate swimming pool or two days a week for black children to use the existing pool. Because of their efforts to desegregate the swimming pool, the Ku Klux Klan tried to force the NAACP out of Monroe by driving through black neighborhoods throwing rocks and bottles and shooting firearms into the air. Williams and other African Americans appealed to the governor, the president, and the city council to stop Klan intimidation. He and other black activists became the subject of death threats. To protect himself, Williams began openly wearing a gun, which was legal at the time. After the Klan threatened to blow up the house of the local black physician, Dr. Albert E. Perry, who they believed financed the NAACP branch, Williams and about sixty other black men decided to defend Perry's house. Mostly World War II veterans, they organized themselves and even built a rifle range for practice. When a Klan motorcade drove by Perry's home and fired shots into it, Williams and his men fired back from fortifications on the property. The Klan quickly retreated and did not return. The rout of the Klan reinforced Williams's belief that African Americans had to stand up for their rights and to defend themselves through the use of violence if necessary.

Williams received national attention when he sought release from juvenile detention of two African American boys, aged eight and ten, who had been given indeterminate sentences by a judge for assaulting and molesting three white girls in what became know as the "kissing case." The black youngsters had joined a group of white kids who were playing. The girls kissed the boys, and one of them kissed one of the black children on the cheek. When the girl's mother heard about this incident, she became furious and called the police, who arrested the black youngsters and brutally beat them in the basement of the jail. The boys' mothers were fired from their jobs as housekeepers, and one was served with an eviction notice from her home. This case went to the heart of southern opposition to desegregation and fear of white women having sex with black men, although white men could sexually compromise black women with impunity. Gunnar Myrdal had identified interracial marriage and sex as the issue that most concerned southern whites in his rank order of discrimination. Sexual taboos in the South had as much to do with the subordination of white women as with the oppression of African Americans. White male supremacy rested as much on sexual as it did on racial grounds.

The NAACP at both the state and national levels initially refused to become involved in this case because of its highly charged sexual connotations and white racist efforts to characterize the civil rights movement as harboring the ultimate objective of black men having sex with white women. Williams and his allies organized the Committee to Combat Racial Injustice to pursue the case. The Socialist Workers Party (SWP) became interested in the case, sent a lawyer to assist with it, and helped Williams to gain national and international publicity against the boys' detention. Protest committees sprang up in several European countries, and petitions flooded the U.S. government. As the case became a cause célèbre, the NAACP took an interest and helped to resolve matters by paying to relocate the boys' families to a new community. Given pressure to free the boys, the North Carolina commissioner of corrections, on February 13, 1959, released them from the correctional facility on the pretext that their home situation had improved and warranted their conditional release.

Williams would again be in the news and in contention with the NAACP when he made a strong statement about the use of violence after two white men were acquitted in Monroe in May 1959 on charges of assaulting black women. Although many black people in Monroe wanted immediate revenge after the assaults, Williams had counseled them to let the legal process take its course.

After the acquittals, black women in the court loudly protested and accused Williams of not protecting them. They exclaimed that the men would have been punished if not for Williams. Ashamed of what had happened and with the haunting memory of Mack Charles Parker's lynching in Mississippi only a month earlier, Williams told the press that black people could not rely on the law and that it was necessary to stop lynching with lynching. When Roy Wilkins heard the statement, he called Williams, who was unrepentant, about the danger such a statement posed for the NAACP that was trying to secure legislation against lynching. Wilkins suspended Williams as branch president. Williams later clarified his statement by announcing that he did not advocate lynching but self-defense. With his new celebrity, Williams sought to reach a larger audience through speeches, publications, and broadcasts. He anticipated many of the tenets of the Black Power movement in the mid-1960s through his focus on economic empowerment, race pride, political self-determination, and self-defense. Many of these elements of black nationalism had their origins in the early nineteenth century and have been a consistent theme in African American history. Williams began publishing the *Crusader Weekly Newsletter* in July 1959, with feature articles on black history, politics, and culture as well as the nexus in the struggle for black liberation between the United States and Africa.

After being charged with kidnapping for shielding a white couple during tense demonstrations in Monroe, Williams fled to Cuba in August 1961. He had worked with the Fair Play for Cuba Committee, had visited Cuba, and had met the nation's president when Fidel Castro came to the United States in 1960 to address the United Nations General Assembly and elated African Americans by moving into the Hotel Theresa in Harlem. Williams started Radio Free Dixie in Cuba and broadcast with a signal that reached as far north as Canada. The program promoted African American music, especially politically conscious jazz and rhythm and blues, and provided news coverage of the black freedom struggle and Williams's commentary against white supremacy. In 1962, he published a book, *Negroes with Guns*, that called for black self-determination and self-defense and became one of the most influential books among black radicals, along with Frantz Fanon's *Wretched of the Earth* (published in French in 1961 and translated into English by 1963) and *The Autobiography of Malcolm X*, which appeared in 1965. In 1963, followers of Williams organized the Revolutionary Action Movement, a Marxist-Leninist group that advocated the need for fundamental change in American society and violence as the means to secure such change. They named Williams as president-in-exile, a title that he also held for the Republic of New Africa, formed in 1968. The Republic of New Africa demanded that five southern states be ceded for an independent black country, as well as $200 billion in reparations for the enslavement and oppression of African Americans. Black veterans of World War II and the Korean War in

1964 founded the Deacons for Defense and Justice in Jonesboro, Louisiana. They later moved their headquarters to Bogalusa, Louisiana. The Deacons for Defense and Justice declared that African Americans had to defend themselves because local law enforcement and the federal government had failed to protect them, especially against Klan violence. They started branches in Alabama, Florida, Mississippi, North Carolina, and South Carolina and claimed fifty chapters across the South by 1965. They primarily protected civil rights workers. Williams returned from exile in 1969 after having spent several years in China in addition to Cuba. The country had undergone tremendous change during his eight years of exile. After his homecoming, he resigned from the Revolutionary Action Movement, which had basically become defunct from FBI infiltration and criminal convictions for alleged conspiracies against the government, and from the Republic of New Africa. According to his biographer, Timothy Tyson, Williams considered himself misunderstood by the militants who did not appreciate that he always thought of himself as an American patriot who believed in the Constitution and fervently thought that the country should live up to it. Williams quietly spent the rest of his life in Michigan, where he died in 1996.[5]

## THE SIT-INS

Before Williams left the country, a new generation had come to the fore of the civil rights struggle with renewed vigor in direct action against racial segregation. On February 1, 1960, four black freshmen from the historically black college, North Carolina A&T in Greensboro, staged a sit-in at the lunch counter of the local Woolworth's department store. African Americans could purchase items in the store and could even take food out, but they could not dine in the store. The four male students, who were neatly dressed, remained in their seats after being refused service until the store closed. Classmates and students from nearby colleges, including some white students, soon joined them. The example of the sit-in spread to other cities in North Carolina and throughout the South. Northern students picketed Woolworth's stores in support of the sit-ins. The sit-down strike was a tactic used by the labor movement during the 1930s and adopted by the Congress of Racial Equality (CORE) at a sit-in in 1943 to desegregate restaurants in Chicago.[6] Two years before the Greensboro sit-in, black high school and college students staged a sit-in on July 19, 1958, in Wichita, Kansas. The four-week sit-in at the Dockum Drugstore lunch counter was led by Ron Walters, a Wichita State College freshman who headed the Wichita NAACP Youth Council. Its success influenced sit-ins in Oklahoma City, which led to desegregation of lunch counters there, although many other restaurants and public facilities in Oklahoma City remained segregated. It would take six years of boycotts, demonstrations, and sit-ins before the Oklahoma City Council passed an ordinance that opened public accommodations to all without regard to race, religion, or color.[7]

Many of the students encountered violence as supporters of white supremacy poured ketchup on their heads, emptied bowls of sugar on them, spat at them, punched them, and even put out lighted cigarettes on their clothes and bare flesh. The disciplined students remained nonviolent. In several cities, they were arrested and imprisoned, but more students joined the demonstrations. Picketing and boycotting the national chains such as Woolworth and Kress soon brought an end to segregated lunch counters. In the May issue of *The Southern Patriot*, Ella Baker wrote that the demonstrations were "concerned with something bigger than a hamburger or even a giant-sized coke." The students, black and white, North and South, were "seeking to rid America of the scourge of racial segregation and discrimination—not only at lunch counters, but in every aspect of life."[8]

Many of the student activists met in March at the Highlander Folk School in Tennessee for the Annual Leadership Workshop for College Students. The Highlander Folk School was established in the 1930s and was run by the white couple, Myles and Zilphia Horton. Initially, it focused on worker education and labor organization but recognized that racism was a major obstacle to economic equality in the South. The school developed a series of workshops to empower community organizers working on adult education, voter registration, and civic participation. Septima Poinsette Clark, who was fired from teaching in the Charleston, South Carolina public schools in 1956 because of her fight for equal pay for black teachers and her membership in the NAACP, became director of education at Highlander and initiated its citizenship schools to promote adult literacy, voter registration, and empowerment of local activists to address problems through community organization. Zilphia Horton helped to popularize the black spiritual "I'll Be Alright," which became "I Will Overcome," and was sung by black women labor organizers during the 1940s who transformed it into "We Shall Overcome." Music was a central part of the struggle for racial equality, and "We Shall Overcome" became an anthem of the movement. It also spread worldwide and could be heard in demonstrations as far away as Poland and China.

## THE STUDENT NON-VIOLENT COORDINATING COMMITTEE

Ella Baker, who served as acting executive director of SCLC, invited the student activists to her alma mater, Shaw University, a historically black college in Raleigh, North Carolina, for an Easter weekend conference. On April 15–16, 1960,

142 students from the South and 30 from the North attended the Student Leadership Conference on Non-Violent Resistance to Segregation. Leaders of SCLC, which helped to finance the meeting, hoped that the students would become the youth wing of their organization. Baker counseled the students to remain independent, to form their own organization, to avoid becoming entangled in the bureaucracy and politics of the older organizations. She encouraged them to look toward "group-centered leadership" rather than a "leadership-centered group" that she thought would only temper movement toward change. The students decided to form the Student Non-Violent Coordinating Committee (SNCC), initially a loose federation of local student protest groups. They selected Marion Barry, a graduate student at Fisk University and future mayor of Washington, D.C., as chairman. They also decided that the movement would be open not just to African Americans but to all people who were willing to fight against injustice. They maintained that freedom for African Americans meant freedom for all Americans.

Within a year, SNCC set up headquarters in Atlanta and appointed James Forman as executive secretary, a position that he held for five years. Forman, who had served a four-year stint in the Air Force and graduated from Roosevelt University in Chicago with a degree in public administration, was older than most of the members of SNCC. He tried to create a more highly structured organization than many of the students desired. As SNCC moved from desegregation demonstrations to voting rights campaigns, grassroots organizing, and community empowerment, full-time field secretaries replaced representatives of the local student protest groups. The field secretaries received subsistence wages of twenty-five to forty dollars a week, depending on whether they were single or married.

## FREEDOM RIDES

In many respects, SNCC would become the shock troops of the civil rights movement, who initially were well schooled in nonviolent direct action and who advocated the principles of "participatory democracy," in which the oppressed had to play a direct role in their own liberation. Members of SNCC would help to sustain the freedom rides after its courageous organizers came under vicious assault. In May 1961, CORE decided to test the recent Supreme Court decision of *Boynton v. Virginia* that had banned separate terminal facilities for interstate passengers. CORE in 1947 had made a "Journey of Reconciliation" through the upper South to test the Supreme Court decision of 1946 in *Morgan v. Virginia* against segregation in interstate transportation. Now the freedom riders would travel through the Deep South to challenge compliance with the Supreme Court decision in access to bus terminal facilities, including lunch counters, rest rooms, and waiting rooms. CORE members planned to journey from Washington, D.C., to New Orleans. CORE was the most interracial of the civil rights organizations and was dedicated to Gandhian principles of nonviolent direct action. The freedom riders encountered little difficulty until they reached Rock Hill, South Carolina, where John Lewis, later chairman of SNCC, and John Bigelow, a white architect, were severely beaten when they attempted to enter the white waiting room of the Greyhound bus terminal. The CORE volunteers continued their journey to Alabama, where a white mob in Anniston beat the freedom riders and burned their bus. At this juncture, CORE decided to terminate the journey, given that its members had brought the nation's attention to white racist resistance to the Supreme Court decision.

SNCC volunteers from Nashville, Tennessee, agreed to complete the freedom ride. Students at Fisk University, Meharry Medical School, the American Baptist Theological Seminary, and Tennessee State University—all historically black schools—had been preparing for some time for nonviolent direct action under the tutelage of James Lawson. A member of the Fellowship of Reconciliation, Lawson served a year of a three-year prison sentence for refusing to register for the draft in 1951, during the Korean War. He was paroled to the Methodist Board of Missions and assigned to India as a missionary. He spent three years in India, where he became more closely acquainted with the nonviolent direct action philosophy of Mohandas Gandhi. Lawson became a strong advocate of nonviolence, not just as a tactic but also as a philosophy and a way of life. On his return to the United States, Lawson attended Oberlin College for graduate study. There he met Martin Luther King Jr., who urged Lawson to move to the South in support of the civil rights struggle. He soon left Oberlin, moved to Nashville as the first southern field secretary for the Fellowship of Reconciliation, and enrolled as a theology student at Vanderbilt University. In Nashville, he organized workshops on nonviolence that attracted stalwarts of the movement such as Marion Barry, John Lewis, Diane Nash, James Bevel, and Bernard Lafayette, who led the sit-in demonstrations in Nashville and continued the freedom rides from Birmingham into Montgomery, where they were again attacked, with John Lewis being knocked unconscious. Given international publicity about the vicious attacks on the freedom riders, President John F. Kennedy and his brother, Attorney General Robert F. Kennedy, tried to persuade the freedom riders to cease their travel. The freedom riders refused to stop, and the Kennedys made arrangements with Mississippi officials to keep their segregated facilities as long as the freedom riders were not harmed. Mississippi law enforcement prevented attacks on the freedom riders but arrested and jailed them. More than three hundred freedom riders spent time in the state's repressive prisons. By the end of the summer, the Interstate Commerce

Commission ruled that all interstate facilities had to comply with the Supreme Court decision.

## DESEGREGATING OLE MISS AND THE UNIVERSITY OF ALABAMA

With students challenging segregation in public accommodations and transportation, school desegregation, especially in higher education, was proceeding very slowly. Although the Supreme Court had ruled in several cases against segregation in graduate and professional education and the 1954 decision overturned the principle of "separate but equal," it became necessary to challenge segregation almost one step at a time. In early 1961, James Meredith, a nine-year veteran of the Air Force, sought to transfer from the historically black Jackson State College to the University of Mississippi. The NAACP obtained a federal district court order for the University of Mississippi to admit Meredith, but Mississippi Governor Ross Barnett responded, "Never." Barnett played to southern resistance and compared the desegregation order to the crisis that led to the Civil War. When federal marshals tried to enroll Meredith in September 1962, Barnett stood in the doorway of the registrar's office to block Meredith's enrollment. Later, a riot broke out, with 150 marshals injured, twenty-five of them shot. President Kennedy had to federalize the Mississippi National Guard to restore order and to enroll Meredith in the university, from which he graduated a year later. A similar, though less violent, drama would play itself out the following year at the University of Alabama, where Governor George C. Wallace blocked the entry of black students. In his inaugural address as governor in 1963, Wallace had promised "segregation now, segregation tomorrow, segregation forever." The black students were subsequently able to enroll at the university with the assistance of a federalized Alabama National Guard. With his reputation as a staunch segregationist, Wallace entered several Democratic Party primaries in 1964 and four years later received a larger percentage of the vote than any third-party or independent candidate since Theodore Roosevelt in 1912.

## STALEMATE IN ALBANY, GEORGIA

Much of the success of the civil rights movement depended on dramatizing segregation, creating a confrontation, and enlisting federal support to enforce the law. The movement faced one of its greatest setbacks in Albany, Georgia, where it failed to achieve its goals. A coalition of SNCC and NAACP Youth Council members sought to test the Interstate Commerce Commission ruling against segregation in interstate transportation facilities. They selected the day before Thanksgiving in 1961, when many students from the historically black Albany State College took the bus home for the holiday. When students entered the white side of the bus terminal and refused to leave, they were arrested. Leaders of what became known as the Albany Movement held a mass rally the evening after Thanksgiving to organize for an end to segregation in the city. The youth were joined by their parents, who were prepared to fight against segregation. To bring attention to their struggle and to spark support, the older members of the movement decided to invite King and SCLC to Albany. SNCC members opposed inviting King and SCLC because they believed that it would take away from grass roots organizing and would highlight celebrity rather than the hard work that needed to be done in developing and sustaining local leadership and involvement. The lack of unity, amorphous target of desegregating the city as a whole, and shrewdness of the chief of police, Laurie Pritchett, led to the failure of the Albany Movement. Pritchett, who did not resort to violence or let an unruly mob create a scene, provided no pretext for federal intervention. SCLC ceased its activities in Albany by the end of 1962, although SNCC organizers remained in the area. But little change had come to the city; its facilities remained segregated.

## BIRMINGHAM

SCLC drew on its experiences in Albany after it entered the struggle in Birmingham at the invitation of Rev. Fred Shuttlesworth, one of its board members. Shuttlesworth had formed the Alabama Christian Movement for Human Rights (ACMHR) in 1956 after the state of Alabama banned the NAACP for conducting an illegal boycott in Montgomery and for failing to turn over its membership lists. ACMHR became an affiliate of SCLC. Shuttlesworth led the campaign for desegregation of the buses in Birmingham and succeeded by 1961, although his home was destroyed by dynamite. Because so many homes and churches of African Americans had been bombed in Birmingham, many referred to the city as "Bombingham."

The year 1963 symbolically marked the hundredth anniversary of the Emancipation Proclamation and the putative end of slavery. African Americans across the country were determined one hundred years after the end of slavery that they should win their full rights as citizens of the United States. It was one of the most active years in the civil rights struggle with thousands of demonstrations throughout the nation. In Birmingham, ACMHR challenged segregation in public facilities. With SCLC, ACMHR devised Project C, a strategy of boycotts, pickets, and demonstrations to end segregation of elevators, fitting rooms, restrooms, drinking fountains, parks, pools, and schools and to improve employment and housing for African Americans. Project C stood for confrontation. Although King was committed to nonviolence, he believed that one of the most effective weapons for African Americans in the South was to provoke opposition in such a manner that the country would see the need to take action for change.

## THE LETTER FROM BIRMINGHAM JAIL

Project C began on April 3 with sit-ins and later marches against which the state court issued an injunction. The demonstrators disobeyed the injunction and were arrested with the goal of filling up the jails. King and Rev. Ralph D. Abernathy, one of his closest friends and allies and secretary-treasurer of SCLC, were arrested and jailed on Good Friday, April 12. Eight local Christian and Jewish clergy wrote a letter to the *Birmingham News*, "An Appeal for Law and Order and Common Sense," that called on King to pursue the movement's concerns in the courts and to obey its decisions while the issues were being litigated. They characterized the demonstrations as "unwise and untimely," and concluded that they were being led by "outsiders." The clergy indicated that they condemned hatred and violence as well as actions, even though they may be peaceful, that incited hatred and violence. King read this statement and wrote his famous "Letter from Birmingham Jail," one of the most important documents of the civil rights struggle, which clearly and distinctly explained the reasons for the movement, the urgency of the moment, and the need sometimes to disobey unjust laws. To the charge of being an outsider, King responded, "Injustice anywhere is a threat to justice everywhere.... Anyone who lives inside the United States can never be considered an outsider anywhere in this country." He chided the clergy for criticizing the demonstrations rather than the underlying causes for them. Moreover, he reminded them, "We know through painful experience that freedom is never voluntarily given by the oppressor.... For years now I have heard the word 'wait!' It rings in the ear of every Negro with piercing familiarity. This 'Wait' has almost always meant 'Never.'" He let them know that African Americans had waited for more than 340 years for their "constitutional and God-given rights." He remarked, "The nations of Asia and Africa are moving with jet-like speed toward gaining political independence, but we still creep at horse-and-buggy pace toward gaining a cup of coffee at a lunch counter." King laid bare the indignities suffered by African Americans and the effects on them. He informed the clergy that "when you are forever fighting a degenerating sense of 'nobodiness'—then you will understand why we find it difficult to wait." The white moderate in his estimation seemed more interested in law and order than in justice. Blaming African Americans for precipitating violence while peacefully demonstrating, Dr. King observed, was like "condemning the robbed man because his possession of money precipitated the evil act of robbery."[9]

Because so many of the demonstrators had been arrested and were either in jail or could not risk another arrest, James Bevel, an SCLC organizer, suggested using schoolchildren to sustain the demonstrations. Bull Connor, Birmingham's public safety commissioner, gave the organizers the images that they needed to rally national and indeed international support for change. When thousands of children, some as young as six, marched in what became known as the "Children's Crusade," Connor's police beat them with nightsticks, let vicious dogs attack them, and had firemen turn hoses on them with a force of water so strong that it tore clothes from their backs and bark from trees. Those images in newspapers and on the evening news forced the Kennedy administration into action. Robert F. Kennedy personally called business leaders with branches of their corporations in Birmingham to put pressure on their companies to end segregation in the city. Almost a month after the demonstrations began, the city reached an agreement to desegregate public facilities and to increase employment opportunities for African Americans. Backlash to the agreement was not long in coming as a bomb damaged the home of King's younger brother, the Rev. A. D. King, and destroyed part of the A. G. Gaston Motel, which King had used as his headquarters. Gaston was a black businessman, a self-made millionaire, with an insurance company, bank, business school, and real estate in addition to the motel. His enterprises depended on a black clientele that had few options for the services he provided. He supported the movement financially, although desegregation would break his hold on black patronage and weaken his economic empire. After the bombings, many African Americans in Birmingham who had sat on the sidelines and did not participate in the nonviolent demonstrations became enraged, took to the streets, threw rocks and bottles at police and state troopers, overturned cars, and set stores on fire. SCLC organizers were able to quiet the crowd, but their retaliation was a harbinger of things to come.

## MALCOLM X

King faced criticism not only from virulent racists as well as conservative and moderate whites but also from some African Americans whom he described in his "Letter from Birmingham Jail" as a "force of bitterness and hatred that comes perilously close to advocating violence. It is expressed in the various black nationalist groups that are springing up over the nation. This movement is nourished by the contemporary frustration over the continued existence of racial discrimination. It is made up of people who have lost faith in America, who have absolutely repudiated Christianity, and who have concluded that the white man is an incurable 'devil.'" Malcolm X was one of the critics who lambasted King and the civil rights organizers in Birmingham for using children in the demonstrations and for not protecting them. Malcolm X was a follower of Elijah Muhammad and the Nation of Islam who transformed his life while in prison and gained dignity and respect for himself as a black man. Upon his release from prison in 1952, he became an organizer and spokesman for the Nation of Islam, a religious group that emerged out of Detroit in the early 1930s. The Nation of Islam was supposedly the true religion of the black man that preached race pride and self-sufficiency. Malcolm X helped to increase its membership from a few temples to a nationwide organization. He started the newspaper, *Muhammad Speaks*, and the policy that each male member had to sell a certain quota of newspapers on the street as a recruiting and fundraising technique. As National Representative for the Nation of Islam, Malcolm X spread the group's influence beyond its estimated 500,000 members at its height before his assassination in 1965. The Nation of Islam emphasized a consciousness of self, clean living, protection of black women, thrift, a nutritious diet, and self-defense. The organization became noted for rehabilitating alcoholics, drug addicts, and criminals. But it also castigated the white man as the devil who was responsible for the impoverishment and oppression of African Americans. Once African Americans knew their real identity and freed themselves from self-hatred imposed on them by white racism, they would no longer be lost. They would find themselves, know who they are, only within the Nation of Islam. In many respects, Malcolm X became a countervailing force to King, especially in the North, where many African Americans were beginning to question the civil rights movement, the goal of integration, nonviolence, and the extent to which their lives had changed.

## THE MARCH ON WASHINGTON FOR JOBS AND FREEDOM

Because of lingering racial inequality, increasing rates of unemployment and underemployment especially in central cities, deindustrialization, poverty, and suburbanization that left most African Americans behind in deteriorating ghettos, A. Philip Randolph and Bayard Rustin proposed a March on Washington for Jobs and Freedom. Black unemployment was three times higher than white unemployment, with as much as 40 percent unemployment in many inner-city areas. Almost half of African Americans were in poverty compared with about 18 percent of white Americans. Randolph and Rustin realized that unless the economic status of African Americans improved, civil rights gains would not be very meaningful. Rustin was a master strategist who devised the logistics for bringing what was initially estimated as 100,000 demonstrators to the nation's capital, a figure that rose to 250,000 when a closer count was taken. After Birmingham, with its horrendous images of white repression as African Americans sought to exercise their fundamental rights of citizenship, the Kennedy administration recognized that something had to be done to avoid adverse publicity for the country, especially abroad. Although the Kennedy administration supported the principle of racial equality, it was also concerned that more violent demonstrations might get out of hand and jeopardize Kennedy's reelection. He therefore proposed civil rights legislation to end segregation in interstate transportation and public accommodations, to make it easier to register and vote, and to terminate federal funds for states and localities that still practiced racial discrimination. Southern members of Kennedy's own Democratic Party resisted the legislation. The March on Washington of August 28, 1963, which gained the endorsement of the major civil rights organizations, CORE, NAACP, SCLC, SNCC, and the National Urban League, would, it was hoped, generate national support for the civil rights bill.

Although the March on Washington caught the nation's attention, it did not have the broad based support that future generations would accord it. The National Baptist Convention, the largest black organization in the United States, with an estimated eight million members, did not support the March on Washington. Its conservative leader, the Rev. Joseph H. Jackson, was cool to the civil rights movement and church involvement in secular affairs. Moreover, many of the activist ministers, including King, had pulled out of the organization in 1961 to form the Progressive National Baptist Convention. Similarly, the labor movement as represented by the AFL-CIO did not encourage the march. African Americans had enjoyed a strained relation with the labor movement. At the beginning of World War II, fourteen major national unions explicitly prohibited black membership. Many others tacitly excluded African Americans. Even during the war, many white workers went on strike rather than accept black workers or agree to their promotion from unskilled and semiskilled to skilled and supervisory positions. The United Auto Workers was the only major union to help finance and organize the March on Washington. Although it began as a demonstration for jobs and freedom, the emphasis slowly shifted away from jobs to freedom and civil rights legislation to avoid antagonizing white workers.

On the eve of the march, W. E. B. Du Bois, the towering figure of the black liberation movement in the United States and Africa, died in Ghana. The federal government had restored his passport in 1958, after which he made an international tour with visits to China, Ghana, and the Soviet Union, among other nations. Kwame Nkrumah, the president of Ghana, invited him to move to Ghana and to publish an *Encyclopedia Africana*, a project he had initiated in the early 1940s but had to abandon because of the war, lack of funding, and ostracism by the U.S. government. In late 1961, Du Bois officially joined the Communist Party and left the United States for Ghana, where he died at age ninety-four and is buried. News of Du Bois's death was announced to the crowd massed in front of the Lincoln Memorial, stretching to the Washington Monument. A hush fell over the audience as it began to listen to the featured speakers. Although Martin Luther King's "I Have a Dream" speech has become the most noted oration of the day, John Lewis, the newly elected chair of SNCC, delivered the most militant address to the audience. Lewis almost did not get a chance to give his speech, which the march organizers felt set the wrong tone. In his prepared remarks, which were distributed in advance, Lewis called Kennedy's civil rights bill "too little, too late," and announced that SNCC could not support it. He criticized Kennedy's appointment of racist judges and excoriated the federal government for not protecting civil rights workers, who were still being beaten in the South. Only two months before the march, Medgar Evers, NAACP field director in Mississippi, was assassinated as he exited his car in the driveway to his home. Lewis was angry and bitter about the inaction of the federal government and suggested that African Americans would have to tear apart the South and put it back together as a democratic society. He referred to marching through the South as General Sherman did during the Civil War, a reference sure to raise the ire of white southerners. Under pressure from march organizers, Lewis delivered a revised text that still conveyed his anger and the need for people of conscience and conviction to force change. He noted that there was little to be proud of with the march, because "hundreds and thousands of our brothers are not here—they have no money for their transportation, for they are receiving starvation wages... or no wages at all." Lewis asked what was being done to "insure the equality of a maid who earns $5.00 a week in the home of a family whose income is $100,000 a year."[10]

## UNDERSTANDING KING'S SPEECH

King struck a similar note in the much overlooked and neglected first part of his speech when he stated that "one hundred years later, we must face the tragic fact that the Negro is still not free," and that "the Negro lives on a lonely island of poverty in the midst of a vast ocean of material prosperity." He referred to coming to the nation's capital to cash a check, a promissory note guaranteed to all Americans through the Constitution and the Declaration of Independence for "the unalienable rights of life, liberty, and the pursuit of happiness." He observed, "It is obvious today that America has defaulted on this promissory note insofar as her citizens of color are concerned. Instead of honoring this sacred obligation, America has given the Negro people a bad check; a check which has come back marked 'insufficient funds.' But we refuse to believe that the bank of justice is bankrupt. We refuse to believe that there are insufficient funds in the great vaults of opportunity of this nation. So we have come to cash this check." King emphasized what he called "the fierce urgency of now" to change the condition and status of African Americans. In words close to what Lewis wanted to say, King promised that there would be neither rest nor tranquility in the country until African Americans enjoyed their rights as American citizens. He warned, "The whirlwinds of revolt will continue to shake the foundations of our Nation until the bright day of justice emerges." But he also urged African Americans not "to satisfy our thirst for freedom by drinking from the cup of bitterness." He reminded them that they needed allies, that the freedom and destiny of African Americans was inextricably bound to that of white Americans. Both Lewis and King captured the mood of black America, which was growing impatient with the pace of change in their lives. Rather than recognize and acknowledge African American's "sweltering discontent," the media and the nation turned attention instead to the part of the speech that King basically extemporized—his vision, his dream, for the future of America, which would "transform the jangling discords of our nation into a beautiful symphony of brotherhood." King later recalled that he started reading his prepared remarks and was then inspired to use the words "I Have a Dream," words and references that he had used before at rallies in Birmingham and in Detroit. The response, of course, was tremendous, so much so that then and now, there has been a tendency to forget the pithy and trenchant earlier part of his speech. After the March on Washington, King became the symbol of the civil rights movement, was named *Time Magazine's* Man of the Year, and nine months later won the Nobel Peace Prize, the youngest person at age thirty-five ever to win the award. King, who lived in a modest rented home and drove a Ford with seventy thousand miles on it, gave all of his $54,000 prize to civil rights organizations, despite his wife's entreaties to use a portion of the money to establish accounts for their children's college education.[11]

## THE "DREAM" OR THE "NIGHTMARE"

Malcolm X was quick to pounce on King's speech, replacing the metaphor of the "dream" with Malcolm X's own metaphor of the American "nightmare." And it was not long before that nightmare resurfaced in Birmingham, Alabama, where barely two weeks after the March on Washington, a bomb rocked the 16th Street Baptist Church, a staging ground for the earlier demonstrations, and snuffed out the lives of four young black girls who were preparing for Sunday school. In a fit of rage and resentment, when asked almost two months later to comment on the assassination of President John F. Kennedy, Malcolm X, perhaps with the murder of the four young girls still in mind, remarked that it was like "the chickens coming home to roost." That statement got Malcolm X into trouble with Elijah Muhammad, the head of the Nation of Islam, who had instructed his ministers not to comment on President Kennedy's death. Members of the Nation of Islam, who did not vote and refused to serve in America's armed forces, distanced themselves from an American society that they believed was doomed to destruction and from which they would be saved. Because of his popularity and engagement with white America, especially in college appearances and on television, Malcolm X encountered jealousy and charges of apostasy by some of Elijah Muhammad's close lieutenants.

To discipline Malcolm X, Elijah Muhammad suspended him from his responsibilities. Malcolm X realized that he had lost the confidence of the man he idolized, who had rescued him and given meaning and purpose to his life. Because of his affection for and allegiance to Elijah Muhammad, Malcolm X had dismissed rumors about Muhammad's infidelity in having sexual relations with and children by his young secretaries, several of whom Malcolm X had personally recommended to Elijah Muhammad. With his eyes now open, Malcolm X recognized that Elijah Muhammad had been hypocritical, preaching family sanctity while practicing promiscuity. Moreover, Malcolm X had chafed at not being able to play a more active role in the black struggle for freedom in the United States. In March 1964, he broke with the Nation of Islam and established the Muslim Mosque Inc. and the Organization of Afro-American Unity, patterned after the Organization of African Unity on the African continent. He pronounced separatism and black nationalism as his cultural and political philosophy, although he modified his ideas after he visited Mecca, changed his name to El-Hajj Malik El-Shabbazz, and concluded that the religion of Islam embraced people of different races and colors. He traveled throughout Africa seeking the support of African nations for a petition to the United Nations that would examine the violation of African American's human rights. He held that African Americans were not free because the country first had to acknowledge their human rights before they could secure civil rights. Moreover, he questioned the strategy of the civil rights movement in appealing to the American government, which he considered judge and jury and before which African Americans could not gain a fair hearing. They had to take their case to a higher body, to the United Nations, where they were more likely to receive justice.

## THE CIVIL RIGHTS ACT OF 1964

Lyndon B. Johnson, who as vice president succeeded John F. Kennedy, sought passage of the civil rights bill as a way to honor his memory and to temper the growing movement. On July 2, 1964, President Johnson signed the Civil Rights

Act into law. The legislation prohibited discrimination in public transportation and in public accommodations such as restaurants, hotels, motels, gas stations, theaters, stadiums, auditoriums, parks, playgrounds, libraries, and swimming pools. It authorized the Justice Department to file school desegregation lawsuits and allowed government agencies to withhold federal funds from programs that practiced discrimination. School districts that failed to comply with Department of Health, Education, and Welfare guidelines would lose federal funds. The federal government had moved beyond school desegregation with "all deliberate speed" to the immediate end of the South's dual school system. The Civil Rights Act also banned discrimination on the basis of race, religion, national origin, or sex by employers, labor unions, and employment agencies. It also created the Equal Employment Opportunity Commission to enforce the law. This agency was an expansion of President Kennedy's executive order 10925, issued on March 8, 1961, which established the President's Committee on Equal Employment Opportunity, required government contractors not to discriminate in employment on the basis of race, creed, color, or national origin, and called on those contractors to "take affirmative action to ensure that applicants are employed, and that employees are treated during employment, without regard to their race, creed, color, or national origin." The Civil Rights Act of 1964 added sex as a category for nondiscrimination and affirmative action in employment. President Johnson's executive order 11246, issued on September 28, 1965, and later amended by executive order 11375, required federal contractors, including colleges and universities, to set goals and timetables for employing women and minorities who were underutilized in the workforce and qualified and available for employment.

## THE VOTER EDUCATION PROJECT

The Kennedy administration had tried to shift the civil rights struggle from demonstrations to voter registration. At a June 16, 1961 meeting, Attorney General Robert F. Kennedy promised civil rights leaders federal protection and financial support for a voter registration drive. CORE, NAACP, SCLC, SNCC, and the National Urban League joined together in 1962 for the Voter Education Project (VEP), headed initially by Wiley Branton, a lawyer who represented the black students in Little Rock, Arkansas, and later by Vernon Jordan, who became head of the National Urban League. The VEP basically provided grants to other organizations for voter registration and voter education. SNCC was one of the most active organizations in this area as its field secretaries worked in some of the most intractable sections of the rural South. After the freedom rides, SNCC developed two wings of the organization, one that focused on direct action and another that focused on voter registration. The voter registration wing did the tedious and dangerous work of convincing rural African Americans to abandon traditions of deference and oppression to register and vote. At great risk to themselves and to those African Americans whom they encouraged to break with the past and to realize that voting was not just "white folks' business," the SNCC workers tried to make a difference in those places where African Americans were often a majority of the population but a tiny fraction of the registered voters, such as southwest Georgia and the Mississippi Delta. In Mississippi, at the suggestion of Robert Moses, they formed the Council of Federated Organizations (COFO) in 1961, a coalition of CORE, NAACP, SCLC, and SNCC. Moses was a graduate of Hamilton College in upstate New York and had studied philosophy as a graduate student at Harvard. Ella Baker influenced him to become involved in the civil rights movement and to move to the South where he became SNCC's first full-time voter registration worker. In 1963, COFO organized a mock gubernatorial election in Mississippi in which black voters through the "Freedom Ballot" could vote for their own candidates, most for the first time in their lives. The success of this campaign, in which more than eighty thousand disfranchised African Americans voted for COFO candidates, inspired Moses to propose Mississippi Freedom Summer for 1964, to challenge disfranchisement through voter registration, education, and the Mississippi Freedom Democratic Party (MFDP).

## MISSISSIPPI FREEDOM SUMMER

COFO invited college students from the North, mainly white students, to participate in the Mississippi Freedom Summer project. The purpose of the project was to improve the lives of African Americans in what most activists considered the most racially repressive state in the country. There were about thirty project sites with healthcare facilities, voter registration clinics, literacy classes, and Freedom Schools. The Freedom Schools, under the direction of Staughton Lynd, a white history professor at historically black Spelman College, sought to empower black youth with a sense of pride, knowledge of their history, and mastery of academic skills. They would be the vanguard of a new generation to break the legacy of white supremacy in Mississippi. COFO relied primarily on white volunteers, some one thousand of whom agreed to participate in the project, with the belief that the government and the country would not tolerate the type of intimidation and violence that confronted black civil-rights workers. Only two days after the project began in Mississippi, following training sessions for the volunteers in Oxford, Ohio, three civil rights workers were reported missing. James Chaney, a twenty-one-year-old black Mississippi native; Andrew Goodman, a twenty-year-old white student from Queens College in New York City; and Michael Schwerner, a twenty-four-year-old white Cornell University graduate, had gone on Sunday, June 21, 1964, to investigate a church bombing near Philadelphia, Mississippi. The county deputy sheriff arrested them for allegedly speeding, took them to jail, released them at about 10:30 that evening, and turned them over to the Klan. The Klan beat, shot them, and buried their bodies under an earthen dam being constructed in a remote area of the county. Although black civil rights workers had been trying in vain to get the federal government involved in investigating beatings and murders for some time, the FBI under adverse publicity and intense pressure entered the case. President Johnson sent former CIA Director Allen Dulles and FBI Director J. Edgar Hoover to Jackson, Mississippi, to speak with the governor and to find the missing civil rights workers. More than 150 federal agents worked on the case in the field. They discovered the bodies of three black civil rights workers, one wearing a CORE T-shirt, but little was done to prosecute their murderers, although the killers of two of them were identified. National, indeed international, attention focused on the missing white volunteers. A $30,000 reward led an informant to tell where the bodies were buried, and the FBI found them six weeks after their disappearance. Nineteen men, including police officers and Klansmen, were indicted by the U.S. Justice Department not for the murders but for violating Chaney, Goodman, and Schwerner's civil rights. Murder, except in bank robbery or kidnapping, was not a federal offense. An all-white jury in 1967 convicted seven of the men, including the county deputy sheriff and the local Klan leader, for violating their civil rights. For the state of Mississippi, this was a victory. The movement, however, paid a terrible toll during Mississippi Freedom Summer, with six civil rights workers murdered, four critically wounded, and eighty beaten, and thirty homes bombed, thirty-seven churches burned, and more than one thousand people arrested.

Mississippi Freedom Summer culminated in the MFDP's delegates to the Democratic Party National Convention in Atlantic City in August 1964. The MFDP delegates challenged the state's lily-white delegation and sought to be seated in the convention as the democratically selected party representatives from Mississippi. Fannie Lou Hamer, a courageous resident of Ruleville, Mississippi, who lost her plantation job for seeking to register to vote and who was severely beaten in a Winona, Mississippi, jail for trying to register others to vote, testified before the convention on why the MFDP delegates should be seated as the state's representatives. She explained that she was "sick and tired of being sick and tired" of fighting for her God-given rights. Because Lyndon Johnson did not want to alienate the white South in his election campaign and because of his desire to win the presidency by a large margin, the Democratic Party put pressure on the MFDP delegation to accept a compromise of two at-large seats with the rest of the group attending the convention as observers. King, Wilkins, Rustin, and others tried to influence the delegation to accept the compromise, but they refused. Many of the young SNCC workers became disillusioned as they played by the rules of the game and found themselves rebuffed. They began to think about building their own political party and taking control of those areas of the South where African Americans were a majority of the population. Moreover, they began to question interracial coalition, and some concluded that African Americans had to rely entirely on themselves, the beginning of Black Power. The growing sense of disunity was compounded when members of the Nation of Islam assassinated Malcolm X on February 21, 1965.

## SELMA

SNCC workers became further discouraged by the voting rights campaign that SCLC organized in Selma, Alabama. The campaign involved daily marches to the county courthouse to register African Americans to vote and where they met resistance and were arrested. To dramatize the campaign, SCLC planned a march from Selma to Montgomery, the state capital. When the marchers led by John Lewis of SNCC and Hosea Williams of SCLC crossed the Edmund Pettis Bridge, state troopers lobbed tear gas and beat the marchers back across the bridge in what became known as Bloody Sunday, March 7, 1965. Vivid pictures of the attack were shown on television across the country as some stations interrupted their regularly scheduled programs to play tapes of the horrible scene. King proposed another march several days later. A federal judge, however, issued an injunction against the march, and King faced a dilemma. Although he had disobeyed state laws he considered unjust, he had never defied a federal injunction, inasmuch as he had basically relied on the federal government to keep the states in check. While SCLC appealed the injunction, there was a clamor, especially among SNCC workers to proceed with the march. On Tuesday, March 9, King led about three thousand marchers across the bridge, where state troopers awaited them, but he had the marchers stop, kneel, pray and turn around and march back to Selma. The SNCC workers felt betrayed by King's not proceeding with the march. King was caught in the middle between the protesters and the federal government, inasmuch as he desired passage of voting rights legislation and did not want to upset President Johnson's plans for introducing such legislation. President Johnson hoped to avoid further violence. During the early stages of the campaign, a young black SNCC worker, Jimmie Lee Jackson, had been shot by a state trooper while trying to protect his mother from the trooper's blows and subsequently died of his wounds. After the march on March 9, James Reeb, a white Unitarian minister from Boston, was attacked and killed by a white mob in Selma. With these deaths and the events of Bloody Sunday, there were protests and demonstrations throughout the country for federal intervention. In a nationally televised address to Congress on March 15, President Johnson condemned the bloodshed in Selma and declared that it was wrong to deny fellow citizens the right to vote. In a statement that brought tears to King's eyes as he watched, Johnson vowed that "we shall overcome" the nation's history of racial discrimination and injustice. He invoked the phrase several times, to the surprise and delight of King and his supporters.

## THE VOTING RIGHTS ACT OF 1965

SCLC succeeded in having the federal injunction against a march from Selma to Montgomery lifted, and two weeks after Bloody Sunday, King and Ralph J. Bunche, the first African American to receive the Nobel Peace Prize in 1950, along with dignitaries and committed citizens from across the country, led a triumphant and symbolic march across the Edmund Pettis Bridge. Only three hundred marchers would make the actual five-day trek to Montgomery, under conditions of the court order that lifted the injunction. After celebrating the march in Montgomery, a white housewife from Detroit, Viola Gregg Liuzzo, who had volunteered to drive marchers back to Selma, was shot and killed that evening by Klansmen. Congress quickly and overwhelmingly passed the Voting Rights Act of 1965, which President Johnson signed into law on August 6. The Voting Rights Act eliminated literacy tests and other devices that had been used to prevent African Americans from registering to vote and authorized the use of federal officials to supervise voter registration in those areas that denied large numbers of African Americans the right to vote. A year earlier, Congress had ratified the Twenty-fourth Amendment to the Constitution, prohibiting the use of the poll tax as a requirement for voting in federal elections. By 1969, for the first time since Reconstruction, more than half the eligible black voters in the South were registered to vote.

## UNDERSTANDING THE CIVIL RIGHTS MOVEMENT

In reviewing the civil rights movement, there is a question of balance and proportion. How much attention do we give to the government and its role as initiator and supporter of legislation and its implementation, as Steven F. Lawson and Charles M. Payne discuss in *Debating the Civil Rights Movement, 1945–68*? How much emphasis do we place on major personalities such as Roy Wilkins, Martin Luther King Jr., A. Philip Randolph, Ella Baker, Bayard Rustin, James Farmer, John Lewis, Fannie Lou Hamer, Whitney Young, Septima Clark, or Robert Moses? Or the central organizations: NAACP, CORE, SCLC, SNCC, and the National Urban League? What about white allies in the Communist Party, labor organizations, pacifist movement, and religious communities? Do we treat the civil rights movement like a series of military campaigns, moving from Montgomery to Little Rock, Greensboro, Albany, Birmingham, Mississippi, and Selma? Should we look more to the everyday people who sustained the movement, as Charles Payne recommends, to gain a better understanding of the complexity of the black community, especially its class, color, gender, ideological, regional, religious, sexual, and political differences? What about the very term "civil rights movement," which Payne suggests was more an issue of white supremacy—not just the separation of the races, but the dominance of one over the other, in which segregation was but an instrument of white supremacy?[12] Or do we adopt Vincent Harding's assessment, in *Hope and History: Why We Must Share the Story of the Movement*, that it was a black-led and inspired "revolution" that challenged the white supremacist and antidemocratic roots of this nation and reverberated around the globe in Europe, Asia, the Caribbean, and South Africa, with "We Shall Overcome" becoming the international anthem of freedom? What about black protest in boycotts, sit-ins, and demonstrations as consumer discontent that affected profit margins and influenced some major businesses to change policies? Where do we begin the story? Where do we end it?

## NOTES

1. L. D. Reddick, "The Bus Boycott in Montgomery," *Dissent* 3 (1956): 107–117.

2. William Julius Wilson, *The Truly Disadvantaged: The Inner City, the Underclass, and Public Policy* (Chicago: University of Chicago Press, 1987).

3. David J. Garrow, *Bearing the Cross: Martin Luther King, Jr., and the Southern Christian Leadership Conference* (New York: William Morrow, 1986).

4. Vincent Harding, *Hope and History: Why We Must Share the Story of the Movement* (Maryknoll, N.Y.: Orbis Books, 1990).

5. Timothy B. Tyson, *Radio Free Dixie: Robert F. Williams and the Roots of Black Power* (Chapel Hill: University of North Carolina Press, 1999).

6. William H. Chafe, *Civilities and Civil Rights: Greensboro, North Carolina and the Black Struggle for Freedom* (New York: Oxford University Press, 1980).

7. Quintard Taylor, *In Search of the Racial Frontier: African Americans in the American West* (New York: Norton, 1998), 285–289.

8. Ella Baker, "Bigger Than a Hamburger," *Southern Patriot* 18 (1960): 4.

9. Martin Luther King Jr., *Why We Can't Wait* (New York: Harper & Row, 1964), 82–83.

10. John Lewis, *Walking with the Wind: A Memoir of the Movement* (New York: Simon & Schuster, 1998), 216–220.

11. Garrow, *Bearing the Cross*, 282–285, 363–369.

12. Steven F. Lawson and Charles M. Payne, *Debating the Civil Rights Movement, 1945–1968* (Lanham, Md.: Rowman & Littlefield, 1998).

# BLACK POWER / BLACK CONSCIOUSNESS, 1965–75

Five days after President Johnson signed the Voting Rights Act into law, the Watts section of South Central Los Angeles exploded into violence. For four days, African Americans vented pent-up anger and frustration at police brutality, unemployment, deteriorated housing, and poor schools. They looted and burned stores, especially those owned by whites, and threw rocks and bottles at passing white motorists. It took the National Guard to calm the area, and in the end there were thirty-four deaths, hundreds of injuries, and more than four thousand arrests. Before the voting rights campaign in Selma, Martin Luther King Jr., who had sensed the deepening dissatisfaction of northern African Americans, planned to devote the attention of the Southern Christian Leadership Conference (SCLC) to the problems of housing, jobs, and schools in the North.

African Americans faced similar problems in the West, where, according to Quintard Taylor, the civil rights struggle focused on "job discrimination, housing bias, and de facto school segregation." One of the largest civil rights protests in the West took place in 1964 against the Sheraton Palace Hotel in San Francisco for its policy against hiring African Americans. As many as 1,500 demonstrators picketed the hotel, and several hundreds staged a sit-in in the hotel lobby until the Sheraton Palace signed an agreement with the city's mayor that was binding on all of San Francisco's major hotels and resulted in about two thousand jobs for people of color. The civil rights movement in the West often involved an uneasy alliance among African Americans, Chicanos, and Asian Americans.[1]

In 1962, SCLC had established Operation Breadbasket as its economic development program. The Rev. Leon Sullivan and other black ministers in Philadelphia, Pennsylvania, had started a "selective patronage" campaign to improve black employment. SCLC invited Sullivan to Atlanta to explain how the campaign worked and adopted it as Operation Breadbasket, which was to address poverty and unemployment, especially in urban areas. Initially, Operation Breadbasket organized black consumers in the South to win jobs and service and supply contracts for black businesses. When SCLC established the project in the North, it gained its greatest success in Chicago, where Jesse Jackson, who joined King's staff in 1965, became director of the local Operation Breadbasket in 1966 and a year later became national director. Jackson developed a strong base in Chicago more than a national movement. The program used boycotts and the threat of boycotts to gain concessions from major corporations. Jackson began the Black Business and Cultural Expositions as a means to strengthen black businesses. Although Operation Breadbasket succeeded in signing agreements for more jobs and use of black businesses by several giant corporations, it did not put systems in place to monitor compliance with the agreements. Jackson resigned from SCLC in 1971 and organized Operation PUSH (People United to Serve Humanity), which became his base of activity for action similar to Operation Breadbasket and for his forays into national politics.

## THE CHICAGO FREEDOM MOVEMENT

King turned his attention to Chicago in 1965 with an ambitious program to improve employment, housing, and schools and to eradicate the slums. SCLC worked closely with the Coordinating Council of Community Organizations (CCCO), formed in 1962 primarily to rehabilitate the deplorable public schools in black neighborhoods, schools that were often overcrowded, with students attending double shifts and classes in trailers. CCCO and SCLC identified neighborhood segregation as the source of the problem of poor schools in black neighborhoods and launched an open housing campaign with marches through all-white neighborhoods to dramatize the issue and to seek concessions from the city government. Chicago had the unenviable reputation of being one of the most segregated cities in the North, with its clearly identified white ethnic and black neighborhoods. Marches through white neighborhoods generated the attention and reaction that SCLC hoped for, with huge counterdemonstrations of angry crowds that threw rocks and bottles at the marchers. King remarked that he saw greater hatred on the faces of white mobs in Chicago than he had seen in the South. What later became known as the Chicago Freedom Movement reached an agreement with the city on August 26, 1966, to promote fair and open housing through real estate agents and mortgage lenders, to limit the height of new buildings in public housing projects, and to seek scattered sites for public housing rather than concentrating such housing in poor neighborhoods.

## THE MEREDITH MARCH AGAINST FEAR

While King was trying to address the underlying causes for violent explosions in the North, James Meredith, the first African American to graduate from the University of Mississippi, decided to undertake a solitary "march against fear" from Memphis, Tennessee, to Jackson, Mississippi. He wanted to encourage black voter registration and to demonstrate that African Americans could enjoy their rights as American citizens without fear of retaliation. On the second day of his well-publicized march, an unknown assailant shot and wounded Meredith. The Congress of Racial Equality (CORE), Student Non-Violent Coordinating Committee (SNCC), and SCLC agreed to complete what they called the Meredith Mississippi Freedom March. There was dissension from the beginning of the March as some of the younger activists declared that they would strike back if anyone attacked them. Not only did they reject nonviolence, but many of them also advocated an all-black march because of their disappointment with white liberals in particular and the glacial pace of change in general.

The march reached Greenwood, Mississippi, an SNCC stronghold, on its tenth day. There Stokely Carmichael, who had become SNCC chairman in 1966, launched into a speech that condemned Mississippi justice for not protecting African Americans against violence. He proclaimed that what African Americans needed was "Black Power." After the speech, Carmichael's lieutenant, Willie Ricks mounted the platform and whipped the crowd into a frenzy, with the chant, "What do we want?" and the response, "Black Power." King, who participated in the march, opposed the term as connoting violence and "black domination rather than black equality." Carmichael defended the term by noting that the issue of violence or nonviolence was irrelevant, that African Americans needed to use their economic and political resources to achieve power similar to white ethnic groups. With racial pride and economic and political power, African Americans would be able to determine their own destiny.

In a book later published with political scientist Charles Hamilton, Carmichael defined Black Power as "a call for black people in this country to unite, to recognize their heritage, to build a sense of community . . . to define their own goals, to lead their own organizations . . . to reject the racist institutions and values of this society. The concept of Black Power rests on a fundamental premise: *Before a group can enter the open society, it must first close ranks.*"[2] Black Power took numerous forms—economic, cultural, educational, political, religious, and social.

## THE BLACK PANTHER PARTY

In October 1966, four months after the Meredith Mississippi Freedom March, Huey P. Newton and Bobby Seale founded the Black Panther Party for Self-Defense in Oakland, California. The party was heavily influenced by Malcolm X, Frantz Fanon, and Karl Marx. It sought to empower dispirited and dispossessed African Americans who were subject to police brutality and exploitation. The Black Panther Party started armed street patrols at a time when it was lawful to carry arms openly in California. They observed the police from a respectable distance and read individuals being detained their legal rights. In several instances, after a person had been arrested, they went to the police station and posted bail. These confrontations led to altercations with the police, the death of an Oakland officer, and Newton's arrest. The campaign to free Newton gave the Panthers a public image that spread throughout the country, an image marked by swaggering military steps, black berets, and leather jackets. With it, the Panthers spread across the country. Given their revolutionary rhetoric and widespread influence on black youth, FBI Director J. Edgar Hoover deemed the Panthers the most dangerous subversive group in the United States. The FBI's Counterintelligence Program (COINTELPRO), together with internal dissension, occasioned the decline and eventual demise of the Panthers by the late 1970s. They had sought greater support from black communities through free breakfast programs, sickle cell anemia clinics, transportation for families to visit prison inmates who were often incarcerated in remote locations distant from urban areas, and educational projects. But legal charges against the Panthers, though they usually resulted in acquittals, drained the Party's resources.

## CULTURAL NATIONALISM

Members of the Black Panther Party, as revolutionary nationalists, advocated a fundamental change in the structure of American society to win freedom, justice, and equality for African Americans. The Panther's major rival on the West Coast, Maulana Karenga, held that African Americans first had to free themselves from an internalization of racial inferiority, that they needed a cultural change before they could initiate fundamental change within the society. In the same year that Newton and Seale founded the Black Panther Party, Karenga started the US (as distinct from "them") Organization to help rescue and rebuild the Watts community and other areas across the country that suffered from the devastation of urban uprisings. Whereas the Panthers primarily took inspiration from leftist ideology, US was heavily influenced by pan-Africanism. Karenga maintained that African Americans needed to reconstruct their African heritage for true liberation. He formulated the theory of Kawaida, a Swahili term meaning "tradition," defined through the Nguzo Saba, "seven principles," an African value system. Karenga initiated the celebration of Kwanzaa, a holiday for African Americans, from December 26 to January 1, which features one of the seven principles of the Nguzo Saba for each day. Kwanzaa, which means "first fruits" in Swahili, was established to counter the materialism that came to symbolize Christmas and that created financial strain for many poor and working-class black families. It was not meant to replace Christmas but to provide an opportunity during the holiday season for African Americans to focus on family and friends, communal values, and celebration of each other rather than material goods. Although Karenga began Kwanzaa in 1966 for African Americans to help them recover their identity and self-worth, Kwanzaa is now celebrated by people of African ancestry worldwide.

Kawaida theory influenced poet, playwright, and author LeRoi Jones, who changed his name to Imamu Amiri Baraka in 1966. Baraka was one of the most prominent writers of the Black Arts movement. Similar to Karenga, he believed that African Americans had to recover and embrace their own culture before they could acquire political liberation. In Chicago, Don L. Lee used Kawaida theory to build the Institute of Positive Education and Third World Press. Lee, who changed his name to Haki R. Madhubuti in 1973, was one of the most popular poets of the Black Arts movement. Paperback volumes of his poetry published by a black company, Broadside Press, sold hundreds of thousands of copies. Dudley F. Randall, a poet in his own right, founded Broadside Press in 1965 to print individual poems and books at affordable prices. In addition to Lee, Broadside Press published such poets as Gwendolyn Brooks, Nikki Giovanni, Robert Hayden, Etheridge Knight, Audre Lorde, Sonia Sanchez, and Margaret Walker.

## THE BLACK ARTS MOVEMENT

The Black Arts movement fostered Black Consciousness and linked art and politics to promote black liberation and self-determination. From the mid-1960s to the mid-1970s, black artists created one of the greatest outpourings of black dance, drama, literature, music, painting, poetry, and sculpture than in any era since the Harlem Renaissance of the 1920s. Inspired in large measure by Malcolm X and Black Power, the Black Arts movement sought to define a black aesthetic, a black vision of beauty and art. The very term "black" took on significance as a positive rather than a negative reference. "Negro" was associated with the old identity that involved self-hatred, dependency, and submissiveness. The new identity was one that African Americans defined for themselves. They were proud, assertive, and self-determining, and they displayed this new attitude in "Afro" hairstyles that featured large, bold, and natural mounds of hair without the use of chemicals that black men and women had previously applied to "straighten" their hair. They wore colorful dashikis or African-style dress with African-inspired pendants and jewelry. Many African Americans adopted Muslim, African, or African-sounding names to express their new identity.

The Black Arts movement drew on the improvisational qualities of jazz and the cadences of the black vernacular. There was an effort to meld black popular culture with African traditions, real or invented. Two publications, *Black World* and *The Black Scholar*, fostered discussion of the Black Arts movement, Black Power, and Black Consciousness. John H. Johnson, publisher of *Ebony Magazine*, began his business in 1942 with *Negro Digest*, a black version of *Reader's Digest*. *Negro Digest* stopped publication in 1951 but reappeared a decade later under the editorship of Hoyt W. Fuller, who shifted its direction from featuring material success and integration to a decidedly black cultural nationalist framework. Fuller changed the name of the journal to *Black World* in 1970 and presented some of the most important debates about black literature, culture, and politics by established and emerging black intellectuals and writers. By 1976, the journal began to lose circulation as the Black Arts movement, Black Power, and Black Consciousness waned, and Johnson decided to cease publication. Fuller, with a cadre of national supporters, published *First World Magazine* until his death in 1981. Robert Chrisman and Nathan Hare started *The Black Scholar* in California in 1969. Although it featured some of the same writers, it had a revolutionary nationalist rather than the cultural nationalist bent of *Black World*. *The Black Scholar* has tried to make the work of the black academy, especially black studies programs, more accessible to the black community.

## BLACK STUDIES

The drive for the institutionalization of black studies, especially on predominantly white college campuses, began during the late 1960s under the influence of the Black Power, Black Consciousness, and Black Arts movements. Black studies, as the multidisciplinary analysis of the lives and thought of people of African ancestry on the African continent and throughout the world, has a lineage in this country dating from the 1830s. The early study of black people took place outside the academy in historical and literary associations. The more academic approach began with W. E. B. Du Bois in the early twentieth century and the Atlanta University Studies, a series of examinations of black life that Du Bois proposed to replicate each decade to provide a record of black history, problems, and accomplishment. Carter G. Woodson, through the Association for the Study of Negro (now African American) Life and History, founded in 1915, promoted the discovery, preservation, writing, and dissemination of information about the African and African American past. He published the *Journal of Negro History* (currently the *Journal of African American History*) in 1916. Woodson began the observance of Negro History Week in 1926, expanded to Black History Month in 1976 during the nation's bicentennial. Beginning in 1939, with the inauguration of Gunnar Myrdal's massive study of black America, *An American Dilemma*, more white scholars began to take note of the African American past. Franz Boas at Columbia University and Robert Park at the University of Chicago were pioneer white scholars in the study of Africans and African Americans. They were followed by Melville Herskovits, Herbert Aptheker, Kenneth Stampp, and August Meier.

As more black students entered predominantly white colleges and universities during the late 1960s, they challenged the prevailing orthodoxies that either ignored black people or characterized them as inferior, deviant, and pathological. The black college population grew dramatically from about 200,000 in 1960 to more than 500,000 by 1970. This increase came in large part from federal legislation during the mid-1960s that barred discrimination in higher education and provided financial-aid programs. Higher education also sought to provide an alternative for black youth from the disorder and violence taking place in urban areas across the country. Black students, first at San Francisco State College and later across the country, demanded courses that were relevant to their experiences. They also demanded black faculty to teach the courses. As a part of black self-determination, they wanted programs, departments, centers, and institutes to house the courses. The students sought black cultural centers and in some instances black dormitories. Colleges and universities accommodated the growing number of black students in various ways. Most schools established black studies programs in which faculty held joint appointments with traditional departments. A few formed black studies departments that gave black studies the same position as traditional departments, with discretion over curriculum, hiring, tenure, and promotion.

These changes did not come without struggle as black students across the country, often with white allies such as the Students for a Democratic Society, conducted strikes and took over buildings to press their demands. By 1973, there were more than two hundred black studies programs and departments. The National Council for Black Studies was organized in 1975 to foster the expansion and development of the field. The movement for black studies during the late 1960s and early 1970s corresponded with the insurgency of African

Americans, especially in northern urban areas. The early proponents of black studies sought to wed the academy with the streets, to make scholarship relevant to the improvement of black communities. In Atlanta, the Institute of the Black World, established in 1969 under the leadership of historian Vincent Harding, promoted the development of black studies and held early discussions about its methods and purposes as well as curriculum development. The Institute of the Black World through research, workshops, and conferences examined the use of education for social change.

## URBAN UPRISINGS, REBELLIONS, OR RIOTS

The rise of Black Power coincided with the outbreak of some of the worst urban uprisings, rebellions, or riots in the history of the United States, which many commentators blamed on the new black consciousness and militancy. There were some 329 riots in 257 cities across the nation between 1964 and 1968. Two of the worse outbreaks of violence after the Watts Riot of 1965 were in Newark, New Jersey, and Detroit, Michigan, in 1967. The precipitant for both of these outbreaks was an encounter with the police. As the National Advisory Commission on Civil Disorders (the Kerner Commission) would later report, police practices were the major grievance for African Americans, more so than unemployment, substandard housing, and inadequate education. The police were symbols of oppression and were emblematic of political repression. In Newark, rumor spread that the police killed a black cabdriver after his arrest for speeding. For three days, African Americans looted stores and set fire to buildings. Twenty-one African Americans lost their lives and 1,600 were arrested, and there was more than $10 million in property damage. Ten days after the Newark uprising, African Americans in Detroit rioted after a police raid on an illegal bar. Before the National Guard and Federal infantry troops quelled the violence, there were forty-three deaths and 7,231 arrests, along with almost $200 million in property damage.

Matters grew worse with the assassination of Martin Luther King Jr. on April 4, 1968, at the hands of a white supremacist named James Earl Ray. African Americans took to the streets throughout the country in anger and frustration. The National Advisory Commission on Civil Disorders, appointed by President Lyndon B. Johnson to examine the causes of the riots, especially after the unprecedented violence in Newark and Detroit, concluded that the uprisings stemmed from African Americans' being left behind in the tide of economic progress sweeping the country. In an oft-quoted statement, the Kerner Commission reported that America was becoming two nations—one black and one white, separate and unequal. The urban rebellions were a form of political insurgency, of collective violence, releasing pent-up resentment over economic exploitation, racial discrimination, and police brutality. Despite civil rights legislation, executive orders, and court decisions, African Americans especially in the North believed that they had experienced little positive change in their lives.

## THE WAR ON POVERTY

Although Lyndon B. Johnson had promised to launch the "Great Society" after being elected president in 1964, the war in Vietnam overshadowed his vaunted War on Poverty. The Economic Opportunity Act of 1964 established the Head Start Program to provide preschool education for poor children, Upward Bound to prepare poor teenagers for college, Volunteers in Service to America (VISTA) to assist poor communities as a type of domestic peace corps, the Legal Services Corporation to give legal assistance to indigent clients, and the Community Action Program to make the services of federally funded antipoverty agencies more accessible to the poor. Other programs—food stamps, free school lunches, Medicare (health care for the elderly), Medicaid (health care for the poor), and federal aid to education—helped to alleviate poverty, especially for the elderly and white Americans. In 1959, 35.2 percent of Americans aged 65 and above were below the poverty line, according to the U.S. Census Bureau. By 1975, the number had dropped to 15.3 percent. 15.2 percent of white families were below the poverty line in 1959, which declined to 7.7 percent by 1975. For African American families, 48.1 percent were in poverty in 1959 and 27.1 percent by 1975. The percentage of impoverished elderly declined by 57 percent; the percentage of white families dropped by 49 percent, and the percentage of black families by 43 percent.

## THE VIETNAM WAR

While a relatively smaller percentage of black families were escaping from poverty, a higher proportion of African Americans were serving in Vietnam. American involvement in the Vietnam War escalated between 1965 and 1968, when the United States took over much of the fighting from the South Vietnamese. Because they were less likely to receive draft deferments for education, medical disability, or conscientious objection, the military drafted black youth at a disproportionate rate, twice as high as white youth. Although African Americans made up only about 12 percent of the population, black men suffered almost a quarter of the casualties in the war. Moreover, the cost of the War against Poverty paled in comparison with the War in Vietnam, some $10 billion to $140 billion. Martin Luther King Jr., who became a vigorous opponent to the war in Vietnam, estimated that it cost almost $500,000 to kill one enemy soldier at a time when the country spent only about $35 a person to relieve poverty. King's opposition to the war brought great criticism from traditional civil rights leaders and supporters. But King questioned the government's willingness to spend enormous sums to kill people abroad rather than to uplift its dispossessed at home. King was not alone in braving opprobrium for opposing the war in Vietnam. Muhammad Ali, formerly known as Cassius Clay, whom Malcolm X had recently converted to the Nation of Islam and who became world heavyweight boxing champion on February 25, 1964, refused induction for the military in 1967 on religious grounds and because he believed that African Americans were being forced to fight a war that was not in their interests. He was convicted of violating the Selective Service Act and sentenced to five years in prison, which he appealed. The Supreme Court overturned his conviction in June 1970, but for three and a half years, at the prime of his career, Ali was prohibited from boxing. He regained the heavyweight title in 1974.

## BENIGN NEGLECT

In March 1968, after U.S. forces suffered tremendous casualties during the Tet Offensive, at the beginning of the Vietnamese New Year, President Johnson announced that the United States would stop bombing North Vietnam and begin peace negotiations. Given growing opposition to the war, failure to achieve the Great Society, white backlash against his civil rights initiatives, and declining popularity, Johnson also announced that he would not seek his party's nomination for the presidency. Richard M. Nixon's election as president in 1968 slowed the momentum that African Americans had gained during the civil rights era. Nixon's domestic policy adviser, Daniel Patrick Moynihan, who had served as assistant secretary of labor in the Johnson administration, called for a period of "benign neglect" for African Americans. He argued that most of the unrest among African Americans, especially the riots, was a result of "rising expectations," that is, the promise of improvement in their lives engendered frustration for many African Americans for whom change was not taking place fast enough. Moreover, Nixon had run as a "law and order" candidate to put an end to violence in the streets and as a promoter of black capitalism as a form of black power to improve the economic condition of African Americans. The tide began to change from the government's role in promoting social justice to the accusation of deficiencies among black people themselves. As assistant secretary of labor in the Johnson administration, Moynihan had produced a study, *The Negro Family: The Case for National Action*, that became known as the

Moynihan Report. The study was controversial, inasmuch as it seemed to affirm the idea of a "culture of poverty." For Moynihan, the explosive growth of black female-headed households after World War II was a primary source of the problems confronting the black poor in juvenile delinquency, teenage pregnancy, illegitimacy, crime, drug addiction, and poor school performance. This breakdown of the lower socioeconomic black family helped to perpetuate a "cycle of poverty." While Moynihan proposed government intervention through food stamps and a guarantee of income that would eliminate the welfare bureaucracy and keep families intact, many social scientists, in particular, focused on alleged deficiencies among African Americans rather than the impact of racial discrimination, poverty, and unequal educational opportunities on black families and individuals.

## AFFIRMATIVE ACTION

Although the Nixon administration initiated the recommended period of benign neglect, it continued the policy of affirmative action that President John F. Kennedy put in place with Executive Order 10925, which required government contractors to take affirmative action to ensure that applicants were employed without discrimination on the basis of race, creed, color, or national origin. Title VII of the 1964 Civil Rights Act barred discrimination in employment on the basis of race, color, religion, sex, or national origin. It empowered federal courts to order "affirmative action as may be appropriate" to remedy past workplace discrimination. President Johnson's Executive Order 11375 obligated government contractors to set goals and timetables for employing previously "underutilized" minority workers who were available and qualified for positions. The Johnson administration urged government, business, and labor to open more jobs to African Americans, to seek qualified employees affirmatively, and to train those who did not meet job qualifications. The Department of Health, Education, and Welfare (HEW) required in 1967 that colleges and universities receiving federal funds set affirmative action goals for employing women and minority faculty. During the Nixon years, HEW stipulated that colleges and universities recruit, employ, and promote members of previously excluded groups, even if prior exclusion could not be traced to past discriminatory actions. The HEW guidelines distinguished between goals that were indicators of compliance and quotas that might exclude others from equal opportunity.

Numerous cases have come before the Supreme Court that have provided a narrower tailoring of affirmative action. In the 1978 *Regents of the University of California v. Bakke* decision, the court ruled against quotas but upheld the use of race as one variable among many in selecting a diverse student body. A year later in *United Steel Workers v. Weber*, the court approved the use of quotas by employers in skill-training programs to increase the number of African Americans eligible for skilled positions. The court in 1980 affirmed congressional legislation that mandated a 10 percent "set aside" of public construction funds for minority firms but rejected in *Richmond v. J. A. Croson Co.* (1989) a municipal set-aside provision of 30 percent for minority contractors. Two Supreme Court decisions, *Shaw v. Reno* (1993) and *Adarand Constructors v. Pena* (1995), suggested that the court might be moving away from affirmative action practices and more toward "colorblind" considerations, especially in the composition of voting districts and the award of contracts. But in *Grutter v. Bollinger* (2003), involving the admissions practices of the University of Michigan Law School, the Supreme Court reinforced *Bakke* and stipulated that race could be one consideration to promote the educational benefits of diversity. In a challenge to the University of Michigan's undergraduate admissions procedures (*Gratz v. Bollinger*), the Court rejected awarding points on the basis of race and ethnicity as being too mechanical, not narrowly tailored, and not providing an individualized review of each applicant. The Court, however, endorsed the compelling need for diversity in higher education and the nation's interest in keeping paths to leadership open for talented and qualified individuals of every race and ethnicity.

## BLACK POLITICAL ACTIVISM

One of the more enduring effects of the Black Power and Black Consciousness movements has been in the political arena. Black nationalists, community activists, and politicians called a series of national conventions during the late 1960s and early 1970s to develop a black agenda and to elect more African Americans to political office. The 1967 Black Power Conference held in Newark called for greater black self-determination in education, community services, and election of black officials. The conference adopted a "Black Power Manifesto" that likened the black population in the United States to a neocolonial people and called for African Americans to unite in common cause for liberation. Some of the black cultural nationalists wanted to consider dividing the United States into separate black and white nations as a means for African Americans finally to escape white domination and oppression. Several other Black Power conferences were held but failed to generate consensus on a black agenda. Some advocates defined Black Power as a form of black capitalism, while others desired a plebiscite to determine whether African Americans wanted to separate from the United States into a distinct part of the country, perhaps in five southern states. This idea was very close to the Nation of Islam, which declared that if the United States would not accord African Americans their rights, then it should set aside land for them in the South where they would be able to take care of themselves. At the Congress of African Peoples convention in 1970 in Atlanta, the delegates adopted the concept of "nation time" to move African Americans forward under the precept of unity without uniformity.

After the riots, white flight from the cities to the suburbs, and black political activism, many cities elected black mayors. In 1967, Carl Stokes of Cleveland became the first black mayor of a major city, with Richard Hatcher elected mayor of Gary, Indiana, the same year. By 1975, there were 135 black mayors, who went on to form the National Conference of Black Mayors. Atlanta, Baltimore, Birmingham, Chicago, Cincinnati, Cleveland, Dayton, Denver, Detroit, Jackson (Mississippi), Kansas City (Missouri), Little Rock, Los Angeles, Minneapolis, New Orleans, Newark, New York City, Oakland, Philadelphia, Richmond (Virginia), Rochester (New York), Seattle, St. Louis, and Washington, D.C., had all elected black mayors by the 1990s. The number of black elected officials swelled to more than eight thousand by 1993. In 1971, there were thirteen black members of Congress, five elected that year. The group formally organized as the Congressional Black Caucus (CBC) on June 18, 1971. The CBC helped to sponsor the 1972 National Black Political Convention in Gary, Indiana, which attracted some eight thousand attendees. The convention discussed political empowerment, coalition building, and the prospect of a black independent party. Disagreements arose over whether African Americans should abandon established labor unions and form their own, a resolution condemning Israel for racist exploitation of Palestinians, and busing for school desegregation. Several other black political conventions were held during the 1970s but with similar results. While most black nationalists sought an independent black political party, black elected officials determined that their interests and those of their constituencies remained within the Democratic Party. The CBC inspired the establishment of TransAfrica in 1977 as a lobby for issues related to American policy toward Africa and the Caribbean. TransAfrica spearheaded the anti-apartheid drive that led to American sanctions against South Africa, Nelson Mandela's release from prison in 1990, the dismantling of apartheid, and South Africa's first democratic elections in 1994 that installed Mandela as president. The CBC also established the Congressional Black Caucus Foundation to undertake studies of issues relating to the black community and congressional policies. The CBC has been a strong advocate for improving education, economic development, employment, health, criminal justice, and housing for African Americans.

Given the drive for greater black political empowerment, Shirley Chisholm, the first black woman elected to Congress, announced her candidacy for the Democratic Party nomination for president in January 1972. She was the first African American to launch a campaign for a major party nomination for president. She expected that she would gain the support of women's groups and of African Americans, but she was not able to energize either. Although she was dedicated to improving conditions for African Americans as she demonstrated while a member of the New York State Legislature, African Americans identified her more with the women's movement as a co-founder of the National Organization for Women (NOW). In one of her speeches before the U.S. House of Representatives, Chisholm declared, "As a black person, I am no stranger to race prejudice. But the truth is that in the political world I have been far oftener discriminated against because I am a woman than because I am black."[3] When she announced her candidacy for the Democratic Party presidential nomination, she said, "I stand before you today as a candidate for the Democratic nomination for the Presidency of the United States. I am not the candidate of black America, although I am black and proud. I am not the candidate of the women's movement of this country, although I am a woman, and I am equally proud of that. I am not the candidate of any political bosses or special interests. I am the candidate of the people." Chisholm did not build a base for her candidacy and garnered only 151 delegate votes for the 1972 Democratic Party National Convention.

By 1975, with the death of Elijah Muhammad and transformation of the Nation of Islam into an orthodox Islamic group (although Louis Farrakhan would revive the old group in 1978), the conservative backlash against social welfare programs, and economic recession, the Black Power / Black Consciousness era came to a close. Although the intensity of the period would fade, currents would persist to the present. With the rise of the black middle class, the persistence of a large black underclass, the strengthening voice of black women, the incorporation of African Americans into mainstream politics, and greater diversification of the black population with black immigration from abroad, African Americans became more multidimensional. The civil rights and Black Power movements opened American society more widely to African Americans. But for the post-1975 period, there were challenges that did not lend themselves to amelioration with the strategies of the past.

## NOTES

1. Quintard Taylor, *In Search of the Racial Frontier: African Americans in the American West* (New York: Norton, 1998), 290–291.

2. Stokely Carmichael and Charles Hamilton, *Black Power: The Politics of Liberation in America* (New York: Random House, 1967), 44.

3. Shirley Chisholm, *The Good Fight* (New York: Harper & Row, 1973).

# A GLASS HALF-FULL OR HALF-EMPTY

In 1989, the National Research Council published *A Common Destiny: Blacks and American Society*, the most comprehensive review of African Americans since the Myrdal study of 1944. The study's editors concluded that the "status of black Americans today can be characterized as a glass half full—if measured by progress since 1939—or as a glass that is half empty—if measured by the persisting disparities between black and white Americans since the early 1970s."[1] The progress that African Americans enjoyed came in large measure from greater opportunity in education and in employment.

## GROWTH OF THE BLACK MIDDLE CLASS

The black middle class, as defined by education, occupation, and income, is primarily a post-1960s development. In 1960, only 20 percent of African Americans completed high school, compared with 43 percent of the white population. African Americans had little access to higher education, except at historically black colleges, and were largely excluded from graduate and professional schools. Only 3 percent of African Americans graduated from college, less than half the white graduation rate of 8 percent. The small number of black professionals was largely confined to serving the black population. They were primarily small businessmen, ministers, teachers, and undertakers, with a few doctors, lawyers, and pharmacists. African Americans found limited white-collar opportunities outside the black community in either the public or private sectors of the economy. The civil rights movement, black skill development, public policy, and economic growth contributed to the emergence of a sizeable black middle class.

As the opportunity structure of the country expanded, African Americans took advantage of the new possibilities. They enjoyed both absolute progress as the nation as a whole prospered and relative progress in relation to the rest of the society. By 1995, African Americans graduated from high school at almost the same rate as white Americans, at about 87 percent. A third of eighteen- to twenty-four-year-old black high school graduates enrolled in college, compared with about 42 percent of whites in the same category. White students, however, graduated with a bachelor's degree or more, about 24 percent, at twice the rate of black students. Today, African Americans hold a wider range of jobs than in 1960. They have been particularly successful in securing middle-income employment in the public sector. African Americans are twice as likely as whites to work for municipal, state, or federal government. Although the public sector has provided African Americans with generally stable middle-income positions, it does not pay as much as the private sector. African Americans in the private sector are less likely than whites to hold executive, administrative, and managerial positions. Black professionals in the corporate world are more apt to hold "soft" positions in personnel and public relations than to have line authority in planning and production, which would help them to move up the corporate ladder.

By the late 1990s, about 40 percent of black households held middle-class status, compared with approximately 60 percent of white households. The Economic Policy Institute defined middle-class status as families earning between $40,000 and $60,000 a year in 1999. The proportion of black middle-class households almost doubled since 1960 and grew at a faster rate than the white middle class. Middle-income status for African Americans, however, required that black women contribute more to household income than white women. Although middle-income status today demands more two-paycheck households, black wives are one and half times more likely than white wives to work full time. Moreover, the median income for black college-educated women is almost the same as that of white women, while black college-educated men earn about $9,000 less than white men. More black women than black men are graduating from college and from graduate and professional schools. Although still significant, the median income gap between black male and female college graduates is closing faster than the gap between black and white male college graduates. The declining number of black male college graduates and the improving economic status of black females help to explain the drop in percentage of female-headed black family households below the poverty line. In 1987, 51 percent of black female-headed households were below the poverty line. A decade later, only 40 percent of such households were impoverished. Although improving, the percentage is still much larger than the 24 percent of all black families in poverty and only 8 percent of two-parent households.

Whether the black middle class can reproduce itself well into the twenty-first century is questionable. Hugh Price, president of the National Urban League, observed in 1998, "Many of us have been laboring under the false comfort that the expansion of the black middle class and the creation of individual black millionaires have moved African Americans closer to economic parity. The reality is, no matter how great incomes become for individual blacks, our wealth is not sustained because we have very few assets that can be passed on." The black middle class rests more on income than on assets. Black married couples have about 80 percent of the income of white married couples but only one-quarter the net worth. Given its net financial assets, a typical middle-class white family can sustain itself at its current standard of living for about four months if it loses its income stream, while the typical middle-class black family could not sustain itself for a month. Among some African Americans, there is the sad but true expression that the difference between being middle class and poor is one paycheck. Although economic prosperity during the 1990s was good for African Americans, they have historically been the last hired and the first fired. Because of its fragility, the black middle class confronts more economic strains than the white middle class and is less able to pass on human and financial capital to the next generation.[2]

## THE PERSISTENCE OF POVERTY

In 1997, the black poverty rate was less than 27 percent, the lowest ever recorded, but still more than twice as high as that among white Americans (about 11 percent). Black unemployment, moreover, remained more than twice as high as white unemployment (about 10 percent against 4.7 percent). The new global economy and the decline of manufacturing jobs in heavy industries such as auto, rubber, and steel have limited the prospects for a further decline in poverty rates for African Americans. Many of the jobs that were a way out of poverty have been relocated not just out of inner city areas with large black populations but out of the country to low-wage areas abroad. The shift to a service-based and high-technology economy has dried up well-paying blue-collar jobs and has created a widening gap between greater skilled professional work and low-paying employment that requires less education. Economists William A. Darity Jr. and

Samuel L. Myers Jr., in their book *Persistent Disparity: Race and Economic Inequality in the United States Since 1945*, argue that earnings for the top strata of society, both black and white, have increased, stagnated for those in the middle, and declined for those at the bottom. African Americans, unfortunately, are disproportionately represented at the bottom of the economic ladder. As white males lose good-paying jobs, they depress the occupational ladder for African Americans, by dominating the remaining well-paid positions. The political commentator and author Kevin Phillips has noted that economic growth for the top 1 percent of the country, during the presidency of Ronald Reagan, increased to 37 percent of private net worth, a figure not reached since 1929 before the nation suffered the Great Depression. Corporate chief executives, whose pay in 1980 was thirty to forty times more than that of the average worker, increased their compensation to 130–140 times more by 1990. Meanwhile, the middle class experienced little growth and even some erosion of its position.[3] Many middle-class white Americans who became nervous about the precariousness of their own economic position began to question and even oppose what they perceived as an advantage for African Americans through affirmative action in education and employment.

## POLITICAL INCORPORATION

African Americans sought to protect the gains of the civil rights era through the political process. In addition to the number of black elected officials that grew from about a hundred in 1964 to more than eight thousand by 1994, African Americans worked primarily through the Democratic Party to secure extending the voting rights act, strengthening federal restrictions against discrimination based on race, gender, age, or handicap, and enforcing fair housing laws. One of the greatest triumphs was President Ronald Reagan's signing into law on November 2, 1983, legislation that established the third Monday in January as an official national holiday in honor of Martin Luther King Jr. To forestall the Reagan agenda to unravel Lyndon Johnson's Great Society, especially its social welfare programs, and advances in civil rights, Jesse Jackson entered the Democratic presidential primary in 1983. His strategy was to energize the black electorate, to register larger numbers to vote, to influence the Democratic Party platform, and to elect more black and progressive white candidates. He sought to forge a "Rainbow Coalition" of voters across racial, ethnic, and gender lines. His appeal was primarily to those who felt shut out of government, who were dispossessed socially and economically. Although Jackson pursued a broad constituency, he carried considerable baggage. He had never been elected to office and lacked experience in foreign affairs. He had upset Jewish voters by meeting with Yasir Arafat, head of the Palestinian Liberation Organization in 1979, and by calling New York City "Hymietown," an obvious ethnic slur. Louis Farrakhan, who had been recruited to the Nation of Islam by Malcolm X and who became national spokesman after Malcolm X left the organization, defended Jesse Jackson and provided bodyguards from the Fruit of Islam. Farrakhan himself became embroiled in controversy when he was accused of making anti-Semitic remarks.

Jackson gained about one-quarter of the votes in the Democratic Party primaries and secured approximately three hundred delegates, only an eighth of the total and not enough to secure the nomination. He was given a prominent time slot to address the Democratic National Convention in San Francisco, which helped to increase his national stature. Jackson did succeed in registering more African Americans to vote and in inspiring more of them to go to the polls, although the Democratic Party nominee, Walter Mondale, lost the election to incumbent President Reagan. Jackson's run, however, involved more African Americans in the political process. He ran again in the 1987 Democratic Party primary and increased his vote total to one-third of the ballots cast and his delegate count to more than a fourth of the total. Jackson's primary candidacy strengthened black influence within the Democratic Party. In 1989, William H. Gray III, from Pennsylvania, became the first African American to serve as majority whip in the House of Representatives. Earlier that year, Ronald H. Brown became the first African American to chair the Democratic National Committee and helped to engineer Bill Clinton's election as president in 1992. L. Douglas Wilder, in 1990, became the first African American ever elected governor when he became Virginia's chief executive. Two years later, Carol Moseley Braun from Illinois became the first black woman elected to the U.S. Senate and only the second African American to serve in that body in the twentieth century, after Edward W. Brooke III, a Republican, who was elected from Massachusetts in 1966. There were seventeen new black members of Congress in 1993, raising the membership of the Congressional Black Caucus from seventeen when it was founded in 1971 to thirty-eight. There were actually thirty-nine black members of the U.S. House of Representatives, but Gary A. Franks, Republican from Connecticut, chose not to join the Congressional Black Caucus. These numbers gave black members of Congress some leverage within the Democratic Party, but not sufficient strength to pass legislation.

African Americans fared fairly well during the Clinton administration as he appointed black Americans in unprecedented numbers to federal and judicial positions. Moreover, the economy prospered during his presidency with record low levels of unemployment and the lowest level of African Americans below the poverty line since the figures were first recorded in the 1960s. President Clinton enjoyed great popularity among African Americans, especially with his comfort in their presence and seeming understanding of their plight. He helped to strengthen historically black colleges and universities and through federal loan programs made college education more accessible. He came under criticism, however, for his welfare reform bill, which required adult welfare recipients to find work within two years, restricted family benefits to five years, and transferred control of welfare programs to the states through block grants. These reforms took place during prosperous times but disturbed many black leaders who feared their effects on African Americans if the economy turned sour.

## ELUSIVE RACIAL EQUALITY

Although African Americans made impressive social, political, and economic gains since 1939, racial equality in relation to the rest of the society remained an elusive goal. Housing segregation actually increased by the end of the twentieth century, and with it the drive for school integration declined. In measures of life span, infant mortality, teenage pregnancy, single-parent households, imprisonment, AIDS infections, poverty, and crime, African Americans suffered by comparison with the rest of the population. At the end of the twentieth century, one in three young black men were under the supervision of the criminal justice system, either under arrest, in prison, or on parole. Black males were ten times more likely than whites to be imprisoned. They were targeted as potential criminals through racial profiling, arrested more frequently, generally had less than adequate legal representation, were convicted at higher rates, and received longer sentences for the same crimes committed by whites. For example, African Americans were 15 percent of the nation's drug users but were a third of those arrested for drug use and almost two-thirds of those convicted on drug charges. Almost half the nation's prison population was black, as were 40 percent of the inmates on death row.

Police brutality, a precipitant of many of the urban uprisings during the mid-1960s, remained a problem for African Americans. The police beating of Rodney King in Los Angeles in 1992 was captured on videotape and outraged many African Americans who assumed that the police would be held accountable. Before the police trial, a Korean storeowner in Los Angeles, who had also been recorded on videotape in the murder of a fifteen-year-old black girl, Latasha Harlins, for allegedly stealing a bottle of orange juice, received only five years probation and community service as punishment. When an all-white jury in Simi Valley, California, to which the police trial had been moved because of pretrial publicity, acquitted the police of excessive force, assault with a deadly weapon, and filing false reports, African Americans in Los Angeles went on a rampage. They especially took out vengeance on Korean storeowners. In lives lost, about fifty-eight, and property damage of about $1 billion, the Los Angeles riot was the worst uprising ever. Later, when African Americans in large measure celebrated the 1994 acquittal of O. J. Simpson, the famous football player, who had been tried for the murder of his ex-wife Nicole Brown and her friend Ronald Goldman, many white Americans found it difficult to understand their joy. In many respects, O. J. Simpson had become demonized during the trial, but the brilliant defense of his attorneys, especially the black lawyer Johnnie Cochran, signaled a victory not just for Simpson but for black America. The issue of police brutality, however, still persisted during the end of the twentieth century with a New York City policeman sodomizing Abner Louima with a broomstick in 1997; Riverside, California police, in 1998, firing twenty-seven shots at Tyisha Miller, who was asleep in her car, hitting her a dozen times and causing her death; and New York City police, in 1999, shooting Amadou Diallo forty-one times and killing him while he stood unarmed in the entrance to his apartment building. Add to these blatant incidents of police brutality, the heinous lynching on June 7, 1998, of James Byrd Jr. in Jasper, Texas, whose white assailants slit his throat and dragged his body for two and a half miles behind a pickup truck, tearing his limbs apart, there was still a question in American society of the extent to which the black body was given equal value or could be violated with impunity.

## RECONCILIATION, RESPONSIBILITY, AND REPARATIONS

For many conservatives, black and white, primary responsibility for African Americans achieving racial equality resided in themselves. Shelby Steele identified black victimization as the primary deterrent to progress. Steele and more recently John McWhorter have suggested that African Americans must rely more on themselves than on government programs, such as affirmative action. They and others have argued that the "victim mentality" has relieved African Americans of responsibility because they have focused more on what has been done to them than on what they can do for themselves. Moreover, the so-called victim mentality has been divisive by looking at everything through the lens of race.

Ironically, the Million Man March of October 16, 1995, almost fit into a similar conservative framework. The Million Man March attracted the largest assembly of African Americans in the nation's history. Manning Marable described the social philosophy of the event as "deeply conservative," because it did not devote major attention to public policy or the need for new legislation to improve the condition of African Americans. Instead, it focused almost entirely on African American men and the need for change from within.[4] Louis Farrakhan, head of the Nation of Islam, issued the call for the Million Man March, in many respects a stroke of genius, to address the despair, alienation, and hopelessness felt by many black men, especially young ones. Drugs, single-parent households, teenage pregnancy, violence, and incarceration were tearing apart many black communities.

Local organizing committees were established in more than three hundred cities largely through the efforts of the Nation of Islam. A range of black men of different religious persuasion and socioeconomic background helped to organize for the march. Louis Farrakhan, who occupied the place of honor at the march and was its main speaker, encountered much criticism for his anti-Semitic remarks, for calling an all-male march, and for homophobic sentiments within the Nation of Islam. Despite the criticism of Farrakhan and the Nation of Islam, black men, out of a deep sense of a need for self-assertion, rallied to the idea of the march. In the words of Ron Daniels, chair of the Campaign for a New Tomorrow, "Farrakhan made the call—but the March belongs to us all."[5] Many black men attended the march as an act of defiance, to demonstrate that they could think for themselves, and to show the nation and each other that black men were not parasites, living off the society and making no positive contribution to it. There were almost as many reasons for attending the march as there were participants. LaRon D. Bennett, a Christian minister from Brunswick, Georgia, joined the march as a statement "that we as a group, black males, and as a people, black Americans, are facing a unique and serious dilemma, and we are committed to doing our part to change it."[6]

Although the official mission statement for the march listed three challenges "to Ourselves, to the Government, and to the Corporations," the published program for the march centered on "The Challenge to Ourselves." The three major themes were atonement for past failings to themselves, their communities, and the environment; reconciliation with their families and communities to achieve operational unity without uniformity; and responsibility "in personal conduct, in family relations and in obligations to the community and to the struggle for a just society and a better world."[7] As part of the Million Man March, the organizing committee called for a Day of Absence for those who could not attend the march, and especially for black women to stay away from work, school, entertainment, and sports and to concentrate on atonement, reconciliation, and responsibility. The Million Man March was to serve as a catalyst for change among African Americans. It is difficult to assess its success or failure. For a time, many black churches and organizations experienced an increase in black male membership and participation. Black male voter turnout was higher in 1996 than four years earlier, although black female voter turnout declined. This may have been a reason for the Million Woman March on October 25, 1997, in

Philadelphia. The Million Woman March mission statement featured family values, education, health, homelessness, and respect for the elderly. The official poster for the march proclaimed repentance, resurrection, and restoration. Numerous other efforts followed the pattern of the Million Man March, including the Million Children's March and the Million Family March. One of the goals of the Million Man March was to create an African American Development Fund, to be administered by the preexisting National Black United Fund, which was organized in 1972 to assist social welfare and social action organizations. The African American Development Fund was to foster business development among African Americans.

Perhaps because of failure to start a significant African American Development Fund, attention during the late twentieth and early twenty-first century turned to reparations. The persistence of poverty, perpetuation of a large black underclass that disproportionately represented about a third of the black population, deteriorating inner city education, declining employment opportunities, and continued disadvantage for African Americans in relation to the rest of the society strengthened the case for reparations. The idea of reparations for African Americans dates back to the end of the Civil War, when many former slaves anticipated that they would receive forty acres and a mule for their unrequited labor. Their anticipation was heightened by the Freedmen's Bureau Bill of March 3, 1865, which provided for settling former slaves and poor whites on forty-acre plots of abandoned land. Few of them received any land as owners of abandoned land reclaimed their property. Marcus Garvey's Universal Negro Improvement Association (UNIA) and the Nation of Islam during the early twentieth century demanded land in compensation for slavery and the oppression of African Americans. Queen Mother Moore, a member of the UNIA and an activist in Harlem, started the Reparations Committee of Descendants of United States Slaves in 1955. One of the most dramatic calls for reparations came in 1969 when James Forman, former executive secretary of the Student Non-Violent Coordinating Committee, disrupted services at New York's Riverside Church and read the Black Manifesto, demanding that white churches and synagogues pay $500 million in compensation for slavery.

The movement for reparations gained steam during the late 1980s when several African American organizations formed the National Coalition of Blacks for Reparations in America (N'COBRA) 1987. Moreover, Jewish organizations since World War II succeeded in securing reparations from the German government for the Holocaust, in which some six million Jews were systematically murdered. Japanese Americans also pressed the case for an apology and restitution for loss of property to those individuals interned in concentration camps during World War II. President Ronald Reagan in 1988 signed an act that apologized for the wrongful internment of Japanese Americans and that provided each surviving internee with a tax-exempt payment of $20,000. During the early 1990s, Jewish groups pressed banks, especially Swiss banks, which illegally held the assets of Holocaust victims and survivors. These organizations also sought compensation from corporations that used Jewish slave labor during World War II. A $1.25 billion settlement was reached in 1998 that included a $100 million payment to low-income, elderly Jewish victims of the Holocaust, especially the use of slave labor.[8]

Former TransAfrica head Randall Robinson made an eloquent and popular case for reparations with his book *The Debt: What America Owes to Blacks*, published in 2000. The book became a national bestseller and creed for the twenty-first-century reparations movement. For Robinson, it was time to address the plight of the millions of African Americans mired in poverty. He argued for restitution to African Americans for the damage done to them psychically, economically, and socially through enslavement and racial segregation and discrimination. The first step for him is for America "to face up to the massive crime of slavery and all that it has wrought."[9] The United States has not acknowledged nor has it apologized for the damage done to African Americans that must come first before trying to right the wrongs of racial oppression. African Americans have occupied a disadvantaged place in American society for so long that it has become structural, deeply embedded in the nation's fabric, and will take dramatic and wide-ranging action to correct it.

## THE COMPLEXITY OF BLACK PROGRESS

The National Urban League labeled its report for 2004 on the state of black America *The Complexity of Black Progress*. Although African Americans have made great strides toward the goal of racial equality, the gap in education, economics, health, social justice, and civic engagement remains wide. The economic boom of the Clinton years subsided after the 2000 elections as the nation entered a recession and African Americans lost ground. The recession was exacerbated by the terrorist attacks of September 11, 2001, on the World Trade Center in New York City and the Pentagon in Washington, D.C., which took more than three thousand American lives. Because of substantial differences in wealth, African Americans experience greater difficulty in weathering an economic recession than white Americans. During the boom years of the 1990s, white wealth grew at a faster rate, and black net worth dropped from 22 percent of white net worth in 1992 to 16 percent by 2001. Moreover, average black household income, which had grown to about 68 percent of average white household income by 1999, dropped to approximately 64 percent by 2001, or about the level that existed in 1975. The deteriorating position of black wage earners was in large measure the result of a general decline in manufacturing jobs.[10]

Black unemployment as well as white unemployment increased after the election of George W. Bush to the presidency in 2000. Bush won the election by carrying the state of Florida by a margin of 537 votes. Black voter turnout in Florida was particularly high because African Americans were disenchanted with the governor, Bush's brother Jeb, for his retreat from affirmative action. The percentage of African Americans registered to vote in 2000 and the percentage that went to the polls were the highest over the past twenty years. In Florida, 16 percent of registered voters in 2000 were African American, compared to 10 percent in 1996, although African Americans were only 13 percent of the state's voting age population. Black voters in Florida, however, found themselves harassed, turned away from the polls, and given misleading ballot instructions. Black voters were ten times more likely than white voters to have their ballots rejected, even if they got the chance to vote. George W. Bush's opponent, Al Gore, would have won the election for president if the black ballots had counted.[11]

A major issue that grew out of the 2000 elections was the disfranchisement of black voters with felony convictions. In Florida, felony convictions were particularly salient because many black men found their names mistakenly on a list that the state paid a private company to cleanse its voting rolls of convicted felons. Twenty-nine states prevent felons from voting during the period of their parole or probation, and eleven states disfranchise felons for life. Because of the disproportionate incarceration of African Americans, they have been deprived the right to vote in much higher percentages than whites, especially in the southern states. 13.8 percent of African Americans have lost the right to vote in Florida compared to 5.0 percent of whites and Latinos. In Alabama, the percentages are 12.4 and 4.3, 13.8 in Virginia and 3.4, 9.7 in Mississippi and 3.1, 16.5 in Nevada and 3.7, and 8.8 in Texas and 2.9. Felony convictions, accurately reported or not, have become a means of limiting the black vote.[12]

## THE CHANGING FACE OF AMERICA

As President Clinton's Advisory Board to the President's Initiative on Race discovered, the United States was a vastly different nation at the beginning of the twenty-first century than it was at the beginning of the twentieth century or even at the beginning of World War II. The Advisory Board, chaired by the venerable African American historian, John Hope Franklin, was to examine "race, racism, and the potential for racial reconciliation in America." It held meetings around the country that explored the way in which race played a role in "civil rights enforcement, education, poverty, employment, housing, stereotyping, the administration of justice, health care, and immigration." The board found that the United States is a racially, ethnically, and culturally diverse nation but with common values and goals for freedom, equal opportunity, fairness and justice. Race and ethnicity, however, play a powerful role in access to equal opportunity and the ability to lead a productive life. Unfortunately, "the absence of both knowledge and understanding about the role race has played in our collective history continues to make it difficult to find solutions that will improve race relations, eliminate disparities, and create equal opportunities in all areas of American life."[13]

The black/white dichotomy that characterized so much of American life has lost much of its significance at the beginning of the twenty-first century. The journalist and author Michael Lind has suggested that the new dichotomy might be between beige and black, that is, a white-Asian-Hispanic majority and a minority of African Americans who have been in large measure excluded from growing rates of intermarriage. There were two million interracial marriages in 1990, compared with 150,000 in 1960. Black and white marriages rose from about 50,000 in 1960, when they were still against the law in many states, to approximately 300,000 by 1990. Still, the percentage of African Americans aged 25–34 taking white spouses was much lower at 6 percent than for Hispanics at 30 percent, Asian Americans at 40 percent, and Native Americans at 53 percent.[14] African Americans are the most racially isolated group in the country as measured by residential and marital segregation.

The new face of America with a Hispanic population (although itself ethnically diverse) that has now become the largest minority and a black population that itself is becoming more diverse poses new challenges for African Americans. The black population at the beginning of the twenty-first century includes more West Indian and African immigrants than ever and is less monolithic. The West Indian population in Miami is 48 percent of the black community and will soon exceed the American-born black population. Almost one-third of the black population in Boston and New York City is foreign-born. The immigrant black population is different culturally, socially, and economically from native-born African Americans. They have not experienced the same legacy of racism in the United States and for the first and second generations often identify themselves more by their ethnicity—Barbadian, Ethiopian, Haitian, Jamaican, Nigerian, Trinidadian, and so forth—than by their race. For many of the new immigrants, class is more of an issue than race because it was the major distinction back home. Many black immigrants believe that African Americans have not taken advantage of the possibilities available to them in the United States and are more likely to focus on opportunities than on grievances.[15] The multidimensionality of the black community, whether in class, ethnicity, gender, region, religion, or sexuality, will open a new chapter in African American history during the twenty-first century, to be written against the backdrop of a changing American and global society.

## NOTES

1. Gerald David Jaynes and Robin M. Williams Jr., eds. *A Common Destiny: Blacks and American Society* (Washington, D.C.: National Academy Press, 1989).

2. Robert L. Harris Jr., "The Rise of the Black Middle Class," *The World & I*, February 1999, 40–45.

3. Kevin Phillips, *Boiling Point: Republicans, Democrats, and the Decline of Middle-Class Prosperity* (New York: Random House, 1993), xix, xxii, 27–31.

4. Manning Marable, *Black Leadership* (New York: Columbia University Press, 1998), 161–162.

5. Haki R. Madhubuti and Maulana Karenga, eds., *Million Man March / Day of Absence: A Commemorative Anthology* (Chicago: Third World Press, 1996), 112–113.

6. LaRon D. Bennett Sr., *The Million Man March (The Untold Story)* (Brunswick, Ga.: BHouse Publishing, 1996), 32.

7. *The Million Man March / Day of Absence Mission Statement* (Los Angeles: University of Sankore Press, 1995).

8. Manning Marable, *The Great Wells of Democracy: The Meaning of Race in American Life* (New York: Basic Civitas Books, 2002), 223–253.

9. Randall Robinson, *The Debt: What America Owes to Blacks* (New York: Dutton, 2000).

10. The *State of Black America 2004* (New York: National Urban League, 2004). See also Manthi Nguyen, ed., *Black Americans: A Statistical Sourcebook* (Palo Alto, Calif.: Information Publications, 2003).

11. Robert Kuttner, "The Lynching of the Black Vote," *Boston Globe*, December 10, 2000.

12. John Mark Hansen, "Task Force on the Federal Election System: Disfranchisement of Felons" (Charlottesville, Va.: Miller Center of Public Affairs, 2001).

13. *One America in the 21st Century: Forging a New Future; The President's Initiative on Race* (Washington, D.C.: U.S. Government Printing Office, 1998).

14. Michael Lind, "The Beige and the Black," *New York Times Magazine*, August 16, 1998.

15. Darryl Fears, "A Diverse—and Divided—Black Community," *The Washington Post*, February 24, 2002.

# PART II

## *Key Themes in African American History Since 1939*

# NAMING OURSELVES

## The Politics and Meaning of Self-designation

ROSALYN TERBORG-PENN

People of African ancestry in the United States have been concerned for more than two hundred years about what to call themselves. This concern has generally been in response to heightened periods of white oppression and ensuing black protest. During the last half of the twentieth century, the issue of "naming ourselves" has recurred every ten to twenty years. There has been a type of "call and response," a rhythm, to self-designation in relation to cultural and political conditions within American society.

Howard University Professor Kelly Miller found in the late 1930s that as some names went out of circulation, such as "African," "darkie," and "freedmen," others resurfaced, such as "black," "Afro-American," "Negro," and "colored." Miller wrote, "Some would wish to abolish all nominal distinction and let the individual be known as an American, regardless of his race or color. The banishment of all nominal distinction is purely idealistic, and will be impossible unless or until all distinction and discrimination, based upon race or color, are completely obliterated."[1] African Americans sought the appropriate designation, rejecting some and affirming others, in response to ways in which the broader society treated them. As long as discrimination and segregation persisted, African Americans needed to define themselves.

This self-definition was not entirely in response to actions of the dominant society but also grew out of pride among African Americans in their own culture.

To use the term "American" did not convey a sense of racial or ethnic identity. Many people of African descent worried about losing their cultural identity through integration into the larger society. Both political (African Americans' relation to the larger society) and cultural (pride in race and heritage) issues animated the debate over self-designation during the late twentieth century.

Although African Americans faced race riots in Detroit, Harlem, Los Angeles, and Beaumont, Texas, during World War II, racial discrimination and segregation were not as blatant during the war as before it, as the country focused its attention on defeating fascism and the Nazi doctrine of Aryan supremacy. Racial repression, however, erupted immediately after the war in competition for employment, housing, and recreation. Because of their more egalitarian experiences abroad, black men returned after the war with a new determination to secure racial equality at home. The white South, in particular, was just as determined to keep African Americans in their traditional place of racial subordination. The Cold War, civil rights struggle, and Black Power movement raised questions about self-identity for African Americans that they did not question during World War II. The quest for an appropriate name corresponded with each of these eras. Despite the gains made by African Americans and a renewed sense of racial pride, the contestation over self-designation resurfaced during the 1980s and 1990s. New social and cultural complications, however, entered the equation as larger numbers of people of African ancestry immigrated to the United States with their own forms of self-designation that challenged the views of native-born blacks.

## POPULAR AND INTELLECTUAL RESPONSES TO SELF-DESIGNATION

Beginning with the late 1930s, there were both popular and intellectual responses to questions of self-designation. The National Association for the Advancement of Colored People (NAACP) represented a broad range of African Americans and their supporters. It had taken the lead in lobbying federal agencies to have the word "negro" officially recognized as a proper noun, spelled uppercase: "Negro." The NAACP's efforts mirrored a growing trend among black institutions such as colleges and universities in using the word "Negro." Howard University considered itself "the capstone of 'Negro' education," and Tuskegee Institute published *The Negro Yearbook*.

Black newspapers, during the 1930s, polled their readers about what they wanted to be called. *The Baltimore Afro-American* sent a reporter on a tour of five eastern cities (Baltimore, Philadelphia, Washington, New York, and Wilmington, Delaware) to poll readers and to determine whether they preferred the terms "Negro" or "Colored" as race designations. Of the 163 black respondents,

58 percent preferred the term "Colored" over "Negro." About 10 percent of the respondents rejected both terms, with "Afro-American" being the most popular alternative. The readers gave a variety of reasons for their choices. Some readers rejected the term "Negro" because it meant "black" to them, and they observed that most people of African ancestry in the United States were not "black" in complexion. For this reason, "Colored" was a more appropriate term for them. Other readers did not like the way the word "Colored" sounded and selected "Negro" instead. Many preferred "Colored" because "Negro" sounded too much like "nigger," especially as pronounced by many white southerners, and was offensive to them.[2]

Black popular preferences for group designation were more culturally and emotionally laden than the preferences of intellectual and organizational leaders. The populace responded more to skin tone and pronunciation than to political implications. They were generally more conservative than their leaders and would remain so until the 1950s, when the term "Negro" became widely accepted by the national media, the U.S. Government Printing Office, and public libraries, where catalogers substituted "Negro" for "Colored." Black intellectual and organizational leaders, despite the name of the NAACP, promoted the term "Negro" because it represented people of African descent around the world. It provided a global identity and corresponded with growing international race consciousness and independence movements. For them, the term "Colored" suggested a type of bastardization, biologically and culturally. "Negro" offered a sense of identity and unity that would help African Americans to free themselves from racial oppression.

As many mainstream black intellectual and organizational leaders embraced the term "Negro," others disparaged it. One of the most vehement opponents of the word "Negro" was the Barbadian-born scholar and activist Richard B. Moore, who owned a bookstore in Harlem. He published a pamphlet in 1960, *The Name "Negro": Its Origins and Evil Use*, which attacked the term as originating in slavery and denoting inferiority and subordination. Moore led a successful campaign to change the name of the venerable Association for the Study of Negro Life and History, which had been organized in 1915 by the reputed "Father of Black History," Carter G. Woodson. In 1973, the organization officially changed its name to the Association for the Study of Afro-American Life and History.

At a time when many intellectual and organizational leaders were moving toward the term "Afro-American," college students, in particular, were advocating "black" as a positive emblem of racial pride that countered popular connotations associated with the word as meaning dirty, evil, impure, repulsive, ugly, and so forth. They turned a term that had been used to demean one another upside down. They rebelled against American society's traditional devaluation of Africans and rejected "black" as the lowest rank in the human color scheme.

They put the term "black" at the top and invested it with new cultural meaning. In large measure, under the influence of the Black Power, Black Consciousness, and Black Arts movements, the youth adopted "black" as a means of self-designation and as a statement of opposition to "white" society and its oppression of African Americans. In *Long Memory: The Black Experience in America*, Mary Frances Berry and John W. Blassingame suggested that "black" and "Afro-American" have been the most popular terms of self-designation over time.[3] Their rise in popularity during the late 1960s indicate the cyclical nature of self-naming, as African Americans have used, abandoned, and revived certain designations.

## NEGRO, BLACK, OR AFRO-AMERICAN

"Afro-American" and "black" vied for acceptance as the most commonly used designation during the late 1960s. In 1967, *Ebony Magazine*, the nation's oldest and most prestigious black popular publication, carried a feature "What's in a Name: Negro vs. Afro-American vs. Black?" Lerone Bennett Jr., who wrote the article, surveyed some of the leading black intellectuals and leaders. Many of the older respondents considered the term "Negro" acceptable, while the younger ones divided over the designations "Afro-American" and "black." The historian Benjamin Quarles leaned toward the term "Negro" because of the usefulness of words for different historical contexts. The actor, playwright, and activist Ossie Davis, however, preferred the term "Afro-American" because it implied a connection to an ancestral land, Africa, and to a history and a culture.[4]

Despite a growing tendency to accept "Afro-American" during the 1970s, "black" remained the designation of choice among the masses of African Americans, according to Bettye Collier-Thomas and James Turner in their article "Race, Class and Color: The African American Discourse on Identity." "Black" became a generic reference for all people of African ancestry and was imbued with cultural meaning through the Black Power, Black Consciousness, and Black Arts movements. Collier-Thomas and Turner noted, "Artists and intellectuals, as cultural workers, advocated the necessity for reclaiming and affirming Africanity and particularly cultural heritage. It was posited that such an objective would enhance the quality of cultural life in the black community and would institutionalize values of self-respect and solidarity."[5]

During the late 1960s and early 1970s, African Americans expressed black consciousness through hairstyles, attire, art, speaking patterns, and naming practices. Even older, more conservative African Americans, both men and women, began to wear their hair "natural," that is, without chemical treatments that had been used to straighten their hair in the past. Younger African Americans on school and college campuses wore what was called the "big bush," natural hair in a neat coiffure that bounced as one walked proudly. There was a new assertiveness, a sense of self-assuredness, in the way that African Americans, particularly young adults, carried themselves.

African-influenced clothing, especially the dashiki, a free-flowing blouse, became fashionable. African-inspired jewelry complemented the attire. Many African Americans decorated their homes with African art, such as masks, fertility dolls, woven baskets, and sculpture. Handshakes became symbolic signs of unity, particularly among black men. African American families gave their children African, Arabic, or African-sounding names. Many African Americans changed their surnames from European-based to African-based names. Black artists in particular made the rhythmic and improvisational elements of jazz part of their creative expression in poetry, prose, and painting. These practices affected black vernacular speech patterns that set African Americans apart from the broader society.

The war in Vietnam and the antiwar movement distracted many African Americans from the Black Power and Black Consciousness movements. Moreover, the rising black middle class began to feel a sense of security that racial prejudice and discrimination were behind them. For a sizeable portion of the black population, who were upwardly mobile, the civil rights struggle had been a great success. As a result of growing middle-class complacency and lower-class apathy, for about a decade, there were few public outcries to rethink the issue of naming and to build a new strategy against a growing conservative American backlash. Many white Americans assumed that African Americans had gotten everything they wanted and more. Several polls in the 1980s revealed that many whites believed that prejudice and discrimination against African Americans was a thing of the past. Most white Americans concluded that affirmative action was no longer necessary and that extension of the Voting Rights Act, first passed in 1965 and renewed in 1970 and 1982, was not needed.

By the mid-1980s, African American leaders recognized that black Americans confronted a new reality, the illusion of progress. Although the black middle class grew to almost 40 percent of the black population, about a third of African Americans were mired in poverty, and there appeared to be a permanent black underclass that had not benefited from earlier progress. Moreover, the black middle class found itself locked into place with glass ceilings in professional and corporate America. Racial profiling, or another form of racial stereotyping that assumed that African Americans were more likely to commit crime, began to affect middle-class African Americans as well as the poor. Given these different conditions, there was a new cry for a self-defining name.

Sociologist K. Sue Jewell revisited the issue of what African Americans should call themselves and the extent to which changes during the 1960s had a lasting influence. She interviewed eighty-seven black college students in the

Midwest. She found that 73.5 percent of these primarily middle-class black men and women identified themselves as "black." The others used a range of terms including "Negro," "Colored," and "Mixed," but none claimed a term with reference to Africa. Moreover, "black" seemed to have lost the cultural and political saliency that it had captured during the 1960s. Jewell discovered that 69 percent of the students did not believe that their parents ever experienced racial prejudice or discrimination in the past. She concluded that there was a breakdown in cultural transmission from one generation of African Americans to the next.[6] The young were ignorant about past injustices and the battles their elders had to wage for advantages that the youth enjoyed. A growing number of scholars, intellectuals, politicians, and activists also noticed these trends and worried that a new generation of African Americans suffered from complacency while their rights were slowly evaporating.

## AMERICAN PLURALISM, ETHNICITY, AND "AFRICAN AMERICAN"

A growing discourse to change "black" and "Afro-American" to "African American" emerged during the late 1980s among black leaders and intellectuals as signs of a plural U.S. society—not just measured in terms of black and white—became more evident. Nonwhite immigration to the United States showed signs of what demographers predicted about the changing composition of the population and the declining status of African Americans as the nation's largest minority. Latinos grew in numbers as did Asian Americans, and people of African ancestry from other parts of the Americas, Europe, and Africa. Many of these new residents similar to immigrants before them identified themselves with both their native land and their newfound home and called themselves Cuban American, Mexican American, Korean American, Haitian American, and so forth. Black leaders representing native-born people of African descent began to urge that black Americans abandon "black" and "Afro-American" for "African American" to convey an ethnic identity.

Like most of the designations that black Americans have used over time, "African American" is generic. It refers to the African continent but not to any specific ethnic or national group. Political scientist Ben L. Martin has observed that these "pluralist, minority-majorities, view and then joined the more traditional black-white, minority-majority imagery with its flashback to slavery and segregation. The African American campaign since 1988 has been less successful in finding African roots than reminders of slavery in the New World."[7]

The term "African" has taken on greater significance in the United States as a means of identifying those individuals from various areas of the African continent who were forcibly brought to North America. In the United States, as historian Sterling Stuckey has noted, the Angolans, Igbo, Senegalese, Ashanti, Yoruba, and other ethnic groups melded into a people with common elements from their cultures to become Africans. For this reason, Martin suggests that the "campaign has been less successful in finding African roots than reminders of slavery," although scholars such as Sterling Stuckey would disagree with him. Stuckey and others argue that the disparate people from the African continent forged a common identity, an African sensibility, that evolved into a distinctive African American culture combining African customs and American practices.

In 1988, as Jesse Jackson campaigned for the Democratic Party presidential nomination, he brought the issue to public attention when he announced through the media that people of African descent preferred to be called "African American," and that he would lead a movement to replace the word "black" with that term. Jackson proposed an ethnic self-descriptor, not a racial one. His call came in the context of several developments. For many years, most scientists questioned race as a scientific category. They found as much variation within so-called races as between them. Race was more a social than a scientific construction. It was a means of convenience to classify the different peoples of the earth into general categories. It provided a hierarchy that came into existence primarily during the sixteenth century to justify European domination over the black, red, and yellow "races." Through pseudoscientific racism in the nineteenth century, apologists for slavery assigned certain characteristics to the different "races." It was assumed, for example, that the white race was the most intelligent, followed by the yellow, the red, and the black. The idea of Aryan or white supremacy received a severe jolt, however, during the 1930s when Jesse Owens won four gold medals at the 1936 Olympic Games, and Joe Louis in 1938 knocked out Max Schmeling, the reputed symbol of Nazi superiority, in the first round of their second bout. Proponents of racial classification have sought other ways to explain differences among human beings—differences that turn out to be more cultural than biological.

Jesse Jackson and others explained the "cultural integrity" of the term "African American," which also placed black Americans in a proper historical context. The term provided African Americans with a land of origin and a history, which extended beyond enslavement in the United States. Thus, African American history did not begin in 1619 with the introduction of the first African captives into what became the United States. It involved a glorious past in Africa and people who were not destined to occupy a subordinate position in American society. The term "African American" offered a means of unity and hope for the future. Through it, black Americans would take their place in American society, as had Asian Americans, Cuban Americans, German Americans, Irish Americans, Italian Americans, and other groups.

The conservative black elite response to changing racial designation was not predictable. More often than not, leaders of African descent were cautious and ambivalent about accepting a new name, but not as resistant as in the past. By the 1990s, the NAACP leadership neither accepted nor rejected the term. The National Urban League, however, adopted it and used "African American" in documents and publications. The black press quickly used the terms "black" and "African American" interchangeably. Most major newspapers employed the term, but the *New York Times* and *Washington Post* were slower in embracing it.

As the twentieth century drew to a close, and as African Americans began to live longer, communities experienced critical masses of at least three generations interacting some times in concert and often in conflict. Many of the octogenarians, in remembering their past, reverted to using self-descriptors such as "Colored" and "Negro." Middle-aged baby boomers used the term "African American" but often slipped into the word "black," reflecting days of the Black Consciousness movement of their youth. Young black college students and professionals employed the term "African American." They represented the elite leadership of the future and appropriated a multicultural approach to a plural American society.

The non-elite younger generation, however, has set its own pace by using a variety of diverse colloquial words to describe themselves and their cohort. They have taken negative terms and converted them into endearing phrases. This practice continues the distinctive cultural pattern among African Americans of subverting a demeaning word or phrase by turning it upside down and investing it with new meaning.

Class and generational differences were not the only distinguishing features of self-identity preferences. First-generation immigrants of African descent and their offspring often made self-descriptive choices based on their place of birth, whether in the Caribbean or in Africa—that is, for instance, Haitian American or Nigerian American. Even as citizens of the United States, they still tended to hold on to their countries of origin. They have sometimes been referred to as "the other African Americans" because of their emphasis on their distinctiveness from native-born people of African ancestry in the United States, as some native-born people of African ancestry become indignant when black immigrants assume an African American identity.

"Other African Americans" who have immigrated to the United States, such as Kenyan-born scholar Ali Mazrui, identify as "American African." Like many others, Mazrui, who holds an endowed chair at Binghamton University, has lived in the United States for many years and has children who were born in this country. His children's generation has basically assimilated into African American culture and is more likely to identify themselves as "African Americans." Because the Americas represent such a broad geographical area, some people of

African descent in the United States have started using the term "U.S. African Americans," in recognition of African descendants in the Americas who can also appropriately use the term "African American."

In times of crisis, however, "black" has been used to unite people of African ancestry across ethnicity and geography. When Abner Louima, a Haitian immigrant, was beaten and sodomized in 1997 by New York City police, and Amadou Diallo, a Guinean immigrant, was shot forty-one times and killed by New York City police while standing unarmed in the entrance to his apartment building, people of African ancestry throughout the United States joined together as blacks to protest these injustices. Racial profiling, moreover, has affected people of African ancestry without class or ethnic distinction. In opposition to this form of racial stereotyping, they have come together as blacks rather than as African Americans. There has been a plural approach to self-description at the beginning of the twenty-first century, and at the same time a need for group identification during times of social distress, revealing the ever-shifting nature of "naming ourselves."

## SOURCES

Henry, Tanu T. "Black Labeling: What's in a Name?" *Africana.com*, March 19, 2001.

Malcolm X and Alex Haley. *The Autobiography of Malcolm X*. New York: Grove Press, 1965.

Stuckey, Sterling. *Slave Culture: Nationalist Theory and the Foundation of Black America*. New York: Oxford University Press, 1987.

Turner, W. Burghardt, and Joyce Moore Turner, eds. *Richard B. Moore, Caribbean Militant in Harlem: Collected Writings 1920–1972*. Bloomington: Indiana University Press, 1988.

## NOTES

1. Kelly Miller, "Negroes or Colored People?" *Opportunity Magazine*, May 1937.

2. *The Baltimore Afro-American Newspaper*, July 24–31, 1937.

3. Mary Frances Berry and John W. Blassingame, *Long Memory: The Black Experience in America* (New York: Oxford University Press, 1982), 393–396.

4. Lerone Bennett Jr., "What's in a Name? Negro vs. Afro-American vs. Black," *Ebony Magazine*, November 1967.

5. Bettye Collier-Thomas and James Turner, "Race, Class and Color: The African American Discourse on Identity," *Journal of American Ethnic History* 14, no. 1 (Fall 1994): 23.

6. K. Sue Jewell, "Will the Real Black, Afro-American, Mixed, Colored, Negro Please Stand Up?: Impact of the Black Social Movement, Twenty Years Later," *Journal of Black Studies* 16, no. 1 (September 1985): 63–67.

7. Ben L. Martin, "From Negro to Black to African American: The Power of Names and Naming," *Political Science Quarterly* 106, no. 1 (Spring 1991): 95.

# LOOKING BACKWARD

## African Americans in the Postindustrial Era

ROBIN D. G. KELLEY

In the first years of this new century, one cannot help but feel a sense of déjà vu. Just as the age of segregation and disfranchisement of black voters followed in the wake of Reconstruction's promise of new democratic order, Black America's Second Reconstruction—the freedom movement of the 1950s and 1960s—gave way to declining job opportunities, greater urban segregation caused by white flight, a reversal of many gains in civil rights, and a sharp increase in racist violence. Events in Florida during the closely contested 2000 presidential race between Republican George W. Bush and Democrat Al Gore taught black voters that their voting rights are not completely protected, despite the Fifteenth Amendment and the Voting Rights Act of 1965. Invoking an 1868 statute denying convicted felons the right to vote, Florida's secretary of state issued a "purge" list of some 700,000 alleged felons to registrars containing many egregious errors, including the names of black citizens who had never committed a crime, had received clemency, or had had their records expunged. In Woodville, Florida, a police roadblock randomly stopped and searched black voters on their way to the polls. All in all, because of an array of technical problems, the state ended up discarding nearly 200,000 votes, most of which were from counties with large black populations. Florida was the key to the election; whoever won there would go to the White House. By one count, Bush won by 537 votes. African Americans were not the only ones complaining about the election, but the National

Association for the Advancement of Colored People (NAACP) filed suit against the Florida Secretary of State for violating the Fourteenth Amendment and the Voting Rights Act of 1965, and the U.S. Civil Rights Commission launched an investigation and found evidence of "prohibited discrimination."

Just as imperialism was a prominent feature of the late nineteenth century, the demands of our new global economy prompted foreign wars and invasions to protect U.S. interests, from Grenada to the Middle East. Just as black convict labor was central to the New South's industrialization in the 1890s, today both state and private institutions are turning to prisoners for light manufacturing, telemarketing, and the more traditional tasks of building and repairing infrastructure. Just as Social Darwinism and the "Negro Question" generated deeply racist books in the name of science, such as Frederick Hoffman's *Race Traits and Tendencies of the American Negro* (1896) and Robert Wilson Shufeldt's *The Negro: A Menace to American Civilization* (1907), we have witnessed the return of scholarly investigations into race and intelligence, most prominently in the publication of Charles Murray and Richard Hernstein's *The Bell Curve* (1995).

And yet, not unlike a century ago, the turn of the new century brought us a kind of renaissance in black arts and letters. The year 1897 marked the founding of the American Negro Academy and beginning of W. E. B. Du Bois's emergence as one of the world's leading intellectuals. Today black intellectuals have been deemed the new "public intellectuals," and Afro-American studies centers such as the Du Bois Institute at Harvard University are seen as the center of a new renaissance. In the midst of Jim Crow and disfranchisement, the works of Paul Laurence Dunbar, Frances Ellen Watkins Harper, Charles Chesnutt, and others flowered. The twentieth century closed with Rita Dove's having enjoyed the honor of being poet laureate of the United States, the late Jean-Michel Basquiat's being selected by European art critics as the century's greatest American artist, and novelist Toni Morrison's earning Pulitzer and Nobel prizes for her complex, magical renderings of black people. And in both eras, black music rests at the center of American popular culture. Today it is hip-hop and rhythm & blues; last century it was ragtime and early blues. The hit song of 1896 was Ernest Hogan's "All Coons Look Alike to Me." Beyond the vaudeville and black musical theater circuit, Sissieretta Jones was a true international star of the opera, despite being banned from the Metropolitan Opera House because of her color.

## FROM THE BEST OF TIMES TO THE WORST OF TIMES

How did we get here . . . again, to this odd Dickensian moment characterized by the best of times and the worst of times? Back in March 1972, when some eight thousand African American men and women gathered in Gary, Indiana, to attend the first convention of the National Black Political Assembly, very few believed that the situation for African Americans could get any worse. On the contrary, the delegates believed that the political winds had shifted, that African Americans were on the road to real political power. Although they disagreed over ideology—radicals demanded fundamental changes in the political and economic system and proposed an independent black political party, while moderates planned to work within the Democratic Party—the overall feeling of the convention was one of optimism. The mood was tempered by the fact that police violence continued to be a source of tension in several cities, many urban schools were still segregated and woefully inadequate, and Richard M. Nixon had just been elected to a second term as president. His 1968 campaign attacked welfare mothers, blamed the black poor for their own poverty, and linked the social movements of the 1960s to criminals and drug addicts. Despite appointing a few African Americans to mid-level federal posts and proposing grants and tax cuts for black-owned businesses, the Nixon administration was hostile to African Americans. Adopting a policy of "benign neglect," Nixon believed that enough progress had been made on civil rights and that there was no need to combat racial inequities. He was not out of step with the white majority, who believed that black people were ungrateful and lazy and received too many government handouts. Fearing the spread of ghetto rebellions to the suburbs and concerned that too large a portion of their taxes was going to support welfare, whites overwhelmingly voted for Nixon, partly reflecting an antiblack backlash.

Still, the activists who gathered in Gary in 1972 were not merely responding to Nixon's policies; they believed that black people were on the move and that, no matter how much repression they faced, the tide was turning in their favor. It was the age when black was beautiful, Afros were in, and militant organizations such as the Black Panther Party and the Black Liberation Front won some local support in urban neighborhoods for their advocacy of black control over political and economic institutions. The civil rights movement could claim some important victories, especially for an expanding black middle class seeking to integrate corporate boardrooms, formerly lily-white suburban communities, and mainstream politics. The electoral victories were stunning: in 1969, 994 black men and 131 black women held public office; by 1975 the number of black elected officials grew to 2,973 men and 530 women. By 1974, more than two hundred African Americans served as state legislators, and seventeen sat in Congress—including four women, Shirley Chisholm of New York, Cardiss Collins of Illinois, Barbara Jordan of Texas, and Yvonne Brathwaite Burke of California. Two years earlier, Chisholm made history by becoming the first black woman to run for president of the United States. Her presidential campaign was more than symbolic; she garnered more than 150 delegates' votes at the Democratic

National Convention on a platform that included support for equal rights, affirmative action, and women's liberation. Unfortunately, most black male leaders were unwilling to endorse a woman for president, and few predominantly white women's organizations came out in support of Chisholm.

The source of hope and optimism lay in the local victories. Black politicians won mayoral races in several major cities, including Los Angeles, Atlanta, New Orleans, Newark, Philadelphia, and Washington. Their victory was bittersweet, however, for they had come to power just as these cities were undergoing profound social and economic changes. Black leaders had not counted on a reduction in federal spending on cities, white and black middle-class flight to the suburbs, a rapid growth in urban poverty and unemployment, and one of the most severe economic recessions in U.S. history. The decade of hope was crushed by what some scholars have called the "postindustrial era"—shifts in the global economy characterized by a greater concentration of wealth in the hands of a few multinational corporations. New developments in communications technology enabled corporations to move manufacturing operations virtually anywhere in the world in order to take advantage of cheaper labor, relatively lower taxes, and a deregulated environment hostile to trade unions. High-paying jobs in America's cities, made possible by decades of unionizing, began to disappear just as the black urban population reached its apex. By 1979, for example, 94 percent of the profits of the Ford Motor Company and 63 percent of the profits from Coca Cola came from overseas operations. Between 1973 and 1980, at least four million jobs were lost to firms moving outside the United States, and during the decade of the 1970s, at least 32 million jobs were lost as a result of shutdowns, relocations, and scaled-down operations.

The jobs created by the transfer of production processes to so-called underdeveloped countries did not improve the standard of living for workers in these countries. Instead, things got worse. The International Monetary Fund and World Bank imposed austerity measures, trade unions were crushed, and undemocratic regimes gained support from corporations and countries with strong economic interests. The deteriorating conditions of labor prompted international immigration and thus created a cheap labor pool for the United States and other metropolitan nations. Many of the new immigrants are also black, hailing from Africa, Latin America, and the Caribbean. By the early 1980s, approximately fifty thousand legal immigrants from the English-speaking Caribbean and some six thousand to eight thousand Haitians were entering the United States annually, about half of whom settled in New York City.

By the end of the 1970s, the U.S. economy appeared to be in a permanent crisis. The decline of manufacturing jobs in steel, rubber, auto, and other heavy industries had a devastating impact on black workers. Although black joblessness had been about twice that of whites since the end of World War II, black unemployment rates increased even more rapidly, especially after 1971. While the number of unemployed white workers declined by 562,000 between 1975 and 1980, the number of black unemployed increased by 200,000 during this period. The loss of manufacturing positions was accompanied by an expansion of low-wage service jobs. The more common service jobs included retail clerks, janitors, maids, computer programmers and data processors, security guards, waitresses, and cooks—jobs with little or no union representation and very little in the way of health or retirement benefits.

Not surprisingly, one of the most striking features of the 1970s and 1980s was the widening income gap between blacks and whites. At the beginning of the 1970s, African Americans in the Northeast made about seventy-one cents for every dollar whites made; by 1979 that ratio dropped to fifty-eight cents. In 1978, 30.6 percent of black families earned income below the official poverty line, compared with 8.7 percent of white families. Black women and children were the hardest hit by the economic crisis. Hemmed in by limited job opportunities, more and more working-class black women found themselves having to raise children without the benefit of a spouse to help pay the bills or participate in childcare. In 1969, women headed 54 percent of all black families below the poverty line; in 1974 this figure rose to 67 percent. Although single parent families (including those run by males) tended to suffer more than two parent families because they lacked a second wage earner, the structure of the family was not the cause of poverty. Most of these households were poor, not because the women were unmarried but because of the lack of employment opportunities for women and inequality in wages as a result of race and sex discrimination. Besides, not all poor African Americans received public assistance, nor were they the primary beneficiaries of welfare. And many who did qualify for some form of public assistance did not always receive it. A 1979 study revealed that more than half of all poor black households received no federal welfare support.

## THE INCOME GAP

A large income gap persisted between blacks and whites and emerged within the black community itself. The expansion of the black poor was accompanied by a small but significant increase in the black middle class. In 1970, 15.7 percent of black families had incomes over $35,000; by 1986 the percentage had grown to 21.2 percent. Black families earning over $50,000 almost doubled, increasing from 4.7 percent in 1970 to 8.8 percent in 1986. The civil rights movement's demands for equal access were partly responsible for the success of the black middle class. Antidiscrimination laws and affirmative action contributed to increasing black enrollment at major colleges and universities, reducing discrimination in hiring, and expanding job opportunities for minorities and women. African Americans employed in the public sector enjoyed even greater benefits since such policies were more strongly enforced at the federal, state, and municipal levels. By 1970, 28 percent of all employed African Americans held government jobs, and governmental agencies employed approximately 60 percent of all black professional workers.

In spite of the statistics, many middle-class black families found themselves living a relatively precarious existence. All economic indicators show that the black middle class, on average, possess substantially less "wealth" than middle class whites who earn the same income. By wealth we mean total assets (savings, home equity, stocks, bonds, retirement accounts, etc.) minus total debts. Many black families reporting middle-class incomes were often the result of two parents' working full-time for fairly low or moderate wages. Black suburban homeowners during the 1970s and 1980s often lived from paycheck to paycheck; one layoff could mean the loss of their home. And racial discrimination continued to persist. A massive study of ten million applications to savings and loan associations between 1983 and 1988 revealed that the rejection rate for blacks was more than twice that of whites, and that high-income African Americans were rejected more frequently than low-income whites. This pattern continued well into the 1990s.

## RESURGENCE OF RACISM

Discrimination in the post–civil rights period sometimes took more blatant forms. By the late 1970s the Ku Klux Klan tripled its membership and initiated a reign of terror against black people, which included the firebombing of homes, churches, and schools in more than a hundred towns and rural areas, and drive-by shootings into the homes of NAACP leaders in the South. Very few of these incidents led to convictions. Nonetheless, white supremacist groups accounted for a small proportion of the rising incidents of racism during the late 1970s and 1980s. Between 1982 and 1989, the number of hate crimes reported annually in the United States grew threefold, and many of these incidents occurred on college campuses. An even bigger problem facing African Americans was the growing number of police killings and nonlethal acts of brutality. Between 1979 and 1982, protests were organized throughout the country around specific cases of police violence, some of the more highly publicized incidents occurring in Philadelphia, New Orleans, Memphis, Miami, Birmingham, Oakland, Detroit, and Washington. The Los Angeles Police Department made headlines after the 1979 killing of Eula Mae Love. Love, a thirty-nine-year-old woman who stood about five feet four inches tall, was shot a dozen times by two LAPD officers who were called to the scene after she tried to stop a utility worker from turning off her gas. When they arrived she was armed with a kitchen knife, but the only thing she had stabbed was a tree in her yard. Three years later, at least fifteen deaths were caused by chokeholds administered by Los Angeles police officers attempting to subdue suspects.

The resurgence of racism, both subtle and blatant, was accompanied by a slow but steady dismantling of legislative gains achieved by the civil rights movement. Affirmative action was challenged both politically and in the courts almost as soon as it was implemented. The first real assault came from a famous Supreme Court case known as *Regents of the University of California v. Bakke* (1978). Bakke claimed that he was discriminated against because the University of California admitted African Americans with lower test scores in order to make their quota of admitting minority students. The Supreme Court ruled that Bakke had been unfairly denied admission to the medical school. The Court did not overturn all forms of affirmative action, but the justices did argue that quotas—a procedure in which a specific number of slots are set aside for designated groups—were unconstitutional and his denial of admission an example of "reverse discrimination." Bakke won the case, but the unspoken facts behind the University of California at Davis's admissions policy call into question the Court's opinion that he was a victim of reverse discrimination. First, the sons and daughters of influential white families—potential donors or friends of the dean of the medical school—were also admitted over Bakke with lower test scores. As has been the case historically, the dean controlled a handful of slots to admit special cases. Second, most minority applicants had higher scores than Bakke. This is an important fact, for the Bakke case left many observers with the wrong impression that the University of California at Davis admitted unqualified minorities. Justice Thurgood Marshall, the first African American to serve on the Supreme Court, who also dissented from the majority opinion, viewed the Bakke decision as a tragedy. He did not believe that America was even close to becoming a color-blind society. "The dream of America as a great melting pot," he wrote in his dissent against the Bakke case, "has not been realized for the Negro; because of his skin color, he never even made it into the pot."

The 1980s reflected the changed mood in the United States toward African Americans and other people of color. The election of former California Governor Ronald Reagan to the White House in 1980 had disastrous consequences for black Americans, especially the poor. During his two terms in office, military spending increased by 46 percent while expenditures for housing were slashed by 77 percent and education by 70 percent. The Reagan administration also succeeded in reducing the number of families eligible for Aid to Families with Dependent Children (AFDC), cutting the Federal Food Stamp program by $2 billion, and reducing federal child nutrition programs by $1.7 billion. By the start of his second term, the condition of poor and working-class blacks was worse than it had been during the 1973 recession. In 1985, about one out of every three African Americans lived below the poverty line. Reagan-era spending cuts were especially hard on cities, where the vast majority of African Americans lived. In addition to closing down the Neighborhood Self-Help and Planning Assistance program, which allotted $55 million to assist inner cities in 1981, grants and aid to cities was reduced to a fraction of what it had been under Nixon. To make matters worse, several cities experienced a "tax revolt" from suburban communities that no longer wanted their property taxes to fund urban schools or city services.

Reagan did win support from a small cadre of black neoconservatives, the more prominent figures among whom included Stanford University professor Thomas Sowell; Robert L. Woodson, head of the National Center for Neighborhood Enterprise; and Roy Innis of the Congress of Racial Equality. Ignoring policy initiatives that eroded urban economies and contributed to the disappearance of high-wage jobs, black Reaganites argued that welfare and affirmative action undermined middle-class values of hard work and thrift by making the black poor dependent on government. The problems of urban poverty cannot be solved with equal opportunity legislation, they insisted, because the only thing holding back poor African Americans are weak cultural values, broken families, and irresponsible parenting. While most African Americans understood that racism alone could not explain all the problems facing their communities, they nevertheless found these characterizations inaccurate if not incomprehensible. Instead, they found themselves in a world where equal opportunity, welfare, civil rights, and black power had become foreign words in the national vocabulary. And if this were not enough, the crumbling cities African Americans and other minorities had inherited turned out not to be the utopia they had hoped for. They were dangerous, difficult places where racist police officers still roamed and well-paying jobs fled the city limits. Despite the rising number of black mayors, it became clear by the 1980s that a new freedom movement was needed.

## THE NEED FOR A NEW MOVEMENT

What a new movement (or movements) would look like was less clear to black activists at the dawn of the postindustrial, post–civil rights era than in the heady days of the southern freedom movement. Although issues of class and gender had always been present in black social movements, the emergence of women's rights, welfare rights, and worker-based organizations during the 1970s made these issues more pronounced. In 1973, a year after Shirley Chisholm's defeat in the Democratic primary, some four hundred African American women gathered in

New York City to attend the first conference of the National Black Feminist Organization (NBFO). The NBFO was formed to combat sexist and racist discrimination against black women and to fight for more participation in the political process. Its founding members included black women from all walks of life, from lawyers to domestic workers, welfare rights organizers to polished elected officials. After its first year, however, welfare rights activists felt the NBFO sidestepped the problems of poor women, and many African American lesbians criticized the NBFO for ignoring homophobia and for speaking only to issues affecting heterosexual women. One particular group that emerged out of these debates was the Combahee River Collective, a gathering of black feminists who had come together initially in response to a string of unsolved murders of black women in Boston. Formed in 1974, they broke with the NBFO and developed a radically different political philosophy, arguing that women could not be completely liberated until racism and homophobia are annihilated, and unless capitalism is replaced by socialism.

The Combahee River Collective was not alone in its support for socialism. A number of predominantly and exclusively black organizations were formed in the 1970s dedicated to some kind of socialist or Marxist-Leninist revolution—organizations bearing names such as the League of Revolutionary Struggle, the Black Workers Congress, the Communist Labor Party, the Revolutionary Workers League, and the All-African People's Revolutionary Party. Some of its members became part of what was known as the "factory" or "industrial concentration" movement. Young activists took jobs in manufacturing in order to organize workers at the point of production, hoping to inspire a radical, multiracial challenge to capitalism and what they saw as a reformist trade union movement. Some of these black trade unionists went on to play key roles in the renewed labor movement under the leadership of AFL-CIO president John Sweeney. During the 1980s and 1990s, unions such as the Service Employees Industrial Union (SEIU) and their "Justice for Janitors" campaign, as well as the Union of Needle Trades, Industrial and Textile Employees (UNITE), brought together black, Asian, and Latino workers in community-based campaigns reminiscent of the civil rights struggles of the previous generation.

Other black activists continued the tradition of pan-Africanism, supporting liberation movements around the globe, especially in Africa and the Caribbean. The armed struggles in southern Africa, in particular, captured the imaginations of black radicals who subsequently founded the African Liberation Support Committee (ALSC) in 1971. On May 27, 1972, the ALSC held the first African Liberation Day demonstration, drawing approximately thirty thousand protesters in Washington, D.C. alone, and an estimated thirty thousand more across the country. The ALSC reflected the radical orientation of the liberation movements in Portuguese Africa; its Coordinating Committee consisted of representatives from several nationalist and black left organizations. Because the ALSC attracted such a broad range of black activists, it became an arena for debate over the creation of a black radical agenda. Unfortunately, it fell apart within three years of its founding because of internal squabbling and sectarianism, exacerbated by state repression. However, the death of the ALSC hardly killed black internationalist politics during this period. By the 1980s, the U.S. anti-apartheid movement, led by college students, radical trade unionists, and independent policy organizations such as Randall Robinson's Trans-Africa, played a critical role in the collapse of white-minority rule in South Africa. Moreover, several black organizations led protests against the U.S. interventions in Third World countries, notably the overthrow of Grenada's socialist government (1983), the invasion of Panama (1989), and the "Persian Gulf War" against Iraq (1991).

Closer to home, Reagan's election prompted black activists from different ideological camps to come together to fight back against his conservative policies. Despite some successes in local elections, the initiatives coming from Gary were never turned into a national movement. In 1980 they tried again, forming the National Black Independent Political Party (NBIPP). Conceived as a mass-based political movement reflecting a diversity of opinion, NBIPP attracted between 1,500 and 2,000 activists to its founding convention. Perhaps NBIPP's most revolutionary proposal was to put in place mechanisms that would ensure gender equality throughout the organization: its charter and constitution called for equal gender representation in all leadership positions. Although NBIPP turned out to be short-lived, it nevertheless set the stage for Jesse Jackson's historic bid for president in 1984.

A veteran civil rights activist and founder of Operation PUSH (People United to Serve Humanity)—an organization whose activities centered on improving black children's academic performance and expanding opportunities for black businesses through the use of boycotts—Jackson was initially dismissed by the media as well as most black politicians. His campaign quickly gained momentum, however, partly because his agenda went well beyond "black" issues. Dubbed the "Rainbow Coalition," the campaign's staff of environmentalists, feminists, labor organizers, as well as Asian and Latino grassroots community activists produced campaign literature in English and Spanish, insisted that the 1965 Voting Rights Act be used in behalf of Latinos, and registered many Puerto Rican and Mexican American voters. Jackson not only supported Native American rights but was also the only candidate to attend the National Congress of American Indians. His opposition to plant closings, his call for federal assistance to struggling farmers, and his promise to cut military expenditures by at least 20 percent, attracted some blue-collar workers, farmers, and peace advocates. Most important, Jackson brought to the presidential race a vision for a new America that challenged politics as usual. Not surprisingly, the Democratic Party leadership believed a vote for

Jackson would undermine efforts to beat incumbent Ronald Reagan. They simply did not believe Jackson had a chance against the frontrunner, Walter Mondale.

Despite inadequate funding and enormous skepticism, Jackson ran a respectable campaign, winning several state primaries and caucuses and garnering 3.5 million popular votes. He might have lost the nomination to Mondale (who was subsequently crushed by Ronald Reagan in a landslide election), but Jackson's Rainbow Coalition made some very important strides. Its massive voter registration drive brought hundreds of thousands of new voters—notably African Americans and Latinos—into the Democratic Party. In five southern states alone, 183,000 new voters were registered between 1983 and 1984. Jackson forced the Democratic leadership to look at foreign policy issues in a different light. He gave the struggle against apartheid in South Africa far more visibility than it had had before, and sharply criticized U.S. military intervention in Central America and the Caribbean.

Jackson attracted quite a few young people to his campaign, but too many poor urban youth felt isolated, disfranchised, and hopeless. Cities were crumbling because of cutbacks and capital flight, job opportunities disappeared, urban schools suffered from overcrowding and declining budgets, and recreational facilities rapidly deteriorated. Beginning in the 1970s, a wave of public recreational-service employees were either laid off or allowed to retire without replacement. Money for service and maintenance of parks and playgrounds evaporated. In New York, for example, municipal appropriations for parks dropped by more than $40 million between 1974 and 1980—a 60 percent cut in real dollars. To make matters worse, a growing number of public schoolyards in inner-city communities had become inaccessible during after-school hours. Increasingly, the urban landscape was filled with idle young bodies with few job prospects and virtually no recreational outlets. In the place of what might have been a vibrant urban economy emerged an informal sector linked to drugs and gangs. Of course, this was not the rule everywhere, and the percentage of young people involved in the underground economy was and remains quite small, but the sense pervaded inner-city communities that there was no future to look forward to.

## NEW CULTURAL MOVEMENTS

In the absence of grassroots political movements in the inner cities, new cultural movements took form. Perhaps the most important development in the late 1970s was the birth of hip-hop, a predominantly black and Latino youth culture that incorporated rap music, graffiti art, and break dancing. The origins of hip-hop music can be traced to the South Bronx, New York, where young DJs (disk jockeys) began mixing together different kinds of dance music at local parties, clubs, and outdoor events. The DJs were followed by MCs (masters of ceremony) whose job was to keep the crowd moving and the parties "jumping" by rhyming on the microphone. Although we associate hip-hop with young black and Puerto Rican men, women had been part of the hip-hop underground from its origins, a fact that is not obvious to most since sexism kept most women rappers from getting record contracts. Some of the pioneering New York women rappers include Lady B, Sweet T, Lisa Lee, Sha Rock, the Mercedes Ladies, Sula, Sequence, and Sweet T. It was not until the appearance of Salt N' Pepa, and later MC Lyte and Queen Latifah, that women rappers gained legitimacy and respect.

Early rap artists such as the Funky Four Plus One, Sugarhill Gang, and Kurtis Blow were known for their humorous or boasting lyrics, as early as 1981, but groups such as Grandmaster Flash & The Furious Five also recorded songs, such as "White Lines" and "The Message," that critiqued contemporary racism, poverty, police brutality, and drug use. Of course, many rappers produced chilling stories of modern "baaad men" tales of street life; an alternative movement emerged devoted to radical political themes. Artists such as Public Enemy, KRS-One, Intelligent Hoodlum, Paris, The Coup, Brand Nubians, X-Clan, and, much later, groups such as Blackstar and Dead Prez were committed to black nationalist or Afrocentric messages. Indeed, black nationalism made a comeback among the 1990s generation—the sons and daughters of the 1960s generation. The militant nationalist and Muslim leader Malcolm X quickly emerged as the decade's central black hero. Kente cloth (a colorful and intricately woven West African fabric), beads, and leather medallions with outlines of Africa became popular consumer items. Membership in the Nation of Islam and other Black Muslim groups rose dramatically during the late 1980s and 1990s.

The resurgence of black nationalism or even mild support for establishing black institutions was more than a fad, and it certainly was not limited to the inner city. In the post–civil rights era, integrating into mainstream white society was simply not a primary goal, if it ever had been. Instead, African Americans fought for equal access to institutions of power, fair wages, equal treatment before the law, decent housing at fair, secure prices, and the right to move in public without harassment from police or racist citizens. African Americans had long turned to the federal government to protect their basic rights as citizens, but under Reagan and his Republican successor, George H. W. Bush, the trend to back away from federal policing of racial discrimination continued unabated. The appointment of conservative justices under Reagan and Bush led to major reversals in laws pertaining to equal rights and affirmative action. In several landmark cases during the 1988–89 term, the Court severely limited some key civil-rights statutes that protected African Americans from discrimination at the workplace, in schools, and at the polls.

## THE CLINTON ADMINISTRATION

Some African Americans believed the election of Democrat Bill Clinton to the White House might offer some relief. His two terms in office turned out to be somewhat of a mixed blessing. While he promoted a "President's Initiative on Race," it resulted in a series of "town hall" meetings about race relations in contemporary America and a published report with no impact on public policy. Instead, some of the trends launched by Reagan and Bush continued under Clinton's watch, including the further rollback of affirmative action. In *Hopwood v. State of Texas* (1996), the Court of Appeals for the Fifth Circuit Court decided to prohibit the use of race-based admissions criteria to achieve diversity at the University of Texas Law School, and Proposition 209 effectively dismantled public affirmative action programs in California. Clinton and his administration continued to offer lukewarm support of affirmative action, but planned to eliminate "minority set-asides" and "quotas" eventually because white voters believed these were unfair advantages resulting in "reverse discrimination."

Clinton focused even more attention on dismantling "welfare as we know it." The 1996 "Personal Responsibility and Work Opportunity Reconciliation Act" abolished Aid to Families with Dependent Children (AFDC), replacing transfer payments with block grants to states, which then could determine how long a family receives support. More important, the new law forced welfare recipients into an extremely low-wage labor market without concern for the needs of children. Under the act, for example, recipients whose youngest child is more than a year old had to do some form of paid or unpaid work after twenty-four months of receiving benefits or lose their benefits altogether. And those required to work but who failed to find jobs within two months of receiving assistance must enroll in a mandatory workfare program. To make matters worse, anyone convicted of a drug felony was denied direct aid or welfare for life. Unemployed adults between eighteen and fifty years of age with no children were limited to just three months of food stamps in any three-year period, which essentially meant that the only safety net available to them was unemployment insurance. By some estimates, the Personal Responsibility Act left some 3.5 million children without any means of support.

The continuing threat of poverty and declining opportunities in business and higher education were just the tip of the iceberg. More and more young African Americans are finding their way into an expanding, increasingly privatized and profit-making prison system. Since 1980 the number of African Americans in prison has tripled; between 1979 and 1992, the percentage of African Americans admitted to state and federal prisons grew from 39 percent to 54 percent. In fact, between 1988 and 1998, New York State's prison budget increased by $761 million, while its expenditures on public universities declined by $615 million. In New York alone, there are twice as many black men in prison as are enrolled in the entire state university system. By the year 2000, the U.S. inmate population reached two million inmates, two-thirds of whom were nonviolent offenders. Today a little over one-third of young urban black men are either incarcerated, on probation, or convicted felons. And yet, despite these numbers, violent crime in general, and crimes committed by African Americans in particular, have declined steadily since the mid-1970s. Between 1976 and 1992, the percentage of black arrests for forcible rape declined by 8.4 percent while the percentage of white arrests increased by 4.3 percent. The percentage of black arrests for robbery, burglary, larceny, and aggravated assault actually decreased from 1988 to 1992.

Racial disparities in sentencing, resulting in part from the "War on Drugs," waged mainly against low-income urban communities where crack cocaine was prevalent, partly explain why the prison population can increase while crime rates fall. The key factor was the passage of a ten-year mandatory sentence for possession of crack cocaine. As a result, drug offenders constituted 22 percent of federal prison admissions in 1980; by 1992, 58 percent of all federal prisoners were drug offenders. Under these laws, sentences for crack were up to a hundred times more severe than for powder cocaine. Because crack is much cheaper than powder cocaine and more pervasive in poor urban communities, it is not surprising that 91 percent of those sentenced for federal crack offenses were black while only 3 percent were white. Yet studies show that whites constitute a higher proportion of crack users: 2.4 million (64.4 percent) for whites compared to 990,000 (26.6 percent) for blacks, and 384,000 (9.22 percent) for Latinos.

## POLICE BRUTALITY, RACIAL PROFILING, AND THE CRIMINAL JUSTICE SYSTEM

The rising prison population represented only one side of the African American community's struggles with the criminal justice system. Police violence, long a source of tension within African American communities, seemed to escalate in the 1990s. The catalyst for the Los Angeles rebellion of 1992 was a police brutality trial that ended in the acquittal of four officers who had brutally beaten Rodney King thirteen months earlier. Unlike most incidents of police brutality, this one was captured on videotape. The entire nation watched King writhe in pain as he was punched, kicked, whacked with a wooden baton, and shocked twice with a high-voltage stun gun. When it was all over, King suffered a broken cheekbone, nine skull fractures, a shattered eye socket, a broken ankle, and the need for twenty stitches in his face. Thus, when the all-white jury handed down a not guilty verdict on April 29, 1992, the city of Los Angeles blew up. When the rioting came to a halt on May 2, at least fifty-eight people had been killed (twenty-six African Americans, eighteen Latinos, ten whites, two Asians, and two persons of unknown ethnicity) and thousands had been injured. The fires left more than five thousand buildings destroyed or badly damaged. The estimated property damage totaled a staggering $785 million. The riots had a rippling effect beyond Los Angeles, as smaller and less volatile protests erupted in San Francisco, Atlanta, Las Vegas, New York, Seattle, Tampa, and Washington.

By the end of the twentieth century, police harassment and brutality became the leading source of protest for African Americans, irrespective of class. The problem of police use of excessive force was dramatized by a series of high-profile beatings and shootings, including the 1997 assault on Haitian immigrant Abner Louima. New York Police Department (NYPD) officers arrested, handcuffed, beat and sexually assaulted Louima in the bathroom of a Brooklyn precinct house. After shoving a broken broomstick into Louima's rectum, a police officer, Justin Volpe, threatened to kill him if he told anyone about the assault. Louima did press charges, which resulted in Volpe's conviction and more investigations into other cases of racism and excessive force in the NYPD. Less than two years later, members of the same NYPD street crimes unit killed another black immigrant, twenty-two-year old street vendor Amadou Diallo. Although he was unarmed, had no criminal record, and looked nothing like the alleged suspect in a Bronx rape case, four officers fired forty-one bullets at him—nineteen of which entered his body. The Diallo killing prompted the largest police brutality protest in New York's history. Tens of thousands of protestors representing the entire spectrum of race, ethnicity, and age, blocked the streets around City Hall and engaged in civil disobedience resulting in hundreds of arrests. Unfortunately, the Diallo killing and Louima beating were just the start. During the first six months of 1999, for example, literally dozens of other people were killed or badly beaten by police under dubious circumstances.

The most notable case highlighting racism in the criminal justice system centers around jailed journalist and activist Mumia Abu-Jamal. A former Black Panther Party member whose exposés on police misconduct and racial discrimination in Philadelphia won awards and national acclaim, Mumia had been convicted of first-degree murder and sentenced to death for the alleged shooting of a white police officer on December 9, 1981. He had no prior criminal record, despite being subject to FBI surveillance since he was sixteen years old, and the evidence against Mumia was questionable, to say the least. An international movement, endorsed by many leading celebrities, lawyers, and social justice activists, demanded that he receive a new trial. Even the Secretary General of Amnesty International expressed concern in a 1997 statement that "Mumia Abu Jamal's original trial may have been contaminated by the deep-rooted racism that appears to taint the application of the death penalty in Pennsylvania."

Many black citizens were moved by these dramatic cases of police abuse, and some took to the streets in protest. But unequal police practices also affected African Americans more subtly in the form of "racial profiling," or what has been called "Driving While Black" (DWB). These are routine traffic stops used as a pretext to search for evidence. It is used ostensibly to target drug dealers and based on the premise that people of color (mainly blacks and Latinos) commit most drug offenses. Although the premise is factually untrue, the vast majority of motorists routinely stopped as alleged drug carriers are African Americans and Latinos. Between January 1995 and September 1996, Maryland state police officers stopped and searched 823 motorists on Interstate 95, of whom 600 were black. Only 19.7 percent of those searched in this corridor were white. Some cases were highly publicized. In 1998, a Liberian student named Nelson Walker was pulled over by state police for not wearing a seatbelt. The officers proceeded to search his car for illegal drugs, weapons, or other contraband to the point of dismantling a door panel, a seat panel, and part of the sunroof. When the officers realized they would not find anything, they handed Walker a screwdriver, said, "You're going to need this," and drove off. The overwhelming number of incidents like these became evident when victims began to sue and concerned politicians supported legislation outlawing racial profiling. The state of New Jersey alone paid out over $800,000 in out-of-court settlements to victims of racial profiling.

## REPARATIONS AND "THE BIG PAYBACK"

That the state of New Jersey could be compelled to make restitution payments to victims of racism is significant, for here is where the comparison with the turn of the last century ends. The demand for some kind of restitution or reparations to compensate for the enslavement, exploitation, and suffering of black people in America is not new and, indeed, was a prominent demand in the nineteenth century. Abolitionist leader Sojourner Truth made the case for reparations through land distribution to ex-slaves, insisting that "America owes to my people some of the dividends. . . . I shall make them understand that there is a debt to the Negro people, which they can never repay. At least, then, they must make amends." In 1890, a black woman named Callie House filed several suits and petitioned Congress for reparations. About the same time, emigrationist leader Bishop Henry McNeal Turner made similar arguments, estimating that black people were owed some $40 billion for unpaid labor.

But today the dream of reparations has spawned a full-blown movement. Pointing to recent precedents in the form of reparations to interned Japanese Americans, Holocaust victims, Native land claims settlements, and isolated black victims of racial violence (for example, in Rosewood, Florida), organizations such as the National Coalition of Blacks for Reparations in America (N'COBRA) and the African Reparations Movement (ARM) have argued strongly that government and private companies return the dividends made from centuries of slavery and institutionalized racism. And they have begun to win support. Lawsuits have been filed against firms that directly benefited from the slave trade. Michigan Representative John Conyers's efforts to get Congress to study the question of reparations has received nationwide support, and not only from other African Americans.

In an age of backlash, when anti–affirmative action sentiment has cast what were once called "rights" as "special privileges" (welfare, antidiscrimination laws, state protection of equal opportunity), the demand for reparations represents a powerful offensive. The arguments for reparations recast these measures not only as rights but also as payback. Rather than blame the victim for their poverty, the reparations movement insists that the impoverished created much of America's wealth, and that unpaid labor and discriminatory legislation—such as federal housing policies that consistently devalued black neighborhoods and subsidized middle-class white suburbs—explain racial disparities in wealth. Moreover, their demands that payments take the form of massive investments in improving housing, schools, and civil society more generally, have the potential to transform the entire nation, not just black communities.

So perhaps this isn't déjà vu all over again. Sure, the problem of the color line is still with us, but perhaps the postindustrial era has not ushered in a new winter in America but a new spring, a new day for emancipatory politics. Perhaps the lesson in this global economy of ours is that equal access and antidiscrimination legislation is not enough; the fundamental problems cannot be solved short of a significant redistribution of wealth as well as a change in the way we think about where wealth comes from. While history is unpredictable and every future uncertain, perhaps we might imagine this new millennium of ours as the era of "The Big Payback." Now wouldn't that be something.

## SOURCES

Amott, Teresa L., and Julie A. Matthaei. *Race, Gender, and Work: A Multicultural History of Women in the United States*. Boston: South End Press, 1991.

Bell, Derrick. *And We Are Not Saved: The Elusive Quest for Racial Justice*. New York: Basic Books, 1987.

Bush, Rod. *We Are Not What We Seem: Black Nationalism and Class Struggle in the American Century*. New York: New York University Press, 1999.

Carroll, Peter N. *It Seemed Like Nothing Happened: The Tragedy and Promise of America in the 1970s*. New York: Holt, Rinehart and Winston, 1982.

Carter, Stephen L. *Reflections of an Affirmative Action Baby*. New York: Basic Books, 1991.

Chisholm, Shirley. *The Good Fight*. New York: Harper & Row, 1973.

Collins, Sheila D. *The Rainbow Challenge: The Jackson Campaign and the Future of U.S. Politics*. New York: Monthly Review Press, 1986.

Cross, Brian. *It's Not About a Salary . . . Rap, Race and Resistance in Los Angeles*. London: Verso Books, 1993.

Davis, Angela. *Women, Culture, and Politics*. New York: Random House, 1989.

Davis, Mike. *City of Quartz: Excavating the Future in Los Angeles*. New York: Verso Books, 1990.

Feagin, Joe R., and Melvin P. Sikes. *Living with Racism: The Black Middle-Class Experience*. Boston: Beacon Press, 1994.

Garwood, Alfred N., ed. *Black Americans: A Statistical Sourcebook 1992*. Boulder, Colo.: Numbers and Concepts, 1993.

Giddings, Paula. *When and Where I Enter: The Impact of Black Women on Race and Sex in America*. New York: William Morrow, 1984.

Gill, Gerald. *Meanness Mania: The Changed Mood*. Washington, D.C.: Howard University Press, 1980.

Gwaltney, John Langston. *Drylongso: A Self-Portrait of Black America*. New York: Vintage Books, 1981.

Harding, Vincent. *The Other American Revolution*. Los Angeles: Center for Afro-American Studies, 1980.

Harris, William H. *The Harder We Run: Black Workers Since the Civil War*. New York: Oxford University Press, 1982.

Hatch, Roger D., and Frank E. Watkins, eds. *Reverend Jesse L. Jackson: Straight from the Heart*. Philadelphia: Fortress Press, 1987.

Henry, Charles. *Jesse Jackson: The Search for Common Ground*. Oakland: Black Scholar Press, 1991.

Jaynes, Gerald David, and Robin M. Williams Jr. *A Common Destiny: Blacks and American Society*. Washington, D.C.: National Academy Press, 1989.

Jennings, James. *The Politics of Black Empowerment: The Transformation of Black Activism in Urban America*. Detroit: Wayne State University Press, 1992.

Jones, Jacqueline. *The Dispossessed: America's Underclasses from the Civil War to the Present*. New York: Basic Books, 1992.

——. *Labor of Love, Labor of Sorrow: Black Women, Work, and the Family from Slavery to the Present*. New York: Vintage Books, 1986.

Kasinitz, Philip. *Caribbean New York: Black Immigrants and the Politics of Race*. Ithaca, N.Y.: Cornell University Press, 1992.

Kelley, Robin D. G. *Yo' Mama's Disfunktional!: Fighting the Culture Wars in Urban America*. Boston: Beacon Press, 1997.

Landry, Bart. *The New Black Middle Class*. Berkeley: University of California Press, 1987.

Lawson, Steven F. *Running for Freedom: Civil Rights and Black Politics in America Since 1941*. Philadelphia: Temple University Press, 1991.

Lipsitz, George. *The Possessive Investment in Whiteness*. Philadelphia: Temple University Press, 1998.

Lusane, Clarence. *African Americans at the Crossroads: The Restructuring of Black Leadership in the 1992 Elections*. Boston: South End Press, 1994.

——. *Pipe Dream Blues: Racism and the War on Drugs*. Boston: South End Press, 1991.

Madhubuti, Haki R., ed. *Why L.A. Happened: Implications of the '92 Los Angeles Rebellion*. Chicago: Third World Press, 1993.

Marable, Manning. *How Capitalism Underdeveloped Black America: Problems in Race, Political Economy, and Society*. Boston: South End Press, 1983.

——. *Race, Reform, and Rebellion: The Second Reconstruction in Black America, 1945–1990*. 2nd ed. Jackson: University Press of Mississippi, 1991.

Mauer, Marc. *Race to Incarcerate: The Sentencing Project*. New York: New Press, 1999.

Munford, Clarence J. *Race and Reparations: A Black Perspective for the 21st Century*. Trenton, N.J.: Africa World Press, 1996.

Nelson, Jill, ed. *Police Brutality*. New York: Norton, 2000.

Oliver, Melvin, and Thomas Shapiro. *Black Wealth / White Wealth: A New Perspective on Racial Equality*. New York and London: Routledge, 1995.

Parenti, Christian. *Lockdown America: Police and Prisons in the Age of Crisis*. New York: Verso Books, 1999.

Piven, Frances Fox. *The New Class War: Reagan's Attack on the Welfare State and its Consequences*. New York: Pantheon Books, 1982.

Rank, Mark Robert. *Living on the Edge: The Realities of Welfare in America*. New York: Columbia University Press, 1994.

Reeves, Jimmie L., and Richard Campbell. *Cracked Coverage: Television News, The Anti-cocaine Crusade, and the Reagan Legacy*. Durham, N.C.: Duke University Press, 1994.

Robinson, Randall. *The Debt: What America Owes Blacks*. New York: Dutton, 2000.

Rose, Tricia. *Black Noise: Rap Music and Black Culture in Contemporary America*. Middletown, Conn.: Wesleyan University Press, 1994.

Simms, Margaret C., and Julianne Malveaux, eds. *Slipping Through the Cracks: The Status of Black Women*. New Brunswick, N.J.: Transaction Books, 1986.

Steinberg, Stephen. *Turning Back: The Retreat from Racial Justice in American Thought and Policy*. Boston: Beacon Press, 1995.

Terkel, Studs. *Race: How Blacks and Whites Think and Feel about the American Obsession*. New York: New Press, 1992.

West, Cornel. *Race Matters*. Boston: Beacon Press, 1993.

White, Deborah Gray. *Too Heavy a Load: Black Women in Defense of Themselves, 1894–1994*. New York: Norton, 1998.

Williams, Patricia. *The Alchemy of Race and Rights: Diary of a Law Professor*. Cambridge, Mass.: Harvard University Press, 1991.

Wilson, William J. *The Truly Disadvantaged: The Inner City, the Underclass, and Public Policy*. Chicago: University of Chicago Press, 1987.

Wright, Bruce. *Black Robes, White Justice*. Secaucus, N.J.: Lyle Stuart, 1987.

# AFRICAN AMERICANS IN THE MILITARY

BRENDA L. MOORE

Before World War II, the American military was staffed almost exclusively by white males. However, the shortage of white manpower during America's major wars, beginning with the Revolution, typically led to the recruitment of racial minorities, particularly African Americans. After the conclusion of these conflicts, most minority servicemen either left the ranks of their own volition or were forced to exit as a matter of policy.

Large numbers of African Americans entered the armed forces during World War II, where they served in segregated units. In 1948, by presidential order, the military services were finally desegregated. Since that time, African Americans have played a critical role in the military, and the military in turn has come to occupy an important place in the postwar black experience. In some ways the military has been at the forefront of social change. Although problems of racial discrimination have not been totally resolved, the American armed services have offered greater opportunities for blacks in recent years than many other sectors of society.

## WORLD WAR II: A SEGREGATED MILITARY

The "recruit / reject syndrome" is a common theme in studies of the early war experiences of African Americans. That is, in times of war African Americans were recruited into the military, and after war their service and their earned benefits as veterans were rejected. This theme is found in studies of the nearly five thousand African Americans who fought on the side of the colonists in the battles of Lexington, Concord, Ticonderoga, and Bunker Hill during the American Revolution; the 390,000 African Americans who fought for the Union during the Civil War; and the first all-black division, the 92nd Infantry, created during World War I.

This trend would begin to change during the years of American involvement in World War II (December 1941–September 1945), as African Americans began to serve in the military in larger numbers and in a variety of roles. There are several reasons for the dramatic increase in the number of African Americans in World War II. For one thing, the country's attitude toward racial oppression was changing. Although African Americans were forced to serve in racially segregated units, racial oppression in the United States and in other parts of the world fell under heavy criticism. From the very beginning, World War II was a battle against racial supremacy; the ideologies of Nazism, fascism, and totalitarianism were under severe attack. And, as in previous battles, African Americans reasoned that through participation in the war effort they would be accepted as first-class citizens after the war.

In addition, many African Americans felt that military service would provide them with training in occupational skills that could be used in the civilian labor market once the war had ended. Educational rewards became even more of an incentive to join the military after President Franklin D. Roosevelt signed into law the Servicemen's Readjustment Act of 1944, providing educational benefits for veterans. The GI Bill, as it was popularly known, was available to women as well as men, and many African Americans, male and female veterans alike, used it after the war to obtain college degrees.

However, the most important factor leading to an increase in the participation rates of African Americans was the War Department's realization that the United States would not be able to fight the war effectively without recruiting from the African American community. In 1937, a plan was devised to mobilize African Americans in proportion to their numbers in the general population. A few years later, the country's first peacetime draft (the Selective Training Act of 1940) prohibited racial discrimination against volunteers and draftees. Because racial segregation was the norm in the United States, the War Department grappled with the challenge of employing large numbers of African American men, and later women, to fill military needs while adhering to the ideology of racial segregation.

Attempting to resolve the race issue, the War Department formulated a seven-point policy outlining how African Americans were to be utilized. The policy specifically stated that (1) the strength of black personnel in the military would be proportionate to the black population of the country (10.6 percent); (2) black units would be established in each major branch of the Army; (3) black reserve officers who were eligible for active duty would be assigned to "Negro units officered by colored personnel;" (4) African Americans would receive the opportunity to qualify for reserve commissions; (5) African Americans were to be given aviation training; (6) black civilians were to be accorded equal opportunity for employment at work; and (7) there would be no intermingling between "colored and white" enlisted personnel in the same regimental organization.[1] The seventh point affirmed racial segregation in the military, to which the African American press and political organizations retorted that it was inconsistent with the ideology of democracy. Moreover, such a policy was costly and inefficient to implement; too much time and too many resources were spent providing racially separate housing, training, eating, and recreational facilities.

Suffice it to mention that some African Americans objected to serving in the U.S. military to fight fascism and Nazism abroad when the issue of racism had not been resolved at home. On April 10, 1943, for example, Edward Strong, national secretary of the National Negro Congress, spoke out against African Americans participating in the war effort while racism still existed in the United States. Most African American leaders, however, encouraged black men and women to enlist in the military, and win a "Double-V": victory against oppression abroad and victory against oppression at home.

An estimated 909,000 African Americans enlisted in the military during World War II; more than 500,000 were stationed overseas. African Americans served in racially segregated engineering, quartermaster, combat support, hospital, aviation, artillery, and armored units around the world. For example, the all-black 810th and 811th Engineer Aviation Battalions were the first large task force deployed to Australia after Pearl Harbor; the 91st and 96th Engineer General Service Regiments arrived in Brisbane on April 6, 1942. The 518th Quartermaster Battalion, the 335th Station Hospital, and the 858th Aviation Battalion were also among the many all-black units serving in the Pacific during the war.

African Americans were also stationed in Europe, serving in the all-black 22nd Quartermaster Group and the 578th and the 969th Field Artillery Battalions, as well as many other units. The 99th Pursuit (Fighter) Squadron, more popularly known as the Tuskegee Airmen, participated in campaigns in North Africa and Europe, earning three Distinguished Unit Citations. The 761st Tank Battalion, the first black unit to go into combat, fought in France, Holland, Belgium, Luxembourg, Germany, and Austria. Owing to the demands of war, a few thousand African American support soldiers were retrained as infantrymen and assigned to serve in divisions with white soldiers in France, Belgium, and Germany; all-black platoons fought alongside white platoons in the Battle of the Bulge. Twenty-two African American combat units served in Europe; these experimental units were lauded for their performance in combat.

An estimated 6,500 African American women served in the Women's Army Corps during the war, 850 of whom were members of the all-black 6888th Central Postal Directory Battalion stationed in Europe. Nearly five hundred African American women served in the Army Nurse Corps, stationed at Fort Bragg, North Carolina; Camp Livingston, Louisiana; and Fort Huachuca, Arizona. Some of these women were deployed overseas in Australia.

Although most African Americans were in the Army, they served in other branches of the military as well. More than 165,000 African Americans were in the Navy during the war, three-quarters of whom served overseas. In 1943, all-black crews were aboard the destroyer escort ship *Mason* and the submarine chaser *PC1264*. There were very few African American women in the Navy during World War II—only an estimated twenty-five—and they were integrated with white women. Approximately 17,000 African American men served in the Marine Corps during the war; 5,000 in the Coast Guard; and 24,000 in the Merchant Marine.

Perhaps the biggest obstacle facing African Americans in uniform during World War II was overcoming the stereotype that they were genetically inferior to whites. And although segregation and racial discrimination sometimes led to boycotts, race riots, and courts-martial, African American military personnel persevered in dispelling racial stereotypes. More than 900,000 African American men and women fought for the "Double V." In many ways, World War II proved to be a metaphoric laboratory in which the capabilities of African Americans were tested. When given the opportunity, many African Americans rose to the task. Among these World War II heroes was Dorie Miller, of Waco, Texas, a Navy cook who fired at Japanese planes in Pearl Harbor and was later awarded the Navy Cross for valor. Leonard Harmon, William Pinkney, and Eli Benjamin were also Navy messmates recognized as heroes during World War II.

In the Army, Benjamin O. Davis Sr. was the first African American to achieve general officer rank. He had initially entered the military in 1898, serving with the 9th and later the 10th Cavalry during the Spanish-American War. He was nominated for promotion to brigadier general on October 25, 1940, and served in Europe and Washington, D.C., during World War II. The only other African American line officer in the army during World War II was his son. A West Point graduate in 1936, Benjamin O. Davis Jr commanded the 99th Pursuit Squadron and later the 332nd Fighter Group in the European theater and was awarded the Distinguished Flying Cross.

African American women also served with distinction in the military. Prudence Burns Burrell was assigned to the all-black 268th Station Hospital at Fort Huachuca, Arizona, and later was one of fourteen African American nurses deployed overseas to Australia to care for wounded soldiers. Several African American women were military leaders in the Women's Army Corps (WAC). Major Charity Adams commanded the 6888th Central Postal Directory Battalion, the largest WAC battalion stationed overseas during the war. Martha Settle (later Putney) was commanding officer of the 55th WAC Hospital Company, assigned to Gardiner General Hospital, Chicago. Settle would later earn a Ph.D. in history from the University of Pennsylvania and become a professor at Howard University. In 1992, Martha Putney's book *When the Nation Was in Need* was published, in which she discussed the various military units and field assignments in which black WACs served during the war, and elaborated on the consequences of a racially segregated military. A. Noel Campbell, Ruth Lucas, Vera Harrison, Corrie Shephard, Margaret Barnes, Blanche Scott, and Ann Hall were among the African American commanding officers in the Women's Army Corps during World War II.

The black press, as well as black political officials such as Mary McLeod Bethune, Congressman Adam Clayton Powell, and War Department Civilian Aide on Negro Affairs William H. Hastie, spoke out against racial segregation in the military throughout the war. Most important, however, African American military personnel succeeded in performing beyond the expectations of a skeptical America.

Before World War II had ended, the U.S. government was taking additional steps to increase the involvement of African Americans in the armed services. In 1944, the Army established a board (the Gillem Board) to determine how best to utilize African Americans. The board recommended that African Americans be given greater opportunities to serve in the military and that black platoons, companies, and battalions be incorporated into larger white units. The board recommended further that the number of African Americans in the military was not to exceed 10 percent of their representation in the larger society. Interestingly, the Navy had integrated crew ships as early as 1946 and the Marine Corps had integrated basic training. Made a separate service branch soon after World War II ended, the Air Force was in favor of integration and was making assignments based on ability. The Army was the only service that advocated racial segregation.

By the end of the war, the entire U.S. military was moving rapidly toward racial desegregation. In July 1948, President Harry S. Truman issued Executive Order 9981 establishing the President's Committee on Equality of Treatment and Opportunity (the Fahey Board). In an effort to convince it to desegregate, the Fahey Board concluded that the Army should establish quotas not on race but achievement, with the understanding that if the number of African Americans were to become disproportionately high, racial quotas would be reinstated. The policies for racial integration were in place shortly before the Korean War.

## THE KOREAN WAR: RACIAL DESEGREGATION

At the onset of the Korean War (1950–53), twenty-one African American pilots from the 99th and the 332nd, along with several African American enlisted men, were deployed in integrated Air Force combat units. The Army, by contrast, was still racially segregated; the 24th Infantry Battalion comprised exclusively African American units. By 1951, however, African American recruits were too numerous to be absorbed by all-black units, so they were integrated into previously all-white units.

The army launched a study in 1951 (Project Clear) to examine the effects of racial integration on military effectiveness. The results of this study, which showed that racial integration enhanced the effectiveness of the army, provided support for the movement to abolish segregation. Although 90 percent of the African Americans were serving in integrated army units by the close of the Korean War, segregated units were not completely abolished until 1954.

Benjamin O. Davis Jr. commanded the 51st Fighter Inceptor Wing and flew an F-86 fighter in Korea. He was promoted to brigadier general and became the highest-ranking black officer in the Air Force. Among the other African Americans with distinguished service during the Korean War were Air Force fighter pilots Maj. (later Gen.) Daniel "Chappie" James and Lt. James Harvey. Col. (later Gen.) Frank Petersen served as a Marine Corps combat fighter pilot. Ens. Jesse L. Brown, killed in the line of duty, was the first African American combat pilot in the Navy. Sgt. Cornelius H. Charlton and Pvt. William Thompson, both of the 24th Infantry Regiment, 25th Division, received the Medal of Honor for service in Korea.

## THE VIETNAM WAR: STRUCTURAL INEQUALITY AND RACIAL TENSION

As racial integration became a reality in the U.S. military, equality of opportunity and treatment surfaced as central issues. In 1964, the President's Committee on Equal Opportunity in the Armed Forces (the Gesell Committee) reported that African Americans were concentrated in low pay grades, as compared to their white counterparts, and that racial discrimination persisted on military installations. One year later, in March 1965, the U.S. government launched a major air strike against North Vietnam and became involved in a war that would deploy more than a half million men and women.

The number of African Americans serving in the military during the Vietnam War (1965–1975) soared after President Lyndon B. Johnson charged the armed services with helping to eradicate poverty. The resulting experimental program,

Project One Hundred Thousand, was designed to induct 100,000 men who would otherwise be ineligible for military service owing primarily to low aptitude scores. Consequently, African Americans were inducted into service and assigned to combat positions in Vietnam at a disproportionately high rate. As Martin Binkin found, blacks were more likely than whites to be drafted, sent to Vietnam, serve in high-risk combat units, and be killed or wounded in battle.

The military came under heavy criticism for the large proportion of black casualties early in the war in Southeast Asia. Civil Rights organizations, such as the Student Non-Violent Coordinating Committee (SNCC), the Congress of Racial Equality (CORE), and the Southern Christian Leadership Conference (SCLC), spoke out against United States involvement in the Vietnam War. Julian Bond, then director of publicity for SNCC, was later denied a seat in the Georgia legislature because he supported those who protested against the war by burning their draft cards. Martin Luther King Jr. declared, "We have been repeatedly faced with the irony of watching Negro and white boys on TV screens as they kill and die together for a nation that has been unable to seat them together in the same school."[2]

Some scholars, such as Charles Moskos and John S. Butler, argue that African Americans did not in fact experience a disproportionate rate of casualties during the Vietnam War as a whole. On the other hand, James Westheider notes that during the years 1965 and 1966, African Americans did indeed die in disproportionately high numbers in Vietnam. He further reports that the Pentagon reacted to the high death rates by reducing the number of African Americans in front-line combat. Thus, Westheider claims, by the end of the war the number of African American deaths was proportionate to the number of African American males of military age in the general population. This issue remains a topic of debate among scholars.

The Vietnam era was also a time when racial tension in the military was at its peak. A study of race relations on Army posts during the 1960s, conducted by then former Army Chief of Staff Gen. William Westmoreland, concluded that an increase in racial tension was widespread; and that unless immediate action was taken to identify the problem at the squad and platoon level, an even greater increase in racial confrontation could be expected. Indeed, race riots occurred among soldiers stationed in Germany and in Vietnam, among marines at Camp Lejeune and Kaneohe Naval Air Station, among airmen at Travis Air Force Base, and among sailors aboard the aircraft carriers *Kitty Hawk* and *Constellation*. Westheider found that most of the riots in Vietnam occurred in rear or support units and in settings where different units congregated, such as mess halls, enlisted men's clubs, civilian bars, and brothels. He further asserted that there were few racial problems in active combat units, because survival in combat forced black and white soldiers to develop the unit cohesion often lacking in support units.

A negative consequence of the racial tension was that more than twenty thousand African American men received less than honorable discharges. "Bad discharges," as they were called, were given for such minor infractions as giving a black power salute, greeting another with the handshake called the dap, or having an Afro-style haircut. Those who received dishonorable discharges lost their veteran privileges, an issue that continues to be raised before Congress by the Black Veterans Braintrust today.

A positive consequence of the racial tension in the military, and indeed the country, during the Vietnam War is that the Department of Defense began to recognize and to address the issue of racial inequality in the armed services. In 1970, Secretary of Defense Melvin Laird established the Domestic Action Council and charged it with developing major race relations programs for the military. This action led to the establishment of the Defense Race Relations Institute (the precursor to the Defense Equal Opportunity Management Institute), which functions primarily to foster equal opportunity in the military through training. The services eventually took a zero-tolerance stand against race discrimination and began taking punitive action against military personnel who committed overt acts of racism.

There were several African American recipients of the Medal of Honor in Vietnam, and African American men and women alike served there with distinction. One was Capt. Colin Powell, who served two tours of duty in Vietnam. He arrived first in 1962, serving as advisor to the Army of the Republic of Vietnam (ARVN) in the A Shau Valley, and later as commander of the Hue Citadel airfield. He returned to Vietnam in July 1968 as a major, assigned to the 23rd Infantry Division. Powell received the Legion of Merit Award and the Soldier's Medal for his performance in a helicopter rescue. He would later become a four-star general, chair the Joint Chiefs of Staff, and serve as secretary of state.

## THE ALL-VOLUNTEER FORCE

On March 27, 1969, President Richard M. Nixon issued an announcement that he had appointed an advisory commission on an all-volunteer force under the chairmanship of former Secretary of Defense Thomas Gates. The commission had been directed to develop a comprehensive plan for eliminating conscription (the military draft). An all-volunteer force, commissioners argued, would strengthen American freedom by removing the inequity imposed on the expression of patriotism. They also declared that an all-volunteer force would promote the efficiency of the armed forces and enhance their dignity.

The Gates Commission recommended that the U.S. government move toward an all-volunteer force by making several structural changes. One recommendation was for the military to raise the average level of basic pay for personnel in their first two years of service. Another suggestion was for the U.S. government to make comprehensive improvements in the conditions of military service. Finally, the commission advised that a standby draft system be established and activated by joint resolution of Congress upon request of the President.

The idea of an all-volunteer force raised concern among many military scholars and government officials. Some feared that an all-volunteer force would be too costly for the nation to afford. Another concern was that it would lack the flexibility to expand rapidly in times of sudden crises. It was also argued that an all-volunteer force would undermine patriotism by weakening the traditional belief that each citizen has a moral responsibility to serve his country. Some made the case that the presence of draftees in a conscripted force guards against the growth of a separate military ethos. Consistent with this argument was the matter that an all-volunteer force could pose a threat to civilian authority, American freedom, and democratic institutions.

Another set of objections centered on the issue of social representation. Critics argued that the higher pay associated with an all-volunteer force would be especially appealing to men from the lowest economic classes, motivated primarily by monetary rewards rather than by patriotism. Similarly, it was argued that African Americans, who have relatively poorer occupational opportunities in the civilian sector, would enroll in disproportionate numbers. These critics claimed that the rate of white enlistment and reenlistment might decline due to a greater presence of African Americans, which could lead to a predominantly black enlisted force. They further argued that the problem would only be exacerbated by a resulting black resentment at bearing an undue share of the burden of defense.

Since the all-volunteer force went into effect, the representation of African Americans in the military indeed increased to disproportionately large numbers. Current statistics show that while African American comprised 12.8 percent of the American population in September 2002, they represented 21.6 percent of the active-duty personnel for the same period. African Americans were overrepresented in all of the services except the Coast Guard. The converse was true for white Americans, who were underrepresented in all of the services except for the Coast Guard.

Today the U.S. military, particularly the Army, is receiving accolades for successfully integrating African Americans at all levels. In the words of Moskos and Butler, the U.S. military "is an organization unmatched in its level of racial integration. It is an institution unmatched in its broad record of black achievement. It is a world in which the Afro-American heritage is part and parcel of the institutional culture." The Army, they assert, is the "only place in American life where whites are routinely bossed around by blacks."[3]

Surely, the United States armed services have come a long way in ameliorating racial tension since the problematic days of the Vietnam War era. Compared to other major institutions in the country, the military is in the vanguard of racial progress. With the lack of economic opportunities in the civilian sector, the military, as the critics of the AVF forecasted, is particularly appealing to many African Americans. There are several economic incentives for joining today's military. One such incentive is the military's standardized pay scale; regardless of race, ethnicity, or gender, service members of the same rank receive the same pay. This stands in contrast to the civilian sector, where, for example, African Americans sometimes receive salaries lower than those of their white counterparts. Another incentive is the fact that, unlike many civilian employers, the armed services are willing to accept applicants without skills or prior work experience. In addition, military personnel receive a competitive salary, housing and subsistence allowance, medical insurance, enlistment bonuses, and post-service education.

The greatest number of African Americans is in the Army's enlisted ranks, where they made up 21.8 percent of the personnel as of September 2002. What is more, African American women outnumbered white women in the enlisted grades of E4 (corporal) through E9 (sergeant major). In other words, there were more African American women in the Army with ranks of corporal and sergeant at all levels than there were white women. By contrast, only 8.5 percent of all active-duty officers and 10.1 percent of Army officers were African Americans. These statistics, obtained from the Defense Manpower Data Center, show that African Americans were underrepresented in the officer corps. However, since officers must have a college degree, this level of officer representation compared favorably with the national proportion of African American college graduates, which was less than 7 percent.

Still, the low representation of African Americans in the officer corps is an issue for African Americans in uniform today, and it may potentially lead to social conflict in the future. Part of the problem is that social class in the military is defined by rank level: enlisted, noncommissioned officer, and officer. Enlisted personnel and noncommissioned officers make up the working class, and officers comprise the managerial class. While the overwhelming majority of officers in today's military are white, what sometimes appears to be racial discrimination is caused by African Americans' class position in the military. In other words, race in today's military is often confounded by class.

Another enduring issue concerning African Americans in the all-volunteer force is the lack of training in military occupations that transfer to the civilian labor market. Concentrated mainly in service, supply, functional support, and administrative jobs, African Americans often do not acquire the skills in the military needed to obtain high paying jobs in the civilian sector. Whites, by contrast, are concentrated in electronics repair and electrical- and mechanical-equipment repair occupations, and they often receive training that prepares them to compete for technical jobs in the civilian sector.

## WAR IN THE PERSIAN GULF

Although African Americans made up 16.6 percent of the total reserve and active force during the Desert Shield and Desert Storm (August 1990–March 1991) operations, they comprised 23.5 percent of the military personnel deployed to the war zone. Therefore, the number of African Americans deployed was disproportionately large compared not only to their percentages in the general population (12.8 percent) but also to their percentages in the military. However, as sociologist Mark Eitelberg observed, blacks served primarily in support units and were less likely to experience combat in the Gulf than were their white counterparts. According to Eitelberg's study of racial and ethnic representation in Desert Shield and Desert Storm, 36 percent of African American enlisted personnel and 31 percent of officers were assigned to combat positions, as compared with 45 percent of white enlistees and 42 percent of officers.

Among the many African American women and men serving in Desert Shield and Desert Storm was Sgt. Lauren Long. She was assigned as a dispatcher and bus driver. Sgt. Shelton Torbert served with the 3rd Armor Division. Many African American officers deployed to the Gulf, such as Lt. Col. James Donald and Maj. Abraham Turner, advanced to general later. The highest ranking and one of the most influential military officers during Operation Desert Shield and Desert Storm was Colin Powell. As chairman of the Joint Chiefs of Staff, he played a pivotal role in the strategic planning of the war. He received the Presidential Medal of Freedom, the country's highest nonmilitary award, for the role he played in the Gulf War.

As the United States began to mobilize for a second war with Iraq in 2003, the issue of black representation in the military once again surfaced. The United States military is not representative of the country; it is disproportionately African American, male, working class, and from the South. To guard against any one segment of the American population shouldering a disproportionate burden of defense, Congressman Charles Rangel of New York proposed reinstating the military draft. This proposal met with a great deal of controversy. Although some Americans supported the idea of reinstating the military draft, others were against it, arguing that obligatory service would be a violation of the American people's civil rights. The debate ceased as the United States began Operation Iraqi Freedom.

By March 2003, the United States had deployed 230,521 active duty military personnel, 19.4 percent of whom were African Americans. Reservists accounted for an additional 38,842, making the total strength of the American armed services 269,363. African Americans accounted for 42,140 (21 percent) of the active duty enlisted ranks, and 2,694 (8.9 percent) of the officers. In each of the service branches, the number of African Americans deployed to the Gulf in March 2003 exceeded their representation in the general population. The number of black active duty enlisted personnel deployed ranged from a high of 28.6 percent in the Army to a low of 12.4 percent in the Marine Corps. The Army deployed the greatest percentage of active-duty black officers (13.4 percent). The Army National Guard and the Army Reserve deployed the largest proportion of African Americans (16.2 percent and 23.8 percent respectively) as compared to other reserve units (Navy Reserve: 14.8 percent, Marine Corps Reserve: 8.1 percent, Air National Guard: 7.7 percent, and Air Force Reserve: 6.6 percent).

The total number of active duty African American women deployed to Iraq in March 2003 was 7,013 (or 3.5 percent of all active duty members deployed), as compared to that of white women (9,611 or 4.8 percent). The number of African American women reservists deployed was 815 (or 2.5 percent of all reservists deployed) as compared to 1,477 (or 4.6 percent) white women reservists deployed. As of August 2003, American military personnel are still deployed in Iraq.

Among the black military personnel deployed to Iraq in 2003 was Command Sergeant Major (CSM) Dwight Brown, responsible for the safety, health, welfare, morale, and discipline of Army troops stationed in the country. One of the seven members of the 507th Maintenance Company taken as a prisoner of war was Spec. Shoshana Johnson, a black woman. A thirty-year-old single mother assigned as a cook, she was captured near the city of Nasiriyah and was released unharmed with other members of her unit after three weeks in captivity.

Perhaps the most visible African American serving in Iraq during the first phase of the war was West Point graduate, Gen. Vincent K. Brooks. During Operation Iraqi Freedom, Gen. Brooks served on the Joint Chiefs of Staff as well as spokesman for the United States Central Command, based in Qatar. His daily briefings to news reporters were televised and could be seen in homes around the world.

## RACIAL CHALLENGES IN THE TWENTY-FIRST CENTURY

Although the services have done well in eliminating overt acts of racism, racial issues—some still unresolved and some newly emergent—continue to challenge the military in the twenty-first century. A recent summary of the Military Equal Opportunity Climate Survey, conducted by the Defense Equal Opportunity Management Institute at Patrick Air Force Base in Florida, shows that, in general, African Americans are less optimistic than whites about equal opportunity in the armed forces. The Armed Forces Equal Opportunity Survey (AFEOS), a random sample of active-duty Army, Navy, Air Force, Marine Corps, and Coast Guard personnel and reservists on full-time duty, provides more details about current racial issues in the contemporary armed services. A summary of data from the AFEOS reveals that one-fifth of the black military personnel experienced career-related discrimination in 1996. Additional findings about black enlisted and officer personnel that year have been summarized in a recent publication as follows: Three-fourths had faced negative and offensive racial encounters during that year: 52 percent had been told offensive racist stories; 49 percent had suffered unwelcome attempts to draw them into offensive discussions of race; 46 percent had endured acts of racial condescension; 37 percent had encountered hostile racial stares; 28 percent had endured racist comments or epithets; and 20 percent had been confronted with racist periodicals or other materials. In addition, 6 percent had been physically threatened or intimidated because of their race.[4]

Yet, African Americans enlist in the military in greater numbers and reenlist more often than do their white counterparts. Although race issues continue to surface in the armed services, blacks still find greater career opportunities in the military than in the civilian sector. As African Americans experience greater opportunities for occupational growth in the broader society, their representation in the military will probably decrease.

## SOURCES

Adams-Ender, Clara, and Blair S. Walker. *My Rise to the Stars: How a Sharecropper's Daughter Became an Army General*. Lake Ridge, Va.: CAPE Associates, 2001.

"African Americans and WWII: 50th Anniversary of World War II Commemorative Issue 1941–1945." *Negro History Bulletin* 51–57, nos. 1–12 (December 1993).

Allen, David, and Rick Chernitzer. "Many Troops, Analysts Say Military Is Ahead of the National Trend on Race Issues." *Pacific Stars and Stripes*, February 28, 2002.

Biggs, Bradley. *The Triple Nickels: America's First All-Black Paratroop Unit*. Hamden, Conn.: Archon Books, 1986.

Binkin, Martin, Mark J. Eitelberg, Alvin Schexnider, and Marvin Smith. *Blacks and the Military*. Washington, D.C.: Brookings Institution, 1982.

Bogart, Leo, ed. *Social Research and the Desegregation of the U.S. Army*. Chicago: Markham, 1969.

Christian, Garna L. *Black Soldiers in Jim Crow Texas 1899–1917*. College Station: Texas A&M University Press, 1995.

Davis, Benjamin O. *Benjamin O. Davis, Jr., American: An Autobiography*. Washington, D.C.: Smithsonian Institution Press, 1991.

Dellums, Ronald. "Don't Slam the Door to the Military." *Focus* 3, no. 8 (1975).

Earley, Charity Adams. *One Woman's Army: A Black Officer Remembers the WAC*. College Station: Texas A&M University Press, 1989.

Eitelberg, Mark J. "A Preliminary Assessment of Population Representation in Operation Desert Shield and Desert Storm." Paper presented at the Biennial Conference of the Inter-University Seminar on Armed Forces and Society, Baltimore, Md., October 1991.

Fletcher, Marvin. *America's First Black General, Benjamin O. Davis, Sr., 1880–1970*. Lawrence: University Press of Kansas, 1989.

Franklin, John Hope. *From Slavery to Freedom: A History of Negro Americans*. 5th ed. New York: Knopf, 1974.

Gewertz, Ken. "A Soldier's Story." *Northeastern Alumni Magazine* 5 (May–June 1986).

Gold, Philip. *Evasions: The American Way of Military Service*. New York: Paragon, 1985.

Homan, Lynn M., and Thomas Reilly. *Black Knights: the Story of the Tuskegee Airmen*. Gretna, La.: Pelican, 2001.

Hope, Richard O. *Racial Strife in the U.S. Military*. New York: Praeger, 1979.

Janowitz, Morris. "The All-Volunteer Military as a Sociopolitical Problem." *Social Problems* 22 (February 1975): 435.

Johnson, Jesse. *Black Women in the Armed Forces: 1942–1974*. Hampton, Va.: Privately published, 1974.

Lee, Ulysses. "The Draft and the Negro." *Current History* 55 (July 1968): 28–48.

——. *United States Army in World War II: Special Studies: The Employment of Negro Troops*. Washington, D.C.: U.S. Government Printing Office, 1966.

Moore, Brenda L. "African American Women in the U.S. Military." *Armed Forces and Society* 17 (1991): 363–384.

——. *To Serve My Country, to Serve My Race: The Story of the Only African American Wacs Stationed Overseas During World War II*. New York: New York University Press, 1996.

Moore, Brenda L., and Schuyler Webb. "Equal Opportunity in the U.S. Navy." In *Women in the Military*, ed. Rita Simon, 83–102. New Brunswick, N.J.: Transaction Publishers, 2001.

Moskos, Charles C. "The American Dilemma in Uniform: Race in the Armed Forces." *Annals of the American Academy of Political and Social Science* 406 (March 1973): 94–106.

——. "From Citizens' Army to Social Laboratory." *The Wilson Quarterly* 27, no. 1 (1993): 83–94.

——. "From Institution to Occupation: Trends in Military Organization." *Armed Forces and Society* 4 (1977): 41–50.

Moskos, Charles C., and John S. Butler. *All That We Can Be: Black Leadership and Racial Integration the Army Way*. New York: Basic Books, 1996.

Moskos, Charles C., and Frank R. Wood. *The Military More Than Just a Job?* McLean, Va.: Pergamon-Brassey's, 1988.

Mullen, Robert W. *Blacks in America's Wars*. New York: Monad Press, 1973.

Nichols, Lee. *Breakthrough on the Color Front*. New York: Random House, 1954.

President's Committee on Equal Opportunity in the Armed Forces. *Equality of Treatment and Opportunity for Negro Military Personnel Stationed Within the United States*. Washington, D.C.: U.S. Government Printing Office, 1964.

Powell, Colin, and Joseph Persico. *My American Journey*. New York: Random House, 1995.

Putney, Martha S. *When the Nation Was in Need: Blacks in the Women's Army Corps During World War II*. Metuchen, N.J.: Scarecrow Press, 1992.

Schexnider, Alvin. "Expectations from the Ranks: Representativeness and Systems." *American Behavioral Scientist* 19, no. 5 (1976): 523–542.

Schexnider, Alvin, and John S. Butler. "Race and the All-Volunteer System." *Armed Forces and Society* 2, no. 3 (1976): 421–432.

Smith, Graham. *When Jim Crow Met John Bull: Black American Soldiers in World War II Britain*. New York: St. Martin's Press, 1987.

Stokes, Louis. "The Black Veteran: Defender of the American Dream." *Cleveland Call and Post*, November 22, 1990.

Terry, Wallace. *Bloods: An Oral History of the Vietnam War by Black Veterans*. New York: Random House, 1984.

U.S. Department of Defense, Office of the Assistant Deputy of Defense for Equal Opportunity and Safety Policy. *Black Americans in the Defense of Our Nation*. Washington, D.C.: U.S. Government Printing Office, 1991.

U.S. Office of the Under Secretary of Defense Personnel and Readiness. *Career Progression of Minority and Women Officers*. Washington, D.C.: Department of Defense, 1999.

U.S. President's Commission. *The Report of the President's Commission on an All-Volunteer Force*. Washington, D.C.: U.S. Government Printing Office, 1970.

Vaughn, Chris. "Military Not Representative of Country." *Fort Worth Star-Telegram*, September 21, 2002.

Westheider, James E. *Fighting on Two Fronts: African Americans and the Vietnam War*. New York: New York University Press, 1997.

## NOTES

1. Ulysses Lee, *United States Army in World War II: Special Studies, The Employment of Negro Troops* (Washington, D.C.: U.S. Government Printing Office, 1966), 76.

2. Quoted in Jack D. Foner, *Blacks and the Military in American History* (New York: Praeger, 1974), 206.

3. Charles C. Moskos and John S. Butler, *All That We Can Be: Black Leadership and Racial Integration the Army Way* (New York: Basic Books, 1996), 2.

4. Joe R. Feagin and Clairece Booher Feagin, *Racial and Ethnic Relations*, 7th ed. (Upper Saddle River, N.J.: Prentice-Hall, 2003), 174.

# AFRICAN AMERICANS IN SPORTS

## The Other Champions

SUNDIATA DJATA

Race has been an important element in black American sport history. Gender, class, and religion have also been significant. Since 1939, black athletes have participated in sporting arenas in increasing numbers. Before World War II, professional and collegiate sports sought to maintain segregation. Even though performances by Jesse Owens and Joe Louis brought attention to the abilities of black athletes, integration came very slowly. For example, it took twelve years for all the major league baseball teams to desegregate, and some southern colleges maintained all-white teams until the 1960s. Even after the modern civil rights movement, racism remained prevalent. As Jack Olson has observed, "Every morning the world of sports wakes up and congratulates itself on its contributions to race relations. The litany has been repeated so often that it is believed almost universally."

### BOXING AND BASEBALL

During the 1940s and 1950s, blacks with the help of white benefactors integrated or reintegrated sports. Black American history in boxing dates to the slavery era, and Joe Louis advanced that tradition; between 1940 and 1942, he was the only black world boxing champion. Soon others followed, including Sidney "Bean Jack" Walker, Bob Montgomery, Ike Williams, Lou Brooks, Jimmy Reeves, Lloyd Marshall, Earl Turner, and Willie White. Since the 1940s, blacks have been prolific in boxing, with Ray Charles "Sugar Ray" Robinson, Johnny Saxton, Bob Foster, Charles "Sonny" Liston, Thomas "Hit Man" Hearns, Joe Frazier, George Foreman, "Marvelous" Marvin Hagler, Michael Spinks, and Mike Tyson, to name a few—though Muhammad Ali captured the imagination of the sport world like no other athlete. By the new millennium, boxing witnessed a new generation of daughters, not sons, as Laila Ali and Jacqui Frazier-Lyde followed their fathers' footsteps.

Jackie Robinson, a Negro League player who played in six World Series, made his minor league debut with the Montreal Royals in 1946, desegregating baseball. After he moved up to the Brooklyn Dodgers the next year, others were signed, including John Wright, Don Newcombe, Roy Campanella, Roy Partlow, Dan Bankhead, Joe Black, and Jim Gilliam. When Larry Doby joined the Cleveland Indians in 1947, he became the first black player in the American League. Henry Thompson joined the St. Louis Browns, and Willie Mays became the third black player to sign with the New York Giants in 1951. Frank Robinson, the fifth black Hall of Fame inductee, began his career with the Cincinnati Reds, winning the Rookie of the Year Award in the National League in 1956. The Boston Red Sox was the last team to desegregate when Elijah "Pumpsie" Green signed in 1959. When black athletes broke the color barrier, they faced "stacking," meaning that they were generally limited to first base or the outfield. Nevertheless, blacks established themselves with exceptional skills in "thinking" positions. For instance, Ernie Banks played shortstop, Don Newcombe and Joe Black were pitchers, and Roy Campanella and Elston Howard were catchers. Scores of others followed, among them Willie McCovey, Richie Allen, Ken Singleton, Dave Winfield, Dwight Gooden, and Ken Griffey Jr. A new generation of players took the game to new heights with record-breaking careers. Rickey Henderson holds the record for stolen bases, and Barry Bonds, who captured the single season homerun record, became the first to hit four hundred home runs and steal four hundred bases. In 1974, Henry "Hank" Aaron broke the home-run record of Babe Ruth, hitting number 715, passed Ty Cobb's record for games played, and became first on the National League runs list, previously held by Willie Mays. The next year, he became the career RBI leader. Despite impressive gains, many who played in the Negro Leagues lost the chance at major league history. Satchel (Leroy Robert) Paige was one of the few Negro League stars who played in the majors long after his prime. With a career that spanned five decades, he was inducted into the Hall of Fame by the Committee on Negro Baseball Leagues.

## BASKETBALL AND FOOTBALL

Basketball and football have been more available to blacks because they are inexpensive sports. The Rens (later the Washington Bears and Dayton Rens) and the Harlem Globetrotters were all-black teams, but no black league existed in basketball. In 1946, the Basketball Association of America was formed to increase attendance at professional games. After Don Barksdale became the first black player on the 1948 Olympic team, the integration of professional basketball soon followed although the first black to play professional basketball was with the Rochester Royals in the National Basketball League in 1946. In 1950, the New York Knicks signed Nat "Sweetwater" Clifton, a member of the Globetrotters, the Washington Capitals signed Earl Lloyd, and Charles Cooper joined the Boston Celtics. Although teams were signing blacks, an unwritten quota limited the number of blacks on any team to four, and only two could start. Professional basketball received little national attention until the battles between the Celtics' Bill Russell and the Philadelphia Warriors' Wilt Chamberlain, beginning in 1959 and continuing to the late 1960s, attracted a generation of fans. According to Richard O. Davies, these players, with Lenny Wilkins, Oscar Robertson, and Elgin Baylor, changed the thinking that blacks "lacked the intelligence and discipline to provide team leadership." Julius "Dr. J" Ervin, Kareem Abdul Jabbar, Earvin "Magic" Johnson, Michael Jordan, and Shaquille O'Neal have taken the sport to a new level. Finally, a women's professional league found support so that players such as Sheryl Swoopes, Lisa Leslie, and Nikki Teasley could demonstrate their prowess. Earlier outstanding collegiate players such as Cheryl Miller had to find other opportunities when women's leagues folded.

When the All-American Football Conference (AAFC) organized in 1946, it allowed teams to sign black players. The Cleveland Rams were first, signing Marion Motley, a running back from the University of Nevada-Reno, the first black inducted in the Hall of Fame in 1968. Meanwhile, the National Football League (NFL) signed fewer blacks, with only three teams doing so—the Los Angeles Rams, New York Giants, and Detroit Lions. The Washington Redskins were the last to sign a black player, Bobby Mitchell, in 1962, taking seventeen years for all the teams to desegregate. Stacking also existed in football, which denied blacks the opportunity to play leadership positions. In 2001, the Dallas Cowboys signed three black quarterbacks in the same season. It took decades before such a feat was possible. Willie Throwers played quarterback for the Chicago Bears in 1953 for a short time, but James Harris became the first black starting quarterback with the Los Angeles Rams in 1978. Warren Moon refused to shift positions as most black quarterbacks had been coerced to do, and signed with the Canadian Football League, but later moved to the

NFL. Post-1970 superstars have included Earl Campbell, Tony Dorsett, Barry Sanders, Emmit Smith, and Reggie White.

Desegregation on the collegiate level was a more difficult process. Coaches typically failed to promote racial reform for fear of alienating boosters, alumni, administrators, and elected officials. When the University of Kentucky played Texas Western College (later the University of Texas at El Paso) for the 1966 NCAA basketball championship, it was a pivotal point in sport history. Kentucky coach Adolph Rupp refused to recruit black players, while Texas Western coach Don Haskins recruited black players because he was unable to compete with major white schools for top white athletes. All of the Texas Western starters and the two leading substitutes were black, and they won the game 72–65. Kentucky left the runner-up trophy in the locker room. Afterward, Vanderbilt announced that a black player had been signed, and other Southeast Conference schools followed suit. In 1971, Southern Methodist of the Southwest Conference signed its first black football player, Jerry Levias, placing pressure on other teams in the conference to do the same.

Before the 1960s, black colleges attracted the top black athletes. Morgan State won the Amateur Athletic Union (AAU) Indoor relay crown in 1955. In 1962 Texas Southern swept to victory in every relay event in the Texas Relays. Between 1946 and 1959, seventeen players from black colleges signed with the NFL. Clarence "Big House" Gaines at Winston-Salem became the first black college coach to win an NCAA title (Division II) in 1967, while Jake Gaither of Florida A&M won twelve conference titles. However, Eddie Robinson of Grambling State compiled more victories in collegiate football and sent more players to the NFL than any other coach.

Black collegiate programs met hard times when major white programs began to woo top black athletes. Nevertheless, players from black programs excelled in the NFL, among them Walter Payton (Jackson State), Jerry Rice (Mississippi Valley State), Doug Williams (Grambling), and Steve McNair (Alcorn State). White schools have increasingly tapped black talent since the 1960s. In 1961 Ernie Davis was the first black awarded the Heisman Trophy, followed by Mike Garrett (1965) and O. J. Simpson (1968). By the 1980s even basketball and football programs at southern schools were predominantly black. However, it took longer for blacks to be play quarterback. Prior to mid-1960s Sandy Stephens (Minnesota), Wilber Hollis (Iowa), Jim Raye (Michigan State), and Ron Burton (Colgate) were among the few who played the position. John McClusky became Harvard's first black quarterback in 1964, and Marlin Briscoe set quarterback records at the University of Omaha. By 1988, fifteen of the thirty-four starting quarterbacks in the bowl games were black, and by the end of the century, many of the collegiate quarterbacks had advanced to the NFL. On the other hand, few quarterbacks from black institutions have been drafted to play the position in the NFL. Williams and McNair have been exceptions.

## TRACK AND FIELD

Track and field was another sport in which blacks excelled. Between 1932 and 1948 blacks established supremacy in the sprints and jumping events. Track programs at black colleges compared favorably with football, but as early as 1948, even the best-equipped black colleges had difficulties competing with programs at white colleges. Although top black trackers were lured to white programs, they continued to focus on certain events. The Olympics provided the best opportunities for black women athletes such as Mae Faggs, Catherine Hardy, and Barbara Jones in 1950s, and Wilma Rudolph's multi-event gold medal performance in 1960. Nell Jackson became the first black head track coach of an U.S. Olympic team in 1956. Since then black American women have set standards for women of other nations. A few with stellar careers include Florence Griffith Joyner, the Associated Press Female Athlete of the Year in 1988; Marion Jones, who won the award in 2000; and Jackie Joyner-Kersee, who ended her brilliant heptathlon career with four consecutive Goodwill Games titles in 1998. Moreover, Jearl Miles-Clark, the U.S. record holder in the 800-meter event, earned four 400-meter titles, while Gail Devers has won eight national titles in the 100-meter event. Meanwhile, black American men such as Carl Lewis, Allen Johnson, Calvin Davis, and Jon Drummond have made track and field history. Maurice Green ran the fastest 100-meter sprint in 1999, while Michael Johnson did the same in the 200-meter event in 1996.

## GOLF AND TENNIS

Certain sports have been out of reach of the mass of black people. Golf and tennis have been prime examples of racism and classism, partly because these sports have been expensive, deemed elitist, and mostly played at private clubs, which typically barred blacks. Golf was desegregated via the courts. The Michigan delegation to the Professional Golfers Association (PGA) annual meeting in 1943 insisted that a "whites only" clause be written in the constitution. The Ladies Professional Golfers Association (LPGA), formed in 1948, also barred blacks. Bill Spiller, a four-time black United Golfers Association (UGA) champion, Ted Rhodes, and Madison Gunter sued the Richmond (California) Golf Club for refusing their entries in 1948. The PGA agreed to drop the "whites only" clause to settle the lawsuit. Lawsuits in other cities followed. Even though public courses were desegregated, many private clubs remained restricted.

Although the number of blacks in golf increased in the 1970s, coinciding with the growth of a black middle class and an interest in individual sports, many were more interested for the social advantages than professional aspirations. Unlike the team sports, there were no well-coached black professionals in golf. The majority of the UGA events were held in the Northeast and Midwest until 1954, when the nationals were played in Dallas, Texas. As with other black leagues, there were outstanding players such as Howard Wheeler, a five-time UGA National Professional champion between 1933 and 1958. Rhodes won the title for the consecutive years 1949–51 and again in 1957. Thelma Cowan won four national titles, and Anne Gregory won it five times. Robert Lee Elder, who turned professional in 1959, was the next great black golfer. He became a thirty-three-year-old rookie in 1967 when he received his PGA card. Pete Brown won the UGA title in 1961, and a PGA satellite event in 1963. After winning the UGA title in 1964, Renee Powell became the first black woman on the LPGA tour in 1967. Charlie Sifford, a six-time winner of the UGA national title, was the most famous black golfer prior to 1970. He began playing in the major league in 1955, and in 1957 was the first black to win a significant title in a predominant white event. When the PGA rescinded its "white only" clause, he became the first black player to receive a PGA card. In addition, he became the first black player to win a major title in 1969. Most of the professionals had been self-taught, and many were former caddies. However, Calvin Peete never caddied, nor played in the UGA, but became the best "black" golfer in history. Eldrick "Tiger" Woods, however, removed that race qualifier when he became potentially the best golfer in history. Woods won several major titles (three Masters), including four consecutive majors (the U.S. Open, British Open, PGA Championship, and the Masters) by the age of twenty-six, creating an unprecedented interest in the sport.

The segregation line in tennis cracked soon after in professional baseball. Since the United States Lawn Tennis Association (USLTA) denied membership to blacks, black players formed the American Tennis Association (ATA). By 1939, 150 black tennis clubs existed with approximately 28,000 players. Although Althea Gibson made tennis history when she entered the 1949 Eastern Indoor Championship, Reginald Weir was the first black player to play the National Indoors. In 1953, Oscar Johnson won a USLTA affiliated event in Los Angeles. That year, as an eighteen-year-old, he applied to a USLTA junior event in St. Louis but was denied entry when he appeared on the site and the directors discovered he was black. Although the USLTA had been desegregated, racism remained at local tournaments and private clubs. Even with additional public courts built during the Roosevelt administration, tennis remained an expensive sport, and many like Gibson, Arthur Ashe, Luis Glass and Bonnie Logan, had the help of benefactors like Dr. Walter Johnson, who coached many black players who also lived in his home. Gibson became the first black professional player, winning the 1956 French and 1957 and 1958 Wimbledon and U.S. Open. Robert Ryland made his professional debut at the Cleveland Arena in 1958. Ashe, however, was the first black male to win a grand slam, the 1968 U.S. Open, later adding Wimbledon in 1975. Ashe's success created a tennis boom among blacks. In the early 1980s, the professional tour had a record number of black players, including Renee Blount, Kim Sands, Lloyd Bourne, and Chip Hooper. However, it was the next generation that had greater success, with Zina Garrison, Lori McNeil, MaliVai Washington, and Chanda Rubin. Despite the gains in professional tennis, only two players have won grand slam titles since Ashe, Venus Williams (2000, 2001 Wimbledon and U.S. Open) and her sister Serena (1999 U.S. Open, 2002 French and Wimbledon). In addition, Venus became the first black player to be ranked number one in the open era.

## BOWLING

Bowling quickly became a popular sport in the United States, mainly as a family activity. In 1947, *Ebony* magazine listed bowling as the number one sport among blacks. In the professional ranks, blacks were forced to form a separate league, the National Negro Bowling Association (NNBA), organized in 1939 in Detroit because the American Bowling Congress (ABC) and the Women's International Bowling Congress (WIBC) had "white only" clauses in their constitutions. The NNBA changed its name to the National Bowling Association in 1944. A few of the top players were Merrit Thomas, Ben Harding, Hazel Lyman, and Virginia Dolphin. After a National Committee for Fair Play in Bowling met in New York City in 1948 to consider ways to achieve integration, the ABC and WIBC repealed their "white only" clauses in 1951. Despite desegregation of the leagues, the number of black professionals has remained low. George Branham III was the first to win a national tour title in 1986. By 1991, only two blacks were among 120 full-time Professional Bowling Association (PBA) bowlers. Kim Terrell and Cheryl Daniels were the only blacks competing full-time on the Ladies Professional Bowling Tour.

## CREW, CYCLING, FIELD HOCKEY, AND FENCING

Olympic sports such as crew, cycling, field hockey, and fencing have attracted few participants at black colleges. Hampton University started a boat club in

1912, but had no other black schools with which to compete. Blacks have had a long but sketchy history in cycling, dating back to the nineteenth century. Oliver "Butch" Martin was on the 1964 Olympic Team and placed twelfth in the American Bicycle League's national road race in 1967. Nelson Vails, who began riding as a messenger, won a silver medal in 1984. In field hockey, black players tended to emerge from white schools. C. Vivian Stringer was on the Mid-East field hockey team. Tina Sloan Green was on the national field hockey team in 1969. She later coached at Temple from 1974 to 1979 and founded the Philadelphia Inner City field hockey program in 1980. Gloria Jean Byard was the first black to earn a position on a national team in 1974.

After World War II, more blacks were drawn to fencing, but most were trained in the YMCA / YWCA or at white colleges. Peter Westbrook believed that few blacks have taken interest in fencing because there was little money to be made. Sophronia Pierce Stent became the first black woman accepted into the Amateur Fencer's League of America (AFLA) in 1951, and Nikki Franke was the 1975 American Fencers League of America Champion. Bruce Davis won the NCAA foil competition for Wayne State in 1957–58. In 1971 Edward Ballinger of NYU was the Intercollegiate Fencing Association champion in foil. Also, Tyrone Simmons of the University of Detroit won the same title in 1972. In 1981 Peter Lewison was an NCAA All American. Michael Lofton was the second black saber NCAA winner in 1984, while Ruth White of NYU was the 1971–72 National Intercollegiate Women's Fencing Association (NIWFA) winner in foil. Sharon Montplaisir won the NIWFA championship in 1984. The first black member of an Olympic team was Uriah Jones, a former AFLA winner, who made the squad in 1968. In 1972 Ruth White, Bart Freeman, and Tyrone Simmons made the team, and Peter Westbrook finished thirteenth in the saber in 1976. In 1984 five blacks competed on the Olympic team, including Michael Lofton and Semyon Pinkhasov.

## GYMNASTICS

Even though public schools used gymnastics more for training than competition, many black public schools lacked gymnastic training in their physical education classes. Eventually, gymnastics was slowly accepted as an Olympic sport, which led to expanded television coverage by 1980. Black gymnasts have been a part of the tremendous growth of the sport. Mike Carter was the first to gain a national reputation, becoming a three-time All-American at Louisiana State. Ron Galimore, son of Chicago Bears star Willie Galimore, became the only gymnast to win NCAA individual titles in four different years; he scored perfect scores in NCAA championships. Diane Durham was the first internationally ranked black woman.

She was the United States Junior Champion in the floor exercises, vault, parallel bars, and balance beam in 1981 and 1982. Finally, Dominique Dawes was an integral part of the gold medal team in the 1992 Olympics.

In the sport of judo, a few names have emerged. George Harris, the first black American to reach the international level, was a member of the 1964 Olympic team. In the 1976 Olympics, Allen Coage won a bronze medal as a heavyweight. Edward Liddie captured a bronze medal in the 132-pound extra-lightweight class in the 1984 Olympics.

## LACROSSE, SOCCER, SOFTBALL, AND VOLLEYBALL

Lacrosse is the oldest organized athletic activity in North America. Ivy League schools, first, and then other colleges and affluent public schools adapted the traditional Native American game. Black Canadian participation dates to the late 1880s, but there was little black American participation until 1939, when Simeon F. Moss played for Rutgers University. In 1941 and 1942 Lucien Victor Alexis Jr. played for Harvard University and was benched in a game against the United States Naval Academy when its team refused to play against a black player. It was in 1976 that the Naval Academy had its first black player, George Moore. Nearly all black players at white colleges had never played the game, as was the case for Jim Brown when he attended Syracuse University in 1955; he became the first black player in a North-South game. The first black player selected to a South All-Star team was John Mackey, three years later. James Ford, who set Rutgers University scoring and assist records, played in high school as did Albert Ray, a two-time high school All-American, who played at Rutgers. Morgan State, a historically black college, developed a major lacrosse program. After six years of intercollegiate play, the team was number ten in the college division in 1975, and Miles Harrison was the first player from a black school to be selected for the North-South Game. Other stars from Morgan State included Wayne Jackson, a College Division Third Team All-America in 1973; and Dave Raymond, College Division Honorable Mention All-America in 1974. Blacks have also been club players. Most clubs were concentrated along the eastern seaboard. Harold Rumsey played for the Manhasset Lacrosse Club in Long Island in the 1940s. Larry Palmer of the Philadelphia Lacrosse Club, Val Emery Jr. of the Mount Washington Club, Dean Rollins of the New York Lacrosse Club, Morgan Holley of the Chesapeake Lacrosse Club, and Wendell Thomas of the Maryland Lacrosse Club have been standouts since 1970.

Soccer, called football outside of the United States, has enjoyed an illustrious history, although American football has overshadowed it in this country.

Blacks played soccer on the collegiate level in the early half of the century. Although Brazilian Edison "Pele" Nascimento has remained the most highly recognized black star, Afro-Caribbeans have made up teams at black colleges like Howard University, which has won national titles (NAIA 1961, NCAA Division I 1974). Black American Alfonso Smith Jr., who played at the University of Tampa, was recruited for the 1984 Olympic team. The United States women's performance in 1996 Olympics, and that of the men in the 2002 World Cup (with star player DaMarcus Beasley) have been instrumental in increasing the popularity of the sport.

Softball has been immensely popular, and a few black players have been inducted into the Softball Hall of Fame like Frankie Williams, Charles Justice and Billie Harris. Williams, who played with the Raybestos Cardinals (Stratford), was American Softball Association (ASA) All-American for three years. Justice, the Satchel Paige of softball, pitched for over thirty years with a record of 873–92. Harris, pitcher and utility player from 1948 to 1975, was a three-time ASA All-American. From 1953 to 1975 she played in the Pacific Coast Women's League.

Volleyball has been a popular nonprofessional team sport. Black players have figured more prominently in the sport after the 1970s. In 1977, the women's team at Tuskegee Institute became the first from a black school to win an AIAW-sanctioned state title. Flo Hyman, Rita Crockett, and Rose Magers helped the U.S. team win a silver medal in the 1984 Olympics. Moreover, Hyman was the top hitter at the 1981 World Cup Tournament. Since then, black women have made the Olympic squad in numbers far greater than the men. Blacks have also begun to compete in beach volleyball.

## SWIMMING

Segregation denied many black children access to public pools, thereby limiting black participation in swimming. Nevertheless, in the 1930s, Morris Jackson and Emily Jeter were prominent swimmers. Walter Hutchinson, a swimming coach at the Los Angeles Twenty-Eight Street YMCA, led his team of junior black swimmers to a second place in the AAU Junior Olympic 200-meter freestyle in the 1950s. The star performer was ten-year-old Charles E. Spann III. Charles Chapman remains the only noted black marathon swimmer; in 1981, he also became the first African American to swim the English Channel. Before the modern civil rights movement, Morgan State, Tennessee State, and Howard had strong swim teams. Frank Stewart specialized in the freestyle at Tennessee State and became an instructor at the Great Lakes Naval Training Center during World War II. Stewart began at Chicago's International YMCA in 1936 at age eleven. Other Tennessee State swimmers were John Swann, who won the

NAIA 100-meter butterfly in 1958, and Clyde James won the NAIA 100-yard backstroke in 1960–61. As in other sports, integration hurt swimming programs at black colleges, and some dropped swimming to save money. Nathan Clark was one of the first to be ranked nationally (fourth) in 1962–63 season while at Ohio State. Rick White, who competed at Long Island University, was a three-time world champion high diver and captain of the United States team at the 1973 International Team Championship. Fred Evans competed at the University of Illinois-Chicago, and became the NAIA and NCAA Division II champion in the 100-meter breast stroke in 1976 and 1977, and was later inducted into the United States Swimming Hall of Fame. Bob Murray (University of Michigan) was the 1978 and 1980 Big Ten champion in the 50-meter freestyle. In 1981, Trent Lyght set an Arizona State University record in the 100-meter breast stroke. Chris Silva of UCLA was a member of the winning 1982 PAC-10 400-meter relay team that won the NCAA title. In addition, he won a silver medal in the 1983 World University Games in the 400-meters. The first black Olympic medalist hailed from Surinam; Anthony Nesty won gold medals in the 1988 and 1992 Olympics. The first black from the United States to medal was Anthony Ervin in the 2000 Olympics.

## TABLE TENNIS, WEIGHTLIFTING, AND WRESTLING

Blacks have also participated in table tennis (ping-pong). Ronnie Hobson, twelve years old at the time, the first black champion, and Sol Hairston, a runner-up, were two of eight black players from Newport News to participate in the 1960 Open. Joy Foster from Jamaica won the girls' title. George Braithwaite, an immigrant from Guyana, won the U.S. National Class "B" championships in 1966 and the Class "A" title in 1968. Although blacks have played table tennis in leagues and recreation centers, they have viewed it merely as a recreational activity.

Blacks have been increasingly drawn to the sport of weightlifting. John Davis won his first world title, the light-heavyweight championship in 1938 at age seventeen. Afterward, he won twelve national titles in two divisions, six world titles, two Olympic gold medals (1948, 1952), and two Pan-American Games titles (1951, 1958). John Terry, the featherweight world record holder in 1938, became the first featherweight to deadlift six hundred pounds in 1939. James Bradford was second to Davis in the 1952 Olympics, but won a silver medal in 1960 when he was national champion.

Unlike most modern sports, largely developed by whites or Native Americans, wrestling has an African antecedent. Moreover, wrestling has long been prominent in the black community. Before 1960, black professional wrestlers competed among themselves until Edward "Bearcat" Wright refused to wrestle in places that barred integrated bouts. The National Association for the Advancement of Colored People (NAACP) supported him, and soon blacks could book matches against white opponents. Black wrestlers were billed as the good guys and the white opponent as the villain in order to avoid possible lynching. Some of the pro wrestlers included Reggie "Sweet Daddy" Siki, Buster "The Harlem Hangman" Lloyd, "Seaman" Art Thomas, and actor Woody Strode.

Among black colleges, Morgan State has perhaps the oldest history in wrestling. Black colleges have produced talented wrestlers like John Organ (Howard), Robert Gardner (Lincoln), Hulon Willis (Virginia State), Thurlis Little (Elizabeth City), James Raglund (South Carolina State), and James Phillips (Morgan State). In 1980, William Smith of Morgan State became the first wrestler from a black college to win the NCAA Division II 158-pound title. His teammate Greg Veale won the 167-pound title in 1983. Black wrestlers have excelled at predominantly white institutions, among them Robert Douglas, who competed at West Liberty State (West Virginia), where he won the 1962 NAIA 130-pound title. He transferred to Oklahoma State and won the Big Eight Championship in 147-pound division in 1965. Later, he landed a position at Arizona State, becoming the first black coach of a major program at a predominantly white school. Don Benning was the first black coach at a predominantly white college, Omaha University, and named Coach of the Year in 1970. Since the 1980s some programs at predominantly white universities have experienced major shifts in the racial composition of their teams. For instance, in the mid-1990s, the Northern Illinois wrestling team was dominated by blacks, among them Llewellyn Ferguson, Demond Rodez, Eric Muhammad, and Lonnie Baxter. By the end of the decade, only one black wrestler was on the team.

## CAR AND MOTORBOAT RACING

Dating back to the late nineteenth century, motor racing has developed into a major sport, although blacks have only slowly adopted it. Black drivers raced before World War II just for the fun of the sport and their interest in automobiles. Motor racing is very expensive, and drivers require major sponsors; the American Automobile Association also had an unwritten rule to ban black drivers. Even after the ban was lifted, racism remained. In 1971, a white promoter of the Charlotte (North Carolina) Motor Speedway promised Wendell Scott a "first-class car," but Scott believed that the promoter relented to pressure from white drivers and gave him with a second-rate car. In Georgia, it took the Chamber of Commerce to grant permission for him to race, and he may have been allowed to do so at least in part because he was light-skinned. Still, he was permitted on the track only after an ambulance for blacks arrived, since no ambulance for whites would take him to the hospital if he wrecked. Due to lack of resources, it was 1961 before Scott could race on the Grand National circuit. His biggest win came in the National Association of Stock Car Auto Racing Grand National in Jacksonville, Florida in 1964. Benny Scott and Willie T. Ribbs have made other advancements. Scott won the 1969 Southern Stock Car Title in 1969. In 1972, he was part of the first integrated corporate effort to win a starting position in the Indianapolis 500. Ribbs, who came from a racing family, won the 1978 Dunlop Championships in Europe, obtained a Budweiser sponsorship in 1983 for the Trans-Am Circuit, and earned Rookie of the Year award. Ribbs became the first black driver to qualify for the Indianapolis 500. In 2002, George Mack also qualified for the Indianapolis 500. By this time, two former NBA players, Larry Nance and Tom Hammonds, were also racing.

The history of powerboat racing has paralleled that of auto racing. In the 1950s, Arthur Kennedy Sr. and Arthur Kennedy Jr. were the only black members of the National Outboard Association (NOA). The senior Kennedy began racing in 1947 at the age of thirty-one, but his son began racing at age eight. The father won twelve of thirteen events in 1954. The son has amassed two NOA records for the one-mile straightaway in 1955, the NOA High-Point Championships in 1968, the Bermuda Four-hour TART marathon, and the Schaeffer Cup for the Mod U Class in 1978. Another competitor, Charles Marks, who sponsored himself in offshore powerboat racing, won the 1989 National Championships.

## ICE HOCKEY, SKATING, AND WINTER OLYMPIC SPORTS

Blacks have had a limited history in winter Olympic sports. Although in 1938, Charles Brooks played ice hockey for Medford (Massachusetts), black Canadians have played a pivotal role in the history of ice hockey. Willie O'Rhee became the first black hockey player in the National Hockey League (NHL) in 1957, followed by Grant Fuhr, Tony McKegney, Ray Neufeld in the mid-1980s. A few blacks from the United States competed in the college ranks. Lloyd Robinson played at Boston University after returning from an all-black unit in World War II, Donald Seale played at Clarkson University from 1954 to 1957, and Ed Wright played at Boston University from 1967 to 1970. Wright later coached at the State University of New York. On the professional level, Val James played in the Eastern Hockey League for the Erie (Pennsylvania) Blades, and the Rochester Americans in the American Hockey League in the mid-1970s.

Black participation in ice skating has been just as meager. Mable Fairbanks won amateur competitions before becoming a professional in 1951. Bobby

Beauchamp was second in the junior world event and the United States junior men's competition in 1979. In 1981 he was seventh among American senior men. The most heralded black skater was Debi Thomas, who won a bronze medal in the 1988 Olympics, after having the lead following the compulsories. The only other black skater with major Olympic success was Surya Bonaly of France.

Black participation in other winter Olympic sports has been sparse, especially in skiing. When the bobsled team from Jamaica first competed, it was considered a joke. Soon, Trinidad entered the competition. When Vonetta Flowers won a gold medal in the two-member bobsled in 2002, and the four-men silver medal team included two blacks, Randy Jones and Garrett Hines, black participation became serious. However, few blacks have competed in speed skating. Gayle Ann Fannin, who won the New York State title, trained for the 1964 Olympics. Erroll Fraser, a cyclist turned speed skater, also trained for the Olympics by watching films of skaters. More recently, Shani Davis has competed in junior speed skating championships.

## CHALLENGES FOR LEADERSHIP POSITIONS

Once black athletes overcame "stacking," they met other challenges. The move into ownership and managing positions proved to be an even more difficult task. In 1987 Al Campanis, vice president of the Los Angeles Dodgers, argued that blacks might not have the necessities to manage a baseball team. Several have proved him wrong, beginning with Frank Robinson, who became the first black manager in baseball in 1974. By 1991 Hal McRae and Cito Gaston were also managers. Other milestones were made in 1989 when Bill White became National League President; the Boston Red Sox hired Elaine Weddington as the first black female assistant general manager. Tracy Lewis served as president of the Savannah Cardinals (1985–1987).

Bertram Lee and Peter Bynoe in 1989 became the first black part-owners of a major sport team, the Denver Nuggets of the National Basketball Association (NBA). After the Charlotte Hornets franchise moved to New Orleans, the NBA Board of Governors on January 10, 2003, approved granting an expansion team to Robert Johnson, the founder of Black Entertainment Television. Johnson paid $300 million for the franchise that included the Charlotte Sting, a women's basketball team. He named the expansion team the Charlotte Bobcats.

Baseball's commitment to diversity came under fire in 1990 when fourteen managerial openings were filled and only one black was hired. Basketball has been the leader in racial hiring. There have been more black coaches in the NBA than any other professional league. On the collegiate level, John Thompson

(Georgetown) became the first black to win the NCAA, later joined by Nolan Richardson (University of Arkansas). C. Vivian Stringer took Delaware State to the final of the first NCAA women's tournament, and Carolyn Peck guided Purdue to the NCAA Women's Championship in 1999.

In 1991, blacks comprised 72 percent of the NBA, 61 percent of the NFL, and 18 percent of the MLB (major league baseball). However, the numbers differed in the front office, where blacks were only 9 percent of the NBA, 6 percent of the NFL, and 4 percent of the MLB. Only 3 percent of the head coaches and 16 percent of assistant coaches in the NFL were black. As for physicians, in 1994 95 percent in the NBA, 97 percent in the NFL, and 95 percent of the MLB were white.

Black quarterbacks have made tremendous leaps since 1990 when there were sixteen black quarterbacks on twelve teams in the CFL (six starters), but only six on 28 teams in the NFL (three starters). Quarterbacks such as James Harris, Vince Evans, and Doug Williams faced greater hardships. For instance, Williams at Tampa Bay was the fifty-fourth highest paid quarterback in the league, although he was one of twenty-four starters. Moreover, any mistake these early quarterbacks made was intensified by their color. The successes of Warren Moon, Rodney Peete, Jay Walker, and Randall Cunningham proved beyond a doubt that black quarterbacks could be what Doug Williams called a CEO (chief executive officer) on the field. Meanwhile, after years of questioning why there were no black head coaches in the NFL, Art Shell became the head coach of the Raiders in 1989, followed by Dennis Green, Ray Rhodes, Tony Dungee, and Herman Edwards. However, there were no black general managers in the NFL by 1990. Harold Henderson, vice president for labor relations, was the highest-ranking black executive in league history. Prior to these developments, Willie Brown, defensive backfield coach for the Raiders, maintained, "I think the owners are uncomfortable with blacks in executive positions. They don't think we can handle the responsibility or provide leadership."

Black women have faced racism and sexism. Although men coach women, rarely have women coached men in individual or team sports. Stephanie Ready, who played basketball and volleyball at Coppin State, became assistant coach of National Basketball Development League's (NBDL) Greenville (South Carolina) Groove in 1999, the first woman to coach a men's professional team.

There have been additional concerns. Some teams find it necessary to reserve spots for whites to appease fans. When the New York Knicks had an all-black team in 1979–80, attendance at the games dropped to a thirteen-year low although the team had improved by eight wins over the previous season. Few people have complained about a quota system that ensures a number white players or limits the number of black players on sport teams.

Blacks have sought other opportunities in the sports world. For example, Johnny Greer and Mike Carey became the first black referees in the NFL. In boxing, Doris Brown became a ringside physician, and Cora Wilds has chaired the DC Boxing Commission. In tennis, Bernard Chavis was the first black to referee a USTA national tournament in 1996. A few in tennis like Benny Sims and Marcel Freeman, both hired by Chanda Rubin, have coached professionals. Ashe served as captain of the Davis Cup Team.

## SPORTS JOURNALISM AND SPORTS AGENTS

In sports journalism, blacks were generally limited to black publications. Sam Lacy has been a "living legend" since he began covering the Negro Leagues for the *Baltimore Afro-American*. Over the decades, black journalists have moved into the mainstream. Doug Smith of *USA Today* has been one of the best-known journalists to cover tennis. In addition, Andre L. Christopher, who reported on tennis for the *Miami Herald*, later became a senior writer for the USTA. Other journalists wrote about various sports, including Solomon Crenshaw Jr. (*Birmingham News*), and Keven B. Blackstone (*Dallas Morning News*). In broadcast journalism, blacks have worked as announcers and analysts, including Pam Oliver, Quinn Buckner, John Saunders, Robin Roberts, and Gus Johnson. In the NFL, blacks and women have been more likely assigned as sideline reporters. Few have had positions like O.J. Simpson on ABC's *Monday Night Football*, or Bryant Gumbel, who anchored the Summer Olympics and now hosts a sports show on the HBO cable network.

In recent years, more blacks have become sport agents, an easier task in football or basketball than in individual sports. Marcus Vickers, Andre Collana, Fletcher Smith, and Eugene Parker have represented players in the NBA and NFL. There have been fewer black woman, but Alicia Boston, a corporate attorney, became one of thirty-three women agents in the NFL. In tennis, agents like Bill Shelton and Carlos Fleming started with major marketing firms.

## SPONSORSHIP AND ENDORSEMENTS

Black athletes have found a major obstacle in finding sponsorship and endorsement. When Doug Williams became the Super Bowl MVP, he earned $175,000 in endorsements—compared to $1,000,000 for Jim McMahon and $750,000 for Phil Simms, white MVPs. Jackie Joyner-Kersee initially received few endorsements, which reflected racism and sexism. Zina Garrison and Lori McNeil failed to profit from commercial endorsements despite their success. Charles Marks stopped competing in offshore powerboat racing in 1991 because he failed to attract major sponsorship. Few black athletes have had the opportunities presented to Michael Jordan, Tiger Woods, or the William Sisters, who have become major crossover personalities.

## CHALLENGES FOR BLACK STUDENT ATHLETES

Blacks in collegiate athletes have had other struggles. In 1968, there were protests at several major universities as black athletes demanded black coaches, black cheerleaders, a black support staff, and increased sensitivity to their issues on the part of white administrators. Black athletes also experienced isolation, particularly those who found few other black students on campus. Interracial dating became a major problem. Despite desegregation in collegiate sports, even in the 1990s, black athletes found themselves as the lone black on teams in certain sports. For example, Tammy Campbell was the only black player on the volleyball squad, while Rucker Odem III was the only black on the baseball team at Northern Illinois University.

Black professional athletes have feared losing endorsements and being highly criticized by white journalists. While most black athletes have remained silent on social issues, few have been as outspoken as Muhammad Ali and Arthur Ashe, the latter arrested for demonstrating against apartheid in South Africa. Jackie Robinson's contract dictated that he remain silent as he suffered racial abuse for the first two years. Later, he was outspoken about racism in the sport. John Carlos and Tommy Smith protested at the 1968 Olympic Games, wearing black gloves in a black power salute during the playing of the National Anthem. They were expelled from the team, and that defiant act has followed them throughout their careers, a clear message to black athletes.

A problem receiving far less attention is that faced by black women athletes. Black colleges have not historically offered equal opportunity to women athletes; some schools even prevented women from joining the marching band. Therefore, Title IX of the Education Amendments of 1972 has affected black schools as well. The irony is that many blacks have attacked Title IX despite the opportunities it has created for black women athletes, preferring to safeguard opportunities for black males. Because of Title IX, Katrina Adams (tennis) could become Northwestern's 1986 Female Athlete of the Year, and Esther Myrick and Gail Myrick (basketball) could play in front of full crowds at Florida A&M. Swin Cash, Asjha Jones, and Tamika Williams played on the University of Connecticut undefeated basketball team that won the NCAA title in 2002. Black women also have used athletic scholarships to finance their education.

Another challenge for colleges was Proposition 48, or NCAA Bylaw 14.3 (1983), which required student athletes to attain a minimum grade point average in a core curriculum and attain a minimum score on the Scholastic Aptitude Test or American College Test. While Arthur Ashe supported this proposal, many other blacks, including several black college coaches, criticized it, believing that it could reduce the enrollment of black athletes, particularly males. Jesse Stone, dean of Southern University Law School, called the proposition "patently racist."

One of the major challenges of the modern black student athlete is the continuing notion of exploitation by predominantly white colleges. Although black athletes have too often gotten the shaft after their years of eligibility, it has been difficult to find solutions. Parents have also played a major role in this situation as they have viewed professional sport, via college, as an ultimate prize, and have pushed their children in that direction. Ernie Banks admitted that he wanted to attend Harvard and become a lawyer, but his father paid him to play baseball. As more black youths have increasingly begun to leave college early for the pros, or skip college altogether to join the professional ranks, many white sport journalists have criticized both developments. The irony is that very little has been said about white athletes in sports like tennis, where most of the top pros have failed even to finish high school. Of course, tennis and golf have not been moneymaking sports for colleges like football and basketball, where the top talent has been necessary to develop winning programs. The fear is that colleges could lose their monopoly on these athletes.

Since 1939, blacks have made great gains in sports. The post-civil rights generation of black athletes has set the bar higher and has helped to create the greatest era in sport history. These accomplishments have generated a rich history, and as sport history becomes more accepted as a central academic field, these successes will help illuminate various economic, political, and social aspects of society.

## SOURCES

Ashe, Arthur R., Jr. A *Hard Road to Glory: A History of the African-American Athlete Since 1946*. New York: Warner Books, 1988.

Blackstone, Kevin B. "Greatest Era in Sports? It's Today." *Dallas Morning News*, June 18, 2002.

Coakley, Jay S. *Sport in Society: Issues and Controversies*. St. Louis: Mosby, 1990.

Davies, Richard O. *America's Obsession: Sports and Society Since 1945*. Orlando, Fla.: Harcourt Brace, 1994.

Dunkel, Tom. "Introducing the First Black Coach in the NFL." *Sport*, February 1986.

Edwards, Harry. *The Revolt of the Black Athlete*. New York: Free Press, 1969.

Lapchick, Richard E. *1994 Racial Report Card*. Boston: Northeastern University Center in the Study of Sport in Society, 1994.

Meadows, Barry. "What's White . . . And White . . . And White . . . And Why?" *World Tennis*, February 1982.

"New Path for College for Women." *Ebony*, April 1987.

Noverr, Douglas A., and Lawrence E. Ziewacz. *The Games They Played: Sports in American History, 1865–1980*. Chicago: Nelson-Hall, 1983.

Olsen, Jack. *The Black Athlete: A Shameful Story*. New York: Time-Life Books, 1968.

Quarles, Benjamin. *The Negro in the Making of America*. New York: Touchstone, 1987.

Reisler, Jim. *Black Writers / Black Baseball: An Anthology of Articles from Black Sports Writers Who Covered the Negro Leagues*. Jefferson, N.C.: McFarland, 1994.

Riess, Steven A., ed. *Major Problems in American Sport History*. Boston: Houghton Mifflin, 1997.

Shropshire, Kenneth L. *In Black and White: Race and Sports in America*. New York: New York University Press, 1996.

Taylor, John. *The Rivalry: Bill Russell, Wilt Chamberlain, and the Golden Age of Basketball*. New York: Random House, 2005.

Wiggins, David K. *Glory Bound: Black Athletes in a White America*. Syracuse, N.Y.: Syracuse University Press, 1997.

# AFRICAN AMERICANS IN LITERATURE AND THE ARTS

KEVIN K. GAINES AND PENNY M. VON ESCHEN

To survey African American literature, art, dance, and film since 1939 is to come to grips with the period's unique constellation of forces that shaped cultural production, for better or worse. Since World War II, African Americans in literature and the arts were inspired and energized by the accelerating movements for African American freedom and African liberation. Indeed, African American literary and cultural production both advanced and reflected the struggle for freedom. As that struggle accelerated, black writers and artists enjoyed unprecedented opportunities in the form of wider audiences and greater freedom to portray the dignity and diversity of black life. At the same time, their creative endeavors were both emboldened and constrained by the simultaneous postwar emergence of the United States as the dominant global superpower.

A greater independence in black literary and cultural expression flourished in the context of struggles for racial justice within radical politics. New Deal sponsorship of the arts carried forward the cultural radicalism of the New Negro renaissance. The engagement with African ancestral arts by black artists that Alain Locke had encouraged in *The New Negro* (1925) was fostered by public sponsorship of the arts. Moreover, black writers, along with artists, captured the popular aspirations for equal citizenship awakened by World War II, and they devoted much attention to the impact of urbanization on the black population. Inevitably, the work of these cultural producers struck a blow against the racial stereotypes and taboos so pervasive in American mass culture. Indeed, the period was marked by an extraordinary explosion of fiction, drama, and poetry, much of it critically acclaimed, which defies canonical narratives. While a degree of autonomous cultural expression flourished within subcultures of cultural radicalism, black writers and visual and performing artists clashed with the prevalence of racial stereotypes in mass cultural industries. They contended, too, with the unexamined racism of a critical establishment whose Anglocentric standards posed formidable obstacles to their careers and visions of black self-determination. While literary critics invoked a spurious universalism as the standard for literature, African American writers employed diverse modes of expression encompassing experimentation, social commitment, affirmations of black cultural distinctiveness, evocations of a heroic African American past, and exploration of existential realities of black urban experience. Throughout, black performing artists labored under conditions all too often characterized by a paucity of resources and a lack of control of cultural production. For all concerned, disinterested creative practice was not an option, as black artistic strategies included struggles over access to publishers, galleries, and audiences as well as battles over representations of African American life.

For their part, African American visual artists selected from myriad influences in their representations of black modernity. In the 1930s, the Federal Artists project and public art commissions enabled artists to enshrine the African past as central to its representation of modern black life, as seen in Charles Allston's *Modern Medicine* (1936). Jacob Lawrence's *Migration* and *John Brown* series and Hale Woodruff's *Amistad* series (1939) foregrounded traditions of black resistance, reflecting the legacy of New Negro radicalism as well as the movement of social realism. In the work of Lawrence, Aaron Douglas, and Romare Bearden, this historicism was complemented by an abiding interest in African American music and renderings of everyday life in contemporary urban milieu, which combined folkloric elements with modernist experimentation. After World War II, however, some black artists sought a greater degree of inclusion into the art establishment by rejecting figurative painting for what they regarded as a more liberating aesthetic practice of abstraction. The motivations for the shift to nonfigurative art were complex, ranging from the pursuit of artistic and ideological freedom to anxieties that black content and realism facilitated the process of ghettoizing African American art.

In the theater, black playwrights and actors struggled to build an independent theater movement in Harlem and other major black urban centers whose dramatic productions would render the complexity—indeed, the social truths—of black life for black audiences. Such a movement would expand the narrow range of portrayals available to actors and audiences in musical comedy productions. In New York, the Negro Unit of the Federal Theater project built on the efforts of the Rose McLendon Players and other short-lived black theater ventures. New Deal sponsorship contributed greatly to the development of black actors, playwrights and audiences, providing support for several productions performed in Harlem's Lafayette Theater. Perhaps the most memorable of these was a 1936 production of *Macbeth* with an all-black cast. Set on a West Indian island, the Negro Unit's *Macbeth* electrified Harlem, and more than 52,000 people saw it. Federal sponsorship aided several productions containing themes of black resistance. William Du Bois's action-packed *Haiti* chronicled that black nation's victorious slave uprising against the French. The political tenor of these productions prompted congressional scrutiny and accusations of Communist influence. In Chicago, federal funds had supported Ted Ward's drama *Big White Fog*, which later was staged for Harlem audiences. Not long afterward, Congress eliminated funding for the Federal Theater, and the struggle for an independent black theater reverted to its precarious state.

The radicalism of what Michael Denning has called the Cultural Front, which marks the conjuncture of New Deal reform, interracial labor organizing drives, and the rise of mass cultural industries, facilitated the staging of some black-oriented theater projects at Broadway's mainstream venues. The adaptation of Richard Wright's *Native Son* for the Broadway stage capitalized on the commercial success of the novel, and it catapulted Canada Lee, a black actor of Caribbean extraction, to stardom. Among this period's many firsts in the realm of black cultural achievement, Paul Robeson played the title role in the landmark Broadway production of *Othello* in 1943, which enjoyed a record run. Robeson and Lee would become inspirational icons for their successors, the next generation of black playwrights and actors, as much for their political integrity as for their formidable talents. Out of these successes, the American Negro Theater was founded, serving as an incubator for some of the black theatrical talent, including Frank Silvera, Ossie Davis, Ruby Dee, Eartha Kitt, Sidney Poitier, Diana Sands, and Harry Belafonte, that would eventually reach millions through Hollywood and television productions. Throughout the 1930s, Robeson had starred in several British films of decidedly uneven quality. His career as film actor and concert singer was defined by the vexing struggle of black artists over control of the representation of their people. His triumph as Othello followed his involvement in a demeaning Hollywood production, *Tales of Manhattan*, that prompted his decision never again to work in films. Robeson's checkered film career was a cautionary lesson for the next generation of black actors and actresses.

## RACISM, EMPIRE, AND URBAN INDUSTRIALISM

African American literary and artistic production also reflected the ongoing confrontation of peoples of African descent with the West, where they experienced racism, empire, and the rigors of urban industrialism. World War II accelerated ongoing processes of urbanization that fueled a unity of purpose for blacks, a burgeoning sense of cosmopolitanism and solidarity that demanded equal rights and informed artistic and literary quests for self-identity. Since the 1920s, African Caribbeans had migrated in substantial numbers to major U.S. cities, helping transform Harlem, in particular, into a global black metropolis. In addition, the interwar years saw Africans and Caribbeans attending historically black colleges in the United States, as well as the universities of England and France. Since the 1920s, Paris, as the world capital of modernism in literature and the arts, became the destination of such prominent black writers as Claude McKay, and later, of artists such as Meta Warrick Fuller, Beauford Delany, Lois Mailou Jones, and Romare Bearden. Stateside, World War II sparked a resurgence in the urban migration of African Americans fleeing racial oppression in the South, with almost three million flocking to urban centers and defense jobs, and helping to make Detroit, Chicago, and other cities rich wellsprings of black literary, artistic, and musical talent. The war, like its predecessor, acquainted New World blacks with the best and worst of Western culture, for some forging alliances with colonized Africans and nonracist Europeans. Mass experiences of military service and labor migrations established pathways for the continuing sojourns of writers and artists to Europe. In the postwar period, African American writers, including James Baldwin and Chester Himes, would flock to Paris, following the celebrated example of Richard Wright.

Wright shared the harrowing quotidian black experiences of migration and flight from exploitation and brutality, and he viewed his writing as a conduit for the democratic aspirations of black peoples worldwide. Wright's unprecedented critical and commercial success with *Native Son* (1940) shifted the landscape of American literature and established him as a controversial figure. Self-taught, Wright had benefited from the New Deal Federal Writers project and had refined his craft under the aegis of the Communist Party, which had exerted a strong influence on American literary culture and black struggles during the Depression. Wright would later break with the party to maintain independence from its ideological strictures. But even as an anticommunist, Wright's blunt criticisms of U.S. domestic and foreign policy issued from self-imposed exile in France gained him the lasting enmity of U.S. officialdom. Wright had been a mentor for aspiring black writers, including James Baldwin, Ralph Ellison, Gwendolyn Brooks, and Margaret Walker. But as much as his exile, the incessant drubbing of attacks on his reputation, combined with the Cold War's repression of dissent, inexorably isolated Wright from his would-be allies. The subversive connotations laid to Wright's exile by the liberal intelligentsia provide a crucial context for Wright's falling out with Baldwin and Ellison.

To some extent, Cold War attacks on Wright's reputation have bequeathed a masculinist narrative of African American literary history, which asserts an aesthetic teleology whose apogee is modernism. By this reckoning, Wright's realism and naturalism, influenced by sociological discourse, is first challenged by Baldwin's critique of *Native Son* as a protest novel deficient in literary merit. Finally, Ellison's signal achievement with *Invisible Man* (1952), which received the National Book Award, marks the arrival of an African American high modernism. Black feminist critics have noted the arbitrariness and exclusionary effect of this masculinist—even oedipal—narrative. Yet this mythic construction also suggests the fraught relationship of African American literary and cultural expression to sociopolitical change. That struggle pitted outspoken black intellectuals such as Wright and Robeson against a liberal establishment hostile to independent black opposition and animated by the deep contempt within Cold War culture for collectivism, racial and ethnic particularity, gender diversity, and homosexuality. Avatars of the Cold War liberal intelligentsia measured black literature against high modernist standards predicated on universal humanism. The white-male particularity of such standards usually remained unspoken, save for critics' occasional gendered diatribes at the expense of women writers. Its counterpart in academic discourse was a standard of liberal objectivity that also was synonymous with Euro-American power and privilege and predicated on the exclusion of the bodies and perspectives of women and people of color.

The demand by black audiences for more dignified portrayals of themselves in film took on a new urgency during World War II. Hollywood responded with a limited inclusiveness, with brief cameo appearances by such stars as Lena Horne that might be excised in deference to white southern audiences, or with its musical comedies featuring all-black casts. Perhaps the most memorable of the latter contained the immortal and improbable dance routines of the elegant and acrobatic Nicholas Brothers. Such cinematic displays of talent likely to elicit unalloyed joy from black audiences remained all too rare, however. Generally, into the 1950s, Hollywood, and to some extent, the popular music industry, envisioned a predominantly white audience, ensuring that black expression or subject matter would be either censored, expropriated (as in the proliferation of cover versions by whites of hit songs originated by blacks) or sentimentalized for white mass consumption. The black dramatic film actors prominently featured in Hollywood, including Ethel Waters, Pearl Bailey, Ruby Dee, and Dorothy Dandridge as well as Belafonte and Poitier, prevailed over flawed material by dint of sheer talent. In 1964, the increasingly bankable Poitier was the first black to win an Academy Award for his leading role in *Lilies of the Field.*

Poitier was vulnerable to criticism from some quarters that many of his roles reflected white fantasies of nonthreatening, sexless black males. Yet his accomplishments inspired the next generation of black male stage and screen actors, and as director and producer of several projects (collaborations with Bill Cosby and Belafonte), he helped showcase several generations of black talent.

In modern dance, there was a burst of innovation by a group of African American choreographers who followed the pioneering efforts of Pearl Primus and Katherine Dunham. Dunham exemplified the engagement with the culture of Africa and its diaspora. A dancer, choreographer, and anthropologist, Dunham explored African-based dance forms, incorporating her work in a Jamaican Maroon community and her initiation into Haitian Vodoun. In 1940, she founded the Katherine Dunham Dance Company and in 1943, established the Dunham School of Arts and Research in New York City. In the 1950s black choreographers Talley Beatty, Donald McKayle (considered the leading black choreographer of the day), and, later, Alvin Ailey fought prevailing (and unfortunately, enduring) stereotypes that black dancers lacked the proper physique for ballet and modern dance and worked to incorporate black themes into dance. Ailey assembled the Alvin Ailey American Dance Theater (AAADT) in 1958. Through such pieces as the celebrated *Blues Suites* (1958), *Revelations* (1960), and *Cry* (1971), Ailey conveyed the richness and beauty of African American culture. More than others, Ailey capitalized on the ironies of racial discrimination in America and the country's increasing need to defend and justify its record before peoples abroad. Beginning with a 1962 tour of East Asia and Southeast Asia, with his collaborator Carmen de Lavallade heading the bill as a guest star, the AAADT made several trips abroad under the auspices of the State Department, including a celebrated African tour in 1967 and culminating in a triumphant 1971 tour of the Soviet Union. Seizing the world stage to promote black culture and civil rights, Ailey spoke forthrightly to audiences abroad about the black American struggle to overcome centuries of discrimination. Arthur Mitchell and the Dance Theater of Harlem (founded in 1969) continued in the tradition of fighting exclusionary stereotypes confronting black ballet dancers. The achievements of these companies helped to lay the foundation for the continuing success of black dance and the birth of a new generation of choreographers such as Judith Jamison, Bill T. Jones, and Ronald K Brown.

In poetry, the work of Margaret Walker, Melvin Tolson, Robert Hayden and Gwendolyn Brooks was distinguished by an exacting formalism and, as often, political protest, as in the case of Hayden's *Heart Shape in the Dust* (1940), Walker's *For My People* (1942), Brooks's *A Street in Bronzeville* (1945), and Tolson's *Rendezvous with America* (1944). The dense historical and literary allusions of Tolson's "Libretto for the Republic of Liberia" (1953), commissioned by President William Tubman, owe more to the modernism of Eliot than that of the Harlem Renaissance. With her command of classic verse forms, Brooks ushered in a new era of critical acclaim for black writers with *Annie Allen* (1949), which won the 1950 Pulitzer Prize.

## THE ROLE OF THE AFRICAN AMERICAN WRITER

The mainstream recognition accorded to Brooks occasioned the renewed discussion of the role of the African American writer. Such manifestos as those of Langston Hughes (1926) and Richard Wright (1937) had emphasized African American writers' obligation to shun dominant bourgeois aesthetics that led them astray from the rich subject material of African American working-class and folk cultures. In a 1951 essay, "Which Way for the Negro Writer," Lloyd Brown took issue with the view advanced by some critics that Negro writing had been "emancipated" from the constrictions of Negro, or racial, subject matter. Brown, author of the socially engaged novel *Iron City* (1953), identified the prescriptive turn to universal standards as indicative of a white supremacist mindset incapable of rendering the Negro with human dignity. While Brown noted that some critics admirably saw no conflict between "racial themes" and literary craft, he disputed the prevailing dichotomies imposed by Cold War culture between form and content, art and politics. From another perspective, Baldwin's critique of *Native Son*, "Everybody's Protest Novel" (1948), seemed to endorse the elevation of art over politics at the expense of Wright's reputation. In fairness to Baldwin, however, his actual complaint with African American fiction was that it generally failed to do justice to the richness, complexity, and beauty of black life. Baldwin believed that writers should emulate the genius of black music in confronting the joys of black experience, as well as what he called the bottomless, ironic, mocking sadness of the likes of Billie Holiday.

Ralph Ellison's *Invisible Man* (1952), in its masterful synthesis of blues, African American cultural history, and Homeric myth, seemed to answer Baldwin's appeal for an illumination of the meanings dormant in black music and culture. And Baldwin's coming-of-age novel *Go Tell It on the Mountain* (1953) was an eloquent evocation of the church as ambiguous haven of repression and redemption for impoverished Harlemites. Then, too, the fiction of black women writers devoted equal attention to the squalid realities, as well as the beauty and resiliency of African American urban existence. Such work by black women writers undermines the masculinist narrative of literary history situating Wright as progenitor. While Ann Petry's *The Street* (1947) has been linked to Wright, it is more appropriate to define black women's writing during the late 1940s and 1950s as inhabiting an ambiguous, though not inhospitable space within African American literature. The most prominent black women writers of the 1950s, and those later to emerge, such as Paule Marshall, Rosa Guy, Maya Angelou, and Audre Lorde, flourished as part of a progressive black literary culture which, though not free of sexism, at least did not elevate patriarchy to a racial imperative, as would become the case during the Black Power era.

Black women's perspectives were elaborated in such works as Dorothy West's *The Living Is Easy* (1948) and Gwendolyn Brooks's *Maud Martha* (1953). Brooks's novel is noteworthy for its imagistic modernism and its near-exclusive focus on Maud's interior life, its critique of class and gender politics within the black community, and its poignant evocation of the angry silences so pervasive in African American existence. Such silences were resoundingly broken, often with trenchant political analysis, by Alice Childress's indomitable domestic worker heroine in *Like One of the Family* (1956). Childress's novel languished while portions of it reached far more readers through serialization in the black press. Lorraine Hansberry's *A Raisin in the Sun* (1959), the classic drama of black life on the south side of Chicago, had as great an impact on African American drama as Wright had exerted on literature. The triumphant Broadway run of Hansberry's play, directed by Lloyd Richards, and its film adaptation with much of its original stage cast, represented a vindication of Ted Ward's Depression-era family melodrama in *Big White Fog*, which was a model for Hansberry's exploration of a black family's reliance on a collective memory of resistance as a bulwark against an uncertain and possibly dangerous future. While the enduring appeal of Hansberry's play stemmed from its meditation on the deferred dreams of African Americans as the bitter underside of the American dream, the play's black feminist subplot suggests a synthesis between black consciousness and black feminism that arguably was not unusual for its time.

At stake here is the need for revisions of literary history that can account for the diversity of black writing, including work too marginalized to warrant in its day any but the most cursory attention of official cultural gatekeepers. Moreover, the nascent black feminism asserted by women writers inspired by black movement activism, raises further questions about the relationship between black feminism and black gay and lesbian subjectivities within African American literary and cultural production. Gay and lesbian writers and artists were unquestionably prominent within African American culture, yet their sexuality remained for the most part invisible or unremarked. This paradox suggests several possible explanations, with possibilities for black gay existence ranging from a minimal toleration conditioned on acquiescent silence to a more open acceptance of women and homosexuals within artistic subcultures. Such explanations, too, would have to account for the individual strategies and negotiations of such prominent black gay figures as Hughes, Baldwin, Hansberry, Billy Strayhorn, Ailey, and Bayard Rustin. No doubt homophobia shaped these negotiations, if not outright silences. No doubt some felt that to break an expedient silence might compromise the struggle for racial equality. Then, too, the absence of a gay liberation movement that might demand or support public outspokenness might also explain their discretion. While it may be impossible to disentangle these possible interpretive scenarios from the pressures of homophobia and the closet, and while homophobia continues to exert a pernicious effect within black communities, it may be misleading to read back into African American cultural history an unbroken narrative of intolerance. It is conceivable that public assertions of homophobia can be traced to such crises as the conformity of the Cold War era, or the post-civil rights assertion of an embattled black nationalism.

## THE LITERARY MAINSTREAM, BLACK COMMUNITIES, AND SOCIOPOLITICAL CHANGE

As the modern civil rights movement came to dominate the nation's, and the world's, headlines, popular demand propelled black writing into the mainstream increasingly on its own terms. For many writers, artists, musicians and dancers, the emergence of new African states from colonial rule fueled an assertion of Afro-diasporic cultural identity against the liberal intelligentsia's ostensibly race-neutral tenets of universalism. This trend was encouraged by the founding of the American Society of African Culture (AMSAC) in New York during the late 1950s, in partnership with the French intellectuals of African descent who had previously established the Société Africaine Culturelle (SAC), with the cooperation of Richard Wright. These groups sought to foster intellectual exchange among writers of African descent on the relationship of culture to the development of independent African nations. In the United States, a 1959 AMSAC conference on "The Negro Writer and His Roots" furthered the debate on black writer's tumultuous relationship to the literary mainstream, black communities, and sociopolitical change. This and other AMSAC events brought together such writers as Hansberry, Baldwin, Marshall, Guy, Angelou, John Oliver Killens, Julian Mayfield, and John Henrik Clarke. Also involved were poets Langston Hughes and Samuel Allen (Paul Vesey). In its early days, AMSAC helped legitimize the assertion of transnational black solidarities, representing a thaw in the government's crackdown on Robeson and Du Bois for their advocacy of African liberation. Ironically, in 1967 it would be disclosed that the CIA covertly funded AMSAC, as well as a number of other international cultural organizations. It is unlikely that many of the participants in AMSAC's programs suspected this at the time. Indeed, the chronic dependency of black communities and colleges, which routinely lost out to elite white institutions in seeking foundation support for the founding of African studies programs, quite likely made black writers, academics, and artists appreciative of the support they needed to visit the continent. Under these circumstances, many tended to be less inquisitive about the source of such support.

Some critics of African American literature have counterposed sociology against literature, with the former perceived as the antithesis of literary achievement. To some degree, this view echoed the Cold War logic that cordoned off art from sociopolitical concerns. In fact, the pervasiveness of sociological discussions of race in America made an engagement with sociopolitical questions inescapable for many. Paule Marshall's *Brown Girl, Brownstones* (1959), for example, was written partly in response to sociological theories of matriarchy as the sign of family disorganization and pathology. Arguably the most influential text in African American letters in the second half of the century was the work of a sociologist, E. Franklin Frazier's *Black Bourgeoisie* (1957). Appearing at the dawn of the mass mobilization for civil rights, Frazier's book galvanized middle-class African American youth who embraced the book's indictment of their elders' political complacency during the Cold War. As much as the militant example of Wright, or the streetwise vernacular voice of Hughes, it was the popularity of Frazier's critique of the black middle class that laid the foundation for the Black Arts movement's rejection of high modernism and its celebration of black folk culture.

Frazier aside, African American writers aspired to much more than exposing the self-delusions and foibles of an uncommitted black bourgeoisie. Such figures as LeRoi Jones, Hansberry, and Baldwin were taking aim at the ideological underpinnings of Cold War liberalism. Emboldened by the freedom movement, they waged a crucial struggle over the terms by which black literature and aspirations would be defined, and over who would do the defining. This struggle, in turn, provided much of the momentum for Black Power and its intellectual extensions, the Black Arts and Black Studies movements. LeRoi Jones's *Blues People* (1963) was a pioneering work of cultural criticism, although its sociological analyses of black music elicited sharp criticism from Ellison. Jones, like Frazier, wrote of the blandness and conformity of American liberalism; his critique of the impact of commodification on black musical expression remains influential. In *The Sign in Sidney Brustein's Window* (1964), Hansberry deplored the cynicism of white liberals browbeaten into acquiescent silence by McCarthyism. *Another Country* (1961) contained Baldwin's indictment of New York City, and by extension, the American nation, as a spiritual wasteland, where pathologies of racism, sexism and homophobia militated against love and human connection. Against the hopelessness of America, Baldwin figured France as an expatriate haven for self-realization, as it had been for the author. Baldwin's best-selling essay *The Fire Next Time* (1963) challenged the unconscious racism of northern liberalism, particularly the widespread contention that black people had to prove themselves "acceptable" for equal citizenship.

With eloquent fury he described the psychic devastation of the North's institutional racism on blacks, and warned of the incendiary consequences of white liberals' determined refusal to accept responsibility for the corrosive effect of racism on human relationships.

As racial confrontations escalated, behind these critiques of American liberalism was a growing disillusionment with the federal government's complacency (if not complicity) in the face of white supremacist violence. In 1963, Hansberry and Baldwin, along with Belafonte and Lena Horne, had joined a group of civil rights activists in a heated exchange with Attorney General Robert Kennedy, at which they excoriated the federal government's inaction. Nation of Islam spokesman Malcolm X pointedly questioned the motives of the government and dismissed the movement's goal of integration as mere tokenism. Malcolm also spoke for those critics of the movement who, outraged by the killing of civil rights workers, came to reject its strategy of nonviolence. Malcolm's assassination came as he was seeking a rapprochement with civil rights leaders and activists, and with progressive whites as well. To be sure, nonviolent protest campaigns and federal civil rights legislation had transformed the political culture of the South. But many blacks in the urban North still faced underemployment, substandard schools, segregated slums, and police brutality. The limited impact of civil rights reforms thus sparked militant demands for "Black Power!" In addition, the entrenched racial inequalities of American society were exacerbated by the escalation of the U.S. intervention in the Vietnam War, with African American soldiers bearing a disproportionate burden in casualties. When heavyweight champion Muhammad Ali refused to serve in the armed forces in Vietnam, claiming that "no Viet Cong ever called me nigger," the government unwittingly created a new popular symbol of antiwar sentiment and black dissent.

## THE BLACK ARTS MOVEMENT

The militancy of the Black Arts movement owed much to these events, and the violence of what was termed the "black revolution." The nation's cities endured successive waves of urban rebellions, including those waged in angry retaliation for the 1968 slaying of Martin Luther King in Memphis. The violent rhetoric of black militants was answered by the deadly force of federal and local campaigns waged by authorities against the Black Panthers and other activists. Without denying its complexity and heterogeneity, much Black Arts literature furthered Malcolm's legacy of uncompromising militancy. The poetry of Amiri Baraka (LeRoi Jones), Mari Evans, Nikki Giovanni, Haki Madhubuti, and other younger writers often deployed ritualized anger, attacked white and Western ideals and institutions, and often portrayed the African American population as divided between those assimilated, "brainwashed" Negro individuals and a saving remnant which had achieved authentic black consciousness. The importance of performative genres of poetry and theater within the Black Arts movement reflected not only a rejection of canonical modernism in favor of popular cultural forms, including jazz, fusion, blues, and soul music, but also the demand that black art contain social relevance and speak directly to black audiences. At its best, for a brief moment the Black Arts movement revitalized black urban public culture, with its proliferation of grass roots literary publications, journals, and magazines, its poetry readings and community theaters, nightclubs and performance spaces where musicians, artists, and writers could collaborate and commune with audiences. Within these spaces artists promoted messages of love, unity, solidarity, cultural nationalism and variants on the slogan "black is beautiful." These affirmations, however, vied with an anger that might overshoot its ostensible target of white society to loose its invective on those blacks perceived as internal threats to community, such as women and homosexuals, for instance. For all its explosive impact, however, it seems useful to consider the movement as, in part, an awakening of black consciousness among middle-class African American youth who in many ways were discovering themselves and their history for the first time. As poet Lucille Clifton recalled, their declarations of black protest, anger, and pride were hardly a revelation to working-class blacks like herself.

As Clifton suggests, while much of the Black Arts movement was believed to be as new as the recently proclaimed designation "black" in place of the outmoded "Negro," there were clear continuities with previous generations of black artists, writers, and musicians. The Black Arts movement made possible the rediscovery of black writers and dramatists, nurtured in the postwar black left, whose militancy and rejection of stereotypes seemed to have anticipated the current mood. Critic Darwin Turner, in an overview of African American drama, pointed out that the playwright William Branch had long ago denounced the hypocrisy of American militarism and racism in *A Medal for Willie* (1951), and had presciently explored the issue of armed resistance in his *In Splendid Error* (1955), which portrayed Frederick Douglass as he deliberates whether to join John Brown's antislavery insurrection. In 1963, Romare Bearden convened three generations of African American artists in Spiral, a New York–based cooperative whose debates over the criteria of black art anticipated and informed those of the 1970s. Editor Hoyt Fuller revived the journal *Negro Digest* during the early 1960s, and by the time of its transformation into *Black World* in the 1970s, it was the major national outlet for black arts and black studies discourse. Such long-established figures as Langston Hughes, Gwendolyn Brooks, and James Baldwin aligned themselves with the movement by producing work that mined the spiritual and cultural resources of black language and by actively mentoring younger writers. Brooks lent moral and material support to younger writers and refused to publish with white-owned firms. She and others supported such black-owned publishing ventures as Chicago's Third World Press, and poet Dudley Randall's Drum and Spear Press, based in Detroit. The viability of black-owned publishing firms sparked mainstream publishers' renewed interest in black writing, making many out-of-print works available, notably those of Zora Neale Hurston and Nella Larsen. While the careers of such prominent figures as Audre Lorde, Paule Marshall, Rosa Guy, and Maya Angelou could be traced back to the Harlem Writer's Group of the early 1950s, the Black Arts movement provided the context for the emergence of these and many other important writers as Henry Dumas, Ishmael Reed, June Jordan, Sonia Sanchez, Wanda Coleman, Toni Cade Bambara, Jayne Cortez, Jay Wright, Michael Harper, John A. Williams, Alice Walker, William Melvin Kelly, Wesley Brown, Leon Forrest, John Edgar Wideman, and Toni Morrison, who in 1993 became the first black woman recipient of the Nobel Prize in literature.

## CULTURAL PRODUCTION IN THE POST-CIVIL RIGHTS ERA

A major legacy of the Black Arts movement is the critical acclaim and commercial success achieved by Morrison, Walker, and other novelists, such playwrights as August Wilson and Adrienne Kennedy, and African American directors of feature films. While unprecedented, the commercial recognition accorded to these and other black writers has outstripped an African American and generally American academic and critical discourse whose preoccupation for canon revision has contributed to the ongoing neglect of many important writers. A vital antidote to this cultural lag is the journal *Callaloo*, a rare outlet for serious engagement with the depth and diversity of black diaspora cultural production. Commercial success for artists occurs at a moment of dwindling government support, and keen competition for scarce resources, particularly for visual artists, dancers and choreographers and theatrical talent. This chronic problem animates Wilson's controversial advocacy of an independent black theater movement, for some a curious position given the acclaim Wilson's frequently staged dramas have received in Broadway productions, two of which, *Fences* (1986) and *The Piano Lesson* (1987), received the Pulitzer Prize. The issue of limited support for black artists was further reflected in the controversy surrounding the major institutional support bestowed on the African American artist Kara E. Walker. Some artists of the Black Arts generation wondered why the art establishment had gotten so solidly behind Walker's ambiguous silhouetted renderings of racial and gendered stereotypes engaged in acts of sexual violence. The issue over the controversy surrounding Walker and other younger artists is not so much their appropriation of stereotypes, understood within the commonplace appeal within black public culture for "positive images." Rather, the controversy is the most recent manifestation of black artists' longstanding struggle for power and control of their work and its reception against an art establishment whose stance toward African American artists remains exclusionary and often ill-informed. Walker's defenders would claim that her use of stereotypes constitutes a transgressive act of satire, a postmodern exercise in parody that divests the stereotype of its oppressive power and thus cannot be seen as anything but an antiracist statement. Her critics contend that at best, Walker's presentation of such volatile material reinforces rather than critiques racial and sexual stereotypes. At worst, it trivializes and dishonors those who endured the rape and debasement her work depicts, and suggests that African Americans derived some pleasure from that debasement.

The profitability of Spike Lee's films has created opportunities for other African American filmmakers, including John Singleton, Carl Franklin, Mario Van Peebles, Forrest Whittaker, and the independent auteurs Julie Dash, Charles Burnett, and Haile Gerima. But the problem of stereotyped and formulaic subject matter and a dearth of challenging roles persist, symptomatic of a lack of African American creative control. Documentary film, however, has been a powerful site of alternative expression and critical reflection on black consciousness, history and memory, with the contributions of Henry Hampton, Isaac Julien, Jacqueline Shearer, Louis Massiah, Toni Cade Bambara, Marlon Riggs, and many others.

In the post-segregation era, and after the Cold War, the conditions of artistic production were no longer shaped by quite the same constraints on expression that confronted black writers and artists of previous generations. Yet in the early twenty-first century, we are at a decidedly ambiguous moment. On one hand, there is a postmodern rupture, largely generational, defined by those black cultural producers who have embraced stereotypical subject matter that many will always consider anathema regardless of the artists' professed transgressive intent. On the other hand, there is another tendency that for all its radical experimentation and emphasis on formalism is still devoted to the ongoing project of limning the complexities of black subjectivity against racial essentialism or reductive notions of blackness, and contesting structures of power shaped by intersections of race, gender, and sexuality. Here, the work of several writers, including science fiction writers Octavia Butler and Samuel Delaney, or legal scholars Derrick Bell and Patricia Williams, provide a variety of historically grounded meditations on the racial past, present, and future. From the standpoint of the dystopian imagination of Butler and Bell, the prospect of an imagined black subject entirely lacking in a historical memory of racial oppression is not so much liberating as it suggests a scenario for postmodern reenslavement.

At the same time, Hollywood, mainstream art institutions and the publishing industry have discovered and catered to African American audiences. The best-selling novels of Walter Mosley and Terry McMillan helped initiate a proliferation of new titles by black writers during the 1990s. Oprah Winfrey has brokered her popularity as daytime television talk show host to bring the acclaimed fiction of Toni Morrison to wider audiences, compelling the publishing industry to take notice of her formidable marketing clout. Yet, as with continuing controversies over the uses of the black image, the newly prominent black cultural presence carries some ironies: for example, Hollywood productions of the 1980s typically represented black freedom struggles from the standpoint of white liberal protagonists. Perhaps the best known of this genre, *Mississippi Burning* (1988), misleadingly portrayed the FBI as the savior of powerless blacks struggling against segregationist terror. Furthermore, with global media corporations assuming a near-monopoly on distribution, black writers, artists, actors, and filmmakers continue to face issues of lack of access to resources and lack of control of production.

In a society that has remained profoundly segregated, integration exists largely in the realm of the symbolic. The newly exoticized (rather than reviled) black male body of the likes of Michael Jordan has become a lucrative commodity in global advertising campaigns, and deceased jazz icons provide the soundtrack in television advertisements of luxury consumer goods. Yet these symbolic appropriations of the black image and sound nevertheless operate within a visual and ideological structure of normative whiteness. Such artists as Lorna Simpson, Adrian Piper, and the late Marlon Riggs deploy experimental and conceptual approaches in work that confronts power relations structured by racism in language and lived experience, including their internalization among black people as manifested in sexism and homophobia. Yet the legacy of independent black cultural production embodied by Robeson, Hansberry, Poitier, Ossie Davis, and Ruby Dee has been carried forward by Winfrey, Quincy Jones, Debbie Allen, Danny Glover, Wesley Snipes, and Bill and Camille Cosby. While corporate control of media industries has always imposed constraints on independent black expression and creativity, those African American cultural producers and entrepreneurs can take some comfort in what remains, for better or worse, the global fascination—and national obsession—with African and Afro-diasporic history and cultures.

## SOURCES

Aschenbrenner, Joyce. *Katherine Dunham: Dancing a Life*. Urbana: University of Illinois Press, 2002.

Baker, Houston A., Jr. *Blues, Ideology, and Afro-American Literature: A Vernacular Theory*. Chicago: University of Chicago Press, 1984.

Baldwin, James. *Another Country*. New York: Dell, 1962.
——. *The Fire Next Time*. New York: Dial Press, 1963.
——. *Go Tell It on the Mountain*. New York: Knopf, 1953.
Bearden, Romare, and Harry Henderson. *A History of African-American Artists from 1792 to the Present*. New York: Pantheon Books, 1993.
Bell, Derrick. *Faces at the Bottom of the Well*. New York: Basic Books, 1992.
Brooks, Gwendolyn. *Annie Allen*. New York: Harper & Brothers, 1949.
——. *Maud Martha*. Chicago: Third World Press, 1994.
Brown, Lloyd. "Which Way for the Negro Writer?" *Masses and Mainstream* (1951).
Butler, Octavia. *The Parable of the Sower*. New York: Four Walls Eight Windows, 1993.
Childress, Alice. *Like One of the Family: Conversations from a Domestic's Life*. Brooklyn: Independence Publishers, 1956.
Chomsky, Noam, et al. *The Cold War and the University: Toward an Intellectual History of the Postwar Years*. New York: New Press, 1997.
Cripps, Thomas. *Making Movies Black: The Hollywood Message Movie from World War II to the Civil Rights Era*. New York: Oxford University Press, 1993.
Cruse, Harold. *The Crisis of the Negro Intellectual*. New York: Morrow, 1967.
Denning, Michael. *Cultural Front: The Laboring of American Culture in the Twentieth Century*. New York: Verso Books, 1996.
Dunning, Jennifer. *Alvin Ailey: A Life in Dance*. New York: Da Capo, 1998.
Edwards, Brent Hayes. *The Practice of Diaspora*. Cambridge, Mass.: Harvard University Press, 2003.
Ellison, Ralph. *Invisible Man*. New York: Random House, 1952.
Frazier, E. Franklin. *Black Bourgeoisie*. Glencoe, Ill.: Free Press, 1957.
Gaines, Kevin. "From Center to Margin: Internationalism and the Origins of Black Feminism." In *Materializing Democracy*, ed. Russ Castronovo and Dana D. Nelson, 294–313. Durham: Duke University Press, 2002.
Gates, Henry Louis, Jr. *Reading Black: Reading Feminism: A Critical Anthology*. New York: Meridian Books, 1990.
Gates, Henry Louis, Jr., and Nellie McKay, eds. *The Norton Anthology of African American Literature*. New York: Norton, 1997.
Griffin, Farah Jasmine. *"Who Set You Flowin'?": The African-American Migration Narrative*. New York: Oxford University Press, 1995.
Hansberry, Lorraine. *A Raisin in the Sun*. New York: Random House, 1959.
——. *The Sign in Sidney Brustein's Window*. New York: Samuel French, 1965.
Jones, LeRoi. *Blues People: Negro Music in White America*. New York: Morrow, 1963.
Jones, LeRoi, and Larry Neal, eds. *Black Fire: An Anthology of Afro-American Writing*. New York: Morrow, 1968.
Kelley, Robin D. G. *Freedom Dreams: The Black Radical Imagination*. Boston: Beacon Press, 2002.
Kinnamon, Keneth, and Michel Fabre, eds. *Conversations with Richard Wright*. Jackson: University Press of Mississippi, 1993.
Locke, Alain. *The New Negro*. New York: Simon & Schuster, 1997.
Marshall, Paule. *Brown Girl, Brownstones*. New York: Random House, 1959.

Mitchell, Loften. *Black Drama: The Story of the American Negro in the Theater*. New York: Hawthorn Books, 1967.
Nichols, Charles, ed. *Arna Bontemps, Langston Hughes Letters, 1925–1967*. New York: Paragon House, 1990.
Petry, Ann. *The Street*. Boston: Houghton Mifflin, 1946.
Pindell, Howardena. "Diaspora/Realities/Strategies." *N.Paradoxa* No. 7 (August 1998).
Poitier, Sidney. *This Life*. New York: Knopf, 1980.
Powell, Richard J. *Black Art and Culture in the 20th Century*. New York: Thames and Hudson, 1997.
Rampersad, Arnold. *The Life of Langston Hughes*. 2 vols. New York: Oxford University Press, 1986–88.
Randall, Dudley, ed. *The Black Poets*. New York: Bantam Books, 1971.
Stovall, Tyler. *Paris Noir: African Americans in the City of Light*. New York: Houghton Mifflin, 1996.
Tolson, Melvin. *Rendezvous with America*. New York: Dodd Mead, 1944.
Turner, Darwin. *Black Drama in America: An Anthology*. Washington D.C.: Howard University Press, 1994.
Walker, Margaret. *For My People*. New Haven, Conn.: Yale University Press, 1942.
West, Dorothy. *The Living Is Easy*. New York: Arno Press, 1969.
Williams, Patricia. *The Alchemy of Race and Rights*. Cambridge, Mass.: Harvard University Press, 1991.
Wright, Richard. *Native Son*. New York: Harper & Brothers, 1940.

# BLACK MUSIC AND BLACK POSSIBILITY

## From Be-Bop to Hip-Hop

CRAIG WERNER

Rising out of the choir lofts of Baptist palaces and the threshing floors of storefront churches; suffusing the communal celebrations at the Apollo, Regal and Uptown Theaters and the dance floors of underground clubs on the wrong side of the tracks; crafted in tiny recording studios in Detroit, Memphis, and New Orleans; downloaded in lonely computer labs where introspective intellectuals commune with the spirits of their West African ancestors; voicing the aspirations of gangbangers, working mothers, and upwardly mobile MBAs banging their heads against the glass ceilings of corporate boardrooms; tapping the feet of the respectable citizens of Sugar Hill and Roxbury and their distant kinfolks scratching out a living in the lumber yards of Georgia and the cotton fields of the Mississippi Delta; black music continues to reflect and shape what Amiri Baraka called the "changing same" of an increasingly complicated and diverse African American community. Drawing on the wellsprings of gospel, jazz, and the blues, musical forms from be-bop, rhythm & blues (R&B), and traditional gospel to soul, funk, and hip-hop offer a historical meditation on black possibility. As it has done since the first moans sounded in the festering holds of the slave ships, music responds to the central questions of African American history: to flee or fight white power, to affirm black identity or assimilate in the larger society, to transcend the material world or try to conquer it, to pursue innovation or pursue tradition. Responding to the calls of ordinary people and charismatic leaders, the music articulates the ongoing drive for freedom that remains the beating heart of African American history.

## BLUES, GOSPEL, AND JAZZ

African American music and African American history are deeply rooted in what the great novelist Ralph Ellison called the underlying "impulses" of African American culture: blues, gospel, and jazz. For Ellison, the terms refer not to specific forms of music but to interrelated ways of dealing with experience. The blues confront the suffering at the center of that history and articulate isolation and despair, the sense that black people have been cast adrift in a world where the devil has taken control. Rather than giving in to those feelings, blues artists "finger the jagged grain" of the "brutal experience" and tell their stories in voices that walk the line between despair and laughter, asserting black humanity in a world predicated, as Martin Luther King Jr. observed, on the "thingification" of human beings. Blues master Willie Dixon summed up the blues response when he sang, "I'm here, everybody knows I'm here." Traditional blues, which developed during the Jim Crow era, are steeped in this stoic sensibility, but the impulse is central to rock 'n' roll, hip-hop, and the gritty side of R&B.

The gospel impulse also bears witness to the burdens of life, often the same experiences that gave rise to the blues. But where the blues celebrate survival, gospel seeks a redemption with both individual and communal dimensions. Whatever its specific form—traditional gospel, reggae, soul, the celebratory moments of disco and house music—gospel reconnects individuals with powers larger than themselves: God and a community committed to, as Mahalia Jackson sang, "moving on up." Small wonder that gospel provided the guiding spirit of the civil rights movement and remains a shelter in times of storm.

Where both blues and gospel are grounded in the way things are, the jazz impulse imagines what might be. Jazz impulse artists, many of whose records will never be filed in the jazz section of the record store, assemble pieces drawn from a limitless range of traditions into models of a new world. New combinations of sounds imply new ways of thinking about self, community, and their role as what Ellison called "link[s] in the chain of tradition."[1] As poet Yusef Komunyakaa wrote, jazz expresses "a synthesis of conflict and beauty. A futuristic maturity. An opening out toward multidimensionality through simplicity."[2] In these terms, George Clinton, Jimi Hendrix, and the enigma intermittently known as Prince belong to the jazz tradition as surely as Miles Davis and Duke Ellington.

## BLUES REALITIES, GOSPEL REDEMPTIVE HOPES, AND JAZZ VISIONS AFTER WORLD WAR II

The modern forms of the complex interplay of blues realities, redemptive hopes, and jazz visions took shape, in black music and black life, in the heady days after the end of World War II. Although the struggle for legal equality would require a string of landmark legal battles, the returning black veterans shared unshakeable determination to bring the walls of segregation tumbling down. Among the songs that greeted them, no song carried more symbolic resonance than Lionel Hampton's "Flying Home." Like much African American music, "Flying Home" spoke differently to black and white audiences. Even as the song signaled the end of conflict for most white veterans, their black counterparts knew that for them, a new battle was just beginning.

Returning to communities that had been transformed by the wartime economy as well as the ongoing Great Migration from the cotton fields of Jim Crow to urban centers, North and South, many black veterans understood World War II as half of a struggle for democracy that was being fought on two fronts. Having helped win the war overseas, the black GIs knew that America stood on the verge of an era of change. As the Freedom Movement gathered energy and transformed the nation over the next three decades, black music would provide the spiritual ammunition for the everyday people determined to, as soul preacher Curtis Mayfield sang, "keep on pushing."

As it had for their ancestors from West Africa and the "black and unknown bards" who transformed the suffering of slavery into the profundity of the spirituals, sacred music played a central role in postwar black life. As the freedom movement gathered energy, the jubilation that shook the rafters of black churches took on a political meaning. Faced with the threat of violent retribution from white supremacists, the movement's foot soldiers drew strength from both the message and the energy of gospel. Mahalia Jackson's "Move On Up a Little Higher," which sold more than two million copies, almost all of them to blacks, when it was released in 1947, was the best known of hundreds of gospel songs that combined spiritual and political determination. The quiet confidence Mahalia expressed in "Move On Up a Little Higher" resonated through Brother Joe May's "Working on a Building," the Radio Four's "Blood Done Signed My Name," the Caravans' "I'm Coming Through," and Dorothy Love Coates and the Original Gospel Harmonettes' "99 1/2." The black community's overwhelming affirmation of the gospel stars expressed a shared determination grounded in the knowledge that God stood with them in history. Studs Terkel, then working as a Chicago radio host, recalled Mahalia's explanation of gospel's political power, which reached back to the spirituals of the slavery era. "She explained to me that the spiritual wasn't simply about Heaven over there, 'A City Called Heaven.' No, the city is here, on Earth. And so, as we know, slave songs were code songs. It was not a question of getting to Heaven, but rather to the free state of Canada or a safe city in the North—liberation here on Earth!"[3] When Mahalia assured them that He *would* calm the raging sea, it helped black folks gather their energy for battle. No one doubted that the higher ground meant a place in the freshman class at the University of Alabama or a job behind the perfume counter of a downtown Detroit department store as well as a seat on the Lord's right hand.

## BE-BOP AND RHYTHM & BLUES

While the gospel vision voiced aspirations that the veterans and their families shared with their elders and ancestors, two new forms of black music—be-bop and rhythm & blues—responded directly to the often disorienting changes reshaping American life. Both rhythm & blues and be bop blossomed in the urban enclaves where migrants gathered as they moved from the feudal agricultural economy of the Black Belt South to growing industrial centers from Atlanta and Louisville to Chicago, Detroit, and Los Angeles. From the beginning, jazz had been an aggressively urban music, thriving in cities where people from radically different backgrounds came together. Louis Armstrong combined the sounds of New Orleans marching bands and barrelhouse pianos with the acoustic blues that arrived on Basin Street with the migrants escaping from the Mississippi Delta. Duke Ellington's 1940s masterpiece "Harlem Air Shaft" provided the definitive soundscape for the World War II migration, sampling the sounds that wafted out of the windows of tenement flats occupied by black folks who'd started out everywhere from Georgia, Jamaica, and the Carolinas to the Everglades, East Texas, and the black hamlets of Kansas and Oklahoma.

For Armstrong, Ellington and their contemporaries, no line separated art from entertainment. Duke and Count Basie were modernist musicians whose sophisticated compositions rivaled those of Igor Stravinsky and Béla Bartok, who also based many of their greatest works on folk dances and tunes whistled in the marketplaces of Russia and Hungary. But Duke and the Count were also great dance-band leaders whose music crossed lines of color, class, gender, and generation.

During World War II, however, jazz began to change. As new social spaces began to open up for African Americans, jazz players such as Charlie Parker and Dizzy Gillespie demanded recognition as serous artists. At a time of African American "firsts"—Jackie Robinson's heroic journey into major league baseball symbolized countless forays across the color line in education, employment, and government service—the be-boppers claimed their place in an avant-garde that had viewed jazz as a primitive alternative to the wasteland rather than a part of the modernist ferment. Explicitly rejecting the idea of jazz as dance music, Bird, Diz, and, in his inimitably quirky way, Thelonious Monk concocted rhythmic and harmonic puzzles that forced their listeners to educate themselves in blues metaphysics as well as musical theory. You couldn't even hear the melody of "Klacktoveedsedstene" or "Bloomdido" unless you kept the chord structure playing in your head.

While most black listeners granted be-bop at least a measure of respect, they overwhelmingly preferred down-home R&B. Even young black intellectuals like Amiri Baraka (then LeRoi Jones) craved gutbucket sax players like Louis Jordan and Earl Bostic. Remembering the complicated cultural mix of his youth, Baraka contrasted what he experienced at home in Newark and across the river where he circulated through the interracial Bohemian scene in Greenwich Village. Baraka paid tribute to be-bop as "a music of rebellion. . . . Black people began breaking out of the ghetto and the music did too."[4] But for him, the language of be-bop would remain an acquired tongue. When he tired of the pressures placed on him as one of the few blacks in the interracial avant-garde, Baraka slipped back to New Jersey where the jukeboxes at the corner tavern poured forth the latest R&B hits, "a place where Black people live" and where they "move in almost absolute openness and strength."[5]

## CROSSING OVER INTO THE ENTERTAINMENT MAINSTREAM

Black musicians and their audiences imagined an exhilarating and sometimes cruelly deceptive array of possibilities. Almost every African American shared the desire to overthrow segregation and claim full access to the same resources as the white veterans whose GI Bill educational benefits and FHA loans paved the way to increasing affluence. But they differed, sometimes sharply, over how to relate to a white world that had provided little evidence of the moral or cultural superiority it claimed. Sharing the ambivalence of their communities, black musicians charted alternatives for a range of possibilities from full immersion in the white mainstream to black nationalist self-determination.

Aware that the one thing white folks definitely possessed was money, some musicians envisioned themselves as sepia Sinatras or ebony Garlands. Setting out to garner their share of the riches waiting in Las Vegas and at upscale nightclubs like the Copacabana, entertainers such as Sammy Davis Jr. and Nat "King" Cole, the first black entertainer to host his own television show, envisioned a world where they could bask in the bright lights and cash the fat checks the Great White Way. Decked out in finely tailored suits and putting on a reassuringly friendly demeanor for white audiences that had grown up with images of animalistic black beasts and comic buffoons, the crossover pioneers embodied what novelist and folklorist Zora Neale Hurston called the Negro's "feather-bed resistance." "We let the probe enter," wrote Hurston, "but it never comes out. It gets smothered under a lot of laughter and pleasantries."[6] Turning philosophical, Hurston concluded, "The theory behind our tactics: 'The white man is always trying to know into somebody else's business. All right, I'll set something outside the door of my mind for him to play with and handle. . . . I'll put this play toy in his hand, and he will seize it and go away. Then I'll say my say and sing my song."[7]

Aware of the danger if he let the mask slip, Sam Cooke pursued the crossover strategy as part of an explicitly political agenda. A constant reader who was a friend of both Malcolm X and Muhammad Ali, Cooke had been a gospel superstar as a member of the Soul Stirrers before charming the white teenager audience with romantic hits like "You Send Me," "Cupid," and "Wonderful World," in which he disingenuously began "don't know much about history." In fact, Cooke knew his history well, and he guarded against losing contact with the fans who had lifted him to stardom by playing gospel versions of his hits when he performed in black clubs. "When the whites are through with Sammy Davis, Jr., he won't have anywhere to play," commented Cooke even as he was preparing to play the Copacabana Club, "I'll always be able to go back to my people 'cause I'm never gonna stop singing to them. . . . I'm not gonna leave my base."[8] Ultimately, Cooke believed, as white audiences grew accustomed to the gospel touches in his crossover hits, they would gradually open up to the real thing. The dollars they funneled into the black music world would help fuel the community's economic development. Cooke founded a record company, SAR, which, if he had lived, might well have been to Chicago what Motown was to Detroit or Stax was to Memphis. Like Cooke's breathtaking movement anthem "A Change Is Gonna Come," the best SAR records—notably the Soul Stirrers' soaring tribute to the movement "Free At Last"—anticipate the gospel soul that would allow Curtis Mayfield, Aretha Franklin, and Al Green to join the white rockers atop the pop charts.

## RHYTHM & BLUES / ROCK 'N' ROLL

Cooke carefully shaped a romantic image that contrasted with the gritty sexuality of his R&B elders in part because he had paid close attention to the early history of rock 'n' roll. The rock 'n' roll explosion of the mid-1950s was really an R&B explosion with a touch of a country drawl. In the early days, there wasn't any easy way to tell the two styles apart. The first generation rock 'n' rollers burst onto the radio and, occasionally, the TV screens of America at almost precisely the same time the Supreme Court's *Brown vs. Board of Education* decision and the triumphant Montgomery Bus Boycott challenged segregation. Ardent segregationists often—and accurately—viewed rock 'n' roll as part of the "problem." Teens attending ostensibly segregated dances and concerts, galvanized by Little Richard's "Rip It Up," Bo Diddley's "I'm a Road Runner," and Chuck Berry's "Brown Eyed Handsome Man," ignored the policies that consigned blacks to the balcony or stomped all over the rope that divided the auditorium into separate but equal seating areas.

It wasn't that the singers had set out to redefine the world around them. As Sam Phillips, whose Sun Records helped break down the racial barriers, commented: "I wasn't looking for no tall stump to preach from."[9] But what happened at Sun, Chess Records in Chicago, and Atlantic Records in New York set the stage for the great soul empires that came close to realizing Sam Cooke's dream of a truly desegregated musical world. Carl Perkins, a Sun rockabilly singer who had grown up in the cotton fields side by side with black sharecroppers, recalled a conversation he had with Chuck Berry. "When you walked up to an old 54 or 55 Wurlitzer jukebox, it didn't say 'Blue Suede Shoes,' Carl Perkins, white. 'Blueberry Hill,' Fats Domino, black. No. There was no difference. Kids danced to Little Richard, Chuck Berry, Elvis, Carl. Chuck Berry said to me one time, he said, 'you know Carl, we just might be doing as much with our music as our leaders are in Washington to break down the barriers.' He was right."[10]

Hypersensitive to the threat of international communism, mainstream politicians painted any challenge to American "normalcy" as part of an all-encompassing communist plot. The new "mongrel music" provided an inviting target. Pictures of Little Richard, eyes rolled back underneath a distinctly bizarre mountain of hair, confronted Cold War America with one of its worst nightmares. It didn't help that Little Richard seemed at least as interested in the white boys as the sisters they were supposed to be protecting. The hysterical tone of the attacks on rock 'n' roll comes through clearly in a pamphlet distributed to white parents: "Help save the youth of America! Don't let your children buy or listen to these Negro records. The screaming idiotic words and savage music are undermining the morals of our white American youth!"[11]

The authorities cracked down on the interracial music scene. In city after city, panicky promoters summoned police to restore order while horrified white parents condemned rock 'n' roll as a communist-sponsored plot to reduce America to an outpost of the rhythm-crazed African jungle. Chuck Berry went to jail on charges of corrupting the morals of a minor; Little Richard was hounded into retirement. Pioneering DJ Alan Freed, who made no distinction between rock 'n' roll and R&B, was exiled in a trumped-up "payola" scandal that somehow let clean-cut pop impresario Dick Clark escape unscathed. And in a series of events that would shape the future of rock 'n' roll, Elvis Presley was drafted, cleaned up, and, after his discharge, transformed from the missionary of musical miscegenation into a safely sanitized matinee idol, the official "King of Rock 'n' Roll."

Elvis provides a case study in the minstrel appropriation of African American styles that works like Eric Lott's *Love and Theft* and W. T. Lhamon's *Raising Cain: Blackface Performance from Jim Crow to Hip-Hop* have placed at the center of American cultural history. *Jet* magazine and almost every black person who actually knew him absolved Elvis of personal racism. His coronation by the white media, however, angered those who knew that Little Richard, Chuck Berry, and Fats Domino, not to mention Louis Jordan, Muddy Waters, and Howlin' Wolf, could make equally legitimate claims to the throne. It wasn't the first or the last time the music industry bestowed the crown on a white contender—or pretender. In the 1920s, the music industry anointed the aptly named Paul Whiteman as the "King of Jazz," and similar patterns have recurred like clockwork, arising in relation to sixties rock (the Rolling Stones), disco (the Bee Gees), R&B (Michael Bolton), funk (the Red Hot Chili Peppers), and hip-hop (Kid Rock and Eminem).

## A RETURN TO THE ROOTS

Not surprisingly, many black musicians responding to minstrelsy and the cultural aridity of the mushrooming suburbs, seconded essayist Julian Mayfield's sardonic identification of "the mainstream" with "oblivion." Their imaginations fired by the African independence movements as well as the news from Greensboro and Selma, the jazzmen of the 1950s and 1960s explored the meaning of freedom in a culture motivated by individualism and greed. Running endless permutations on the possible combinations of the jazz impulse variables of self, community, and tradition, the major stylistic schools—hard bop, cool jazz, free jazz, soul jazz, "freedom music"—gave serious consideration to every alternative from integration to intransigent separatism.

Hard boppers such as Horace Silver and soul jazzman Jimmy Smith summoned be-bop abstraction back to earth, rooting the soloists' individual explorations in the soil of gospel and the blues. The interracial cool jazz community, conversely, contemplated the possibility of a new modernist style combining jazz with European and classical traditions. Redefining their communities and choosing their weapons to meet the ever-changing needs of the moment, Charles Mingus and Max Roach yoked the music and political struggles of Ghana and Cuba with those of Montgomery, Little Rock, and Birmingham. Probably the most revered jazzman of his time, John Coltrane dreamed a transcendent sphere where the echoes of the spirituals and the laments for the young girls murdered in the bombing of the 16th Street Baptist Church could come together with the strains of Nigeria and India in a hymn to the Love Supreme. As Miles Davis demonstrated by gliding effortlessly from the bluest blues to cool abstraction, from "My Funny Valentine" and *Kind of Blue* to *Sketches of Spain*, the only limits on black people's imagination of freedom were those they placed on themselves.

Back in the world where this week's paycheck never seemed to cover next week's bills, the limits on living out those dreams remained all too real. That was why the visions that attracted the most enthusiastic chorus of "Amens" were those rooted most deeply in gospel and the blues: R&B and its younger sibling, soul. R&B split the difference between Saturday night and Sunday morning. Even as their voices soared with the promise of redemption they'd felt growing up in the church, pioneers such as Ray Charles, Sarah Vaughan, Dinah Washington, and Clyde McPhatter shared the razor-edged realism of blues singers such as Muddy Waters, John Lee Hooker, and Etta James. Identifying the theory behind the fusion of the sacred and secular that would flow from Sam Cooke and Lavern Baker through the Temptations and Staple Singers to Prince, Anita Baker, and R. Kelly, Ray Charles, who Andrew Young anointed the "Bishop of Atlanta," observed, "Gospel and the blues are really, if you break it down, almost the same thing. It's just a question of whether you're talkin' about a woman or God."[12]

At a time when the movement sought to promote "positive" images of blackness, the results didn't always go down well with respectable black churchgoers who had long considered the blues to be "devil's music." Yet, despite the disapproving looks of their elders and the risk of rekindling white stereotypes of black sexuality, Brother Ray and his acolytes introduced a large audience to the emotional intensity they had learned from gospel singers such as Reverend Claude Jeter of the Swan Silvertones, Clara Ward, and the incomparable Archie Brownlee of the Five Blind Boys of Mississippi. The economic incentives were substantial. The crossover success of Motown, Aretha Franklin, and Michael Jackson—not to mention disco and hip-hop—provided suggestive evidence that, however problematic their taste in political leaders, a surprisingly large number of whites might in fact be able to tell the difference between filet mignon and refried spam. Motown's Berry Gordy Jr. stated the underlying theory behind the practice, if not always the rhetoric, of the vast majority of black record label owners and producers from Duke Robey, the gangster-slick scion of Houston's R&B powerhouse Peacock Records, to hip-hop empire builders Russell Simmons and Master P. "In the music business there had long been the distinction between black and white music, the assumption being that R&B was black and Pop was white," Gordy wrote in his autobiography, *To Be Loved*. "But with Rock 'n' Roll and the explosion of Elvis those clear distinctions began to get fuzzy. Elvis was a white artist who sang black music. What was it? (a) R&B, (b) Country, (c) Pop, (d) Rock 'n' roll or (e) none of the above. If you picked C you were right, that is, if the record sold a million copies. 'Pop' means popular and if that ain't, I don't know what is. I never gave a damn what else it was called."[13]

Even though almost every secular singer pursued crossover success, few abandoned the black audiences back home at the Apollo Theater in New York, the Regal in Chicago or its namesake in Baltimore, the Howard in Washington, the Hippodrome in Richmond and the countless less prominent venues that made up the Chitlin Circuit. Harlem-born novelist James Baldwin reflected on the differences between the downtown clubs where blacks and whites mingled and the uptown clubs where whites were rarely seen. "It's not that the music is intrinsically better—always," wrote Baldwin, "But the people playing it and the people hearing it have more fun with it, and with each other. They know, on one level, everything concerning each other that there is to know: they are all black. And this produces an atmosphere of freedom which is exactly as real as the limits which have made it necessary. And what they don't know about each other, like who works where, or who sleeps with whom, doesn't matter. No one gives a damn because they know exactly how rough it is out there, when the club gates close. And while they are dancing and listening to the music and drinking and joking and laughing, with all of their finery on, and looking so bold and free, they know who enters, who leaves, and on what errands: they are aware of the terrible and unreachable forces which yet rule their lives."[14]

## MUSIC AND THE CIVIL RIGHTS MOVEMENT: GOSPEL AND SOUL

At the same time that the R&B and jazz performers were reshaping the history of American music, a different kind of music played a crucial role in the freedom movement that was reshaping American society. The most familiar, and officially sanctioned, version of the civil rights movement story revolves around the heroic campaigns organized by Martin Luther King Jr.: a series of hard-won victories beginning in Montgomery and climaxing at the March on Washington and the legislative breakthroughs of 1964 and 1965. In that story, music occupies a peripheral place, providing a background soundtrack for the real political story. The montage of overly familiar highlights include "We Shall Overcome," the earnest political ballads strummed by the followers of Bob Dylan and Joan Baez during Freedom Summer, and Mahalia's mournful version of "Take My Hand Precious Lord" montaged against the mule-driven wagon carrying the body of the fallen leader to his martyr's grave.

The emergence of a new school of movement historians inspired by John Dittmer's *Local People*, Charles Payne's *I've Got the Light of Freedom*, and Timothy Tyson's *Radio Free Dixie* opens the possibility of a deeper understanding of the centrality of music to the movement. Repositioning the legal battles at the center of the civil rights movement in relation to a longer history of African American freedom struggles, the new historians take their cue from Ella Baker's credo, "Strong people don't need strong leaders." Without denying the contributions of King, Thurgood Marshall, and their white liberal sometimes-allies, the new movement historians center attention again on Baker's "beloved community," the ordinary people who forged a new social order in defiance of white supremacist bombs and bombast. Living in communities whose names would never grace the lips of Walter Cronkite or Bobby Kennedy, the local people relied equally on the sense of moral rectitude they shared with King and on the shotguns and revolvers with which they had defended themselves since Reconstruction.

And they sang. Somehow, communities had to find a way to break the old patterns, transform fear into resistance. SNCC field secretary Phyllis Martin pointed to music's central role: "The fear down here is tremendous. I didn't know whether I'd be shot at, or stoned, or what. But when the singing started, I forgot all that. I felt good within myself. We sang 'Oh Freedom' and 'We Shall Not Be Moved,' and after that you just don't want to sit around anymore. You want the world to hear you, to know what you're fighting for."[15] Bernice Johnson Reagon, then a member of the SNCC Freedom Singers and later presiding spirit of the black womanist group Sweet Honey in the Rock, remembered how music had empowered the beloved community in Dawson, Georgia. "I sat in a church and felt the chill that ran through a small gathering of Blacks when the sheriff and his deputies walked in. They stood at the door, making sure everyone knew they were there. Then a song began. And the song made sure that the sheriff and his deputies knew we were there. We became visible, our image was enlarged, when the sound of the freedom songs filled all the space in that church."[16] As the movement reached its high water mark in the 1960s, the sounds of freedom spread throughout the nation via the soul music that filled the airwaves, the Top Forty charts, and the hearts and minds of young Americans of all colors. The churchy pop music emanating from Motown, Stax, and hundreds of other ramshackle studios in every corner of black America made huge inroads into the pop market. Beginning in 1962, *Billboard* magazine discontinued its separate chart for black music for almost two years on the grounds that it essentially duplicated the Top 100.

Even more explicitly than R&B in the 1950s, soul provided the soundtrack for the freedom movement as it gathered energy from the sit-ins, the freedom rides, and the hard-fought campaigns in the streets of Birmingham and the halls of Congress. Mavis Staples, who had begun her career singing gospel but gradually shifted over into the world of soul, explained it best. "We were singing about freedom," she recounted. "We were singing about when will we be paid for the work we've done. We were talking about doing right by us. We were down with Martin Luther King. Pops said this is a righteous man. If he can preach it, we can sing it."[17]

Heeding Sam Cooke's crossover strategy, 1960s soul music typically told upbeat fables of true love. But for those who responded fully to the redemptive strains of Martha and the Vandellas' "Dancing in the Streets," Wilson Pickett's "In the Midnight Hour," and the Temptations' "Get Ready," soul music helped forge the sense of community that made the movement possible. While only a few first-generation soul stars followed Nina Simone and Curtis Mayfield in addressing political issues directly, the music of Smokey Robinson and the Miracles, Sam and Dave, Dionne Warwick, Stevie Wonder, Otis Redding, and, above all, James Brown and Aretha Franklin animated the spirits and soothed the souls of the freedom warriors and those who dreamed of joining their ranks. The widow of Medgar Evers recalled that in the days before he was gunned down outside their home near Jackson, Mississippi, they rarely spoke, preferring to hold each other while listening to their favorite music.

Curtis Mayfield articulated the connection between soul music and the movement perfectly when he observed that the Impressions' classics like "People Get Ready," "Keep on Pushing," and "We're a Winner" were "locked in with Martin Luther King. It took something from his inspiring message. I was listening to all my preachers and the different leaders of the time. You had your Rap Browns and your Stokely Carmichaels and Martin Luther Kings, all of those people were there right within that same era. They get their credit and rightfully so."[18] But, Mayfield insisted, the movement's driving power came from the "invisible heroes," the common people who made the movement real in the small towns of the South and the ghettos of the North. After all, black America had never been short of soaring orators. But when local people from Watts to Detroit heeded Martha and the Vandellas' call to go "dancing in the streets" a whole new sense of nationhood was born.

No one gave that nation more strength than Aretha Franklin. Raised in a household where Mahalia Jackson, Marion Williams, and Clara Ward were frequent visitors, Aretha had grown up in a house where gospel music and the freedom movement were synonymous. Nothing expressed the connection between culture and politics more powerfully than Aretha's music. Black comedian Dick Gregory wasn't exaggerating when he compared her political impact with that of Martin Luther King Jr. "You'd hear Aretha three or four times an hour. You'd only hear King on the news."[19] Soul music historian Peter Guralnick describes the scene outside Skippy White's Record Store in Boston's Roxbury ghetto the day "I Never Loved a Man" was released. "People were dancing on the frosty street with themselves or with one another and lining up at the counter to get a purchase on that magic sound as the record kept playing over and over. It was as if the millennium had arrived."[20]

## THE RISE OF BLACK POWER

The millennial moment lasted less than a decade. Even as Aretha's "Respect" and James Brown's "Papa's Got a Brand New Bag" served notice that a new breed of brothers and sisters was ready to take control, the shaky civil rights coalition had begun to collapse along with the sense of shared purpose that had allowed the beloved community to overthrow Jim Crow. As the chants of "Freedom Now!" gave way to the uncompromising demands for "Black Power," and the war in Vietnam gutted the domestic programs that might have given substance to President Lyndon Johnson's War on Poverty, a growing sense of betrayal swept over the northern and western ghettos. Just as their fathers and uncles had shaped the post-World War II freedom movement, black Vietnam veterans played a central role in defining Black Power. Their story awaits adequate treatment from historians, but it is richly chronicled in Marvin Gaye's *What's Going On*, Curtis Mayfield's *Back in the World*, and Funkadelic's "Maggot Brain" and "March to the Witch's Castle."

Politically, the meaning of Black Power remained notoriously hard to pin down. For the Nation of Islam, Black Power meant an Islamic theocracy. For Coleman Young, it meant control of Detroit's Democratic Party. For some black Vietnam veterans, it meant applying the lessons they had learned in the Mekong Delta to the Mississippi Delta and the streets of Watts. For the Dodge Revolutionary Union Movement (DRUM), it meant equal access to supervisory positions on the assembly line. For the Republic of New Africa, it meant a communal society founded on African principles. For the Black Panthers, it meant an international revolution against capitalism. Musically, however, the message was clearer. Repudiating the masks that had seemed an intractable part of black expression, the seventies soul stars combined the rhythmic drive of James Brown and George Clinton's P-Funk empire, the searing vocals of Patti LaBelle and Chaka Khan and the sultry sophistication of Barry White and Isaac Hayes.

While the street corner orators and ghetto revolutionaries invoked Patrice Lumumba and Malcolm X, the music coalesced around messages that grew directly out of sixties-style gospel soul. When Stevie Wonder invited his people to claim "the higher ground," Curtis Mayfield urged them to "Get On Up," and the Cornelius Brothers and Sister Rose proclaimed that it was "Too Late to Turn Back Now," they were tuning in with the deepest impulses of African

American music. The cost of redemption was, as Earth, Wind & Fire put it, "true devotion": to the salvation of your soul and the liberation of your people.

From a gospel perspective, that meant *all* of the people. Sometimes Black Power had trouble living up to the ideal, and the failure contributed to the movement's political collapse. Most Black Power theorists called for a radical break with a past they defined in terms of slavery and submission. For those who subscribed to the values of Marxism or the Nation of Islam, that meant rejecting both Christianity, defined as the slaveholder's religion, and the blues. Maulana Karenga, whose primary contribution to the movement was advancing Kwanzaa as a black alternative to Christmas, openly repudiated the blues. "The blues are invalid; for they teach resignation, in a word acceptance of reality—and we have come to change reality."[21]

The words sounded righteous, but their simplistic militancy didn't ring true to many African Americans, especially the older generation that understood the difference between veiled resistance and abject surrender. Not even the youthful members of Karenga's US organization were about to give up Ray Charles or Muddy Waters, let alone Aretha's "Spirit in the Dark" or Marvin Gaye's "Inner City Blues." The most powerful albums of the Black Power era—Sly and the Family Stone's *There's a Riot Goin' On*, Mayfield's *Roots*, Franklin's *Spirit in the Dark*, Earth, Wind & Fire's *Spirit*, and the barrage of Stevie Wonder albums that culminated in *Innervisions* and *Songs in the Key of Life*—combined blues realism and gospel aspiration in a way that clarified, rather than betrayed, the meaning of Black Power.

## BLACK WOMEN'S LIBERATION

For reasons both commendable and dubious, Black Power emphasized the recovery of black manhood. When some men bought the supposed glamour of the pimp lifestyle at face value, however, numerous black women responded enthusiastically to the measured feminism (or, for those who hesitated to embrace a term they associated with a white middle class agenda, womanism) of June Jordan, Alice Walker, Audre Lorde, and Toni Morrison. The womanist writers were literary heirs to a musical tradition that extended from Dinah Washington's "Baby Get Lost" and Big Mama Thornton's "Hound Dog" through Nina Simone's "Four Women" and Aretha's "Chain of Fools" to Ann Peebles's "I'm Gonna Tear Your Playhouse Down," Jean Knight's "Mr. Big Stuff," and Laura Lee's "Women's Love Rights." The best disco records—Gloria Gaynor's "I Will Survive," Donna Summer's "Bad Girls," and Sister Sledge's "We Are Family"—chimed right in with what amounted to a collective sermon on the theme of black women's liberation. In fact, both the centrality of women and the form's origins in interracial gay dance clubs contributed to the ferocious antidisco backlash that would play a key role in the resegregation of American music in the early 1980s.

## THE MULTIDIMENSIONAL BLACK COMMUNITY

As the 1970s neared their end, the two-decade long call and response between black music and the pop mainstream lurched toward collapse. Black America was changing fast and, as always, the music moved with the people. Some of the changes reflected the weariness that descended in the wake of Watergate and Vietnam. But several disturbing trends had been set in motion, ironically, by the successes of the freedom movement. The first generation of R&B artists grew up and played their music in a world where the vast majority of black people lived, worked, and played in the same communities. Duke Ellington, Louis Jordan, and Ray Charles knew that their audience included black surgeons and insurance executives as well as women who spent their days scrubbing the white folks' floors and men who woke at dawn to empty white folks' garbage. Brothers and sisters scratching out a living on the streets shared neighborhoods with postal workers and teachers. The idea of a "black community"—which came in different flavors depending on whether you were in the North, South, or West—wasn't entirely an abstraction.

When the freedom movement began to open areas of American society that had been reserved for "whites only," many blacks jumped at the chance to raise their children in a better world. Ironically, the movement's success in breaking some racial barriers contributed to the fractures that would threaten to make a mockery of the gospel dream of communal redemption. As more black college graduates entered the professional world and moved to suburbs or integrated middle-class neighborhoods, the inner cities became more and more isolated. The collapse of the industrial economy and an increasingly hostile political climate made it ever more difficult for those who remained behind to follow their fortunate kinfolk out of the ghetto.

The fault lines appeared early in the music of the late 1970s and 1980s, first in the divergence between disco and funk, and later in the open antagonism between rap and R&B. When disco first appeared, it was just another part of the black dance mix that made no distinction between funk, soul, and the imported novelty records that took their name from the European discotheques where they had first been played. After *Saturday Night Fever* sparked the disco craze, however, the novelty developed disturbing undercurrents. As upscale clubs such as Studio 54 opened their doors to interracial coteries of celebrities and thrill-seekers, disco stars found it lucrative to cater to an audience dedicated to narcissistic hedonism rather than communal uplift. Disco represented a deliriously illogical extension of the fundamental premise of gospel soul. Gospel music sang about salvation through God; soul music sang about the power of love. Taking the progression another step into the secular world, disco translated "love" as "sex." If respectable black churchgoers had expressed their doubts about Ray Charles and the Staple Singers, many shared Jesse Jackson's condemnation of the disco scene as a moral cesspool. While local disco scenes—most notably the house music communities of Chicago and New Jersey—maintained their vitality, disco culture gradually lost contact with the black clubs and audiences in the rural South and the urban ghettos where hip-hop would soon fill the cultural vacuum.

## THE RISE OF HIP-HOP

Originating in the South Bronx and spreading rapidly to other cities in the northeast and on the west coast, early hip-hop provided a blues chronicle of a community ravaged by deindustrialization and a political backlash that, as Dan Carter demonstrates in *From George Wallace to Newt Gingrich: Race in the Conservative Counterrevolution, 1963 1994*, allowed Ronald Reagan to win the White House with a rhetoric and an agenda only once removed from arch-segregationist George Wallace. The pioneering rappers updated the verbal pyrotechnics of Cab Calloway and Chuck Berry as part of a call and response with DJs who manipulated modern electronic(s) to create shimmering montages of the urban soundscape. The vibrant culture mix around them included breakdancing and graffiti art. Growing out of the musical and social confusion of the late 1970s, the first hip-hop hits had clear affinities with funk ("Looking for the Perfect Beat" by the revered "Godfather of Hip-Hop," Afrika Bambaata) and disco ("Rapper's Delight" by the Sugarhill Gang, a middle-class New Jersey group marketing party-friendly versions of raps they'd picked up second- or thirdhand on forays into Harlem.) But the record that would define the blues heart of hip-hop was "The Message" by Grandmaster Flash & The Furious Five, a cinema vérité report from the urban jungle. Sounding a warning of the bitter day dawning in Reagan's America, the song's chorus would elicit cries of "Amens" for the rest of the century: "Don't push me 'cause I'm close to the edge / I'm trying not to lose my head / It's like a jungle sometimes / makes me wonder how I keep from goin' under."

At its best, 1980s hip-hop kept faith with "The Message." The blues realities were clear. As the Reagan tax cuts drained resources from social programs, a voting majority embraced a political rhetoric organized around baseless anecdotes of welfare queens riding in Cadillacs to purchase porterhouse steaks. Run-D.M.C. stripped the music down to its minimalist core behind images of street violence, resurgent racism and dysfunctional schools. KRS-One and Eric B and Rakim (whose dazzling lyrical virtuosity marked him as hip-hop's heir to Charlie Parker) seconded Run-D.M.C.'s no-nonsense response to those who denied or distorted the blues realities hammering poor black Americans: "It's like that and that's the way it is." Wu-Tang Clan would provide the definitive economic critique of the Reagan era in their classic, "C.R.E.A.M. (Cash Rules Everything Around Me)."

If hip-hop was, as rapper Chuck D of Public Enemy called it, "Black America's CNN," the reports portrayed a community that had lost its political bearings. While Public Enemy called for a renewed black revolution, Jesse Jackson's Rainbow Coalition and Louis Farrakhan's increasingly self-assured Nation of Islam competed for the support of a community divided along lines of class, gender, and generation. The root of the tensions lay in the social paradox that created a black middle class of unprecedented size at the same time many inner city residents were dropping off the edge of the economic world. Feelings of political betrayal and nihilistic anger spread through the ghettos. Afrocentric identity politics attracted thousands who had little interest in academic critiques of a movement that rarely bothered to distinguish between history and inspirational mythology. Afrocentrism was only the most popular flavor of identity politics; by the midpoint of the 1980s, the conservative counterrevolutionaries had succeeded in dividing their opposition into warring camps divided by ethnicity and sexual orientation as well as ideological hair-splitting.

As Nelson George observed in *The Death of Rhythm and Blues*, the 1980s marked a watershed in African American music: for the first time, the most popular forms of black music did not appeal to both young and old. Especially after the rise of "West Coast" gangsta rappers like N.W.A., Ice Cube, and Tupac Shakur, who had plenty of cousins back east and down south, many older blacks echoed media condemnations of hip-hop as an unholy alliance of pornographers, misogynists, and straight-out thugs. It didn't help that many of the gangstas were willing to market cartoon versions of their blues-based reports on ghetto life to young white males unable to distinguish between simple fact and minstrel hallucination. When the gangstas ushered the word "nigga" back into the American mainstream, it raised specters of a buried past that few who had been there wanted to revisit.

The fragmentation of the African American community was clear in the unprecedented hostility directed against R&B by substantial numbers of hip-hop fans, according to whom, R&B stood for "Romance & Bullshit." All too often, the musical conflict played out in terms of class, gender, and cultural identity. Venting misogynist and homophobic feelings that scandalized those who shared the freedom movement's commitment to universal human dignity, numerous hip-hop fans claimed possession of an authentic blackness (young, male, ghetto) while dismissing R&B as the feminized voice of a middle class that might as well be white. While the underground house music scene attracted fewer direct attacks, the unapologetically homophobic gangstas wanted no part of a latter-day disco scene that welcomed gays and lesbians. While church-raised R&B singers such as Anita Baker and Luther Vandross maintained their distance from the polemics, a group of black intellectuals led by jazz trumpeter Wynton Marsalis and his house theorist Stanley Crouch missed no opportunity to dismiss hip-hop as a subliterate betrayal of black music's great tradition.

Fixated on the gangstas, Marsalis seemed unaware of the richness and variety of the self-proclaimed "hip-hop nation" of the nineties. A plethora of stylistic schools reminiscent of midcentury jazz engaged in a dynamic call and response on the age-old questions at the heart of gospel and the blues, questions that remained unanswered at the dawn of the new millennium. Following in the footsteps of the "Native Tongues" movement of the 1980s (De La Soul, A Tribe Called Quest), the "conscious rappers" and underground poets affiliated with the Lyricist's Lounge wove surrealistic verbal tapestries while Jay-Z and Juvenile issued updates on the blues realities in the projects of Brooklyn and New Orleans; Missy Elliott and Lauryn Hill put to rest the persistent rumors that women couldn't rap; cartoon thug Eminem became the first white rapper to earn the general respect of his black peers; and movements based in Virginia (Timbaland), New Orleans (home base for rhythmic genius Mannie Fresh), and Atlanta (Goodie Mob, Outkast) added southern spice to the hip-hop stew. The fact that Marsalis, despite the achievements of, say, Louis Armstrong and Duke Ellington, was the first African American honored with the Pulitzer Prize in music did little to enhance his street credibility.

The endlessly inventive hip-hop production styles blurred into an international DJ culture that generated an array of new forms: acid jazz, drum and bass, trip hop, jungle, ambient, dub. Reflecting the demographic changes that would soon make Latinos the largest minority in the United States, a multiracial computer-literate cast including Tricky, Goldie, Talvin Singh and DJs Shadow, Krush, Quik, and Spooky had thoroughly deconstructed and reconstructed musical tradition with an eye toward the coming day when no group, including whites, would be able to claim majority status. By the end of the 1990s, hip-hop and its offshoots occupied the center of youth culture from Toronto to Tokyo.

Even as African Americans adjusted to their changing place in a nation transformed by immigration and globalization, the lingering echoes of the freedom movement grew louder in a gospel music scene rejuvenated by Kirk Franklin, whose crossover strategy summoned memories of Sam Cooke. Astonishing young black women inspired by the examples of Whitney Houston and Natalie Cole quietly reintegrated the pop music charts during the Clinton years. Stylistically, the new R&B varied from Mariah Carey's pop confections and Faith

Evans's gospel love songs to the street-wise hip-hop fusions of Mary J. Blige and TLC. Commercially, it dominated the charts from the mid-1990s on, shaping the daily experience of young Americans of all races much as Motown had done thirty years earlier. Whether the cultural victories of hip-hop and R&B would have a meaningful political impact remained unclear.

## BACK TO THE FUTURE

As the hostility between hypermasculine hip-hop and bourgeois R&B faded into a bad memory, D'Angelo, Erykah Badu, India.Arie, Angie Stone, and R. Kelly forged a neo-soul movement, applying balm to their listener's aching souls. Determined to prove themselves worthy of the legacies of Martin, Malcolm, and Ella Baker as well as Mahalia, Aretha, and Stevie Wonder, the new soul stirrers challenged their people to remember the redemptive visions of the ancestors: to look a brutal history in the eyes like the blues; to transcend it like gospel; to find new ways to confound it like jazz. Everything had changed, and it was still the same.

### SOURCES

Brewster, Bill, and Frank Broughton. *Last Night a DJ Saved My Life: The History of the Disc Jockey*. New York: Grove Press, 2000.

Carter, Dan T. *From George Wallace to Newt Gingrich: Race in the Conservative Counterrevolution, 1963–1994*. Baton Rouge: Louisiana State University Press, 1996.

Corbett, John. *Extended Play: Sounding Off from John Cage to Dr. Funkenstein*. Durham, N.C.: Duke University Press, 1994.

Cross, Brian. *It's Not About a Salary: Rap, Race and Resistance in Los Angeles*. New York: Verso Books, 1993.

Dittmer, John. *Local People: The Struggle for Civil Rights in Mississippi*. Urbana: University of Illinois Press, 1994.

Ellison, Ralph. *Shadow and Act*. New York: Random House, 1964.

Escot, Colin, and Martin Hawkins. *Good Rockin' Tonight: Sun Records and the Birth of Rock 'n' Roll*. New York: St. Martin's, 1991.

Fernando, S. H. *The New Beats: Exploring the Music, Culture, and Attitudes of Hip-Hop*. New York: Anchor Books, 1994.

George, Nelson. *The Death of Rhythm & Blues*. New York: Omnibus, 1988.

———. *Where Did Our Love Go?: The Rise and Fall of the Motown Sound*. New York: St. Martin's, 1985.

Giddins, Gary. *Visions of Jazz: The First Century*. New York: Oxford University Press, 1999.

Gillett, Charles. *The Sound of the City: The Rise of Rock and Roll*. 2nd ed. New York: Da Capo, 1996.
Gordy, Berry. *To Be Loved: The Music, The Magic, The Memories of Motown*. New York: Warner, 1994.
Guralnick, Peter. *Sweet Soul Music: Rhythm and Blues and the Southern Dream of Freedom*. New York: Harper & Row, 1986.
Heilbut, Anthony. *The Gospel Sound: Good News and Bad Times*. Rev. ed. New York: Limelight, 1985.
Jones, LeRoi (Amiri Baraka). *Blues People: Black Music in White America*. New York: Morrow, 1963.
———. "The Changing Same: R&B and New Black Music." In *The Black Aesthetic*, ed. Addison Gayle Jr., 118–131. Garden City, N.Y.: Anchor Books, 1972.
Kelley, Robin. *Race Rebels: Culture, Politics and the Black Working Class*. New York: Free Press, 1996.
Kofsky, Frank. *Black Nationalism and the Revolution in Music*. New York: Pathfinder, 1970.
Lhamon, W. T., Jr. *Raising Cain: Blackface Performance from Jim Crow to Hip Hop*. Cambridge, Mass.: Harvard University Press, 1998.
Lott, Eric. *Love and Theft: Blackface Minstrelsy and the American Working Class*. New York: Oxford University Press, 1993.
Marcus, Greil. *Mystery Train: Images of America in Rock 'n' Roll Music*. New York: Dutton, 1977.
Marsh, Dave. *The Heart of Rock and Soul*. New York: Plume, 1989.
Morgan, Joan. *When Chickenheads Come Home to Roost: A Hip-Hop Feminist Breaks It Down*. New York: Touchstone, 2000.
Murray, Albert. *Stomping the Blues*. New York: Viking, 1976.
Murray, Charles Shaar. *Crosstown Traffic: Jimi Hendrix and the Rock 'n' Roll Revolution*. New York: St. Martin's, 1989.
Neal, Mark Anthony. *Soul Babies: Black Popular Culture and the Post-Soul Aesthetic*. New York: Routledge, 2002.
———. *What the Music Said: Black Popular Music and Black Public Culture*. New York: Routledge, 1998.
Nissenson, Eric. *Ascension: John Coltrane and His Quest*. New York: St. Martin's, 1993.
O'Brien, Lucy. *She Bop: The Definitive History of Women in Rock, Pop & Soul*. New York: Penguin, 1996.
Palmer, Robert. *Deep Blues*. New York: Viking, 1981.
———. *Rock & Roll: An Unruly History*. New York: Harmony, 1995.
Payne, Charles M. *I've Got the Light of Freedom: The Organizing Tradition and the Mississippi Freedom Struggle*. Berkeley: University of California Press, 1995.
Reagon, Bernice Johnson. *We Who Believe in Freedom*. New York: Anchor Books, 1993.
Ritz, David. *The Divided Soul of Marvin Gaye*. New York: Da Capo, 1991.
Rose, Tricia. *Black Noise: Rap Music and Black Culture in Contemporary America*. Middletown, Conn.: Wesleyan University Press, 1994.
Sidran, Ben. *Black Talk*. New York: Da Capo, 1981.

Small, Christopher. *Music of the Common Tongue: Survival and Celebration in African-American Music*. Middletown, Conn.: Wesleyan University Press, 1998.

Smith, Susan. *Dancing in the Street: Motown and the Cultural Politics of Detroit*. Cambridge, Mass.: Harvard University Press, 2000.

Spencer, Jon Michael. *Protest and Praise: Sacred Music of Black Religion*. Minneapolis: Fortress Press, 1990.

Toop, David. *Rap Attack 2: African Rap to Global Hip Hop*. London: Serpent's Tail, 1991.

Tyson, Timothy. *Radio Free Dixie: Robert F. Williams and the Roots of Black Power*. Chapel Hill: University of North Carolina Press, 1999.

Van Deburg, William. *New Day in Babylon: The Black Power Movement and American Culture*. Chicago: University of Chicago Press, 1992.

Vincent, Ricky. *Funk: The Music, the People, and the Rhythm of the One*. New York: St. Martin's, 1995.

Ward, Brian. *Just My Soul Responding: Rhythm and Blues, Black Consciousness, and Race Relations*. Berkeley: University of California Press, 1998.

Werner, Craig. *A Change Is Gonna Come: Music, Race & the Soul of America*. New York: Plume, 1998.

Wexler, Jerry. *Rhythm and Blues: A Life in American Music*. New York: Knopf, 1993.

Wolff, Daniel. *You Send Me: The Life and Times of Sam Cooke*. New York: Morrow, 1995.

## NOTES

1. Ralph Ellison, *Shadow and Act* (New York: Vintage Books, 1972), 234.

2. Yusef Komunyakaa, "It's Always Night," *Caliban* 4 (1988): 52.

3. Julie Schwerin, *Got to Tell It: Mahalia Jackson, Queen of Gospel* (New York: Oxford University Press, 1992), 65.

4. Amiri Baraka, *The Music: Reflections on Jazz and the Blues* (New York: Morrow, 1987), 184.

5. Amiri Baraka, "The Changing Same (R&B and Black Music)," in *Selected Plays and Prose of Amiri Baraka/LeRoi Jones* (New York: Morrow, 1979), 161.

6. Zora Neale Hurston, *Mules and Men* (Bloomington: Indiana University Press, 1978), 5.

7. Ibid.

8. Daniel Wolff, *You Send Me: The Life and Times of Sam Cooke* (New York: Morrow, 1995), 100.

9. *Good Rockin' Tonight* (Time-Life Video 13861).

10. Ibid.

11. Philip Norman, *Symphony for the Devil: The Rolling Stones Story* (New York: Linden, 1998), 89.

12. Quoted in the liner notes to Ray Charles, *The Birth of Soul* (Atlantic Records 82310).

13. Berry Gordy, *To Be Loved: The Music, The Magic, The Memories of Motown* (New York: Time Warner, 1994), 95.

14. James Baldwin, "Color," in *The Price of the Ticket* (New York: St. Martin's, 1985), 320.

15. Quoted in Jon Michael Spencer, *Protest and Praise: Sacred Music of Black Religion* (Minneapolis: Fortress Press, 1990), 91.

16. Quoted in the liner notes to *Voices of the Civil Rights Movement: Black American Freedom Songs, 1960–1966* (Smithsonian CD 40084).

17. Mavis Staples, interview with Craig Werner, March 1998.

18. Curtis Mayfield, interview with Craig Werner, February 1998.

19. Ann Powers, "Aretha Franklin," in *The Rolling Stone Book of Women in Rock*, ed. Barbara O'Dair (New York: Random House, 1997), 93.

20. Peter Guralnick, *Sweet Soul Music: Rhythm and Blues and the Southern Dream of Freedom* (New York: HarperCollins, 1986), 345.

21. Maulana (Ron) Karenga, "Black Cultural Nationalism," in *The Black Aesthetic*, ed. Addison Gayle (Garden City, N.Y.: Anchor Books, 1972), 36.

# BLACK BUSINESS DEVELOPMENT

JULIET E. K. WALKER

Before the late 1930s, black business existed primarily in a race-based, black-consumer market economy. Black business development was essentially in the service sector and depended almost exclusively on an African American clientele. Restaurants, grocery stores, barber and beauty shops, taxicabs, taverns, mortuaries, and newspapers catered to the needs of black consumers. Some black entrepreneurs established larger businesses, such as savings banks, insurance enterprises, real estate ventures, construction firms, hotels, business schools, and cosmetic and hair-care companies. The largest black business in total employees before World War II was the North Carolina Mutual Insurance Company in Durham. Insurance was a lucrative market for black entrepreneurs, since mainstream companies refused to write policies on African Americans. Although few black businesses were located in white business districts or had white clientele, there were many white enterprises, such as clothing and furniture stores, in black business districts that relied solely on black customers.

The post–civil rights era marked the slow expansion of black business enterprise into the mainstream American economy. With federal government programs that promoted minority business expansion, black entrepreneurs gained access to government contracts and black companies became more involved in manufacturing. The federal government, especially during the Nixon administration, promoted "black capitalism." At the same time, many traditional black businesses, especially in the customary "goods" manufacturing sector, started to decline in competition with multinational corporations, which began to cater to an African American market they had previously ignored. Yet, most distinctive, in black business history in the closing decades of the twentieth century were the successes made by black entrepreneurs who packaged and marketed black culture, in particular black music, to a broad audience. A few superstar black athletes also emerged as leading entrepreneurs.

## BLACK BUSINESS DEVELOPMENT DURING WORLD WAR II

Black business development changed significantly during World War II as African American entrepreneurs broadened the scope of their enterprises, especially in the manufacturing arena, with the assistance of government contracts. Before World War II, black manufacturing was limited primarily to cosmetic and hair-care products. The twenty-odd black businesses that received defense contracts during the war enjoyed total revenues in the millions, much higher than those of enterprises that were limited to supplying goods and services to black consumers with average revenues in the tens of thousands. In 1941, the McKissick Brothers Construction Company of Nashville, Tennessee, founded in 1909, won a $4 million defense contract to construct a two-thousand-acre airfield at Tuskegee Institute in Alabama. During construction, the company employed some 1,900 black workers. This new, segregated base was used to train black pilots, subsequently known as the Tuskegee Airmen.

Black businesses also gained contracts to manufacture military uniforms, parachutes, and the like. California-based black architect Paul R. Williams signed defense contracts worth millions of dollars to design naval airbases and the housing on those bases. The Kerford Quarry Stone Mining Company in Atchison, Kansas, was one of the largest black-owned businesses during the war. Some three hundred men, black and white, worked for the company mining nonmetallic limestone. Kerford leased storage space for food supplies in its limestone caves to the federal government.[1] These enterprises were the exception. Most black businesses remained small and continued to provide goods and services to a black consumer market. Still, new employment opportunities for blacks that developed during the war increased their consumer spending, which contributed to an increase in profits made by these enterprises.

## BLACK BUSINESS EXPANSION AFTER WORLD WAR II

With a disposable income of $7 billion, the increase in black consumer spending after World War II helped several black businesses to prosper.[2] Arthur G. Gaston, of Birmingham, Alabama, established the Booker T. Washington Insurance Company in 1932, the profits from which he used to establish the Booker T. Washington Business College, the Gaston Motel, the Citizens Savings and Loan Association, a radio station, a soft-drink bottling company, and the Vulcan Realty and Investment Corporation, which financed and constructed apartment buildings, office space, and homes. In Chicago, S.B. Fuller built a business empire that included health and beauty products, cleaning aids, a department store, real estate, and livestock operations. He began his career in the 1930s as a door-to-door salesman. As the company expanded, Fuller employed more than five thousand workers in his cosmetics business, and the firm earned over $10 million a year in sales. Fuller had also secretly purchased a white cosmetics factory. Several of his products were sold to southern white consumers, but during the early 1960s, when they discovered that the company was black-owned, they boycotted those products.[3]

While Fuller never fully recovered from the downturn in business and was forced to declare bankruptcy, his contemporary, black publishing giant John H. Johnson, relying primarily on black consumers, had remarkable success. Johnson began his publishing company in 1942 with *Negro Digest*, a magazine patterned after *Reader's Digest*, but which carried news for blacks about the struggle for racial equality. *Negro Digest* became an instant success, with sales of $50,000 a month after its first eight months of existence. In 1945, Johnson started his flagship publication, *Ebony* magazine, which followed the format of *Life*, the popular picture magazine. *Ebony* featured the lifestyles of the black middle class and became both a showcase of black achievement and an incentive for material success. In 1951 he launched *Jet*, a pocket-sized weekly magazine that provided current events information on black America. In diversifying, with book publishing, an insurance company, radio stations, television specials, and hair and beauty products, Johnson emerged as one of the most successful black entrepreneurs in America.

The hair-care and cosmetics industry continued to be a base for black business development until the end of the twentieth century, when it encountered competition from mainstream cosmetics firms. Still, black hair salons provided opportunities for many black women to own their own business.[4] Rose Morgan and Olivia Clark began the Rose Meta House of Beauty in Harlem in 1947 and within three years had sales of $3 million a year for their hair-care and beauty products. They also established a chain of beauty shops throughout the

United States and in British Guiana, Cuba, Jamaica, Liberia, and Puerto Rico. Sarah Spencer Washington, of Atlantic City, New Jersey, employed some five hundred workers in a factory that produced Apex hair-care products. She also invested in real estate, started beauty colleges, and built a black resort. By the 1970s, Chicago was the center of black hair-care product manufacturing; Johnson Products, Soft Sheen, and Luster were among the nation's largest black businesses until the 1990s.

## BLACK BUSINESS DEVELOPMENT DURING THE CIVIL RIGHTS ERA

Initially the civil-rights movement had a deleterious effect on black businesses. The drive for racial equality opened previously segregated hotels, restaurants, theaters, banks, and insurance companies to African Americans, but it did not generate reciprocity in white patronage of black businesses. The federal government had provided a boost for some black businesses with defense contracts during World War II, but it was slow to encourage black business development along with desegregation and the right to vote. After the urban rebellions and violence during the 1960s in Harlem (1964), Watts (1965), Detroit (1967), and many other cities, tension ran high among African Americans, some of whom identified capitalism as the root of the problem of racial subordination.

The Black Panther Party advocated that the means of production should be taken from white businessmen and placed in black communities for the organization of cooperatives and employment for black Americans. Black nationalists such as Malcolm X argued that African Americans had to gain control over the economy of their communities and provide for themselves rather than boycotting and picketing white businesses for employment. The NAACP and the National Urban League called for the creation of more black capitalists but opposed the development of a separate black economy. They advocated incorporation of African American business development within the capitalist system. Martin Luther King Jr., however, had criticized American capitalism for its inequities. In 1967, he stated, "The profit motive, when it is the sole basis for an economic system, encourages cut-throat competition and selfish ambition."[5]

Still, King promoted the development of black business through Operation Breadbasket. Jesse Jackson in Chicago was its national director, with a mandate to influence corporations to use black contractors, suppliers, and banks, and to employ black workers. King's assassination in 1968 and subsequent rioting prompted both the government and corporate America to promote black business development as a means of providing a greater economic stake in American society.

## THE FEDERAL GOVERNMENT AND BLACK BUSINESS DEVELOPMENT

Richard Nixon ran for president in 1968 on a platform of nurturing black capitalism. During the campaign, he described the need for technical assistance and loan guarantees for African Americans to start new businesses in inner-city areas. After his election, Nixon issued executive order 11458, which established the Office of Minority Business Enterprise (OMBE), later renamed the Minority Business Development Agency (MBDA). He also strengthened the Small Business Administration (SBA) to provide federal support for black business development. These initiatives helped to give life to Title IV of the 1964 Civil Rights Act, which required government agencies to seek the fullest possible use of minority businesses in purchasing goods and services. SBA programs offered guarantees against loan defaults by minority businesses and mandated that a percentage of government contracts go to minority businesses. State and municipal governments seeking federal grants had to set aside at least ten percent of procurement contracts for minority firms. In 1978, during the Carter presidency, Congress enacted Public Law 95–907, which required companies bidding for prime government contracts to submit plans that included subcontracting to minority businesses.

Government contracts, especially in the defense industry, helped African American businesses to expand beyond the traditional race-based markets. H. F. Henderson Industries, Inc., in New Jersey, was founded in 1954 and prospered from the manufacture of electronics for the military. In 1987, Henderson received a $125 million defense contract to manufacture spare parts for an artillery-battery computer system. South Carolina-based American Development Corporation (ADCOR) was started in 1972 and received Department of Defense contracts to supply hi-tech manufacturing equipment. During Operation Desert Storm in the Persian Gulf, the Department of Defense awarded the company ten contracts for military hardware. The Red River Shipping Company, started in 1983, became one of the top one hundred black enterprises. In 1990, during the Gulf War, it was awarded contracts to ship soybean oil and military cargo for the United States Agency for International Development.

Jackson and Tull, a Maryland-based electrical engineering firm founded in 1974, grew by securing government contracts from the National Aeronautics and Space Administration (NASA) and the Department of Defense. It supplied a broad array of services to high technology industries, including advanced computers and unmanned system technologies. The company received a Lockheed Martin subcontract for the Hubble Space telescope. The Air Force Research Laboratory at Kirkland Air Force base granted Jackson and Tull a $49 million contract for spacecraft research and development.

Defense contracts also provided a start for a new group of black entrepreneurs who had achieved distinguished careers in professional sports. Former Pittsburgh Steelers player John Stallworth (inducted into the Football Hall of Fame in 2002) founded Madison Research Corporation in Alabama. He secured contracts from NASA and the Department of Defense for missile defense programs.

St. Louis–based World Wide Technology (WWT) was the leading black business at the end of the twentieth century and owed much of its success to defense contracts. Founded in 1990 by David L. Stewart, WWT secured a contract to package and ship computer hardware to the U.S. military in Bosnia. Subsequent contracts with Hansom Air Force base in Massachusetts, the Army Corps of Engineers in Nebraska, and with Boeing and Lockheed launched WWT into prominence as one of the top one hundred federal prime contractors in information technology. WWT also expanded with contracts from Fortune 500 hi-tech companies, including Oracle, Cisco, Dell, Compaq, Gateway, Microsoft, and Lucent. In 2002, with sales of $716 million, WWT ranked as the nation's second-largest black business.

Although the federal government gave a boost to black business development and expansion, especially through defense contracts, assistance to black businesses was a small fraction of the annual defense budget. Many black businesses rose and fell on participation in federal programs. The SBA set-aside programs supported businesses for only eight years. Once companies lost their "protected" status, many were not able to compete in the general market. While many new companies promoted themselves as black businesses and are considered black-owned, too, some have only minority interests in those enterprises. Still, there was an expansion of black business activity. Earl Graves, in the magazine that he started in 1970, *Black Enterprise*, has chronicled the rise of the largest enterprises with annual lists of the top black firms in areas such as industry, service, auto dealerships, advertising, banks, and insurance.

## POST–CIVIL RIGHTS BLACK BUSINESS

With the election of black mayors in most of the major cities, municipal contracts further contributed to the development and growth of black businesses. Herman J. Russell in Atlanta started his construction company in 1952 but did not realize earnings in the hundreds of millions of dollars until the 1970s, after the election of Maynard Jackson in 1973 as Atlanta's first black mayor. Jackson insisted on black businesses gaining a share of the city's economic development, especially expansion of its airport. Subsequently, the H. J. Russell Construction Company received a contract to build the airport's parking deck. The company was also involved as contractor or subcontractor for the Atlanta Stadium, the

Martin Luther King, Jr. Community Center, the Carter Presidential Center, the Atlanta Merchandise Mart, and the fifty-two-story Georgia Pacific office building. Russell joined forces with black-owned C. D. Moody Construction Company to win the bid for the $209 million Olympic Stadium in Atlanta for the 1996 games. It was during Maynard Jackson's second term as mayor (1989–93) that Atlanta secured the Olympic Games.

Though black mayors made a difference for their communities for a time by making sure that black businesses had access to lucrative government contracts and subcontracts, it was not long before white construction firms challenged the set-asides for minority companies. In *Richmond v. J. A. Croson Co.*, the Supreme Court in 1989 ruled against a minority set-aside program in Richmond, Virginia, that required contractors to subcontract at least 30 percent of contracts to minority firms. In 1995, the Supreme Court determined in *Adarand Constructors v. Pena* that the federal government's affirmative-action programs should be subject to the same strict scrutiny as applied to state and local programs. In effect, the government at the federal, state, and local levels could not advantage one group based on race, ethnicity, or gender over others.

## BLACK ENTREPRENEURSHIP AND MAINSTREAM AMERICA

Many African American businesses no longer rely almost exclusively on race-based markets. Reginald F. Lewis, a graduate of historically black Virginia State College and Harvard Law School, started the first black law firm on Wall Street in 1973 and specialized in corporate law and venture capitalism. Ten years later, he established the investment firm, the TLC Group (The Lewis Company), that purchased the McCall Pattern Company in 1984, a 117-year-old firm. The TLC Group turned the company around and sold it for an 800 percent profit three years later. With venture capital financing, Lewis purchased through a leveraged buyout Beatrice International Foods, which had annual sales of more than $1 billion, making TLC the largest majority black-owned company in the United States until Lewis's death of brain cancer in 1993.

Other black businesses also entered the food industry. The La-Van Hawkins Food Group in Detroit, with 7,319 workers, had the largest number of employees for a black business in the United States in 2001. One of the most successful black businesses in the food industry, with annual sales of approximately $419 million, is the Philadelphia Coca-Cola Bottling Company. It was founded in 1985 by its chief executive officer, J. Bruce Llewellyn, as a joint venture with entertainer Bill Cosby and basketball star Julius "Dr. J" Erving. Llewellyn achieved initial success in the food industry in 1969 when he purchased the

Bronx-based Fedco Foods Store and expanded it from ten to twenty-seven stores. In 1990, Llewellyn, along with investors Camille Cosby (the wife of Bill Cosby), Julius Erving, and members of Michael Jackson's family, purchased New York Times Cable for $125 million.

Not only have many African American–owned businesses entered the mainstream, but black executives have also attained positions of prominence and power in major corporations. Franklin D. Raines became chairman and CEO of Fannie Mae, in 1999, the largest non-bank financial services company in the world and the largest source for financing home mortgages in the United States. In 2001, Kenneth Chenault became CEO of American Express Company and Richard Parsons was appointed CEO of AOL-Time Warner. A year later, Stanley O'Neal became CEO of Merrill Lynch & Co., the nation's largest stock brokerage firm. Although great progress was made by the end of the twentieth century, impediments still stood in the way against the advancement of women and minorities in corporate America. The Federal Glass Ceiling Commission in 1995 reported that 97 percent of senior managers in Fortune 500 companies were white, and 95 percent were male.

## THE COMMODIFICATION OF BLACK SONG

One means to business success during the late twentieth and early twenty-first centuries has been the merchandizing of black music, especially to a mainstream audience. African American music, more than a cultural expression, has become an important commodity, a product to be packaged and sold. Berry Gordy Jr. became the first black entrepreneur to make a major breakthrough in the music industry with Motown Records, a company he founded in 1959. With Motown, African Americans as artists, writers, and producers began to profit from the production of black music. Gordy developed soul music in the 1960s, a new style that combined popular music and rhythm and blues, and marketed it to a white audience, while retaining a black consumer base. He sold Motown to Music Corporation of America in 1988 for $61 million. *Forbes Magazine* estimated his net worth that year as more than $180 million from sale of the company and from music publishing, film, and television subsidiaries that Gordy still controlled.

By the 1990s, a major growth area had emerged in the promotion of black culture, especially in the "hip-hop" music industry. Much of the financial success of the nation's first black billionaire, Robert Johnson, must be attributed to the products of black music impresarios and entrepreneurs who provided the song, the music videos, the style, and the personalities that generated huge profits for Black Entertainment Television (BET). Johnson started BET, the first black-owned cable television network, in 1980 and sold it two decades later to Viacom for nearly $3 billion. BET opened a national market for hip-hop music and culture. Hip-hop emerged around "rap" music that came out of the Bronx, New York, during the 1970s with influences from the Caribbean. Rap music was a part of African American culture that drew on the practice of boasts, signifying, and testifying in rhymes. Many black disk jockeys rhymed introductions to their shows and the songs that they played on the radio. The "hip hop" scene captured this tradition with a DJ who introduced rhythms from records by "scratching" them on turntables, stopping, starting, and repeating beats. It was this quality that gave the style its name.

Graffiti art and break dancing also contributed to the style that soon included forms of verbal and nonverbal expression, clothing, and philosophy. Russell Simmons, who began Def Jam Records in 1984, was a pioneer entrepreneur of the hip-hop industry. His company produced and marketed music for some of the major rap artists and became the largest black-owned music business in the country. In 1992, Simmons's film and television division produced *Def Comedy Jam*, a popular entertainment television show. His Broadway show *Def Poetry Jam* won a Tony Award in 2003 as the best theatrical event. His company, Phat Fashions, manufactures clothing for urban youth, while Sean "P Diddy" Combs, who has produced the music of many major rappers, especially on the East Coast, through his Bad Boy Entertainment, has branched into the clothing market with his Sean John label. Several other black-owned companies have created fashions for the hip-hop generation, such as FUBU (For Us, By Us), which had gross earnings of $380 million in 2000. Karl Kani Infinity, established in 1989, had sales of its urban fashions of $71.2 million in 2002.

Sports and entertainment became major vehicles for wealth accumulation and black business development at the turn of the century. The 2002 issue of *Fortune* magazine list of "America's 40 Richest Under 40" included six African Americans, all from the world of sports and entertainment. Michael Jordan (39) ranked ninth at $408 million; Percy Miller, "Master P" (33), eleventh at $293.8 million; Combs (32), twelfth at $293.7 million; Tiger Woods (26), sixteenth at $212 million; Shaquille O'Neal (30), twenty-second at $171 million; and Will Smith (33), thirty-ninth at $113 million. Earvin "Magic" Johnson, at age forty-three, missed the list, but he had amassed a $500 million empire that consisted of movie theaters, restaurants, shopping malls, and athletic clubs. Most of the former basketball star's businesses involve joint ventures and have brought new goods and services to inner-city neighborhoods.

Bill Cosby, sixty-five years old in 2002, was one of the nation's wealthiest African Americans, possessing assets in excess of $500 million from his popular *Cosby Family* television show and other entertainment programs, product endorsements, and publications. Although these African Americans accumulated great wealth, only two made *Forbes* magazine's September 30, 2002, list of the "400 Richest People in America." Robert Johnson of BET was number 149 on the list with $1.3 billion. While Oprah Winfrey was 229 in 2002, with $975 million, in 2003 she was ranked 427 with $1 billon.

Oprah Winfrey capitalized on what is called "black girlfriend talk" to become the nation's number one confidant. She quickly became America's top talk-show host and established a media conglomerate through joint ventures and strategic alliances. She has diversified into film, cable TV, and the publishing industry, and her book club has made instant best sellers of books she has recommended to her audience. In 1999, her Harpo Entertainment Group reached a licensing agreement with Hearst Corporation to create a new magazine. *O, the Oprah Magazine*, which features Winfrey on the cover of each issue, has become one of the most successful periodicals in the country. Her reach and influence are enormous, and she consistently tops lists of the most admired Americans.[6]

Other black women have achieved notable business success. Cathy Hughes's Radio One consists of twenty-seven stations in nine major markets, with a staff of about 1,550. In 1999, she took her company public with an initial public stock offering that raised $1.2 billion. She retained control of 56 percent of the voting stock in the company, which is the sixteenth largest media company in the United States. Hughes has expanded her interest in the communications industry by investments in cable television. Ernesta G. Procope, the founder, CEO, and president of E. G. Bowman Co., Inc. heads the largest minority-owned and female-owned insurance brokerage firm in the country. She started in business by opening her own insurance company in Brooklyn, New York, in 1952. Later, she expanded to Wall Street and now heads a company that is licensed in all fifty states and that includes some of the country's top corporations as its clients.

## MULTINATIONAL CORPORATIONS AND BLACK BUSINESSES

The race-based market has been the engine that has driven black business development, especially in beauty and hair-care products. The rise of global capitalism, however, has weakened that traditional black industry. The black hair-care market was a $1 billion industry in the late 1980s, when white-owned companies began to vie for the business and soon controlled half of the market. While Chicago-based Alberto Culver purchased the Dallas-based Pro-Line, founded by Comer Cottrell, the multinational pharmaceutical corporation company, IVAX Corporation purchased Johnson (George S. Johnson) Products, maker of the Ultra-Sheen hair-care line, in 1993. French-based L'Oreal, the world's largest cosmetics company, bought Soft Sheen Products (started in 1964 by Edward Gardner) in 1998. With the purchase of Carson Products, Inc., in 2000, L'Oreal gained control of 50 percent of black women's hair-relaxer kits and 62 percent of the black women's hair-coloring market. African Americans comprise 12.3 percent of the nation's population but 37 percent of the hair-care product consumer market. Only John H. Johnson's Fashion Fair Cosmetics remained at the end of the twentieth century as a major black-owned beauty and hair-care products company.

Multinational corporations also made inroads into the black advertising industry. New York-based UniWorld Group was the largest African American–owned advertising agency. In 1999, UniWorld sold 49 percent of the company to a London-based firm, while Burrell Communications Group in Chicago the following year sold 49 percent of its business to a French-based agency. Essence Communications Inc., publisher of *Essence* magazine, a very successful publication geared to black women, sold 49 percent of the business to AOL–Time Warner, which explained that the purchase would facilitate the company's expansion into the African American market and strengthen its presence in the beauty and fashion advertising categories.

## THE DEBATE OVER RACE, CAPITALISM, AND BLACK BUSINESS

African Americans have historically debated the purpose of black entrepreneurship and business development in the United States. Should African Americans be involved in business in a capitalist economic system that exploited black labor during slavery and segregation? Should black entrepreneurs have a special commitment to use their profits for the economic and social advancement of African Americans? Black intellectuals and activists have given these issues some attention but have provided few viable solutions.

On the radical left, black intellectuals and activists have denounced capitalism and the free-enterprise system and have maintained that working-class solidarity should take precedence over questions of race, ethnicity, or gender. Rather than consider the socioeconomic system as the source of the problem, the political right has identified certain self-defeating attitudes and behaviors among African Americans themselves as contributing to the absence of economic equality. Black conservatives consider lack of motivation, refusal to work hard, and self-destructive behaviors such as having children outside of wedlock, drug addiction, and crime, not capitalism itself, as the problem. They oppose affirmative action as a program that casts African Americans as victims. Black conservatives urge African Americans to take their place in the "race for success" alongside other Americans without the crutch of government assistance or the so-called victim's complaint that they are owed something because of past discrimination.

Economists such as Thomas Sowell and Walter Williams, as well as literary critic Shelby Steele and linguist John McWhorter, celebrate capitalism and free enterprise and view the marketplace as basically race-neutral, as a common ground where everyone with dedication and hard work can succeed. Glenn Loury, once a leading conservative voice, has identified "racial stigma" against African Americans as contributing to racial inequality. Although he opposed affirmative action throughout the late 1980s and early 1990s, Loury has since concluded that it is necessary to open doors of opportunity previously closed to African Americans and to change a socioeconomic system that has traditionally excluded them. Consequently, Loury now joins black economists such as Thomas D. Boston, William Darity, Julianne Malveaux, and Samuel L. Myers Jr., who have attributed the advances made by black businesses to affirmative action.

Black organizations also have made efforts to promote business development. The National Urban League announced in 1998 that one of its goals for the twenty-first century is to foster a new civil-rights movement to focus on economic empowerment. The National Black Chamber of Commerce has also provided support for black business development. National networking conferences offer opportunities for black business owners. George Fraser, who publishes *Success Guide Worldwide—The Networking Guide to Black Resources*, has sponsored an annual Power Networking Conference since 1988. The publisher of *Black Enterprise* magazine, Earl Graves, since 1995 has organized an annual Black Enterprise Entrepreneurs Conference. In 1997, Jesse Jackson initiated his Wall Street Economic Summit Conference / Wall Street Project, dedicated to helping African Americans gain full access to capital, industry, and technology. Through his National Action Network, Al Sharpton has launched his Madison Avenue initiative to challenge racial bias in advertising. These initiatives have placed African Americans more firmly within the American economy. In many respects, African Americans have moved from criticism of the capitalist economy to a drive for inclusion within it, especially through business development.

## THE FUTURE OF BLACK BUSINESS DEVELOPMENT

Despite the new forms of black business ownership, strategic alliances, and joint ventures, aggregate black business receipts have not increased much as a percentage of all American business receipts. While black businesses have developed new markets in technology and in the commodification of black music, they have lost many of their traditional markets. Black businesses have not been able to compete, for example, with the industry giants and multinational corporations in insurance and hair-care products. Also, while some black businesses continue to thrive, others, especially small enterprises in urban neighborhoods have never recovered from the urban riots of the 1960s. Immigrants from Asia and the Middle East have filled the vacuum left by black storeowners who were unable or unwilling to reestablish their businesses, usually grocery stores, restaurants, cleaners, and liquor stores, after the urban devastation. Moreover, middle-class African Americans have increasingly moved to the outer rings of cities and the inner suburbs, where they shop at malls that contain few, if any, black-owned stores.

The future course of black business development will likely depend in large measure on access to the sorts of defense and government contracts that helped to stimulate black business growth after World War II, on participation in municipal construction contracts, and on provision of goods and services to traditional markets. The Houston-based Aztec Facility Company, founded in 1981 by a leading black woman entrepreneur, Sherra Aguirre, expanded from its core janitorial and housekeeping services to environmental management and hazardous-waste disposal. With contracts from corporate, industrial and government clients, including the military, and one thousand employees, the company has receipts of more than $25 million. Also, supplier contracts from the nation's leading automakers marked an expansion of blacks in auto-parts manufacturing. While the Detroit-based Bing Group (started in 1980 by former basketball star Dave Bing as a steel-processing and metal-distribution company for the auto industry) emerged as one of the nation's leading businesses, several black auto-parts manufacturers, to remain competitive, merged to form Global Automotive Alliance LLC, under the leadership of William F. Pickard.

In the twenty-first century, African American businesses will have to become more innovative in reaching consumers, whether in the mainstream economy or in traditional markets. Earvin "Magic" Johnson demonstrates the viability of business development in inner-city areas, especially with joint ventures, while the young entertainment entrepreneurs are reaching consumers in traditional, national, and international markets with their music, clothing, and videos. Hip-hop entrepreneur Master (Percy Miller) P, whose record company No Limit produces rap artists, has moved into the telecommunications industry with his prepaid cell phones, while Russell Simmons's new Visa prepaid debit card marks this hip-hop entrepreneur's entry into the financial industry. Primarily, these enterprises developed by Johnson, Miller, and Russell are joint ventures with white corporate America and provide examples of the types of innovation that will influence the future development of black business.

Increasingly, white corporate America will become a significant factor in black business activity not only for blacks who work in it, but also for black entrepreneurs.[7] Gale Sayers, former Chicago Bears running back and a member of the Football Hall of Fame, developed a technology solutions firm in 1984 with offices across the country. In 2002, with revenues of $225 million, the Sayers Group was the fifteenth-ranking black business in the nation. George Foreman, the former heavyweight champion, viewed as "America's Salesman," has earned almost $200 million from his grill endorsements alone. Still, notwithstanding the expansion of black business into mainstream American business and the rise of superstar black entrepreneurs, the state of black business in America was comparatively grim at the end of the twentieth century.

In the aggregate, as the following table demonstrates, black businesses have not been as successful as other minority businesses. At the end of the twentieth century, while black business ranked second in the number of minority firms, it was next to last in sales and receipts. Why? Almost half of the number of black businesses had gross receipts of less than $10,000; 23 percent had gross receipts from $10,000 to $25,000, and, only 8,600 had gross receipts of more

Minority-Owned Business Enterprises, 1997

| | All firms | | Firms with paid employees | | | |
|---|---|---|---|---|---|---|
| **Group** | *Firms (number)* | *Sales & Receipts ($1,000)* | *Firms (number)* | *Sales & Receipts ($1,000)* | *Employees* | *Payroll ($1,000)* |
| Universe (all firms) | 20,821,935 | 18,553,243,047 | 5,295,152 | 17,907,940,321 | 103,359,815 | 2,936,492,940 |
| Total minorities | 3,039,033 | 591,259,123 | 615,222 | 516,979,920 | 4,514,699 | 95,528,782 |
| Black | 823,499 | 71,214,662 | 93,235 | 56,377,860 | 718,341 | 14,322,312 |
| Hispanic | 1,199,896 | 186,274,582 | 211,884 | 158,674,537 | 1,388,746 | 29,830,028 |
| American Indian & Alaska Native | 197,300 | 34,343,907 | 33,277 | 29,226,260 | 298,661 | 6,624,235 |
| Asian & Pacific Islander | 912,960 | 306,932,982 | 289,999 | 278,294,345 | 2,203,079 | 46,179,519 |

*Source*: 1997 Surveys of Minority- and Women-Owned Business Enterprises Company Summary, U.S. Bureau of the Census (http://www. census.gov/epcd/mwb97/group.htm)

than $1 million. In 1997, black business receipts amounted to $71.2 billion, while Hispanic receipts totaled $186.3 billion and Asian and Pacific Islanders totaled $306.9 billion. Notwithstanding a $593 billion consumer market, black business receipts of $71.2 billion amounted to only .4 percent of total American business receipts.

At the dawn of the twenty-first century, a few black businesses had gained spectacular success in new areas of enterprise, not only WWT in technology but also the sixth-ranked Barden Company in casino gaming. The Houston-based CAMAC Holdings, Inc., an international oil and refining company established by Nigerian born Kase Lawal, however, was the only black business in 2002 with receipts of over $1 billion. Black business development in the twenty-first century will differ dramatically from the traditional enterprises of the past.

## SOURCES


Bailey, Ronald W., ed. *Black Business Enterprise: Historical and Contemporary Perspectives*. New York: Basic Books, 1971.

Ballard, Donna. *Doing It for Ourselves: Success Stories of African American Women in Business*. New York: Berkley Books, 1997.

Bell, Gregory S. *In the Black: A History of African Americans on Wall Street*. New York: John Wiley, 2002.

Boston, Thomas D. *Affirmative Action and Black Entrepreneurship*. New York: Routledge, 1999.

Butler, John Sibley. *Entrepreneurship and Self-Help Among Black Americans*. Albany: State University of New York Press, 1991.

Darity, William A., and Samuel L. Myers. *Persistent Disparity: Race and Economic Inequality in the United States Since 1945*. Lyme, N.H.: Elgar, 1998.

Dingle, Derek. *Black Enterprise Titans of the B.E. 100s: Black CEOs Who Redefined and Conquered American Business*. New York: John Wiley & Sons, 1999.

Drake, St. Clair, and Horace R. Cayton. *Black Metropolis: A Study of Negro Life in a Northern City*. New York: Harcourt, Brace, 1945.

Fraser, George C. *Success Runs in Our Race: The Complete Guide to Effective Networking in the African-American Community*. New York: Morrow, 1994.

Henderson, Alexa Benson. *Atlanta Life Insurance Company: Guardian of Black Economic Dignity*. Tuscaloosa: University of Alabama Press, 1990.

House-Soremekun, Bessie. *Confronting the Odds: African American Entrepreneurship in Cleveland, Ohio*. Kent, Ohio: Kent State University Press, 2002.

Ingham, John N., and Lynne B. Feldman, *African American Business Leaders: A Biographical Dictionary*. Westport, Conn.: Greenwood, 1994.

Johnson, John H., and Lerone Bennett Jr. *Succeeding Against the Odds*. New York: Warner Books, 1989.

King, Martin Luther, Jr. *Where Do We Go From Here: Chaos or Community?* New York: Bantam Books, 1968.

LaFeber, Walter. *Michael Jordan and the New Global Capitalism*. New York: Norton, 1999.

Lewis, Reginald F., with Blair S. Walker. *"Why Should White Guys Have All the Fun?": How Reginald Lewis Created a Billion-Dollar Business Empire*. New York: Wiley, 1995.

Loury, Glenn C. *The Anatomy of Racial Inequality*. Cambridge, Mass.: Harvard University Press, 2002.

Marable, Manning. *How Capitalism Underdeveloped Black America: Problems in Race, Political Economy, and Society*. Cambridge, Mass.: South End Press, 1983.

McWhorter, John. *Losing the Race: Self-Sabotage in Black America*. New York: HarperCollins, 2001.

Ogg, Alex. *The Men Behind Def Jam: The Radical Rise of Russell Simmons and Rick Rubin*. New York: Omnibus Press, 2002.

Posner, Gerald. *Motown: Music, Money, Sex and Power*. New York: Random House, 2002.

Sowell, Thomas. *The Economics and Politics of Race: An International Perspective*. New York: Morrow, 1983.

Steele, Shelby. *The Content of Our Character: A New Vision of Race in America*. New York: St. Martin's Press, 1990.

Walker, Juliet E. K. *The History of Black Business in America: Capitalism, Race, Entrepreneurship*. New York: Macmillan, 1998.

——, ed. *Encyclopedia of African American Business History*. Westport, Conn.: Greenwood, 1999.

Weare, Walter B. *Black Business in the New South: A Social History of the North Carolina Mutual Life Insurance Company*. Urbana: University of Illinois Press, 1973.

Weems, Robert E. *Black Business in the Black Metropolis: The Chicago Metropolitan Assurance Company, 1925–1985*. Bloomington: Indiana University Press, 1996.

——. *Desegregating the Dollar: African American Consumerism in the Twentieth Century*. New York: New York University Press, 1998.

Williams, Walter E. *The State Against Blacks*. New York: New Press, 1982.

## NOTES

1. Juliet E. K. Walker, *The History of Black Business in America: Capitalism, Race, Entrepreneurship* (New York: Macmillan, 1998), 244.

2. Robert E. Weems Jr., *Desegregating the Dollar: African American Consumerism in the Twentieth Century* (New York: New York University Press, 1998), 37.

3. Walker, *History of Black Business*, 296–301.

4. Tiffany Gill, "'I Had My Own Business... So I Didn't Have to Worry': Beauty Salons, Beauty Culturists, and the Politics of African American Female

Entrepreneurship," in *Beauty and Business: Commerce, Gender, and Culture in Modern America*, ed. Phillip Scranton, 164–194 (New York: Routledge Press, 2001).

5. Martin Luther King Jr., *Where Do We Go From Here: Chaos or Community?* (New York: Harper & Row, 1967), 186.

6. Juliet E.K. Walker, "Oprah Winfrey, The Tycoon: Contextualizing the Economics of Race, Class, Gender in Black Business History in Post-Civil Rights America," in *Black Business and Economic Power*, ed. Alusine Jalloh and Toyin Falola, 484–525 (Rochester, N.Y.: University of Rochester Press, 2002).

7. Juliet E.K. Walker, "White Corporate America: The New Arbiter of Race," in *Constructing Corporate America: History, Politics, Culture*, ed. Kenneth Lipartito and David Scilica, 246–293 (New York: Oxford University Press, 2004).

PART III

# *Chronology, 1939–2005*

ROBERT L. HARRIS JR.

1939

The National Association for the Advancement of Colored People (NAACP) Legal Defense and Educational Fund is established as a distinct organization

The National Negro Bowling Association is founded in Detroit, Michigan

Germany invades Poland, leading to the outbreak of World War II

More than 75,000 people attend Marian Anderson's concert at the Lincoln Memorial

1940

Richard Wright's *Native Son* is published

Benjamin O. Davis Sr. becomes the highest-ranking African American in the armed services with appointment as brigadier general

Hattie McDaniel is the first African American to win an Academy Award as best supporting actress for *Gone with the Wind*

1941

The 99th Pursuit Squadron, an all-black air combat unit, is established at the Tuskegee Institute

A major race riot breaks out in East St. Louis, Illinois

A. Philip Randolph, founder of the Brotherhood of Sleeping Car Porters, schedules the March on Washington for July 1

President Franklin D. Roosevelt issues Executive Order 8802 barring discrimination in employment in defense industries and setting up a Committee on Fair Employment Practices

Japanese attack Pearl Harbor; Dorie Miller, a black cook without training as a gunner, shoots down four planes and is later awarded the Navy Cross

**1942**

William L. Dawson of Illinois is elected to the U.S. House of Representatives

Hugh N. Mulzac is the first African American to become captain of a U.S. merchant ship, the *Booker T. Washington*

**1943**

Race riot in Detroit, Michigan

Paul Robeson appears in *Othello* on Broadway, the first black actor to play a title role

The Professional Golfers Association approves white-only membership

Adam Clayton Powell Jr. of New York is elected to the U.S. House of Representatives

**1944**

The United Negro College Fund is founded by the president of the Tuskegee Institute, Frederick Douglass Patterson

The U.S. Supreme Court, in *Smith v. Allwright*, overturns the white primary and rules that African Americans cannot be denied the right to vote in primary elections

**1945**

The 332nd Fighter Squadron, called the Tuskegee Airmen, participate in an air raid over Berlin and later win a Distinguished Unit Citation

Mary McLeod Bethune, W. E. B. Du Bois, and Walter White attend the United Nations Organizing Conference in San Francisco, California

World War II ends

John H. Johnson publishes the inaugural issue of *Ebony Magazine*

**1946**

The Supreme Court rules against segregation in interstate bus travel in *Morgan v. Virginia*

Ralph J. Bunche is appointed director of the Trusteeship Division at the United Nations

The National Negro Congress petitions the United Nations against racial discrimination and brutality in the United States

1947

The NAACP petitions the United Nations against racial discrimination in the United States

The Congress of Racial Equality (CORE) initiates its Journey of Reconciliation to test compliance with the Supreme Court decision in *Morgan v. Virginia*

Rosa Lee Ingram, a Georgia tenant farmer, is convicted with two of her sons and sentenced to death for killing a white man whom she charged attacked her

Jackie Robinson crosses the "color line" to play for the Brooklyn Dodgers of the National League, desegregating major league baseball; Larry Doby plays for the Cleveland Indians of the American League

President Harry S. Truman's Commission on Civil Rights issues its report *To Secure These Rights*

John Hope Franklin's *From Slavery to Freedom: A History of Negro Americans* is published

1948

The United Nations General Assembly adopts the Universal Declaration of Human Rights

The U.S. Supreme Court rules in *Sipuel v. University of Oklahoma* that states must offer equal legal education for African Americans

The U.S. Supreme Court rules in *Shelly v. Kramer* against restrictive covenants in housing deeds

A. Philip Randolph threatens civil disobedience against segregation and discrimination in the Selective Service System

President Harry S. Truman issues Executive Order 9980 to develop a Fair Employment Practices Board to end racial discrimination in federal employment and Executive Order 9981 to end racial segregation in the military

Alice Coachman becomes the first African American woman to win an Olympic medal, for the high jump

William T. Coleman Jr. is the first black law clerk in the U.S. Supreme Court

Edward R. Dudley is the first African American appointed as an ambassador and is posted to Liberia

1949

Wesley A. Brown becomes the first black graduate of the U.S. Naval Academy at Annapolis, Maryland

"Rhythm & blues" comes to be used to describe a style of commercial black music, taking the place of the term "race records"

Jackie Robinson of the Brooklyn Dodgers becomes the first African American to win the National League's Most Valuable Player Award

William Still's *Troubled Island* is the first opera written by an African American to be produced by a major opera company, premiering at the New York City Opera

Paul Robeson, speaking at the Paris Peace Conference, states that African Americans are not likely to go to war on behalf of the United States, which had oppressed them for generations, against the Soviet Union, which had elevated them to human dignity in one generation

**1950**

Ralph J. Bunche becomes the first black person to win the Nobel Peace Prize, for mediating the crisis in Palestine

Gwendolyn Brooks is the first African American to win a Pulitzer Prize for her book of poetry, *Annie Allen*

Juanita Hall is the first African American to win a Tony Award for her portrayal of Bloody Mary in the Broadway musical *South Pacific*

The U.S. Supreme Court rules in *McLaurin v. Board of Regents* against segregating students in classrooms at the University of Oklahoma

In *Sweatt v. Painter*, the U.S. Supreme Court rules that equality of education means more than comparable facilities and provides a precedent that "separate" is in itself "unequal"

The U.S. Supreme Court rules in *Henderson v. United States* that black passengers on railroad dining cars cannot be forced to eat behind a partition

Earl Lloyd is the first African American to play in a National Basketball Association game as a member of the Washington Capitols

Arthur Dovington of the Eastern Amateur League Atlantic City Seagulls is the first African American to play organized ice hockey

Althea Gibson is the first African American to play tennis in the U.S. Open

The U.S. State Department revokes Paul Robeson's passport for his refusal to sign an affidavit denying that he had ever been a member of the Communist Party

The American Medical Association admits its first black delegate to its annual meeting

Helen O. Dickens becomes the first black woman admitted to the American College of Surgeons

W. E. B. Du Bois runs for the U.S. Senate from New York as the American Labor Party candidate

**1951**

Janet Collins becomes the first black prima ballerina as a member of the Metropolitan Opera

A race riot erupts in Cicero, Illinois, over African Americans moving into a white neighborhood

The U.S. Department of State denies W. E. B. Du Bois a passport, alleging that he is an unregistered agent of a foreign government

Sugar Ray Robinson becomes the world middleweight boxing champion

**1952**

Ralph Ellison's novel *Invisible Man* wins the National Book Award

Charlotta Bass, editor of the *California Eagle*, is the first black woman to run for vice president of the United States as a candidate of the Progressive Party

The Tuskegee Institute's Department of Records and Research notes that for the first time in seventy-one years there is no reported lynching in the United States

**1953**

James Baldwin's first novel, *Go Tell It on the Mountain*, is published

Willie Mae "Big Mama" Thornton's "Hound Dog," later popularized by Elvis Presley, is number one on the *Billboard* Rhythm & Blues chart for seven weeks

The U.S. Supreme Court rules against segregation in Washington, D.C. restaurants

James Carter, Vivian Carter Bracken, and Calvin Carter start Vee Jay Records in Chicago, recording many popular rhythm and blues groups and later helping introduce The Beatles to American audiences

**1954**

Ralph J. Bunche becomes the highest-ranking American citizen at the United Nations as Undersecretary

In *Brown v. Board of Education*, the U.S. Supreme Court rules that separate schools are inherently unequal and overturns the 1896 *Plessy v. Ferguson* decision that validated "separate but equal"

Malcolm X becomes minister of Nation of Islam Temple No. 7 in Harlem

Martin Luther King Jr. is appointed pastor of the Dexter Avenue Baptist Church in Montgomery, Alabama

The National Negro Network began broadcasting as the first black-owned radio network

Benjamin O. Davis Jr. becomes the first black general in the U.S. Air Force

Charles C. Diggs Jr. is elected to the U.S. House of Representatives from Michigan

**1955**

Emmett Till, a fourteen-year-old African American from Chicago, is lynched in Money, Mississippi

Rosa Parks's arrest for refusing to give up her seat sets off the Montgomery, Alabama, bus boycott

Marian Anderson becomes the first African American to sing in the New York City Metropolitan Opera House

Alice Childress is the first black woman to win an Obie Award for her play *Trouble in Mind*

Roy Wilkins becomes executive secretary of the NAACP after the death of Walter White

The Interstate Commerce Commission bars segregation on buses, in waiting rooms, and on railroad coaches in interstate transportation

### 1956

More than one hundred members of Congress sign the "Southern Manifesto," which denounces the Supreme Court decision in *Brown v. Board of Education* and calls on states to resist desegregation

Autherine Lucy becomes the first black student to enroll at the University of Alabama

The Montgomery bus boycott ends when a federal court rules that racial segregation on the buses is unconstitutional

The Colored Methodist Episcopal Church changes its name to the Christian Methodist Episcopal Church

Floyd Patterson becomes the youngest world heavyweight boxing champion at age twenty-one

Nell C. Jackson becomes the first African American named as head coach of a U.S. Olympic team, track and field

Robert N. C. Nix is elected to the U.S. House of Representatives from Pennsylvania

### 1957

The Southern Christian Leadership Conference (SCLC) is founded in New Orleans and headquartered in Atlanta

Ghana becomes an independent nation

The Prayer Pilgrimage for Justice is held at the Lincoln Memorial in Washington, D.C.

President Dwight D. Eisenhower sends troops into Little Rock, Arkansas, to protect the black youngsters who desegregated Central High School

President Dwight D. Eisenhower signs into law the first civil rights bill since 1875; it authorizes the federal government to intervene on behalf of citizens denied the right to vote, makes the civil rights section of the Justice Department a division, and establishes the U.S. Commission on Civil Rights

Malcolm X starts the newspaper *Muhammad Speaks*

Charles Sifford is the first African American to win a major professional golf tournament

Althea Gibson becomes the first African American tennis player to win the singles and doubles title at Wimbledon, England

1958

Martin Luther King Jr. is stabbed in Harlem while autographing copies of his book *Stride Toward Freedom*

Paul and Eslanda Robeson leave the United States for the Soviet Union, where they reside for five years

Clifton W. Wharton Sr. becomes the first African American to head a European embassy, in Romania

Alvin Ailey founds the Alvin Ailey Dance Theatre

1959

Lorraine Hansberry's *Raisin in the Sun* is produced on Broadway

Berry Gordy starts Motown Records in Detroit, Michigan

W. E. B. Du Bois receives the Lenin Peace Prize

Martin Luther King Jr. travels to India to learn more about Mohandas Gandhi and nonviolent direct action

Dorothy Dandridge wins a Golden Globe Award as best actress in a musical, *Porgy and Bess*

1960

Four black students from North Carolina A&T University in Greensboro, North Carolina, sit in at a Woolworth's lunch counter that has refused service to African Americans, inaugurating the sit-in movement

President Dwight D. Eisenhower signs into law the Civil Rights Act of 1960, authorizing federal courts to help register voters in areas where they had been denied the right to vote because of racial discrimination

Harry Belafonte becomes the first African American to win an Emmy Award for his television special *Tonight with Harry Belafonte*

Wilma Rudolph becomes the first woman from the United States to win three gold medals for track and field in the Olympics

The Student Non-Violent Coordinating Committee (SNCC) is founded at Shaw University in Raleigh, North Carolina

Martin Luther King Jr. is arrested with fifty demonstrators at Rich's Department Store in Atlanta and sentenced to four months at the Reidsville State Prison; Robert F. Kennedy telephones the Georgia judge who sentenced King and asks for his release, which happens the following day

The Sharpeville Massacre in South Africa leaves seventy-two dead and more than two hundred injured

Albert Luthuli of South Africa wins the Nobel Peace Prize

1961

The Congress of Racial Equality (CORE) begins the "freedom rides," to designate buses and terminals

Ernie Davis, a running back at Syracuse University, becomes the first African American to win the Heisman Trophy as the nation's best college football player

Charlayne Hunter and Hamilton Holmes are the first black students to enroll at the University of Georgia

Whitney M. Young Jr. becomes executive director of the National Urban League

James B. Parsons is appointed the first black federal district judge

W. E. B. Du Bois joins the American Communist Party and leaves the country for Ghana, where the President Kwame Nkrumah asks him to coordinate publication of the *Encyclopedia Africana*

1962

Jackie Robinson becomes the first African American inducted into the Baseball Hall of Fame in Cooperstown, New York

The National Baptist Progressive Convention breaks away from the National Baptist Convention

James Meredith becomes the first black student to attend the University of Mississippi

Edward Brooke is elected Attorney General of Massachusetts

Marjorie Lawson is the first black woman elected a judge in Washington, D.C.

John "Buck" O'Neill becomes the first black coach of a major league baseball team, heading the Chicago Cubs

Wilt Chamberlain is the first National Basketball Association player to score one hundred points in a game

Mel Goode, with ABC, becomes the first African American television news commentator

Augustus F. Hawkins is elected to the U.S. House of Representatives from California

1963

Medgar Evers, NAACP Field Secretary in Mississippi, is assassinated outside his home in Jackson

Vivian Malone and James Hood enroll at the University of Alabama despite the effort of Governor George Wallace to block their entrance

Arthur Ashe becomes the first African American to join the U.S. Davis Cup tennis team

Martin Luther King Jr. writes his famous "Letter from Birmingham City Jail"

In Birmingham, Alabama, Chief of Police Eugene "Bull" Conner uses high-powered water hoses and dogs against demonstrators

More than 250,000 attend the March on Washington, at which Martin Luther King Jr. delivers his renowned "I Have a Dream" speech

Four young black girls are killed in the bombing of the Sixteenth Street Baptist Church in Birmingham, Alabama

Elijah Muhammad suspends Malcolm X as a minister in the Nation of Islam because of his saying about the assassination of President John F. Kennedy that the chickens had come home to roost

## 1964

The Civil Rights Act of 1964 outlaws discrimination in most places of public accommodation, establishes the Equal Employment Opportunity Commission, and requires the end of racial discrimination in all federally assisted programs

The Twenty-fourth Amendment to the Constitution, which bans use of the poll tax in federal elections, is ratified

Malcolm X breaks with the Nation of Islam and starts the Muslim Mosque and the Organization of Afro-American Unity

Carl T. Rowan becomes director of the United States Information Agency and a member of the National Security Council

James E. Chaney, Andrew Goodman, and Michael Schwerner, civil rights workers, are murdered in Philadelphia, Mississippi

Sidney Poitier is the first African American to win an Academy Award for best actor, for *Lilies of the Field*

Muhammad Ali (Cassius Clay) wins the world heavyweight boxing title

Martin Luther King Jr. is awarded the Nobel Peace Prize

John Conyers is elected to the U.S. House of Representatives from Michigan

Nelson Mandela is sentenced to life imprisonment in South Africa

Samuel Kountz is one of the surgeons who performs the first successful kidney transplant for individuals who are not identical twins

Mississippi Freedom Summer organizes freedom schools and registers voters for the Mississippi Freedom Democratic Party, which unsuccessfully challenges the whites-only Mississippi Democratic Party at the national convention in Atlantic City, New Jersey

## 1965

Malcolm X is assassinated at the Audubon Ballroom in Harlem

Alex Haley publishes *The Autobiography of Malcolm X*

The Selma to Montgomery march for voting rights is staged

The Voting Rights Act provides for suspension of literacy tests, appointment of federal examiners to insure equitable voting registration, and federal protection for citizens seeking the right to vote

Thurgood Marshall is appointed Solicitor General of the United States

Joan Murray, at WCBS in New York, becomes one of the first black women newscasters

The Watts Riot in Los Angeles, California, leaves 34 dead and 900 injured; more than 3,500 are arrested

1966

Milton Olive becomes the first African American to win the Medal of Honor for heroism in the Vietnam War

Robert C. Weaver becomes the first African American member of the Cabinet as secretary of Housing and Urban Development

Bill Cosby is the first African American to win an Emmy for best actor in a dramatic series for *I Spy*

Floyd McKissick becomes director of the Congress of Racial Equality (CORE)

Andrew Brimmer becomes the first African American governor of the Federal Reserve Bank

Kwame Toure (Stokely Carmichael) becomes chairman of the Student Non-Violent Coordinating Committee (SNCC)

Bill Russell becomes the first black National Basketball Association head coach with the Boston Celtics

Emmett Ashford, of the American League, becomes the first black major league baseball umpire

During the James Meredith March Against Fear through Mississippi, Willie Ricks and Stokely Carmichael issue a call for "Black Power"

Huey P. Newton and Bobby Seale organize the Black Panther Party in Oakland, California

Edward W. Brooke is elected to the U.S. Senate from Massachusetts, the first African American elected to the Senate since Reconstruction

Constance Baker Motley becomes the first black woman appointed to the federal bench

1967

Riots in Newark, Detroit, Chicago, and thirty-seven other cities

President Lyndon B. Johnson appoints Thurgood Marshall the first black Supreme Court Justice

The U.S. Supreme Court rules in *Loving v. Virginia* that the state law against interracial marriage is unconstitutional

The Black Power Conference is held in Newark

Martin Luther King Jr. announces his opposition to the Vietnam War

Muhammad Ali has his heavyweight championship title removed after refusing induction into the military

The U.S. House of Representatives votes to expel Adam Clayton Powell on charges of misappropriation of funds; he is reelected by his district in Harlem, and the U.S. Supreme Court rules in 1968 that Congress cannot deny him his seat

Carl B. Stokes is elected the first black mayor of Cleveland, Ohio, and Richard B. Hatcher becomes the first black mayor of Gary, Indiana

1968

Martin Luther King Jr. is assassinated in Memphis, Tennessee

Violence disrupts 125 cities across the nation

The Kerner Commission, appointed by President Lyndon B. Johnson after the riots during the summer of 1967, reports that the nation is becoming two societies, one white and one black, separate and unequal

Elizabeth D. Koontz is elected the first black president of the National Education Association

The Poor Peoples' Campaign is organized by the Southern Christian Leadership Conference (SCLC)

The Housing Rights Act of 1968 prohibits discrimination in the sale or rental of housing

Henry Lewis becomes the first African American to lead a symphony orchestra as director of the New Jersey Symphony

At the Olympic Games in Mexico City, Tommie Smith and John Carlos give the Black Power salute on the medal stand and are followed later by Lee Evans, Larry James, and Ron Freeman, who wear black berets and give the Black Power salute

Arthur Ashe wins the U.S. Open Tennis Championship

O.J. Simpson wins the Heisman Trophy

The American Football League's Marlin Briscoe of the Denver Broncos becomes the first black starting quarterback in professional football

Shirley Chisholm of Brooklyn, New York, becomes the first black woman elected to the U.S. Congress

Fashion model Naomi Sims is the first black woman to appear on the cover of *Ladies Home Journal*; the following year, she appears on the cover of *Life Magazine*

1969

Chicago police officers kill Black Panther Party members Fred Hampton and Mark Clark

Clifton R. Wharton Jr. becomes the first African American to head a major predominantly white university as president of Michigan State University

Patricia Roberts Harris becomes the first black woman to head a law school as dean of the Howard University School of Law

Angela Davis is dismissed from her faculty position at the University of California at Los Angeles for membership in the Communist Party; she appeals the dismissal and is reinstated by the courts

Louis Stokes is elected to the U.S. House of Representatives from Ohio

Gwendolyn Brooks succeeds Carl Sandburg as poet laureate of Illinois

Molefi Asante and Robert Singleton start the *Journal of Black Studies*

*The Learning Tree*, by Gordon Parks, is the first film directed for a major studio, Warner Brothers, by an African American

Arthur Mitchell and Karel Shook found the Dance Theatre of Harlem

The Studio Museum in Harlem is established to provide working space for black artists

**1970**

Cheryl A. Brown, Miss Iowa, is the first African American to compete in the Miss America Beauty Pageant

Kenneth Gibson becomes the first black mayor of Newark, New Jersey

Two black students at Jackson State College in Jackson, Mississippi, are killed in a police attack and another twelve are injured

*Essence Magazine*, geared to black women, begins publication

*Black Enterprise Magazine*, with a focus on economic development, begins publication

Charles Gordon wins the Pulitzer Prize for his play *No Place to Be Somebody*

Daniel Patrick Moynihan, domestic policy adviser to President Richard M. Nixon, suggests a period of "benign neglect" on the issue of race

Charles Rangel defeats Adam Clayton Powell for a seat in the U.S. House of Representatives from New York

George W. Collins is elected to the U.S. House of Representatives from Illinois

Ronald V. Dellums is elected to the U.S. House of Representatives from California

Ralph H. Metcalfe is elected to the U.S. House of Representatives from Illinois

Norma Holloway Johnson, who later presided over the grand jury investigation of President William Jefferson Clinton, is appointed to the U.S. District Court in Washington, D.C.

**1971**

In a raid on the Republic of New Africa headquarters in Jackson, Mississippi, by local police and FBI agents, one police officer is killed

The U.S. Supreme Court rules in *Swann v. Charlotte-Mecklenburg* that busing schoolchildren for racial integration is constitutional

*Sweet Sweetback's Baadassss Song*, a black independent film by Melvin Van Peeples, influences a wave of "blaxploitation" films

Jesse Jackson founds People United to Save Humanity (PUSH)

Walter Fauntroy is elected to the House of Representatives from Washington, D.C.

Parren J. Mitchell is elected to the U.S. House of Representatives from Maryland

Charles C. Diggs Jr. becomes the first chairman of the Congressional Black Caucus

1972

Benjamin Hooks becomes the first black member of the Federal Communication Commission

Shirley Chisholm seeks the Democratic Party Presidential nomination

Vernon Jordan becomes executive director of the National Urban League

The U.S. Supreme Court overturns the 1967 conviction of Muhammad Ali for draft evasion

The first Black National Political Convention is held in Gary, Indiana

Frank Willis, a security guard at the Watergate Offices, discovers men breaking into the Democratic Party National Headquarters; the ensuing scandal ends two years later in Richard M. Nixon's resignation from the presidency

James M. Rodger Jr. of Durham, North Carolina, becomes the first black Teacher of the Year

Yvonne Braithwaite Burke is elected to the U.S. House of Representatives from California

Barbara Jordan is elected to the U.S. House of Representatives from Texas

1973

Tom Bradley becomes the first black mayor of Los Angeles, California

Marian Wright Edelman founds the Children's Defense Fund

Barbara Sizemore, of Washington, D.C., becomes the first black woman to be named superintendent of schools for a major city

Andrew Young is elected to the U.S. House of Representatives from Georgia

Cardiss Collins is elected to the U.S. House of Representatives from Illinois

1974

Henry "Hank" Aaron breaks Babe Ruth's record for most career home runs

Elaine Brown becomes chairperson of the Black Panther Party

Maynard Jackson becomes the first black mayor of Atlanta

Harold E. Ford is elected to the U.S. House of Representatives from Tennessee

Frank Robinson of the Cleveland Indians becomes the first black manager of a major league baseball team

Fashion model Beverly Johnson becomes the first black woman on the cover of *Vogue* magazine

**1975**

President Gerald Ford appoints William T. Coleman to serve as secretary of transportation

Margaret Bush Wilson becomes the first woman to head the NAACP board of directors

Daniel "Chappie" James becomes the first black four-star general

Gloria Randle Scott becomes the first black woman to serve as national president of the Girl Scouts, U.S.A.

Marva Collins founds the Westside Preparatory School in Chicago

Arthur Ashe becomes the first black male to win the Wimbledon Tennis Championship

Elijah Muhammad dies and is succeeded by his son Wallace D. Muhammad as head of the Nation of Islam; Wallace D. Muhammad moves the group more closely to orthodox Islam

Mervyn Dymally is elected lieutenant governor of California

The Combahee River Collective, a black feminist organization, is founded in New York City and raises the issue of homophobia among African Americans

**1976**

Barbara Jordan becomes the first African American to deliver the keynote address at a major party political convention

Pauli Murray is ordained as the first black woman priest in the Episcopal Church

Alex Haley publishes *Roots*

Unita Blackwell, of Mayersville, becomes the first black woman mayor in Mississippi

Mary Frances Berry is named chancellor of the University of Colorado at Boulder

Kenneth Gibson becomes the first black president of the U.S. Conference of Mayors

The Association for the Study of Afro-American Life and History extends Negro History Week (established in 1926) to Black History Month

**1977**

Clifford Alexander Jr. becomes the first black secretary of the army

Mary Frances Berry becomes assistant secretary for education in the Department of Health, Education, and Welfare

Louis Farrakhan breaks with Wallace D. Muhammad and revives the Nation of Islam

The television miniseries *Roots* attracts the largest audience in television history

Eleanor Holmes Norton becomes the first black woman to head the Equal Employment Opportunity Commission

Clifton R. Wharton is named Chancellor of the State University of New York, the nation's largest university

Andrew Young becomes the first black U.S. Ambassador to the United Nations

Patricia Roberts Harris, secretary of housing and urban development is the first black woman appointed to the Cabinet; President Jimmy Carter later appoints her as secretary of health, education, and welfare

Benjamin L. Hooks becomes executive director of the NAACP

1978

The U.S. Supreme Court rules in *Regents of the University of California v. Bakke* that race might be considered in college admissions, but that quotas for minority students are illegal

Religious leader Jim Jones leads his followers, most of them African American, in mass suicide in Guyana

James Alan McPherson's book of short stories, *Elbow Room*, wins the Pulitzer Prize in fiction

Toni Morrison wins the National Book Critics Circle Award for *Song of Solomon*

Sonia Sanchez wins the American Book Award for *I've Been a Woman*, a book of poems

The U.S. Postal Service issues its first stamp, honoring Harriet Tubman, in the Black Heritage Series

Faye Wattleton, at age twenty-five, becomes president of Planned Parenthood, the first black woman and the youngest person to hold the position

Muhammad Ali, in defeating Leon Spinks, becomes the first boxer to win the heavyweight championship three times

Guion S. Bluford Jr., Frederick D. Gregory, and Ronald E. McNair become the first African Americans in the astronaut program

The Church of Jesus Christ of Latter-Day Saints (Mormons) removes its 148-year ban against black men becoming clergy

Ernest Morial becomes the first black mayor of New Orleans

Bennett Stewart is elected to the U.S. House of Representatives from Illinois

Julian Dixon is elected to the U.S. House of Representatives from California

George "Mickey" Leland is elected to the U.S. House of Representatives from Texas

Melvin H. Evans is elected to the U.S. House of Representatives as a nonvoting delegate from the Virgin Islands

1979

Amalya L. Kearse is the first woman appointed to the U.S. Court of Appeals for the Second Circuit

Lucille Clifton becomes poet laureate of Maryland

Max Robinson, with ABC, becomes the first black news anchor

"Rapper's Delight," by the Sugar Hill Gang, gains national radio airplay and sparks interest in rap music

Karen Stevenson, a student at the University of North Carolina at Chapel Hill, becomes the first African American woman to be named a Rhodes Scholar

Franklin A. Thomas becomes the first African American to head a major foundation as president of the Ford Foundation

Arthur Lewis, a Princeton University professor born in St. Lucia, becomes the first black man to win a Nobel Prize in economics

Richard Arrington becomes the first black mayor of Birmingham, Alabama

William H. Gray III is elected to the U.S. House of Representatives from Pennsylvania

1980

Toni Cade Bambara wins the National Book Award for *The Salt Eaters*

Robert L. Johnson starts a cable company, Black Entertainment Television, in Washington, D.C.

Levi Watkins, of Johns Hopkins University Hospital, makes the first surgical implant of a battery-operated heart-regulating device

Mervyn Dymally is elected to the U.S. House of Representatives from California

George W. Crockett is elected to the U.S. House of Representatives from Michigan

Gus Savage is elected to the U.S. House of Representatives from Illinois

Harold Washington is elected to the U.S. House of Representatives from Illinois

The National Black Independent Party is formed and requires equal male and female representation in all leadership positions

1981

President Ronald Reagan appoints Samuel Pierce Jr. to serve as secretary of housing and urban development

Bryant Gumbel becomes co-anchor of television's "Today" on NBC

The Morehouse School of Medicine is started in Atlanta

Jewel Jackson McCabe founds the National Council of 100 Black Women

Arnetta R. Hubbard becomes the first woman president of the National Bar Association

Edolphus "Ed" Towns is elected to the U.S. House of Representatives from New York

Andrew Young is elected mayor of Atlanta

1982

Alan Wheat is elected to the U.S. House of Representatives from Missouri

John E. Jacob becomes President of the National Urban League

Charles Fuller wins the Pulitzer Prize for *A Soldier's Play*

Louis Gossett Jr. wins the Academy Award for best supporting actor in *An Officer and a Gentleman*

Quincy Jones wins five Grammy Awards for *The Dude*

Hershel Walker wins the Heisman Trophy

1983

Harold Washington is elected the first black mayor of Chicago

Alice Walker wins the Pulitzer Prize for *The Color Purple*

Gloria Naylor wins the National Book Award for *The Women of Brewster Place*

Martin Luther King Jr.'s birthday, January 15th, becomes a national holiday

Vanessa Williams becomes the first African American to be named Miss America, but resigns ten months later after *Penthouse Magazine* publishes nude photos of her; Suzette Charles, also an African American, who is first runner-up, becomes Miss America

Guion S. Bluford Jr. becomes the first black astronaut in space aboard the *Challenger*

Jesse L. Jackson successfully negotiates with President Hafez al-Hassad to release Lt. Robert Goodman, a navigator-bombardier whose plane was shot down over Syria

Katie Hall is elected to the U.S. House of Representatives from Indiana

Charles Hayes is elected to the U.S. House of Representatives from Illinois

Major Robert Owens is elected to the U.S. House of Representatives from New York

1984

Jesse L. Jackson wins 17 percent of the Democratic Party Presidential Primary vote

W. Wilson Goode is elected the first black mayor of Philadelphia

Shirley Chisholm starts the National Political Caucus of Black Women

Rev. Leontine T. C. Kelly becomes the first black woman bishop of a major religious denomination as bishop of the United Methodist Church in the San Francisco area

Bishop Desmond Tutu of South Africa wins the Nobel Peace Prize

Octavia Butler wins the Hugo Award for science fiction writing

*The Cosby Show* premieres and becomes the most watched situation comedy in television history

Michael Jackson wins eight Grammy Awards

Wynton Marsalis becomes the first musician to win Grammy Awards for both jazz and classical recordings

John Thompson becomes the first black coach to win the NCAA Basketball Championship with Georgetown

Carl Lewis wins four gold medals at the Olympics, equaling Jesse Owens's record

Washington, D.C., Delegate Walter Fauntroy, TransAfrica President Randall Robinson, and civil rights activist Mary Frances Berry are arrested for sitting in at the South African Embassy and spark nationwide protests against American policy toward South Africa

### 1985

Rita Dove wins the Pulitzer Prize for her collection of poetry, *Thomas and Beulah*

Bo Jackson wins the Heisman Trophy

Eddie Robinson of Grambling University becomes college football's top winning coach

Seven adults and four children are killed in the Philadelphia police raid on MOVE, a black radical group, in which a state police helicopter drops a bomb on the organization's house

Sherian Cadoria becomes a brigadier general, the highest rank held by a woman in the U.S. Army

Sharon Pratt Kelly becomes the first woman treasurer of the National Democratic Party

### 1986

Wole Soyinka of Nigeria is the first black writer to win the Nobel Prize in literature

Sidney Barthelemy is elected mayor of New Orleans

Floyd Flake is elected to the U.S. House of Representatives from New York

John Lewis is elected to the U.S. House of Representatives from Georgia

Martin Luther Kings Jr.'s bronze bust, by sculptor John Wilson, is the first statue of an African American placed in the U.S. Capitol

Mike Tyson becomes the youngest world heavyweight boxing champion at age twenty

Oprah Winfrey becomes the first black woman to host a nationally syndicated television talk program

Edward Perkins becomes the first black U.S. ambassador to the Republic of South Africa

Ronald McNair and fellow crewmembers perish in the explosion of space shuttle *Challenger*

Michael Griffith is hit by a car and killed in Howard Beach, a section of Queens, New York, when he tries to escape from a gang of white youths who attack him and two companions as they seek help for their disabled car

1987

Johnetta B. Cole becomes the first woman president of Spelman College, an all-female, historically black college in Atlanta

Niara Sudarkasa becomes the first woman president of Lincoln University in Pennsylvania, the oldest historically black college in the United States

Mae Jemison becomes the first black female astronaut

Reginald F. Lewis purchases the multinational food company Beatrice International in a leveraged buyout, and as head of TLC Beatrice becomes the wealthiest black businessman in the country

Walter E. Massey becomes the first African American to head the American Association for the Advancement of Science

African Americans riot in Tampa, Florida, after a twenty-three-year-old black man dies while police try to subdue him with a chokehold

Kurt Schmoke is elected the first black mayor of Baltimore, Maryland

Mike Espy is elected to the U.S. House of Representatives from Mississippi

Kweisi Mfume is elected to the U.S. House of Representatives from Maryland

August Wilson's *Fences* wins a Pulitzer Prize for drama and four Tony Awards for best play, best director (Lloyd Richards), best actor (James Earl Jones), and best actress (Mary Alice)

1988

Colin Powell becomes a four-star general and the first black chief of staff for the U.S. Armed Forces in 1989

Toni Morrison wins the Pulitzer Prize for her novel *Beloved*

Jesse Jackson places second at the Democratic National Convention with 1,218 votes to the party's presidential nominee Michael Dukakis's 2,876

Temple University becomes the first university to offer a doctorate in African American studies

Rep. John Conyers of Michigan introduces legislation calling for Congress to consider reparations for enslavement and segregation

Donald M. Payne is elected to the U.S. House of Representatives from New Jersey

Debi Thomas becomes the first African American figure skater to win an Olympic medal

Florence Griffith-Joyner becomes the first American woman to win four medals in the Olympic Games

Eugene Marino in Atlanta becomes the first African American archbishop in the Roman Catholic Church

Naquib Mahfouz of Egypt is the second black writer to win the Nobel Prize in literature

1989

The U.S. Supreme Court, ruling in *City of Richmond v. Croson*, strikes down the city's minority set-aside program

Ronald H. Brown becomes the first black chairman of the Democratic National Committee

David Dinkins becomes the first black mayor of New York City

Yusef Hawkins, sixteen years old, is shot to death in the Bensonhurst section of Brooklyn, New York, by white youths who attack him and three friends who had traveled there to consider buying a used car

President George H. W. Bush appoints Louis Sullivan to serve as secretary of health and human services

Although acquitted by a jury, the U.S. Senate tries and convicts U.S. District Court Judge Alcee Hastings on articles of impeachment for fraud, corruption, and perjury

Arsenio Hall becomes the first African American to host a late night television talk show

Barbara Harris becomes the first woman bishop in the Episcopal Church

Andre Ware from the University of Houston is the first black quarterback to win the Heisman Trophy

Art Shell, of the Los Angeles Raiders, becomes the first black head coach in the National Football League

Bill White is named president of the National League in baseball, the first African American to head a major sports league

1990

Nelson Mandela is released from prison in South Africa after serving twenty-seven years

L. Douglas Wilder becomes the first black governor of Virginia and the first African American ever elected as a governor

Sharon Pratt Kelly becomes the first woman mayor of Washington, D.C.

William J. Jefferson is elected to the U.S. House of Representatives from Louisiana

Craig Washington is elected to the U.S. House of Representatives from Texas

Maxine Waters is elected to the U.S. House of Representatives from California

Barbara Rose-Collins is elected to the U.S. House of Representatives from Michigan

Gary Franks, a Republican, is elected to the U.S. House of Representatives from Connecticut

Eleanor Holmes Norton is elected to the U.S. House of Representatives as delegate from the District of Columbia

Marguerite Ross Barnett becomes president of the University of Houston

Carole Gist becomes the first African American to be crowned Miss USA

Debbye Turner is named Miss America

Richard Parsons, chief executive officer of the Dime Savings Bank in New York City, is the first black executive of a nonminority savings bank

Denzel Washington wins an Academy Award for best supporting actor in *Glory*

Charles Johnson wins the National Book Award for his novel *Middle Passage*, the first black male since Ralph Ellison to win the award

August Wilson wins a second Pulitzer Prize for drama for his play *The Piano Lesson*

**1991**

Emmanuel Cleaver is elected the first black mayor of Kansas City, Missouri

Wellington Webb is elected the first black mayor of Denver, Colorado

Willie Herenton is elected the first black mayor of Memphis, Tennessee

Roland Burris becomes the first African American attorney general for the state of Illinois

Marjorie Vincent is named Miss America

William H. Gray III becomes president of the United Negro College Fund

Thurgood Marshall announces his retirement from the U.S. Supreme Court

Anita Hill, in the confirmation hearings of Clarence Thomas for appointment to the U.S. Supreme Court, charges Thomas with sexual harassment

Clarence Thomas is confirmed as a U.S. Supreme Court Justice

Whoopi Goldberg wins an Academy Award for best supporting actress in *Ghost*

Shelby Steele wins the National Book Critics Circle Award for his book *The Content of Our Character*

Los Angeles police are videotaped beating motorist Rodney King

Workers excavating a construction site in lower Manhattan, New York City, uncover a historic African burial ground

Basketball star Earvin “Magic” Johnson announces that he had the AIDS virus and retires from the NBA

**1992**

Carol Moseley Braun from Illinois becomes the first black woman elected to the U.S. Senate

Alcee Hastings is elected to the U.S. House of Representatives from Florida
Lucien Blackwell is elected to the U.S. House of Representatives from Pennsylvania
Sanford Bishop is elected to the U.S. House of Representatives from Georgia
Corrine Brown is elected to the U.S. House of Representatives from Florida
Eva Clayton is elected to the U.S. House of Representatives from North Carolina
Jim Clyburn is elected to the U.S. House of Representatives from South Carolina
Cleo Fields is elected to the U.S. House of Representatives from Louisiana
Earl F. Hilliard is elected to the U.S. House of Representatives from Alabama
Eddie B. Johnson is elected to the U.S. House of Representatives from Texas
Cynthia A. McKinney is elected to the U.S. House of Representatives from Georgia
Carrie Meek is elected to the U.S. House of Representatives from Florida
Melvin J. Reynolds is elected to the U.S. House of Representatives from Illinois
Bobby Rush is elected to the U.S. House of Representatives from Illinois
Robert C. Scott is elected to the U.S. House of Representatives from Virginia
Walter Tucker III is elected to the U.S. House of Representatives from California
Melvin Watt is elected to the U.S. House of Representatives from North Carolina
Albert Wynn is elected to the U.S. House of Representatives from Maryland
Former U.S. Representative Barbara Jordan, from Texas, is keynote speaker at the Democratic National Convention in New York City
Mae Jemison becomes the first black woman in space aboard the shuttle *Endeavor*
Arthur Ashe, former tennis star, announces that he has the AIDS virus
Heavyweight boxing champion Mike Tyson is found guilty of raping an eighteen-year-old Miss Black America contestant and sentenced to six years in an Indiana prison
Fifty-two people are killed after rioting and looting breaks out in South Central Los Angeles following the acquittal of four Los Angeles police officers accused of beating Rodney King
Vernon Jordan becomes chairperson of president-elect Bill Clinton's transition team
Cito Gaston, of the Toronto Blue Jays, becomes the first black manager of a major league baseball team to win the World Series
Jackie Joyner-Kersee becomes the first woman to win consecutive gold medals for the heptathlon
Boston University professor and poet Derek Wolcott, a native of St. Lucia, wins the Nobel Prize in Literature

1993

Toni Morrison becomes the first African American writer and the second American woman to win the Nobel Prize in Literature

Nelson Mandela of South Africa shares the Nobel Peace Prize with South African President F. W. de Klerk

Rita Dove is named the first African American poet laureate of the United States

President Bill Clinton appoints Ron Brown to serve as secretary of commerce, Hazel O'Leary to serve as secretary of energy, Mike Espy to serve as secretary of agriculture, and Jesse Brown to serve as secretary of veteran affairs

Rodney Slater becomes the first African American appointed as head of the Federal Highway Administration

Drew Days is named Solicitor General

Benjamin Chavis becomes NAACP executive director

Mary Frances Berry becomes head of the U.S. Commission on Civil Rights

Joycelyn Elders is appointed surgeon general of the United States

Bill Campbell becomes mayor of Atlanta

Dennis Archer becomes mayor of Detroit

Freeman Bosley Jr. is elected the first black mayor of St. Louis

Benny Thompson is elected to the U.S. House of Representatives from Mississippi

Sharon Sayles Belton becomes the first African American and the first woman to be elected mayor of Minneapolis

William R. Johnson becomes the first black mayor of Rochester, New York

Kenya Moore becomes the second black woman to be crowned Miss USA

Kimberly C. Aiken becomes the fifth black woman to be crowned Miss America

David Satcher becomes the first African American to head the Centers for Disease Control in Atlanta

Barbara Ross-Lee is named dean of the Ohio University College of Osteopathic Medicine, the first black woman to head a predominantly white medical school

1994

Spencer Crew becomes the first black director of the Smithsonian Institution's National Museum of American History

Deval L. Patrick is appointed assistant attorney general for civil rights

Charles F. Bolden Jr. commands the space shuttle *Discovery* and is the fifth African American to fly a shuttle mission

Marc Morial is elected mayor of New Orleans

Whitney Houston wins eight American Music Awards, the most ever by a female performer

Survivors of Rosewood, a black town near Gainesville, Florida, completely destroyed by a white mob in 1923, are awarded $150,000 each by the state

Sheila Jackson Lee is elected to the U.S. House of Representatives from Texas

Chaka Fattah is elected to the U.S. House of Representatives from Pennsylvania

J. C. Watts, a Republican, is elected to the U.S. House of Representatives from Oklahoma

Marion Barry is reelected mayor of Washington, D.C., after spending six months in prison on a drug conviction; he previously served as mayor from 1979 to 1991

Four African Americans win Pulitzer Prizes, the most ever in a single year: William Raspberry for Commentary, Isabel Wilkerson for Reporting, David Levering Lewis for Biography, and Yusef Komunyakaa for Poetry

Nelson Mandela is inaugurated as president of South Africa

Hugh B. Price is named president of the National Urban League

O. J. Simpson is arrested and accused of killing his ex-wife, Nicole Brown Simpson, and her friend Ronald Goldman

Beverly Harvard becomes chief of police in Atlanta, the first woman to head a major police department

**1995**

Lonnie R. Bristow is elected the first African American president of the American Medical Association

Richard Parsons becomes president of Time Warner, Inc., one of the world's top media and entertainment companies

Ruth Simmons is named president of Smith College in Northampton, Massachusetts, one of the elite women's colleges

Lenny Wilkens becomes the coach with the most wins in the history of the National Basketball Association

Astronaut Bernard A. Harris Jr. becomes the first African American to walk in space

Myrlie Evers-Williams, wife of slain civil rights leader Medgar Evers, is elected chair of the NAACP

Ron Kirk is elected first black mayor of Dallas, Texas

Eighty-seven-year-old Oseola McCarty of Hattiesburg, Mississippi, who made a living washing laundry, donates $150,000 to the University of Southern Mississippi for scholarships

Million Man March in Washington, D.C., drew over a million participants

LaSalle Lefall Jr., Howard University School of Medicine professor, is installed as president of the American College of Surgeons

Kweisi Mfume becomes president of the National Association for the Advancement of Colored People

1996

Jesse Jackson Jr. is elected to the U.S. House of Representatives from Illinois

Willie Brown becomes the first black mayor of San Francisco, California

Floyd Adams Jr. is elected the first black mayor of Savannah, Georgia

Danny Davis is elected to the U.S. House of Representatives from Illinois

Carolyn Kilpatrick is elected to the U.S. House of Representatives from Michigan

Julia Carson is elected to the U.S. House of Representatives from Indiana

Juanita Millender-McDonald is elected to the U.S. House of Representatives from California

Harold Ford Jr. is elected to the U.S. House of Representatives from Tennessee, and at age twenty-six is the youngest member of the 105th Congress

Elijah Cummings is elected to the U.S. House of Representatives from Maryland

Lloyd D. Ward is named president of Maytag Appliances

Margaret A. Dixon becomes the first black president of the American Association of Retired Persons

President Bill Clinton appoints Franklin Raines Head of the Office of Management and Budget, the first African American to hold the position

California voters ratify Proposition 209, which prohibits state and local government as well as colleges and universities from discriminating against or giving preferential treatment to any individual or group in public employment, public education, or public contracting on the basis of race, sex, color, ethnicity, or national origin; it effectively ends affirmative action in the state

J. Paul Reason is appointed the first black four-star admiral in the U.S. Navy

Some thirty-two black churches are mysteriously burned in the South over the period 1995–96

Muhammad Ali lights the flame for the Summer Olympic Games in Atlanta

Michael Johnson becomes the first male athlete to win gold medals at the Olympics in both the 200- and 400-meter races

1997

President Bill Clinton names Alexis Herman to serve as secretary of labor and Rodney Slater as secretary of transportation

Maxine Waters is selected to chair the Congressional Black Caucus

Kenneth I. Chenault is named president and chief operating officer of American Express Company

President Bill Clinton nominates Eric H. Holder Jr. to serve as deputy attorney general, the second-highest position in the U.S. Justice Department; Holder becomes the highest-ranking black law enforcement official in the nation's history

Cuba Gooding Jr. wins an Academy Award for best supporting actor in *Jerry Maguire*

Tiger Woods becomes the first black golfer and the youngest to win the Masters Tournament

Sidney Poitier becomes Bahamian ambassador to Japan

Harvey Johnson is elected the first black mayor of Jackson, Mississippi

Abner Louima, a Haitian immigrant, is sodomized with a broomstick by a New York City police officer while being held in the police station

Betty Shabazz, widow of Malcolm X, dies from burns suffered in a fire set by her grandson

David Satcher, head of the Centers for Disease Control, is named Surgeon General

Robert G. Stanton becomes the first black head of the National Park Service

President Bill Clinton names historian John Hope Franklin to head the national advisory board "One America in the 21st Century: The President's Initiative on Race"

The Million Woman March in Philadelphia attracts over a million participants

Lee Brown is elected the first black mayor of Houston, Texas

1998

Adam W. Herbert Jr. is named chancellor of the State University System of Florida, the first African American to hold the position

Gregory Meeks is elected to the U.S. House of Representatives from New York

Julian Bond is elected to chair the NAACP board of directors

Three white men kill James Byrd Jr., of Jasper, Texas, by dragging his body behind a pickup truck

Acquired Immune Deficiency Syndrome (AIDS) is the leading killer of black males aged 25–44 and the second leading killer of black women in that age group

Stephanie Tubbs-Jones is elected to the U.S. House of Representatives from Ohio

Joe Rogers, a Republican, is elected lieutenant governor of Colorado

J. Kenneth Blackwell, a Republican, becomes the first African American elected as Ohio's secretary of state

Henry Louis Gates Jr., a Harvard University professor, is awarded the National Humanities Medal

Mark Whitaker becomes the first black editor of *Newsweek Magazine*

Tyisha Miller is shot at twenty-seven times and killed by police in Riverside, California, as she sleeps in a locked car with a gun on her lap

1999

Almost three thousand black farmers who brought a suit against the U.S. Department of Agriculture for unfairly denying them government loans are awarded a settlement of $50,000 each and cancellation of debts owed the government

Amadou Diallo, an immigrant from Guinea, West Africa, is shot at forty-one times and killed by policemen in New York City as he stands in the vestibule of his apartment building

Maurice Ashley of Brooklyn, New York, becomes the first black grandmaster of chess

William Julius Wilson, a Harvard University professor, receives the National Medal of Science

Ronald K. Noble, a New York University law professor, is named head of the International Criminal Police Organization (INTERPOL), the first American to hold the position

Lauryn Hill wins five Grammy Awards and sets a record for a female recording artist

Serena Williams wins the U.S. Open Women's Tennis Singles Championship, the first black woman since Althea Gibson in 1958

Michael Coleman is elected the first black mayor of Columbus, Ohio

Andrew Young is named president of the National Council of Churches, representing thirty-five Protestant denominations and some fifty million members

A. Barry Rand becomes chairman and chief executive officer of Avis Rent-a-Car

2000

Rev. Michael Curry is elected bishop of the Episcopal Diocese of North Carolina, the first African American Episcopal bishop in the South

Marlon St. Julien becomes the first black jockey in seventy-nine years to race in the Kentucky Derby

The Chicago city council joins Detroit, Cleveland, and Dallas in urging Congress to hold federal hearings on reparations

Venus Williams wins the Women's Wimbledon Tennis Championship, the first black woman to do so since Althea Gibson in 1957

Vashti Murphy McKenzie is elected a bishop in the African Methodist Episcopal Church, the first woman to hold the position in the 213-year history of the denomination

Tiger Woods becomes the youngest golfer to win all four major championships: the British Open, Masters, PGA, and U.S. Open

James Perkins is elected the first black mayor of Selma, Alabama

Marion Jones becomes the first woman to win five medals in track and field at the Olympics

On the fifth anniversary of the Million Man March, Louis Farrakhan organizes the Million Family March

Viacom acquires Black Entertainment Network and its holdings for $3 billion

**2001**

President George W. Bush names Colin Powell to serve as secretary of state, the first African American to hold the position

Condoleezza Rice is selected as President George W. Bush's national security advisor, the first African American woman to serve in the position

President George W. Bush appoints Roderick Paige to serve as secretary of education

Ossie Davis and Ruby Dee receive the Screen Actors Guild Lifetime Achievement Award

President George W. Bush names Ruth Davis director general of the U.S. Foreign Service, a position that supervises thousands of diplomatic personnel; she is the first African American to hold the position

David L. Lewis, biographer of W. E. B. Du Bois, wins a second Pulitzer Prize, the first time a recipient's second volume wins the award

Former Ku Klux Klan member Thomas Blanton Jr. is convicted for the 1963 bombing of the 16th Street Baptist Church in Birmingham, Alabama, that led to the death of four young black girls preparing for church services

Diane Watson is elected to the U.S. House of Representatives from California

In a survey conducted by the *Washington Post*, 52 percent of black men report that they had been the victims of "racial profiling" by the police, questioned or detained primarily because of race

E. Stanley O'Neal becomes the first black president and chief operating officer of Merrill Lynch, the investment firm

Barry Bonds of the San Francisco Giants captures the single season home run record

Ruth Simmons is installed as president of Brown University, the first African American to head an Ivy League school

Bishop Wilton Gregory is elected president of the U.S. Conference of Catholic Bishops, the first African American to hold the position

William Burrus becomes the first black president of the American Postal Workers Union

AOL Time Warner names Richard D. Parsons chief executive officer of the world's largest media company

**2002**

Shirley Franklin becomes Atlanta's first female mayor

Alicia Keys ties Lauryn Hill's record five Grammy Awards

Halle Berry wins the Academy Award for best actress in a leading role, for *Monster's Ball*, the first black woman to win in that category

Denzel Washington wins the Academy Award for best actor in a leading role, for *Training Day*, the second black male after Sidney Poitier to win in that category

Tiger Woods wins his third Masters Golf Championship in six years and becomes only the third player to win the tournament two years in a row

Lerone Bennett Jr. receives the American Book Awards Lifetime Achievement award

Former Detroit Mayor Dennis Archer, is named president-elect of the American Bar Association, the first African American slated to head the group

David Scott is elected to the U.S. House of Representatives from Georgia

Denise Majette is elected to the U.S. House of Representatives from Georgia

Artur Davis is elected to the U.S. House of Representatives from Alabama

Frank Ballance is elected to the U.S. House of Representatives from North Carolina

Kendrick Meek is elected to the U.S. House of Representatives from Florida

There are thirty-nine black members of Congress, all Democrats

2003

Black Entertainment Television founder Robert Johnson becomes the first black majority owner of a major professional sports team with the Charlotte Bobcats

Beverly W. Hogan is the first woman president of Tougaloo College, outside Jackson, Mississippi

U.S. Representative Elijah Cummings (D-Md.) heads the Congressional Black Caucus with thirty-nine members

Jennette Bradley, lieutenant governor of Ohio, becomes the first black woman to hold a statewide number two position

Elson Floyd is the first African American to head the University of Missouri system

Michael Steele becomes Maryland's first black lieutenant governor

The U.S. Supreme Court rules in *Gratz v. Bollinger* that the University of Michigan cannot use an undergraduate admissions process with racial preferences that give automatic points to African American, Hispanic, and Native American applicants

In *Grutter v Bollinger*, the U.S. Supreme Court approves the University of Michigan Law School's use of race and ethnicity in admissions as serving a compelling national interest to achieve a diverse student body; the admissions process is considered narrowly tailored in evaluating individual applicants without automatic racial preferences

1st Lt. Vernice Armour is the first black female combat pilot in the U.S. Marine Corps

Colbert I. King, a *Washington Post* columnist, wins a Pulitzer Prize for commentary

Marc Morial, former New Orleans mayor, heads the National Urban League

Ann Fudge, former president of Kraft Foods, becomes chair and CEO of Young & Rubicam

Navy Rear Admiral Barry Black is the first African American chaplain of the U.S. Senate

Ericka Dunlap of Florida becomes the seventh African American crowned Miss America

2004

Alphonso Jackson becomes Secretary of Housing and Urban Development

Heather McTeer Hudson is the first African American mayor of Greenville, Mississippi

Beyonce Knowles ties Lauryn Hill, Norah Jones, and Alicia Keys with five Grammy Awards

Michael L. Lomax, former President of Dillard University, becomes head of the United Negro College Fund

Willie Adams Jr. is the first black mayor of Albany, Georgia

Novelist Edward P. Jones wins the Pulitzer Prize for fiction, and journalist Leonard Pitts of the *Miami Herald* wins the award for commentary

Phylicia Rashad is the Tony Award winner for best leading actress on Broadway; Audra McDonald wins for best performance by a featured actress in a play; Anika Noni Rose wins for best performance by a featured actress in a musical

Simmie Knox is the first African American artist to paint official White House portraits of a former president and first lady, Bill and Hilary Clinton

President George W. Bush awards former U.S. Senator Edward W. Brooke the Presidential Medal of Freedom, the nation's top civilian honor

Hazel O'Leary, former U.S. secretary of energy, becomes president of Fisk University

U.S. Representative Cynthia McKinney (D-Ga.) regains her seat in Congress

Barack Obama (D-Ill.) is the third African American elected to the U.S. Senate since Reconstruction and the second from Illinois

Emanuel Cleaver (D-Mo.), former mayor of Kansas City, is elected to the U.S. Congress

Gwen Moore (D) is the first African American elected to the U.S. Congress from Wisconsin

Al Green (D-Tex.) wins a seat in the U.S. Congress

Former Virginia Governor L. Douglas Wilder becomes the first black mayor of Richmond, Virginia

Charles Steele Jr. is president of the Southern Christian Leadership Conference

2005

Melvin Watts (D-N.C.) heads the Congressional Black Caucus, with forty-three members, all Democrats

Condoleeza Rice becomes the first African American woman to serve as U.S. secretary of state

African American entertainers receive five Academy Award nominations

Jamie Foxx receives the Academy Award for best actor (*Ray*) and Morgan Freeman the Academy Award for best supporting actor (*Million Dollar Baby*)

Bruce Gordon is the fifteenth president of the NAACP

Edgar Ray Killen is convicted of killing James Chaney, Andrew Goodman, and Michael Schwerner in Philadelphia, Mississippi, in 1964

Hurricane Katrina, one of the worst natural disasters in the nation's history, devastates New Orleans with its 68 percent black population; hundreds die and hundreds of thousands are left homeless

# PART IV

## *A–Z Entries*

ROBERT L. HARRIS JR.
WITH THE ASSISTANCE OF MICHELLE R. SCOTT

**Aaron, Henry "Hank"** (1934– ) Professional baseball player Hank Aaron, the son of Pearl and Edwin Caldwell, was born in Mobile, Alabama, on February 5, 1934. After attending the Josephine Allen Institute in 1951, Aaron slowly rose to prominence as a ball player for the Atlanta Braves between 1954 and 1965. He later joined the Milwaukee Brewers in 1966 and was an integral part of the player development staff of the Atlanta Braves between 1976 and 1990. The highlight of his baseball career occurred on April 18, 1974, when Aaron broke baseball legend Babe Ruth's home run record. Aaron holds eighteen major league records and was inducted into the Baseball Hall of Fame in 1982.

**Abdul-Jabbar, Kareem** (1947– ) Born on April 16, 1947, in New York, Lewis Ferdinand Alcindor led the University of California at Los Angeles basketball team to three national championships during his three varsity years and was named first team All-American for all three years. At the time, freshmen were ineligible. After his sophomore season, the National Collegiate Athletic Association banned dunking; the so-called Alcindor Rule lasted for ten years. In 1968, he converted to Islam and changed his name to Kareem Abdul-Jabbar. He played professional basketball first with the Milwaukee Bucks, with whom he won the National Basketball Association (NBA) championship in 1971, and the Los Angeles Lakers, with whom he won three national titles. At the time of his retirement in 1989, he held NBA records for the most seasons, games, and minutes played, most points scored, and the most blocked shots.

**Abernathy, Ralph David (1926–90)** Born on March 11, 1926, in Linden, Alabama, Ralph Abernathy served from 1951 to 1961 as pastor of the First Baptist Church in Montgomery. He became a close friend of Martin Luther King Jr., who was pastor of Dexter Avenue Baptist Church in that city. They became leaders of the Montgomery Improvement Association, which coordinated the Montgomery bus boycott (1955–56). With the establishment of the Southern Christian Leadership Conference (SCLC) in 1957, King became president and Abernathy secretary-treasurer. After King settled there in 1960, Abernathy moved to Atlanta and became pastor of West Hunter Street Baptist Church (1961–90). He often accompanied King on demonstrations and was placed in the same jail cells with him. After King's assassination in 1968, Abernathy became head of SCLC and held the position until 1977. He died on April 17, 1990.

**Alabama Christian Movement for Human Rights** Rev. Fred Shuttlesworth, former chairperson of the Birmingham Chapter of the NAACP, brought together several ministers to start the Alabama Christian Movement for Human Rights (ACMHR) after the state of Alabama banned the NAACP in 1956. The ACMHR fought against segregation in Birmingham through lawsuits and direct action campaigns. In 1963, Shuttlesworth invited the Southern Christian Leadership Conference to assist in the movement to desegregate public facilities in the city.

**Ali, Muhammad (1942– )** Born on January 17, 1942, in Louisville, Kentucky, Cassius Marcellus Clay became the first boxer to win the heavyweight title three times. During his career, he won fifty-six fights, thirty-seven by knockout, and lost only five bouts. After he defeated Sonny Liston for the heavyweight championship in 1964, he announced that he had converted to the Nation of Islam and had taken the name Muhammad Ali. He had been studying Islam under the tutelage of Malcolm X for three years before the announcement. In 1967, he refused induction into the military on religious grounds and because he believed that African Americans were being forced to fight a war that was not in their interests. He was convicted of violating the Selective Service Act and sentenced to five years in prison, which he appealed. The Supreme Court overturned his conviction in June 1970, but for three and a half years, at the prime of his career, Ali was prohibited from boxing. He regained the heavyweight title in 1974. By the time of his retirement from the ring in 1981, he was one of the most recognized and respected men in the world. Slowed by Parkinson's disease, Ali has been honored around the world. Having won a gold medal as a light heavyweight at the 1960 Olympics in Rome, he lit the torch for the 1996 Summer Olympic Games in Atlanta, Georgia.

**Ailey, Alvin** (1931–89) Internationally renowned modern dancer and choreographer Alvin Ailey was born in Rogers, Texas, on January 5, 1931. He studied under the famed choreographer Lester Horton and formed the interracial Alvin Ailey American Dance Theater company in New York in the late 1950s. Ailey's bold, dramatic signature dance style is most visibly present in the dance suite *Revelations*, which was choreographed to the music of traditional African American spirituals. Other of his signature pieces include *Blues Suite* and *Cry*, a solo dedicated to his mother and black women worldwide. Ailey remained the executive director of his world acclaimed dance company until his death in New York in 1989.

**Anderson, Marian** (1902–93) Marian Anderson, an internationally known contralto opera singer, was born to John and Annie Anderson in Philadelphia, Pennsylvania, on February 17, 1902. She attended William Penn and South Philadelphia High Schools and began to study with vocal teacher Giuseppe Boghetti in her senior year. After completing high school, she traveled through Europe, perfecting her craft, and performed with acclaimed African American tenor Roland Hayes. Anderson's eventual fame helped to break some racial barriers and raised awareness about racial inequality in the United States. Upon being denied to perform in Constitution Hall by the Daughters of the American Revolution in 1939, Anderson, with the help of Eleanor Roosevelt, held a legendary concert in front of the Lincoln Memorial on April 9. In the 1950s Anderson became the first African American permanent member of the Metropolitan Opera Company and the first African American to perform at the White House.

**Angelou, Maya** (1928– ) Poet, essayist, actress, and screenwriter, Angelou was born Marguerite Annie Johnson on April 4, 1928, in St. Louis, Missouri. She has chronicled her life story through biographical installments beginning with *I Know Why the Caged Bird Sings* in 1970. She wrote and recited the poem "On the Pulse of Morning" for President Bill Clinton's first inauguration in January 1993.

**Armstrong, Louis "Satchmo"** (1900–71) Louis Armstrong, a virtuoso jazz trumpeter, singer, and bandleader, was born in New Orleans in 1900. Armstrong learned to play the trumpet in the band of a children's home and later joined King Oliver's Creole Jazz Band in 1922. Armstrong formed his own jazz ensembles, including "Louis Armstrong and His Hot Five." Armstrong is most remembered as an initiator of the jazz improvisational solo and one of the first to mimic the phrasing of a brass instrument through song—a precursor to "scat" singing. Throughout his career he worked with countless artists, including Earl Hines, Ella Fitzgerald, Bessie Smith, and Sidney Bechet. Armstrong also performed in international jazz festivals, Broadway shows, and American and foreign films before his death in 1971.

**Ashe, Arthur (1943–93)** The first African American male to win the Wimbledon tennis title (1975), Arthur Ashe was born on July 10, 1943, in Richmond, Virginia. His tennis mentor, Dr. Walter Johnson, was the same coach who had discovered and tutored Althea Gibson, the first African American woman to win the Wimbledon title. Ashe was a strong supporter of TransAfrica and the struggle against apartheid in South Africa. He retired from tennis in 1979 at age thirty-six after suffering heart disease and having bypass surgery. Ashe contracted AIDS in 1983 through a blood transfusion during a second heart operation. He became a spokesman against AIDS until his death on February 6, 1993.

**Ashford, Evelyn (1957– )** Olympian runner Evelyn Ashford was born in California in 1957. She attended UCLA in the 1970s and went on to compete in the Summer Olympics in Montreal in 1976, the Los Angeles Olympics in 1984 and the Seoul Olympics in 1988. She has four World Cup titles, two Olympic gold medals, and one Olympic silver medal. She was the first African American woman to bear the American flag at the Olympic opening ceremonies in 1988.

**Association for the Study of African American Life and History** Founded in Chicago on September 9, 1915, by Carter G. Woodson and others, the Association for the Study of African American (formerly Negro) Life and History (ASALH) began the observance of Negro History Week in 1926 as the second week in February to embrace the birthdays of Abraham Lincoln (February 12) and Frederick Douglass (February 14). ASALH expanded the observance to Black History Month in 1976 during the nation's bicentennial. Woodson began publishing the *Journal of Negro History* (now the *Journal of African American History*) in 1916, started Associated Publishers as a book company in 1922 to disseminate research on black people, and initiated the *Negro* (now Black) *History Bulletin* in 1937 to reach a popular audience, especially schoolchildren. ASALH has been the premier organization for promoting the discovery, preservation, publication, and discussion of black life and culture.

**Attica Prison Uprising** On September 13, 1971, after several attempts to have prison officials improve conditions, especially terrible overcrowding, largely black and Latino inmates took control of Attica state prison in upstate New York. An outside committee of politicians, journalists, and activists requested by the inmates drafted a proposal for changes in the prison. After four days of negotiations, Governor Nelson Rockefeller authorized the National Guard to seize the prison. Thirty-nine people were shot during the raid, including ten hostages. The inmates were brutally beaten and forced to run a gauntlet of state troopers, who hit them with nightsticks. Although state officials blamed inmates for deaths of the hostages, it was later demonstrated that all the deaths were caused by the police during the raid on the prison.

**Baker, Ella (1903–86)** Ella Josephine Baker, educator and political activist, was born in Norfolk, Virginia, in 1903. She was raised in Littleton, North Carolina, by her parents, Blake Baker and Georgianna Ross Baker. Young Baker attended Shaw Boarding School and later graduated from Shaw University. She played a pivotal role in political movements from the 1930s through the 1970s. In the 1930s she moved to New York and served as the national director of the Young Negroes Cooperative League, and worked with the Workers Education Project and the Works Project Administration (WPA). In the 1940s Baker worked as a field secretary and a director of branches in the NAACP. She desired to democratize the NAACP more fully and make it more active in grassroots activity. As the civil rights era dawned, Baker tried to infuse her egalitarian principles into the leadership practices of the Southern Christian Leadership Conference (SCLC) and was an instrumental advisor and mentor to members of the Student Nonviolent Coordinating Committee (SNCC). Baker was also active in the Mississippi Freedom Democratic Party, the Southern Conference Education Fund and served as an advisor to countless other political organizations until her death in 1986.

**Baker, Josephine (1906–75)** Dancer and entertainer Josephine Baker was the toast of Paris during the 1920s and 1930s. She was a staunch advocate of human rights and won the Croix de Guerre and Legion d'Honneur for her work with the French Resistance during World War II. Born in St. Louis, Missouri, on June 6, 1906, Baker lived most of her life in France, where she adopted as many as twelve children of different races and made her home an ideal multiracial community. She refused to perform before segregated audiences in the United States. She attended the 1963 March on Washington. On April 14, 1975, she died in Paris and was given a state funeral.

**Baldwin, James (1924–87)** Novelist, essayist, and playwright James Baldwin was born in Harlem, New York, on August 2, 1924, to Emma Birdis Jones. He was later adopted by Daniel Baldwin, his stepfather. Baldwin attended DeWitt

Clinton Public High School and as a high school student became deeply involved in the Pentecostal faith. He was ordained as a Pentecostal minister at age fourteen, but at age seventeen he turned away from the church and began to explore writing. Baldwin eventually moved to Paris to become a professional writer. He made racial strife in the United States his central subject matter. He returned to the United States briefly during the civil rights movement and gave several talks on racial injustice. His most famous works include the autobiographical novel *Go Tell It on the Mountain* (1953), a collection of essays entitled *The Fire Next Time* (1963), and the plays *The Amen Corner* (1950) and *Blues for Mister Charlie* (1964). Baldwin died in Paris in 1987.

**Baraka, Amiri (LeRoi Jones) (1934– )** Imamu Amiri Baraka, a poet, writer, and educator, was born on October 7, 1934, in Newark, New Jersey, to Anna Jones and Coyette LeRoi. Baraka received a B.A. in English from Howard University in 1954 and a M.A. from Columbia University. He served in the Air Force between 1954 and 1957. Best known for works that criticize the racial stratification system in the United States and celebrate African American culture, Baraka is the author of such signature texts as *The Dutchman and the Slave* (1964) and the book *Blues People* (1963). He has also written several other plays, nonfiction works, and books of poetry. Some of Baraka's honors include an Obie award for the *Dutchman*, a Guggenheim Fellowship, an American Book Award, and a National Endowment for the Arts Grant. He retired in 1999 as professor of Africana studies at the State University of New York, Stony Brook.

**Basie, William "Count" (1904–84)** Jazz pianist, composer, and bandleader William "Count" Basie was born in Red Bank, New Jersey, in 1904. Influenced by the stride pianists James P. Johnson and Fats Waller, Basie developed his predominant right hand piano style in the jazz clubs of New York and later resettled in Kansas City in the mid-1920s. He joined Bennie Moten's band in 1924; by 1936 the group had transformed into Count Basie and His Orchestra. The signature driving rhythm section of the Basie Orchestra helped it become one of the leading groups of the Swing Era. Basie infused the sounds of classic blues into his jazz and popular pieces and his group rose to international prominence with tunes like *Lil Darlin'*, *One o'Clock Jump*, and *April in Paris*. Basie worked with hundreds of talented musical artists including Billie Holiday, Jimmy Rushing, Lester Young, Quincy Jones, and Joe Williams. He continued to lead the band until his death in 1984.

**Bates, Daisy Gaston (1914–99)** With her husband, L. C. Bates, Daisy Gaston Bates published the weekly newspaper *Arkansas State Press*, which examined the issues of the day for African Americans, especially racial discrimination and segregation in the state. She served as president of the NAACP state conference and provided transportation for the nine black students who desegregated Little Rock's Central High School in September 1957. The state of Arkansas later arrested, convicted, and fined her one hundred dollars for not turning over the NAACP membership roster and financial information. The U.S. Supreme Court later overturned her conviction. She was born in Huttig, Arkansas, on November 11, 1914, and died on November 4, 1999.

**Battle, Kathleen** (1948– ) Soprano opera singer Kathleen Battle was born in Portsmouth, Ohio, in 1948. She earned bachelor's and master's degrees in music at Cincinnati College-Conservatory. She made her debut as a soloist in Spoleto, Italy, in 1972 and made her first appearance at the Metropolitan Opera in 1976. She has performed such roles as Despina in *Cosi fan tutte* and Zerlina in *Don Giovanni*. Battle has sung in the central opera houses of Europe and often includes traditional African American spirituals in her repertoire.

**Bearden, Romare** (1912–88) Born in Charlotte, North Carolina, on September 2, 1912, Bearden is one of the most famous African American artists of the twentieth century. His collages reflect the cultural complexity of African American life. He organized a group of black artists in New York called Spiral to capture the momentous activities of the civil rights movement. He died on March 12, 1988.

**Belafonte, Harry** (1927– ) Singer, actor, producer, and activist Harry Belafonte was born in New York on March 1, 1927. His parents were Malvene Love Wright and Harold Belafonte Sr. He attended the Manhattan New School for Social Research Dramatic Workshop from 1946 to 1948. He has appeared in several plays, films, and television specials, including *Carmen Jones* (1954), *Island in the Sun* (1957), *Uptown Saturday Night* (1974), and *White Man's Burden* (1995). Belafonte often uses his position as an entertainer to raise awareness around pressing global issues as evidenced in his production of the *We Are the World* album and video (1985), which raised funds for famine victims in Africa. His honors include a 1953 Tony Award, a 1960 Emmy Award, a 1985 Grammy Award, and a 1994 National Medal of Arts Award.

**Bennett, Lerone, Jr.** (1928– ) Editor and historian Lerone Bennett Jr. was born on October 28, 1928, in Clarksdale, Mississippi. After graduating from Morehouse College, he became city editor of the black newspaper *The Atlanta Daily World*. After a year with the paper, he was hired by Johnson Publishing Company as associate editor of *Jet Magazine* and subsequently became senior editor of the flagship publication *Ebony Magazine*. His book *Before the Mayflower: A History of Black America* and other publications have explored the meaning of the black experience in the United States.

**Berry, Halle** (1968– ) The first African American woman to win an Academy Award for best actress, Halle Berry was born on August 14, 1968, in Cleveland, Ohio, to an interracial couple. Raised by her mother in the predominantly white suburb of Bedford, Berry attended a predominantly white high school, where she encountered racial prejudice. She was determined to succeed and became class president as well as head cheerleader. She won the Miss Teen Ohio and Miss Teen America beauty contests and was first runner-up in the Miss USA competition. Berry studied journalism at Cleveland's Cuyahoga Community College before moving to New York, where she became a model. She appeared in a couple of television series, including *Knot's Landing*, before she made her movie debut in Spike Lee's *Jungle Fever*. Several other movie roles followed, including her portrayal of Dorothy Dandridge in the HBO television film *Introducing Dorothy Dandridge*, for which Berry won a Golden Globe and an Emmy for best actress in a made-for-television film. She won an Academy Award in 2002 for her role in *Monster's Ball*.

**Berry, Mary Frances** (1938– ) Mary Frances Berry is a historian, lawyer, and political activist. She was born in Nashville, Tennessee, on February 17, 1938, to Frances Southall Berry and George Ford Berry. She graduated from Pearl High School in 1956 and pursued her B.A. and M.A. at Howard University, a Ph.D. in constitutional history at the University of Michigan, and a J.D. at the University of Michigan Law School. Berry has taught at such institutions as Central Michigan University, Eastern Michigan University, and the University of Maryland. She served as provost at the University of Maryland from 1974 to 1976 and became the first African American woman to lead a major research institution when she became the chancellor of the University of Colorado at Boulder in 1976. Berry fuses her role of educator with that of political activist and has acted as the assistant secretary for education in the Department of Health, Education, and Welfare under the Carter administration and as a member of the U.S. Commission on Civil Rights. Most recently Berry has been a professor of history at the University of Pennsylvania.

**Bethune, Mary McLeod** (1875–1955) The renowned educator, political activist, and government official Mary McLeod Bethune was one of seventeen children born to Patsy McIntosh McLeod and Sam McLeod in Sumter County, South Carolina. McLeod attended Chicago's Bible Institute for Home and Foreign Missions in 1894 and prepared to be a missionary to Africa. She then attended

Haines Institute in Augusta, Georgia, and joined the faculty of Presbyterian Kendall Institute upon graduation. In 1904, Bethune founded Daytona Educational and Industrial College, a professional and vocational school for black women. Bethune's college merged with the coeducational Cookman Institute in 1923, which was later renamed Bethune-Cookman College. Bethune was a pivotal figure in the Black Women's Club Movement and was elected president of the National Association of Colored Women in 1924. She later founded the National Council of Negro Women in December 1935. Bethune took her leadership skills to a broader national level and became a leader of the National Youth Administration under the Roosevelt administration. When Bethune became the director of the Division of Negro Affairs in 1936 she held the highest political office of any black woman of her era. Bethune was also fervently interested in international affairs and was one of the few African Americans, along with W.E.B. DuBois and Walter White, to attend the United Nations Organizing Conference in 1945. Bethune wrote columns for the *Pittsburgh Courier* and several articles for black periodicals throughout the nation. She continued her educational and political activities until her death on May 18, 1955.

**Black Panther Party for Self-Defense** Huey P. Newton and Bobby Seale founded the Black Panther Party for Self-Defense in Oakland, California, in October 1966. The aim of the Black Panther Party, through its ten-point platform, was self-determination for African Americans, an end to police brutality, trials for black people by juries of their peers, full employment, reparations, decent housing, a relevant education system, exemption from military service, freedom for black people held in prison, and a plebiscite for African Americans to determine their destiny in the United States or elsewhere. The image of armed black men in black jackets and berets as well as several well-publicized shootouts with the police brought the Panthers to national attention and attracted many adherents across the country. The Panthers also became a target of the FBI's Counterintelligence Program (COINTELPRO), which led to the death and imprisonment of many of its members. The Black Panther Party turned to the black community for support through its survival programs, such as free breakfasts for children, sickle cell anemia testing, free health clinics, transportation for families to visit prison inmates, and educational projects. Due to police repression and internecine conflict, the Panthers declined and virtually disappeared after Newton's death on August 22, 1989.

**Blackwell, Unita (1933– )** Born on March 18, 1933, in Lula, Mississippi, Unita Blackwell chopped cotton until inspired by the Student Non-Violent Coordinating Committee (SNCC) to become involved in the civil rights movement. She was fired from her job because of her efforts to register African

Americans to vote. She initiated a lawsuit, *Blackwell v. Board of Education*, to advance school desegregation in Mississippi. In 1976, she became the first black woman mayor in the state, as mayor of Mayersville, where she once had been denied the right to vote.

**Blaxploitation Films** A new genre of film that corresponded to the rise of the Black Power movement emerged during the late 1960s. Hollywood supplied the black moviegoing audience with images of black men who came out on top through violence. These were action films that generally had simple plots and stereotyped African Americans as pimps, hustlers, and thieves—thus "blaxploitation," short for black exploitation. The low-budget films found a ready audience, especially among young African Americans who sought release and escape from their inner-city surroundings. The popularity of the genre brought needed dollars into Hollywood during the difficult economic period of the late 1960s and early 1970s.

**Bluford, Guion S. (1942– )** Astronaut, pilot, and business executive Guion Stewart Bluford was born in Philadelphia, Pennsylvania, on November 22, 1942, to Lolita and Guion Bluford Sr. He received a B.A. in aerospace engineering at Pennsylvania State University (1964), an M.S. and Ph.D. in aerospace engineering and laser physics at Air Force Institute of Technology (1974 and 1978, respectively), and an M.B.A. at the University of Houston-Clear Lake (1987). Bluford served in the Air Force from 1965 to 1993, including duty in Vietnam, and retired as a colonel. He was the first African American to travel to space and made his first space shuttle mission in August 1983 as a mission specialist. Bluford became the vice president and general manager of NYMA, an aerospace consulting firm.

**Bond, Julian (1940– )** Born in Nashville, Tennessee, on January 14, 1940, Julian Bond became communications director of the Student Non-Violent Coordinating Committee (SNCC) in 1962. The Georgia state legislature tried to prevent him from taking his seat in that body in 1966 when he refused to abandon his opposition to the war in Vietnam and support of draft resistance. The U.S. Supreme Court ruled his exclusion from the Georgia legislature as unconstitutional. He was later elected to the state senate but lost a bitterly contested race for the U.S. Congress to John Lewis, a former ally in SNCC. Bond narrated the popular television series on the civil rights movement, *Eyes on the Prize*; taught at the University of Virginia; hosted a syndicated television program, *TV's Black Forum*; and became chair of the board of the NAACP in 1998.

**Bradley, Tom** (1917–98) Tom Bradley, law enforcement officer, politician, and lawyer, was born on December 29, 1917, in Calvert, Texas. After attending the University of California at Los Angeles, Bradley joined the Los Angeles police and served as an officer between 1940 and 1962. He then had a private law practice between 1960 and 1963 before he was elected council member for the Tenth District of Los Angeles. In 1973, Bradley was elected mayor of Los Angeles, a position that he held until 1993. He later served as senior counsel to the Brobeck, Phleger & Harrison law firm until his death on September 29, 1998.

**Braun, Carol Moseley** (1947– ) The first African American woman elected to the U.S. Senate, Carol Moseley Braun was born in Chicago on August 16, 1947. She graduated from the University of Illinois and the University of Chicago Law School. Before her election to the U.S. Senate in 1992, Braun served in the Illinois House of Representatives. She served only one term in the U.S. Senate before losing her bid for reelection. President Bill Clinton appointed her ambassador to New Zealand, a post that she held from 1999 to 2001.

**Brimmer, Andrew F.** (1926– ) Born in Newellton, Louisiana, on September 13, 1926, Andrew F. Brimmer became the first black member of the Board of Governors of the Federal Reserve Bank when President Lyndon B. Johnson appointed him to the position in 1966. Holding a Ph.D. in economics from Harvard University, Brimmer taught at Michigan State University, the University of Pennsylvania, and Harvard's Graduate School of Business. He served twice as president of the Association for the Study of African American Life and History and heads an economic consulting firm, Brimmer & Co., in Washington, D.C.

**Brooke, Edward W., III** (1919– ) The first African American elected to the U.S. Senate in the twentieth century, Brooke was born in Washington, D.C., on October 26, 1919. A graduate of Howard University and Boston University Law School, he served as Massachusetts attorney general before being elected as a Republican to the U.S. Senate in 1966. He served two terms in the U.S. Senate before losing his bid for a third term. He was often at odds with the Republican Party and President Richard Nixon over issues of civil rights, the Vietnam War, and economic policy. Brooke was one of the first senators to call for Nixon's resignation after Watergate.

**Brooks, Gwendolyn** (1917–2000) Poet Gwendolyn E. Brooks was born in Topeka, Kansas, on June 17, 1917. Her parents, David A. Brooks and Keziah

Wims Brooks, raised her in Chicago. She attended Woodrow Wilson Junior College and published her first book of poetry, *A Street in Bronzeville*, in 1941. Brooks received two Guggenheim fellowships and completed her next book, *Annie Allen* (1950). It was awarded the Pulitzer Prize in poetry that year, making Brooks the first African American in history to be so honored. In the 1960s, Brooks was influenced by the rise of black consciousness and began to write poetry to reflect the experiences of the black masses. In 1968, she succeeded Carl Sandburg as poet laureate of the state of Illinois and became consultant in poetry to the Library of Congress in 1985–86 before that title was changed to poet laureate. She died on December 3, 2000, in Chicago.

BROWN V. BOARD OF EDUCATION The U.S. Supreme Court decided unanimously in 1954 that separate educational facilities were inherently unequal and violated the equal protection clause of the Fourteenth Amendment. *Brown v. Board of Education* effectively overturned the U.S. Supreme Court decision in *Plessy v. Ferguson* that affirmed segregation and the doctrine of "separate but equal."

**BROWN, HUBERT G. "H. RAP" (1943– )** In 1966, H. Rap Brown became national chairman of the Student Non-Violent Coordinating Committee (SNCC) and became noted for his advocacy of black self-defense. He was born in Baton Rouge, Louisiana, on October 4, 1943, and was active in the civil rights movement as a high school student and as a student at Southern University. The FBI's Counterintelligence Program (COINTELPRO) targeted Brown for inciting African Americans to violence. One of Brown's favorite slogans was, "Violence is as American as apple pie." He served time in jail for transporting weapons across state lines and for being a fugitive from justice. For a time, he was on the FBI's Ten Most Wanted List. While in prison, he converted to Islam and took the name Jamil Abdullah Al-Amin. After his release from prison, he moved to Atlanta, where he owned a grocery store and became a spiritual leader (imam) for Muslim families across the country. On March 21, 2000, Al-Amin was arrested for murdering a sheriff and wounding a deputy. He had fled from Atlanta to Lowndes County, Alabama, the site of much of his work for SNCC. Two years later, he was convicted of murder and sentenced to life imprisonment.

**BROWN, JAMES (1934– )** Musical entertainer James Brown, son of Susie and Joseph Brown, was born on June 17, 1934, in Augusta, Georgia. Known as the "Godfather of Soul," Brown was the leader of the Famous Flames and eventually became an internationally acclaimed solo artist. He has forty-four gold records and won Grammy Awards in 1965 and 1986. Some of his hit records include "Please, Please, Please," "I Feel Good," "Cold Sweat," and "Say It Loud, I'm

Black and I'm Proud." He continues to tour the world with his signature style of soul music.

**Brown, Ronald H. (1941–96)** In 1989, Ronald Brown became the first African American chair of the Democratic Party National Committee. Born on August 1, 1941, in Washington, D.C., he graduated from Middlebury College and St. John's University School of Law. Brown served as general counsel for the National Urban League, chief counsel to the U.S. Senate Judiciary Committee, and staff director for Senator Edward M. Kennedy. He helped to elect Bill Clinton as president in 1992 and was appointed secretary of commerce. He died in a plane crash on April 3, 1996, while on a trade mission to Bosnia. The U.S. Department of Commerce's National Oceanic and Atmospheric Administration named a ship after him in July 1997.

**Brown, Sterling (1901–89)** Born in Washington, D.C., on May 1, 1901, Sterling Brown taught at Howard University from 1929 to 1969. A renowned poet, he drew on the blues tradition for much of his work, such as *Last Ride of Wild Bill* and *Southern Road*. Brown influenced many of the writers of the Black Arts movement such as Amiri Baraka and A. B. Spellman. He was one of the first academics to make a systematic and scholarly study of African American literature, with *The Negro in American Fiction* and *The Negro Caravan*. He died on January 13, 1989.

**Butler, Octavia (1947– )** Science fiction author Octavia E. Butler, daughter of Octavia Margaret Butler and Laurice Butler, was born in Pasadena, California, on June 22, 1947. She received her associate's degree at Pasadena City College and attended California State University and the University of California at Los Angeles. Butler was one of the first African American women to win acclaim in the science fiction genre. Some of her novels include *Mind of My Mind* (1977), *Kindred* (1979), and *Parable of the Talents* (1998). Her honors include a MacArthur Foundation Fellowship, which she was awarded in 1995.

**Bunche, Ralph Johnson (1904–71)** Born on August 7, 1904, in Detroit, Ralph Bunche grew up in Los Angeles, where he attended the University of California and played football, baseball, and basketball. Graduating summa cum laude, he pursued a doctoral degree in political science at Harvard University, which he received in 1934, after interrupting his study to start the political science department at Howard University. His dissertation at Harvard on European colonial administration in Africa won the best dissertation award for 1934 in political science. He was the first African American to receive a Ph.D. in political science in the United States. Bunche was a major researcher and consultant to Gunnar Myrdal for his study *An American Dilemma: The Negro Problem and Modern Democracy*. During World War II, he headed the Africa section of the Office of Strategic Services, the forerunner of the Central Intelligence Agency (CIA). He later worked for the U.S. State Department on post-war planning, especially for dependent areas. He became head of the United Nations Trusteeship Department in 1946 and a year later served on the UN Commission on Palestine. After the assassination of United Nations mediator Folke Bernadotte, Bunche became acting mediator and negotiated an armistice between Arabs and Israelis. He became the first African American to receive the Nobel Peace Prize in 1950. Appointed Undersecretary General for Special Political Affairs, he remained at the United Nations until shortly before his death on December 9, 1971.

**Carmichael, Stokely (1941–98)** Born in Port of Spain, Trinidad, on July 29, 1941, Stokely Carmichael attended high school in New York and graduated from Howard University in 1964. He became a Student Non-Violent Coordinating Committee (SNCC) volunteer after college and worked in Lowndes County, Alabama, registering African Americans to vote. He was selected to head SNCC in 1966 and raised the cry for Black Power during the Meredith March. With Charles Hamilton, he wrote *Black Power: The Politics of Liberation in America*, published in 1967. Carmichael moved to Conakry, Guinea, in West Africa in 1969, changed his name to Kwame Toure, and became a proponent of pan-Africanism. He died of prostate cancer on November 16, 1998.

**Carroll, Diahann [Carol Diahann Johnson] (1935– )** Diahann Carroll, singer and actress, was born on July 17, 1935, in New York. She is the daughter of Mabel Faulk and John Johnson. Carroll attended New York University before embarking on a career on the stage, screen, and television. She has appeared in such films as *Carmen Jones*, *Porgy and Bess*, *Paris Blues*, *The Five Heartbeats*, and most recently *Eve's Bayou*. In 1968, Carroll made her mark in television when she became one of the first African Americans to star in her own television comedy, *Julia*. She returned to television in the primetime 1980s drama *Dynasty*. Carroll won a Tony Award for her play *No Strings* in 1962 and received an Academy Award nomination for *Claudine* in 1974. She continues to make occasional film and television appearances.

**Carson, Benjamin (1951– )** Benjamin Carson has become one of the world's foremost experts on brain surgery, especially the delicate operation involved in separating Siamese twins joined at the head. Born in Detroit on September 18, 1951, he was raised in poverty by a single mother. She insisted that Carson do well in school after he was labeled a slow learner. He improved his grades and won a scholarship to Yale University. Carson received an M.D. degree from the University of Michigan School of Medicine and became director of the Division of Pediatric Surgery at Johns Hopkins Medical School, where he is a professor of neurosurgery, plastic surgery, oncology, and pediatrics.

**Catlett, Elizabeth (1915– )** Elizabeth Catlett, sculptor and printmaker, was born on April 15, 1915, in Washington, D.C. She is the daughter of Mary Carson Catlett and John H, Catlett. Young Catlett earned her B.S. at Howard University in 1935 and her MFA at the State University of Iowa in 1940. She then attended the Art Institute of Chicago, studied privately with Ossip Zadkine, and attended Escuela de Pintura y Escultura in Mexico City in 1948. Catlett has taught at several public schools in the United States, at the National School of Fine Arts, and at the National Autonomous University of Mexico. She works in the mediums of marble, limestone, bronze, terracotta, and wood and her commissioned works include *Olmec Bather* (1966, National Polytechnic Institute in Mexico), *Phyllis Wheatley* (1973, Jackson State University), *Louis Armstrong* (1975–76, New Orleans), and *Mother and Child* (1992, Colgate Palmolive). Her prints can be found in institutions such as the Metropolitan Museum of Art in New York, the National Museum of American Art in Washington, and the Museo de Arte Moderno in Mexico City.

**Chamberlain, Wilt (1936–99)** Professional basketball player Wilt Chamberlain was born in Philadelphia, Pennsylvania, on August 21, 1936. He attended Kansas University between 1954 and 1958. Chamberlain began his professional career as a Harlem Globetrotter in 1958. He subsequently played for the Philadelphia Warriors (1959–65), the Philadelphia 76ers (1965–68), and the Los Angeles Lakers (1968–73). Chamberlain was named most valuable player in the NBA four times and holds records for the most points scored by an individual in a one game (100) and all-time professional lead in points scored (30,000). He was inducted into the Basketball Hall of Fame in 1978. He died unexpectedly at the age of sixty-three in 1999.

**Charles, Ray (1930–2004)** Born on September 23, 1930, in Albany, Georgia, Ray Charles was one of the most influential musicians of the post–World War II era. His combination of blues, gospel, and jazz generated a popular following. Charles's career was almost ended by a seventeen-year addiction to heroin that he overcame by 1966. His rendition of Hoagy Carmichael's "Georgia on My Mind" became the state's official song in 1979. Ray Charles was among the first ten recording artists inducted into the Rock and Roll Hall of Fame in 1986. He died on June 10, 2004, at his home in Beverly Hills, California, of acute liver disease.

**Chisholm, Shirley (1924–2005 )** A cum laude graduate of Brooklyn College, Shirley Chisholm earned a master's degree from Columbia University Teacher's College and taught nursery school. She was born Shirley St. Hill in Brooklyn on November 30, 1924, and lived with her family for several years in Barbados. Married to Conrad Chisholm in 1949, she rose in politics from election to the New York State Assembly to the U.S. House of Representatives and became the first African American woman in the House in 1969. She ran for the Democratic Party nomination for president in 1972. After retiring from Congress in 1982, she taught at several colleges and helped to form the National Political Congress of Black Women. She died on January 1, 2005, in Ormond, Florida.

**Civil Rights Congress** The Civil Rights Congress was organized in 1946 through a merger of several communist-affiliated organizations. It fought for African American rights as well as the civil liberties of those individuals being silenced by the McCarthy era's suppression of communism in the United States. In 1951, William L. Patterson, executive director of the Civil Rights Congress, and Paul Robeson, the noted actor and singer, presented a petition to the United Nations on behalf of the organization. The petition charged the United States with genocide in the conditions inflicted on African Americans through systematic executions, lynchings, and terrorism that were calculated to bring about their physical destruction. The Civil Rights Congress was also noted for its defense of Rosa Lee Ingram, a widowed black tenant farmer, who was convicted along with her two sons for killing a white farmer after the sons came to her defense and hit the farmer on the head while he was sexually harassing their mother. Ingram and her sons were acquitted in 1954. The Civil Rights Congress folded in 1956, unable to pay the legal bills incurred in defending itself against the Subversive Activities Control Board and other government agencies that labeled it a communist organization.

**Clark, Kenneth Bancroft (1914–2005 )** Born on July 24, 1914, in the Panama Canal Zone, Kenneth B. Clark became known for work on the psychological damage to black youth caused by segregation and racism, work that was used in the 1954 *Brown v. Board of Education* Supreme Court decision. Clark graduated from Howard University and received his doctorate from Columbia University. From 1942 to 1975 he taught at the City College of New York, from which he retired as professor emeritus of psychology. He helped to organize the Harlem Youth Opportunities Unlimited program in the 1960s to increase educational and economic opportunities. He also founded the Metropolitan Applied Research Center to study and to publish work on race relations in the United States. He died of cancer on May 1, 2005, at his home in Hastings-on-Hudson, New York.

**Clark, Septima** (1898–1987) Educator and civil rights activist Septima Poinsette Clark was the daughter of former slave Peter Poinsette and free black Victoria Anderson Poinsette. Clark was born in Charleston, South Carolina, on May 3, 1898. She attended Avery Institute and later taught there and raised her family before earning her B.A. at Benedict College in 1942 and her M.A. from Hampton University in 1945. When the civil rights era began, Clark traveled throughout the South and established citizenship schools that instructed African Americans in life skills and the logistics of voting. Clark joined the Southern Christian Leadership Conference (SCLC) in 1961 and continued to promote the merits of citizenship training. She continued her educational and activist efforts until her death in 1987.

**Clarke, John Henrik** (1915–98) A self-taught writer and historian, John Henrik Clarke was born on January 1, 1915, in Union Springs, Alabama. He dropped out of school after the eighth grade and later traveled to New York, where he joined the Harlem History Club and the Harlem Writers Guild. He was a mentor and friend to Kwame Nkrumah, who became the first president of Ghana in 1957, and to Malcolm X, among others. He helped to shape the black studies movement as a faculty member in the Africana Studies and Research Center at Cornell University and in the Black and Puerto Rican Studies Department at Hunter College in New York, from which he retired in 1985 as the Thomas C. Hunter Distinguished Professor Emeritus. He coordinated the CBS television series *Black Heritage: The History of Afro-Americans* in 1968, which stimulated broad interest in African American history. Clarke remained an active intellectual even after losing his eyesight. He died on July 16, 1998.

**Cochran, Johnnie L., Jr.** (1937–2005) Born in Shreveport, Louisiana, on October 2, 1937, Johnnie Cochran graduated from the University of California at Los Angeles and received a law degree from Loyola University. He served as deputy city attorney for Los Angeles and as assistant district attorney for Los Angeles County before entering private practice. Cochran represented numerous high profile clients including former Black Panther Geronimo Pratt, James Brown, Michael Jackson, O. J. Simpson, and Abner Louima. The Simpson case, nationally televised, brought him to fame. Cochran and Simpson's legal team secured an acquittal in the famous case that divided the nation. The *National Law Journal* named him one of the best trial lawyers in the country in 1994. In 2001 he announced the formation of the Reparations Coordinating Committee with noted lawyers and scholars to bring legal action for the enslavement and segregation of African Americans. He died of a brain tumor on March 29, 2005.

**Cole, Nat "King"** (1919–65) Jazz pianist, vocalist, and composer Nat "King" Cole was born Nathaniel Adams Coles on March 7, 1919, in Montgomery, Alabama. He was the son of Edward James Coles and Pertina Adams Coles, who later moved to Chicago, where he attended Wendell Phillips High School and studied music under Walter Dyett. Cole formed the King Cole Trio in 1938, which had such hits as "Straighten Up and Fly Right." Cole won international acclaim when he became a solo vocalist in the mid-1940s. Praised for his smooth and precise lyric quality, Cole appeared in several films, traveled throughout the United States, Europe, and Mexico, and made television history when he became the first African American to host his own variety show on CBS in 1955. Owing to lack of commercial sponsorship, Cole's show was canceled after ten episodes. Cole's vocal hits include "The Christmas Song," "Mona Lisa," "Unforgettable," "Route 66," and "When I Fall in Love." Cole continued to perform until he died of lung cancer in Santa Monica, California, on February 15, 1965.

**Coleman, William T., Jr.** (1920– ) William T. Coleman graduated summa cum laude from the University of Pennsylvania in 1941 and magna cum laude from Harvard University Law School in 1946 after service in the Army Air Corps. He became the first African American Supreme Court Law Clerk when appointed by Justice Felix Frankfurter. Coleman later worked for the NAACP Legal Defense and Educational Fund and helped to write the brief for the 1954 *Brown v. Board of Education* Supreme Court case. President Gerald Ford named him secretary of transportation in 1975. After his stint in the cabinet, Coleman became a senior partner in a Washington, D.C., law firm.

**Collins, Marva** (1936– ) Marva Nettles Collins, a Chicago educator, was born in Monroeville, Alabama, on August 31, 1936. She is the daughter of Bessie Maye Nettles and Alex L. Nettles. Collins received her B.A. from Clark College in 1957 and attended Northwestern University. After teaching in the Chicago public school system for several years Collins grew dissatisfied with the process and results of traditional education and in 1975 established Westside Preparatory School, an alternative school for impoverished Black youth. Westside's curriculum was based on interdisciplinary study in a non-tracked or grade-level environment. Collins was offered the position of secretary of education in the administrations of both Ronald Reagan and George H. W. Bush. She declined both times. Subsequently, she established the Marva Collins Preparatory School in Cincinnati, Ohio, and aided in state educational planning in Oklahoma.

**Coltrane, John** (1926–67) John William Coltrane, jazz musician, bandleader, and composer, was born to John Robert and Alice Blair Coltrane on September 23, 1926, in Hamlet, North Carolina. Musical instruction was a part of his upbringing at home, and he later attended Philadelphia's Ornstein School of Music and studied with Mike Guerra. Coltrane joined the Jimmy Johnson Big Band and later played clarinet in the U.S. Navy Band from 1945 to 1946. He perfected his skills in local Philadelphia bands and went on to play with Dizzy Gillespie between 1949 and 1951. Coltrane developed an innovative style of playing that was influenced by African rhythms and the harmony, melody, tonality and modes of such composers as Debussy, Ravel, and Bartok. Coltrane worked with such artists as Charlie Parker, Thelonious Monk, Miles Davis, Pharaoh Sanders, Ravi Shankar, and Cannonball Adderly. He continued to record and perform his signature style of jazz until his death from liver disease on July 17, 1967, in New York.

**Communist Party USA** The Communist Party of the United States of America (CPUSA) was organized in 1921 and played an important role in the struggle for racial equality. Communists supported the rights of working class African Americans, especially in union organization. They were major backers of the National Negro Congress (1935–46), the Southern Negro Youth Congress (1937–48), and the Civil Rights Congress (1946–56). The Communist Party lost much African American support after the Nazi-Soviet Pact of 1939 and the organization's criticism of the war against fascism. Once Germany invaded the Soviet Union in 1941, the CPUSA changed its position. It opposed African Americans' "Double V" campaign for victory at home and abroad for fear that it would detract from the war effort. After World War II, the CPUSA came under great scrutiny and harassment by the United States government. It never recovered its strength. The fall of the Soviet Union in 1991 led to the virtual end of the CPUSA.

**Congressional Black Caucus** The Congressional Black Caucus (CBC) was formally established in 1971 with Congressman Charles Diggs of Michigan as its first chairman. The CBC formed the Congressional Black Caucus Foundation in 1976 to study issues related to congressional politics and African Americans. A year later, it founded TransAfrica to lobby in Washington, D.C., for the interests of Africa and the Caribbean, especially an end to apartheid in South Africa. The CBC has worked in Congress and in Washington to improve the social and economic position of African Americans.

**Congress of Racial Equality** The Congress of Racial Equality (CORE) was founded in Chicago in 1942. The group was dedicated to social change through interracial organizing and nonviolent direct action. CORE used the sit-in technique borrowed from the labor movement to protest segregation in public accommodations, primarily in the North. In 1947, after the Supreme Court decision in *Morgan v. Virginia* outlawing segregation in interstate transportation, CORE decided to test the case by organizing freedom rides through the upper South. CORE revived the freedom rides in 1961 when it challenged segregation in interstate transportation in the Deep South. CORE worked with other civil rights organizations in the South during the mid-1960s, especially on voter registration. The interracial coalition within CORE fell apart after 1966 when the organization endorsed Black Power and deleted the word "multiracial" from its constitution. Under the leadership of Roy Innis, who initially focused on black self-determination and economic development, CORE became increasingly conservative during the 1980s.

**Cosby, William Henry, Jr. "Bill"** (1937– ) Born in Germantown, Pennsylvania, on July 12, 1937, Bill Cosby became one of America's favorite comedians and entertainers. As co-star with Robert Culp of the television series *I Spy* (1965–68), Cosby became the first African American to play a lead in a dramatic series that did not have a predominantly black cast. He used success in that series to produce numerous television programs such as *The Bill Cosby Show, Fat Albert and the Cosby Kids, The Cosby Show,* and *You Bet Your Life.* Through *The Cosby Show,* about an upper middle-class black family, he was able to project positive images of black life and to attract a large audience; the program was often rated number one. Cosby also became a national spokesman for major products such as Jell-O, Coca-Cola, and Kodak. In addition to his comedy record albums, he has written numerous books. With his publications, comedy performances, and television series, he gained a reputation as America's favorite "dad." In the process, he has become one of the country's wealthiest African Americans and a major philanthropist. He and his wife, Camille, contributed $20 million to Spelman College to build the Camille O. Hanks Cosby Academic Center.

**Council on African Affairs** Organized in 1937, the Council on African Affairs (CAA) sought to inform American citizens about the African continent, especially the problems of colonial exploitation of its people and its resources. The CAA was often the major source of information in the United States about Africa. It provided news releases to key newspapers across the country and internationally. Because of the left-wing leanings of many of its members, including its chair, Paul Robeson, the Office of the U.S. Attorney General placed it on the list of subversive organizations. W. E. B. Du Bois became vice chair after leaving the NAACP in 1948. The CAA ceased operations in 1956 under pressure from the U.S. Subversive Activities Control Board.

**Dandridge, Dorothy (1923–65)** Actress and singer Dorothy Dandridge, the daughter of Ruby and Cyril Dandridge, was born in Cleveland, Ohio, on November 9, 1922. As a young girl, Dandridge and her older sister Vivian performed in a child vaudeville act that evolved into a musical trio known as the Dandridge Sisters. In the 1930s the Dandridge Sisters performed on the New York club circuit and appeared at the Cotton Club. By the 1950s, Dandridge was a popular solo nightclub performer. She rose to prominence as one of the most acclaimed African American actresses of her time with her performance in *Carmen Jones* (1954). The performance earned her an Academy Award nomination for best actress, a first for an African American. Dandridge's other key films include *Bright Road* and *Porgy and Bess*. Despite the prospects of a resurgence in her career, Dandridge reportedly committed suicide on September 4, 1965.

**Davis, Angela Yvonne (1944– )** Born in Birmingham, Alabama, on January 26, 1944, Angela Davis rose to prominence in 1969 when the California Board of Regents and Governor Ronald Reagan fired her from her teaching position at the University of California at Los Angeles for being an avowed member of the Communist Party. The U.S. Supreme Court overturned her dismissal. Davis again became the center of national attention when she was placed on the FBI's Ten Most Wanted list for being a fugitive from justice after allegedly supplying Jonathan Jackson with weapons that he used in an attempt to free his brother George Jackson, a member of the Black Panther Party, from prison. Davis was apprehended and served sixteen months in jail, during which time there was an international "Free Angela Davis" campaign. She was subsequently acquitted of murder and conspiracy charges. She currently teaches at the University of California at Santa Cruz and has written books on political prisoners and women's issues.

**Davis Jr., Benjamin O. (1912–2002)** Benjamin O. Davis Jr., military officer, government official, and business executive, was born on December 18, 1912, in Washington, D.C. He graduated in 1936 from the United States Military Academy and was commissioned a second lieutenant. He commanded the Tuskegee Airmen during World War II. Davis was the first African American to become a general in the Air Force. After retiring from the military as a lieutenant general, Davis served as the director of public safety for Cleveland, Ohio, and director of the Office of Civilian Transportation. He was the state's secretary of transportation from 1970 to 1971 and assistant secretary of transportation for environmental safety and consumer affairs. He died July 4, 2002, at Walter Reed Army Hospital in Washington, D.C., after suffering from Alzheimer's disease.

**Davis, Miles (1926–91)** Jazz trumpeter, bandleader, and composer Miles Davis was born in Alton, Illinois, in 1926 and was raised in East St. Louis. He attended Julliard in 1945 and began his professional career playing with such musicians as Benny Carter, Billy Eckstine, and Charlie Parker. Davis excelled in a variety of jazz styles and led the development of "cool jazz" in the mid-1950s, modal jazz in the late 1950s, and rock-jazz fusion in the 1960s. Some of Davis's most influential albums include *The Birth of the Cool, Kind of Blue, Sketches of Spain*, and *Bitches Brew*. He continued to experiment with various jazz styles and recorded until his death on September 28, 1991.

**Davis, Ossie (1917–2005)** Ossie Davis and Ruby Dee, whom he married in 1948, were the royal couple of black theater. Born in Cogdell, Georgia, on December 18, 1917, Ossie Davis rose to prominence as an actor and a playwright. He was also an activist in the struggle for human rights and was blacklisted from the stage during the 1950s for left-wing affiliations. His appearances on stage, in film, and on television won him great notice and awards. With Ruby Dee, he gave readings and dramatic performances across the country, especially on college campuses. He and Ruby Dee received the National Medal for the Arts in 1995 and the Screen Actor's Guild Lifetime Achievement Award in 2001. He died on February 4, 2005.

**Davis, Sammy, Jr. (1925–90)** A singer, dancer, actor, musician, impersonator, and comic of enormous talent, Sammy Davis Jr. was born on December 8, 1925, in Harlem into a stage family. By the time he was four years old he was performing with his father. They toured the country as the Will Mastin Trio, which included Davis, his father, and his adopted uncle Will Mastin. Davis soon became a recording artist and an actor. In 1954, he survived a serious car accident that cost him his left eye. After this brush with death, he converted to Judaism, which he maintained had lessons for African Americans as an oppressed people. Davis rose to fame during the 1960s, appearing in several films with fellow "Rat Pack" members Frank Sinatra, Dean Martin, Peter Lawford, and Joey Bishop. He supported civil rights causes and received the NAACP's Spingarn Medal in 1968. He later had his own television show and performed frequently in Las Vegas. A heavy smoker, he died of throat cancer on May 19, 1990.

**Dawson, William L. (1886–1970)** A graduate of Fisk University and Northwestern University Law School, William L. Dawson became a political kingpin on the south side of Chicago. He was born in Albany, Georgia, and settled in Chicago after college. Initially a Republican, he became a Democrat in 1939 as African Americans became attracted to the party by Franklin D. Roosevelt and the New Deal. Dawson won election to the House of Representatives in

1942, where he became the first African American to head a congressional committee, as chair of governmental operations. He was a cautious politician who played patronage politics but who did not advance the cause of civil rights in a manner similar to his more flamboyant colleague in Congress, Adam Clayton Powell. Dawson remained in Congress until his death on November 9, 1970.

**Deacons for Defense** The Deacons for Defense and Justice were organized in Jonesboro, Louisiana, in 1964 to defend African Americans seeking to register to vote against Ku Klux Klan violence. Many of its members were Korean War veterans who believed that African Americans should protect themselves because southern law enforcement officials failed to do so. The Deacons established their headquarters in Bogalusa, Louisiana, in 1965 and started branches throughout the South. Because of ongoing violence against civil rights workers and lack of protection by the government—local, state, and federal—many African Americans became critical of the civil rights movement's nonviolent philosophy and technique. The Deacons provided protection during the Meredith March through Mississippi in 1966. The organization had faded away by 1968, after the major gains of the civil rights movement.

**Dellums, Ronald V. (1935– )** Congressman Ronald V. Dellums was born in Oakland, California, on November 24, 1935, to Vernie and Willa Dellums. After attending Oakland Technical High School, he enlisted in the U.S. Marine Corps. After his military service, Dellums earned an associate's degree from Oakland City College in 1958, a bachelor's degree from San Francisco State College in 1960, and a master's degree in social work from the University of California at Berkeley in 1962. He worked as a social worker for Bay Area institutions until he began his political career in 1967 by running for the Berkeley city council. Dellums was elected to Congress in 1970, representing the Oakland-Berkeley area. With his appointment to the House Armed Services subcommittee in 1980, Dellums became the first African American to head a defense congressional committee. Dellums was the chair of the Congressional Black Caucus from 1988 to 1991, the chair of the House Armed Services Committee in 1993. He retired from Congress in 1998.

**Dinkins, David (1927– )** David Norman Dinkins, public official, lawyer, and educator, was born on July 10, 1927, in Trenton, New Jersey. His parents were Sally and William H. Dinkins. After serving in the military, Dinkins earned his B.A. in mathematics at Howard University in 1950, and a law degree at Brooklyn Law School in 1956. He worked with the Dyett, Alexander, and Dinkins law firm until 1971, when he began to enter New York politics. Dinkins served as the president of the City Board of Elections and the Manhattan borough president before becoming the first African American mayor of New York, a position he held from 1989 until 1993. Most recently, Dinkins has been a professor in the practice of public affairs at Columbia University's School of International and Public Affairs and a fellow at the Barnard-Columbia Center for Urban Policy.

**Doby, Lawrence Eugene "Larry" (1923–2003)** Larry Doby was the first African American to play baseball in the American League and the second black major league baseball player after Jackie Robinson in the National League. Doby was born in Camden, South Carolina, on December 13, 1923. He played for the Newark Eagles in the Negro National League and with the San Juan Senators in Puerto Rico before joining the Cleveland Indians on July 4, 1947. Playing with the Cleveland Indians, Chicago White Sox, and Detroit Tigers, Doby led the league in home runs twice and made the all-star team six times. He became the second black manager of a major league baseball team after Frank Robinson. Doby managed the Chicago White Sox for eighty-seven games in 1978. Despite his accomplishments, he was not inducted into the Baseball Hall of Fame until 1998. He died after a long illness on June 19, 2003, at his home in Montclair, New Jersey.

**Dove, Rita (1952– )** Born in Akron, Ohio, on August 28, 1952, Rita Dove graduated summa cum laude from Miami University of Ohio and received a master's in fine arts degree from the Writers' Workshop at the University of Iowa. She received the Pulitzer Prize for poetry in 1987 and served as poet laureate of the United States (1993–95), the first African American to hold that title. (Gwendolyn Brooks held a similar position before it was given the official title.) Dove's poetry and fiction reveal the beauty and significance of ordinary events in everyday lives. She is Commonwealth Professor of English at the University of Virginia.

**Drake, St. Clair (1911–90)** Born on January 2, 1911, in Suffolk, Virginia, St. Clair Drake graduated from Hampton Institute, where he came under the tutelage of Allison Davis, who introduced him to anthropology. While teaching high school in Virginia, Drake conducted research for Davis and helped to write the manuscript that became the book *Deep South*. Drake studied intermittently at the University of Chicago, where he received his Ph.D. in 1952. Before that, he published the pioneering study *Black Metropolis*, with Horace Cayton, about the African American community in Chicago. Drake began teaching at Roosevelt University in Chicago in 1946, where he developed a strong program in African Studies. He was an adviser to Kwame Nkrumah and taught at the University of Ghana after the country became independent, while retaining his position at Roosevelt. He went to Stanford University in 1969, where he headed the African and African American Studies Program. After completing his two-volume study *Black Folk Here and There*, he stayed at Stanford until his death on June 14, 1990.

**Drew, Charles Richard** (1904–50) A graduate of Amherst College and McGill Medical School in Montreal, Canada, Charles Drew was born on December 6, 1904, in Washington, D.C. At McGill, he studied the chemical composition of blood and blood group types. The medical profession faced the problem of not having enough whole blood to match needs for blood transfusion. He discovered that blood plasma rather than whole blood could be preserved for transfusions and established a blood bank at Columbia-Presbyterian Hospital in New York, where he conducted research with a fellowship from the Rockefeller Foundation. Drew was teaching surgery at Howard University when the British Red Cross asked him to become medical director of its blood bank program. He soon became medical director of both the British and the American Red Cross programs. Drew resigned his position after the military insisted on storing blood donated by blacks separately and using it only for black patients. He returned to Howard University, where he headed the department of surgery until his death in an automobile accident on April 1, 1950.

**Du Bois, William Edward Burghardt** (1869–1963) W. E. B. Du Bois was born in Great Barrington, Massachusetts, on February 23, 1869. He was raised by his mother after his father deserted the family soon after his birth. His mother encouraged his education. Du Bois attended Fisk University in Nashville, Tennessee, and became the first African American to receive a Ph.D. degree in history from Harvard University in 1895. His dissertation, *The Suppression of the African Slave Trade to the United States*, became the first volume published in the Harvard Historical Studies series. Du Bois became a pioneer in the study of sociology with his book, *The Philadelphia Negro*, published in 1899. He taught at Atlanta University, where he conducted an annual study of different aspects of black life that he planned to complete each decade for a comprehensive analysis of Black America. With William Monroe Trotter, he started the Niagara Movement in 1905 to demonstrate that African Americans were not satisfied with their condition and were determined to protest racial injustice. The Niagara Movement was a precursor to the National Association for the Advancement of Colored People (NAACP), which was organized in 1909. Du Bois was a founder of the NAACP and became director of research and editor of the *Crisis Magazine* in 1910. He remained with the NAACP until 1934, when he resigned under pressure, but returned in 1944 to prepare the organization for the postwar world in the struggle for racial equality in the United States and decolonization of Africa. Du Bois left the NAACP again in 1948 over political differences. The U.S. government indicted Du Bois in 1950 for not registering as the agent of a foreign power in his role as chair of the Peace Information Center. For eight years, he could not travel outside the United States. Although he was considered the father of pan-Africanism, Du Bois was not able to attend the independence ceremonies for Ghana, the first modern independent African nation. With his passport restored in 1958, Du Bois traveled abroad and was honored by China and the Soviet Union. He accepted an invitation from Kwame Nkrumah to live in Ghana and to write an *Encyclopedia Africana*, a project that Du Bois initiated in the 1940s. Before leaving for Ghana in 1961, Du Bois became a member of the Communist Party, renounced his American citizenship in 1963, and died in Ghana on August 27, 1963, on the eve of the momentous March on Washington.

**Dunham, Katherine** (1909– ) Katherine Dunham, dancer and choreographer, was born on June 22, 1909, in Chicago to Fanny June Dunham and Albert Dunham Sr. She attended Joliet Township Junior College and later transferred to the University of Chicago. She combined her studies in dance with cultural anthropology and eventually studied with Melville Herskovits. In 1937, Dunham earned a Guggenheim Fellowship to study the dances of Haiti, Jamaica, Martinique, and Trinidad and subsequently developed a dance style known as the Dunham technique, which combines Western modern dance with Afro-Caribbean stylings. Dunham developed her own professional dance company in 1939 and established the Katherine Dunham School of Arts and Research in 1943. She continues to lecture and offer master classes on Afro-Caribbean dance and culture. Dunham earned her Ph.D. from Northwestern University in 1947.

**Edelman, Marian Wright** (1939– ) Born in Bennetsville, South Carolina, Marian Wright Edelman graduated from Spelman College and Yale Law School. She became the first black woman to pass the bar exam in Mississippi, where she headed the NAACP Legal Defense and Education Fund. She founded the Children's Defense Fund in 1973 to promote the improvement of health, education, and welfare for America's youth.

**Ellington, William "Duke"** (1899–1974) Jazz composer, bandleader, and pianist Edward Kennedy Ellington was born in Washington, D.C., on April 29, 1899, to James Edward Ellington and Daisy Kennedy Ellington. He began taking music lessons at the age of seven and formed his first band, the Duke's Serenaders, in 1917. By the 1920s Ellington and his ensemble, the Washingtonians, moved to New York. Soon renamed the Duke Ellington Orchestra, Ellington's band grew to be one of the most popular bands in the nation and it played for the Cotton Club and Broadway musicals. A prolific and innovative composer, Ellington wrote many of the jazz tunes that characterized the popular music of the 1930s, 40's, and 50's. Some of his famed works include "Take the 'A' Train, " Satin Doll," "In a Sentimental Mood," and "Sophisticated Lady," among many other compositions, sacred as well as secular. Ellington's honors and awards include three Grammy Awards, a Spingarn Medal, and the Presidential Medal of Freedom. He continued to compose and perform until he succumbed to lung cancer on May 24, 1974.

**Ellison, Ralph (1914–94)** Novelist and essayist Ralph Waldo Ellison was born on March 1, 1914, in Oklahoma City to Ida Milsap Ellison and Lewis Ellison. He attended Frederick Douglass High and majored in music at Tuskegee Institute between 1933 and 1936. Ellison wrote essays and short stories for the *New Challenge* periodical and served as editor for the *Negro Quarterly*. Ellison rose to prominence with *Invisible Man*, his signature work about the physical and emotional journey of a young black man who migrates from the rural South to the urban North. Ellison's other works include the collection of essays *Shadow and Act* and the posthumously published novel *Juneteenth*. He continued to write until his death in 1994.

**Erving, Julius (1950– )** Popularly known as Dr. J., Julius Erving was born in East Meadow, New York, on February 22, 1950. He played professional basketball first with the Virginia Squires in the American Basketball Association (ABA), where he became Rookie of the Year in 1972. After being traded to the New York Nets, he led the team to the ABA Championship and led the league in scoring. He played with the Philadelphia 76ers in the National Basketball Association (NBA) from 1976 until he retired in 1987. Before he retired, he became the third player in NBA history to score 30,000 points. He was a member of the NBA All-Star team each year from 1977 to 1987 and two times was voted the All-Star Game's most valuable player. He mesmerized crowds with his acrobatic slam-dunks. After retiring from basketball, he developed numerous business enterprises in beverage distribution and cable television.

**Evers, Medgar (1925–63)** Born on July 2, 1925, in Decatur, Mississippi, Medgar Evers became the first field director in Mississippi for the National Association for the Advancement of Colored People. He served in the military during World War II and graduated from Alcorn Agricultural and Mechanical College in Mississippi. Evers investigated the murder of African Americans that were often dismissed as accidents. He organized voter registration campaigns and led boycotts against segregation in public facilities and transportation. On June 12, 1963, he was shot dead in the driveway of his home by Byron De La

Beckwith, who twice was freed by all-white juries. De La Beckwith boasted at a Ku Klux Klan rally that he killed Evers. He was finally convicted and sentenced to life in prison in 1994.

**Farmer, James L. (1920–99)** James Leonard Farmer Jr., civil rights activist and educator, was born on January 12, 1920, in Marshall, Texas, to James L. Farmer Sr. and Pearl Houston Farmer. Praised for his oratorical skills, Farmer entered Wiley College in Marshall at the age of fourteen. He later studied religion at Howard University and worked with the theological scholar Howard Thurman. In 1941, after completing his theological studies, Farmer became a part-time secretary for the Fellowship of Reconciliation (FOR), an interracial civil rights organization. Farmer's work with FOR prompted him to develop the Committee (later Congress) of Racial Equality (CORE) in the early 1940s. CORE was originally a branch of FOR that went into various communities and participated in direct civil rights activism. Farmer's fight against segregation led him to become the program director of the NAACP in 1955 and the national director of CORE by 1961. In the 1960s, Farmer and CORE were instrumental in the Freedom Rides, the March on Washington, and voting rights activities. In the 1970s and 1980s, Farmer acted as the assistant secretary of the administration for Health, Education, and Welfare and developed the Council on Minority Planning and Strategy. Before his death on July 9, 1999, he received the Presidential Medal of Freedom, the nation's highest civilian award.

**Farrakhan, Louis (1933– )** Born Louis Eugene Wolcott on May 17, 1933, in Bronx, New York, Louis Farrakhan grew up in Boston. He graduated with honors from Boston English High School and attended Winston-Salem College in North Carolina but dropped out to pursue a career as a calypso singer. Malcolm X converted him to the Nation of Islam in 1955. Farrakhan studied under Malcolm X and became leader of the Boston Mosque. When Malcolm X left the Nation of Islam, Farrakhan succeeded him as head of the Harlem Mosque and as National Spokesman for Elijah Muhammad, the organization's founder. After Elijah Muhammad's death in 1975, his son, Wallace Dean Muhammad, succeeded him and moved the organization toward orthodox Islam. Farrakhan revived the old Nation of Islam in 1978 with an emphasis on black self-determination. He involved the organization in politics in 1984 when he endorsed Jesse Jackson's campaign for the Democratic Party's presidential nomination. The Nation of Islam had previously avoided involvement in the politics of a system that it considered doomed for destruction. Farrakhan, who defended Jackson after he came under harsh criticism for a reference to New York that was considered offensive to Jews, soon made remarks himself that were deemed anti-Semitic. In 1995, Farrakhan issued a call for a march for atonement and reconciliation. The success of the resulting Million Man March boasted Farrakhan's standing in the United States and some Muslim nations.

**Fitzgerald, Ella** (1918–96) Jazz vocalist Ella Fitzgerald was born in 1918 in Newport News, Virginia, and was raised in New York. Known as the "First Lady of Song," Fitzgerald began her career by winning an amateur contest at the famed Apollo Theater in New York. In 1935, she became the featured vocalist in the Chick Webb Band and recorded national hit tunes such as 1938's "A Tisket, A Tasket." Fitzgerald became the director of the band after Webb's death in 1939 and led it until 1941. By the 1950s she became a solo artist and toured the world with her renditions of George Gershwin, Cole Porter, Jerome Kern, and Johnny Mercer songs. Fitzgerald performed with Duke Ellington, Louis Armstrong, Count Basie, and countless other musical artists. She won thirteen Grammy Awards and continued to perform until the late 1980s. Fitzgerald died in Los Angeles on June 16, 1996.

**Foreman, George** (1949– ) George Foreman was born in Marshall, Texas, on January 10, 1949, and raised in Houston. As a young man, he had frequent run-ins with the police; a judge recommended that he join the Job Corps, where he developed his emerging talent as a boxer. He fought several amateur bouts before winning the heavyweight class gold medal at the 1968 Olympic Games in Mexico City, where he refused to join protests by other black athletes; indeed, he held an American flag while receiving his medal. That refusal led to strong criticism in the black press and within the black community. Foreman turned professional in 1969 and by 1971 had accrued a 32–0 record, earning number-one ranking in the World Boxing Association. In 1974, he fought what was arguably his most famous fight against Muhammad Ali in Zaire; his loss marked his first defeat. Foreman has retired from boxing several times since, become an ordained minister, and earned a sizable income as a spokesperson for several companies and as an entrepreneur marketing his famed kitchen grill. In June 2003, he was inducted into the International Boxing Hall of Fame.

**Forman, James** (1928–2005 ) The first executive secretary of the Student Non-Violent Coordinating Committee (SNCC), James Forman was born on October 4, 1928, in Chicago, Illinois. He served in the Air Force from 1947 to 1951 and entered Roosevelt University in 1953, graduating four years later. He taught in the Chicago public schools. As executive secretary of SNCC, he helped to bring some structure to the organization. He encountered some resistance from members of SNCC who did not want a tightly structured bureaucracy. Forman resigned as executive secretary in 1966. He started the National Black Development Conference in 1969 and issued the Black Manifesto that demanded $500 million in reparations from white churches and synagogues. He remained active in issues related to African American economic empowerment. Forman died in Washington, D.C., on January 10, 2005, of colon cancer.

**Franklin, Aretha (1942– )** Gospel and rhythm & blues vocalist Aretha Louise Franklin was born on March 25, 1942, in Memphis, Tennessee. As the daughter of the renowned pastor and evangelist C. L. Franklin, young Franklin began her career as a gospel music performer in the mid-1950s before signing as a jazz vocalist with Columbia Records in 1960. Franklin achieved greater success when she joined Atlantic Records in 1967 and recorded the national hit "I Never Loved a Man." Known as the "Queen of Soul," Franklin followed with such hits as "Respect," "Chain of Fools," and "I Say A Little Prayer." She continued to record both sacred and secular works and her efforts were rewarded with fifteen Grammy Awards and more than twenty number one R&B hit records. She was the first woman to be inducted into the Rock & Roll Hall of Fame and was honored with a Grammy Legends Award, a Kennedy Center Honors Award, and a Grammy Lifetime Achievement Award. Franklin continues to record and tour.

**Franklin, John Hope (1915– )** Born on January 2, 1915, in Rentiesville, Oklahoma, John Hope Franklin became one of the foremost American intellectuals of the twentieth century. A brilliant scholar and respected academician, he has also devoted himself to advancing racial equality. He prepared background material on the Fourteenth Amendment for the legal brief in the *Brown v. Board of Education* Supreme Court case. His survey of African American history, *From Slavery to Freedom: A History of African Americans*, has been the standard textbook in the field since its first publication in 1947. His scholarship has been deliberately revisionist to set the story straight about the role that African Americans have played in the development of the United States. A recipient of the nation's highest civilian award, the Presidential Medal of Freedom, President Bill Clinton selected Franklin in 1997 to head his Initiative on Race—One America for the Twenty-First Century.

**Fuller, Hoyt W. (1923–81)** A major architect of the Black Consciousness movement, Fuller was born September 10, 1923, in Atlanta, Georgia, and grew up in Detroit, Michigan, in an aunt's home. His father died when he was four years old, and his mother later became an invalid. Fuller graduated from Wayne State University and worked as a journalist in Ohio, West Virginia, and Michigan before joining *Ebony* magazine in 1954. He left the United States three years later in disgust over the lynching of Emmett Till and white resistance to desegregation. Fuller settled in Europe, where he no longer felt the need constantly to affirm his identity; later he visited Africa and determined that the African independence movement would influence the freedom of African Americans. With this confidence, he returned to the United States in 1960 and became editor of *Negro Digest* a year later. Fuller made *Negro Digest* the most widely read and influential black literary magazine. He changed the name to *Black World* in 1970 to reflect its international role as a voice of black artistic, cultural, and intellectual expression. Fuller helped to found the Organization of Black American Culture (OBAC) in Chicago to develop black creative talent and to improve the black community. Fuller promoted the idea of a black aesthetic and the importance of black culture to advance the cause of black people in the United States and internationally. When Johnson Publications discontinued *Black World* in 1976, black artists, intellectuals, and activists rallied to launch *First World* magazine, which Fuller published from Atlanta while commuting to teach in the Africana Studies and Research Center at Cornell University. He died of a heart attack in Atlanta on May 11, 1981.

**Gates, Henry Louis, Jr. (1950– )** Born on September 16, 1950, in Keyser, West Virginia, Henry Louis Gates Jr. is the leading proponent of African American studies. One of the first winners of the MacArthur Foundation "genius awards," he has devoted himself to uncovering, recording, and disseminating information about African and African American culture. He is general editor of the fifty-two volume series *African American Women Writers of the Nineteenth Century* and author or editor of some fifty volumes, including *Africana: The Encyclopedia of the African and African American Experience*, *African American Lives*, and the *Norton Anthology of African American Literature*. He has received the George Polk Award for Social Commentary and a National Humanities Medal, and was elected to the American Academy of Arts and Letters. In 2002, he was selected to deliver the Jefferson Lecture in the Humanities by the National Endowment for the Humanities.

**Gibson, Althea (1927–2003)** Althea Gibson was born on August 25, 1927, in Silver, South Carolina. She played tennis initially on the black circuit through the American Tennis Association, an African American organization formed in 1916 and the oldest noncollegiate black sports group in the United States. Prior to 1950, when Gibson broke the barrier, African Americans could not enter U.S. Lawn Tennis Association events. She became the first African American to win a Wimbledon title in 1957 and was named Babe Didrickson Zaharias Female Athlete of the Year, the first black female athlete to win the award. After retiring from tennis, she took up golf and toured with the Ladies Professional Golfers Association. She died on September 28, 2003.

**Gillespie, John Birks "Dizzy" (1917–93)** Jazz musician, bandleader, and composer John Birks Gillespie was born on October 21, 1917, in Cheraw, South Carolina. The youngest of nine children, Gillespie was the son of James and Lottie Powe Gillespie. Known as one of the founders of bebop jazz, Gillespie began playing piano and trumpet at the age of twelve and joined his first professional group at eighteen. Gillespie developed his signature style of playing the trumpet while working with Cab Calloway's and Earl Hines's bands in the late 1930s and early 1940s. In the 1930s, Gillespie, Charlie Parker, Thelonious Monk, and others began experimenting with the rhythms and harmonies of more traditional swing music and developed bebop. Gillespie formed his own big band in 1945 and later fused the new sounds of bebop with Afro-Cuban music. In the 1950s and 1960s Gillespie's band was one of the jazz ensembles funded by the State Department to travel through Europe, Africa, and the Middle East on goodwill tours. Gillespie's career spanned almost sixty years; some of his prominent compositions include "A Night in Tunisia" and "Manteca." He died in 1993.

**Giovanni, Nikki (1943– )** A major poet of the Black Arts movement, Nikki Giovanni was born Yolanda Cornelia Giovanni on June 7, 1943, in Knoxville, Tennessee. Her early poetry reflected the racial pride and assertiveness of the era. Her later work focused less on politics and more on interpersonal relations. She made a series of recordings in which she read her poetry to musical accompaniment. Those recordings heightened her popularity.

**Gordy, Berry (1929– )** Entrepreneur and songwriter Berry Gordy III, the son of Berry Gordy II and Bertha Ida Fuller Gordy, was born in Detroit on November 28, 1929. After serving in the Army during the Korean War, Gordy returned to Detroit to become a songwriter. Although he achieved moderate success with songs that he wrote for Jackie Wilson and The Miracles, Gordy's rise to fame came with his development of Motown Records in 1959. At its height Motown encompassed eight record labels, a management service, and a publishing company. Gordy and Motown helped promote some of the most popular R&B groups of the 1960s and 1970s, including The Temptations, The Supremes, Mary Wells, Marvin Gaye, Stevie Wonder, and The Jackson 5. Gordy was inducted into the Rock & Roll Hall of Fame in 1990.

**Graves, Earl G., Jr. (1935– )** Earl Graves Jr., the founder and publisher of *Black Enterprise Magazine*, was born on January 9, 1935, in Brooklyn. The first black business magazine, *Black Enterprise* has recorded the diversification and progress of black business in America since its first issue in 1970. It has fostered economic growth and development among African Americans. Graves has expanded his business interests to include broadcasting, market research, and beverage distribution.

**Gray, William H., III (1941– )** William H. Gray III was born in Baton Rouge, Louisiana, on August 20, 1941. A Baptist minister, he was active in community development, especially low-income housing. In 1978, he was elected to the U.S. Congress from Philadelphia. He rose to the position of majority whip for the Democratic Party in 1989, the number three leadership position in the House of Representatives and the highest position ever held in Congress by an African American. He resigned from Congress in 1991 to become president of the United Negro College Fund (UNCF). He initiated a drive to raise $250 million for UNCF by the beginning of the new century.

**Gregory, Frederick Drew (1941– )** On November 22, 1989, Frederick Gregory became the first African American to command a space flight with the launch of the space shuttle *Discovery*. He was born on January 7, 1941, in Washington, D.C. Gregory graduated from the U.S. Air Force Academy in 1964. He served as a helicopter pilot in the Vietnam War. Before joining the astronaut program in 1978, he was a National Aeronautics and Space Administration (NASA) research test pilot at Langley Research Center in Virginia. In addition to serving as commander of *Discovery*, he also commanded the space shuttle *Atlantis* in 1991.

**Gregory, Dick (1932– )** Born on October 12, 1932, in St. Louis, Missouri, Dick Gregory became one of the first top black nightclub comedians. He attended Southern Illinois University on a track scholarship, served in the Army, and moved to Chicago, where he honed his craft in small black clubs. His breakthrough came in January 1961, when the Playboy Club in Chicago hired him for one night as a replacement for a white comedian who had become ill. Gregory was a hit with an all-white audience that included many southern salesmen in town for a convention. He became a master satirist who poked fun at segregation. He also became a participant in the civil rights movement and used his talent to raise funds for civil rights organizations. Gregory opposed the war in Vietnam and was a popular speaker on college campuses. He wrote several books about race relations and the assassination of Martin Luther King Jr. He has promoted vegetarianism and founded a company to distribute diet products. Gregory has been active in human rights issues in the United States and abroad and has often conducted fasts to make his point.

**Haley, Alexander Murray Palmer (1921–92)** Alex Haley was born in Ithaca, New York, on August 11, 1921, while his father studied agriculture at Cornell University and his mother took courses at the Ithaca Conservatory of Music (later Ithaca College). His parents took him to Henning, Tennessee, six weeks after his birth, where he grew up with his grandmother, Cynthia Murray Palmer. It was on her front porch that Haley heard stories about the family, and especially about "the African." After a mediocre college career without receiving a degree, Haley joined the Coast Guard and remained in the service for twenty years. He developed and honed skills as a journalist and short story writer while in the Coast Guard. After retiring in 1959, he embarked on a career as a writer. His break came when *Reader's Digest* asked him to write a piece on Elijah Muhammad and the Nation of Islam. *Playboy* later commissioned him to conduct an interview with Miles Davis. After Haley's appearance, the interview became a regular feature of the magazine. His second assignment for *Playboy* was an interview with Malcolm X, which led to his collaboration on the *Autobiography of Malcolm X*. Haley later spent eight years researching his family's history and four years writing *Roots: The Saga of an American Family*, published in 1976. The television dramatization of *Roots*, a twelve-hour miniseries broadcast over eight nights, was a stunning success as over half the nation watched at least one episode. The Pulitzer Prize committee gave Haley a special award for *Roots* because it could not place the book in the traditional categories of fiction or history. Haley referred to the work as "faction," a combination of fact and fiction. Most historians considered the book a historical novel. *Roots* rekindled pride in African Americans and influenced the growth of interest in genealogy by all Americans. After facing several legal complaints that he plagiarized parts of the book, as well as an exhausting lecture schedule, Haley died of a heart attack in Seattle on February 10, 1992.

**Hamer, Fannie Lou (1917–77)** Born in Montgomery County, Mississippi, on October 6, 1917, Fannie Lou (Townsend) Hamer was the child of sharecroppers. She had to work in the cotton fields during her youth and completed only the sixth grade. After marrying Perry Hamer, they moved to Ruleville, Mississippi, where she worked as sharecropper and became recordkeeper on a plantation. She lost her job after she attempted to register to vote during a Student Non-Violent Coordinating Committee (SNCC) voter registration campaign. She later became a SNCC field secretary. She was an organizer and vice-chairperson of the Mississippi Freedom Democratic Party, which sought to replace the Mississippi Democratic Party delegates, with no African Americans, at the Party's National Convention in 1964, in Atlantic City, New Jersey. Fannie Lou Hamer testified in a nationally televised session about the problems that African Americans encountered in seeking to register and to vote in Mississippi.

She described a beating that she and others received in a Winona County, Mississippi, jail in 1963 for trying to exercise their rights as American citizens. She became famous for her statement that she was "sick and tired of being sick and tired." She worked tirelessly for black educational, economic, and political progress in Mississippi until her death from breast cancer on March 14, 1977.

**Hampton, Lionel (1908–2002)** Lionel Hampton made the vibraphone an important jazz instrument through his innovative style. He was born on April 12, 1908, in Louisville, Kentucky and raised in Birmingham, Alabama, and Chicago. He played with numerous major bands during his career until forming his own group in 1940. President Dwight D. Eisenhower made him a goodwill ambassador for the United States and he performed around the world. President Bill Clinton honored Hampton with the National Medal of Arts. Slowed by a series of strokes in 1992 and 1995, Hampton died of heart failure on August 31, 2002.

**Harris, Patricia Roberts (1924–85)** Born on May 31, 1924, in Mattoon, Illinois, Patricia Roberts Harris became the first African American woman appointed an ambassador of her country, in her case to Luxembourg. She graduated from Howard University and from George Washington Law School. She briefly served as dean of Howard University Law School, the first black woman to head a law school, but she resigned after only a month because of differences with the faculty and the president. When President Jimmy Carter appointed her as secretary of the Department of Housing and Urban Development in 1976, she became the first black woman to hold a cabinet position. She later became Secretary of Health, Education, and Welfare. She ran for mayor of Washington, D.C. in 1982 but lost to Marion Barry. She died on March 23, 1985.

**Hastie, William H. (1904–76)** Born on November 17, 1904, in Knoxville, Tennessee, William H. Hastie became the first African American appointed a federal judge in 1937 with the U.S. District Court for the Virgin Islands. Hastie graduated magna cum laude, Phi Beta Kappa, and class valedictorian from Amherst College. At Harvard University Law School, he was the second African American to serve as editor of the *Harvard Law Review* after his cousin Charles Hamilton Houston. Hastie also taught at Howard University Law School and helped Houston to make it a top-flight institution. He served as dean of the Law School from 1939 to 1946, the year that he became the first black governor of the Virgin Islands. He later became a judge on the Third Circuit Court of Appeals and served as its chief justice for three years before he retired in 1971. Hastie was given serious consideration for appointment to the U.S. Supreme Court, a position that later went to his former student Thurgood Marshall. Hastie died on April 14, 1976.

**Hayes, Roland** (1887–1976) Roland Hayes was widely recognized as one of the greatest classical singers of the twentieth century. He was born on June 3, 1887, in Curryville, Georgia. He studied classical music in America and in Europe before making his breakthrough in 1921, at age thirty-four, in London. Hayes was also responsible for bringing the spirituals to the concert stage by a solo performer. He became the first African American classical singer to perform with the major orchestras and conductors of the time. He later taught at Boston University before his death on December 31, 1976.

**Height, Dorothy** (1912– ) Born in Richmond, Virginia, on March 24, 1912, Dorothy Height became a social reformer interested in the progress of black women, and through them all African Americans. She was executive secretary of the Phillis Wheatley Young Women's Christian Association (YWCA) in Washington, D.C., and served on the YWCA national board during the 1940s. Height was president of Delta Sigma Theta Sorority from 1947 to 1956, during which time she strengthened its community involvement. She became president of the National Council of Negro Women (NCNW) in 1957 and held the position until 1997. She has been active in the struggle for racial and gender equality and influenced the YWCA to take a strong stand against racism. Under her leadership, the NCNW acquired a national headquarters building on Washington's Pennsylvania Avenue, near the Capitol.

**Highlander Folk School** Founded in 1932 by Myles Horton and Don West in Monteagle, Tennessee, the Highlander Folk School trained community activists initially in union organizing and later in civil rights strategies. Its workshops addressed voter education, adult literacy, and interracial cooperation. Many leaders of the civil rights movement attended its Citizenship Schools throughout the South. Both the state and federal governments suspected the Highlander Folk School of subversive activity, and agents harassed its staff and students. The state revoked the school's charter in 1962 and confiscated its property. The school transferred most of its programs to the Southern Christian Leadership Conference, reorganized as the Highlander Research and Education Center, and relocated to New Market, Tennessee, in 1971.

**Holiday, Billie** (1915–59) Born on April 7, 1915, in Philadelphia, Pennsylvania, Billie Holiday set the standard for jazz vocalists. Her life experiences of poverty and child abuse influenced her haunting interpretation of jazz songs that she infused with a blues sensibility. Her interpretation of "Strange Fruit," written by Abel Meerpol, a Jewish high school English teacher in the Bronx, made it an anthem for racial justice with its dramatic depiction of lynching. Holiday recorded "Strange Fruit" in 1939 with a small label, Commodore, after major record labels refused the song. Many radio stations banned the song as incendiary. Holiday, who battled drug addiction most of her life and spent eight months in prison in 1947 for heroin possession, died on July 17, 1959.

**Hooks, Benjamin L. (1925– )** Executive director of the National Association for the Advancement of Colored People (NAACP) from 1977 to 1992, Benjamin L. Hooks was born on January 31, 1925, in Memphis, Tennessee. He graduated from Howard University and earned a law degree from DePaul University in Chicago. A Baptist minister, Hooks served on the board of directors of the Southern Christian Leadership Council. He became the first black criminal court judge in Tennessee in 1965. A member of the Republican Party, he nominated Richard Nixon for president at the Republican National Convention in 1972 and later became the first African American appointed to the Federal Communications Commission. He led the NAACP during a difficult period in its history and sought to involve the organization in community development and social welfare rather than just legal and political issues. After resigning the position of executive director in a dispute with the chairman of the NAACP board, William F. Gibson, Hooks was chairman of the Leadership Council on Civil Rights, a position he held until 1994. He then returned full time to his position as pastor of the Middle Street Baptist Church in Memphis.

**Horne, Lena (1917– )** At age sixteen, Lena Horne, who was born on June 30, 1917, in New York, became a dancer with the chorus line at the Cotton Club in Harlem. She performed in major nightclubs across the country and was the first black performer to sign a contract with a Hollywood studio, MGM. She starred in several films during the 1940s but was blacklisted during the 1950s for her friendship with Paul Robeson and support of the African independence movement. She returned to the stage during the late 1950s and appeared in the movie *The Wiz* in 1978. Her 1981 one-woman Broadway show, *Lena Horne: The Lady and Her Music,* was a stunning success. She symbolized black feminine beauty but also the problem of black women's securing leading roles in mainstream films.

**Houston, Charles Hamilton (1895–1950)** Born in Washington, D.C., on September 3, 1895, Charles Hamilton Houston graduated Phi Beta Kappa from Amherst College and cum laude from Harvard University Law School, where he was the first African American editor of the *Harvard Law Review*. He practiced law in Washington with his father, William L. Houston. In 1929, he became head of the law school at Howard University. He transformed the law school from an evening school that students attended part-time to a full-fledged legal program. Houston believed that the law and the black lawyer as a social engineer would lead to racial equality. He trained law students at Howard, among them Thurgood Marshall, to use the legal system against racial segregation. Houston became the first full-time legal counsel for the National Association for the Advancement of Colored People (NAACP) and laid the groundwork to defeat the doctrine of "separate but equal." Because of health problems, he resigned as NAACP chief counsel in 1938 but remained active in civil rights litigation. Houston suffered a heart attack in 1948 and died of complications on April 22, 1950.

**Houston, Whitney** (1963– ) In 1994, Whitney Houston became the first female performer to win eight American Music Awards. She was born on August 9, 1963. Her mother, Cissy Houston, was a noted gospel singer. Whitney began singing in a gospel choir at eleven and eventually became a backup singer to Chaka Khan and Lou Rawls. Her debut album in 1985 was the most commercially successful recording by a female artist at that time. She made her film debut in 1992 in *The Bodyguard*. The single from the soundtrack *I Will Always Love You* became the best-selling single of all time. Houston married pop star Bobby Brown in 1992 and had her first child, Bobbi Kristina, a year later. She has made several more films and signed a record-breaking recording contract for $100 million in 2001.

**Hughes, Langston** (1902–67) Born in Joplin, Missouri, on February 1, 1902, Langston Hughes became a major poet of the Harlem Renaissance during the 1920s. His famous poem "The Negro Speaks of Rivers," published in 1921 and dedicated to W. E. B. Du Bois, reveals his interest and pride in black history and culture. Hughes drew deep from the well of African American culture and employed the blues, jazz, and the black vernacular in his poems. He graduated from Lincoln University in 1929 and went on to write novels and plays. His newspaper column for the *Chicago Defender* introduced the character, Jesse B. Semple, who had a strong racial consciousness but who delighted readers with his humor. Hughes came under investigation during the early 1950s for his left-wing views and affiliations. He later toured in Africa and other areas for the U.S. State Department. He continued to write plays and poetry as well as an anthology of black humor. He died in New York on May 22, 1967.

**Hunton, William Alphaeus, Jr.** (1903–70) A graduate of Howard University, William Alphaeus Hunton earned a master's degree in literature from Harvard University and a Ph.D. from New York University in 1938 while teaching at Howard. He was born on September 18, 1903, in Atlanta. Because of Hunton's affiliation with the National Negro Congress, which was considered communist-dominated, the House Un-American Activities Committee investigated him. He later became director of education for the Council on African

Affairs (CAA) and worked for an end to apartheid in South Africa. The federal government harassed the CAA, ordered it to register as a subversive organization, and forced its disbanding in 1956. After several tours of Africa, Europe, and the Soviet Union, Hunton and his wife moved first to Conakry, Guinea, and then to Accra, Ghana, where he assisted W. E. B. Du Bois with the planned *Encyclopedia Africana*. After the overthrow of Kwame Nkrumah in 1966, the Huntons moved briefly to the United States before settling in Lusaka, Zambia, where he died of cancer on January 13, 1970.

**Hurston, Zora Neale (1891–1960)** Zora Neale Hurston was born on January 7, 1891, in Notasulga, Alabama, although she often listed her birth as in 1901 or 1910. She grew up in Eatonville, Florida, an all-black town. She attended Howard University and graduated in 1928 from Barnard College, where she studied with Columbia University anthropologist Franz Boas. With the support of Charlotte Osgood Mason, a wealthy white patron, who also assisted Langston Hughes, Hurston collected black folklore in the South and later in Haiti and Jamaica. Her collection *Mules and Men* was the first published compilation of black folklore by an African American. She became a prominent writer of the Harlem Renaissance era and continued her work after its decline. Despite her numerous publications, Hurston died impoverished on January 28, 1960, in a welfare home in Florida.

**Jackson, Jesse Louis (1941– )** Born on October 8, 1941, in Greenville, South Carolina, Jesse Jackson attended the University of Illinois on a football scholarship but left the school after he learned that African Americans were not permitted to play quarterback. He went to North Carolina Agricultural and Technical College in Greensboro, where he became a star athlete and civil rights activist. After graduating in 1964, he attended Chicago Theological Seminary, was ordained a minister, and left the seminary in 1965 to work with the Southern Christian Leadership Conference (SCLC). Martin Luther King Jr. asked him to lead the Chicago branch of Operation Breadbasket, which SCLC started as an economic initiative to secure greater employment for African Americans by America's businesses. Jackson later became national director of Operation Breadbasket and succeeded in gaining agreements with businesses, often under threat of boycott, to employ more African Americans, use black suppliers, deposit funds in black banks, and advertise in black media. Jackson left SCLC in 1971. He had been restless with the organization after King's assassination in 1968 and differed with its leadership. Jackson founded Operation PUSH (People United to Save—later changed to Serve—Humanity). Under PUSH, he continued many of the programs started by Operation Breadbasket and added a focus on improving black self-esteem and educational achievement. Jackson ran for the Democratic Party presidential nomination in 1984 and 1988. In the process, he registered large numbers of African Americans to vote that helped to put more black officials in office. He was plagued, however, by remarks that he made in the 1984 campaign about going to "Hymietown," an anti-Semitic reference to New York. In 1988, he organized the National Rainbow Coalition to bring together and to empower the dispossessed in American society. He has launched a Wall Street project to bring African Americans more firmly into the economy of the United States.

**Jackson, Joseph H. (1900–90)** President (1953–82) of the National Baptist Convention, the largest black organization in the country, Joseph H. Jackson was born on September 11, 1900, in Jamestown, Mississippi. He graduated from Jackson College (now Jackson State University) and received a bachelor of divinity degree from Colgate-Rochester Divinity School. In 1941, he became pastor of Olivet Baptist Church in Chicago, one of the largest black Baptist congregations in the country. Jackson was a conservative in the tradition of Booker T. Washington and believed that African Americans should focus on self-help and economic progress. He opposed civil rights demonstrations preferring to work through the legal system and criticized the planned 1963 March on Washington. In 1960, Martin Luther King Jr. supported Jackson's opponent to head the National Baptist Convention. A split ensued that led to formation of the Progressive National Baptist Convention, which supported civil rights demonstrations. Jackson never forgave King for his opposition. Even after King's assassination in 1968, when a street was named in his honor in Chicago that included the address of Olivet Baptist Church, Jackson changed the official address of the church so that it would not carry King's name. Joseph H. Jackson died on August 18, 1990.

**Jackson, Mahalia (1911–72)** Perhaps the greatest gospel singer of all time, Mahalia Jackson was born on October 26, 1911, in New Orleans. Blues singers Bessie Smith and Ma Rainey, the Sanctified Church, and the Baptist Church influenced her style of phrasing, emotion, and tone. Jackson moved to Chicago in 1927 and rose to fame first as part of an a cappella quartet and later as a soloist. She became the song demonstrator for Thomas A. Dorsey, the father of gospel, who was most noted for his composition, "Precious Lord, Take My Hand." In 1954, she was the first gospel performer to have a network radio program with CBS. She refused lucrative contracts to become a popular music singer and remained committed throughout her life to gospel. She sang just before Martin Luther King Jr. delivered his famous address at the March on Washington in 1963 and performed "Precious Lord, Take My Hand" at King's funeral service in 1968. Mahalia Jackson died in Chicago on January 27, 1972.

**Jackson, Michael** (1958– ) Born on August 29, 1958, in Gary, Indiana, Michael Jackson became one of the major popular singers in the United States. He began singing with his brothers in amateur contests and won the prestigious amateur night contest at the Apollo Theater in Harlem. Under the tutelage of Berry Gordy, the founder of Motown Records, The Jackson Five rose to fame. Michael began recording solo in 1971, although the brothers continued also to perform together. In 1975, they left Motown and signed with Epic Records. Because Motown owned the name The Jackson Five, the group changed its name to The Jacksons. In 1982, Michael collaborated with Quincy Jones to make the album *Thriller*, which became the best-selling recording of all time, with sales of more than forty million. Because of his huge success, MTV reversed its ban on playing black musical videos. Michael Jackson has become more known as an eccentric star of American popular culture than as a musical genius who innovated popular dance and music during the 1980s. His extensive plastic surgery and skin lightening has brought him under considerable criticism for trying to escape his racial identity.

**Jackson, Shirley Ann** (1946– ) A graduate of the Massachusetts Institute of Technology with a doctoral degree in physics, Shirley Ann Jackson was born in Washington, D.C., on August 5, 1946. She was the first African American female to receive a Ph.D. in physics and the first to earn a doctoral degree at MIT. She served as a research associate at the Fermi National Accelerator Laboratory in Batavia, Illinois, a visiting scientist at the European Center for Nuclear Research, and a researcher at the Stanford Linear Accelerator and Aspen Center for Physics before she began work at Bell Laboratories on electrical and optical properties of semiconductors. In 1991, she became professor of physics at Rutgers University. She was appointed chair of the U.S. Nuclear Regulatory Commission in 1995 and became the eighteenth president of Rensselaer Polytechnic Institute in Troy, New York, in 1999.

**Jamison, Judith** (1943– ) Born on May 10, 1943, in Philadelphia, Pennsylvania, Judith Jamison became the principal dancer with the Alvin Ailey American Dance Theater. She has appeared as a guest artist with major dance and ballet companies nationally and internationally. She danced with ballet star Mikhail Baryshnikov in 1976 in a performance choreographed by Alvin Ailey and set to Duke Ellington's music. After Ailey's death in 1989, Jamison became artistic director of the theater.

**Jemison, Mae** (1956– ) The first African American woman astronaut, Mae Jemison was born in Decatur, Alabama, on October 17, 1956, and grew up in Chicago. She graduated from Stanford University and received a medical degree from the Cornell University Medical College. She became the first African American female in space in 1992 aboard the space shuttle *Endeavor.* Jemison left the National Aeronautics and Space Administration in 1993 to start her own company, the Jemison Group, which specializes in use of technology for development in Third World nations. She has taught at Dartmouth College and served as Andrew D. White Professor-at-Large at Cornell University.

**Johnson, Earvin "Magic" (1959– )** Magic Johnson changed the game of basketball. His ability to score, assist, and rebound brought the term "triple double" into the sports lexicon as he was able to make double figures in each area of the game. Born on August 14, 1959, in Lansing, Michigan, Johnson attended Michigan State University and turned professional after his sophomore year when he led his team to the National Collegiate Athletic Association championship. His dynamic play and electrifying smile earned him the nickname "Magic." Johnson held the National Basketball Association (NBA) record for assists when he retired in 1991, had won five NBA titles with the Los Angeles Lakers, and was named the NBA's most valuable player three times and the All-Star Game's twice. He was inducted into the Basketball Hall of Fame in 2002. Johnson retired from basketball after he discovered he had contracted AIDS. He established the Magic Johnson Foundation for education, prevention, research, and treatment of AIDS. In retirement, he has worked on economic development for black communities through the Johnson Development Corporation that manages theaters, shopping malls, retail complexes, and franchises with Starbucks and T.G.I. Fridays. He has demonstrated the viability of business enterprise in inner city neighborhoods.

**Johnson, John H. (1918–2005)** Born on January 19, 1918, in Arkansas City, Arkansas, John H. Johnson moved to Chicago in 1933 to further his education because African Americans were not able to attend school beyond eighth grade in his hometown. He graduated from DuSable High School in Chicago and attended the University of Chicago. He dropped out of college and went to work for Supreme Liberty Life Insurance Company, where he prepared a weekly digest of information on black America for the company president. That experience led to publication of *Negro Digest*, which Johnson started with a $500 loan against his mother's furniture. From *Negro Digest,* Johnson built the largest black publishing company in the United States, with *Ebony Magazine* and *Jet*. He also ventured into the beauty products industry with Fashion Fair Cosmetics, radio broadcasting, and insurance. He became one of the wealthiest black men in America and one of the few African Americans on *Forbes Magazine*'s list of the wealthiest Americans. In 1972, he officially opened an eleven-story office building to house his business, the first black-owned building constructed in downtown Chicago. Johnson contributed $4 million to Howard University in 2003, and the university named its new School of Communications building in his honor. He died in Chicago on August 8, 2005, after an extended illness.

**Johnson, Robert** (1946– ) The first African American billionaire, Robert Johnson was born on April 8, 1946, in Hickory, Mississippi. He graduated from the University of Illinois and earned a master's degree in Public Administration at Princeton University. Johnson served as press secretary to Walter E. Fauntroy, the Washington, D.C., delegate to Congress, before becoming vice president of government relations for the National Cable Television Association in 1976. In 1980, he started Black Entertainment Television (BET), the first black-owned cable television network, which he sold to VIACOM in 2000 for about $3 billion. He made history again in January 2003 when he purchased the Charlotte, North Carolina, National Basketball Association franchise and became the first African American to have majority ownership in a major sports team.

**Jones, Quincy** (1933– ) Quincy Jones was born on March 14, 1933, in Chicago and grew up in Seattle. He attended Seattle University and the Berklee School of Music in Boston. He played trumpet but soon found his calling in composing, arranging, and conducting music. He worked with some of the major bands and artists, such as Dizzy Gillespie, Lionel Hampton, Count Basie, and Frank Sinatra. Jones became one of the first African American music composers for Hollywood films. He also wrote and arranged music for television. He produced several of Michael Jackson's best-selling albums. Jones put together the *We Are the World* album and video in 1985 for famine relief in Africa. Jones has won more than two dozen Grammy Awards for his work.

**Jordan, Barbara** (1936–96) Barbara Jordan was born on February 21, 1936, in Houston, where she graduated from Texas Southern University. She received a law degree in 1959 from Boston University. After several losing campaigns for the Texas House of Representatives, she became the first black woman elected to the Texas state senate in 1966. In 1972, she became the first African American elected from the South to the U.S. Congress. She rose to fame during the 1974 Watergate Hearings that led to the impeachment of President Richard M. Nixon. She eloquently defended the U.S. Constitution in the serious deliberations over impeachment. Jordan opposed the war in Vietnam during her years in Congress. She delivered a rousing keynote address to the 1976 Democratic Party National Convention. Hobbled by knee problems, she decided not seek reelection in 1978. She taught at the Lyndon Baines Johnson School of Public

Affairs at the University of Texas in Austin and held the LBJ Chair in National Policy from 1982 to 1986. Jordan suffered from multiple sclerosis and contracted leukemia shortly before her death on January 17, 1996.

**Jordan, Michael** (1963– ) A five-time National Basketball Association (NBA) Most Valuable Player, Michael Jordan led the Chicago Bulls to six NBA titles during the 1990s. He was born on February 17, 1963, in Brooklyn but grew up in North Carolina, where he attended the University of North Carolina at Chapel Hill. He turned professional after his junior year but continued to take courses to earn a bachelor's degree there. He retired from basketball in 1993 to play professional baseball with the Chicago White Sox. Having turned in a less than average performance as a baseball player, he returned to the Chicago Bulls in 1995 and retired again in 1999, though he returned to play for two seasons with the Washington Wizards. Jordan was not only a successful sports figure but also an international spokesman for numerous commercial products.

**Jordan, Vernon E., Jr.** (1935– ) Born in Atlanta on August 15, 1935, Vernon Jordan graduated from DePauw University in Indiana as the only black student in his class. He received his law degree from Howard University in 1960. He served as NAACP field secretary in Georgia from 1961 to 1963 and as head of the Voter Education Project from 1965 to 1969. He became head of the United Negro College Fund in 1970 and executive director of the National Urban League (NUL) from 1972 to 1981. In 1980, he was shot in the back by a sniper on the way to his hotel after giving a speech in Fort Wayne, Indiana. He was hospitalized for more than three months but fully recovered from his near-fatal wounds. After resigning as executive director of the NUL, Jordan joined a powerful Washington, D.C., law firm and served on the board of major corporations. He became one of the nation's most influential African Americans and headed President Bill Clinton's transition team after the 1992 election.

**Joyner-Kersee, Jacqueline** (1962– ) The first woman to win gold medals in multisport (heptathlon) and individual (long jump) events in the 1988 Olympics in Seoul, South Korea, Jacqueline Joyner-Kersee was born on March 3, 1962, in East St. Louis, Illinois. She was a gifted athlete who graduated in the top 10 percent of her high school class and played basketball and ran track at the University of California at Los Angeles, from which she earned a bachelor's degree in history in 1985. She dominated her sports events well into the 1990s.

**Karenga, Maulana** (1941– ) The founder of Kwanzaa, an African American celebration held between December 26 and January 1, Maulana Karenga was born Ronald Everett in Parsonburg, Maryland, in 1941. He graduated from the

University of California at Los Angeles with a bachelor's degree in 1963 and a master's degree in 1964, both in political science. He earned two doctoral degrees, one in political science from United States International University and the other in ethics of Africa and ancient Egypt from the University of Southern California. He founded the US (as distinct from them) Organization in 1966. Karenga developed Kawaida theory to reclaim an African value system for black liberation in the United States from racial domination and oppression. He was convicted of aggravated assault on two female US members in the early 1970s and served time in prison. The US organization has served as a catalyst for cultural change among African Americans, with the belief that black people in the United States will not free themselves until they first free their minds. Karenga has been a strong supporter of black studies, as chair of the department at the University of California at Long Beach, and of Afrocentricity, or an African-centered approach to knowledge. He was a member of the executive council of the organizing committee for the Million Man March in 1995 and helped to write its mission statement.

**Killens, John Oliver** (1916–87) Born in Macon, Georgia, on January 14, 1916, John O. Killens graduated from Howard University. He became a labor organizer of black and white workers for the Congress of Industrial Organizations but became discouraged about white working-class interest in an interracial society. He founded the Harlem Writers Guild in the early 1950s to promote its members' creativity and social change. Killens believed that art should contribute to black liberation. His novels focused on racism in American society and the black struggle for freedom. He also wrote plays and children's literature. At the time of his death on October 27, 1987, he was working on a novel about the great nineteenth-century Russian poet and dramatist Alexander Pushkin, whose great-grandfather was a black African. The work was published posthumously in 1988.

**King, Martin Luther, Jr.** (1929–68) Martin Luther King Jr., who was born Michael King Jr. on January 15, 1929, in Atlanta, became the symbol of the civil rights movement. He grew up in a solidly middle-class black household and attended Morehouse College, as did his father and his maternal grandfather. His maternal grandfather built Ebenezer Baptist Church, which both his son-in-law and his grandson would later pastor, into one of Atlanta's strongest black churches. After a trip to Germany in 1934, King's father changed his name and that of his son to Martin Luther King. King's grandfather and father were both involved in the struggle for racial equality in Atlanta, primarily through the National Association for the Advancement of Colored People. Benjamin E. Mays, the president of Morehouse College, had a strong influence on King. He showed him that he could become a minister without sacrificing a commitment to social justice. King graduated from Crozer Theological Seminary in Chester, Pennsylvania, in 1951 and received a Ph.D. in theology from Boston University in 1955. He married Coretta Scott, who was studying music at the New England Conservatory of Music in Boston, in 1953.

They moved to Montgomery, Alabama in 1954, where King became pastor of Dexter Avenue Baptist Church. King rose to prominence as president of the Montgomery Improvement Association (MIA), organized to conduct the Montgomery bus boycott. Dr. King was only twenty-six years old when selected to head the MIA, a position that several ministers shunned because of fear of reprisals. King had to weather threats on his life and the bombing of his home. But he matured as a leader during the boycott and developed an understanding of guiding people to change nonviolently first through his Christian faith and later through his understanding of the Gandhian philosophy of nonviolent direct action. After the success of the Montgomery bus boycott, King founded the Southern Christian Leadership Conference (SCLC) to coordinate direct action campaigns throughout the South. SCLC organized the Prayer Pilgrimage for Freedom in 1957 before the Lincoln Memorial in Washington to dramatize the need for the enfranchisement of African Americans. In his speech before about 27,000 people, King intoned, "Give us the ballot and we will no longer have to worry the Federal Government about our basic rights." It was on the same spot six years later, after protests in Atlanta and Albany, Georgia, and Birmingham, Alabama, that King rose to oratorical heights with his "I Have a Dream" speech.

In 1964, King became the second African American after Ralph Bunche to receive the Nobel Peace Prize. He continued to press for African American voting rights with the March from Selma to Montgomery that led to passage of the Voting Rights Act of 1965. King turned his attention North in 1966 to address residential segregation, substandard housing, and poor schools in Chicago. He also became outspoken about the war in Vietnam in the face of persistent poverty in the United States. King inaugurated a Poor People's Campaign to force the federal government to end poverty in the United States and traveled to Memphis, Tennessee, to support garbage workers in a strike for better wages and working conditions. There James Earl Ray, a white supremacist, shot and killed Martin Luther King Jr. on April 4, 1968, as King was standing on the balcony of the Lorraine Motel.

**KING, RILEY B. (1925– )** Born on September 16, 1925, in Itta Bena, Mississippi, B. B. King, as he was popularly called, became a renowned blues guitarist and singer who influenced many of the major rock musicians of the late twentieth century. The initials stood for Blues Boy, a name that he adopted while working as a disk jockey in Memphis, Tennessee. With his growing popularity in Europe, especially in England, during the 1960s, he developed a broader following in the United States.

**Lawless, Theodore K. (1892–1971)** A noted dermatologist, Theodore K. Lawless was born on December 6, 1892, in Thibodeaux, Louisiana. He graduated from Talladega College in Alabama and earned an M.D. degree from Northwestern University Medical School in Chicago. After postgraduate research in the United States and Europe on skin diseases, he established his practice in the black community on the south side of Chicago. Because of his expertise, he attracted patients of all racial and ethnic backgrounds. Lawless was a smart businessman and philanthropist. He made gifts for research laboratories in the United States and Israel. He made contributions to Israeli organizations in appreciation for the support he received from Jewish physicians when he sought to conduct research in Europe during the 1920s. He built Lawless Memorial Chapel at Dillard University in New Orleans in honor of his father. Lawless died on May 1, 1971.

**Lawrence, Jacob (1917–2000)** Born in Atlantic City, New Jersey, on September 7, 1917, Jacob Lawrence became one of the most noted black painters of the twentieth century. His work of historical narrative, with impressionistic renderings of Toussaint L'Ouverture, Frederick Douglass, and Harriet Tubman, reveal a series of powerful tributes to black heroes. His *Migration Series*, the story of the black trek out of the South to the North and West, won him fame in 1941. This work was the first by an African American artist to be featured in a major New York Art Gallery. Lawrence taught at the University of Washington from 1971 until he retired in 1987. He died on June 9, 2000.

**Leadership Conference on Civil Rights** Organized in 1950 by an interracial coalition of religious, political, and civil rights groups, the Leadership Conference on Civil Rights (LCCR) became a major lobby organization in Washington, D.C., for civil rights legislation. Clarence Mitchell, legislative chair of the LCCR, was known as the "101st Senator" for his tireless efforts on Capitol Hill in support of civil rights. The organization was initially located in New York and moved to Washington in 1963. Under the guidance of Ralph Neas, the first white executive director of the LCCR, the group grew to 185 member organizations by the early 1990s. LCCR played a key role in blocking the confirmation of Robert Bork as a Supreme Court Justice in 1987.

**Lee, Shelton Jackson "Spike" (1957– )** Director, writer, actor, and producer of his own films, Spike Lee was born in Atlanta on March 20, 1957. He graduated from Morehouse College in Atlanta and New York University with a master of fine arts degree in filmmaking. Lee's films have generally been made with low budgets and have grossed considerable income. Perhaps his best-known is Malcolm X (1992), made with a $34 million budget. Lee went over his initial Warner Bros.–approved budget of $28 million and secured the funds needed to complete the film from black celebrities such as Bill Cosby, Oprah Winfrey, Magic Johnson, Michael Jordan, and Janet Jackson. The film, which was three hours long, recouped its investment but did not make the profit that was predicted for it. Young filmgoers did not relate to it as much as the generation of the 1960s.

**Lewis, John** (1940– ) John Lewis was a founding member of the Student Non-Violent Coordinating Committee (SNCC) and was its national chairman from 1963 to 1966. He was born in Pike County, Alabama, on February 21, 1940, and graduated from the American Baptist Theological Seminary in Nashville, Tennessee, in 1957. He participated in the 1961 Freedom Rides and was viciously attacked. He was also beaten during "Bloody Sunday," March 7, 1965, in Selma, Alabama, when demonstrators were brutally turned back from the Edmund Pettis Bridge. After he resigned as chairman of SNCC in 1966, Lewis worked on community organization and voter registration. He was elected to the Atlanta city council from 1981 to 1986 and defeated Julian Bond in 1986 for election to the U.S. House of Representatives. He has been an outspoken advocate of human rights in the Congress.

**Lewis, Reginald** (1942–93) Born in Baltimore, Maryland, on December 7, 1942, Reginald Lewis graduated from Virginia State College and Harvard Law School. He started the first black law firm on Wall Street in 1973 and specialized in corporate law and venture capitalism. He organized an investment firm, TLC (The Lewis Company) in 1983 and purchased the McCall Pattern Company, a 117-year-old company. Lewis sold McCall three years later at a tremendous profit, and in 1987 made a leveraged buyout of Beatrice International Foods, which became the largest black-owned company in the United States. Lewis, with personal wealth of nearly half a billion dollars, was one of the richest African Americans. Before his death on January 19, 1993, of brain cancer, he made a $3 million bequest to Harvard Law School to endow the Reginald F. Lewis Fund for International Study and Research.

**Louis, Joe** (1914–81) The first black heavyweight boxing champion since Jack Johnson in 1915, after a ban on African Americans fighting for the title, Joe Louis was born Joe Louis Barrow on May 13, 1914, in Chambers County, Alabama. He was the seventh of eight children in a sharecropping family. After his father's death, his mother remarried and the family moved to Detroit, where his stepfather worked for the Ford Motor Company. During the Depression, Louis took up boxing to help support his family. His managers were two black numbers men, John Roxborough and Julian Black, who had to form a partnership with a white fight promoter, Mike Jacobs, to secure major bouts for Louis. He soon became a symbol for African Americans of what they could do if given an opportunity. African Americans throughout the country faithfully followed his bouts on radio and placed their own fortunes on his success in the ring. If he won, they walked taller. In his second fight with the German fighter, Max Schmeling in 1938, Louis also became the symbol of American democracy. His defeat of Schmeling in the first round was seen as a vindication of democracy over fascism.

Louis was drafted into the Army in 1942 but continued to fight professionally during World War II. He donated most of his earnings to the Army and Navy Relief Funds. Louis retired from boxing in 1949 but had to return to the ring a year later because of financial problems. He lost a fifteen-round decision to Ezzard Charles in September 1950 and lost his last fight, an eight-round knockout, to Rocky Marciano in October 1951. But he won sixty-three of sixty-six professional bouts, forty-nine by knockout. Louis, one of the most popular heavyweight champions, was plagued by debt, especially to the Internal Revenue Service, became addicted to drugs for a time and suffered several nervous breakdowns. He became a greeter for the casinos in Las Vegas, where high rollers could fraternize with him and later brag to their friends that they knew the "champ." Louis died of a heart attack in Las Vegas on April 12, 1981.

**Malcolm X (1925–65)** Malcolm Little was born in Omaha, Nebraska, on May 19, 1925. His parents were members of Marcus Garvey's Universal Negro Improvement Association. After his father's death, probably at the hands of white racists, and his mother's nervous breakdown, Malcolm lived in foster care. He was a brilliant student but had his ambitions thwarted by the low expectations for black students in his predominantly white school. He drifted to Boston and to New York, where he became involved in petty crime. He served time in prison for burglary and transformed his life through the teachings of Elijah Muhammad and the Nation of Islam. He took the symbol X as a reminder of the last name that had been stripped from his slave ancestors. After his release from prison in 1952, Malcolm X became an indefatigable organizer for the Nation of Islam. He became minister of its important Temple #7 in Harlem and National Representative for Elijah Muhammad and the organization. Malcolm X helped to develop temples across the country and started the newspaper *Muhammad Speaks* in his basement.

Malcolm X was very much influenced by Elijah Muhammad and the Nation of Islam. He fostered black pride and the need for African Americans to do for themselves. He opposed integration and preached that the struggle should be for human rights rather than civil rights. The United States did not recognize the African American's very humanity. If the country acknowledged their human rights, according to Malcolm X, it was possible for African Americans to acquire rights as citizens. But the United States had the power to make the decision to recognize their human rights, which Malcolm X considered to be God-given and protected by the United Nations Charter. Although he adhered to the Nation of Islam's belief that the United States was doomed and that African Americans should seek their own self-determination, he believed that the Nation of Islam should become more involved in the struggle for black freedom and equality. He broke with the Nation of Islam in large measure because of this position. He also became disillusioned with Elijah Muhammad who fathered several children with his secretaries, several of whom had been recommended by Malcolm X.

After his break with the Nation of Islam, Malcolm X made a pilgrimage to Mecca and changed his name to El-Hajj Malik El-Shabbazz. He traveled extensively throughout Africa and sought to bring the denial of African American human rights before the United Nations through his fledging group, The Organization of Afro-American Unity, and with the assistance of African nations. On February 21, 1965, he was assassinated at the hands of members of the Nation of Islam at the Audubon Ballroom in Harlem.

**Marsalis, Wynton (1961– )** A talented classical and jazz musician, Wynton Marsalis was born on October 18, 1961, in New Orleans. He came from a musical family. Marsalis played trumpet with Art Blakey's Jazz Messengers before starting his own group in 1982. He became the first musician in 1984 to win Grammy Awards for both jazz and classical recordings. Since becoming artistic director of the jazz program at Lincoln Center in 1991, he has worked to preserve and to promote jazz music as a national and international treasure.

**Marshall, Thurgood (1908–93)** The first African American appointed to the U.S. Supreme Court, Thurgood Marshall was born on July 2, 1908, in Baltimore, Maryland. He graduated from Lincoln University in Pennsylvania and wanted to attend the University of Maryland Law School, but was denied admission because of his race. He went to Howard University Law School, where he came under the influence of Charles Hamilton Houston. Marshall graduated first in his class from Howard Law School in 1933. He worked in private practice before joining Houston as counsel to the National Association for the Advancement of Colored People (NAACP). In 1939, Marshall succeeded Houston as special counsel for the NAACP. During the 1940s and early 1950s, Marshall won a series of cases before the U.S. Supreme Court that set the stage for the 1954 *Brown v. Board of Education* decision that overturned the doctrine of "separate but equal." President Lyndon B. Johnson in 1965 appointed Marshall solicitor general, the first African American to hold the position, and two years later nominated him for the U.S. Supreme Court. Marshall was a strong opponent of the death penalty on the Supreme Court, supporter of civil liberties, and advocate for labor, the poor, women, and oppressed minorities. He retired from the Court in 1991 and died on January 24, 1993.

**Massey, Walter E. (1938– )** Born in Hattiesburg, Mississippi, on April 5, 1938, Walter E. Massey graduated from Morehouse College and received his doctorate in physics from Washington University. He worked for the Argonne National Laboratory and was later professor of physics and dean of the College at Brown University. He returned to Argonne in 1979 as its director and professor of physics at the University of Chicago, where he also served as vice president for research. He was director of the National Science Foundation (1991–93) and provost and senior vice president for academic affairs for the University of California system (1993–95). He became president of Morehouse College in 1995.

**Mays, Benjamin E. (1894–1984)** Benjamin E. Mays, who served as president of Morehouse College for twenty-seven years, was born on August 1, 1894, in Ninety-Six, South Carolina. He graduated from Bates College in Maine and received a master's degree from the University of Chicago Divinity School, where he also earned a doctorate. After teaching at several historically black colleges, in 1934, Mays became dean of the School of Religion at Howard University. Six years later, he became president of Morehouse College in Atlanta. Mays helped to persuade Martin Luther King Jr., while at Morehouse, to join the ministry and to work for social change. Mays was a force in church circles and helped to organize the World Council of Churches. He influenced the new organization to adopt a resolution defining racism as a divisive element among Christians. Mays was a noted scholar of the black church and the significance of religion in the lives of African Americans. After retiring in 1967, he was elected to the Atlanta School Board in 1969 and became its president in 1970. He died in Atlanta on March 28, 1984.

**Mays, Willie (1931– )** The first player in major league baseball to hit three hundred home runs and steal three hundred bases, Willie Mays was one of the most versatile baseball players of all time. His 7,095 putouts were a record for an outfielder. Joe DiMaggio said that Mays had the greatest throwing arm in baseball. Mays was born on May 6, 1931, in Westfield, Alabama, and grew up in Fairfield, Alabama. At age sixteen, he became a professional baseball player with the Birmingham Black Barons of the Negro Southern League. The New York Giants signed him to a contract on the day he graduated from high school and called him up to the major leagues a year later. He was named Rookie of the Year in his first season. He played in nineteen All-Star Games and four World Series and won twelve consecutive Gold Glove Awards. Mays retired from baseball in 1973 with 660 home runs and a lifetime batting average of .302. He was inducted into the Baseball Hall of Fame in 1979.

**McNair, Ronald** (1950–86) Ronald McNair was a crewmember on the space shuttle *Challenger* in 1984. He was born on October 21, 1950, in Lake City, South Carolina. He graduated magna cum laude from North Carolina Agricultural and Technical State University and received a doctoral degree in physics from MIT. He worked as a physicist at Hughes Research laboratories in California before joining the space program in 1978. He died in the explosion of the *Challenger* on January 28, 1986. MIT named its Center for Space Research in his honor. The U.S. Department of Education designated its initiative to encourage students from disadvantaged backgrounds to pursue advanced degrees the Ronald McNair Scholars Program.

**Meredith, James** (1933– ) Born in Kosciusko, Mississippi, on June 25, 1933, James Meredith was the first African American to graduate from the University of Mississippi in 1963. His enrollment at the university in 1962 came despite opposition from the governor. President John F. Kennedy had to send federal marshals to protect Meredith. In 1966, Meredith launched his famous "March Against Fear," from Memphis, Tennessee, to Jackson, Mississippi, during which he was shot and wounded. Civil rights organizations took up his march. As they continued the trek, Stokely Carmichael made his call for "Black Power." Meredith earned a law degree from Columbia University in 1968 and unsuccessfully ran for office. For a time, he served as domestic policy adviser to the conservative South Carolina senator Jesse Helms.

**Metcalfe, Ralph** (1910–78) The winner of silver medals in the 1932 and 1936 Olympics (finishing second to Jesse Owens) for 100 meters and a gold medal on the 4 × 100 meter relay team in 1936, Metcalfe was born on May 30, 1910, in Atlanta, Georgia. He graduated from Marquette University in Milwaukee, Wisconsin. He coached track at Xavier University in New Orleans before serving in the Army during World War II. After the war, he became the first black state athletic commissioner in Illinois, became an alderman in 1955, and was elected to the U.S. Congress in 1970. Initially a member of the Democratic Party political machine in Chicago, he broke with the machine in 1972 over the issue of police brutality. He handily defeated an opponent handpicked by the machine to run against him in the election. Metcalfe died of a heart attack on October 10, 1978, as he sought his fifth term in Congress.

**Mfume, Kweisi** (1948– ) Born on October 24, 1948, in Baltimore, Maryland, Kweisi Mfume graduated magna cum laude from Morgan State University, where he edited the school newspaper and headed the Black Student Union. He later earned a master's degree in international studies from Johns Hopkins University. In 1979, he was elected to the Baltimore city council and to the U.S. Congress in 1986. He became chair of the Joint Economic Committee of the House and the Senate. In the Congress, he promoted minority business and civil rights legislation. The National Association for the Advancement of Colored People (NAACP) selected him as president and chief executive officer in 1996. He helped to pull the NAACP out of debt and to restore its reputation as the premier civil rights organization. His agenda has focused on civil rights, political empowerment, educational excellence, economic development, health, and youth outreach. He resigned as president on December 31, 2004, and launched a campaign for the U.S. Senate from Maryland.

**Mississippi Freedom Democratic Party** The Student Non-Violent Coordinating Committee (SNCC) organized the Mississippi Freedom Democratic Party (MFDP) in 1964 to challenge the state Democratic Party that excluded black voters. During Mississippi Freedom Summer, SNCC registered black and white voters in the MFDP and sought to have its slate of delegates replace the state Democratic Party delegates at the National Convention in Atlantic City, New Jersey. Lyndon B. Johnson, who was running for reelection as president, through his emissaries proposed a compromise whereby the state delegates would be seated if they swore allegiance to the National Party, and the MFDP would receive two at-large seats. Although Hubert Humphrey, organized labor, and Martin Luther King Jr. exerted great pressure on the MFDP, it refused to compromise. The MFDP protest laid the foundation for the state Democratic Party opening participation to African Americans.

**Montgomery Improvement Association** The Montgomery Improvement Association (MIA) was organized to coordinate the bus boycott after Rosa Parks was arrested for refusing to give up her seat on December 1, 1955. The MIA developed car pools as an alternative system of transportation for African Americans in Montgomery, Alabama. The MIA filed suit in federal court challenging the constitutionality of the city's laws upholding segregation on the buses. It sustained the boycott for more than a year, despite threats, intimidation, and bombings, until the U.S. Supreme Court ruled in *Browder v. Gayle* on December 21, 1956, that the bus segregation violated the Fourteenth Amendment. The MIA continued to exist for several more years but never regained the strength that it displayed during the boycott under the leadership of Martin Luther King Jr.

**Morrison, Toni (1931– )** Born Chloe Anthony Wofford on February 18, 1931, in Lorain, Ohio, Toni Morrison became the second American woman and the first African American to win a Nobel Prize for Literature in 1993. She graduated from Howard University and received an M.A. from Cornell University. Her marriage to Harold Morrison ended in divorce after seven years and two sons. In 1964, Morrison began working for Random House, where she became a senior editor while also teaching at the State University of New York at Albany and later at Princeton University. Her novels have been incisive explorations of black identity, gender relations, family interactions, and cultural practices.

**Moses, Robert Parris (1935– )** Born in New York on January 23, 1935, Robert Moses graduated from Hamilton College in upstate New York and received a master of art degree in philosophy from Harvard University. He joined the Student Non-Violent Coordinating Committee (SNCC) soon after its organization in 1960. He became its first full-time voter registration organizer in the Deep South. In 1962, he was named project director of the Congress of Federated Organizations (COFO), a coalition of the major civil rights organizations in Mississippi. He helped to organize the Mississippi Freedom Democratic Party (MFDP) in 1964 and became disillusioned by its failure to be seated as the official delegation at the National Party Convention in Atlantic City, New Jersey. He resigned from SNCC and used the name Robert Parris to avoid recognition. To escape the draft, he fled in 1966 to Canada and then to Tanzania, where he taught mathematics. He returned to the United States in 1976 and founded the Algebra Project in 1980 to help inner city youngsters learn mathematics. This project earned him a MacArthur Foundation "genius" award. Moses took the project to rural Mississippi in 1992. He considered the work an extension of his earlier civil rights career and his efforts to empower African Americans to achieve racial equality.

**Motley, Constance Baker (1921–2005)** The first black woman to be appointed a federal judge, Constance Baker Motley was born on September 14, 1921, in New Haven, Connecticut. She graduated from New York University and received her law degree from Columbia University. After finishing law school, she became a law clerk for Thurgood Marshall at the NAACP Legal Defense and Educational Fund and later became an associate counsel. She tried many of the desegregation cases in the South, including James Meredith's suit against the University of Mississippi. She also helped to prepare legal briefs for the *Brown v. Board of Education* U.S. Supreme Court case in 1954. In 1964, she became only the second woman and the first black woman to be elected to the New York state senate. A year later, she became the first black woman elected president of the borough of Manhattan. In 1966, President Lyndon B. Johnson appointed her to the U.S. District Court for the Southern District of

New York, the first African American and the first woman to serve on that court. She died of congestive heart failure in New York on September 28, 2005.

**Muhammad, Elijah (1897–1975)** Born Robert Poole in Sandersville, Georgia, on October 10, 1897, Elijah Muhammad became head of the Nation of Islam after the mysterious disappearance in 1934 of Wallace Fard, its founder. Fard converted Elijah Muhammad to the Nation of Islam and gave him his name. After Fard's disappearance, Muhammad moved from Detroit to Chicago, where he established Temple #2. Chicago became the headquarters for the organization as Muhammad proclaimed Fard as Allah and himself the Messenger of Allah. Muhammad developed a black nationalist ideology that brought together elements of Islam, Christianity, Marcus Garvey's Universal Negro Improvement Association, and the Moorish Science Temple. His message characterized the white man as the devil, an invention of a mad black scientist, and the cause of the black man's plight. Once black people discovered true knowledge of themselves, separated from white society, and built their own society, they would be free. The Nation of Islam made many converts from downtrodden African Americans who had become addicted to drugs or were incarcerated in prison. Through the total submission to the Nation of Islam and change of lifestyle, they were able to gain some respectability and material improvement in their lives. The Nation of Islam promoted economic self-sufficiency among African Americans and owned farms, a bank, clothing stores, restaurants, bakeries, grocery stores, a printing and storage plant, airplanes, and an import business for fresh fish sold in their outlets. The organization also conducted its own elementary and secondary schools, known as the University of Islam.

The Nation of Islam had an influence, especially during the 1960s, beyond its membership, as it preached black pride, self-determination, and a healthy diet without pork, drugs, alcohol, or tobacco. At its height, the Nation of Islam had an estimated membership of 500,000. After Muhammad's death on February 25, 1975, it was discovered that the economic assets of the Nation of Islam, valued at almost $80 million, were in the name of Elijah Muhammad and his family rather than the organization itself.

**National Association for the Advancement of Colored People** The National Association for the Advancement of Colored People (NAACP) was organized in 1909 by a merger of the Niagara Movement, which had been formed by W. E. B. Du Bois in 1905, and a group of white liberals who were shocked by the vicious race riot in 1908 that took place in Springfield, Illinois, the burial place of Abraham Lincoln. The NAACP's purpose was to "fix beyond question the status of the American citizen of Negro descent." The NAACP fought for racial equality through legislative, judicial, and educational means. Its campaign against lynching led to a decline in this brutal form of social control and oppression of African Americans. After the decline in lynching during the 1930s, the NAACP turned its attention to segregation in education. Its greatest accomplishment was the U.S. Supreme Court's decision in *Brown v. Board of Education*, which overturned the separate-but-equal doctrine that had underpinned racial segregation in the United States. Southern reaction to this decision almost crippled the NAACP as southern states tried to secure its membership rolls for retaliation, charged that it was infiltrated by communists, and sought to ban it outright. During the 1960s and 1970s, the NAACP continued to work through the legislative and judicial branches while other civil rights organizations developed more direct action programs in boycotts, picketing, and demonstrations. The NAACP shifted its attention during the 1980s and 1990s to economic progress, educational excellence, and community development. The organization moved its headquarters from Manhattan to Brooklyn Heights in 1982 because of escalating costs and then to its own building in Baltimore, Maryland, in 1986.

**NAACP Legal Defense and Educational Fund** The NAACP created the NAACP Legal Defense and Educational Fund (LDF) in 1939 as a tax-exempt corporation to fund the NAACP's litigation and education programs. Thurgood Marshall was its first director. The LDF was closely associated with the NAACP and was represented on its national board. It was the LDF that brought most of the important cases that culminated in *Brown v. Board of Education* in 1954, after which the two organizations split in 1956 over differences in priorities. The NAACP saw the LDF as its mechanism for litigating civil rights cases, while the LDF considered its mission to achieve educational equality. The LDF angered many African Americans during the 1960s when it refused to defend black radicals. It has been involved primarily in affirmative action, employment discrimination, and capital punishment cases. More recently, it has focused on environmental and health care discrimination.

**National Negro Congress** The National Negro Congress (NNC) was organized in 1936 after a conference at Howard University on the status of African Americans during the Great Depression and their access to New Deal programs. It was an umbrella organization of churches, unions, fraternal organizations, businessmen, and political groups. Its purpose was to unite black organizations in the fight against racial segregation. A. Philip Randolph served as president until 1940, when he resigned over growing Communist Party influence in the organization. In 1946, before it was absorbed by the Civil Rights

Congress, the NNC issued a petition to the United Nations on the denial of African American human rights in the United States.

**National Urban League** The National Urban League was founded in 1911 to address the urban condition of African Americans who were beginning to migrate to the cities, especially in the North. It focused on employment opportunities, housing, and social welfare. The Urban League has traditionally sponsored job-training programs and encouraged the education of black social workers. During the 1960s, its executive director, Whitney M. Young, called for a Marshall Plan to rebuild urban America, similar to the one after World War II that helped to rebuild Western Europe. Since 1976, it has published a widely publicized annual report, *The State of Black America*. The Urban League has also devoted attention recently to strengthening black families and encouraging educational achievement.

**Newton, Huey P.** (1942–89) Co-founder of the Black Panther Party with Bobby Seale, Huey Newton was born on February 17, 1942, in Monroe, Louisiana, and grew up in Oakland, California. Newton attended Merit Community College in Oakland, where he joined the Afro-American Association together with Bobby Seale and Ron Everett (Maulana Karenga). Robert Williams, the Revolutionary Action Movement, and Malcolm X had a profound influence on Newton, as did the works of Frantz Fanon and Mao Zedong. Newton believed that African Americans had to use violence if necessary to free themselves from white capitalist and racist domination. Newton was convicted of voluntary manslaughter in 1968 after the death of one police officer and the wounding of another in a shootout with the Black Panthers. He was imprisoned for two years, when his conviction was overturned because of procedural errors in his trial. Newton claimed that the Black Panther Party had changed during his incarceration and had become more remote from the black community. He ordered a number of purges that weakened and factionalized the organization. Accused of murder in 1974 in the death of a black woman, Newton fled to Cuba, where he remained until 1977, when he returned to a moribund party. He was tried for murder, but the charges were dropped after two hung juries. Newton earned a doctorate from the University of California at Santa Cruz in 1980. Before his death on August 22, 1989, allegedly at the hands of a drug dealer whom he had robbed, Newton, who had become addicted to drugs, faced numerous criminal charges, including embezzlement, possession of firearms, and the murder of a teenage prostitute.

**Nixon, Edgar Daniel** (1899–1987) Born in Robinson Springs, Alabama, on July 12, 1899, E. D. Nixon became a prominent civil rights advocate in nearby Montgomery. He worked as a Pullman car porter and learned about racial discrimination and segregation through his travels throughout the country as well as the opportunities that African Americans enjoyed in the North and the West. He became president of the Montgomery branch of the NAACP in 1945 and state president two years later. With not more than a sixth-grade education, Nixon rubbed many of the middle-class black members of the NAACP the wrong way, and they caused his defeat as state president of the NAACP and even as president of the Montgomery branch. He was a close friend, however, of Rosa Parks, and when she was arrested on December 1, 1955, for refusing to relinquish her seat on a Montgomery bus, she called Nixon. He arranged for her bail and helped to call for a boycott. Nixon was elected treasurer of the Montgomery Improvement Association, organized to coordinate the boycott. Nixon retired as a Pullman porter in 1964 and worked organizing recreational activities for poor youth in Montgomery before his death on February 25, 1987.

**Norton, Eleanor Holmes (1937– )** A leader of the Student Non-Violent Coordinating Committee, Eleanor Holmes Norton was born in Washington, D.C., on June 13, 1937. She graduated from Antioch College in Ohio and completed a master's degree in American history and a law degree at Yale. She worked with the Mississippi Freedom Democratic Party in 1964 before becoming a civil rights attorney for the American Civil Liberties Union. She became chair of the New York City Human Rights Commission in 1970, and President Jimmy Carter appointed her chair of the Equal Employment Opportunity Commission in 1977. After five years in the position, she taught law at Georgetown University Law School before being elected in 1990 as Washington, D.C. delegate to the U.S. House of Representatives.

**Obama, Barack (1961– )** Born in Hawaii on August 4, 1961, to a black African father and a white American mother, Barack Obama has brought a multidimensional background to the meaning of being an American. Obama electrified the 2004 Democratic Party National Convention in Boston as its keynote speaker with his personal references to the American dream and a United States of America united in the final analysis across lines of race, ethnicity, political party, religion, region, and socioeconomic status. The second African American elected to the U.S. Senate from Illinois and the third African American to serve in the Senate since Reconstruction, Obama graduated from Columbia University and Harvard Law School, where he was the first African American to serve as president of the *Harvard Law Review*. He was a community organizer, civil rights attorney, lecturer at the University of Chicago Law School, and member of the Illinois state senate before being elected to the U.S. Senate in 2004.

**O'Leary, Hazel (1937– )** Born on May 17, 1937, in Newport News, Virginia, Hazel Rollins graduated from Fisk University and completed a law degree at Rutgers University. She was an assistant state attorney general and county prosecutor in New Jersey before becoming a member of the Federal Energy Administration under President Gerald Ford. During Jimmy Carter's administration, she served as head of the Economic Regulatory Administration in the Department of Energy. She married John O'Leary, the deputy energy secretary, in 1980 and they later formed an energy consulting firm, O'Leary Associates. Hazel O'Leary shut down the firm in 1987 after John O'Leary's death. In 1989, she became executive vice president of Northern States Power Company in Minneapolis and was named in 1993 by President Clinton as the first woman and the first African American to serve as secretary of energy. In 2004, she became president of Fisk University.

**Organization of Black American Culture (OBAC)** Founded in Chicago in 1967, OBAC was the brainchild of Hoyt W. Fuller, editor of *Negro Digest/Black World*, poet Conrad Kent Rivers, and scholar-activist Gerald McWorter (Abdul Alkalimat). The purpose of OBAC was to nurture black creative talent to improve the black community. It had three workshops for writers, visual artists, and community relations and cooperated with already existing musicians and theater groups. The visual arts workshop became an independent group, African Commune of Bad Relevant Artists (AFRICOBRA), under the leadership of artist Jeff Donaldson. AFRICOBRA painters sought to combine traditions of African art with the work of artists in the United States to develop an African diasporic aesthetic. OBAC soon became a writers' workshop that influenced such writers as Johari Amini, Cecil Brown, Angela Jackson, Haki Mahdubuti (Don L. Lee), Sterling Plumpp, and Carolyn Rodgers.

**Owens, Jesse (1913–80)** At the 1936 Olympics in Berlin, Germany, Jesse Owens won four gold medals and shattered the premise of Aryan supremacy that black people were inferior. He was born James Cleveland Owens on September 12, 1913, in Oakville, Alabama. He attended Ohio State University and starred in track and field but did not graduate. Although he was hailed as a champion and a symbol of American democracy, Owens was never able to translate his fame into fortune. To earn a living, for a time, he took on the humiliating job of running against racehorses. He later became a business consultant in Chicago and made a number of goodwill trips abroad for the United States. He believed in concentrating on opportunity rather than racial obstacles and often was at odds with the civil rights and later the Black Power movements. He died of lung cancer on March 31, 1980.

**Parker, Charles Christopher (1920–55)** Born in Kansas City, Missouri, on August 29, 1920, "Charlie" Parker helped to revolutionize jazz with his bebop style. He became a professional musician at age fifteen and moved to New York in 1939, where he played with a number of major bands and orchestras. Popularly known as "Bird" or "Yardbird," supposedly because of his fondness for chicken, Parker made the alto saxophone a great improvisational instrument. John Coltrane allegedly switched from alto to tenor saxophone because Parker had done all there was to do on the alto. Parker's bouts with alcohol and drugs, however, ruined his physical and mental health. He died of a heart attack on March 23, 1955.

**Parks, Gordon (1912– )** The first African American photojournalist for a mainstream magazine, *Life*, and the first African American director of a major Hollywood film, Gordon Parks was born on November 30, 1912, in Fort Scott, Kansas. He worked a number of odd jobs to support himself after his mother died when he was sixteen years old. Largely self-taught, Parks was a voracious reader and a quick study. He bought his first camera in 1937 and soon became a fashion photographer. Parks won a Rosenwald Fellowship in 1942 and used it to study under Roy Stryker in Washington, D.C. He later worked for Stryker at the Office of War Information and for Standard Oil. Parks began working for *Life* in 1948, primarily on fashion and celebrities. During the 1960s, he turned more of his attention to the civil rights movement and to slum conditions in Brazil and the United States. He published two books on photographic technique and an autobiography, *The Learning Tree*, which he directed in 1969, as the first black director of a major Hollywood film. He later directed other films, wrote poetry, composed music, and painted.

**Parks, Rosa (1913–2005)** Born on February 4, 1913, in Tuskegee, Alabama, Rosa McCauley married Raymond Parks, a barber, in 1932. They were both active in the struggle for racial equality and protested against the Scottsboro convictions in 1931, when nine young black men were quickly convicted of allegedly raping two white women on a freight train. Rosa Parks served as secretary of Montgomery branch of the National Association for the Advancement of Colored People from 1943 to 1956. On December 1, 1955, she was arrested for refusing to give up her seat on a Montgomery bus not so that a white passenger could sit down but so that he would not have to sit across from a black passenger as was the custom and the law. Her courageous act led to the Montgomery bus boycott, which began the end of bus segregation throughout the South. She had worked as a seamstress at a department store in Montgomery but lost her job because of the bus boycott. She and her husband moved to Detroit in 1957, where she became an administrative assistant to Congressman John Conyers until 1988. She actively supported the civil rights movement and the struggle against apartheid in South Africa. She also sought to address the problem of black high school dropouts and established the Rosa and Raymond Parks Institute for Self-Development in Detroit. She died at her home in Detroit at age 92 on October 24, 2005.

**Patterson, Frederick Douglass** (1901–88) The founder of the United Negro College Fund in 1943, Frederick Patterson was born on October 10, 1901, in Washington, D.C. He graduated from Prairie View College in Texas, received a degree in veterinary medicine at Iowa State College, and earned a doctoral degree in agriculture from Cornell University. He taught at Virginia State College and at Tuskegee Institute, where he became president in 1935. He later founded the United Negro College Fund as a means to secure outside funds for the schools. After retiring as president of Tuskegee, he became president of the Phelps-Stokes Fund, which was started in 1911 to increase educational opportunities for American Indians, Africans, and African Americans. From 1970 to 1980, he headed the Robert R. Moton Memorial Institute, named after the successor to Booker T. Washington as head of Tuskegee Institute. The Moton Institute was established to advance the work of black scholars and scholarship on African Americans, especially education. Patterson was dedicated to building financial security and to making black colleges less dependent on federal funding. He died in New Rochelle, New York, on April 26, 1988.

**Patterson, William** (1891–1980) Born on August 27, 1891, in San Francisco, William Patterson attended the University of California at Berkeley and received a law degree from Hastings College of Law. He moved to New York after World War I, where he practiced law. Viewing capitalism as the cause of black oppression, he joined the Communist Party in 1927. He studied in Moscow for three years, declaring Russian society free of racial prejudice. After returning to the United States in 1930, he became a member of the Central Committee of the Communist Party. He was director of the International Labor Defense from 1932 to 1946, an organization that rivaled the National Association for the Advancement of Colored People, especially in defense of the Scottsboro Boys, who had been convicted in 1931 of allegedly raping two white women on a freight train, with eight of the nine young men sentenced to death. One was spared the death sentence only because he was a minor. Patterson later became executive director of the Civil Rights Congress. He and Paul Robeson presented a petition to the United Nations in 1951 that charged the United States with genocide against African Americans. Patterson served three months in prison before his conviction was overturned for being held in contempt by the House Un-American Activities Committee. He published his autobiography, *The Man Who Cried Genocide*, in 1971. Patterson died on March 5, 1980.

**Pierce, Samuel** (1922–2000) A graduate of Cornell University, where he starred in football, Samuel Pierce was the only black cabinet member during Ronald Reagan's presidency. He was born on September 8, 1922, in Glen Cove, New York. He earned a law degree from Cornell and a master of laws degree from New York University. He served as an assistant U.S. attorney general for New York, assistant U.S. Undersecretary of Labor, New York state judge, general counsel for the U.S. Department of Treasury, and in private practice before being named secretary of housing and urban development in 1981, a position he held until 1989. He was accused of influence peddling and favoritism in providing government contracts to powerful Republicans. Although several of his aides were found guilty of fraud, he was not charged. Pierce, whom J. Edgar Hoover, head of the Federal Bureau of Investigation, once identified as a leader for Black America rather than more "radical" individuals such as Martin Luther King Jr., died of complications from a stroke on October 31, 2000.

**Poitier, Sidney** (1927– ) The first African American to win the Academy Award for best actor, Sidney Poitier was born in Miami, Florida, on February 20, 1927, and grew up in the Bahamas. After military service in the Army during World War II, he settled in New York and joined the American Negro Theatre Company. During the 1950s, he starred in several films and was the first African American nominated for best actor for his role in *The Defiant Ones* in 1958. He won the Oscar for best actor in 1964 for *Lilies of the Field*. He directed his first film in 1972 with *Buck and the Preacher*. He directed several films during the 1980s. The Screen Actors Guild honored him with a Lifetime Achievement Award in 1999.

**Powell, Adam Clayton, Jr.** (1908–72) Born on November 29, 1908, in New Haven, Connecticut, Adam Clayton Powell became known as "Mr. Civil Rights" in the U.S. Congress largely because of what was labeled as the "Powell Amendment," which he attached to legislation and that denied federal support for any segregated facilities. His amendment later became part of the Civil Rights Act of 1964, which barred use of federal funds for any institution that discriminated on the basis of race, creed, or color. Powell graduated from Colgate University and received a master's degree in religious education from Columbia University Teacher's College. He served as assistant pastor to his father at Abyssinian Baptist Church in Harlem, one of the oldest and largest black churches in the country. The church had a long history of serving the black community with a senior citizens home that it opened in 1926. The church also sponsored a credit union, nursery school, adult education center, soup kitchen, and employment bureau. Adam Clayton Powell Jr. succeeded his father as pastor in 1937. He was a strong advocate of racial equality and led "Don't Buy Where

You Can't Work" campaigns in Harlem to foster black employment by department stores, the bus company, and public utilities. In 1941, he became the first African American elected to the New York city council. Three years later, he became the first black congressman from New York. Powell was a political maverick, although he was a member of the Democratic Party. He rose to become chairman of the House Education and Labor Committee and exercised great influence on legislation. He authored some sixty pieces of legislation during his congressional career from 1944 to 1970. Because of what he termed his "peccadilloes"—among them lavish trips at taxpayer expense, having his wife on his payroll, and kickbacks—Congress in 1967 voted to expel Powell. Two years later, Supreme Court Justice Earl Warren, after Powell had been reelected to the seat, which had been declared vacant, ruled that his expulsion from Congress was unconstitutional. Powell no longer had his seniority and lost his bid for reelection in 1970 by 150 votes. He died of cancer on April 4, 1972.

**Powell, Colin Luther (1937– )** The first African American to be named secretary of state, Colin Powell was born on April 5, 1937, in New York. He graduated from City College of New York, where he was a member of the Reserve Officer Training Corps (ROTC) and achieved the highest rank possible, that of cadet colonel. He served in West Germany, then in Vietnam, receiving a Purple Heart for wounds suffered there. After a second tour of duty in Vietnam, Powell earned an M.B.A. from George Washington University and became a White House Fellow in the administration of Richard M. Nixon. With several military commands behind him and rise to the rank of brigadier general, he was appointed military assistant to Secretary of Defense Casper Weinberger. After being named lieutenant general, he served as national security adviser to President Ronald Reagan in 1987. He then became a four-star general and was selected by President George H. W. Bush to become the first black chairman of the Joint Chiefs of Staff. He oversaw the strategy for Operation Desert Storm in 1991 to remove the Iraqis from Kuwait. Powell retired from the military in 1993 and has received two Presidential Medals of Freedom, one from President Bush and one from President Bill Clinton. On January 20, 2001, he was named secretary of state by President George W. Bush. He left office in 2005.

**Price, Leontyne (1927– )** Born on February 10, 1927, in Laurel, Mississippi, Mary Violet Leontyne Price enjoyed a stellar operatic career from 1952 to 1985. She attended Central State College in Ohio before enrolling at Julliard in 1949. Her formal debut at the Metropolitan Opera in 1961 inspired the audience to give her an unprecedented forty-two minute ovation. She toured the world and excelled in Italian, German, French, Spanish, and Slavic repertory in addition to spirituals and other American songs. Her work has been recorded extensively and her legacy has been unmatched in versatility, power, and longevity.

**PRYOR, RICHARD** (1940–2005) As a nightclub performer, movie star, and television host, Richard Pryor used humor, often raunchy, to explore the underside of black life. He was born on December 1, 1940, in Peoria, Illinois. He dropped out of school and joined the military. After military service, he worked in the Caterpillar factory in Peoria and began honing his comedic skills. He appeared in many small clubs before making a breakthrough with a television appearance in 1964. Soon he performed on many national television shows and debuted in the movies in 1967. He acted, produced, wrote, and directed some forty films during his career. He had his own television program in 1977, which lasted for a brief time because the network executives found it too risky. Pryor was diagnosed with multiple sclerosis in 1986. He died of a heart atack on December 10, 2005.

**QUARLES, BENJAMIN** (1904–96) Born on January 28, 1904, in Boston, Massachusetts, Benjamin Quarles graduated from Shaw University in Raleigh, North Carolina, and earned a doctorate in history from the University of Wisconsin. He taught at Shaw, was dean at Dillard University in New Orleans, and chaired the history department at Morgan State University in Baltimore from 1953 to 1967. He was one of the first black historians to publish in the *Mississippi Valley Historical Review* (which became the *Journal of American History*). Quarles was a very productive historian who spent his academic career at historically black colleges and universities. His work on eighteenth- and nineteenth-century African American history set a standard for scholarship that unearthed the key roles that African Americans played in the inception, development, and preservation of the United States. Quarles died at age ninety-two on November 16, 1996.

**RANDALL, DUDLEY** (1914–2000) The founder of Broadside Press in 1965, poet and author Dudley Randall was born in Washington, D.C., on January 14, 1914. His family moved to Detroit when he was nine, and he later graduated from Wayne State University. He worked as a librarian for most of his career. Randall founded Broadside Press to publish and to promote the work of black poets and writers. He started by printing broadsides or poetry on shingle sheets of paper that he sold for fifty cents each. Later, he printed small pamphlets that were reasonably priced at one to two dollars. These small publications became very popular and helped to spread the work of some of the major poets and authors of the Black Arts movement. Because of persistent debt due in large part to the low prices that he charged for the publications, Randall sold Broadside

Press. He remained as a consultant. In 1981, Mayor Coleman Young appointed Randall as Detroit's first poet laureate. Randall died on August 5, 2000.

**Randolph, Asa Philip (1889–1979)** Born on April 15, 1889, in Crescent City, Florida, A. Philip Randolph completed his secondary education at Cookman Institute in Jacksonville, Florida. He traveled to New York in 1911 and attended City College of New York. He worked at odd jobs to support himself and joined the Socialist Party. With Chandler Owen, he started the *Messenger Magazine* in 1917 as a radical journal to examine the subordinate position of African Americans in American society. During World War I, the *Messenger* advised African Americans to resist the draft, and Randolph served a short prison term for his opposition to the war. Randolph severed his ties to the Socialist Party during the early 1920s because it did not engage the exclusion of African Americans from the trade-union movement. Although he was not a Pullman car porter, the porters asked him to help organize a union for them. In many respects, the fact that he did not work for the company made him less vulnerable to retaliation. From 1925 to 1937, he worked to organize the Brotherhood of Sleeping Car Porters, which the company recognized only after Congress passed enabling labor legislation. Randolph served as president of the National Negro Congress from 1936 until his resignation in 1940 over growing Communist Party influence in the organization. In 1941, he threatened a March of Washington that led to President Franklin D. Roosevelt's issuing Executive Order 8802 to ban discrimination in defense industries. He threatened another March on Washington in 1948, which pressured President Harry S. Truman to issue Executive Order 9981 to desegregate the armed forces. Randolph became the elder statesman of the civil rights movement and was an architect of the 1963 March on Washington for Jobs and Freedom. He died on May 16, 1979, at the age of ninety.

**Republic of New Africa** Gaidi Obadele (Milton Henry) and Imari Obadele (Richard Henry) created the Republic of New Africa (RNA) at a 1968 meeting in Detroit. They attracted several hundred delegates who demanded the establishment of a black nation in five states of the South (Alabama, Georgia, Louisiana, Mississippi, and South Carolina). Gaidi Obadele was an attorney and had worked closely with Malcolm X. The call for an independent black nation in five states of the South was very close to the Nation of Islam's vision. The RNA saw itself organizing on the principle of Ujamaa, the Tanzanian example of cooperative economics. The group asked the U.S. government to provide $400 billion in reparations for enslavement and racial oppression and to set aside the five states for the RNA. In 1969, a police officer was killed and four RNA members were wounded in a shootout at New Bethel Baptist Church in Detroit. Two years later, the RNA sought to purchase land in Hinds

County, Mississippi, for its capital but again became involved in a shootout that resulted in the death of a police officer. Imari Obadele, the provisional president of the RNA, and ten other members were arrested and convicted of several charges. One member was convicted of firing the shot that killed the officer and was sentenced to life in prison. Imari Obadele served nine years in prison for his involvement in the murder and for federal conspiracy charges. The RNA has continued the struggle for reparations and the establishment of an independent socialist black nation.

**Revolutionary Action Movement** Founded in 1963, the Revolutionary Action Movement (RAM) advocated a fundamental restructuring of American society to achieve black liberation from racial domination and oppression. RAM justified the use of violence if necessary to achieve the necessary change. The organization was influenced by Robert F. Williams, a leader of the National Association for the Advancement of Colored People (NAACP), who became disillusioned with the government's unwillingness to protect the lives of African Americans. The NAACP expelled Williams, who fled to Cuba in 1961, where he wrote the book *Negroes with Guns*. Although in exile, Williams helped to form RAM as a Marxist-Leninist organization to build a revolutionary army of young African Americans. Under attack from the Federal Bureau of Investigation's Counterintelligence Program (COINTELPRO), RAM members were often arrested and convicted of conspiracy charges based on the FBI's infiltration of the organization and RAM's rhetoric more than its actions. RAM had basically been destroyed by 1968.

**Rice, Condoleezza (1954– )** Appointed by President George W. Bush as national security adviser in 2001 and as secretary of state in 2005, Condoleezza Rice was born on November 14, 1954, in Birmingham, Alabama. She enrolled at the University of Denver at age fifteen and graduated cum laude and Phi Beta Kappa with a degree in political science. She earned a master's degree from the University of Notre Dame and a Ph.D. degree in international studies from the University of Denver in 1981. She taught at Stanford University and served as senior director of Soviet and European affairs for the National Security Council in the administration of President George H. W. Bush. She returned to Stanford, where she became provost in 1993 and was responsible for the academic program and annual budget of some $1.5 billion. She is the author of several books on international relations and foreign affairs.

**Robertson, Oscar (1938– )** A three-time All-American and captain of the 1960 United States gold medal winning Olympic team, Oscar Robertson was born on November 24, 1938, in Charlotte, Tennessee. He grew up in Indianapolis, where he led his high school team to two state basketball championships. Robertson starred in basketball at the University of Cincinnati, from which he graduated in 1960. Popularly known as the "Big O," Robertson was one of the best guards to play professional basketball with the Cincinnati Royals and later the Milwaukee Bucks. He served as president of the National Basketball Players Association from 1965 to 1972 and helped to establish free agency that allowed players to join other teams at the end of their contracts. Robertson retired from professional basketball in 1974 and started a chemical manufacturing company in Cincinnati.

**Robeson, Paul** (1898–1976) A standout student and athlete at Rutgers University, Paul Robeson was born on April 9, 1898, in Princeton, New Jersey. He won thirteen varsity letters in four sports, was named All-American in football twice, and was elected to Phi Beta Kappa in his junior year. He attended Columbia University Law School and and earned money to support himself by playing semiprofessional football on the weekends. Despite his brilliant academic record, he could not secure employment with a major law firm after graduation. He did practice law for a brief time but left the field after less than a year because of racial discrimination. Robeson began acting and singing and enjoyed immense success. He also appeared in almost a dozen films but abandoned a film career at the height of his fame because of Hollywood's stereotypical portrayal of black people on the screen. Robeson was a staunch supporter of African liberation and improvement of living conditions for oppressed people throughout the world. He was attracted to the Soviet Union and its work uplifting the common man and woman. Robeson supported the battle against fascism during World War II and gave many concerts to benefit the American military.

After World War II, Robeson came under government scrutiny during the Cold War because of his left-wing politics. He testified before a California State Legislature committee in 1946 that he had not been a member of the Communist Party, but subsequently refused to answer the question on the principle that the government had no right to intrude into a person's political affiliation and ideology. At the World Congress of the Defenders of Peace conference in Paris, 1949, Robeson stated, "It is unthinkable that the American Negroes would go to war on behalf of those who have oppressed us for generations against a country which in one generation has raised our people to full human dignity of mankind." Those words, which seemed to favor the Soviet Union, created a furor of opposition to Robeson, leading to cancelled concerts and the forfeiture of his passport. The United States Supreme Court ruled in 1958 that the government's requirement that he sign an oath that he was not a communist was unconstitutional. With his passport reinstated, Robeson traveled abroad, especially to the

Soviet Union where he was considered a hero. He remained abroad for five years and returned to the United States in declining health. Robeson died in Philadelphia on January 23, 1976.

**Robinson, Frank (1935– )** The first black manager of a major league baseball team, Frank Robinson was born on August 31, 1935, in Beaumont, Texas. He grew up in Oakland, California. He was the only player to win the Most Valuable Player Award in both the National League (with the Cincinnati Reds) and in the American League (with the Baltimore Orioles). He became player/manager of the Cleveland Indians in 1975. At the time of his retirement in 1977, he had hit the fourth-highest number of home runs in a career at 586. He later managed the San Francisco Giants, the Baltimore Orioles, the Montreal Expos, and the Washington Nationals. Robinson was elected to the Baseball Hall of Fame in 1982.

**Robinson, Jack Roosevelt (1919–72)** Jackie Robinson was the first African American to play professional baseball in the twentieth century. A talented athlete in football, basketball, track, and baseball, Robinson was born on January 31, 1919, in Cairo, Georgia. He grew up in Pasadena, California, where he attended Pasadena Junior College before transferring to UCLA, where he was an All-American in football. Robinson was drafted into the Army in 1942 and wanted to attend Officer Candidates School (OCS). Denied access to OCS, he complained to Joe Louis, the heavyweight boxing champion, who intervened on his behalf. Robinson became a commissioned officer and was later court-martialed for refusing to move to the back of a bus near Fort Hood, Texas. He was acquitted of the charges. After his separation from the military in 1944, Robinson joined the Kansas City Monarchs of the Negro American League. Branch Rickey of the Brooklyn Dodgers signed him to a major league contract in 1945. He played with their minor league team, the Montreal Royals in 1946, and helped them to win the International League Championship. A year later, he was brought up to the Dodgers. As the first black player in the major leagues, he had to endure racial insults from fans and opposing players. Robinson answered with his stellar play and determination to win. He led the Dodgers to six National League titles and one World Series Championship. He retired in 1956 with a .311 lifetime batting average and was elected to the Baseball Hall of Fame in 1961. In retirement from baseball, Robinson became a successful businessman, supporter of the Republican Party, and advocate for African Americans in management positions in sports. He died of a heart attack on October 24, 1972.

**Robinson, Jo Ann Gibson (1912– )** An English teacher at Alabama State University in Montgomery, Alabama, Jo Ann Gibson Robinson became president of the Women's Political Council (WPC) in 1950. She was born in Culloden, Georgia, on April 17, 1912. The WPC had been organized in 1946 by Mary Fair Burks, also an English professor at the college. Its purpose was to promote voter registration and civic involvement among African American women. Given the mistreatment of black women on the buses of Montgomery, the WPC sought to change the seating policy so that black passengers would not have to give up their seats if the white section was full. After Rosa Parks's arrest on December 1, 1955, Robinson circulated fliers calling for a boycott and a mass meeting at Dexter Avenue Baptist Church. The WPC had prepared African Americans for action against the bus company and their groundwork helped to initiate and to sustain the boycott. Robinson served on the board of the Montgomery Improvement Association. She left Alabama State College in 1960, taught at Grambling State College in Louisiana for a year, and moved to Los Angeles, California, where she taught English in the public schools until she retired in 1976. She published her memoir in 1987, *The Montgomery Bus Boycott and the Women Who Started It.*

**Robinson, Randall (1941– )** Born in Richmond, Virginia, on July 6, 1941, Randall Robinson graduated from Virginia Union University in Richmond and earned a law degree at Harvard University. He worked as an administrative assistant to Rep. Charles Diggs of Michigan, who was one of the foremost members of Congress seeking an end to apartheid in South Africa. Robinson became head of TransAfrica in 1977 to lobby for Africa and the Caribbean. He organized daily protests in 1984 in front of the South African embassy in Washington, D.C. In 1986, he succeeded in having the U.S. Congress impose sanctions on South Africa that led to the release of Nelson Mandela from prison in 1990, an end to apartheid, and South Africa's first multiracial elections in 1994, which elevated Mandela to the presidency. Robinson turned his attention to other issues in Africa and the Caribbean and in 1994 went on a hunger strike for twenty-seven days to protest U.S. policy toward Haiti, which denied Haitians fleeing to the United States political refugee status. He became a major advocate for reparations with the publication in 2000 of his book *The Debt: What America Owes Blacks*.

**Robinson, Sugar Ray (1921–89)** Sugar Ray Robinson was born Walker Smith Jr. on May 3, 1921, in Detroit. He moved with his mother to Harlem in 1933 and began boxing under the name Ray Robinson. He was so smooth in the ring that a reporter described him as "sweet as sugar." Robinson held the welterweight and later the middleweight title. He became middleweight champion a record five times. Robinson's fancy footwork and lightening hand speed influenced Muhammad Ali. He retired from the ring in 1965 after an amazing

201 professional bouts, of which he won 174. He died on April 12, 1989, after suffering from diabetes and Alzheimer's disease.

**Rudolph, Wilma** (1940–94) At the 1960 Olympics in Rome, Rudolph was the first woman to win three gold medals and was named Athlete of the Year by United Press. She was born on June 23, 1940, in Bethlehem, Tennessee, the twentieth of her father's twenty-two children (from two marriages). Rudolph suffered from polio and had to wear a brace until she was nine, when she regained strength in her legs. She trained at Tennessee State University and at age sixteen won a bronze medal in the 4 x 100 meter relay race at the Olympics in Melbourne, Australia. She later graduated from Tennessee State in 1963, where she trained for the 1960 Olympic Games in Rome. She retired from track in 1962 and worked in education and youth programs. Her autobiography, *Wilma: The Story of Wilma Rudolph*, was made into a television movie and has inspired many women and people with physical disabilities to overcome obstacles. She died on November 12, 1994, of brain cancer.

**Rustin, Bayard** (1910–87) Born in West Chester, Pennsylvania, on March 17, 1910, Bayard Rustin joined the Communist Party as a young man in Harlem during the 1930s but left the Party in 1941 when it first opposed and then supported World War II after Hitler attacked the Soviet Union. Rustin worked with A. Philip Randolph on the threatened March on Washington in 1941 and later became an organizer for the Fellowship of Reconciliation (FOR), which was formed by Christian pacifists during World War I to promote integration and tenets of nonviolence. He also served with the Congress of Racial Equality (CORE), which members of FOR created in 1942 to desegregate public facilities through nonviolent resistance. Rustin was a Quaker and opposed the draft in World War II for which he served twenty-eight months in prison. He proposed the Journey of Reconciliation that CORE undertook in 1947 through the Upper South to test the recent U.S. Supreme Court decision against segregation in interstate transportation. Given his organizing experience, he volunteered to assist Martin Luther King Jr. with the Montgomery bus boycott, but had to resign after word leaked about his homosexuality and previous ties to the Communist Party. Rustin later served as coordinator of the 1963 March on Washington. He became executive director of the A. Philip Randolph Institute in 1964 and later worked for Freedom House monitoring elections and investigating human rights abuses in Chile, El Salvador, Grenada, Haiti, Poland, and Zimbabwe. He died on August 24, 1987, of cardiac arrest after being hospitalized for a perforated appendix.

**Sanchez, Sonia** (1934– ) Born on September 19, 1934, in Birmingham, Alabama, Wilsonia Benita Driver used the name Sonia Sanchez after her marriage to Albert Sanchez, whom she later divorced. She graduated from Hunter College and studied poetry at New York University. Her poetry reflects the rhythms of black speech and music. For a time, she belonged to the Nation of Islam because she believed that it was doing the most to address African American oppression. Her work speaks to the condition of black people in the United States. She left the Nation of Islam because of its sexism. In addition to her published poetry, she has written plays and children's literature. She was one of the major artists of the Black Arts Movement. Her collection of poems, *Homegirls and Handgrenades*, won an American Book Award in 1985. She has taught in the English Department at Temple University since 1975.

**Seale, Bobby (1936– )** The co-founder of the Black Panther Party was born Robert George Seale on October 22, 1936, in Dallas, Texas. After high school, he joined the Air Force and served for four years. He attended Merrit Community College in Oakland, California, after his discharge, where he was a student with Ron Everett (Maulana Karenga) and Huey Newton. They were members of the Afro-American Association, which grappled with the best ways to achieve black liberation from poverty and racial oppression in the United States. Seale helped to establish a branch of the Revolutionary Action Movement on the West Coast. With Huey Newton, he formed the Black Panther Party to end white racial oppression and police brutality. Seale was tried in 1968 as part of the Chicago Eight for conspiracy to disrupt the Democratic National Convention and was later charged with the murder of a Black Panther Party member in New Haven, Connecticut. He was acquitted in both instances, although he had been bound and gagged during the Chicago Eight trial for disrupting the court in asserting his rights. He ran for mayor of Oakland in 1973 and forced a runoff, which he lost. In his later years, he has become an entrepreneur with his cookbooks and has sought to advance black education.

**Sharpton, Al (1954– )** Known as the "Wonder Boy Preacher" when he began preaching at the age of four, Al Sharpton was born Alfred Sharpton Jr. on October 3, 1954, in Brooklyn, New York. He became an ordained minister at age ten and at age fifteen was appointed by Jesse Jackson as youth director of Operation Breadbasket. In 1973, he began promoting singer James Brown's tours while also heading the National Youth Movement, which he founded in 1971. Sharpton ran unsuccessfully for the New York state senate in 1978 but rose to national prominence after leading demonstrations to protest a number of high profile racial assault and murder cases. He organized the National Action Network in 1991. Its Madison Avenue Initiative has challenged racial bias in advertising. Sharpton ran against incumbent Daniel Patrick Moynihan in the 1994 Democratic Party primary and received 26 percent of the primary vote. He finished second in the Democratic Party primary for mayor of New York in 1997 and ran for president in the 2004 Democratic Party primary.

**Simmons, Russell** (1957– ) Born in Queens, New York, Russell Simmons attended City College of New York but left school to promote local rap artists. In 1984, he joined with Rick Rubin to form Def Jam Records. He also started Rush Artist Management and has produced music for some of the major rap singers. Simmons has grown his company to become the largest black-owned music business in the country with its own film and television division. He has also produced Def Comedy Jam, a popular entertainment television show. A major interpreter and promoter of the Hip Hop culture, Simmons owns PHAT fashion, which produces urban youth–oriented clothing.

**Simmons, Ruth** (1945– ) The first African American president of an Ivy League University, Ruth Simmons was born on July 3, 1945, in Grapeland, Texas, the twelfth child in a sharecropping family. She grew up in Houston and graduated summa cum laude from Dillard University in New Orleans. She earned a doctorate in Romance languages and literature at Harvard University. She taught at University of New Orleans and California State University at Northridge before becoming assistant and then associate dean of graduate studies at the University of Southern California. In 1983, she became director of Afro-American studies at Princeton University and served as provost of Spelman College before returning to Princeton as vice provost in 1992. She was named president of Smith College in 1995. She became president of Brown University in 2001.

**Simpson, O. J.** (1947– ) Born on July 9, 1947, in San Francisco, Orenthal James Simpson won the Heisman Trophy as the nation's top college football player in 1968. After starring at San Francisco Community College, he transferred to the University of Southern California and led the team to a national championship. He was the top choice in the 1969 professional football draft and went to the Buffalo Bills. He became the first player in professional football to rush for more than two thousand yards in a season. After being traded to the San Francisco Forty-Niners in 1977, Simpson retired two years later. He was inducted into the National Football League Hall of Fame in 1985. After retiring from football, he began a career as an actor and starred in several films. He also appeared in commercials for several major companies. The brutal stabbing and death of his ex-wife, Nicole Brown, and a friend on June 12, 1994, made Simpson the center of national attention. He led the police on a nationally televised car chase before being arrested at his suburban Los Angeles home. He was tried for murder but acquitted on October 3, 1995. His case split the nation racially, as most whites assumed his guilt and most African Americans his innocence.

**Southern Christian Leadership Conference** The Southern Christian Leadership Conference (SCLC) was organized in 1957 by Martin Luther King Jr. and grew out of the Montgomery bus boycott. It brought together southern black ministers to fight for economic, political, and social change. It was initially called the Southern Negro Leaders Conference on Transportation and Nonviolent Integration. The organization became more active in civil rights demonstrations after King moved from Montgomery to Atlanta, where SCLC was headquartered, in 1960. SCLC helped to coordinate the movement in Birmingham in 1963 and influenced passage of the Civil Rights Act of 1964 that outlawed segregation in public accommodations and transportation. SCLC engaged in other demonstrations but often clashed over tactics with the Student Non-Violent Coordinating Committee. SCLC's activities in Selma, Alabama, led to the Voting Rights Act of 1965. Given northern unrest and violence, SCLC moved North in 1966 to Chicago to protest poor schools and housing. King was convinced that poverty was one of the worst ills facing the country and planned a Poor People's Campaign despite the opposition of some members of SCLC. After King's assassination on April 4, 1968, SCLC carried out the Poor People's Campaign, in large measure to honor their slain leader. They constructed Resurrection City in Washington, D.C., which housed some 2,500 people, who marched daily to federal agencies seeking policies that would end poverty. About 100,000 people gathered on June 19 in front of the Lincoln Memorial to press the case for economic justice. But enthusiasm for the Poor People's Campaign dwindled as Resurrection City lost residents and local and national leaders criticized the effort. Moreover, the Justice Department refused to extend Resurrection City's permit. On June 24, the police evacuated and sealed off Resurrection City, ending the Poor People's Campaign. Rev. Ralph David Abernathy, King's longtime companion, succeeded him as president of SCLC, followed by Rev. Joseph E. Lowery, and later Martin Luther King III.

**Stokes, Carl** (1927–96) Born on June 21, 1927, in Cleveland, Ohio, Carl Stokes became the first black mayor of Cleveland in 1967 and the first black mayor of a major American city. He attended West Virginia State College and Cleveland College of Western Reserve University and graduated from University of Minnesota. He completed a law degree at Marshall Law School of Cleveland State University. He became assistant city prosecutor in Cleveland and in 1962 the first black Democrat elected to the Ohio General Assembly. He later served two terms, from 1967 to 1971, as mayor of Cleveland. After leaving the mayor's office, he became a reporter and news anchor for WNBC-TV in New York. He returned to Cleveland in 1980 and was subsequently elected a municipal court judge. He served from 1994 to 1995 as ambassador to the Seychelles, a nation of islands in the Indian Ocean off the coast of Africa and northeast of Madgascar. He died on April 4, 1996.

**Student Non-Violent Coordinating Committee** The Student Non-Violent Coordinating Committee (SNCC) grew out of the sit-ins that began on February 1, 1960, in Greensboro, North Carolina. Ella Baker invited student protest leaders to an Easter weekend conference at Shaw University in Raleigh, North Carolina. She was an acting executive director of the Southern Christian Leadership Conference (SCLC) whose leaders, including Martin Luther King Jr., tried to convince the students to become an affiliate of SCLC. Baker counseled the students to form their own group and to develop an organization with a broadly democratic decision-making process. SNCC elected Marion Barry, then a student at Fisk University and later mayor of Washington, D.C., as its chairman. SNCC became the shock troops of the civil rights movement in continuing the Freedom Rides when the buses were attacked and by working in some of the most dangerous areas of the Deep South. SNCC through the Council of Federated Organizations in Mississippi organized Mississippi Freedom Summer, which brought hundreds of white students to the South in 1964. The experience of working with the white students to whom many rural African Americans showed traditional deference convinced many SNCC members of the need for all-black organizers. Their disappointment at the 1964 Democratic Party National Convention when the Mississippi Freedom Party delegates were not seated to replace the Mississippi State Party delegates who discriminated against black voters furthered estranged them from liberal whites. As SNCC became more radical in its position and adopted Black Power, Stokely Carmichael replaced John Lewis as chairman. H. Rap Brown became chairman in 1967 and sought an alliance with the Black Panther Party. The short-lived merger of the two organizations led to the demise of SNCC by the early 1970s.

**Thomas, Clarence (1948– )** Born on June 23, 1948, in Pin Point, Georgia, Clarence Thomas became the second African American to serve on the U.S. Supreme Court. He grew up with his grandparents in Savannah, Georgia, and attended Catholic schools. He entered the seminary in 1967 to become a priest but left after some white classmates cheered the assassination of Martin Luther King Jr. He graduated cum laude from Holy Cross College, in Worcester, Massachusetts, where for a time he was a member of the Black Panther Party, and received a law degree from Yale University Law School. He joined the staff of John Danforth, attorney general of Missouri, and became a member of his staff when Danforth was elected to the U.S. Senate. An opponent of affirmative action and social welfare programs, Thomas became assistant secretary for civil rights in the Department of Education during the administration of President Ronald Reagan. He was later appointed chair of the Equal Employment Opportunity Commission. Many of his critics blamed him for lax enforcement of antidiscrimination laws. President George H. W. Bush appointed him to the

U.S. District Court of Appeals for the District of Columbia in 1989 and nominated him to replace Thurgood Marshall after he retired from the Supreme Court in 1991. Thomas's hearing before the U.S. Senate Judiciary Committee was stormy after Anita Hill, his former assistant, accused him of sexual harassment. Given the publicity around the hearings, Thomas accused the senators of an "electronic lynching," which gained him some sympathy and stifled some of his opponents in the Senate. He was narrowly confirmed and has become a member of the conservative wing of the Court.

**Till, Emmett Louis (1941–55)** Born in Chicago on July 25, 1941, Emmett Till served as a powerful symbol for the early civil rights movement. African Americans throughout the nation became incensed at the brutal slaying of the fourteen-year-old Till. He had gone to visit his uncle for the summer in LeFlore County, Mississippi. Being from the North, Till was not accustomed to the racial etiquette of the South and bragged to his cousins about having a white girlfriend. They dared him to ask the white female clerk at a small store in nearby Money, Mississippi, for a date. Till went into the store, allegedly grabbed Carolyn Bryant by the waist, asked her for a date, said "bye baby," and "wolf whistled" at her on his way out of the store. Because of this infraction that went to the core of the white male's obligation to protect his women, Bryant's husband and his half brother abducted Till from his uncle's home, beat him, shot him in the head, tied a cotton gin fan around his neck, and dumped his body into the Tallahatchie River. The body surfaced three days later, and Bryant and his half brother were arrested and tried for murder but acquitted by an all-white jury. Till's mother insisted on an open-casket wake and funeral. Thousands of black Chicagoans viewed the body and hundreds of thousands more saw the picture of Till's mangled face on the cover of *Jet Magazine*. African Americans around the country resolved that something had to be done to change the racial status quo.

**Walker, Alice (1944– )** Alice Walker was born on February 9, 1944, in Eatonton, Georgia, the eighth child of sharecropper parents. She lost sight in her right eye at age eight when her brother shot her with a BB gun. She attended Spelman College and later transferred to Sarah Lawrence College. She traveled in Africa during college and moved to Mississippi after graduation to participate in the civil rights movement. While conducting research for a short story, Walker discovered Zora Neale Hurston and helped to rescue her from oblivion. She purchased a tombstone for her unmarked grave. Walker's work has explored sexism and the "womanist" rather than "feminist" sensibility of black women. Her novel *The Color Purple* won the National Book Award and the Pulitzer Prize. It was made into a movie that featured Oprah Winfrey.

**Walker, Margaret** (1915–98) Born in Birmingham, Alabama, on July 7, 1915, Margaret Walker graduated from Northwestern University at age nineteen. After graduation, she worked for the Federal Writer's Project. She completed a master's degree in creative writing at the University of Iowa in 1942, the same year that she won the Yale Award for Young Poets with her poem *For My People*. She began teaching at Jackson State University in Mississippi and founded the Institute for the Study of the History, Life and Culture of Black People in 1968. She published the acclaimed *Jubilee* in 1966, based on her grandmother's stories about slavery and emancipation. In 1988, she sued Alex Haley for plagiarizing material from *Jubilee* for his book *Roots*. The case was dismissed. She retired from teaching in 1979 and published a long-awaited biography of Richard Wright, whom she knew in Chicago during the 1930s. Walker died of cancer in Chicago on November 30, 1998.

**Washington, Denzel** (1954– ) The winner of two Academy Awards, one for best actor in 2002 and the other for best supporting actor in 1990, Denzel Washington was born on December 28, 1954, in Mount Vernon, New York. He graduated from Fordham University, where in his senior year he received a small part in a made-for-television movie on the life of Wilma Rudolph, the great sprinter. Washington acted on the stage before gaining the role of a surgeon for the television series *St. Elsewhere*, which ran for six years. He has acted in productions of Shakespeare and continued to appear in film with a powerful performance as Malcolm X in Spike Lee's movie of the same name. Washington turned his hand to directing in 2002 with the film *Antwone Fisher*. He is considered one of America's leading actors and has refused roles that he thinks are degrading to black people.

**Washington, Harold** (1922–87) The first black mayor of Chicago, Harold Washington was born there on April 15, 1922. He graduated from Roosevelt University, where he was the first black student to be elected class president, and earned his law degree at Northwestern University. He was elected to the Illinois House of Representatives in 1965 and to the state senate in 1976. He broke with the Chicago political machine in 1977 when he ran an unsuccessful campaign for mayor in a special election after the death of longtime mayor Richard J. Daley. Washington was elected to the U.S. Congress in 1980. He won the Democratic Party primary for mayor in 1983 with a plurality of 38 percent. He defeated his Republican Party opponent in an acrimonious general election where he was booed in some white areas. Record-breaking turnouts in black neighborhoods and strong support from Latinos and liberal whites secured his victory. He handily won reelection in 1987. Washington did much to end patronage politics in Chicago and to open opportunities for minorities and women.

He died of a heart attack on November 25, 1987, just as he was beginning his second term in office.

**Weaver, Robert C. (1907–97)** Born on December 29, 1907, Robert C. Weaver became the first black cabinet member when President Lyndon B. Johnson appointed him secretary of housing and urban development in 1965, the first head of the newly established agency. Weaver graduated cum laude from Harvard University, where he also earned a Ph.D. in economics, and became an assistant to Secretary of Interior Harold Ickes. The so-called Black Cabinet to which he then belonged was an unofficial group of African Americans in the Roosevelt administration who sought ways to combat racial discrimination and segregation in New Deal programs. He held numerous government posts during and after World War II before being tapped by the governor of New York, Averell Harriman, to become state rent commissioner, the first African American to hold a cabinet position in New York. After serving as secretary of housing and urban development, Weaver became president of Baruch College of the City University of New York for two years and then distinguished professor of Urban Affairs at Hunter College until his retirement in 1978. He died in New York on July 17, 1997.

**Wesley, Charles Harris (1891–1987)** The third African American to receive a doctorate in history from Harvard University after W. E. B. Du Bois and Carter G. Woodson, Charles H. Wesley was born on December 2, 1891, in Louisville, Kentucky. He graduated from Fisk University, received a master's degree from Yale University, and went on for his doctorate before becoming an ordained minister and a presiding elder of the African Methodist Episcopal (AME) Church. Wesley taught at Howard University from 1913 to 1942, when he became president of Wilberforce University, an AME school in Ohio. The trustees dismissed him in 1947 after he sought to liberalize the administration and curriculum, leading to student protests and the eventual establishment of Wilberforce State College (later Central State University). He retired as president of Central State in 1965 and became executive director of the Association for the Study of Negro Life and History (ASNLH). He had also served as general president of Alpha Phi Alpha fraternity from 1931 to 1946 and had authored the first edition of its history in 1929.

Wesley's first book, *Negro Labor in the United States, 1850–1925*, drawn from his dissertation, was a pioneering study of black workers in slavery and freedom. He collaborated on several projects with Carter G. Woodson, founder of the ASNLH. Wesley published histories of major black religious, fraternal, and women's organizations. He died on August 16, 1987, in Washington, D.C.

**West, Cornel (1953– )** Born in Tulsa, Oklahoma, on June 2, 1953, Cornel West grew up in Sacramento, California. He graduated magna cum laude within three years from Harvard University with a degree in Near Eastern Languages and Literature and received a doctoral degree in philosophy from Princeton University. The author or editor of more than two dozen books, West is a leading public intellectual and activist scholar. He advocates pragmatism, Marxism, and prophetic Christianity to address inequality in American society, and is an exponent of radical participatory democracy. He has tried to reach out from academia to the public in his publications, lectures, sermons, and performances, most recently through spoken-word recordings. He has taught at Union Theological Seminary, Harvard, and Princeton.

**Wilder, L. Douglas (1931– )** Born on January 17, 1931, in Richmond, Virginia, Lawrence Douglas Wilder became the first African American ever elected governor of any state. Wilder graduated from Virginia Union University, was drafted into the Army during the Korean War, and received a Bronze Star for bravery. After the war, he earned a law degree at Howard University Law School. He became a millionaire from his law practice and in 1969 was the first African American elected to the Virginia state senate since Reconstruction. He became a powerful legislator and successfully ran for lieutenant governor in 1985. Four years later, he was elected governor from a state with only an 18 percent black population. He served as governor for one term as the Virginia state constitution prohibited the governor from running for a second term. Wilder ran for the U.S. Senate against his political nemesis, Charles Robb, in 1994, but later withdrew from the contest, leading to Robb's reelection in a tough race. In 1995, he became Distinguished Professor in the Center for Public Policy at Virginia Commonwealth University in Richmond. He became the first African American elected mayor of Richmond in 2004.

**Wilkins, Roy (1901–81)** Born on August 30, 1901, in St. Louis, Missouri, Roy Wilkins graduated from the University of Minnesota. He became a journalist and was editor of the *Kansas City Call*, a black newspaper, for eight years. In 1931, he became assistant secretary of the National Association for the Advancement of Colored People (NAACP) and succeeded W. E. B. Du Bois as editor of the *Crisis Magazine*. After Walter White, who served as NAACP executive secretary from 1931 to 1955, died in 1955, Wilkins became head of the organization. He was considered a moderate in relation to the other civil rights leaders but fought to retain the NAACP's status as "the" civil rights organization. He was a frugal and effective administrator, who was dedicated to the integration of African Americans into American society. Wilkins criticized Black Power, Black Studies, and opposition to the War in Vietnam; the latter placed him at odds with Martin Luther King Jr. He retired as executive director of the NAACP in 1977. He died on September 8, 1981, in New York.

**Williams, Robert Franklin (1925–96)** Known for his advocacy of violence, especially for African Americans to defend themselves, Robert F. Williams was born on February 26, 1925, in Monroe, North Carolina. He gained notoriety when the NAACP expelled him in 1959 for advocating the use of violence. Williams fled to Cuba in 1961 after he was indicted for kidnapping a white couple, whom he claimed he protected from angry demonstrators protesting the segregated white swimming pool. While in Cuba, he published the book *Negroes with Guns*, an account of his experiences in Monroe that became a bible for militant black nationalists who advocated fundamental and violent change in American society. He also broadcast Radio Free Dixie, with commentary on what he considered to be America's hypocrisy in her professed ideals and racist practices. Williams lived in China from 1966 to 1969, when he returned to the United States, where he became a research associate in the Institute for Chinese Studies at the University of Michigan. He became disillusioned with the movement in the United States and resigned from leadership positions in those organizations that he spawned such as the Revolutionary Action Movement and the Republic of New Africa. He died on October 15, 1996.

**Williams, Serena (1981– )** Born on September 26, 1981, in Saginaw, Michigan, Serena Williams grew up in the Los Angeles suburb of Compton. Her father, Richard Williams, was determined to develop champion tennis players among his children. He and his wife, Oracene, had five daughters, but only Serena and Venus displayed the talent and inclination to fulfill his dreams. They started on the public tennis courts of Compton and rather than hone their skills on the junior tennis circuit, their father sent them to a tennis academy in Florida to work with a coach who had trained several women professionals. Serena made her professional debut at age fourteen in Canada. She steadily moved up in the rankings and won the U.S. Open in 1999, the first African American woman to win a Grand Slam singles title since Althea Gibson in 1958. In 2002, she and her sister ranked one and two among women players in the world, the first siblings to do so.

**Williams, Venus (1980– )** Born on June 17, 1980, in Lynwood, California, Venus Williams grew up in the Los Angeles suburb of Compton. Like her sister Serena Williams, she made her professional debut in 1994 at age fourteen. In 1998, she clocked a 127 mph serve, a women's world record. She and Serena became the first sisters to win a Grand Slam crown together when they won the French Open doubles title. Venus had won twenty-five career titles and was ranked number one in the world by 2002, but her sister was fast approaching her with fifteen career titles and number two ranking.

**Wilson, August (1945–2005)** The winner of two Pulitzer Prizes for his plays, August Wilson was born Frederick August Kittel on April 27, 1945, in Pittsburgh, Pennsylvania. His father was a German baker whom he seldom saw, so Wilson adopted his mother's maiden name during the 1970s in protest. He dropped out of school at age fourteen because of racial taunts from his white classmates. He became largely self-taught by reading at the library, especially the work of African American writers and the poetry of Dylan Thomas. He started the Black Horizons Theatre in Pittsburgh in 1968 and wrote one-act plays for it. Wilson lived in St. Paul, Minnesota, in the late 1970s, continued to write, and achieved national acclaim in 1984 with *Ma Rainey's Black Bottom*, which was performed on Broadway. Blues music has been a major influence on his work. *Ma Rainey's Black Bottom* became the beginning of a ten-play series that Wilson planned with a setting in each decade of the twentieth century. His work explores the inner conflict of black life, especially the struggle of black men to achieve human dignity and respect. Wilson died of liver cancer on October 2, 2005, in Seattle. That month, the Virginia Theater, on Broadway, was renamed in his honor, joining venues named for such theater greats as Eugene O'Neill, Richard Rodgers, George Gershwin, and Helen Hayes.

**Winfrey, Oprah (1954– )** The most popular talk show host on television during the late twentieth and early twenty-first century, Oprah Winfrey was born on January 29, 1954, in Kosciusko, Mississippi. Her parents never married, and Winfrey lived with her mother in Milwaukee, Wisconsin, where she was sexually abused by male relatives and friends of her mother. At age fourteen, she went to live with her father in Nashville, Tennessee. Winfrey had experimented with drugs and had given birth to a premature baby before moving in with her father. He was a strict disciplinarian, and under his care, Winfrey changed her life and began to do well in school. She attended Tennessee State University and won the Miss Black Nashville and Miss Black Tennessee beauty contests. With a job offer from a local television station, she dropped out of school and became a television reporter and anchor. She moved to Baltimore in 1976, where she hosted *People Are Talking*. The talk show was a hit, and she was recruited by a station in Chicago to host her own morning program against the very popular Phil Donahue. Her show soon moved from last to first place in the ratings. Two years later, she launched the *Oprah Winfrey Show* as a nationally syndicated program. She purchased a warehouse near downtown Chicago that she converted into a production facility and started Harpo Productions. Her empathy with her audiences, sharing of her own story, superb talent, and shrewd business sense made her the world's highest paid entertainer and one of the wealthiest women in the country. When she began her book club, the books that she selected became instant bestsellers. She has produced television miniseries and movies and is working on cable and internet programming for women. Her publication *O: The Oprah Magazine* debuted in April 2000, features her picture on each issue thus far, and has been a huge success in a very competitive industry. In 2002, she was the first recipient of the Academy of Television Arts & Sciences Bob Hope Humanitarian Award.

**Wonder, Stevie** (1950– ) Born on May 13, 1950, in Saginaw, Michigan, and blind since infancy, Steveland Judkins (later Morris), became known as "Little Stevie Wonder" when he began to record for Motown Records; his album *Twelve-Year-Old Genius* in 1963 was Motown's first number one hit. In 1971, at age twenty-one, he negotiated a new contract with Motown that gave him artistic control of his productions. He plays several instruments and has used electronic technology, especially synthesizers, to enhance his sound. Stevie Wonder was a major force behind the drive to make Martin Luther King Jr.'s birthday a national holiday and recorded "Happy Birthday" as part of that effort in 1980. He has supported numerous humanitarian causes.

**Woods, Tiger** (1975– ) Eldrick "Tiger" Woods was born on December 30, 1975, in Orlando, Florida. His father, Earl Woods, trained him to become a golfer from the time that he began to walk. He won his first junior world title when he was eight years old and became an amazing amateur golfer. Woods won the U.S. Junior Amateur Championships for three years in a row (1991–93) and the U.S. Amateur title three years straight (1994–96) while attending Stanford University. He left school in 1996 to turn professional after winning the National Collegiate Athletic Association title. Woods became the youngest player to win the Masters Championship in 1997, and the first golfer of African or Asian descent (his father is African American and his mother is from Thailand) to win a major golf championship. In 1999, he became the first golfer in twenty-five years to win eight Professional Golf Association tour events in a single season. He was the youngest golfer to win all four major titles in 2000 with the Professional Golfers Association Championship, the Masters, the U.S. Open, and the British Open. The following year, he became the first player in the history of the sport to take four major tournaments in a row. He won his second Masters title in 2002. Many consider him the greatest golfer of all time.

**Woodson, Carter Godwin** (1875–1950) Often called the "Father of Black History," Carter G. Woodson was born on December 19, 1875, in New Canton, Virginia. He worked at different jobs to help support his family, including in the coalmines of West Virginia. Woodson began high school when he was twenty years old and finished within two years. He graduated from Berea College in Kentucky, taught for a while in the United States and the Philippines, earned bachelor's and master's degrees from the University of Chicago, and became the second African American after W. E. B. Du Bois to receive a doctoral degree in history from Harvard University. He taught at Howard University and West Virginia Collegiate Institute before devoting full time to the Association for the Study of Negro Life and History that he helped to found in Chicago in 1915. He started the *Journal of Negro History* in 1916 and the *Negro History Bulletin* in 1937. Woodson established Associated Publishers in 1922 to promote books about African and African American history that corrected the errors, omissions, and distortions of previous work. He began Negro History Week in 1926 to inform the nation about the black past and to inspire black youth to greater achievement. His textbook *The Negro in Our History* was widely used, especially by black schools in the South. During his career, he published and edited numerous books on African and African American history that set a foundation for study of the black experience. He died of a heart attack in Washington, D.C., on April 3, 1950.

**Wright, Richard** (1908–60) Born near Roxie, Mississippi, on September 4, 1908, Richard Wright became the first best-selling black author with the publication of *Native Son* in 1940. Wright grew up under the intellectually stifling direction of his grandmother, a Seventh Day Adventist, in Jackson, Mississippi, who discouraged his reading and listening to the radio. To escape his grandmother and the South, Wright moved first to Memphis and then at age nineteen to Chicago. He worked in the Post Office, where he met members of the John Reed Club, a communist organization. Wright joined the Communist Party because its members accepted him without regard to race and encouraged his writing. He later left the Communist Party as it tried to dictate his writing along the party line. Wright moved to New York in 1937 and published a collection of short stories, *Uncle Tom's Children*, about racial injustice and violence in the South. *Native Son* won Wright critical acclaim. He moved to Paris in 1947, where he felt that he could be free from the racism of the United States. The French existentialists whom he met in Paris influenced his writing and his novel *The Outsider*. Wright supported pan-Africanism and decolonization in Africa. He died of a heart attack in Paris on November 28, 1960.

**Young, Andrew** (1932– ) Born in New Orleans on October 23, 1932, Andrew Young became the first African American elected to Congress from Georgia since Reconstruction. Young graduated from Howard University, received a bachelor of divinity degree from Hartford Theological Seminary, and was ordained a Congregational minister. He worked in Georgia and Alabama, where he observed poverty and racial inequality. In 1959, he became assistant director of the National Council of Churches in New York, which financially supported civil rights activities in the South. He joined the Southern Christian Leadership Conference (SCLC) in 1961 and administered its Citizenship Education program, to increase black voter registration. He was appointed executive director of SCLC in 1964, a position he held until 1970. Two years later, he was elected to Congress. President Jimmy Carter appointed him to serve as ambassador to the United Nations, a post that he had to resign in 1979 over a controversy about meeting with representatives of the Palestinian Liberation Organization (PLO). Many supporters of Israel at the time believed that the United States should not recognize the PLO. He ran successfully for mayor of Atlanta in 1982 and served two terms. In 1990, he waged an unsuccessful campaign in the Democratic Party primary for governor of Georgia. He helped Atlanta secure the 1996 Summer Olympics and was co-chairman of the Atlanta Olympic Committee.

**Young, Coleman (1919–97)** The first black mayor of Detroit, Coleman Young was born on May 18, 1919, in Tuscaloosa, Alabama. He grew up in Detroit and worked for Ford Motor Company after graduating from high school. Young became an organizer for the United Auto Workers. He was drafted during World War II, commissioned a second lieutenant in the infantry, and later transferred to the Air Corps. He became a member of the Tuskegee Airmen. After the war, he became the first black paid staff member for the Wayne County AFL-CIO. He was also a leader of the National Negro Labor Council and came under scrutiny of the House Un-American Activities Committee. He refused to identify any of his associates as Communists and was blacklisted. The United Auto Workers dropped him as an organizer. He worked numerous odd jobs to earn a living. He ran unsuccessfully for the Michigan House of Representatives in 1962 but was elected to the state senate two years later. In 1974, he became mayor of Detroit, a city devastated by the riots in 1967 and the oil embargo in 1974. The city lost population as whites fled to the suburbs. Young saved the city from bankruptcy and helped to develop its riverfront. After retiring from office in 1993, he became a professor at Wayne State University. He died on November 29, 1997 after a long bout with emphysema.

**Young, Whitney M., Jr. (1921–71)** Born in Lincoln Ridge, Kentucky, on July 31, 1921, Whitney M. Young Jr. graduated from Kentucky State College, served in the military during World War II, and earned a master's degree in social work from the University of Minnesota. He began work for the National Urban League (NUL) in Minnesota and became head of the Urban League in Omaha, Nebraska. In 1954, he was named dean of the School of Social Work at Atlanta

# PART V

## *Resource Guide*

DEBRA NEWMAN HAM

## AFRICAN AMERICAN HISTORY

### *Textbooks*

#### SURVEYS

Bennett, Lerone. *Before the Mayflower: A History of Black America*. 7th ed. Chicago: Johnson Publishing Company, 2002.

*This very readable survey of African American history is an important introduction to the subject and the role that African Americans have played in building the United States.*

Franklin, John Hope, and Alfred A. Moss Jr. *From Slavery to Freedom*. 8th ed. New York: McGraw-Hill, 2000.

*A comprehensive historical survey of the African American experience that chronicles the struggles of blacks for full citizenship throughout American history. The last chapters address the period from World War II to the Clinton presidency.*

Hine, Darlene Clark, William C. Hine, and Stanley Harrold. *African-American Odyssey with Audio CD: The Combined Volume*. Englewood Cliffs, N.J.: Prentice-Hall, 2003.

*This work provides a general survey of African American history placing events in the context of U.S. history and demonstrating the pivotal role played by blacks particularly in the post–World War II era.*

Hine, Darlene Clark, ed. *The State of Afro-American History: Past, Present and Future*. Baton Rouge: Louisiana State University Press, 1986.

*Some of the essays in this volume explain the trends in black history since the World War II era. John Hope Franklin's essay, "On the Evolution of Scholarship in Afro-American History," discusses four generations of historians.*

Holt, Thomas C., and Elsa Barkley Brown, eds. *Major Problems in African-American History. Volume II: From Freedom to "Freedom Now," 1865–1990s*. Boston: Houghton Mifflin, 2000.

*Documents and essays in this volume provide the sociopolitical background for changes in the African American community from the World War II era to the turn of the twenty first century.*

Horton, James Oliver, and Lois E. Horton. *Hard Road to Freedom: The Story of African America*. New Brunswick, N.J.: Rutgers University Press, 2001.

*This survey of African American history focuses on the pursuit of freedom and civil rights and the challenge that African Americans have posed to the United States to live up to its principles.*

Kelley, Robin D. G., and Earl Lewis, eds. *To Make Our World Anew: A History of African Americans*. New York: Oxford University Press, 2000.

*The period since 1930 is covered in essays by Joe Trotter, Vincent Harding, and Robin Kelley. The essays are entitled "Raw Deal to the New Deal," "We Changed the World," and "Into the Fire."*

Meier, August, and Elliott Rudwick. *Black Historians and the Historical Profession, 1915–1980*. Urbana: University of Illinois Press, 1986.

*The background, education, training, and scholarly work of some black historians such as Carter G. Woodson, Benjamin Quarles, and John Hope Franklin are discussed in this volume.*

Palmer, Colin A. *Passageways: An Interpretive History of Black America*. 2 vols. Fort Worth, Tex.: Harcourt Brace College, 1998.

*Volume 2 of this work covers the period from 1863 to 1965. The World War II and postwar period primarily deal with African American battles for freedom and equality.*

Spivey, Donald. *Fire from the Soul: A History of the African-American Struggle*. Durham, N.C.: Carolina Academic Press, 2003.

*A text with the African American struggle against racism as its organizing principle.*

Trotter, Joe William, Jr. *The African American Experience*. Boston: Houghton Mifflin, 2001.

*The last several chapters cover World War II, civil rights, and black power. The final section is entitled "Redefining the Boundaries of Black Culture and Politics."*

## Black Women

Collins, Patricia Hill. *Black Feminist Thought: Knowledge, Consciousness and the Politics of Empowerment*. Boston: Unwin Hyman, 1990.

*This work explores the words and ideas of black feminist academicians as well as those of African American women outside of academic institutions.*

Gates, Henry Louis, Jr., ed. *Reading Black, Reading Feminist: A Critical Anthology*. New York: Meridian Books, 1990.

*Essays examine black women's literature in the twentieth century and deal with a variety of subjects including feminism. Essayists include Barbara Christian, Rita Dove, Houston A. Baker, and Gwendolyn Brooks.*

Giddings, Paula. *When and Where I Enter: The Impact of Black Women on Race and Sex in America*. Rev. ed. New York: Morrow, 1996.

*Chapters 14–20 document the role of women leaders and activists, particularly organizational leaders such as Mary McLeod Bethune and Fannie Lou Hamer. Giddings covers the 1960s, the Student Non-Violent Coordinating Committee, and the women's movement.*

Harley, Sharon, and Rosalyn Terborg-Penn, eds. *The Afro-American Woman: Struggles and Images*. Rev. ed. Baltimore: Black Classic Press, 1997.

*Several of the essays deal with women in the post-1939 period in the areas of poetry, blues, politics, and education. Authors include Terborg-Penn, Harley, Cynthia Neverdon-Morton, Gerald Gill, Andrea Rushing, and Daphne Harrison.*

Hine, Darlene Clark, and Kathleen Thompson. *A Shining Thread of Hope: The History of Black Women in America*. New York: Broadway Books, 1998.

*The last four chapters of this survey—"The Great Depression," "Towards Freedom," "The Caged Bird Sings," and "A New Era for Black Women"—cover the period since 1939.*

Hudson-Weems, Clenora. *Africana Womanism: Reclaiming Ourselves*. Troy, Mich.: Bedford Publishers, 1994.

*Challenges conventional definitions of feminism and their applicability to African American women with the argument that black women should employ their own definition—that is, Africana Womanism.*

Jones, Jacqueline. *Labor of Love, Labor of Sorrow: Black Women, Work, and the Family from Slavery to the Present*. New York: Basic Books, 1985.

*The last two chapters discuss how black working women were affected by the civil rights and the women's rights movements in the post–World War II era.*

Vaz, Kim Marie, ed. *Black Women in America*. Thousand Oaks, Calif.: Sage, 1995.

*Vaz arranged the essays into four sections: organizing activities, images of black women, and contemporary psychosocial challenges. There is an essay about black women in sports and others on the performing arts and labor.*

White, Deborah G. *Too Heavy a Load: Black Women in Defense of Themselves, 1894–1994*. New York: Norton, 1999.

*A study of black women in the struggle for equality during the twentieth century through their clubs and organizations.*

## GENERAL RESOURCES

### *Almanacs and Atlases*

Asante, Molefi K., and Mark T. Mattson. *Historical and Cultural Atlas of African Americans*. New York: Macmillan, 1992.

*The last chapter of the atlas provides maps, demographic information, photographs, and narratives about African American defiance of segregation, "demonstrative protest," and resultant changes in the social and economic realities.*

Cantor, George. *Historic Landmarks of Black America*. Detroit: Gale Research Inc., 1991.

*A guide to major black history sites throughout the country with brief summaries of their significance.*

Curtis, Nancy C. *Black American Historical Sites: An African American Odyssey and Finders Guide*. Chicago: American Library Association, 1996.

*The guide provides the location and background information for black history sites.*

Smith, Jessie Carney, and Joseph M. Palmisano, eds. *The African American Almanac*. 8th ed. Detroit: Gale, 2000.

*Topics include African American firsts, historic landmarks, civil rights, black nationalism, laws, employment education, entrepreneurship, literature, music, film, television, the military, sports, science and technology, and the arts.*

## *Bibliographies*

Abajian, James de T. *Blacks in Selected Newspapers, Censuses, and Other Sources: An Index to Names and Subjects*. Boston: G. K. Hall, 1977.

*This multivolume source identifies articles, reports, and images by and about African Americans.*

*Dictionary Catalog of the Schomburg Collection of Negro Literature and History*. 9 vols. Boston: G. K. Hall, 1962; supplement, 1976.

*The catalog reproduces about 200,000 cards in the Schomburg Center for Research in Black Culture collection. It includes cataloging information about books, periodicals, microfilm, sound recordings, and films, in the Schomburg's holdings.*

Gubert, Betty K., and Richard Newman. *Nine Decades of Scholarship: A Bibliography of Writings, 1892–1983 of the Staff of the Schomburg Center for Research in Black Culture*. New York: New York Public Library, 1986.

*This bibliography includes references to other bibliographies, articles, anthologies and some books by Schomburg Center for Research in Black Culture staff members relating to a variety of areas of black studies, including the African disapora, civil rights, and black librarianship.*

Ham, Debra Newman, ed. *The African American Mosaic: A Library of Congress Resource Guide for the Study of Black History and Culture*. Washington, D.C.: Library of Congress, 1993.

*Bibliographical essays entitled "The Depression, The New Deal, and World War II," and "The Civil Rights Era" describe Library of Congress manuscripts, microforms, bibliographies, books, films, prints and photographs, and sound recordings relating to black history.*

Higginbotham, Evelyn, Leon F. Litwack, Darlene Clark Hine, and Randall K. Burkett, eds. *The Harvard Guide to African-American History*. Cambridge, Mass.: Harvard University Press, 2001.

*Bibliographic essays, books and articles focus on African American art, music, oral history, photography, film, government documents, manuscript collections, internet resources, newspapers, periodicals and gender and regional studies.*

Hine, Darlene Clark, Patrick Kay Bidelman, and Shirley M. Herd, eds. *The Black Women in the Middle West Project: A Comprehensive Resource Guide, Illinois and Indiana*. Indianapolis: Indiana Historical Bureau, 1986.

*The guide includes historical essays, oral histories, biographical profiles, and information about document collections.*

Hodge, Ruth E. *Guide to African American Resources at the Pennsylvania State Archives*. Harrisburg: Pennsylvania Historical and Museum Commission, 2000.

*Many records relating to the life and history of blacks in Pennsylvania relate to the post-World War II period and cover topics such as economics, legislation, affirmative action, and equal opportunity.*

*Kaiser Index to Black Resources 1948–1986 from the Schomburg Center for Research in Black Culture of the New York Public Library*. 5 vols. Brooklyn: Carlson, 1992.

*This is a comprehensive listing of the resources available at the Schomburg Center.*

Malval, Fritz. *A Guide to the Archives of Hampton Institute*. Westport, Conn.: Greenwood Press, 1985.

*Some of the black studies archival resources at Hampton Institute in Virginia relate to students, faculty, and educational programs for black World War II veterans, who took advantage of the educational benefits of the GI Bill to get further education.*

Moorland Spingarn Research Center, Howard University, Manuscript Division. *Guide to the Processed Collection in the Manuscript Division of the Moorland Spingarn Research Center*. Washington, D.C.: Howard University, 2000.

*Howard collections, especially the Bunche Oral History materials, relate to African Americans who were active during the World War II years and the latter half of the twentieth century, especially in the civil rights movement.*

New York Public Library, Schomburg Collection of Negro Literature and History, Black Studies on Disk, 1999.

*This reference tool provides bibliographic citations to articles, book reviews, books, videos, and other materials pertaining to African American and African diaspora studies. The database includes the Index to Black Periodicals.*

Schatz, Walter, ed. *Directory of African American Resources*. New York: Bowker, 1970.

*This guide gives brief descriptions of archival resources throughout the country for the study of African American history and culture.*

Strickland, Arvarh E., and Robert E. Weems, eds. *The African American Experience: An Historiographical and Bibliographical Guide*. Westport, Conn.: Greenwood Press, 2001.

*A comprehensive bibliographical work arranged by topics with analyses of how the study of the African American experience has changed over time.*

## *Biographical Sources*

*African American Biography*. 4 vols. Detroit: Gale, 1984.

*These volumes profile three hundred African Americans in civil rights, athletics, politics, literature, entertainment, science, religion, and the military.*

Bearden, Romare, and Harry Henderson. *A History of African American Artists from 1792 to the Present*. New York: Pantheon Books, 1993.

*This work provides biographical sketches of artists. Section titles include "The Emergence of African-American Artists During the Depression," "Art Departments in African-American Colleges," and "Post World War II African-American Artists."*

Burkett, Randall K., Nancy Hall Burkett, and Henry Louis Gates Jr., eds. *Black Biography, 1790–1950: A Cumulative Index*. Alexandria, Va.: Chadwyck-Healy, 1991.

*This reference book guides the researcher to a wide variety of black biographical indexes.*

*Contemporary Black Biography: Profiles from the International Black Community*. 29 vols. Detroit: Gale, 2002– .

*Volumes in this ongoing reference include biographical sketches, sources (with some Internet sites), and cumulative indexes. Athlete Henry Aaron, comedian Bill Cosby, actor Hattie McDaniel, and political figure Condoleezza Rice are a few of the names.*

*Index to Personal Names in the National Union Catalog of Manuscript Collections, 1959–1984*. Washington, D.C.: Library of Congress, 1988.

*This guide leads researchers to the papers of various individuals who were involved with race relations. The Union Catalog is available on line.*

Johnson, Harry Alleyn, ed. *Multimedia Materials for Afro-American Studies: A Curriculum Orientation and Annotated Bibliography of Resources*. New York: Bowker, 1971.

*This book offers information about the use of films, audiotapes, slides, transparencies, and videos in the development of curricula for black history. It includes an essay by Charles Wesley about the need for a multimedia approach.*

Mitchell, Sara. *Afro-American Biographies: A Bibliography*. Huntington, N.Y.: Nova Science, 2000.

*This bibliography is divided into several categories: general; science, engineering and invention; entertainers; sports figures-general; baseball players; basketball players; football players; civil rights; women; and the arts.*

Russell, Dick. *Black Genius and the American Experience*. New York: Carroll & Graf, 1998.

*This work presents biographies of artist, Romare Bearden; sculptor, Meta Warwick Fuller; writers Ralph Ellison, James Baldwin, and Toni Morrison; educators, Mary McLeod Bethune and Cornel West; spiritual leaders Howard Thurman, Benjamin Mays and Martin Luther King; musicians Will Marion Cook, Duke Ellington, Louis Armstrong, and Wynton Marsalis; and more.*

Salem, Dorothy C. *African American Women: A Biographical Dictionary*. New York: Garland, 1993.

*Each biographical sketch includes a bibliography, and Salem provides a bibliography of other sources for black women's history in her introduction.*

Smith, Jessie Carney, *Black Heroes of the Twentieth Century*. Detroit: Visible Ink Press, 1998.

*Bibliographic sketches focus on African American leaders in politics, education, the arts and sciences, entertainment and sports. Resources for further study are included with each sketch.*

Smith, Jessie Carney, ed. *Notable Black American Men*. Detroit: Gale Research, 1999.

*Many leaders of the World War II and the postwar period, who were the vanguard in the effort to obtain equal rights in all variety of fields for African Americans, are included in this volume. Each biographical essay includes bibliographic information.*

Smith, Jessie Carney, ed. *Notable Black American Women Detroit*: Gale Research, 1992.

*This encyclopedia has biographical entries about many women who have been active in a variety of endeavors during and since World War II. Each essay includes a list of references.*

Southern, Eileen. *Biographical Dictionary of Afro-American and African Musicians*. Westport, Conn.: Greenwood Press, 1982.

*Southern's work provides biographical information about black musicians and sources where more information can be found.*

## *Chronologies*

Collier-Thomas, Bettye, and V. P. Franklin. *My Soul Is a Witness: A Chronology of the Civil Rights Era in the United States, 1954–1965*. New York: Henry Holt, 2000.

*Lists and explains the trajectory of the civil rights movement from Brown v. Board of Education to the Voting Rights Act.*

Harley, Sharon. *The Timetables of African-American History: A Chronology of the Most Important People and Events in African-American History*. New York: Simon & Schuster, 1995.

*A guide by year and month of developments in African American history from 1619 to the 1990s.*

Hornsby, Alton. *Chronology of African American History*. Detroit: Gale, 1997.

*The bulk of this 720-page volume covers the period from 1939 to 1996. Appendices include historical documents, bibliographic aids and a subject index.*

## *Demography*

Ernst, Robert T., and Lawrence Hugg, eds. *Black America: Geographic Perspectives*. New York: Doubleday, 1976.

*This is a social geography of ethnic and racial minorities in the United States. It assesses some significant works concerning demographic aspects of black America. Topics include the geography of black American and ghetto space, race, economics, and the city.*

Farley, Reynolds. *Growth of the Black Population: A Study of Demographic Trends*. Chicago: Markham Publishing, 1970.

*Subjects include the growth of the black population, changes in Negro fertility, marital status and fertility, family formation, use of birth control, and the effects of changes in health conditions and standards of living.*

Hornor, Louise L. *Black Americans: A Statistical Sourcebook*. Palo Alto, Calif.: Information Publications, 2002.

*Covers demographics, health, education, politics, crime and law enforcement, labor, income, and housing.*

Smith, Jessie Carney, and Carrell P. Horton, eds. *Statistical Record of Black America*. 4th ed. Detroit: Gale, 1997.

*Statistics relate to attitudes, values, economics; crime, law enforcement, education; health, housing, income, spending, employment; politics, population, human services; sports and leisure; the family, and vital statistics.*

## *Encyclopedias*

Appiah, Kwame Anthony, and Henry Louis Gates Jr. *Africana: The Encyclopedia of the African and African American Experience*. New York: Basic Books, 1999.

*The encyclopedia covers a wide variety of subjects, including black consciousness in the United States, the Motown recording company, Paul Robeson, Bill "Bojangles" Robinson, the decolonization of Africa, Ralph Bunche, and sports.*

Hine, Darlene Clark, ed. *Black Women in America* 3 vols. 2nd ed. New York: Oxford University Press, 2005.

*African American women in a wide variety of fields—education, politics, entertainment, literature, science, and medicine—are included in these volumes. Each entry includes a bibliography.*

Salzman, Jack, David Lionel Smith, and Cornel West, eds. *Encyclopedia of African-American Culture and History*. 5 vols. New York: Macmillan, 1996.

*Two-thirds of the 2,200 entries are biographical with topical essays and entries for geographical areas of the United States; includes more than a thousand illustrations.*

## *Film*

Cripps, Thomas. *Making Movies Black: The Hollywood Message Movie from World War II to the Civil Rights Era*. New York: Oxford University Press, 1993.

*Cripps provides an analysis of the types of films that included black stars and appealed to African American audiences. He contends that the war years gave African Americans more access to the centers of popular culture, including film.*

Hyatt, Marshall, ed. *The Afro-American Cinematic Experience: An Annotated Bibliography and Filmography*. Wilmington, Del.: Scholarly Resources, 1983.

*Hyatt provides information on written sources about blacks in films as well as listings of films with African American casts.*

Klotman, Phyllis R. *Frame by Frame—A Black Filmography*. Bloomington: Indiana University Press, 1979.

*This filmography includes an alphabetical listing of feature films and documentaries, indexes of black performers, authors, screenplay writers, producers, and directors. It is a compendium of over three thousand film items.*

Klotman, Phyllis R., and Janet K. Cutler. *Struggles for Representation: African American Documentary Film and Video*. Bloomington: Indiana University Press, 1999.

*Essays focus on pioneers in black documentary films, military and social films, black "high-tech documents," and black diaspora documentaries. It includes interviews with filmmakers, a filmography, a filmmaker index, and a bibliography.*

Klotman, Phyllis R., and Gloria J. Gibson. *Frame by Frame II: A Filmography of the African American Image, 1978–1994*. Bloomington: Indiana University Press, 1997.

*Information includes roles played by African Americans in each film, a list of films, name of black cast members, Oscar winners and nominees, directors, executive producers, musicians, producers, screenwriters, film archives and distributors.*

### *Literature*

Andrews, William L., Frances Smith Foster, and Trudier Harris-Lopez, eds. *The Oxford Companion to African American Literature*. New York: Oxford University Press, 1997.

*This 866-page volume provides biographical sketches of African American writers, synopses of their work, and articles about people, places, and terms relevant to the African American experience. The foreword is by Henry Louis Gates Jr.*

Arata, Esther Spring, and Nicholas John Rotoli. *Black American Playwrights, 1800 to the Present: A Bibliography*. Metuchen, N.J.: Scarecrow Press, 1976.

*The first part of this work provides an alphabetical listing of 560 black playwrights and their works. The second provides a general bibliography of works by the playwrights and section three is an index of play titles.*

French, William P., and Frank Deodene. *Black American Poetry Since 1944: A Preliminary Checklist*. Chatham, N.J.: Chatham Bookseller, 1971.

*This is an alphabetical listing by poet with bibliographical information for each work.*

Hogue, W. Lawrence. *Race, Modernity, Postmodernity: A Look at the History and the Literatures of People of Color Since the 1960s*. Albany: State University of New York Press, 1996.

*This work discusses and compares eight works by authors of African American, Asian American, Native American and Latin American heritage. Hogue discusses the dialogs between creative intellectuals of color and the intellectual trends of three decades.*

McDowell, Deborah E. *"The Changing Same": Black Women's Literature, Criticism, and Theory*. Bloomington: Indiana University Press, 1995.

*The author compares contemporary black women novelists with earlier generations of women writers. She argues that the works have a common concern with the struggle for self-realization, wholeness, and autonomy in a racist, sexist world.*

### *Manuscript Collections*

Burton, Dennis A., James B. Roads and Raymond Smock, eds. *A Guide to Manuscripts in the Presidential Libraries*. College Park, Md.: Research Materials Corporation, 1985.

*Records for U.S. Presidents from Herbert Hoover through Lyndon Johnson are covered in this guide. It describes records and oral histories relating to many aspects of black history. Interviewees include Pauli Murray, Roy Wilkins, and many more.*

Newman, Debra L., ed. *Black History: A Guide to Civilian Records in the National Archives*. Washington, D.C.: National Archives Trust Fund Board, 1984.

*Many federal government records relating to blacks from World War II to the 1980s are listed in this volume. Records relate to legislation, labor, voting rights, black activism, the military, and education.*

Newman, Debra L., ed. *Selected Documents Pertaining to Black Workers Among the Records of the Department of Labor and Its Component Bureaus, 1902–1969*. Washington, D.C.: National Archives and Records Administration, 1977.

*Subject headings in this guide relate to fair employment practices, training for defense industries, black government workers, government contracts, migrant workers, black labor migration, unemployment, relief, women, and labor statistics.*

Paul, Karen Dawley, ed. *Guide to Research Collections of Former U.S. Senators, 1789–1995.* Senate Doc. 103–35. Washington, D.C.: Government Printing Office, 1995.

*Many U.S. Senators were actively involved with racial issues in the World War II and postwar periods. This guide indicates where the papers of various senators are housed.*

U.S. House of Representatives. *Guide to the Records of the United States House of Representatives at the National Archives.* 100th Congress, 2nd session, House of Representatives Doc. No. 100–245, 1989.

*Many post-World War II topics relate to race, racial discrimination, desegregation, and racial violence.*

U.S. House of Representatives, Office of the Bicentennial. *A Guide to Research Collections of Former Members of the U.S. House of Representatives, 1789–1987.* Washington, D.C.: U.S. House of Representatives, 1988. House Document No. 100–171, 100th Congress, Second Session.

*By 1987, more than over ten thousand men and women had served in the House of Representatives. This listing provides the locations of their papers. The records include information about blacks and as well as listing the location of the papers of African American representatives.*

U.S. Senate, *Guide to the Records of the U.S. Senate at the National Archives* compiled by Robert W. Coren, Mary Rephlo, David Kepley and Charles South. Senate Doc. 100–42, U.S. Senate Bicentennial Publication no. 7, 1989.

*Much of the work of some Senate committees involved matters pertaining to African Americans, particularly segregation, discrimination, civil rights, housing, and labor.*

## *Newspapers and Periodicals*

Danky, James P., and Maureen E. Hady, eds. *African-American Newspapers and Periodicals: A National Bibliography.* Cambridge, Mass.: Harvard University Press, 1998.

*African American–owned newspapers and periodicals have vigorously advocated for equal rights for blacks in all fields of endeavor. This volume provides information about the date spans and availability of black newspapers and periodicals.*

Farrar, Hayward. *The Baltimore Afro-American, 1892–1950.* Westport, Conn.: Greenwood Press, 1998.

*The Afro was in the vanguard of the civil rights struggle, particularly under the leadership of Carl Murphy. This volume traces the Afro's campaigns for justice in education, housing, business, employment, and law.*

## *Photography*

Willis, Deborah, ed. *Picturing Us.* New York: New Press, 1994.

*In this volume, a variety of authors, including bell hooks, Angela Y. Davis, and E. Ethelbert Miller, discuss aspects of photographic images of blacks through history and the impact of that imagery on African Americans.*

Willis, Deborah. *Reflections in Black: A History of Black Photographers, 1840 to the Present.* New York: Norton, 2000.

*Willis selected more than six hundred pictures by African American photographers for this volume. Many depict blacks in ordinary pursuits at home, in church, at weddings, or simply in their finest clothes for family and individual portraits.*

### *Web Sites*

Alkalimat, Abdul. *The African American Experience in Cyberspace: A Resource Guide to the Best Web Sites on Black Culture and History*. London: Pluto Press, 2004.

*A rich guide to Internet sources on black history and culture.*

Gumbs, Bob. *Internet Directory to Black Web Sites*. New York: Cultural Expressions, 1999.

*A reference to "Black Cyberspace" for individuals, families, students, educators, researchers, businesses, and historians.*

Westbrooks, Elaine, and Eric Acree. *African American History and Culture on the Web: A Guide to the Very Best Sites*. Wilmington, Del.: Scholarly Resources, 2004.

*This guide reviews the most informative web sites on black history and culture.*

## GENERAL MILITARY RESOURCES

### *Histories*

Astor, Gerald. *The Right to Fight: A History of African Americans in the Military*. Novato, Calif.: Presidio Press, 1998.

*Astor provides an account of the service of black troops.*

Buckley, Gail Lumet. *American Patriots: The Story of Blacks in the Military from the Revolution to Desert Storm*. New York: Random House, 2001.

*Buckley traces the participation of African Americans in every American war since the Revolution.*

Dornbusch, Charles E., *Histories of American Army Units, World Wars I and II and Korean War Conflict*. Washington, D.C.: Office of the Adjutant General, 1956.

*Because units were usually segregated by race, it is possible to identify most African American troops and study their official performance records. Many of their white officers believed that African Americans were inferior to whites.*

Edgerton, Robert B. *Hidden Heroism: Black Soldiers in America's Wars*. Boulder, Colo.: Westview, 2001.

*This book is about the heroism of African Americans throughout the history of America's armed forces. It covers the period from the Revolutionary War through the conflicts in Grenada, Panama, the Persian Gulf, Bosnia, and Kosovo.*

Foner, Jack D. *Blacks and the Military in American History: A New Perspective*. New York: Praeger, 1974.

*Chapter 7 relates to black servicemen in World War II, chapter 8 addresses military desegregation, and chapter 9 looks at the role of black servicemen in Vietnam. Each chapter ends with a bibliographical essay.*

Lee, Ulysses. *The Employment of Negro Troops*. Washington, D.C.: Center of Military History, 1994.

*Written from 1946 to 1952, this military history covers a wide array of topics for all the services with information about units, men, training, physical fitness, quotas, overseas deployment, combat, housing, camp locations and selective service.*

Nalty, Bernard C. *Strength for the Fight: A History of Black Americans in the Military*. New York: Free Press, 1986.

*More than half of this book covers the period from World War II through Vietnam. It includes many photographs of black soldiers and copious notes. The author deals with black militancy in the military and social upheavals during the 1960s and 1970s.*

Phelps, J. Alfred. *They Had A Dream: The Story of Afro-American Astronauts.* Novato, Calif.: Presidio Press, 1994.

*Phelps examines the history of blacks who have participated in the U.S. space program. Readers learn the motivations of these young men and women and the way in which they overcame obstacles.*

Shaw, Henry I., Jr., and Ralph W. Donnelly. *Blacks in the Marine Corps.* Washington, D.C.: History and Museum Division, U.S. Marine Corps, 1988.

*This book reviews the efforts to admit blacks into the Marine Corps and discusses their roles from World War II through the post-Vietnam era.*

U.S. Department of Defense. *Black Americans in Defense of Our Nation.* Washington, D.C.: Government Printing Office, 1991

*Information about blacks in World War II, Korea, Vietnam, and the space program is covered in this Defense Department publication. There is a chapter relating to black females in the military.*

## *Bibliographies*

Davis, Lenwood, and George Hill, *Blacks in the U.S. Armed Forces, 1776–1983: A Bibliography.* Westport, Conn.: Greenwood Press, 1985.

*Chapters 7 through 10 of this bibliography include books, articles, and official government publications relating to black participation in World War II, the Korean War, and the Vietnam War as well as the post-Vietnam era up to 1985.*

Slonaker, John. *The U.S. Army and the Negro: A Military History Research Collection Bibliography.* Carlisle Barracks, Pa.: U.S. Army Military Research Collection, 1972; supplement 1975.

*Sources listed in this bibliography cover World War II, Korea, and military integration. Many of the sources listed are reports available in the Army Military Research Collection in Carlisle, Pennsylvania.*

## *Biographical Sources*

Hawkins, Walter L. *African American Generals and Flag Officers: Biographies of Over 120 Blacks in the United States Military.* Jefferson, N.C.: McFarland, 1993.

*Biographies relate to officers in the U.S. Army, Air Force, Marines, and Navy.*

## *Documents*

MacGregor, Morris J., and Bernard C. Nalty, eds. *Blacks in the Military: Basic Documents.* 13 vols. Wilmington, Del.: Scholarly Resources, 1977.

*Volumes 5 and 6 include documents about black soldiers and sailors in World War II. Volumes 7 through 13 relate to the postwar use of black service personnel, segregation, integration, and equal opportunity.*

## *Records*

Mulligan, Timothy P. *Guide to Records Relating to U.S. Military Participation in World War II.* 2 vols. Washington, D.C.: National Archives and Records Administration, 1996.

*The official records of the U.S. government include military service records, correspondence, reports, printed materials, press releases, and other documents relating to the war. Materials relating to blacks are interspersed.*

Penn, Lisha B. *Records of Military Agencies Relating to African Americans from the Post-World War I Period to the Korean War*. Washington, D.C.: National Archives and Records Administration, 2000.

*Penn provides descriptions of more than 145 series of textual records that include information about African Americans from the end of World War I through the Korean War. Records relate to the Army, Air Force, Navy, and Marine Corps.*

Seely, Charlotte Palmer. *American Women and the U.S. Armed Forces: A Guide to the Records of Military Agencies in the National Archives Relating to American Women*. Washington, D.C.: National Archives and Records Administration, 1992.

*These archival documents reflect the ambivalence in the military leadership about the use of black female enlistees. Records relate to the various services and include topics such as recruitment, promotion, and living conditions.*

U.S., Records of the Air Force, Record Group 18, National Archives and Records Administration.

*Film footage for the period 1942 to 1945 in "Combat Film Subjects" relate to blacks in the Air Force.*

U.S., Records of the Department of the Navy, Record Group 428, National Archives and Records Administration.

*Some Naval records relate to racial policies and the role of blacks in the Navy. Some film footage for 1968 documents the Naval Reserved Officers Training Corps at Prairie View A&M, a historically black college in Texas.*

U.S., Records of the Office of the Chief Signal Officer, Record Group 111, National Archives and Records Administration.

*These records include 9,000 reels of unedited film footage, some of which documents the activities of black troops in the Pacific and European theaters of World War II and in the Korean conflict.*

U.S., Records of the Judge Advocate General, Record Group 53. Washington, D.C.: National Archives and Records Administration.

*Many black soldiers were court-martialed during World War II and Korea. Probably the most famous case is that of Jackie Robinson. The NAACP Legal Defense Fund, directed by Thurgood Marshall became very involved in these cases.*

U.S., Records of the Office of the Inspector General (Army), Record Group 159, National Archives and Records Administration.

*World War II records relate to discrimination, black Army officers, investigations of racial incidents, and reports relating to Tuskegee Army Flying School.*

## WORLD WAR II

### *Histories*

Abdul-Jabbar, Kareem, and Anthony Walton. *Brothers in Arms: The Courageous Story of WWII's 761st "Black Panthers."* New York: Broadway Books, 2004.

*Retired basketball great Abdul-Jabbar, a longtime amateur historian, and journalist Walton recount the career of the storied all-black tank battalion, one of the most highly decorated units in WWII. One high point of Abdul-Jabbar and Walton's narrative is the resistance to prejudice on the part of several members of the 761st, including Lt. Jackie Robinson.*

Allen, Robert L. *The Port Chicago Mutiny: The Story of the Largest Mass Mutiny Trial in U.S. Naval History*. New York: Amistad, 1993.

*After an explosion killing several hundred people at Port Chicago in California, some black seamen refused to work loading explosives. They were court-martialed. Allen provides an exposé of the largest mass mutiny trial in U.S. Naval history.*

American Battle Monuments Commission, *92nd Division Summary of Operations in the World War*. Washington, D.C.: U.S. Government Printing Office, 1977.

*An official history of the service of this segregated division.*

American Battle Monuments Commission, *93rd Division Summary of Operations in the World War*. Washington, D.C., U.S. Government Printing Office, 1977

*An official treatment of the service of the men in this segregated division.*

*Annals of the American Academy of Political and Social Science* 223. Philadelphia: Academy of Political and Social Science, 1942.

*This volume includes a series of articles with the general heading "Minority Peoples in a Nation at War." Article authors include William H. Hastie, Robert Weaver, Walter White, Lester Granger, and Horace Mann Bond.*

*Army Talk* 170 (April 12, 1947). War Department, Sup. Docs. # WIII.7:170.

*This issue of the War Department newsletter includes a series of articles relating to black manpower in the army and black platoons in rifle companies.*

Blackboard, Mandel G., ed. *On Board the USS Mason: The World War II Diary of James A. Dunn*. Columbus: Ohio State University Press, 1996.

*Dunn's diary recounts his experiences aboard the USS Mason, a ship that was manned by African American seamen. The Mason escorted merchant ships from the U.S. to Great Britain and northern Africa from 1944 to 1945.*

Bray, Mayfield and William T. Murphy. *Audiovisual Records in the National Archives of the U.S. Relating to World War II*. Washington, D.C.: National Archives and Records Administration, 1974.

*This reference information paper describes films, still pictures, and sound recordings about World War II. Materials relating to blacks include military service, combat, defense industries, and government work.*

Buchanan, A. Russell. *Black Americans in World War II*. Santa Barbara, Calif.: Clio Books, 1983.

*African American involvement in civilian and military life and their struggle to gain equality during World War II are addressed. Topics include African American protests, racial conflict, and labor relations.*

Bureau of Naval Personnel. *Guide to Command of Negro Naval Personnel*. Washington, D.C.: Navy Department, 1944.

*This handbook reflects attitudes toward black service by the naval establishment and the method the leaders recommended for management of African American personnel.*

Burger, Barbara Lewis. *Pictures of African Americans during World War II*. Washington, D.C.: National Archives and Records Administration, 1998.

*Describes photographs that document the roles of over two and a half million blacks who served in World War II. Many of the photos are from the Army Signal Corps, the Navy, Coast Guard, Marine Corps, and the Office of War Information.*

Byers, Jean. *A Study of the Negro in Military Service*. Washington, D.C.: U.S. Department of Defense, 1950.

*At the request of the NAACP, Byers did this study of blacks in the military, which describes their treatment and the roles they were allowed to play in the war.*

Caliver, Ambrose, ed. *Post War Education of Negroes: Educational Implications of Negro Veterans and War Workers*. Washington, D.C.: Federal Security Agency, U.S. Office of Education, 1945.

*Many African American veterans took advantage of the educational benefits accorded them by the military.*

Carter, Allene G., and Robert L. Allen. *Honoring Sergeant Carter: Redeeming a Black World War II Hero's Legacy*. New York: Amistad / HarperCollins, 2003.

*A well-grounded exposé of the official racism that kept a black combat hero from due honor for more than half a century. As Carter and Robert Allen observe, none of the 294 specimens of the Medal of Honor awarded in World War II went to any of the 1.2 million African Americans who served. In 1992, following pressure by veterans' groups, the Army investigated this inequity, and seven years later President Bill Clinton awarded one to Carter posthumously.*

Converse, Elliott V., et al. *The Exclusion of Black Soldiers from the Medal of Honor in World War II*. Jefferson, N.C.: McFarland, 1997.

*The authors identified some African Americans who distinguished themselves in combat but were overlooked. Several were eventually awarded the Medal of Honor posthumously. One received his award during a White House ceremony.*

Davis, Benjamin O., Jr. *Benjamin O. Davis, Jr.* Washington, D.C.: Smithsonian Institution Press, 1991.

*General Davis, West Point graduate and leader of the Tuskegee Airmen, relates his experiences in a segregated military and the efforts to integrate the U.S. Air Force.*

DeWhitt, Benjamin L. *American Military Casualties and Burials*. Washington, D.C.: National Archives and Records Administration, 1993.

*DeWhitt describes records pertaining to military enlistees and civilian employees who were casualties of World War II. The records provide information (sometimes coded) on the deceased's religion, race, discharge status, and cemetery location.*

DeWhitt Benjamin L., ed. *Personal Participation in World War II*. Washington, D.C.: National Archives and Records Administration, 2000.

*The compiler describes documents pertaining to individuals serving in the U.S. military who received awards and decorations, including Dorie Miller and other African American awardees.*

DeWhitt, Benjamin L., and Heidi Ziemer. *Records Relating to Personal Participation in World War II, "The American Soldier" Surveys*. Washington, D.C.: National Archives and Records Administration, 1997.

*The authors list surveys of opinion conducted among U.S. Army personnel during World War II by the Army Research Branch of the Army Services Forces. Subjects include race relations, the enemy, training, women, and demobilization.*

Douglass, Helen Gahagan. *The Negro Soldier: A Partial Record of Negro Devotion and Heroism Gathered from the Files of the War and Navy Department*. Washington, D.C.: Government Printing Office, 1946.

*Helen Gahagan Douglass, a congresswoman from California, read these laudatory remarks in the House of Representatives on February 1, 1946. Her statements were later printed as a pamphlet.*

Earley, Charity Adams. *One Women's Army: A Black Officer Remembers the WAC*. College Station: Texas A&M University Press, 1989.

*The author, who served from 1942 to 1945 and rose to the rank of lieutenant colonel, was the first black officer in the Women's Army Corps. She led the 6888 Central Postal Battalion—composed entirely of black females—in Europe.*

Evans, James C. *The Negro in the Army, Policy and Practice*. Washington, D.C.: U.S. Department of the Army, 1948.

*Evans was one of several successive civilian aides to the secretary of war who handled affairs relating to black soldiers.*

Finkle, Lee. *Forum for Protest: The Black Press During World War II*. Rutherford, N.J.: Fairleigh Dickinson University Press, 1975.

*This study outlines the role of the black press during the war and addresses black civilian sentiment as well as the views of black soldiers and veterans. Finkle analyzes newspapers, academic journals, and organizational publications.*

Francis, Charles E. *Tuskegee Airmen*. Boston: Bruce Humphries, 1956.

*Because many whites did not feel that blacks could fly planes, the military establishment media closely monitored the first black pilots in the Army Air Corps. This book focuses on the 99th Fighter Squadron and the 332nd Fighter Group.*

Fritz, Ernest W., ed. *393rd Infantry (99th Division) in Review: A Pictorial Account of the 393rd Infantry Regiment in Combat, 1944–1945*. Salt Lake City: Robert E. Freed, 1946.

*This work provides pictorial documentation of the service of this segregated unit.*

Gravely, V. Admiral Samuel L. "Oral History Interview." Navel Historical Center, Operational Archives Branch, 1988.

*Adm. Gravely, one of the first black officers in the Navy, discusses his thirty-four years of service.*

Hargrove, Hondon B. *Buffalo Soldiers in Italy: Black Americans in World War II*. Jefferson, N.C.: McFarland, 1985.

*Hargrove's work documents the service of the 92nd Infantry and the 366th Regiment, African American units that served under adverse conditions in Italy during the war.*

Hastie, William H., *On Clipped Wings: The Story of Jim Crow in the Army Air Corps*. New York: NAACP, 1943.

*Hastie served briefly as the Civilian Aide to the Secretary of War during World War II but quit to protest the treatment of African American military personnel.*

Henri, Florette. *Bitter Victory: A History of Black Soldiers in World War II*. Garden City, N.Y.: Doubleday, 1970.

*This is a highly readable general survey of African American participation in World War II.*

Hine, Darlene Clark. *Black Women in White: Racial Conflict and Cooperation in the Nursing Profession, 1890–1950*. Bloomington: Indiana University Press, 1989.

*U.S. legislators and military leaders considered drafting white nurses in order to avoid using African American nurses in large numbers during World War II. Hine addresses the efforts of black leaders to integrate the military nurse corps.*

Jakeman, Robert J. *Divided Skies: Establishing Segregated Flight Training at Tuskegee*. Tuscaloosa: University of Alabama Press, 1992

*Jakeman discuses the racial policies that affected the recruitment and commissioning of African Americans into the Army Air Corps and the establishment and operation of Tuskegee combat units.*

James, C. L. R. *Fighting Racism in World War II*. New York: Monad Press, 1980.

*Using articles, pamphlets, letters, and resolutions from the press of the Socialist Workers Party, this book presents the African American struggle against racism. James presents various aspects of black protest during the war.*

Jefferson, Alexander. *Red Tail Captured, Red Tail Free: Memoirs of a World War II Tuskegee Airman and POW*. New York: Fordham University Press, 2005.

*Jefferson, one of the Tuskegee Airmen, spent the last months of World War II in a German prison camp after having been shot down over southern France. He remained in the service after the war and retired as an Air Force colonel.*

Johnson, Charles, Jr. *African American Soldiers in the National Guard*. Westport, Conn.: Greenwood Press, 1992.

*This work explains the organization, mobilization of deployment of African American National Guardsmen from the late nineteenth century through 1949. Johnson discusses their military service records in World War II.*

Johnson, Charles. *African Americans and ROTC: Military, Naval and AeroScience Programs at Historically Black Colleges, 1916–1973*. Jefferson, N.C.: McFarland, 2002.

*Johnson explains the establishment and development of Reserve Officer Training Corps (ROTC) detachments at African American colleges. He discusses the role of these programs in providing officers in the modern military.*

Johnson, Jesse J. *Black Armed Forces Officers, 1936–1971*. Hampton, Va.: Hampton Institute, 1974.

*Whites were reluctant to allow blacks to become commissioned officers. However, political pressure from the black leaders and the African American press led to their training and use. Johnson gives a partial listing of black officers.*

Kelly, Mary Pat. *Proudly We Served: The Men of the USS Mason*. Annapolis, Md.: Naval Institute Press, 1995.

*This is the history of the black crew of the USS Mason. Their experiences were compiled through extensive oral interviews with surviving crewmembers. It explains the ship's role in the war and addresses racial relations.*

Lee, Ulysses. *The Employment of Negro Troops*. Washington, D.C.: Office of the Chief of Military History, 1966.

*Using military records, this study provides a history of the role of black soldiers in World War II. Lee focuses on the use of African American troops overseas.*

Louis, Joe. *My Life Story*. New York: Duell, Sloan and Pearce, 1947.

*The author discusses his military experiences as well as his professional boxing career.*

MacDonald, Nancy, and Dwight MacDonald. *The War's Greatest Scandal: The Story of Jim Crow in Uniform*. New York: The March on Washington Movement, 1943.

*Protests led by labor leader A. Philip Randolph led to the beginning of desegregation in defense industries. There are statistics on the number of black troops and their mistreatment, including lynching of black servicemen.*

McGuire, Philip. *He, Too, Spoke for Democracy: Judge Hastie, World War II and the Black Soldier*. New York: Greenwood Press, 1988.

*Hastie, serving as civilian aide to the secretary of war, was an uncompromising advocate of equality for black troops. Hastie soon quit his position as civilian aide because of the unwillingness of the military leaders to democratize their ranks.*

McGuire, Philip, *Taps for a Jim Crow Army: Letters from Black Soldiers In World War II*. Santa Barbara, Calif.: ABC-Clio, 1983.

*McGuire's work is a compilation of letters from black soldiers. The soldiers often describe their racist and violent treatment at the hands of white officers and troops.*

Moore, Brenda L. *To Serve My Country, To Serve My Race: The Story of the Only African-American WACs Stationed Overseas During World War II*. New York: New York University Press, 1996.

*One all-black Women's Army Corps (WAC) unit, the 6888 Central Postal Battalion, served as mail handlers in France. The author's research included interviews with some of those who were a part of the battalion.*

Morehouse, Maggie M. *Fighting in the Jim Crow Army: Black Men and Women Remember World War II*. Lanham, Md.: Rowan and Littlefield, 2000.

*Morehouse studies black men and women who fought for democracy in a segregated Army without receiving proper recognition. She deals with segregation, discrimination, race relations, and the desegregation of the armed forces.*

Motley, Mary Penick, ed. *The Invisible Soldier: The Experience of the Black Soldier, World War II*. Detroit: Wayne State University, 1975.

*Motley collected oral histories from black veterans about their wartime experiences in the preparation of this work.*

Nalty, Bernard C. *The Right to Fight: African-American Marines in World War II*. Washington, D.C.: Marine Corps Historical Center, 1995.

*This work is a part of a series commemorating the fiftieth anniversary of World War II. The Marines allowed no blacks for 150 years and integrated in 1942 only because of political pressure. Nalty provides a brief history of black Marines.*

*Negro History Bulletin* 51/57 (December 1993).

*This was the "50th Anniversary of World War II Commemorative Issue" of the Negro History Bulletin. Some of the articles pertain to the service of black soldiers, blacks in the Corps of Engineers in Alaska, and the role of the black press.*

Nelson, Dennis D. *The Integration of the Negro into the U.S. Navy*. New York: Farrar, Straus, 1951.

*Nelson, a lieutenant in the U.S. Naval Reserve commissioned in 1944, wrote the first comprehensive history of the employment of blacks in the U.S. Navy. It spans the period from the Revolutionary War through 1948.*

*Opinions About Negro Infantry Platoons in White Companies of Seven Divisions Based on a Survey Made in May-June, 1945*. Washington, D.C.: Information and Education Division, Army Service Forces, 1945.

*This study provides information about racial attitudes in the U.S. during the war era.*

Osur, Alan M. *Blacks in the Army Air Force During World War II: The Problem of Race Relations*. Washington, D.C.: Office of Air Force History, 1977.

*Relates the history of black flying units and details the decision making process in allowing blacks to fly and the subsequent use of black airmen.*

Peery, Nelson. *Black Fire: The Making of an American Revolutionary*. New York: New Press, 1994.

*In this autobiography, Peery recounts his personal encounter with racism especially during his service with the 93rd infantry division. His experiences ignited in him a desire to fight social injustice everywhere.*

Poulos, Paula Nassen, ed. *A Woman's War Too: U.S. Women the Military in World War II*. Washington, D.C.: National Archives and Records Administration, 1996

*This study provides an examination of women's roles from many different perspectives. Articles discuss the Air Force, medical services, Marines, and the roles of African American women.*

Purdon, Eric. *Black Company: The Story of Subchaser 1264*. Annapolis, Md.: Naval Institute Press, 2000.

*This is a naval commander's account of one of the two naval shops assigned a mostly black enlisted crew during World War II.*

Putney, Martha. *When the Nation Was in Need: Blacks in the Women's Army Corps During World War II*. Metuchen, N.J.: Scarecrow Press, 1992.

*Putney, a World War II veteran, provides a history of the recruitment, training, and employment of black women during World War II.*

Robinson, Jackie. *I Never Had It Made*. New York: G. P. Putnam, 1972.

*Robinson discusses his World War II experiences as well as his sports career.*

Roth, David. *Sacred Honor: A Biography of Colin Powell*. Grand Rapids, Mich.: Zondervan, 1993.

*Roth looks at Powell's life from his childhood to his distinguished military and civilian career.*

Sandler, Stanley. *Segregated Skies: All Black Squadron of World War II*. Washington, D.C.: Smithsonian Institute Press, 1993.

*Sandler describes the roles of African American troops from early noncombat roles to the efficient service of the 99th Pursuit Squadron and the 332nd Fighter Group.*

Scott, Lawrence P. and William M. Womack. *Double V: The Civil Rights Struggle of the Tuskegee Airmen*. East Lansing: Michigan State University Press, 1998.

*Double V stood for victory abroad and at home. The authors provide a description and analysis of the discrimination that the Tuskegee airmen suffered during and after World War II and their struggle for equal rights as citizens.*

Silvera, John Douglas. *The Negro in World War II*. New York: Arno Press, 1969.

*This is a general survey of African American participation in the war.*

Smith, Steven D. *A Historic Context Statement for a World War II Era Black Officers' Club at Ft. Leonard Wood, Missouri*. Washington, D.C.: U.S. Department of Defense and the U.S. Army Corps of Engineers, 1998.

*A survey of surviving World War II buildings included this segregated black officers' club in Missouri. Efforts to preserve the history of the building included the preparation of a historical account of the building's use.*

Society for the Psychological Study of Social Issues. *Opinions About Negro Infantry Platoons in White Companies of Seven Divisions*. Washington, D.C.: U.S. War Department, 1947.

*During the post–World War II period, military leaders were concerned about the psychological effects of integration. This study examines various aspects of interracial relations.*

Staupers, Mabel. *No Time for Prejudice: A Story of the Integration of Negroes in Nursing in the U.S.* New York: Macmillan, 1961.

*Both the Red Cross and the U.S. military resisted the employment of black nurses. Staupers details the various strategies utilized by these nurses to tear down the walls of discrimination in World War II.*

Stevens, John D. "From the Back of the Foxhole: Black Correspondents in World War II." *Journalism Monographs* 27 (February 1973).

*This study addresses the accomplishments and working conditions of black press correspondents on duty overseas.*

Stillwell, Paul, ed. *The Golden Thirteen: Recollections of the First Black Naval Officers*. Annapolis, Md.: Naval Institute Press, 1993.

*Historically, naval vessels were rigidly segregated, with blacks performing only menial roles. During World War II this system began to change. In this volume, some of the first black naval officers relate their accomplishments and their trials.*

U.S. Department of the Army. *A Historical Analysis of the 364th Infantry in World War II, 1941 to 1945*. Washington, D.C.: Department of the Army, 2001.

*In response to a 1998 book by Carroll Case entitled* The Slaughter, *which alleged that a thousand men of the 364th infantry were killed by the Army in 1943, the Army Center of Military History undertook this study. It includes oral histories.*

Urban Colored Population Commission. *New Jersey Negro in World War II*. Trenton: State of New Jersey, 1945.

*Sara S. Washington was the chair of the Urban Colored Population Commission of the National Baptist Convention, which requested this report from Governor Walter Edge. It includes population statistics, service records, medal winners, and officers.*

Wynn, Neil A. *The Afro-American and the Second World War*. New York: Holmes and Meier, 1976.

*This is a general history of black participation in the war effort.*

Zumwalt, Elmo R., Jr. *On Watch: A Memoir*. New York: Times Books, 1976.

*Admiral Zumwalt addresses issues relating to race relations in the Navy and reviews his own efforts to assure racial and gender equality.*

## *Archive and Manuscript Sources*

Hastie, William H. Papers, Harvard University Library, Cambridge, Mass.

*Hastie was chosen as the civilian aide to the Secretary of War during World War II but resigned in 1943 because the unfair treatment of black troops by the military and the news media.*

"Listing of African-American Units in World War II." U.S. War Department General and Special Staffs, Record Group 165, G-1, Decimal File, 1942–1946, 219.2, Box 443. National Archives and Records Administration.

Logan, Rayford W. *Papers*. Library of Congress, Washington, D.C.

*Logan's diaries discuss his role in convincing President Franklin D. Roosevelt and the U.S. government to train and utilize blacks as pilots during World War II and his participation in the Pan African Congresses organized by W. E. B. Du Bois.*

National Association for the Advancement of Colored People Records, Manuscript Division, Library of Congress, Washington, D.C.

*Soldiers who were mistreated during World War II sent letters detailing their treatment to the NAACP. Most of the pertinent files are called "Soldier Troubles."*

NAACP, 1940–1955, *General Office File. Office of War Information—Negroes and The War, 1941–1943, 1945, 1947*. 2 reels. Frederick, Md.: University Publications of America, 1989.

*These records document the closeness with which the NAACP monitored the actions of the federal government during the war years. The NAACP argued that the U.S. government falsely represented its treatment of conditions affecting black troops.*

NAACP, 1940–1955. *General Office File. United States Air Force, 1940–1943, 1950–1955*. Frederick, Md.: University Publications of America, 1989.

*The records document World War II efforts to secure admission of black candidates to the Aviation Cadet Training Division and other branches of the military. Later files concern discrimination against blacks at Air Force bases.*

National Urban League Records, Manuscript Division, Library of Congress.

*These records primarily concern the availability of employment opportunities for blacks, their working conditions, and adequate housing for them.*

Naval Historical Center Oral History Collection. Operational Archives Branch, Washington Navy Yard, Washington, D.C.

*African Americans discuss their service during World War II including work as messmates and stewards, discrimination on ships, and work with Filipinos.*

Parrish, Noel. *Papers*. Manuscript Division, Library of Congress.

*Parrish was the commander of the Tuskegee Airmen. His papers cover the training and performance of the men and include photographs, camp newsletters, articles, memoirs, and correspondence about the camp and the community.*

Patterson, Frederick D. *Papers*. Manuscript Division, Library of Congress.

*Patterson, as president of Tuskegee Institute, established a school for commercial and military aviation. He was president during the time that the Tuskegee Airmen were training. Some of his records relate to this period of his life.*

Randolph, A. Philips. *Papers*. Manuscript Division, Library of Congress.

*Randolph, a labor leader, threatened a march on Washington by 100,000 blacks to protest discriminatory treatment of blacks in defense industries. In response, President Roosevelt established the Committee on Fair Employment Practices.*

U.S., General Records of the Department of Health, Education, and Welfare. Record Group 235, National Archives and Records Administration.

*Some records address recreational facilities for black soldiers during the war, employment of African Americans in the federal government, and blacks in health professions.*

U.S., General Records of the Department of the Navy, Record Group 80, National Archives and Records Administration.

*The correspondence of the Secretary of the Navy and Assistant Secretary of the Navy includes information relating to the Navy's racial policies.*

U.S., General Records of the Department of State, Record Group 59, National Archives and Records Administration.

*State Department Decimal files include letters of protests from prominent black leaders, the NAACP, and others about the treatment of black soldiers.*

U.S., National Archives Gift Collection, Record Group 200, National Archives and Records Administration.

*Some of the records pertain to World War II blood programs and include information about Charles Drew, a black physician who pioneered work with blood plasma. The gift collection also includes some film footage of black paratroopers.*

U.S., Office of Government Reports, Record Group 44, National Archives and Records Administration.

*These records contain many investigative reports relating to the protests and political activities of blacks at home and the morale of black soldiers abroad during World War II. The government was especially concerned about the black press.*

U.S., Records of the Army Air Forces, Record Group 18, National Archives and Records Administration.

*Records relating to the Tuskegee Airmen (the 99th, 100th, 301st, and 302nd Fighter Squadrons) include sortie reports, aircraft type, captain and crew, flight times, weather, narratives, daily reports, commander's records, and flying school reports.*

U.S., Records of the Bureau of Agricultural Economics, Record Group 83, National Archives and Records Administration.

*The project files of the Division of Program Surveys includes information on "Negro Rationing," sharecropping, peonage, urban problems caused by racism, and black Americans' reactions to World War II.*

U.S., Records of the Bureau of Employment Security, Record Group 183, National Archives and Records Administration.

*Labor market area reports generated by this agency from 1941 to 1949 include information about the utilization of black workers in the defense industry.*

U.S., Records of the Committee for Congested Production Areas, Record Group 212, National Archives and Records Administration.

*Records relating to black people in congested urban areas concern lack of housing and recreational areas, which sometimes led to interracial tensions and racial violence.*

U.S., Records of the Committee on Fair Employment Practices, Record Group 228, National Archives and Records Administration.

*This committee formulated and interpreted policies to combat racial discrimination in employment and investigated and adjusted complaints. Eighty percent of the records pertain to black workers in defense industries.*

U.S., Records of the Foreign Broadcast Intelligence Service, Record Group 262, National Archives and Records Administration.

*Files relating to "Japan's Race Propaganda" give information about Japanese radio broadcasts criticizing U.S. and British race prejudice toward darker races. The Japanese referred repeatedly to the exploitation of blacks in the United States.*

U.S., Records of the Office of Censorship. Record Group 216, National Archives and Records Administration.

*Some records relate to "inflammatory racial references" in black newspapers, which affected racial relations in overseas theaters of operations and leaking of information about troop movement. Reports cover morale, riots, and discrimination.*

U.S., Records of the Office of Civilian Defense, Record Group 171, National Archives and Records Administration.

*Records cover information about the proposed March on Washington planned by A. Philip Randolph and the government's response to it in the records of Crystal Bird Fauset, Director of the Racial Relations Division.*

U.S., Records of the Office of Community War Services. Record Group 215, National Archives and Records Administration.

*Because many war services were segregated, there are separate files relating to African Americans in health, welfare, and recreation.*

U.S. Records of the Office of Emergency Management, Record Group 214, National Archives and Records Administration.

*Files contain information about blacks in defense industries and the establishment of the Fair Employment Practices Committee. Other materials pertain to housing, discrimination, health contractors, and the role of Robert C. Weaver.*

U.S., Records of the Office of the Housing Expediter, Record Group 252, National Archives and Records Administration.

*Records include reports on housing programs for black veterans, rent prices, tenant conditions, and rationing in various major cities.*

U.S., Records of the Office of Labor (War Food Administration), Record Group 224, National Archives and Records Administration.

*Frederick D. Patterson and Claude A. Barnett worked as special assistants to the director of the War Food Administration. The agency operated camps for migratory and foreign farm laborers.*

U.S., Records of the Office of the Secretary of War, Record Group 107, National Archives and Records Administration.

*The records of the Civilian Aide to the Secretary of War include materials generated by William H. Hastie and Truman Gibson and their successors relating to the treatment and utilization of black service members.*

U.S., Records of the Office of War Information, Record Group 208, National Archives and Records Administration.

*The agency generated many reports, press releases, films, newsreels, and sound recordings relating to blacks in the war effort. Records include an illustrated OWI publication by Chandler Owen entitled Negroes and the War.*

U.S. Records of the War Manpower Commission, Record Group 211, National Archives and Records Administration.

*Much of the material about black workers pertains to fair employment practices, manpower allocation, women's work, and government policies in hiring. Records include correspondence and labor reports by Robert C. Weaver.*

## *Film and Video*

*African-Americans in World War II: A Legacy of Patriotism and Valor*. Produced by Milton Thomas of the Joint Visual Information Activity, Alexandria, Va. 1997.

*This 65-minute film documents the service of more than 1.2 million African Americans who served during World War II.*

*The American Experience. Liberators—Fighting on Two Fronts in World War II.* Produced by William Miles and Nina Rosenblum in association with WNET-13, New York. 1992.

*This film, narrated by Denzel Washington and Louis Gossett Jr., focuses on regiments of black soldiers and the racism they faced. It depicts the horrors of the concentration camps from which the soldiers liberated other victims of racism.*

*Henry Brown, Farmer.* Record Group 16, Records of the Department of Agriculture, National Archives and Records Administration, 1942.

*Soldiers on the battlefield are compared with "soldiers of production." Black farmer Henry Brown and his family travel to visit his son, a cadet in the 99th Pursuit squadron. Canada Lee narrates the film.*

*The Invisible Soldiers: Unheard Voices.* Marlboro, Mass.: Com Tel Productions, 2000.

*This video investigates the role of black soldiers in World War II.*

*The Meaning of V-E Day to Negroes.* Mutual Broadcasting System, New World A-Coming, No. 048, 1945. National Archives and Records Administration.

*Oliver Harrington interviews prominent African Americans about their postwar expectations.*

*Negro Colleges in Wartime.* Record Group 208, Office of War Information, National Archives and Records Administration, 1943.

*The film shows how historically black colleges adjusted to war needs by preparing students for various military and civilian occupations. There are scenes at Tuskegee Institute, Hampton Institute, Howard University, and Prairie View College.*

*The Negro Sailor.* Record Group 80, Department of the Navy, National Archives and Records Administration, 1945.

*This 26-minute film is a promotional documentary emphasizing integration, advancement based on ability rather than race, equal treatment, and teamwork. It shows a ship with a predominantly black crew and names medal winners.*

*The Negro Soldier.* Film, Records of the Office of the Chief Signal Officer, Record Group 111, National Archives and Records Administration, 1944.

*This film, directed by Frank Capra, documents the participation of black soldiers in American wars from the Revolution to World War II. Although it was a government documentary, it also became a popular theater film.*

*To Serve My Country, To Serve My Race.* 1997.

*This documentary, directed by Lawrence Walker, shows the commitment of African American women to the World War II military in spite of sexism, racism, and traditionalism in the armed services.*

*Teamwork.* Film, Records of the Office of the Chief Signal Officer, Record Group 111, National Archives and Records Administration.

*This 1946 film deals with interracial cooperation in the Army.*

*Tuskegee Trains Airmen.* Harmon Foundation Gift Collection, National Archives and Records Administration.

*The film shows aviation training at Tuskegee with demonstrations of how parts operate, use of charts and maps. Many scenes include the students. The footage is from the period 1940 to 1949.*

*Wings for This Man.* Records of the U.S. Air Force Commands, Record Group 342, National Archives and Records Administration.

*This 10-minute film describes the organization and training of the Tuskegee Airmen at Tuskegee Air Base in Alabama and shows some of their aerial operations in Europe.*

## DESEGREGATION OF THE ARMED FORCES

Ansel, Raymond B. *From Segregation to Desegregation: Blacks in the U.S. Army 1703–1954*. Carlisle, Pa.: U.S. Army War College, 1990.

*This is a study of the contributions of African Americans in the military and the gradual integration of white and black forces in the post–World War II era.*

Bogart, Leo. *Social Research and the Desegregation of the U.S. Army: Two Original 1951 Field Reports*. Chicago: Markham, 1969.

*Bogart addresses the reactions of white and African American troops to desegregation efforts in the early 1950s.*

Dalfiume, Richard M. *Desegregation of the U.S. Armed Forces: Fighting on Two Fronts, 1939–53*. Columbia: University of Missouri Press, 1969.

*This book discusses the U.S. military's policies on race and reactions to those policies. The author details the way in which the military changed from segregation to integration.*

Gropman, Alan L. *The Air Force Integrates, 1945–1964*. Washington, D.C.: Smithsonian Institution Press, 1998.

*Gropman outlines the attitudes, policies, and procedures used during the integration of the Air Force.*

MacGregor, Morris J. *Integration of the Armed Forces, 1940–1965*. Washington, D.C.: Center of Military History, U.S. Army, 1981.

*African American participation in the Army, Navy, Marine Corps, Coast Guard, and Air Force before, during, and after desegregation is covered in this 647-page work.*

Stillman, Richard Joseph. *Integration of the Negro in the U.S. Armed Forces*. New York: Praeger, 1968.

*Stillman provides information about military plans for integration and the obstacles encountered before achieving success.*

## KOREA

Appleman, Roy E. *Disaster in Korea: The Chinese Confront MacArthur*. Washington, D.C.: Office of the Chief of Military History, 1986.

*This is a general history of the Korean conflict but includes some information about African American troops. Appleman criticizes their performance.*

Appleman, Roy E. *U.S. Army in the Korean War: South to the Naktong, North to the Yalu*. Washington, D.C.: U.S. Government Printing Office, 1961.

*This is a general history of the Korean conflict and both the black and white units that participated in it.*

Bowers, William T., William M. Hammond, and George L. MacGarrigle. *Black Soldier, White Army: The 24th Infantry Regiment in Korea*. Washington, D.C.: Center of Military History, U.S. Army, 1996.

*This study compares and contrasts the performances of white and African American troops in Korea and provides information about the occupation of Japan. The authors emphasize the wartime conditions that black troops faced.*

Bussey, Charles M. *Firefight at Yechon: Courage and Racism in the Korean War*. New York: Brassey's, 1991.

*This is a personal account of a member of an African American unit that fought in the battle of Yechon.*

David, Allan A., ed. *Battleground Korea: The Story of the 25th Infantry Division*. Tokyo: Kyoto Co., 1952.

*The 25th was an African American division that was accused of cowardice before the enemy. The book provides a forum for discussion of this view.*

*Forgotten Warriors*. WGBH. 2001.

*This 29-minute program was aired on WGBH in Boston on May 27, 2001. It addresses the role of black troops in the Korean conflict.*

Jacobs, Bruce. *Soldiers: The Fighting Divisions of the Regular Army*. New York: Norton, 1958.

*Chapter 13 in this volume, "Tropical Lightning (25th Infantry Division)," discusses the service of African American soldiers.*

Petersen, Frank. "Oral History Interview." Naval Historical Center, Operational Archives Branch, 1995.

*Petersen discusses his family background, his decision to join the Navy and then the Marine Corps, and his service in Korea, Japan, and Vietnam. Transcript is available.*

Petersen, Lt. General Frank E. with J. Alfred Phelps. *Into the Tiger's Jaw: America's First Black Marine Aviator: The Autobiography of Lt. Gen. Frank E. Petersen*. Novato, Calif.: Presidio Press, 1998.

*Before 1942 there were no blacks in the Marine Corps. Petersen began his three-star, thirty-eight year Marine Corps career during the Korean War when the Marines, the last service to integrate, became the first to abolish overt segregation.*

## VIETNAM

Binkin, Martin, et al. *Blacks in the Military*. Washington, D.C.: Brookings Institution, 1982.

*This is a part of the Brookings Institution series of "Studies in Defense Policy." This study gives some historical background "from Bunker Hill to Vietnam" and deals with issues relating to blacks in the post-Vietnam army.*

Burkett, B. G. *Stolen Valor: How the Vietnam Generation Was Robbed of Its Heroes and Its History*. Dallas: Verity Press, 1998.

*A chapter in this volume is entitled, "Minority Myth: Blacks in Vietnam."*

Daly, James A. *Black Prisoner of War: a Conscientious Objector's Vietnam Memoir*. Lawrence: University Press of Kansas, 2000. Originally published in 1975 by Bobbs-Merrill as *A Hero's Welcome*.

*This is an autobiographical account of a black Jehovah's Witness who was denied conscientious objector status, then denied noncombatant assignment and ultimately found himself a prisoner of the North Vietnamese.*

Moser, Richard R. *The New Winter Soldiers: G.I. and Veteran Dissent During the Vietnam Era*. New Brunswick, N.J.: Rutgers University Press, 1996.

*Moser's work examines dissent within the military to the Vietnam War, placing considerable emphasis on the black soldiers who contributed to that dissent.*

Olson, James Stuart. *The Vietnam War: Handbook of the Literature and Research*. Westport, Conn.: Greenwood Press, 1993.

*A chapter in this handbook, "Blacks and the Vietnam War," by Ernest M. B. Obadele-Starks and Amilcar Shabazz, provides a bibliographic essay and a book list relating to the service of blacks in the war.*

Powell, Colin, and Joseph E. Persico. *My American Journey*. New York: Random House, 1995.

*Powell discusses his youth, his education and military training, and his professional military career including his time in Vietnam.*

Shuffer, George M. *My Journey to Betterment: An Autobiography*. New York: Vantage Press, 1999.

*Shuffer served in World War II, Korea and Vietnam and retired with the rank of brigadier general. His autobiography recounts the adversity that he and his family had to overcome in the military.*

Taylor, Clyde, ed. *Vietnam and Black America: An Anthology of Protest and Resistance*. Garden City, N.Y.: Anchor Books, 1976.

*Taylor collected the writings of a number of authors who protested against African American participation in another war while being denied equal rights at home.*

Terry, Wallace, ed. *Bloods: An Oral History of the Vietnam War by Black Veterans*. New York: Ballantine Books, 1984.

*Terry interviewed twenty African American men who called themselves by the slang term "bloods." The men describe their experiences in Vietnam particularly in the light of the societal problems blacks faced as citizens in the United States.*

Westheider, James E. *Fighting on Two Fronts: African Americans and the Vietnam War*. New York: New York University Press, 1997.

*This study focuses on the forms racial discrimination took in the U.S. military in the Vietnam era and the ways in which blacks responded to such discrimination.*

## THE CIVIL RIGHTS MOVEMENT

### *Historiographies*

Lawson, Steven F., and Charles Payne. *Debating the Civil Rights Movement, 1945–1968*. Savage, Md.: Rowan and Littlefield, 1998.

*The authors explore the evolution, impact, and consequences of the movement, presenting differing perspectives on issues of causation and concepts of "leadership."*

Meier, August, and John H. Bracey. A *White Scholar and the Black Community, 1945–1965: Essays and Reflections*. Amherst: University of Massachusetts Press, 1992.

*August Meier, a white historian, taught at several historically black colleges and took courses at Howard University. In these essays, he analyzes the development of the civil rights movement and its leaders.*

Robinson, Armstead L., and Patricia Sullivan, eds. *New Directions in Civil Rights Studies*. Charlottesville: University Press of Virginia, 1991.

*This is a collection essays by movement participants and historians assessing the results and long-term implications of the civil rights movement.*

Stanfield, John H., ed. A *History of Race Relations Research: First-Generation Recollections*. Newbury Park, Calif.: Sage, 1993.

*Several historiographical essays provide direction for study and teaching methods on the subject of race relations.*

Stanfield, John H., and Rutledge M. Dennis, eds. *Race and Ethnicity in Research Methods*. Newbury Park, Calif.: Sage, 1993.

*The essays suggest various methodologies for research and writing about race and ethnic relations.*

### *Surveys*

Cook, Robert. *Sweet Land of Liberty? The African-American Struggle for Civil Rights in the Twentieth Century*. New York: Longman, 1998.

*This history concentrates on the period from World War II to the end of the 1960s. Cook, a British historian, stresses the actions of the ordinary men and women who participated in the movement.*

Lawson, Steven F. *Running for Freedom: Civil Rights and Black Politics in America Since 1941*. New York: McGraw-Hill, 1997.

*This work provides a synthesis of the research of the 1980s and 1990s on the civil rights movement emphasizing the interplay between national politics and local insurgency.*

Marable, Manning. *Race, Reform and Rebellion: the Second Reconstruction in Black America, 1945–1990*. 2nd ed. Jackson: University Press of Mississippi, 1991.

*Marable provides an interpretation that credits black nationalist groups and thinkers as the original and innovative political theorists. He emphasizes economic issues.*

Sitkoff, Harvard. *The Struggle for Black Equality, 1954–1992*. New York: Hill and Wang, 1993.

*Sitkoff provides a detailed overview and analysis of the civil rights movement and U.S. race relations.*

Van Deburg, William L. *Black Camelot: African-American Culture Heroes in Their Times, 1960–1980*. Chicago: University of Chicago Press, 1997.

*The author examines the rise of black leaders and role models in sports, film, and the performing arts all of whom exemplified aspects of black power and black aesthetic movements.*

## *Roots of the Movement*

Clark, Kenneth B. *Dark Ghetto: Dilemmas of Social Power*. New York: Harper & Row, 1965.

*Clark's research explores the sociology, psychology, and pathology of the ghetto. He also investigates ghetto schools, power structure, strategies for change, and race relations.*

Du Bois, W. E. B. *W. E. B. Du Bois: A Reader*. Ed. David Levering Lewis. New York: Holt, 1995.

*This reader includes articles by DuBois in sections on "The Niagara Movement, the NAACP and Civil Rights, "Social Science and Civil Rights," and "War and Peace." DuBois presents a numerous arguments against white domination.*

Egerton, John. *Speak Now Against the Day: The Generation Before the Civil Rights Movement in the South*. New York: Knopf, 1994.

*This 627-page history presents individuals and organizations (mostly white) in the American South who wrestled with their virulently racist society in the two decades preceding the civil rights movement of the 1950s and '60s.*

Franklin, John Hope. *Race and History: Selected Essays, 1939–1988*. Baton Rouge: Louisiana State University Press, 1989.

*In this collection of his own essays, Franklin argues that scholars who try to understand race relations in the 1950s must be able to understand the United States in the 1850s. One essay is entitled, "The South and the Problem of Change."*

Kelley, Robin D. G. *Race Rebels: Culture, Politics and the Black Working Class*. New York: Free Press, 1996.

*Demonstrates that black working-class social protests, while outside the boundaries of the organized civil rights movement, are nonetheless a powerful component of the black freedom struggle.*

Moreno, Paul D. *From Direct Action to Affirmative Action: Fair Employment Law and Policy in America, 1933–1972*. Baton Rouge: Louisiana State University Press, 1997.

*Identifies the roots of the affirmative action concepts and policies that emerged in the 1960s in New Deal and black protest initiatives of the 1930s and 1940s.*

Reed, Merle E. *Seedtime for the Modern Civil Rights Movement: The President's Committee on Fair Employment Practice, 1941–1946*. Baton Rouge: Louisiana State University Press, 1991.

*A study of the origins and operations of the Fair Employment Practices Committee.*

Robinson, JoAnn Ooiman. *Abraham Went Out: A Biography of A. J. Muste*. Philadelphia: Temple University Press, 1981.

*Muste was a nonviolent activist in the areas of civil rights, civil liberties, and antiwar action. He was a founder of the interracial Christian group called the Fellowship of Reconciliation. Some of the members of FOR formed Congress of Racial Equality.*

Sitkoff, Harvard. *A New Deal for Blacks: The Emergence of Civil Rights as a National Issue*. New York: Oxford University Press, 1978.

*Sitkoff provides a useful starting point for an overview of the benefits and disappointments of the New Deal from the perspective of African Americans.*

Sullivan, Patricia. *Days of Hope: Race and Democracy in the New Deal Era*. Chapel Hill: University of North Carolina Press, 1995.

*Sullivan studies the New Deal's effects and civil rights trends in the Deep South during 1930s and 1940s, when, in the author's words, "activists . . . tilled the ground for future change."*

## *International Context*

Anderson, Carol. *Eyes Off the Prize: The United Nations and the African American Struggle for Human Rights, 1944–1955*. New York: Cambridge University Press, 2003.

*Cogently tells the story of why the struggle for racial equality focused more on civil than human rights given opposition to international agreements that might interfere with states' rights in particular and the rise of Cold War hysteria.*

Borstelmann, Thomas. *The Cold War and the Color Line: American Race Relations in the Global Arena*. Cambridge, Mass.: Harvard University Press, 2001.

*This work demonstrates the relationship between civil rights in the United States and anticolonial struggles around the world. The book analyzes both foreign and domestic policies during the Cold War.*

Dudziak, Mary L. *Cold War Civil Rights: Race and the Image of American Democracy*. Princeton, N.J.: Princeton University Press, 2000.

*This study places the history of civil rights in the United States in an international framework, examining the impact of international scrutiny on U.S. racial policies and protests and the impact of those policies and protests on America's standing in the world.*

Fredrickson, George. *Black Liberation: A Comparative History of Black Ideologies in the U.S. and South Africa*. New York: Oxford University Press, 1996.

*The author examines black responses to policies and practices mandating white racial domination and discusses the evolution of black resistance movements. He shows how U.S. and South African black nationalists influenced one another.*

Fredrickson, George. *White Supremacy: A Comparative Study in American and South African History*. New York: Oxford University Press, 1989.

*Frederickson analyzes similarities and differences between South Africa and the United States on a wide variety of racial issues. He compares and contrasts racial attitudes and government policies.*

Kapur, Sudarshan. *Raising Up a Prophet: The African-American Encounter with Gandhi*. Boston: Beacon Press, 1992.

*This work traces the history of African American interest in the Indian freedom movement and the nonviolent methods of Mohandas Gandhi, long before those methods became associated with Martin Luther King Jr.*

Smith, Jennifer B. *International History of the Black Panther Party*. New York: Garland, 1999.

*Smith places the Black Panther Party in the context of global freedom struggles.*

## *Autobiographies*

Abernathy, Ralph David. *And the Walls Come Tumbling Down.* New York: Harper and Row, 1989.

*Abernathy, a Baptist preacher, was a civil rights leader and a close friend and confident of Martin Luther King Jr. This autobiography covers Abernathy's childhood, education, and career.*

Bates, Daisy. *The Long Shadow of Little Rock.* Fayetteville: University of Arkansas Press, 1987.

*Bates's memoir relates the dramatic encounter of the nine black students who integrated Central High School in Little Rock, Arkansas, in 1957. Bates spearheaded the provision of a support network for the students as they faced the hatred of whites.*

Beals, Melba Pattillo, and Anne Greenberg, eds. *Warriors Don't Cry: A Searing Memoir of the Battle to Integrate Little Rock's Central High.* New York: Pocket Books, 1994.

*One of the Little Rock Nine relates her memories, drawing on journals she kept at the time of the school integration crisis.*

Brown, Cynthia Stokes, ed. *Ready from Within: A First Person Narrative.* Trenton: Africa World Press, 1990.

*This work provides an autobiography of Septima Clark, who, through her work with the Highlander Folk School and the Southern Christian Leadership Conference, fostered "citizenship education" and grass roots voter registration campaigns throughout the South.*

Browning, Joan, et al. *Deep in Our Hearts: Nine White Women in the Freedom Movement.* Athens: University of Georgia Press, 2000.

*The nine authors all worked with the Student Non-Violent Coordinating Committee during the 1960s. Each writes about the movement, and issues such as gender and the emergence of black power.*

Chafe, William H, ed. *Remembering Jim Crow: African Americans Tell About Life in the Segregated South.* New York: New Press, 2001.

*Chafe spearheaded a two-CD and book project at Duke University to capture the memory of southern segregation. Remembering is part of a larger oral history project at Duke that includes more than 1,300 oral histories.*

Farmer, James. *Freedom—When?* New York: Random House, 1965.

*As national director and spokesman for the Congress of Racial Equality, Farmer presents an insider's view of the organization and its objectives. He also provides autobiographical information.*

Farmer, James. *Lay Bare the Heart: An Autobiography of the Civil Rights Movement.* New York: Arbor House, 1985.

*Farmer discusses his life as a "preacher's kid" in the South, his education, the founding of Congress of Racial Equality, its evolution over two decades, and his leadership of that organization during the civil rights struggle in the South.*

Franklin, Buck Colbert. *My Life and an Era: The Autobiography of Buck Colbert Franklin.* Ed. John Hope Franklin and John Whittington Franklin Baton Rouge: Louisiana State University Press, 1997.

*Franklin discusses his life as an African American lawyer in Oklahoma from the turn of the century through the onset of the civil rights movement.*

Greenberg, Jack. *Crusaders in the Courts: How A Dedicated Band of Lawyers Fought for the Civil Rights Revolution.* New York: Basic Books, 1994.

*Greenberg, former director-counsel of the NAACP Legal Defense Fund, wrote this account of the civil rights cases. He discusses the strategy that led to the 1954 Brown decision and the plan of action that followed that case.*

Jordan, Vernon E., Jr., and Annette Gorgon-Reed. *Vernon Can Read! A Memoir*. New York: Public Affairs, 2001.

*In this memoir, Jordan describes his youth in Atlanta detailing relationships with friends who later became civil rights activists. He discusses his higher education, his induction into the civil rights arena through work with a law firm, and his employment with the NAACP and the National Urban League.*

King, Coretta Scott. *My Life with Martin Luther King, Jr.* New York: Holt, Rinehart, and Winston, 1969.

*King describes her life as the wife of a much-loved and much-hated leader of the civil rights movement. The family was under the constant threat of danger, both physical and emotional.*

King, Martin Luther, Jr. *The Trumpet of Conscience*. New York: Harper & Row, 1967.

*In this book, King commits himself to battles against racism, poverty, and war. The book is a compilation of five talks King gave in 1967 over the Canadian Broadcasting Corporation radio network.*

King, Mary. *Freedom Song: a Personal Story of the 1960s Civil Rights Movement*. New York: William Morrow, 1987.

*Memoir of a white woman's experience in the Student Non-Violent Coordinating Committee.*

Lewis, John, and Michael D'Orso. *Walking with the Wind: A Memoir of the Movement*. San Diego: Harcourt, 1998.

*Congressman Lewis, who was a student demonstrator in the 1960s, became the chairman of the Student Non-Violent Coordinating Committee. He led the organization using nonviolent tactics during freedom rides, demonstrations, and the March on Washington.*

Meredith, James. *Three Years in Mississippi*. Bloomington: Indiana University Press, 1966.

*This is Meredith's own account of his experiences as the first African American to enter the University of Mississippi. It details his battle to enroll at "Ole Miss" and the resistance he faced at the hands of segregationists.*

Motley, Constance Baker. *Equal Justice Under Law*. New York: Farrar, Straus and Giroux, 1998.

*As a civil rights lawyer for the NAACP Legal Defense Fund, Motley, the first black woman appointed to a federal judgeship, worked with Thurgood Marshall on numerous cases, including that of James Meredith.*

Murray, Pauli. *The Autobiography of a Black Activist, Feminist, Lawyer, Priest, and Poet*. Knoxville: University of Tennessee Press, 1989.

*While attending Howard University, Murray pioneered in desegregation campaigns in Washington, D.C., and corresponded about racial issues with Eleanor Roosevelt. By the 1960s, she was a lawyer challenging race and gender discrimination.*

Parks, Rosa. *Quiet Strength: The Faith, the Hope and the Heart of a Woman Who Changed a Nation*. Grand Rapids, Mich.: Zondervan, 1994.

*Parks, whose refusal to give up her bus seat to a white rider in Montgomery, Alabama, in 1955 led to a boycott of the buses there by blacks, relates how she had the strength to face adversity.*

Parks, Rosa, with Jim Haskins. *Rosa Parks: My Story*. New York: Dial Books, 1992.

*Parks's autobiography provides information about her youth, education and training, and active involvement in the civil rights movement.*

Patterson, Frederick D., and Martia Graham Goodson, ed. *Chronicles of Faith: The Autobiography of Frederick D. Patterson*. Tuscaloosa: University of Alabama Press, 1991.

*Patterson, the third president of Tuskegee Institute, helped develop the aviation program and schools of veterinary medicine, engineering, and commercial food preparation. Patterson also was the organizer of the United Negro College Fund.*

Peck, James. *Freedom Ride*. New York: Simon and Schuster, 1962.

*Peck, a white rider, was badly beaten in 1961 when his bus reached Birmingham. He is the only person to have participated in both the 1961 Freedom Rides and the 1947 Journey of Reconciliation, when he was also attacked by racist whites.*

Robeson, Paul. *Here I Stand*. Boston: Beacon Press, 1958.

*Robeson was a star in education, football, music, movies, and politics. His international performances ended in 1950s when the U.S. government denied him a passport because of his radical political views and his open admiration of the Soviets.*

Robinson, JoAnn Gibson, and David J. Garrow, eds. *The Montgomery Bus Boycott and the Women Who Started It: The Memoir of Jo Ann Gibson Robinson*. Knoxville: University of Tennessee Press, 1987.

*Robinson relates the way that the women in Montgomery, Alabama, their families, and their churches rallied their community in the yearlong bus boycott.*

Wilkins, Roger. *A Man's Life: An Autobiography*. Woodbridge, Conn.: Ox Bow, 1991.

*Wilkins, a lawyer, writer, and Pulitzer Prize–winning journalist, describes his participation in the civil rights movement and his battles against racism in the United States.*

Wilkins, Roy with Tom Matthews. *The Autobiography of Roy Wilkins: Standing Fast*. New York: Penguin Books, 1984.

*Wilkins, grandson of an emancipated slave and a journalist, became the leader of the NAACP and was a major force in that organization for over fifty years.*

Young, Andrew. *An Easy Burden: The Civil Rights Movement and the Transformation of America*. New York: HarperCollins, 1997.

*As a close friend and aide to Martin Luther King Jr., Young was present at the heart of every campaign of King's Southern Christian Leadership Conference and recounts and interprets those experiences in this memoir. He documents the evolution of the movement.*

## *Biographies*

Anderson, Jervis. *Bayard Rustin: Troubles I've Seen*. New York: HarperCollins, 1997.

*Anderson provides a portrait of a brilliant and controversial civil rights thinker, strategist, and activist whose association with black protest began with the March on Washington Movement and the Congress of Racial Equality in the 1940s.*

Bass, Jack. *Taming the Storm: The Life and Times of Judge Frank M. Johnson, Jr. and the South's Fight Over Civil Rights*. New York: Anchor Books, 1994.

*Johnson was the federal judge whose vote ended segregated seating on the buses in Montgomery, Alabama, in 1956. He continued for three decades to hand down decisions that proved pivotal for the civil rights of minorities.*

DeLeon, David. *Leaders from the 1960s: A Biographical Sourcebook of American Activism*. Westport, Conn.: Greenwood, 1994.

*This volume includes blacks in categories such as racial democracy, peace and freedom, sexuality and gender, radical culture, and visions of alternative societies.*

Dickerson, Dennis C. *Militant Mediator: Whitney M. Young, Jr.* Lexington: University Press of Kentucky, 1998.

*Examines the life and work of the National Urban League director, analyzing his efforts to mediate between white elites and black communities.*

Fleming, Cynthia Griggs. *Soon We Will Not Cry: The Liberation of Ruby Doris Smith Robinson*. Savage, Md.: Rowan and Littlefield, 2000.

*Robinson was a highly regarded leader in the Student Nonviolent Coordinating Committee. This study of her contributions and struggles illuminates the role of women in that organization.*

Garrow, David. *Bearing the Cross: Martin Luther King, Jr. and the Southern Christian Leadership Conference*. New York: William Morrow, 1986.

*This 800-page work covers King's career from the Montgomery bus boycott and the birth of the Southern Christian Leadership Conference, through his murder in Memphis in 1968.*

Gilliam, Dorothy Butler. *Paul Robeson: All-American*. Washington, D.C.: New Republic, 1976.

*Robeson struggled for artistic and political freedom. The book discusses his international singing career, his love of Russia, and the political atmosphere during the Cold War that signaled his forced retirement.*

Goldman, Peter. *The Death and Life of Malcolm* X. Urbana: University of Illinois Press, 1973.

*Goldman's focuses heavily on Malcolm's last years during which he was estranged from the Nation of Islam and attempted to create a new politics of blackness in America and Africa.*

Grant, Joanne. *Ella Baker: Freedom Bound*. New York: John Wiley and Sons, 1998.

*Baker, who worked with both the NAACP and Southern Christian Leadership Conference, arranged the founding conference of the Student Non-Violent Coordinating Committee, counseled the young activists against affiliating with the Southern Christian Leadership Conference, and served as a role model and mentor to them.*

Halberstam, David. *The Children*. New York: Ballantine Books, 1999.

*Halberstam studies the eight original members of the Nashville student movement, their training by James Lawson in nonviolence, their bravery as pioneers in the sit-ins and freedom rides, and their lives down to the present time.*

Haskins, James. *Profiles in Black Power*. Garden City, N.Y.: Doubleday, 1972.

*Haskins provides biographical sketches of Adam Clayton Powell Jr., Albert B. Cleage, Floyd McKissick, Nathan Wright Jr., Malcolm X, James Forman, Eldridge Cleaver, Huey P. Newton, Stokely Carmichael, Ron Karenga, and H. Rap Brown.*

Hudson-Weems, Clenora. *Emmett Till: The Sacrificial Lamb of the Civil Rights Movement*. Troy, Mich.: Bedford Publishers, 1994.

*Till's brutal lynching on August 28, 1955, emboldened African Americans to take action against racial segregation.*

Janken, Kenneth R. *Rayford W. Logan and the Dilemma of the African American Intellectual*. Amherst: University of Massachusetts Press, 1993.

*Logan, a rights activist, served as a World War I officer, a translator at the Pan African Congresses, a journalist, author, historian, president of a fraternal order. This biography details his struggles with discrimination and his efforts to combat it.*

Lee, Chana Kai. *For Freedom's Sake: the Life of Fannie Lou Hamer*. Urbana: University of Illinois Press, 1999.

*From sharecropper to field secretary for the Student Non-Violent Coordinating Committee to candidate for Congress of the Mississippi Freedom Democratic Party, Hamer emerged as a strong force in the southern freedom movement.*

Levine, Daniel. *Bayard Rustin and the Civil Rights Movement*. New Brunswick, N.J.: Rutgers University Press, 2000.

*Levine gives a scholarly assessment of Rustin's role in the nonviolent civil rights movement and his differences with the leaders of that movement in the era of Black Power and Vietnam.*

Lewis, David Levering. *King: A Critical Biography*. New York: Praeger, 1970.

*Written soon after his assassination in 1968, this volume analyzes King's life and work, particularly his ascendancy from an unknown preacher in Montgomery, Alabama, to a world-renowned civil rights advocate.*

Lewis, David Levering. *W. E. B. Du Bois: The Fight for Equality and the American Century, 1919–1963*. New York: Bowker, 2001.

*Levering's biography documents Du Bois's ceaseless struggle against bigotry in all forms.*

Longenecker, Stephen L. *Selma's Peacemaker: Ralph Smeltzer and Civil Rights Mediation*. Philadelphia: Temple University Press, 1987.

*Smeltzer, a white preacher, kept a detailed record of his efforts in Selma, Alabama, to mediate and diffuse racial tensions in the months preceding the 1965 attack by white policemen on nonviolent demonstrators.*

McKinney, Richard I. *Mordecai, The Man and His Message: The Story of Mordecai Wyatt Johnson*. Washington, D.C.: Howard University Press, 1977.

*Johnson, the first black president of Howard University, appointed and supported many scholars and civil rights activists. Scholars from Howard, particularly in the law school, were instrumental in developing strategies for the civil rights movement.*

McNeil, Genna Rae. *Groundwork: Charles Hamilton Houston and the Struggle for Civil Rights*. Philadelphia: University of Pennsylvania Press, 1983.

*McNeil analyzes Houston's role in the evolution of civil rights litigation as dean of Howard University's Law School and as NAACP general counsel. He mentored Thurgood Marshall and others in the intricacies of constitutional law.*

Oates, Stephen B. *Let the Trumpet Sound: The Life of Martin Luther King, Jr*. New York: HarperPerennial, 1994.

*Oates looks at King's private and public life, his ministry, and his rise to leadership in the civil rights movement during the turbulent era of the 1950s and 1960s.*

Rampersad, Arnold. *The Life of Langston Hughes: 1914–1967*. New York: Oxford University Press, 2002.

*In addition to producing many works of literature, Hughes was an active supporter of the NAACP and a variety of other civil rights initiatives.*

Ransby, Barbara. *Ella Baker and the Black Freedom Movement: A Radical Democratic Vision*. Chapel Hill: University of North Carolina Press, 2003.

*Explores Ella Baker's long-term commitment to social change that focused attention on the process of change, and the protracted struggle, which had to involve those who suffered the brunt of oppression, the everyday person.*

Reddick, Lawrence D. *Crusader Without Violence: A Biography of Martin Luther King, Jr*. New York: Harper and Brothers, 1959.

*This early biography of King discusses his childhood, education, family, ideology, and the Montgomery bus boycott. Reddick was an eyewitness of some of the events in Montgomery and occasionally spoke with King during the boycott.*

Rowan, Carl T. *Dream Makers, Dream Breakers: The World of Justice Thurgood Marshall*. New York: Little, Brown and Company, 1993.

*Benefiting from many hours of interviews with Marshall and use of the NAACP Legal Defense Fund records, Rowan provides a biographical account of Marshall's life and work.*

Shepperd, Gladys Byram. *Mary Church Terrell: Respectable Person*. Baltimore, Md.: Human Relations Press, 1959.

*Terrell, a women's rights and civil rights activist, became involved in the 1950s with the "Co-Ordinating Committee for the Enforcement of District of Columbia Anti-Discrimination Laws." This group was successful in desegregating some sites.*

Watson, Denton L. *Lion in the Lobby: Clarence Mitchell, Jr.'s Struggle for the Passage of Civil Rights Laws*. New York: Morrow, 1990.

*Mitchell, as a lobbyist for the NAACP, worked closely for effective civil rights legislation. He played an important role in the passage of the 1964 Civil Rights Act and the 1965 Voting Rights Act.*

Webb, Sheyann, Rachel West Nelson, and Frank Sikora. *Selma, Lord, Selma: Girlhood Memories of the Civil Rights Days*. University: University of Alabama Press, 1980.

*In 1975, Sikora began interviewing Webb and Nelson, who had been elementary school children at the time of the 1965 Selma civil rights campaign led by Martin Luther King Jr. They discuss their recollections.*

Weiss, Nancy J. *Whitney M. Young, Jr. and the Struggle for Civil Rights*. Princeton, N.J.: Princeton University Press, 1989.

*This biography of Young includes information about his leadership of the National Urban League during the height of the civil rights movement.*

Whitfield, Stephen J. A *Death in the Delta: The Story of Emmett Till*. Baltimore, Md.: Johns Hopkins University Press, 1988.

*This volume recounts the circumstances surrounding the 1955 lynching in Mississippi of fourteen-year-old Emmett Till, and the trial, acquittal, and subsequent confession of his murderers and the impetus the murder gave to the movement.*

Williams, Juan. *Thurgood Marshall: American Revolutionary*. New York: Times Books, 1998.

*Williams traces the influences on Marshall's life and career from his formative years through his terms as a Justice of the Supreme Court.*

Yarbrough, Tinsley E. A *Passion for Justice: J. Waties Waring and Civil Rights*. New York: Oxford University Press, 1990.

*As a federal judge, Waring authored decisions and opinions that helped to destroy the legal underpinnings of segregation. Yarbrough examines Waring's judicial activism, the flouting of southern racial customs by him and his wife.*

## Documents

Aptheker, Herbert C. A *Documentary History of the Negro People in the U.S. 1951–1959: From the Korean War to the Emergence of Martin Luther King, Jr.* Vols. 6 and 7. New York: Citadel Press, 1993–94.

*These documents trace the evolution and progress of the civil rights movement.*

Bass, S. Jonathan, *Blessed Are the Peacemakers. Martin Luther King Jr., Eight White Religious Leaders, and the "Letter from Birmingham Jail."* Baton Rouge: Louisiana State University Press, 2001.

*King's "Letter from Birmingham Jail" is a classic statement of the ethos of the civil rights movement. Bass provides historical background and analysis of this letter.*

Carson, Clayborne, ed. *Malcolm X: The FBI File*. New York: Carroll & Graf, 1995.

*Carson provides portions of the 3,600-page file compiled by the FBI on Malcolm X from the time he emerged from prison until his assassination. There is information about the Nation of Islam and Malcolm's speeches.*

Garrow, David J. *The FBI and Martin Luther King, Jr.* New York: Penguin Books, 1983.

*Garrow documents and analyzes the FBI surveillance of King. He demonstrates that the FBI efforts to document King's life were ceaseless.*

Hampton, Henry, Steve Fayer, and Sarah Flynn. *Voices of Freedom: An Oral History of the Civil Rights Movement from the 1950s through the 1980s*. New York: Bantam, 1990.

*This volume includes transcripts from oral accounts about the murder of Emmett Till, the Montgomery bus boycott, Little Rock, sit-ins, freedom rides, James Meredith, the March on Washington, Mississippi Freedom Summer and more.*

Heath, G. Louis, ed. *The Black Panther Leaders Speak: Huey P. Newton, Bobby Seale, Eldridge Cleaver and Company Speak Out Through the Black Panther Party's Official Newspaper.* Metuchen, N.J.: Scarecrow Press, 1976.

*The Black Panther was the name of the Panther Party's newspaper. The paper recorded the politics of the party and was a forum for the leaders' views. This book provides a chronology of the newspaper and publication and subscription data.*

Levy, Peter B., ed. *Documentary History of the Modern Civil Rights Movement.* Westport, Conn.: Greenwood Press, 1992.

*Levy includes statements from various leaders such as A. Philip Randolph, Paul Robeson, Eslanda Robeson, John Hope Franklin, Septima P. Clark, Charles Houston, Rosa Parks, E. D. Nixon, Diane Nash, Ella Baker, and James Foreman.*

McKnight, Gerald D. *The Last Crusade: Martin Luther King Jr., the FBI and the Poor People's Campaign.* Boulder: Westview Press, 1998.

*McKnight focuses on the last period of King's life as he worked with striking sanitation workers in Memphis and struggled to establish a "Poor People's" encampment in Washington, D.C.*

O'Reilly, Kenneth, ed. *Racial Matters: The FBI's Secret File on Black America 1960–1972.* New York: Free Press, 1991.

*This volume provides a selection of files, transcripts of tapped phone conversations of African Americans, and other FBI material, supplemented by interviews with former FBI employees.*

Singletary, Ra'chel. *Martin Luther King on Film and Video: Documentaries in the Library of Congress.* Library of Congress Motion Picture Division, 1995.

*This is a compilation of television documentaries, plays and television broadcasts with or about Martin Luther King Jr. in the collections of the Motion Picture, Broadcasting and Recorded Sound Division of the Library of Congress.*

Sutherland, Elizabeth, ed. *Letters from Mississippi.* New York: McGraw-Hill, 1965.

*During the summer of 1964 about 650 youths, "mostly Northerners and mostly white and mostly students," went to Mississippi to establish freedom schools, voter education projects, and other services. The letters detail their reactions.*

Washington, James M., ed. *A Testament of Hope: The Essential Writings and Speeches of Martin Luther King, Jr.* New York: HarperCollins, 1991.

*King's speeches and writings are divided into nonviolent philosophy, integration, democracy and black nationalism, sermons, public addresses, historic essays, interviews, and books.*

## *Dictionaries and Encyclopedias*

Burke, Joan Martin, ed. *Civil Rights: A Current Guide to the People, Organizations and Events.* New York: Bowker, 1974.

*Burke's useful reference tool includes a guide to acronyms of the names of civil rights organizations, an alphabetical guide to individuals and organizations, and congressional voting records on civil rights acts from 1957 to 1970.*

Lowery, Charles D., and John F. Marszalek. *Encyclopedia of African-American Civil Rights from Emancipation to the Present.* Westport, Conn.: Greenwood Press, 1992.

*Entries on individuals, events, publications, and organizations that pertain to civil rights.*

Luker, Ralph E. *Historical Dictionary of the Civil Rights Movement.* Lanham, Md.: Scarecrow Press, 1977.

*This dictionary provides a chronology for the civil rights movement, brief biographies of participants in the movement, descriptions of major events and civil rights legislation and a thirty-page bibliography.*

Martin, Waldo, and Patricia Sullivan, eds. *Civil Rights in the U.S.* 2 vols. Farmington Hills, Mich.: Gale Publishing Group, 1999.

*An encyclopedia of articles by established scholars on multiple aspects of the civil rights movement.*

Powers, Roger S., and William B. Vogele. *Protest, Power and Change: An Encyclopedia of Nonviolent Action from ACT-UP to Women's Suffrage.* New York: Garland Publishing, 1997.

*This encyclopedia includes case studies of nonviolent social, political, and economic struggles and profiles of nonviolent activists, organizations, and scholars.*

## *Histories*

Birnbaum, Jonathan, and Clarence Taylor. *Civil Rights Since 1787: A Reader on the Black Struggle.* New York: New York University Press, 2000.

*Birnbaum and Taylor take an all-encompassing view of the movement and redefine civil rights to include many critical struggles for social justice.*

Bracey, John H., Jr., August Meier, and Elliot Rudwick, eds. *Conflict and Competition: Studies in the Recent Black Protest Movement.* Belmont, Calif.: Wadsworth, 1971.

*The articles in this work are divided into two sections, "Nonviolent Direct Action," and "By Any Means Necessary." An article by Allen Matusow is entitled "From Civil Rights to Black Power: The Case of SNCC, 1960–66."*

Branch, Taylor. *Parting the Waters: America in the King Years, 1954–63.* New York: Simon and Schuster, 1988.

*This biography of Martin Luther King Jr. covers his early life and education, family, pastorates, leadership of the Montgomery bus boycott, the founding of the Southern Christian Leadership Conference, and his interaction with Herbert Hoover, John F. Kennedy, and Robert F. Kennedy,*

Branch, Taylor. *Pillar of Fire: America in the King Years, 1963–65.* New York: Simon and Schuster, 1998.

*Volume two of Branch's life of King covers King's leadership in the civil rights movement during the Vietnam War and the Lyndon Baines Johnson presidency.*

Brisbane, Robert H. *Black Activism: Racial Revolution in the U.S., 1954–1970.* Valley Forge, Pa.: Judson Press, 1974.

*This book assesses the impact of the 1954 Supreme Court Brown decision, Martin Luther King, Mississippi Freedom Democrats, Malcolm X, black power, riots, black nationalism, black studies, black politics and black literature.*

Broderick, Francis L., and August Meier, eds. *Negro Protest Thought in the Twentieth Century.* New York: Bobbs-Merrill, 1965.

*Most of the writings relate to the period during and after World War II. Includes essays by William Hastie, Ralph J. Bunche, A Philip Randolph, Thurgood Marshall, and Henry Lee.*

Crawford, Vicki L., Jacqueline Anne Rouse, and Barbara Woods, eds. *Women in the Civil Rights Movement: Trailblazers and Torchbearers, 1941–1965.* New York: Carlson Publishing, 1990.

*This volume addresses the roles of women civil rights leaders such as Fannie Lou Hamer, Ella Baker, Septima P. Clark, Rosa Parks, Gloria Richardson, and a host of unnamed women who provided both leadership and support in the movement.*

Fager, Charles E. *Selma, 1965: The March that Changed the South*. 2nd ed. Boston: Beacon Press, 1985.

*In 1965, demonstrators in Selma, Alabama, gathered for a nonviolent march to the state capital at Montgomery to demand voter rights. White policemen, attempting to stop the march, attacked them. Subsequently, Congress passed the Voting Rights Act.*

Forman, James. *The Making of Black Revolutionaries*. New York: Macmillan, 1972.

*Forman, emerging as a leader of the Student Non-Violent Coordinating Committee, discusses various aspects of the civil rights movement in the South and the emergence of the militant black power movement. Forman includes oral testimonies of various eyewitnesses.*

Franklin, John Hope, and Isidore Starr, eds. *The Negro in Twentieth Century America: A Reader on the Struggle for Civil Rights*. New York: Vintage Books, 1967.

*This volume includes a definition of "race" in the United States, including state laws on race. Other sections relate to the "Nature of the Negro Problem," black protests, black leaders, organizations, methods, goals, and white reactions.*

Geschwender, James A., ed. *The Black Revolt: The Civil Rights Movement, Ghetto Uprisings, and Separatism*. Englewood Cliffs, N.J.: Prentice-Hall, 1971.

*Essays in this volume provide background for the civil rights movement, and its organization, leadership, and tactics. Sections on black power and riots deal with characteristics of cities, participants, attitudes toward riots and separatism.*

King, Martin Luther, Jr. *Why We Can't Wait*. New York: Harper & Row, 1964.

*King analyzes the impatience of the black population with the slow pace of change in racial justice since the 1954 Brown decision. He discusses the Birmingham civil rights campaign and suggests strategy for future actions.*

Kotlowski, Dean J. *Nixon's Civil Rights: Politics, Principle, and Policy*. Cambridge, Mass.: Harvard University Press, 2001.

*The author examines Nixon's policies on school desegregation, fair housing, voting rights, affirmative action, and minority businesses. Kotlowski argues that Nixon recast the civil rights debate from integration to economic empowerment.*

Lewis, Anthony, ed. *Portrait of a Decade: The Second American Revolution*. New York: Random House, 1964.

*Lewis wrote several chapters and compiled many articles from The New York Times dating from the Brown decision of 1954 and on various aspects of the civil rights movement through the mid-1960s.*

Lomax, Louis E. *The Negro Revolt*. New York: Signet, 1963.

*Lomax explains the impetus for change within the black community. He discusses the 1950s, the NAACP, the Urban League, sit-ins, freedom rides, white liberals, Black Muslims, and the "crisis in Negro leadership."*

Meier, August, and Elliott Rudwick, eds. *Black Protest in the Sixties*. Chicago: Quadrangle Books, 1970.

*Articles examine the sit-in movement, the Black Muslims, the NAACP, voting rights, the 1963 March on Washington, Martin Luther King Jr., Bayard Rustin, and Roy Wilkins.*

Meier, August, and Elliott Rudwick, eds. *The Making of Black America*, vol. 2, *The Black Community in Modern America*. New York: Atheneum, 1971.

*The three sections in the collection of essays address the black community, the making of the black ghetto, and the new militancy and the enduring ghetto. Essays address gains and losses in the civil rights movement.*

Miller, Keith D. *Voices of Deliverance: The Language of Martin Luther King, Jr. and Its Sources*. New York: Free Press, 1992.

*Recent scholarship has attributed much of King's writing and speaking to sources other than King himself. This author explores King's background, education, and training to discover the roots of his expression and the extent of his originality.*

Morris, Aldon D. *The Origins of the Civil Rights Movement: Black Communities Organizing for Change*. New York: Free Press, 1984.

*The author, a sociologist, wrote that the purpose of his book was to explain how the civil rights movement became a major force in American society from 1953 to 1963.*

Nossiter, Adam. *Of Long Memory: Mississippi and the Murder of Medgar Evers*. New York: Da Capo, 2002.

*Nossiter provides an examination of the transformation of race relations in the South, as seen through the trial of Medgar Evers.*

Raines, Howell. *My Soul Is Rested: The Story of the Civil Rights Movement in the Deep South*. New York: Putnam, 1977.

*Alabama-born Raines was a reporter for several black-owned newspapers but wrote for many others. Interviewees include E. D. Nixon, Rosa Parks, Bayard Rustin, Julian Bond, Lonnie King, John Lewis, and Autherine Lucy Foster.*

Robnett, Belinda. *How Long? How Long? African-American Women in the Struggle for Civil Rights*. New York: Oxford University Press, 1997.

*Robnett provides an analysis of women participants and leaders in seven civil rights organizations. Information from interviews with the women is included.*

Warren, Robert Penn. *Who Speaks for the Negro?* New York: Random House, 1965.

*Warren presents transcripts of interviews with various individuals about race questions, providing information about the individuals interviewed, the settings for the interviews, and some commentary.*

Williams, Juan. *Eyes on the Prize: America's Civil Rights Years, 1954–65*. New York: Viking, 1987.

*This is the companion volume to the PBS series of the same name. It provides a time-line of the civil rights movement, discusses many topics such as school desegregation, the Emmett Till case, and the Montgomery bus boycott.*

## *Local Studies*

Broussard, Albert S. *Black San Francisco: The Struggle for Racial Equality, 1900–1954*. Lawrence: University of Kansas Press, 1993.

*Examines race relations in San Francisco at the beginning of the twentieth century and the black freedom struggle to the Brown v. Board of Education decision.*

Burns, Stewart. *Daybreak of Freedom: The Montgomery Bus Boycott*. Chapel Hill: University of North Carolina Press, 1997.

*A documentary history of the landmark boycott of 1955–56, with an interpretive introduction and notes for each group of documents.*

Chafe, William H. *Civilities and Civil Rights: Greensboro North Carolina and the Black Struggle for Freedom*. New York: Oxford University Press, 1980.

*Chafe studies the changing nature of black protest from 1940s to the 1960s in a community whose white residents prided themselves on being progressive in matters of race and where real change required breaking through a heavy veneer.*

Dittmer, John. *Local People: the Struggle for Civil Rights in Mississippi*. Urbana: University of Illinois Press, 1994.

*Dittmer locates the roots of the Mississippi freedom struggle in the return of World War II veterans determined to exercise their rights of citizenship. He analyzes the multiple forces, local and national, which shaped that struggle.*

Eick, Gretchen Cassel. *Dissent in Wichita: The Civil Rights Movement in the Midwest, 1954–72*. Urbana: University of Illinois Press, 2001.

*Black students in Kansas organized the first successful sit-ins of the 1950s, two years before the famous sit-ins in Greensboro, North Carolina. And Kansas was a site for other challenges to racial inequality.*

Eskew, Glenn T. *But for Birmingham: the Local and National Movements in the Civil Rights Struggle*. Chapel Hill: University of North Carolina Press, 1997.

*Eskew presents a complex account of events leading to the 1963 civil rights demonstrations in Birmingham, Alabama.*

Fairclough, Adam. *Race and Democracy: the Civil Rights Struggle in Louisiana, 1915–1972*. Athens: University of Georgia Press, 1999.

*Fairclough, a British historian, provides a detailed study of civil rights organizing in one state. The Louisiana movement included a bus boycott in Baton Rouge in 1953 that served as a reference point for the Montgomery boycott leaders.*

Garrow, David J. *Protest at Selma: Martin Luther King Jr. and the Voting Rights Act of 1965*. New Haven, Conn.: Yale University Press, 1978.

*Garrow provides a detailed history of the planned march from Selma to Montgomery to demand voting rights for blacks, the violent reaction by Alabama police, and the subsequent passage of the Voting Rights Act.*

King, Martin Luther, Jr. *Stride Toward Freedom: The Montgomery Story*. New York: Harper & Brothers, 1958.

*King was twenty-nine when he wrote about the Montgomery bus boycott of 1955–56. He provides biographical materials about his early life and explains how he became involved with the boycott.*

McAdam, Doug. *Freedom Summer*. New York: Oxford University Press, 1988.

*This work focuses on the white volunteers who joined the Student Non-Violent Coordinating Committee and Congress of Racial Equality veterans in Mississippi in the summer of 1964 to augment voter registration efforts and staff "freedom schools" and community centers for local blacks.*

Norrell, Robert J., and Arieh J. Kochavi. *Reaping the Whirlwind: The Civil Rights Movement in Tuskegee*. Chapel Hill: University of North Carolina Press, 1998.

*The landmark Supreme Court decision of 1960, Gomillion v. Lightfoot, which prohibited racial gerrymandering, was a major achievement of the Tuskegee movement.*

Payne, Charles. *I've Got the Light of Freedom: The Organizing Tradition and the Mississippi Freedom Struggle*. Berkeley: University of California Press, 1995.

*This book documents the way in which protestors organized their efforts to fight discrimination and segregation.*

Ralph, James. *Northern Protest: Martin Luther King, Jr., Chicago, and the Civil Rights Movement*. Cambridge, Mass.: Harvard University Press, 1993.

*Ralph describes and analyzes King's attempt to apply the tactics of the southern movement to a northern urban setting.*

Rogers, Kim Lacy. *Righteous Lives: Narratives of the New Orleans Civil Rights Movement*. New York: New York University Press, 1993.

*Rogers's work centers on oral histories of twenty-five black and white civil rights leaders in New Orleans, representing three generations of the civil rights movement in that city.*

Youth of the Rural Organizing and Cultural Center. *Minds Stayed on Freedom*. Boulder: Westview Press, 1991.

*This volume preserves the voices of black Mississippians who struggled for justice. Their words are recorded by young black students from the same community.*

## *Labor*

Arnesen, Eric. *Brotherhoods of Color: Black Railroad Workers and the Struggle for Equality.* Cambridge, Mass.: Harvard University Press, 2002.

*Arnesen documents the successful struggle of black railroad men to achieve worker's rights, a movement parallel to the civil rights movement.*

Brazeal, Brailsford R. *The Brotherhood of Sleeping Car Porters: Its Origin and Development.* New York: Harper, 1946.

*The conclusion of this work reports the culmination of the equal employment opportunity struggle of the Brotherhood of Sleeping Car Porters under the leadership of A. Philip Randolph during the World War II period.*

Harris, William H. *The Harder We Run: Black Workers Since the Civil War.* New York: Oxford University Press, 1982.

*Analyzes the relationship of black workers to organized labor and their uphill struggle for equal employment opportunity.*

Honey, Michael Keith. *Black Workers Remember: An Oral History of Segregation, Unionism, and the Freedom Struggle.* Berkeley: University of California Press, 1999.

*Interviewees document their struggle for equal rights in labor unions.*

Honey, Michael Keith. *Southern Labor and Black Civil Rights: Organizing Memphis Workers.* Urbana: University of Illinois Press, 1993.

*The author finds that the civil rights movement of the 1960s originated in part in the interracial industrial union organizing in the South in the 1930s and 1940s.*

Nelson, Bruce. *Divided We Stand: American Workers and the Struggle for Black Equality.* Princeton, N.J.: Princeton University Press, 2002.

*Nelson offers a revisionist interpretation of the American labor movement in the nineteenth and twentieth centuries that emphasizes how organized labor repeatedly undermined the struggle of black workers for freedom and equality.*

Pfeffer, Paula F. *A. Philip Randolph, Pioneer of the Civil Rights Movement.* Baton Rouge: Louisiana State University Press, 1990.

*Pfeffer looks at labor leader Randolph as a tactician who advocated the nonviolent direct action tactics that characterized black protest in the 1950s and 1960s.*

Santino, Jack. *Miles of Smiles, Years of Struggle: Stories of Black Pullman Porters.* Urbana: University of Illinois Press, 1989.

*Santino's interviews with railroad porters provide a history of their labor struggles from 1920 to 1960. Chapters cover the historic setting, unionization, A. Philip Randolph's role and leadership, and popular images and stereotypes of porters.*

Tucker, Susan, ed. *Telling Memories Among Southern Women: Domestic Workers and their Employers in the Segregated South.* New York: Schocken Books, 1988.

*This collection of oral histories relates the stories of white employers and their African American domestic workers from the turn of the twentieth century through the 1960s.*

## *Music*

Carawan, Guy, and Candie Carawan, eds. *Sing for Freedom: the Story of the Civil Rights Movement Through Its Songs.* Bethlehem, Pa.: Sing Out! Publications, 1997.

*This volume includes 115 annotated songs with music and 135 photos from the civil rights movement.*

Guralnick, Peter B. *Sweet Soul Music: Rhythm and Blues and the Southern Dream of Freedom.* New York: Little Brown, 1998.

*Guralnick provides a history of black soul music in the 1950s and 1960s and its relationship to the black community and to the world of white music in the civil rights era.*

Keil, Charles. *Urban Blues*. Chicago: University of Chicago Press, 1966.

*Keil provides the background for the evolution of blues and closely examines a number of artists, including Bobby Blue Bland and B. B. King. The author analyzes the musicians and their music to provide a cultural backdrop for U.S. racial unrest.*

Reagon, Bernice Johnson. *If You Don't Go, Don't Hinder Me: The African American Sacred Song Tradition*. Lincoln: University of Nebraska Press, 2001.

*Four essays that trace the evolution of black sacred music through the great migration of blacks to the North during the war years and the civil rights struggles of the succeeding decades.*

Reagon, Bernice Johnson, ed. *We'll Understand It Better By and By: Pioneering African American Gospel Composers*. Washington, D.C.: Smithsonian Institution Press, 1992.

*The essays provide biographical sketches of black gospel writers. The volume also includes an annotated bibliography of African American gospel music.*

Sanger, Kerran L. *When the Spirit Says Sing!: The Role of Freedom Songs in the Civil Rights Movement*. New York: Garland Publications, 1995.

*Sanger analyzes the lyrics of freedom songs to give insight into civil rights activists' experiences in the movement.*

Seeger, Pete, and Bob Reiser. *Everybody Says Freedom*. New York: Norton, 1989.

*The authors focus on highpoints of the civil rights movement, using songs, photos, and quotations from movement participants to provide an upbeat narrative of the struggles of the 1950s and 1960s.*

Ward, Brian. *Just My Soul Responding: Rhythm and Blues, Black Consciousness, and Race Relations*. Berkeley: University of California Press, 1998.

*Ward examines African American popular culture in the context of the civil rights and black power movements and, as Julian Bond's comment on the cover suggests, describes "how movement and music shaped each other."*

## *Organizations*

Bell, Inge Powell. *CORE and the Strategy of Nonviolence*. New York: Random House, 1968.

*The Congress of Racial Equality attempted direct action initiatives before the 1950s but did not receive popular support. By the 1960s CORE's strategies became increasingly popular first among blacks but then among protesters of various races.*

Carson, Clayborne. *In Struggle: SNCC and the Black Awakening of the 1960s*. Cambridge, Mass.: Harvard University Press, 1995.

*This volume discusses sit-ins, Student Non-Violent Coordinating Committee ideology and leadership, freedom rides, the March on Washington, racial separatism, black power, voter registration, and education.*

Fairclough, Adam. *To Redeem the Soul of America: The Southern Christian Leadership Conference and Martin Luther King, Jr.* Athens: University of Georgia Press, 1987.

*A comprehensive study of the Southern Christian Leadership Conference's origins and development by a British historian.*

Finch, Minnie. *The NAACP: Its Fight For Justice*. Metuchen, N.J.: Scarecrow, 1981.

*Finch provides a general survey of the history of the NAACP.*

Glen, John M. *Highlander: No Ordinary School*. Knoxville: University of Tennessee Press, 1996.

*Glen recounts the history of the school, founded in Monteagle, Tennessee, in the 1930s. In the 1950s and 1960s, its workshops inspired numerous activists such as Rosa Parks, Septima Clark, and some Student Non-Violent Coordinating Committee leaders.*

Greenberg, Cheryl Lynn, ed. A *Circle of Trust: Remembering SNCC*. New Brunswick, N.J.: Rutgers University Press, 1998.

*This work is an edited transcript of a Student Non-Violent Coordinating Committee twenty-fifth year reunion, held at Trinity College in Connecticut in 1995. Participants included a range of personalities, from the best known and legendary to virtually unknown.*

Hughes, Langston. *Fight for Freedom: The Story of the NAACP*. New York: Norton, 1962.

*Chapters 3–6 explain NAACP efforts to protect African American soldiers during World War II, the battle against segregation, education cases, and the legal aspects of the nonviolent protest movement of the early 1960s.*

Jack, Robert L. *History of the National Association for the Advancement of Colored People*. Boston: Meador Press, 1943.

*Jack provides the history of the organization of the NAACP, its growth and the development of branches, types of publicity, the antilynching crusade, and the fight against segregation and discrimination in education and the political arena.*

Joint Center for Political Studies. *Black Elected Officials: A National Roster*. 10 vols. New York. Unipub, 1984–94.

*The volumes provide names of black elected officials arranged by state. There is also statistical information such as the black population of the state and the black electorate, female black elected officials, and black municipal officers.*

Kellogg, Charles Flint. *NAACP: A History of the National Association for the Advancement of Colored People*. Baltimore, Md.: Johns Hopkins University Press, 1967.

*Kellogg provides a history of the founding, the leaders, organizational development, and strategies for racial justice.*

McMillen, Neil R. *The Citizens' Council: Organized Resistance to the Second Reconstruction 1954–64*. Urbana: University of Illinois Press, 1971.

*McMillen details the founding and operations of the Citizens' Councils of America, a key factor in the rise of white resistance to the Brown V. Board of Education decision. Updated in 1994.*

Meier, August, and Elliott Rudwick. *CORE: A Study of the Civil Rights Movement, 1942–1968*. New York: Oxford University Press, 1973.

*This is a study of the development of the Congress of Racial Equality. It utilizes archival materials, manuscript collections, newspaper articles and over two hundred oral interviews. The authors explain tactics, strategies, ideologies, and organizational structure.*

Moore, Jesse T. A *Search for Equality: the National Urban League, 1910–1961*. University Park: Pennsylvania State University Press, 1989.

*Distinguishes the specific work of the National Urban League in addressing urban conditions of African Americans.*

National Urban League. *Black Americans and Public Policy: Perspectives of the National Urban League*. New York: The League, 1988.

*This work chronicles the League's role in influencing public laws and programs in housing, employment, and other areas to provide equal opportunities for African Americans.*

Parris, Guichard, and Lester Brooks, *Blacks in the City: A History of the National Urban League*. Boston: Little, Brown, 1971.

*This 534-page volume provides the history of the founding and development of the National Urban League and the efforts of this group to provide equal opportunities in employment, housing, and social services for blacks.*

Sellers, Cleveland with Robert Terrell. *The River of No Return: The Autobiography of a Black Militant and the Life and Death of SNCC*. New York: William Morrow, 1973.

*Sellers was raised in a South Carolina town where racial segregation ruled. Sellers describes his joy when blacks began to protest their treatment, and relates his participation in the student movement, and his work with the Student Non-Violent Coordinating Committee.*

Zangrando, Robert L. *The NAACP Crusade Against Lynching, 1909–1959*. Philadelphia: Temple University Press, 1980.

*The author addresses lynching in the World War II and postwar years and the efforts of the NAACP to ensure that the U.S. judicial system provided equal protection under the law to all citizens regardless of color.*

Zinn, Howard. *SNCC: The New Abolitionists*. Boston: Beacon Press, 1964.

*Zinn compiled this history of the Student Non-Violent Coordinating Committee from personal observation, interviews, and SNCC Atlanta office files. He addresses the sit-ins and freedom rides and white activists as well as civil rights campaigns in Mississippi, Georgia, and Alabama.*

## School Desegregation

Bell, Derrick A. *Silent Covenants: Brown v. Board of Education and the Unfulfilled Hopes for Racial Reform*. New York: Oxford University Press, 2004.

*Bell examines school desegregation and focuses more attention on effective schools than integrated ones.*

Cashin, Sheryll. *The Failures of Integration: How Race and Class Are Undermining the American Dream*. New York: Public Affairs, 2004.

*Against the backdrop of the Brown v. Board of Education decision, Cashin analyzes the current state of race relations and argues that the United States has to renew an integrationist vision to resolve racial inequality.*

Cecelski, David S. *Along Freedom Road: Hyde County, North Carolina and the Fate of Black Schools in the South*. Chapel Hill: University of North Carolina Press, 1994.

*An account of a yearlong boycott of schools by blacks in Hyde County, N.C., who resisted a desegregation plan that would have closed two black schools.*

Kluger, Richard. *Simple Justice*. New York: Vintage Books, 2004.

*Kluger provides a detailed study of the litigation strategy that led to the 1954 Supreme Court case Brown v. Board of Education. He explains the state of race relations and provides detailed information about the people who were involved. This edition includes a new chapter to mark the fiftieth anniversary of Brown.*

Ogletree, Charles J., Jr. *All Deliberate Speed: Reflections on the First Half Century of Brown v. Board of Education*. New York: Norton, 2004.

*Ogletree considers the legacy of segregation and the struggle against it as a context for the challenges by Martin Luther King Jr. and Thurgood Marshall. He examines the measure of progress toward racial equality fifty years after the Brown decision.*

Orfield, Gary, and Susan E. Eaton. *Dismantling Desegregation: the Quiet Reversal of Brown v. Board of Education*. New York: New Press, 1997.

*Case studies of "resegregation" in ten school districts throughout the United States.*

Patterson, James T., and William W. Freehling. *Brown v. Board of Education: A Civil Rights Milestone and Its Troubled Legacy*. New York: Oxford University Press, 2000.

*The authors review the results of school desegregation since 1954, reassess the decision's legacy, and place continuing debates over mandated busing, affirmative action and other types of "social engineering" in a historical context.*

Tushnet, Mark V. *Making Civil Rights Law: Thurgood Marshall and the Supreme Court, 1936–1961*. New York: Oxford University Press, 1996.

*Tushnet, a former law clerk of Thurgood Marshall, focuses on Marshall's central role in the Brown v. Board of Education decision and the cases that led to it.*

Walker, Vanessa Siddle. *Their Highest Potential: An African American School Community in the Segregated South*. Chapel Hill: University of North Carolina Press, 1996.

*Walker studies a community that did not welcome desegregation brought about in 1969 by the NAACP and the federal government but thrived in spite of the changes that integration brought.*

## *Sports*

Ashe, Arthur R., Jr., Kip Branch, Ocania Chalk, and Francis Harris. *A Hard Road to Glory: A History of the African-American Athlete*. 3 vols. New York: Amistad Press, 1988–93.

*Volume 2 covers 1919 to 1945 and volume 3 the period since 1946. The chapters deal with baseball, basketball, boxing, football, golf, tennis, track, and the Olympics. The set includes statistics, records, and lists of players.*

Astor, Gerald. *". . . And A Credit to His Race": The Hard Life and Times of Joseph Louis Barrow, a.k.a. Joe Louis*. New York: Dutton, 1974.

*Astor discusses the experiences—especially the racial conflicts—of Joe Louis during his professional boxing career. He also addresses Louis's observations about the civil rights movement especially in the area of blacks in sports.*

Chalk, Ocania. *Black College Sport*. New York: Dodd, Mead, 1976.

*Chalk discusses black stars on white college teams as well as those at black colleges. He covers men in baseball, basketball, football, track and field, and black Olympians.*

Chalk, Ocania. *Pioneers of Black Sport*. New York: Dodd, Mead, 1975.

*Chalk's work is a historical treatment of black athletes in baseball, basketball, boxing, and football. His book relates not only the growing role of blacks in professional sports but also the evolution of the mass audience.*

Falkner, David. *Great Time Coming: The Life of Jackie Robinson from Baseball to Birmingham*. New York: Simon & Schuster, 1995.

*Robinson not only excelled in many sports but also was an outspoken civil rights advocate.*

Frommer, Harvey. *Ricky and Robinson: The Men Who Broke Baseball's Color Barrier*. New York: Macmillan, 1992.

*The first black players in the major leagues faced both prejudice and adoration. This volume discusses the struggles of both blacks and whites who pioneered in integrating U.S. sports.*

Gibson, Althea. *I Always Wanted to Be Somebody*. New York: Harper, 1958.

*Gibson, an African American tennis player, made a name for herself by winning the major women's amateur tennis championships and then retired from tennis to pursue professional golf.*

Henderson, Edwin B., and the Editors of *Sport* Magazine. *The Black Athlete: Emergence and Arrival*. New York: Publishers Company, Inc., 1970.

*This volume provides historical background about blacks in sports, then addresses the breakthrough in baseball by Jackie Robinson, and examines "Negro Domination" in basketball, boxing, football, tennis, track, and golf.*

Holway, John. *Voices from the Great Black Baseball Leagues*. New York: Da Capo, 1992.

*This oral history includes interviews with former players in the Negro Leagues as well as their friends and relatives.*

Page, James A. *Black Olympian Medalists*. Englewood, Colo.: Libraries Unlimited, 1991.

*In addition to biographical sketches, the author provides bibliographic information for each entry and provides statistics indicating the Olympic year, the place, event, and the athlete's name and type of medal.*

Rampersad, Arnold. *Jackie Robinson: A Biography*. New York: Random House, 1997.

*Rampersad provides an authoritative biography of Robinson. The author relates information about Robinson's early life, his military service, the Negro Baseball Leagues, the Brooklyn Dodgers, and his postathletic career.*

Russell, Bill, and Taylor Branch. *Second Wind: The Memoirs of an Opinionated Man*. New York: Random House, 1979.

*Russell discusses his own career with the Boston Celtics and the plight of blacks in professional basketball.*

Sammons, Jeffrey T. *Beyond the Ring: The Role of Boxing in American Society*. Chicago: University of Illinois Press, 1988.

*Chapters 5–7 discuss boxers from Joe Louis to Muhammad Ali. The author discusses the relationship between boxing and the law, organized crime, race, and public opinion.*

Tygiel, Jules. *Baseball's Great Experiment: Jackie Robinson and His Legacy*. New York: Oxford University Press, 1983.

*This work explores the life of Jackie Robinson in the context of the racially polarized society of the United States.*

Tygiel, Jules, ed. *The Jackie Robinson Reader: Perspectives on an American Hero*. New York: Dutton, 1997.

*Tygiel explores the outstanding events and issues of Robinson's life through a broad variety of authors.*

Wiggins, David K. *Glory Bound: Black Athletes in a White America*. Syracuse, N.Y.: Syracuse University Press, 1997.

*Part II of this volume covers civil rights and the quest for equality in sports and all of American life. Part III covers race relations and the ideology of sports.*

## *Film, Video, and Audio*

*A. Philip Randolph: For Jobs and Freedom*. WETA. 1996.

*This is a 90-minute film biography of Randolph, a labor activist and civil rights pioneer. It uses archival photos and films of Randolph from the 1960s and interviews with contemporaries in the labor and civil rights movements*

*The American Experience: Adam Clayton Powell*. Channel Four Television, Cine Information, and WETA. 1989.

*The film profiles Powell's life as a pastor and a U.S. Congressman. He served long enough to lead powerful congressional committees. He fought for civil rights for all Americans and for programs to alleviate poverty.*

*The American Experience: Freedom on my Mind*. WGBH. 1996.

*The film focuses on Mississippi in the 1960s and the lives of black residents of that region as they unite with the Student Non-Violent Coordinating Committee to establish the Council of Federated Organizations and the Mississippi Freedom Democratic Party.*

*The American Experience: The Kennedys*. WGBH Educational Foundation. 1992.

*The film includes discussion of the Kennedys' civil rights activism.*

*The American Experience: Malcolm X—Make It Plain*. Blackslide, Inc., and Roja Productions. 1994.

*This biographical film, narrated by Alfre Woodard, includes interviews with Alex Haley, Ossie Davis, Maya Angelou, and Malcolm's family. The film documents Malcolm's life from prison to the Nation of Islam and from Mecca to his assassination.*

*The American Experience: Simple Justice*. New Images Productions. 1993.

*This film shows the legal struggle that led to the historic Brown v. Board of Education Supreme Court ruling in 1954. The film focuses on the NAACP, and the leadership of Charles Hamilton Houston and his protégé, Thurgood Marshall.*

*Black Panthers: Huey Newton and Black Panther Newsreel*. International Historic Films. 1968.

*The video provides self-portraits of the Panthers. Speakers include Huey Newton, James Forman, Eldridge Cleaver, Bob Avakian, Ron Dellums, Bobby Seale, H. Rap Brown, Stokely Carmichael, and Eldridge Cleaver.*

*The Black Theatre Movement—A Raisin in the Sun to the Present*. Woodie King Jr. 1978.

*The civil rights movement went forward on many fronts. This film documents the advances of blacks in the theater world.*

*The Black Press: Soldiers Without Swords*. A Half Nelson Production. 1999.

*This documentary shows the central role of the black press in the civil rights struggle.*

*Eyes on the Prize—America's Civil Rights Years, 1954–1965*. Blackside, Inc. 1989.

*This five-episode series chronicles the struggle by black and white Americans to gain full citizenship for African Americans. Two of the series titles are, "Ain't Scared of Your Jails" and "Mississippi—Is This America?"*

*First Person Singular: John Hope Franklin*. Dick Young Productions. 1997.

*Charles Kuralt narrates this one-hour documentary on Franklin's remarkable life and work. Franklin talks about the discrimination he faced as an African American scholar and details his role as a strategist with the NAACP Legal Defense Fund.*

*Freedom Never Dies: The Legacy of Harry T. Moore*. The Documentary Institute. 2000.

*The Mims, Florida, home of civil rights activist Harry T. Moore was bombed on Christmas Day, 1951. Moore, a schoolteacher who led a crusade against the white supremacists, died on his way to the hospital. His wife, Harriett, died nine days later.*

*Frontline: Racism 101*. PBS. 1988.

*This program explores the increase in racial incidents and violence on America's college campuses. The attitudes of black and white students reveal increasing tensions at various campuses, many of which are still not fully integrated.*

*Fundi: The Story of Ella Baker*. First Run Icarus Films. 1986.

*Baker, an organizer for the NAACP since the 1930s, mentored the generation that created the Student Non-Violent Coordinating Committee, advised and worked with King and the Southern Christian Leadership Conference. Baker, Bob Moses, Marion Barry, and others appear.*

*In Remembrance of Martin*. Idanha Films. 1987.

*Coretta Scott King is joined by public figures celebrating the life and work of Martin Luther King Jr. Interviewees include Ralph Abernathy, Jimmy Carter, Jesse Jackson, John Lewis, Andrew Young, Jesse Jackson, and Julian Bond.*

*Jazz*. PBS. 2001.

*Episodes 8 through 10 cover the period from 1940 through 2001. Ken Burns uses jazz as a vehicle for explaining the evolution of the music as well as the American cultural scene, especially in the light of the civil right struggle.*

*Like it Is: Angela Davis*. American Documentary Films. 1971.

*Davis, a black militant and self-avowed Communist, speaks from prison in December 1970 shortly after her arrest on charges of conspiracy to commit murder. Members of her defense committee also appear.*

*Like It Is: Converging Thoughts of Malcolm X and Martin Luther King, Jr*. ABC. 1990.

*Gil Noble hosts this program about nonviolent and violent freedom strategies in the African American community.*

*Like It Is: Paul Robeson—The Tallest Tree in Our Forest*. ABC. 1976.

*Robeson, an African American singer, actor, lawyer, scholar, and athlete, pioneered in many areas and was among the vanguard in the struggle for civil rights.*

*Living History: Women from Civil Rights to Black Power*. The Stanford Channel, Stanford University. 2001.

*The panel: Victoria Gray Adams, congressional candidate for the Mississippi Freedom Democratic Party; Constance Curry, a white participant in the Student Non-Violent Coordinating Committee; Ericka Huggins, a member of Black Panther Party; and Dorothy Cotton of Southern Christian Leadership Conference.*

*Mandela Through the Eyes of Harlem*. Light Action Production, 1990.

*South African freedom leader Nelson Mandela's visit to Harlem to speak on behalf of the African National Congress and the Mass Democratic Movement against apartheid in South Africa. His wife, Winnie, also speaks about Africa.*

*Marian Anderson*. WETA. 1991.

*Anderson, a contralto, became a symbol of the civil rights movement when the Daughters of the American Revolution refused to allow her to appear in Constitution Hall in 1939. Officials of the Roosevelt administration allowed her to perform at the Lincoln Memorial.*

*Mississippi, America*. WSIU / PBS. 1996.

*Ossie Davis and Ruby Dee narrate this documentary about the participation of whites and blacks in "Freedom Summer of 1964." Civil rights groups and interested individuals went to Mississippi to assist blacks in their fight for the right to vote.*

*Nashville: "We Were Warriors."* WETA. 2000.

*This film reviews the training and preparation of students in 1959 and 1960 for desegregating downtown Nashville, Tennessee. James Lawson, a Methodist minister who had studied Gandhian methods in India, guided the students.*

*Oh Freedom Over Me*. Minnesota Public Radio. 2001.

*The audiotape recounts Mississippi Freedom Summer of 1964, based on interviews with participants—local activists, leaders from the Student Non-Violent Coordinating Committee and the Congress of Racial Equality, and white volunteers from the north.*

*Rosa Parks: The Path to Freedom*. Kingberry Productions / WDIV-TV. 1996.

*This 20-minute videocassette is a review of Parks's central role in the 1955–1956 Montgomery bus boycott.*

*The Songs Are Free: Bernice Johnson Reagon*. PBS. 1991.

*This 58-minute film is part of Bill Moyers's biography series. It profiles Reagon, who presents an historical discussion of African American sacred music. She discusses the origins of civil rights "freedom songs" in the sacred music tradition.*

*We Are Universal*. Nommo Productions. 1971.

*Various black leaders discuss discrimination against blacks in the arts—jazz, poetry, art—and in society. Jesse Jackson, Quincy Jones, Nikki Giovanni, Freddie Hubbard, and others appear.*

W. E. B. *Du Bois: A Biography in Four Voices*. Scribe Video Center. 1996.

*A documentary biography of Du Bois, a scholar and political activist who became an international leader of the struggle against oppression and colonialism. Toni Bambara, Imamu Baraka, Thulani Davis, and Wesley Brown wrote and narrated.*

*Will the Circle Be Unbroken? An Audio History of the Civil Rights Movement in Five Southern Communities and the Music of Those Times*. Southern Regional Council. 1997.

*Clarendon County, South Carolina; Montgomery, Alabama; Jackson, Mississippi; Atlanta, Georgia; and Little Rock, Arkansas are the five communities in question. In the words of narrator Verda May Grovner, the racial history of these communities is told "through the words of the men and women who watched and made, and sometimes tried to stop, one of the most powerful movements in America."*

*You Don't Have to Ride Jim Crow*. New Hampshire Public Television. 1996.

*In 1947, the Congress of Racial Equality sent sixteen black and white men on a bus trip through the upper South to test new federal law prohibiting segregation in interstate transportation. Nearly fifty years later, the seven surviving participants in that "Journey of Reconciliation" reunited to travel the same route again. The 60-minute video also includes footage of the original trip, which was the prototype for the more famous 1960 Freedom Rides. A. Leon Higginbotham narrates.*

## *Manuscripts*

Alpha Kappa Alpha Papers, Moorland Spingarn Research Center, Howard University, Washington, D.C.

*This black women's sorority helped insure that black women had equal opportunity both in military and civilian life.*

Alpha Phi Alpha Papers, Moorland Spingarn Research Center, Howard University, Washington, D.C.

*The first black fraternity organized in 1906 at Cornell University and dedicated to social service and the advancement of humanity.*

Bethune, Mary McLeod. Papers. Bethune Foundation, Bethune-Cookman College, Daytona Beach, Fla.; Amistad Research Center, New Orleans, La.; National Association of Colored Women's Clubs, Washington, D.C.; Bethune Museum and Archives, Washington, D.C.; Fisk University, Nashville, Tenn.; Roosevelt Presidential Library, Hyde Park, N.Y.

*Bethune was an educator and a leader in the civil rights and women rights movements. She worked with the National Council of Negro Women, NAACP, National Urban League, and the Association for the Study of Negro (later Afro-American) Life and History.*

Brooke, Edward William. Papers. Manuscript Division, Library of Congress. Washington, D.C.

*Brooke, a lawyer and public official, served as the attorney general of Massachusetts, and as a U.S. senator from that state. His papers cover civil rights issues, affirmative action measures, and the Watergate cover-up.*

Brotherhood of Sleeping Car Porters. Records. Manuscript Division, Library of Congress, Washington, D.C.

*This union was founded by labor leader A. Philip Randolph in 1925. The records document the growth and functions of the union and reflect its various activities in the areas of civil rights and equal employment opportunity.*

Bunche, Ralph. Papers. Special Collections, Research Libraries, University of California at Los Angeles.

*Bunche, who was both a scholar and a diplomat, was a human rights activist. A Nobel Prize winner for his mediation of the 1948 Palestinian dispute, Bunche became United Nations Undersecretary for Special Political Affairs.*

Burroughs, Nannie Helen. Papers. Manuscript Division, Library of Congress, Washington, D.C.

*Burroughs was an educator and a civil rights and women's rights advocate. Most of her papers consist of materials relating to her establishment and operation of a trade school for young black girls in Washington, D.C., in 1909.*

Center for National Policy Review. Records, Manuscript Division, Library of Congress, Washington, D.C.

*The Center for National Policy Review (CNPR) was a nonpartisan civil rights advocacy group established in 1970 at Catholic University in Washington, D.C. Its staff monitored the efforts of government agencies to enforce the antidiscrimination laws of the 1960s.*

Christopher, Warren Minor. Papers. Lyndon B. Johnson Presidential Library, Austin, Texas.

*As deputy attorney general under Johnson, Christopher generated office files concerning riots, civil rights demonstrations, and task forces on civil disorders and crime.*

Civil Rights Congress. *Papers of the Civil Rights Congress, 1946–1956*. Schomburg Center for Research in Black Culture. Microfilm, 125 reels.

*The Civil Rights Congress issued the "We Charge Genocide" petition to the United Nations in 1951. It fought for the civil liberties of African Americans, labor leaders, and communist party members.*

*Civil Rights During the Johnson Administration, 1963–1969*. Microfilm, 69 reels. Lyndon Baines Johnson Presidential Library, Austin, Texas.

*Johnson was in office during the height of the civil rights movement and signed the Civil Rights Act of 1964 and the Voting Rights act of 1965. He also nominated Thurgood Marshall to the Supreme Court.*

*Civil Rights During the Kennedy Administration, 1960 to 1963*. John F. Kennedy Presidential Library, Boston, Massachusetts

*Kennedy and his brother, attorney general Robert Kennedy, were in regular contact with civil rights leaders, especially Martin Luther King Jr.*

*Civil Rights During the Nixon Administration, 1969–1974*. Microfilm, 46 reels. National Archives and Records Administration, Washington, D.C.

*The Nixon administration was tasked with enforcing much of the civil rights legislation that was passed during the Johnson administration.*

Clark, Kenneth Bancroft. Papers. Manuscript Division, Library of Congress, Washington, D.C.

*Clark is a social psychologist whose concern with the psychology of racism brought him into national prominence in the post–World War II era. His findings were cited in the 1954 Supreme Court decision Brown v. Board of Education.*

Congress of Racial Equality. Records. State Historical Society of Wisconsin in Madison, and the Martin Luther King, Jr. Center for Nonviolent Social Change in Atlanta, Georgia.

*Congress of Racial Equality activities included freedom rides, voter registration projects, sit-ins, and sponsorship of political groups like the Mississippi Freedom Democratic Party. James Farmer became the national director in 1961 and Floyd McKissick in 1966.*

Davis, Angela, *Case Collection*. Microfilm, 23 reels. Meiklejon Civil Liberties Institute, Berkeley, Calif.

*Davis, a militant black power advocate, was tried for conspiracy in a Marin County, California, courthouse shootout. She was on FBI's most wanted list for several months in 1970. She was acquitted.*

Delta Sigma Theta Sorority Papers, Moorland Spingarn Research Center, Howard University, Washington, D.C.

*Members of this black women's sorority often acted as lobbyists in matters relating to the African American community.*

*Detroit Urban League*, 1916–1950. Microfilm, 35 reels. University of Michigan Library, Ann Arbor.

*The records chronicle the role of the Urban League in the national and local Detroit civil rights and equal rights struggle.*

DuBois, William Edward Burghardt. Papers. University of Massachusetts at Amherst.

*The DuBois papers reflect his academic and political endeavors to achieve equal treatment for blacks in the United States, Africa, and other parts of the world. He was an early participant in the work of the NAACP and the editor of its organ, The Crisis.*

Hamer, Fannie Lou. Papers. Amistad Research Center. Tulane University, New Orleans.

*Hamer, who worked for many years as a sharecropper, became an outspoken leader in the southern civil rights movement. Her papers document her work with organizations such as the Mississippi Freedom Democratic Party.*

Harris, Patricia Roberts. Papers. Manuscript Division, Library of Congress.

*Harris was a lawyer, civil rights advocate, public official, and ambassador. She was the first African American woman to serve in a presidential cabinet. These papers relate principally to her cabinet service in the Carter administration.*

Houston, Charles Hamilton. Papers. Moorland Spingarn Research Center, Howard University, Washington, D.C.

*Houston, a Harvard-trained lawyer, served as dean of Howard's law school and as general counsel of the NAACP. Houston trained many of the lawyers who would become active in the civil rights movement, including Thurgood Marshall.*

Houston, William LePre. Papers. Manuscript Division, Library of Congress, Washington, D.C.

*William LePre Houston was a lawyer. His son, Charles Hamilton Houston, served as general counsel of the NAACP. The papers show the firm's work in behalf of black labor and civic organizations and the Houstons' active role in politics and civil rights.*

Hughes, Langston. *Langston Hughes Collection*. Schomburg Center for Research in Black Culture, Lincoln University, and Yale University.

*Hughes, a poet, essayist, and humorist, fought for civil rights along with artistic freedom.*

Johnson, Frank M. Papers. Manuscript Division, Library of Congress, Washington, D.C.

*Johnson was the white federal judge whose vote ended segregated seating on the buses in Montgomery, Alabama, in 1956. He continued for three decades to hand down decisions that proved pivotal for the civil rights of minorities.*

King, Martin Luther. Papers. Special Collections, Boston University Mugar Library and King Center, Atlanta, Georgia.

*The King Papers project at Stanford University is assembling and publishing historical information on Dr. King, including materials in manuscript collections.*

Leadership Conference on Civil Rights. Records. Manuscript Division, Library of Congress. Washington, D.C.

*The Leadership Conference on Civil Rights (LCCR), organized in 1949, is a coalition of more than one hundred national civil rights, religious, labor, civic, professional, and fraternal organizations.*

Logan, Rayford W. Papers, Moorland Spingarn Research Center, Howard University, Washington, D.C., and Library of Congress.

*Logan, a Harvard-trained historian, pioneered in the study of black history and served as chairman of the history department at Howard University. He was a civil rights activist. Logan was also a participant in the Pan-African Congresses.*

Malcolm X. *Transcripts of the Malcolm X Assassination Trial*. Microfilm, 3 reels. New York State Superior Court, New York.

*On February 21, 1965, within a year after Malcolm X disassociated himself from the Nation of Islam, he was assassinated.*

Marshall, Thurgood. Papers. Manuscript Division, Library of Congress, Washington, D.C.

*Although most of these records relate to Justice Marshall's tenure on the Supreme Court, some relate to his work as a federal court judge and his years as solicitor general.*

*Mississippi Oral History Collection*. Microfilm 163 Reels. University of South Mississippi Library.

*These reels provide transcripts of some civil rights leaders and activists.*

National Association for the Advancement of Colored People. Records. Library of Congress, Washington, D.C.

*The Library holds NAACP headquarters and Washington Bureau records. Although the headquarters records include information about NAACP branches, the branch records themselves are located in various repositories.*

*National Association of Colored Graduate Nurses, 1908–1951*. Microfilm, 4 reels. Schomburg Center for Research in Black Culture, New York.

*This group, under the leadership of Mabel Staupers, was active in efforts to desegregate the nurse corps in the U S. armed forces.*

*National Association of Colored Women's Clubs, 1895–1992*. Microfilm, 41 reels. National Association of Colored Women's Club Headquarters, Washington, D.C.

*Many women in this group were active supporters of the civil rights movement and donors of funds for protesters' legal expenses and bail.*

National Urban League Records. Manuscript Division, Library of Congress.

*Founded in 1910 through a merger of several welfare organizations, the National Urban League's aim was to promote the improvement of the industrial, economic, social, and spiritual conditions in black communities.*

National Urban League, Southern Regional Office, Manuscript Division. Library of Congress.

*In 1919, a growing concern for the welfare of blacks in the South prompted NUL officials to hire Jesse O. Thomas, an educator and labor specialist, to open an office in Atlanta, Georgia, to serve as an adjunct to the national office.*

National Urban League, Washington Bureau. Records. Manuscript Division, Library of Congress.

*The Washington Bureau, organized in 1961, provides the NUL with information on legislation pending in Congress and lobbies for League interests and programs before many government agencies.*

Randolph, A. Philip. Papers. Manuscript Division, Library of Congress, Washington, D.C.

*Randolph was a labor union organizer and officer and a civil rights leader. His papers unions, fair employment practices, the March on Washington movement during World War II, the March on Washington for Jobs and Freedom in 1963.*

Rauh, Joseph. Papers. Manuscript Division, Library of Congress.

*Rauh, a lawyer, civil libertarian, and civil rights activist, was a co-founder of the Americans for Democratic Action in 1947. He served as general counsel for the Leadership Conference on Civil Rights.*

Robinson, Jackie. Papers, Manuscript Division, Library of Congress, Washington, D.C.

*Robinson and his wife Rachel carefully kept these papers. They were donated to the Library of Congress in 2001.*

Southern Regional Council. Records. Atlanta University, Atlanta, Georgia.

*From its origin as the Commission on Interracial Cooperation, the Southern Regional Council since 1944 gathered data and provided financial support to help confront social and economic problems in the South since World War II.*

Spingarn, Arthur B. Papers. Manuscript Division, Library of Congress, Washington, D.C.

*Spingarn, a lawyer, served as the NAACP's third president from 1945 to 1965 and in numerous other capacities in the organization during his lifetime.*

Terrell, Mary Church. Papers. Manuscript Division, Moorland Spingarn Research Center, Howard University, Washington, D.C. and Manuscript Division, Library of Congress, Washington, D.C.

*Terrell, a feminist, was an author, lecturer, educator, and civil rights advocate. Her papers focus primarily on her career as an advocate of both women's rights and equal treatment for blacks.*

U.S. General Records of the Department of State, Record Group 59, National Archives and Records Administration.

*Many records relate to the efforts of diplomats around the world to explain and justify U.S. racial conflicts to foreign governments.*

U.S. FBI, Martin L. King Assassination Investigation. National Archives and Records Administration.

*This collection includes FBI records released under the Freedom of Information Act relating to the congressional investigation of the assassination of nonviolent civil rights leader Martin Luther King Jr.*

U.S. FBI. Centers of the Southern Struggle: FBI Files on Selma, Memphis, Montgomery, Albany, and St. Augustine edited by David Garrow. 21 microfilm reels University Publications of America.

*The FBI blots out parts of documents that are not open to the public. Garrow has arranged the remaining available data for use in the study of the civil rights movement.*

U.S. FBI, Communist Infiltration of the Southern Christian Leadership Conference FBI Investigation File. 9 microfilm reels. U.S. FBI Central Files

U.S. FBI, MIB URN (Mississippi Burning), the Investigation of the Murders of Michael Henry Schwerner, Andrew Goodman, and James Earl Chaney, June 21, 1964. 1 microfilm reel. U.S. FBI Central Files.

U.S. FBI, Microfilm series published by Scholarly Resources, Wilmington, Delaware.

*Many of the pages in these investigative files are blacked out for security reasons, but some useful information is available. The series of files relating to civil rights activists and black militants is listed below:*

*FBI File on A Philip Randolph, 1922–1964. 1 microfilm reel. FBI Central Files.*

*FBI File on Elijah Muhammad* 3 microfilm reels. FBI Central Files.

*FBI File on Malcolm* X. 10 microfilm reels. FBI Central Files.

*FBI File on Paul Robeson*. 2 microfilm reels. FBI Central Files.

*FBI File on Roy Wilkins* 1 microfilm reel. FBI Central Files.

*FBI File on the Black Panther Party, North Carolina*. 2 microfilm reels. FBI Central Files.

*FBI File on the* KKK *Murder of Viola Liuzzo*. 1 microfilm reel. FBI Central Files.

*FBI File on the Moorish Science Temple of America (Noble Drew Ali)*. 3 microfilm reels. FBI Central Files.

*FBI File on the Muslim Mosque, Inc* 3 microfilm reels. FBI Central Files.

*FBI File on the NAACP*. 4 microfilm reels. FBI Central Files.

*FBI File on the National Negro Congress*. 2 microfilm reels. FBI Central Files.

*FBI File on the Organization of Afro-American Unity (OAAU)*. 1 microfilm reel FBI Central Files.

*FBI File on the Reverend Jesse Jackson*. 1 microfilm reel. FBI Central Files.

*FBI File on the Student Nonviolent Coordinating Committee*. 3 microfilm reels. FBI Central Files.

*FBI File on W. E. B. Du Bois. 1 microfilm reel. FBI Central Files.*

U.S., Records of the Supreme Court of the United States, Record Group 267. National Archives and Records Administration.

*For the period from 1955 audio tape recordings of oral arguments before the Supreme Court are available. Civil rights cases address education, due process, legal status of blacks, forced confessions, housing, voting rights and more,*

U.S. Records of the Office of Education, Record Group 12, National Archives and Records Administration.

*Many records related to segregated schools. A sound recording of the 1965 White House Conference on Education includes a two-hour discussion of school desegregation.*

U.S. Records of the White House Office, Record Group 130, National Archives and Records Administration.

*A sound recording of President Harry Truman's address at a Howard University commencement on June 13, 1952, is primarily devoted to a review of his administration's accomplishments in the field of civil rights.*

Weaver, Robert C. Papers. Microfilm, 1903–1970. Schomburg Center for Research in Black Culture, New York.

*Weaver was a strategist for the civil rights movement who worked for the federal government for much of his career. He was the first African American to hold a cabinet-level position, Secretary of Housing and Urban Development.*

Wilkins, Roy. Papers. Manuscript Division, Library of Congress, Washington, D.C.

*Wilkins, a civil rights leader and journalist, worked with the NAACP in various capacities from 1931 until he retired as executive director in 1977.*

## BLACK NATIONALISM

### *Black Power*

Brown, Elaine. *Taste of Power: A Black Woman's Story*. New York: Doubleday, 1993.

*Brown gives an account of growing up black in North Philadelphia, and of joining and for a time working at the highest levels of the Black Panther Party.*

Brown, Scot. *Fighting for Us: Maulana Karenga, the US Organization and Black Cultural Nationalism*. New York: New York University Press, 2003.

*Brown studies the black cultural nationalist organization that emerged in Southern California during the mid-1960s and that established a small but effective network throughout the country. As a catalyst group, its "programmatic influence" was much greater than its actual membership.*

Bush, Roderick D. *We Are Not What We Seem: Black Nationalism and Class Struggle in the American Century*. New York: New York University Press, 1999.

*Bush places black power in the context of the history of poor blacks in urban America impacted by issues of both class and race.*

Carmichael, Stokely, and Charles V. Hamilton. *Black Power: The Politics of Liberation in America*. New York: Random House, 1967.

*The authors state that the book gives a framework for preventing "destructive guerrilla warfare" in the United States. Chapters address white power, black power, Mississippi Freedom Democrats, black-belt elections, ghettos, and coalitions.*

Cleaver, Eldridge. *Soul on Ice*. New York: McGraw-Hill, 1968.

*Cleaver's essays address a variety of subjects such as the Watts uprising, the "White Race and Its Heroes," "The Black Man's Stake in Vietnam," domestic law and the assassination of Malcolm X, and relations between men and women.*

Cleaver, Eldridge. *Post-Prison Writings and Speeches*. Ed. Robert Scheer. New York: Random House, 1967–69.

*Cleaver analyzes the decline of the Black Muslims, Robert Kennedy, Huey Newton, Stokely Carmichael, Martin Luther King, Ronald Reagan, the Black Panthers, and the "Shoot-out in Oakland."*

Cone, James H. *Martin & Malcolm & America: A Dream or a Nightmare*. New York: Orbis Books, 1991.

*This work examines the lives and beliefs of Martin Luther King Jr. and Malcolm X as representing the struggle between integrationism and nationalism.*

Franklin, V. P. *Black Self-Determination: A Cultural History of African-American Resistance*. 2nd ed. Brooklyn, N.Y.: Lawrence Hill, 1992.

*Franklin identifies a tradition in the quest for self-determination among African Americans who have defined themselves as a "people" or a "nation."*

Herod, Augustina, and Charles C. Herod. *Afro-American Nationalism: An Annotated Bibliography of Militant, Separatist and Nationalist Literature*. New York: Garland Publishing, 1986.

*Chapters 5 and 9 provide sources with annotations about black nationalist thought from 1945 to 1986. Other chapters cover religious black nationalism, black power, self-determination, and cultural and economic black nationalist thought.*

Hilliard, David with Lewis Cole. *This Side of Glory: The Autobiography of David Hilliard and the Story of the Black Panther Party*. Chicago: Chicago Review Press, 2001.

*An insider's account of the Black Panther Party by its chief of staff.*

Jones, Charles Colcock, ed. *Black Panther Party Reconsidered*. Baltimore, Md.: Black Classic Press, 1998.

*The essays by former Panther party members and scholars sympathetic to its aims includes a review of the party's history, "reflections from the rank and file," reflections on "gender dynamics," and analyses of the Panthers' decline and legacy.*

Lincoln, C. Eric. *The Black Muslims in America*. Boston: Beacon Press, 1961.

*Using information gained from oral interviews, visits to mosques, and Black Muslim literature, Lincoln discusses the history, leaders, rituals, and beliefs of the Black Muslims.*

Malcolm X. *By Any Means Necessary*. New York: Pathfinder, 1992.

*This is a collection of Malcolm X's speeches, interviews, and statements, first published in 1970. All of its contents are from the last year of his life, following his announcement that he was no longer a member of the Nation of Islam.*

Malcolm X. *The Autobiography of Malcolm X*. New York: Grove Press, 1965.

*As told to Alex Haley, Malcolm X discusses his childhood, his life of crime, his conversion to the Nation of Islam, his rise to prominence within that organization, and his eventual rivalry with the Nation's leader, Elijah Muhammad.*

Seale, Bobby. *Seize the Time: The Story of the Black Panther Party and Huey P. Newton*. New York: Random House, 1970.

*Seale wrote this book in San Francisco State Prison with the purpose of explaining the history, programs, and goals of the Black Panther Party at a time when it was under attack by police and federal agencies. Reprinted in 1994.*

Stuckey, Sterling. *Slave Culture: Nationalist Theory and the Foundations of Black America.* New York: Oxford University Press, 1987.

*Stuckey suggests that black culture in the United States since slavery has remained largely African.*

Tyson, Timothy B. *Radio Free Dixie: Robert F. Williams and the Roots of Black Power.* Chapel Hill: University of North Carolina Press, 2001.

*Tyson places Williams's controversial advocacy of armed self-defense in the context of a tradition of black resistance to white racism. He argues that the civil rights and the black power movements grew out of the same soil.*

Van Deburg, William L., ed. *Modern Black Nationalism: From Marcus Garvey to Louis Farrakhan.* New York: New York University Press, 1997.

*This collection provides nationalist thought from a number of black theorists and activists including J. A. Rogers, A. Philip Randolph, Richard B. Moore, Elijah Muhammad, Assata Shakur, Mulana Karenga, and Frances Cress Welsing.*

Van Deburg, William L. *New Day in Babylon: the Black Power Movement and American Culture, 1965–1975.* Chicago: University of Chicago Press, 1992.

*Van Deburg discusses black power on college campuses, and in sports, labor, and the cultural establishment. He reviews the evolution of "soul" food, style, talk, and theology. His examination encompasses art, music, religion, and politics.*

### *Black Arts and Black Aesthetics*

Baker, David N., Lida M. Belt, and Herman C. Hudson, eds. *The Black Composer Speaks.* Metuchen, N.J.: Scarecrow Press, 1978.

*This book consists of interviews with fifteen black composers about their backgrounds, philosophies, motivations, and attitudes. Among the composers interviewed are Herbie Hancock, Ulysses Kay, Archie Shepp, and Noel Da Costa.*

Fowler, Carolyn. *Black Arts and Black Aesthetics: A Bibliography.* Atlanta: First World, 1981.

*The bibliography lists articles, essays and books relating to the "black person as aesthetic object," culture theory, dance, drama, music, Negritude, plastic arts, poetry and fiction.*

Morse, David. *Motown and the Arrival of Black Music.* New York: Macmillan, 1971.

*Morse traces the rise of Motown during its first decade under the leadership of Berry Gordy. He also traces the careers of Martha Reeves, Smokey Robinson, the Supremes, the Temptations, and the Four Tops.*

Neal, Larry. *Visions of a Liberated Future: Black Arts Movement Writings with Commentary by Amiri Baraka, Stanley Crouch, Charles Fuller, and Jayne Cortez.* Ed. Michael Schwartz. New York: Thunder's Mouth Press, 1989.

*This anthology collects Neal's essays, poetry, and drama, with commentary by those who knew him. His essays relate to the black writer's role, the black arts movement, Zora Neale Hurston, Malcolm X, and black power in the international context.*

## URBAN REBELLIONS/RIOTS

Boskin, Joseph, ed. *Urban Racial Violence in the Twentieth Century.* Beverly Hills: Glencoe Press, 1976.

*Boskin provides the historical background of racial violence in America and a variety of authors examine "World War II: The Internal Race War," the Detroit riots of 1943, the Zoot Suit Riots in Los Angeles in 1943, and Harlem uprisings.*

Boutelle, Paul, ed. *The Black Uprisings: Newark, Detroit, 1967*. New York: Merit Publishers, 1967.

*Boutelle introduces eyewitness accounts of the Newark and Detroit riots by Lawrence Stewart and George Novack. This thirty-page pamphlet includes some photographs.*

Canot, Robert. *Rivers of Blood, Years of Darkness: The Unforgettable Classic Account of the Watts Riot*. New York: William Morrow, 1968.

*A race riot in Watts, a section of Los Angeles, took place in August 1965. The study examines the relations between whites and blacks in Watts, especially the relationship with the police force.*

Cohen, Nathan, ed. *The Los Angeles Riots: A Socio-Psychological Study*. New York: Praeger, 1970.

*The authors discuss participants in the riots, attitudes of merchants, social and economic conditions, "police malpractice," physical characteristics of the riot, social services in Watts, the arrest's, the curfew zone, and the "politics of discontent."*

Fine, Sidney. *Violence in the Model City*. Ann Arbor: University of Michigan Press, 1989.

*Study of the racial uprising in Detroit in 1967.*

Grimshaw, Allen D., ed. *Racial Violence in the U.S.* Chicago: Aldine, 1969.

*Chapter 7 includes articles and reports that address "racial readjustment" from 1942 to 1954. Other writings relate to patterns of violence, its underlying causes, psychological factors, and attitudinal patterns.*

Hayden, Tom. *Rebellion in Newark: Official Violence and Ghetto Response*. New York: Vintage Books, 1967.

*Hayden describes the riot in Newark, New Jersey, from July 12 to 17, 1967. The book provides some historical background and gives a day-to-day account of the violence. The account supplies a list of the "dead and the brutalized."*

Horne, Gerald. *Fire This Time: The Watts Uprising and the 1960s*. Charlottesville: University Press of Virginia, 1995.

*Analyzes the Watts community in all its racial, political, social, and ideological complexity, before, during, and after the 1965 uprising.*

Porambo, Ron. *No Cause for Indictment: An Autopsy of Newark*. New York: Holt, Rinehart and Winston, 1971.

*This 398-page work examines in detail the causes and the effects of the 1967 race riot. It includes statements from many eyewitnesses.*

Sauter, Van Gordon, and Burleigh Hines. *Nightmare in Detroit: A Rebellion and Its Victims*. Chicago: Henry Regnery Company, 1968.

*This is a day-by-day chronicle of the July 1967 riot in Detroit.*

*U.S. National Advisory Commission on Civil Disorders Report*. New York: Dutton, 1968.

*This official report on the disorders examines riots in Tampa, Cincinnati, Atlanta, Newark, northern New Jersey, Plainfield, New Brunswick, and Detroit. It details the riots, the participants, background, aftermath, and economic trends.*

Waskow, Arthur I. *From Race Riot to Sit-In, 1919 and the 1960s: A Study in the Connections between Conflict and Violence*. Garden City, N.Y.: Doubleday, 1966.

*Waskow looks at riots in cities such as Washington, Little Rock, and Chicago; "jailhouse riots"; and the role of police. This book was completed just before the 1965 Watts riot.*

## POST–CIVIL RIGHTS

### *Affirmative Action*

Belz, Herman. *Equality Transformed: A Quarter Century of Affirmative Action*. New York: Basic Books, 1996.

*Belz traces the history of affirmative action policies and the race and gender problems related to the policies that affect government agencies and employers.*

Bergmann, Barbara R. *In Defense of Affirmative Action*. New York: Basic Books, 1996.

*Bergman takes a critical look at the advantages, disadvantages, and effectiveness of affirmative action as well as alternatives to the current system.*

Bowen, William G., and Derek Bok. *The Shape of the River: Long Term Consequences of Considering Race in College and University Admissions*. Princeton, N.J.: Princeton University Press, 1998.

*This work analyzes affirmative-action admissions policies by looking at the personal histories of more than sixty thousand black and white students. The authors measure academic success, employment, earnings, and job satisfaction.*

Chavez, Lydia. *The Color Bind: California's Battle to End Affirmative Action*. Berkeley: University of California Press, 1998.

*Chavez details the strategy and motivations behind California Proposition 209, which ended affirmative action in that state. Chavez documents the role of individuals, organizations, and politicians on the state and national level.*

Drake, W. Avon, and Robert D. Hollsworth. *Affirmative Action and the Stalled Quest for Black Progress*. Urbana: University of Illinois Press, 1996.

*The author traces black politics and affirmative action in Richmond, Virginia, from 1945 to 1989.*

Edley, Christopher, Jr. *Not All Black and White: Affirmative Action and American Values*. New York: Hill and Wang, 1996.

*In this evaluation of affirmative action programs, Edley discusses the legality and effectiveness of various programs, investigates their value, and proposes reforms.*

Fleming, John, and Gerald Gill. *The Case for Affirmative Action in Higher Education*. Washington, D.C.: Howard University Press, 1978.

*This study uses a historical approach to address the importance and constitutionality of affirmative action in higher education.*

Garcia, Mildred, ed. *Affirmative Action's Testimony of Hope*. Albany: State University of New York Press, 1997.

*Focusing on race and gender, these essays examine the impact of affirmative action in higher education from the perspective of faculty and students.*

Greene, Kathanne W. *Affirmative Action and Principles of Justice*. Westport, Conn.: Greenwood Press, 1989.

*Greene examines Supreme Court affirmative action rulings specifically examining five cases. She also includes a history of Title VII of the Civil Rights Act of 1964.*

Lawrence, Charles R., III, and Mari J. Matsuda. *We Won't Go Back: Making the Case for Affirmative Action*. Boston: Houghton Mifflin, 1997.

*The authors weave the history of affirmative action and public reaction to it along with individual stories of its benefits.*

Moreno, Paul D. *From Direct Action to Affirmative Action: Fair Employment Law and Policy in America, 1933–1972*. Baton Rouge: Louisiana State University Press, 1997.

*Moreno provides a history of affirmative action as well as the crusade for equal hiring practices decades before 1963. He describes the legal and political responses to racial bias and the remedies provided by civil rights policies.*

Robinson, JoAnn Ooiman. *Affirmative Action: A Documentary History*. Westport, Conn.: Greenwood Press, 2001.

*Robinson carefully traces the evolution of affirmative action strategies, struggles, and victories for blacks, women, and the disabled. This chronological treatment provides the contextual framework for understanding public policies.*

Schwartz, Bernard. *Behind Bakke: Affirmative Action and the Supreme Court*. New York: New York University Press, 1988.

*Allan Paul Bakke, a white unsuccessful applicant to the medical school at the University of California at Berkeley, argued before the Supreme Court that he was discriminated against because less qualified blacks were admitted. He won.*

Wallace, Phyllis A., ed. *Equal Employment Opportunity and the AT&T Case*. Cambridge, Mass.: MIT Press, 1976.

*This study specifically focuses on the landmark decision in the American Telephone and Telegraph case that reinforced equal employment opportunity legislation and opened better jobs within AT&T to minorities and women.*

Weiss, Robert John. *We Want Jobs: A History of Affirmative Action*. New York: Garland, 1997.

*Weiss documents the struggle of blacks for economic equality by focusing on the policies of presidents from Roosevelt to Reagan.*

## Business

Gordy, Berry. *To Be Loved: The Music, the Magic, the Memories of Motown*. New York: Warner Books, 1994.

*Gordy, the chief architect of the Motown music empire, explains the steps that led to the growth and development of the company. He relates finding and developing acts like Smokey Robinson and the Miracles, the Jackson Five, and the Supremes.*

Graves, Earl. *How to Succeed in Business without Being White: Straight Talk on Making It in America*. New York: HarperBusiness, 1997.

*Graves, an entrepreneur and the editor of Black Enterprise magazine, provides insights to African Americans who want to build their own businesses.*

Jenkins, Carol, and Elizabeth Gardner Hines. *Black Titan: A. G. Gaston and the Making of a Black Millionaire*. New York: One World, 2004.

*The story of A. G. Gaston's rise to success in Birmingham, Alabama, where he filled a void during the era of segregation in meeting the banking, construction, insurance, media, motel, and business school needs of African Americans.*

Johnson, John H., and Lerone Bennett Jr. *Succeeding Against the Odds: The Autobiography of a Great American Businessman*. New York: Warner Books, 1989.

*The Johnson Publishing Company founder relates his struggles as an African American businessman. His company publishes Ebony and Jet. Both magazines address present and past issues relating to the black community.*

Pulley, Bret. *The Billion Dollar BET: Robert Johnson and the Inside Story of Black Entertainment Television*. New York: John Wiley & Sons, 2004.

*Pulley reveals the life and business acumen of the first black billionaire.*

Weems, Robert E., Jr. *Desegregating the Dollar: African American Consumerism in the Twentieth Century*. New York: New York University Press, 1998.

*Examines the huge black consumer market and the way in which racism has influenced advertisers and businesses in seeking access to it.*

## *Film*

*Affirmative Action: The History of an Idea*. Films for the Humanities and Sciences. 1996.

*This film explores the historical roots of affirmative action and the current debate over its usefulness.*

*Affirmative Action and Reaction*. Films for the Humanities and Sciences. 1995.

*Lani Guinier, President Clinton's unsuccessful nominee for assistant attorney general, examines affirmative action policies and programs and explores the difference between whites and blacks in their understanding of affirmative action.*

*Affirmative Action Under Fire: When Is It Reverse Discrimination?* Films for the Humanities and the Social Sciences. 1997.

*In 1969, a New Jersey high school had to lay off one of two teachers of equal tenure and equivalent credentials—one white and one black. The black teacher was retained, and the white teacher brought a case of reverse discrimination.*

*Forgotten Fires*. University of California at Berkeley, Independent Television Service. 1998.

*The 57-minute film investigates the burning of two African American churches in rural South Carolina by a member of the Ku Klux Klan. It was filmed over a one-year period.*

*Freedom Bags*. WETA. 1990.

*Even after World War II, only domestic and service jobs were open to black women in many areas. This film consists of interviews with elderly black women who describe the changes in their work from live-in domestics to day laborers.*

*From Fields of Promise*. University of California at Berkeley, Films for Humanities and Social Sciences. 1995.

*Ossie Davis and John O'Neal narrate the story of African American farmers in Gee's Bend, Alabama, who have owned and lived on the same land since the days of slavery.*

*Hate Crime*. Films for the Humanities and Sciences. 1999.

*Part 1 of this program shows how the New South has found some answers to the old problem of racial violence specifically in relation to church burnings. Part 2 documents a pioneering high school class on tolerance.*

*I Remember Harlem*. Films for the Humanities and Sciences. 1980.

*Part 3 of this film, "Towards Freedom, 1940–1965, describes Harlem's politics of protest. Part 4, "Toward a New Day, 1965–1980," depicts Harlem's decline and rebirth, Harlem churches and community life.*

*The Last Graduation*. Films for the Humanities and Social Sciences. 1995.

*This film documents the effectiveness and cost of educating U.S. prisoners. Even though education in prison has proved to be one of the few effective tools for reducing recidivism, funding for such programs is a problem.*

*Miles of Smiles, Years of Struggle: The Untold Story of the Black Pullman Porter*. California Newsreel. 1982.

*This film documents the struggle of black railroad porters and maids to obtain equal treatment and opportunity with the nation's railroads. It parallels the African American labor struggle in other industries.*

*The Second City: Inside the World's Largest Jail*. Films for the Humanities and Social Sciences. 1999.

*This film about the Los Angeles county jail documents racial and gender tensions between the inmates.*

*Sermons and Sacred Pictures*. Films for the Humanities and Social Sciences. 1991.

*This documentary profiles the life and work of L. O. Taylor, a black Baptist minister from Memphis, Tennessee. The film presents clips taken by Taylor in the 1930s and 1940s and contrasts them with contemporary Memphis churches.*

## *Race Relations*

Asante, Molefi. *Erasing Racism: The Survival of the American Nation*. Amherst, N.Y.: Prometheus Books, 2003.

*Asante examines the status of African Americans since the mid-1970s and the case for reparations.*

Bartley, Numan V. *The New South, 1945–1980*. Baton Rouge: Louisiana State University Press, 1995.

*Bartley focuses on the reformation of the South from the end of World War II through the 1970s. He analyzes changes in the economy, government, and urban development, as well as other cultural and social factors.*

Blauner, Bob. *Still the Big News: Racial Oppression in America*. Philadelphia: Temple University Press, 2001.

*Blauner discusses the climate of race relations in the late 1960s, white privilege, colonialism, racism, and black culture. Other issues addressed include institutionalized racism, and immigrant minorities.*

Cose, Ellis. *Color Blind*. New York: HarperPerennial, 1998.

*The topics Cose addresses include racial classification, discrimination, genetics, educational parity, and affirmative action. He studies race relations and attitudes and speculates about a U.S. race-neutral society.*

Cose, Ellis. *The Rage of the Privileged Class*. New York: HarperPerennial, 1997.

*The author discusses the anger of the African American intelligentsia with the racial realities in the United States at the end of the twentieth century.*

Ellis, Carl F., Jr. *Beyond Liberation: The Gospel in the Black American Experience*. Downers Grove, Ill.: Intervarsity Press, 1983.

*Ellis traces the maturing of black consciousness and traces the theological dynamic from slavery to the present, noting especially the contribution of Martin Luther King Jr. and Malcolm X.*

Franklin, John Hope, and Genna Rae McNeil, eds. *African Americans and the Living Constitution*. Washington, D.C.: Smithsonian Institution Press, 1995.

*Essays discuss the evolution of constitutional interpretation in matters relating to African Americans.*

Gates, Henry Louis, Jr. *America Behind the Color Line: Dialogues with African Americans*. New York: Warner Books, 2004.

*A readable companion, in the oral-history tradition of Studs Terkel, to the PBS documentary series, peeking behind the veil "that still, far too often, separates black America from white."*

Gates, Henry Louis, Jr., ed. *Thirteen Ways of Looking at a Black Man*. New York: Random House, 1997.

*Essays chronicle the challenges and triumphs of various successful black men who have challenged conventional ideas of the significance of being a black man in the United States.*

Gates, Henry Louis, Jr., and Cornel West. *African-American Century: How Black Americans Have Shaped Our Country*. New York: Vintage Books, 1997.

*Gates and West assess social conditions for blacks at the end of the twentieth century and analyze race relations by highlighting black achievements.*

Gates, Henry Louis, Jr., and Cornel West. *The Future of the Race*. New York: Knopf, 1996.

*The authors provide an assessment of race relations and social conditions for blacks since 1975 by looking at black leaders and intellectuals. They predict the results of current trends in racial policies.*

Gilroy, Paul. *Against Race: Imagining Political Culture Beyond the Color Line*. Cambridge, Mass.: Belknap Press, 2000.

*Gilroy speculates about dismissing race as a "toxic" concept and criticizes "race thinking."*

Graham, Hugh Davis. *Civil Rights and the Presidency*. New York: Oxford University Press, 1992.

*The author looks at the impact of race and gender in the development of civil rights and provides a history of U.S. policies on civil rights.*

Graham, Lawrence Otis. *Our Kind of People: Inside America's Black Upper Class*. New York: HarperCollins, 1999.

*Graham describes the world of the black elite—their professions, homes, clubs, physical preferences, and their relationship to whites and other blacks. He provides a history of the select black children's organization, Jack and Jill.*

Higham, John, ed. *Civil Rights and Civil Wrongs: Black-White Relations Since World War II*. University Park: Pennsylvania State University Press, 1999.

*The essays detail various trends in U.S. race relations and the history of affirmative action, multiculturalism, and diversity.*

Kelley, Robin D. G. *Freedom Dreams: The Black Radical Imagination*. Boston: Beacon Press, 2002.

*Kelley emphasizes the power of imagination as a revolutionary tool to change society. He examines intellectuals and artists throughout the African diaspora who, drawn by their hope of a better world, led radical movements.*

Kelley, Robin D. G. *Race Rebels: Culture, Politics, and the Black Working Class*. New York: Free Press, 1996.

*Kelley analyzes race issues focusing on cultural and political dynamics especially among the black working class. One chapter is entitled, "The Riddle of the Zoot: Malcolm Little and Black Cultural Politics During World War II."*

Kelley, Robin D. G. *Yo' Mama's Disfunktional!: Fighting the Culture Wars in Urban America*. Boston: Beacon Press, 1997.

*Kelley explores the ways in which misunderstandings of black culture have contributed to the failure of public policy, scholarship, the labor movement, and other social movements. He offers a new analysis of urban multicultural roots.*

Layton, Azza Salama. *International Politics and Civil Rights Polities in the United States, 1941–1960*. New York: Cambridge University Press, 2000.

*Layton argues that racism in the United States harmed the national image abroad and provided impetus for communist propaganda. Because of this tarnished image, the U.S. government was forced to confront racial injustice.*

Loury, Glenn C. *The Anatomy of Racial Inequality*. Cambridge, Mass.: Harvard University Press, 2001.

*Loury uses an interdisciplinary approach to trace the effects of racial stigmatization on relations between blacks and whites in the United States and on the economic condition of blacks.*

Lubiano, Wahneema, ed. *The House That Race Built: Black Americans, U.S. Terrain*. New York: Pantheon Books, 1997.

*Toni Morrison, Angela Y. Davis, Cornel West, and others contributed essays in this volume relating to power, gender, race, and society.*

Maguire, Daniel C. *A New American Justice: Ending the White Male Monopolies*. New York: Doubleday, 1980.

*Maguire investigates equality of education, political and legal rights of African Americans. He addresses housing and employment and explores routes of empowerment for women, American Indians, and Hispanics.*

National Urban League. *The State of Black America*. New York: National Urban League, 2001.

*Each year since 1976, the NUL has published essays relating to conditions among black Americans. Topics in this volume are blacks under thirty-five, affirmative action in higher education, home ownership, the digital divide, and hip-hop.*

Pinkney, Alphonso. *Black Americans*. 5th ed. Upper Saddle River, N.J.: Prentice-Hall, 2000.

*Pickney assesses the characteristics of the black community, including development, socioeconomic status, education, social institutions, family, health, and problems such as homelessness and substance abuse.*

Robinson, Randall. *The Debt: What America Owes to Blacks*. New York: Dutton, 2000.

*Robinson analyzes the long-term effects of racism and ignorance of history on individual psyches, communities, and economic resources.*

Rymer, Russ. *American Beach: How "Progress" Robbed a Black Town—and Nation—of History, Wealth, and Power*. New York: HarperPerennial, 2000.

*American Beach, Florida, once a prosperous African American resort town, has declined as a direct result of integration. Rymer examines positive and negative effects of integration.*

Shabazz, Ilyasah, and Kim McLaurin. *Growing Up X*. New York: Ballantine, 2002.

*Shabazz, the daughter of Malcolm X, pays tribute to her father's legacy but focuses on her mother, Betty, who was left with the responsibility of raising six daughters after Malcolm was assassinated.*

Steele, Shelby. *A Dream Deferred: The Second Betrayal of Black Freedom in America*. New York: HarperPerennial, 1999.

*Steele presents essays that seek answers to questions relating to affirmation action, racial justice, and government and institutional racial policies.*

Stern, Mack. *Calculating Visions: Kennedy, Johnson and Civil Rights*. New Brunswick, N.J.: Rutgers University Press, 1992.

*Stern examines the motivations for the civil rights policies advocated by the Kennedy and Johnson administrations.*

Wicker, Tom. *Tragic Failure: Racial Integration in America*. New York: Quill, 1997.

*Thirty years after the judicial and legislative achievements of the civil rights movement, Wicker analyzes the intent of the laws and the actual situation for blacks. He assesses welfare reform, crime, employment, and affirmative action.*

## *Education*

Allen, Walter R., Edgar G. Epps, and Nesha Z. Haniff, eds. *College in Black and White: African American Students in Predominantly White and in Historically Black Public Universities*. Albany: State University of New York Press, 1991.

*The essays address race and gender as they relate to educational performance, predictors of college student achievement, student support networks, determinants of success for black males and females, desegregation, and student achievement.*

Bobo, Jacqueline, et al., eds. *The Black Studies Reader*. New York: Routledge, 2004.

*A comprehensive examination of black studies as a socially engaged field of scholarly inquiry.*

Du Bois, W. E. B. *The Education of Black People: Ten Critiques, 1906–1960*. Ed. Herbert Aptheker. Amherst: University of Massachusetts Press, 1973.

*Several of Du Bois's articles are "The Future of the Negro State University," 1941, "The Future and Function of the Private Negro College," 1946, and "Whither Now and Why," 1960. Aptheker provides an introduction, editorial notes, and a bibliography of Du Bois's published writings on education.*

Formisano, Ronald P. *Boston Against Busing: Race, Class, and Ethnicity in the 1960s and 1970s*. Chapel Hill: University of North Carolina Press, 1991.

*Court-ordered desegregation of public schools began in Boston in the fall of 1974 igniting racial bigotry and violence. The author argues that racial conflict had been escalating in the city for over a decade.*

Hale, Janice E. *Unbank the Fire: Visions for the Education of African American Children*. Baltimore, Md.: Johns Hopkins University Press, 1994.

*Chapters include "Understanding African American Children in the Context of Their History," "Cultural Styles of African American Children," and "Social Context: Historical and Cultural Factors."*

Ihle, Elizabeth L., ed. *Black Women in Higher Education: An Anthology of Essays, Studies, and Documents*. New York: Garland Publishing, 1992.

*The essays show the range of experiences in African American women's pursuit of higher education. They discuss women's college experiences in general and include biographical essays on women such as Autherine Lucy and Nikki Giovanni.*

Robinson, Armstead L., Craig C. Foster, and Donald H. Ogilvie, eds. *Black Studies in the University: A Symposium*. New Haven, Conn.: Yale University Press, 1969.

*This volume is a record of one of the first comprehensive attempts to thrash out the intellectual and political issues concerned with implementing a program of African American studies in U.S. colleges and universities.*

Tatum, Beverly Daniel. *Why Are All the Black Kids Sitting Together in the Cafeteria? And Other Conversations about Race*. New York: Basic Books, 2003.

*Tatum explains racial awareness and identity among college students in a multicultural society.*

## *Family*

Billingsley, Andrew. *Climbing Jacob's Ladder: The Enduring Legacy of African-American Families*. New York: Simon & Schuster, 1992.

*Billingsley looks at the evolution of African American families from ancient times to the 1990s. He describes the major forces shaping these families and the major patterns of adaptation they made to conditions in the United States.*

Hesslink, George K. *Black Neighbors: Negroes in a Northern Rural Community*. 2nd edition. New York: Bobbs-Merrill, 1974.

*Hesslink argues that racially mixed Cass County, Michigan, provides an example of a stable and egalitarian rural community. He documents the history and development of this county where white Quakers encouraged free blacks and ex-slaves to live among them.*

Stack, Carol B. *All Our Kin: Strategies for Survival in a Black Community*. New York: Harper & Row, 1974.

*Stack entered a black urban community to find out firsthand about black urban poor families, particularly family structures, kin networks, child rearing, childcare, and the impact of welfare.*

## Politics

Dawson, Michael C. *Behind the Mule: Race and Class in African-American Politics*. Princeton, N.J.: Princeton University Press, 1994.

*Dawson contends that being black affects the economic and social opportunities of most African Americans so profoundly that they are usually motivated by racial group concerns rather than class interests.*

Duckett, Alfred, ed. *Changing of the Guard: The New Breed of Black Politicians*. New York: Coward, McCann and Geoghegan, 1972.

*Duckett includes articles by Percy Sutton, Clarence Mitchell, Julian Bond, Charles Evers, Shirley Chisholm, and his own essays on black mayors ("Soul Sisters in Politics") and the Congressional Black Caucus.*

Franklin, V. P., Nancy L. Grant, Harold M. Kletnick, and Genna Rae McNeil, eds. *African Americans and Jews in the Twentieth Century: Studies in Convergence and Conflict*. Columbia: University of Missouri Press, 1998.

*Essays include "The Civil Rights Movement and the Reemergence on the Left," "The Southern Jewish Community and the Struggle for Civil Rights," and "The Increasing Significance of Class: Black-Jewish Conflict in the Postindustrial Global Era."*

Gordon, Ann D., Bettye Collier-Thomas, John H. Bracey, Arlene Voski Avakian, and Joyce Avrech Berkman. *African American Women and the Vote, 1837–1965*. Amherst: University of Massachusetts Press, 1997.

*The authors discuss black women's quest for the vote. Essays include "Shining in the Dark: Black Women and the Struggle for the Vote, 1955–1965 and "From Progressive Republican to Independent Progressive: The Political Career of Charlotta A. Bass."*

Lawson, Steven F. *Black Ballots: Voting Rights in the South, 1944–1969*. New York: Columbia University Press, 1976.

*This study explores the process by which a majority of southern blacks gained the right to vote and the way in which the legal and political institutions of the United States responded to post–World War II demands for the enforcement of the Fifteenth Amendment.*

Lawson, Stephen F. *In Pursuit of Power: South Blacks and Electoral Politics, 1965–1982*. New York: Columbia University Press, 1985.

*Lawson charts the efforts of civil rights forces to redress grievances through federal action. He demonstrates that the commitment to protect the ballot has survived despite changes in partisan control of the White House and the Congress.*

Marable, Manning. *Black American Politics: From the Washington Marches to Jesse Jackson*. London: Verso, 1985.

*Marable looks at the Marches on Washington, D.C., in 1941, 1963 and 1983. He also analyses black politicians and bourgeois democracy, black power in Chicago, and Jesse Jackson's Presidential campaign.*

McAdam, Doug. *Political Process and the Development of Black Insurgency, 1930–1970*. Chicago: University of Chicago Press, 1982.

*The author proposes a "political process" model for the analysis of the efforts by blacks to effect basic changes in the political and economic structures of U.S. society and to redefine minority status from 1930 to 1970.*

Reuter, Theodore, ed. *The Politics of Race: African Americans and the Political System*. Armonk, N.Y.: M. E. Sharpe, 1995.

*These essays examine the major issues involving race and American politics. The theme of the book is that race is a critical element in American politics. Authors include former President Bill Clinton and Congressman William Clay and Senator Bill Bradley.*

Wolters, Raymond. *Right Turn: William Bradford Reynolds, the Reagan Administration, and Black Civil Rights*. New Brunswick, N.J.: Transaction Publishers, 1996.

*Wolters's work covers issues relating to voting rights, affirmative action, and school desegregation during the Reagan administration, especially Assistant Attorney General William Reynolds' role as principal architect of civil rights policies.*

## *Religion*

Collier-Thomas, Bettye, ed. *Daughters of Thunder: Black Women Preachers and Their Sermons, 1850–1979*. San Francisco: Jossey-Bass Publishers, 1998.

*This work provides the text of post-1939 sermons by Florence Spearing Randolph, Quinceila Randolph, F. E. Redwine, and Pauli Murray. The introductory essays are entitled "The Power of Black Women Preachers," and "Rising Above Adversity: The Struggle to Preach."*

Paris, Peter J. *Black Leaders in Conflict: Joseph H. Jackson, Martin Luther King, Jr., Malcolm X, Adam Clayton Powell, Jr.* New York: Pilgrim Press, 1978.

*This book provides a comparative analysis of the thoughts of Jackson, King, Malcolm, and Powell. Though all four were opposed to racism, they disagreed on the forms that opposition should take.*

Sleeper, C. Freeman. *Black Power and Christian Responsibility: Some Biblical Foundations for Social Ethics*. New York: Abingdon Press, 1969.

*Essays in this volume relate to topics such as "Black Power: The Birth of an Image," "'Black and White Together': The Death of a Dream?" and "The Proliferation of Black Power."*

West, Cornel. *Prophesy Deliverance: An Afro-American Revolutionary Christianity*. Philadelphia: Westminster Press, 1982.

*West discusses the African American experience in the light of the social and intellectual currents that shaped American culture. He analyzes race relations by examining the roots of racism and outlining four traditional black responses to white supremacy.*

## *Science and Technology*

Jay, James M. *Negroes in Science: Natural Science Doctorates, 1876–1969*. Detroit: Balamp Publishing, 1971.

*The author includes biographical information as well as some tables and illustrations about individuals who received doctorates in the physical sciences, chemistry and pharmaceutical sciences, agricultural sciences, and biosciences. There is also a listing of female scientists.*

Krapp, Kristine, ed. *Notable Black American Scientists*. Detroit: Gale Research, 1999.

*This book profiles some 250 black inventors, researchers, award winners, and educators in the sciences.*

Pearson, Willie, Jr., and H. Kenneth Bechtel, eds. *Blacks, Science, and American Education*. New Brunswick, N.J.: Rutgers University Press, 1989.

*Topics include black high school students and mathematics education and science, black science majors in colleges and universities and statistics about black Ph.D.s. There are many tables and figures about blacks in higher education.*

Sammons, Vivian O. *Blacks in Science and Medicine*. New York: Hemisphere, 1990.

*Sammons provides biographies of black scientists and physicians.*

Warren, Wini. *Black Women Scientists in the United States*. Bloomington: Indiana University Press, 1999.

*Biographical sketches of more than a hundred black women scientists cover their work in the fields of anatomy, anthropology, astronautics, space science, biochemistry, biology, botany, chemistry, geology, marine biology, mathematics, nutrition, pharmacology, physics, psychology, and zoology.*

## THE 1980S

Amaker, Norman C. *Civil Rights and the Reagan Administration*. Washington, D.C.: Urban Institute, 1988.

*Part 1 is the "Evolution of the Executive Role in Civil Rights Enforcement"; part 2 is the "Reagan Record" in education, federally assisted programs, housing, employment, and voting.*

Barker, Lucius J., and Ronald W. Walters, eds. *Jesse Jackson's 1984 Presidential Campaign: Challenge and Change in American Politics*. Urbana: University of Illinois Press, 1989.

*The authors provide the context for Jackson's presidential bid and describe his campaign style, constituents, voters, the Democratic convention, and Jackson's impact on the United States.*

Omi, Michael, and Howard Winant. *Racial Formation in the United States from the 1960s to the 1980s*. New York: Routledge & Kegan Paul, 1986.

*This work is a synthetic treatment of race that incorporates the progress made by blacks, Hispanics, Asians. It analyzes the current and emerging conditions of racial and ethnic groups and presents a picture of how the United States has related to its minorities.*

Walton, Hanes, Jr. *When the Marching Stopped: The Politics of Civil Rights Regulatory Agencies*. Albany: State University of New York Press, 1988.

*Walton documents the institutionalization of civil rights enforcement agencies within the federal government but argues that once the movement gained legislation and a bureaucracy to enforce it, a perceptible decline in commitment resulted.*

## THE 1990S

Ashmore, Harry S. *Civil Rights and Wrongs: A Memoir of Race and Politics, 1944–1994*. New York: Pantheon Books, 1994.

*Ashmore gives a retrospective view of the causes and effects of the post-World War II civil rights movement in the context of the political developments that both advanced and hindered its effectiveness. One chapter is entitled "Postmortem: The Reagan Counterrevolution."*

Chideya, Farai. *Don't Believe the Hype: Fighting Cultural Misinformation about African-Americans*. New York: Plume, 1995.

*The author states that her work is designed to give readers a chance to question the depictions of African Americans that are standard in the media, specifically modern misconceptions about race.*

Guinier, Lani. *The Tyranny of the Majority: Fundamental Fairness in Representative Democracy*. New York: Free Press, 1994.

*This collection of Guinier's articles challenges the civil rights movement to progress beyond the tactics of the 1960s. Essays include "Keeping the Faith: Black Voters in the Post-Reagan Era" and "The Triumph of Tokenism: The Voting Rights Act and the Theory of Black Electoral Success."*

Kitwana, Bakari. *The Hip Hop Generation and the Crisis in African American Culture*. New York: Basic Civitas, 2002.

*Identifies those African Americans born between 1965 and 1984 as the Hip Hop generation, a cohort that came of age in the post–civil rights era, who confronted and defined a different cultural reality.*

Morrison, Toni, and Claudia Brodsky Lacour, eds. *Birth of a Nation'Hood: Gaze, Script, and Spectacle in the O. J. Simpson Case*. New York: Pantheon Books, 1997.

*This is a collection of twelve essays remarking on the O. J. Simpson trial to determine his guilt or innocence in the murder of his wife. The authors discuss the marketing of the Simpson trial and the perception of race in the media.*

O'Brien, Gail Williams. *The Color of the Law: Race, Violence, and Justice in the Post–World War II South*. Chapel Hill: University of North Carolina Press, 1999.

*O'Brien relates 1946 racial violence in Columbia, Tennessee, to the "politics of policing" in the 1990s.*

Rose, Tricia. *Black Noise: Rap Music and Black Culture in Contemporary America*. Middletown, Conn.: Wesleyan University Press, 1994.

*Rose describes, theorizes, and analyzes elements of rap, including lyrics, music, culture, style, and social context. She examines the relationships between racial and sexual domination, black cultural priorities, and popular resistance.*

Wickham, Dewayne, ed. *Bill Clinton and Black America*. New York: One World, 2002.

*Wickham provides works by a collection of African American authors—including Mary Frances Berry, Johnnie Cochran, and Kweisi Mfume—about the Clinton presidency.*

## LIBRARIES, MUSEUMS, AND HISTORICAL SITES

### *Alabama*

Alabama State Black Archives and Research Center, Normal
Birmingham Civil Rights Institute, Birmingham
Birmingham Museum of Art, Birmingham
George Washington Carver Museum, National Park Service, Tuskegee
Museum of Mobile, Mobile
National African American Archives and Museum, Mobile
Southeastern Center for Afro-American Architecture, Tuskegee
Tuskegee Human and Civil Rights Multicultural Center, Tuskegee
Tuskegee Institute Archives, Libraries and Historical Sites, Tuskegee

### *Arkansas*

Delta Cultural Center, Little Rock
Emoba, Little Rock
Old State House Museum, Little Rock

### *Arizona*

George Washington Carver Museum and Cultural Center, Phoenix

### *California*

Allensworth State Park, Allensworth
California Afro-American Museum, Los Angeles
Ebony Museum of Art, Oakland
St. Andrew's African Methodist Episcopal Church, Sacramento

### *District of Columbia*

Anacostia Neighborhood Museum
Frederick Douglass Home, National Park Service

Library of Congress
Moorland-Spingarn Research Center, Howard University
National Air and Space Museum
National Archives and Records Administration
National Museum of African American History
Smithsonian Institution

## *Florida*

Afro-American Museum of the Arts, Deland
Black Archives, Research and Museum, Tallahassee
Black Heritage Museum, Miami
Broward County Library and Museum, Ft. Lauderdale
Clara White Mission, Jacksonville
Joseph E. Zee Memorial Library, Jacksonville
Museum of African American Art, Tampa
Old Dillard Museum, Ft. Lauderdale
Polk County Historical Museum, Barlow

## *Georgia*

Apex Museum (Afro-American Panoramic Experience), Atlanta
Atlanta College of Arts, Atlanta
Auburn Avenue Research Library, Atlanta
Clark-Atlanta University Libraries and Art Gallery, Atlanta
Hammond House Gallery, Atlanta
Herndon Home, Atlanta
High Museum of Art, Atlanta
Laney Walker Museum, Augusta
Martin Luther King Center for Non-Violent Social Change, Atlanta
Martin Luther King Jr. National Park Site, Atlanta

## *Illinois*

A. Philip Randolph Pullman Porter Museum, Chicago
Bronzeville Children's Museum, Evergreen Park
Chicago Historical Society, Chicago
DuSable Museum of African American History, Chicago
Museum of Science and Industry, Chicago
Museum of Contemporary Art, Chicago

## *Indiana*

Children's Museum of Indianapolis
Conner Prairie Historic Site, Fishers
Crispus Attucks Museum, Indianapolis
Freetown Village Historic Site, Indianapolis
Indianapolis Art Center, Indianapolis
Indianapolis Museum of Art, Indianapolis

### *Iowa*

African American Heritage Foundation, Cedar Rapids

### *Kansas*

Archives of Mid America, Kansas City
Kansas African American Museum, Wichita
Ouindano Town Underground Railroad Site, Kansas City

### *Kentucky*

African American Heritage House, Louisville
The Kentucky Derby Museum, Louisville

### *Louisiana*

Amistad Research Center, New Orleans
Arna Bontemps African American Museum and Cultural Center, Alexandria
Black Arts National Diaspora, Inc., New Orleans
Louisiana State Museum, New Orleans
Musee Rosette Rochon, New Orleans
News Orleans African American Museum of Art, Culture and History, New Orleans
New Orleans Museum of Art, New Orleans
West Baton Rouge Museum, Port Allen
Womanmuse Institute for the Study of Arts, Culture and Ethnicity, Opelousas

### *Maryland*

African American Museum of Maryland, Columbia
Baltimore Museum of Art, Baltimore
Banneker Douglass Museum, Annapolis
Charles H. Chipman Cultural Center, Salisbury
Eubie Blake National Jazz Museum, Baltimore
Faxon Company, Westwood
Great Blacks in Wax Museum, Baltimore
Howard County Center of African American Culture, Inc., Columbia
James E. Lewis Museum of Art, Morgan State University, Baltimore
James J. Davis and Associates, Fort Washington
Maryland African American Museum Corporation, Crownsville
PROUN, Somerville
Reginald H. Lewis Museum of Maryland African American History and Culture, Baltimore

### *Massachusetts*

Children's Museum, Boston
Museum of African American History, Boston
Museum of African American History, Roxbury
Museum of Afro American History, Brookline
National Center for Afro-American Artists, Boston

Old Sturbridge, Village, Sturbridge

## *Michigan*

African American Cultural and Historical Museum, Ann Arbor
Charles H. Wright Museum of African American History, Detroit
Detroit Institute of Art, Detroit
Henry Ford Museum and Greenfield Village Research Center, Dearborn
Michigan Ethnic Heritage Study Center, Harper Woods
Motown Historical Museum, Detroit
Museum of Afrikan American History, Flint

## *Minnesota*

Minnesota Historical Society, St. Paul
Minnesota Institute of Art, Minneapolis

## *Mississippi*

Lawrence C. Jones Museum, Piney Woods
Smith Robertson Black Cultural Center, Jackson

## *Missouri*

American Jazz Museum, Kansas City
Black World History Museum, St. Louis
Bruce R. Watkins Cultural Center, Kansas City
18th and Vine Museum, Kansas City
Missouri Historical Society, St. Louis
Saint Louis Art Museum, St. Louis
Saint Louis Science Center, St. Louis

## *Nebraska*

Great Plains Black Museum, Omaha

## *New Hampshire*

African Arts Resource Center, Portsmouth

## *New Jersey*

African Arts Museum, Tenafly
Ancestral Spirits, Convent Station
Newark Museum, Newark

## *New York*

Bill Hodges Gallery, New York
Brooklyn Children's Museum, Brooklyn
Community Folk Art Gallery, Syracuse

Metropolitan Museum of Art, New York
New York Public Library for the Performing Arts, New York
Schomburg Center for Research in Black Culture, New York
Strong Museum, Rochester
Studio Museum in Harlem, New York

### *North Carolina*

Afro American Cultural Center, Charlotte
Diggs Gallery, Winston Salem State University, Winston Salem
North Carolina Central University Art Museum, Durham
North Carolina Museum of History—Library, Raleigh
North Carolina Transportation Museum, Spencer
Old Salem, Winston-Salem.

### *Ohio*

Art Tatum African American Resource Center, Toledo
Arts Consortium, Cincinnati
Black Studies Museum and Library, Cleveland
Cincinnati Art Museum, Cincinnati
Cleveland African American Museum, Cleveland
Dayton Art Institute, Dayton
Dunbar House, Dayton
King Arts Complex, Columbus
National Afro-American Museum and Cultural Center, Wilberforce
National Underground Railroad Freedom Center, Cincinnati

### *Oklahoma*

SANAMU African Gallery, Oklahoma City
NTU Art Association, Oklahoma City

### *Pennsylvania*

African American Museum in Philadelphia
Carnegie Institute, Pittsburgh
Philadelphia Doll Museum, Philadelphia
Please Touch Museum, Philadelphia
Sen. John Heinz Pittsburgh Regional History Center and Museum, Pittsburgh

### *Rhode Island*

Center for the Study of Race and Ethnicity in America, Providence
Rhode Island Black Heritage Society, Providence

### *South Carolina*

Avery Research Center for African American History and Culture, College of Charleston, Charleston

Briggs-Delaplane Cultural Center, Summerton
I. P. Stanback Museum and Planetarium, Orangeburg
Mann-Simmons Cottage, Columbia
Penn Center, Inc., St. Helena Island

### *Tennessee*

Beck Cultural Exchange Center, Knoxville
Chattanooga Afro American Museum, Chattanooga
National Civil Rights Museum, Memphis

### *Texas*

George Washington Carver Museum, Austin
Gov. Bill and Vara Daniel Historic Village, Rio Vista
Texas Heritage Museum, Rio Vista

### *Virginia*

Alexandria Black Resources Center, Alexandria
Black History Museum and Cultural Center, Richmond
Colonial Williamsburg Foundation, Williamsburg
Hampton University Museum, Hampton
Harrison Museum of African American Culture, Roanoke
Mariners Museum, Newport News
Newsome House Museum and Cultural Center, Newport News
Petersburg Museum Fine, Petersburg
Sixth Mt. Zion Baptist Church Historic Site, Richmond
Virginia Museum of Arts, Richmond

### *Washington*

African American Heritage Museum, Seattle

### *West Virginia*

Harpers Ferry National Park, Harpers Ferry
Stephen T. Mather Training Center, Harpers Ferry

### *Wisconsin*

America's Black Holocaust Museum, Milwaukee
Old World Wisconsin, Engle
Wisconsin Historical Society, Madison

## NEWSPAPERS, PERIODICALS, AND JOURNALS

*About . . . Time* (Rochester, New York)
*African American Review* (Terre Haute, Indiana)

*Africo-American Presbyterian* (Charlotte, North Carolina)
*Afro-American* (Baltimore, Maryland)
*Age* (New York)
*Alabama Tribune* (Montgomery)
A.M.E. *Church Review* (Philadelphia, Pennsylvania)
*American Legacy* (New York)
*American Unity: A Monthly Education Guide* (New York)
*American Visions* (Washington, D.C.)
*Amsterdam News* (New York)
*The Appeal* (St. Paul, Minnesota)
*Arkansas State Press* (Little Rock)
*Arkansas Survey* (Little Rock)
*Atlanta World* (Atlanta, Georgia)
*Baptist Vanguard* (Little Rock, Arkansas)
*Bay State Banner* (Dorchester, Massachusetts)
*Bibleway News Voice* (Washington, D.C.)
*Black Beat* (New York)
*Black Books Bulletin* (Chicago)
*Black Careers* (Philadelphia, Pennsylvania)
*The Black Panther* (Oakland, California)
*The Black Dispatch* (Oklahoma City)
*Black Enterprise* (New York)
*Black Issues in Higher Education* (Fairfax, Virginia)
*The Black Scholar: Journal of Black Studies and Research* (Oakland, California)
*Black Secrets* (New York)
*Black World / Negro Digest* (Chicago)
*Boston Chronicle* (Boston)
*Brown American* (Philadelphia, Pennsylvania)
*The Bulletin* (Sarasota, Florida)
*California Eagle* (Los Angeles)
*California Voice* (San Francisco)
*Campus Chats* (Tuskegee, Alabama)
*Charlotte Post* (Charlotte, North Carolina)
*Chicago Defender* (Chicago)
*The Chicago Gazette* (Chicago)
*The Christian Index* (Memphis, Tennessee)
*The Christian Recorder* (Philadelphia, Pennsylvania)
*Cleveland Call and Post* (Cleveland, Ohio)
*Cleveland Gazette* (Cleveland, Ohio)
*Colorado Statesman* (Denver)
*The Columbus Challenger* (Columbus, Ohio)
*Columbus Times* (Columbus, Georgia)
*The Crisis* (Baltimore, Maryland)
*Dance Herald: A Journal of Black Dance* (New York)
*Dayton Forum* (Dayton, Ohio)
*Denver Starr* (Denver)

*Detroit Tribune* (Detroit)
*Ebony* (Chicago)
*Emerge* (Washington, D.C.)
*The Evening Whirl* (St. Louis)
*Final Call* (Chicago)
*Freedom Call* (Milwaukee)
*Gary American* (Gary, Indiana)
*The Guardian* (Boston)
*Harlem Quarterly* (New York)
*Harvard Journal of Afro-American Affairs* (Cambridge, Massachusetts)
*Houston Defender* (Houston, Texas)
*Indianapolis Recorder* (Indianapolis)
*Informer and Texas Freeman* (Houston, Texas)
*Inglewood Hawthorne Wave* (Los Angeles)
*Iowa Bystander* (Des Moines)
*Jet* (Chicago)
*Journal of African American History* (Washington, D.C.)
*Journal of Negro Education* (Washington, D.C.)
*Journal of Negro History* (Washington, D.C.)
*Kansas City Globe* (Kansas City, Missouri)
*The Lamp* (Miami, Florida)
*Liberator* (New York)
*Los Angeles Sentinel* (Los Angeles)
*Louisiana Weekly* (New Orleans)
*Louisville Leader* (Louisville, Kentucky)
*Madison Times* (Madison, Wisconsin)
*The Miami Times* (Miami, Florida)
*Missionary Lutheran* (St. Louis)
*Missionary Seer* (New York)
*NAACP Bulletin* (New York)
*National Baptist Union Review* (Nashville, Tennessee)
*National Bar Journal* (St. Louis)
*National Negro Health News* (Washington, D.C.)
*Negro History Bulletin* (Washington, D.C.)
*Negro Star* (Wichita, Kansas)
*New Day* (Philadelphia, Pennsylvania)
*New Jersey Herald News* (Newark)
*Ohio State News* (Columbus)
*Opportunity: Journal of Negro Life* (New York)
*The People's Voice* (New York)
*Philadelphia Tribune* (Philadelphia, Pennsylvania)
*Pittsburgh Courier* (Pittsburgh, Pennsylvania)
*Quarterly Black Review of Books* (New York)
*Quarterly Review of Higher Education among Negroes* (Charlotte, North Carolina)
*Richmond Planet* (Richmond, Virginia)
*St. Louis American* (St. Louis)

*St. Louis Argus* (St. Louis)
*Saint Paul Sun* (St. Paul, Minnesota)
*Savannah Tribune* (Savannah, Georgia)
*The Sepia Socialite* (New Orleans)
*Transition* (Durham, North Carolina)
*Tri-State Defender* (Memphis, Tennessee)
*Twin Cities Courier* (Minneapolis)
*The Union* (Cincinnati, Ohio)
*Voice of Missions* (New York)
*The Waco Messenger* (Waco, Texas)

## SELECTED WEB SITES

| | |
|---|---|
| Africa/African American Library | homestead.com/wysinger/africana.html |
| African Americans in Army History, U.S. Center for Military History | army.mil/cmh-pg/topics/afam/afam-usa.htm |
| African-American Mosaic Exhibition through the Library of Congress | loc.gov/exhibits/african/intro.html |
| African American Odyssey, Library of Congress | lcweb2.loc.gov/ammem/aaohtml/aohome.html |
| African American Theses and Dissertations: 1907–1997, University of California, Berkeley | sunsite.berkeley.edu/bibliographies/africanamerican |
| Africana.Com: The Gateway to the Black World | africana.com |
| Afro-American Almanac | toptags.com/aama |
| Afro-American Historical and Genealogical Society | rootsweb.com |
| Amistad Research Center | tulane.edu/~amistad/ |
| Association for the Study of African-American Life and History | asalh.org |
| Black Facts Online | blackfacts.com |
| Black History Pages | blackhistorypages.com |
| Christian Science Monitor Black History Project | csmonitor.com/atcsmonitor/specials/bhmonth/bhindex.html |
| Encyclopedia Britannica Guide to Black History | blackhistory.eb.com |
| History Net at About.Com | thehistorynet.com/NationalHistoryDay/index.html |
| Jackson Davis Collection of African American Educational Photographs | lib.virginia.edu/speccol/davis |
| James Branch Cabell Library Virginia Black History Archives | library.vcu.edu/jbc/speccoll/vbha/l vbha.htm |
| John Henrik Clark Africana Library | library.cornell.edu/africana |
| Library of Congress | loc.gov |
| Martin Luther King, Jr. Center for Nonviolent Social Change | thekingcenter.com |

| | |
|---|---|
| Media Business Solutions Presents: The African American Registry | aaregistry.com |
| Museum of Afro American History Boston | afroammuseum.org/trail.htm |
| National Archives and Records Administration | nara.gov |
| National Association for Equal Opportunity in Higher Education | nafeo.org |
| National Civil Rights Museum | civilrightsmuseum.org |
| National Park Service nps.org | |
| Negro League Baseball | negroleaguebaseball.com |
| New York Institute for Special Education | nyise.org/blackhistory/index.html |
| Our Shared History: African American Heritage (The National Park Service) | nps.gov/aahistory |
| Public Broadcasting Station | pbs.org |
| Schomburg Center for Research in Black Culture | nypl.org/research/sc/sc.html |
| Seacoast, New Hampshire Black History | seacoastnh.com/blackhistory/index.html |
| Smithsonian Institution | si.edu |

# CONTRIBUTORS

**Sundiata Djata** is associate professor of African and African American History at Northern Illinois University. He is the author of *The Bamana Empire in the Niger: Kingdom, Jihad, and Colonialism* (Markus Wiener, 1997) and *Blacks at the Net: The Black Experience in the History of Tennis* (Syracuse University Press, 2005).

**Kevin K. Gaines** directs the Center for Afroamerican and African Studies and is professor of history at the University of Michigan. He is the author of *Uplifting the Race: Black Leadership, Politics, and Culture in the Twentieth Century* (University of North Carolina Press, 1996). He is completing a book on the African American experience in Ghana during the civil rights era.

**Debra Newman Ham** served as curator of the NAACP Papers at the Library of Congress. She is professor of history at Morgan State University. She has edited *African American Mosaic: A Library of Congress Resource Guide for the Study of Black History and Culture* (Library of Congress, 1993), among other works.

**Robert L. Harris Jr.** is vice provost for diversity and faculty development and professor of African American history in the Africana Studies and Research Center at Cornell University. He is the author of *Teaching African American History* (American Historical Association, 1992).

**Robin D. G. Kelley,** professor of anthropology and African American studies at Columbia University, has published seven books. He is preparing a biography of jazz musician Thelonious Monk.

**Brenda L. Moore** has been a member of the Defense Advisory Committee on Women in the Services and is associate professor of sociology at the State University of New York at Buffalo. She is the author of *To Serve My Country, to Serve My Race: The Story of the*

*Only African American WACs Stationed Overseas During World War II* (New York University Press, 1996) and *Serving Our Country: Japanese American Women in the Military During World War II* (Rutgers University Press, 2003).

**Michelle R. Scott** is assistant professor of history at the University of Maryland/Baltimore County. Her forthcoming book is *The Realm of a Blues Empress: Blues Culture and Bessie Smith in Black Chattanooga, Tennessee, 1880–1923* (University of Illinois Press).

**Rosalyn Terborg-Penn** is professor and coordinator of graduate programs in history at Morgan State University. A founder of the Association of Black Women Historians, she has coedited three books, including *Black Women in America: An Historical Encyclopedia* (Oxford University Press, 1994), and is the author of *African American Women in the Struggle for the Vote, 1850–1920* (Indiana University Press, 1998).

**Penny M. Von Eschen** is associate professor of history and member of the Center for Afroamerican and African Studies at the University of Michigan. She is the author of *Race Against Empire: Black Americans and Anticolonialism, 1937–1957* (Cornell University Press, 1997) and *Satchmo Blows Up the World: Jazz Ambassadors Play the Cold War* (Harvard University Press, 2004).

**Juliet E. K. Walker,** the founder and director of the Center for Black Business History, Entrepreneurship and Technology, is professor of history at the University of Texas at Austin. She is the author of *The History of Black Business in America: Capitalism, Race, and Entrepreneurship* (Palgrave Macmillan, 2005) and editor of *The Encyclopedia of African American Business History* (Greenwood, 1999).

**Craig Werner** is professor of Afro-American studies at the University of Wisconsin at Madison. He is the author of *A Change Is Gonna Come: Music, Race & the Soul of America* (Plume, 1999; University of Michigan Press, 2005) and *Higher Ground: Aretha Franklin, Stevie Wonder, Curtis Mayfield & the Rise and Fall of Soul* (Crown, 2004).

# INDEX